DICTIONARY OF MARITIME
AND TRANSPORTATION TERMS

D0813225

DICTIONARY OF MARITIME AND TRANSPORTATION TERMS

Jeffrey W. Monroe, MM
Robert Stewart, MM, PhD

CORNELL MARITIME PRESS
Centreville, Maryland

Library of Congress Cataloging-in-Publication Data

Monroe, Jeffrey W., 1954-
    Dictionary of maritime and transportation terms / Jeffrey W. Monroe, Robert Stewart.
    p. cm.
    Includes bibliographical references.
    ISBN-13: 978-0-87033-569-3
    1. Naval art and science—Dictionaries. 2. Shipping—Dictionaries. I. Stewart, Robert. II. Title.
    V23.M645 2005
    387.5'03—dc22
                        2005014460

Manufactured in the United States of America
First edition, 2005

To Clarence Monroe, my father, crewman, SS *MORRO CASTLE* 1934, who knew the language of the sea and was a professional in every regard.

To Cindy Stewart, my wife, the support for my every endeavor.

CONTENTS

ACKNOWLEDGMENTS

Katie, Deb, and Tami, your skills were invaluable
in putting the words together.

Tom and Bob, your skills allowed me to bring the product together.

A

2BI Business to Business Integration (form of supply chain).

2H Second Half.

3PL Third-Party Logistics. An organization that manages and executes a particular logistics function, using its own assets and resources on behalf of another company.

4PLP Fourth-Party Logistics Providers. The term "4PL" was introduced into the supply chain to convey that deep informational technology skills and deeper analytical skills were required to achieve supply chain leadership. But the true evolution of the 4PL term is better defined in context of the global marketplace where outsourced logistics creates more of a partnership critical to success than a supplier/customer relationship. Companies in the global marketplace are finding that supply chain engineered logistics is not a commodity, and understanding it is a vital means to boost their cost savings, enhancing their cash flow and improving servicing levels for getting their products to market.

A1 First Class Condition. The highest classification given to a vessel. The letter refers to her construction and the figure refers to equipment.

AA Always Afloat (In some ports, the ship is aground when approaching, or at berth.)

AAAA Always Accessible Always Afloat.

AAOSA Always Afloat or Safe Aground.

AAPA American Association of Port Authorities.

AAR Against All Risks (insurance clause); Association of American Railroads.

AARA Amsterdam-Antwerp-Rotterdam Area.

AB Able-Bodied seaman: a person who should be capable of doing all work required of a seaman.

ABACK A vessel whose yards are trimmed where the wind is on her forward side and tending to drive her astern.

A point beyond the midpoint of a ships length. A relative term used to describe the location of one object in relation to another, in which the object described is farther aft than the other. Thus, the mainmast is abaft the foremast. Toward the stern of a ship, back, behind, further aft.

ABAFT THE BEAM Any direction between the beam and the stern on either side of the vessel.

ABANDON For all hands to leave, as abandon ship. A proceeding wherein a shipper/consignee seeks authority to abandon all or parts of its cargo.

ABANDONED GOODS Articles declared by an importer, consignee, or representative to be abandoned and, therefore, the property of the U.S. government. Also applies to goods left too long in a bonded warehouse and,

1

therefore, become the property of the U.S. government. (19CFR127.11-127.13).

ABANDONMENT (APPLICATION FOR) A proceeding wherein a carrier seeks authority to stop service over all or part of its route or to give up ownership or control of cargo or vessel.

ABATEMENT A discount allowed for damage or overcharge in the payment of a bill.

ABC ANALYSIS Classification of items in an inventory according to importance defined in terms of criteria such as sales volume and purchase volume.

In inventory management, the placing of items into categories A, B, and C with respect to monitoring stock levels.

ABEAM The bearing of an object 90 degrees from ahead. At right angles to the keel.

ABEL TESTER A closed-cup flash tester for kerosene and other oils.

ABI U.S. Customs' "Automated Broker Interface," by which brokers file importers' entries electronically.

ABLATION The disappearance of an ice or snow surface by melting and/or evaporation.

ABLE-BODIED SEAMAN AB; a member of the deck crew, ranking higher than ordinary seaman.

ABOARD In or on the vessel. Referring to cargo being put, or laden, onto a means of conveyance.

ABOUT SHIP On the other tack or to reverse as the position of the vessel.

ABOVE A location aboard ship higher than where a person is at a moment in time. To move vertically upward aboard ship.

ABOVEBOARD Above decks without concealment or deceit.

ABOVE DECK On the deck.

ABOX Said of yards when one mast is braced in a direction opposite to that of yards on the next mast.

ABRASION The act or process of rubbing or wearing away, as the abrasion of rock or earth by glaciers. Also, the resulting injury or other effects of abrading; an abraded place, as the abrasion left by glacial action.

ABREAST Side by side; over against; opposite to.

ABS American Bureau of Shipping: a U.S.-based private classification or standards setting society for merchant ships and other marine systems.

ABSENT FLAG A small square blue signal flag flown from a yacht's starboard spreader to signify that the owner is not aboard.

ABSOLUTE ACCURACY The accuracy of a position compared to the actual geographic coordinates of the earth, as measured by Loran C.

ABSOLUTE PRESSURE Total pressure equal to gauge pressure plus 14.7 lb/sq in at sea level.

ABSOLUTE VISCOSITY The force required to move a plane surface of one square centimeter over another plane surface at the rate of one centimeter per second when the two surfaces are separated by a layer of liquid one-centimeter in thickness.

ABSORPTION The physical assimilation of one or more components of a gaseous or vapor phase into a second phase (liquid or solid), the equilibrium distribution of absorbed material in absorbent tending toward homogeneity, as contrasted to the surface phenomenon of adsorption. Also, the movement of a hazardous chemical through the skin and into the blood stream.

One carrier assumes the charges of another without any increase in charges to the shipper.

ABSORPTION OIL An oil with a high solvent power for light hydrocarbons that are present in natural or refinery gas.

ABSORPTION PLANT A plant for recovering the condensable portion of natural or plant gas, by absorbing these hydrocarbons in an absorption oil (often under pressure), followed by separation and fractionation of the absorbed material.

ABT About.

ABURTON Casks, barrels, etc., stowed end-to-end athwartship.

ABUSIVE DRAW Drawing on a standby letter of credit/demand guarantee when no violation of the underlying contract has occurred.

AC Alternating Current.

ACCELERATED DISPOSITION A formal supplication to the district director requesting that the review be hastened and a response received within the allotted time.

ACCELERATION The increasing of speed or velocity.

ACCELERATION TABLES Shows the amount by which any mean time value of an interval must be increased to give the sidereal time value.

ACCEPTANCE An agreement to purchase goods at a stated price and under stated terms. A time draft (or bill of exchange) that the drawee (payer) has accepted and is unconditionally obligated to pay at maturity. Broadly speaking, any agreement to purchase goods under specified terms.

ACCEPTANCE OF GOODS The process of receiving a consignment from a consignor, usually against the issue of a receipt. As from this moment and on this place the carrier's responsibility for the consignment begins.

ACCEPT/REJECT ADVISE A standard notice sent to vendors advising that a shipment has been accepted or rejected.

ACCESS HOLE Opening in any part of ship's plating used as a passageway while ship is under construction.

ACCESSIBILITY A carrier's ability to provide service between an origin and a destination point.

ACCESSORIAL CHARGES Charges that are applied to the base tariff rate or base contract rate, e.g., bunkers, container, currency, and destination/delivery.

ACCIDENT (INS) An unexpected fortuitous event, unforeseen and unintended, not under the control of an insured and resulting in a loss.

ACCIDENT FREQUENCY (INS) The number of times an accident occurs. Used in predicting losses upon which premiums are based.

ACCOMMODATION LADDER A portable set of steps suspended over the ship's side for the accommodation of people boarding from small boats. A permanently mounted access ladder to a ship. Usually running nearly parallel to ship's side.

ACCOMMODATION SPACES Spaces designed for living purposes for passengers and crew aboard a vessel.

ACCOMPANIED TRANSPORT The transport of complete road vehicles by another means of transport (e.g., train, ferry) accompanied by the driver.

ACCOUNT An individual, institution, or organization that purchases a company's products, or the general category of customer service as listed on the company books.

ACCOUNTABILITY Judging the responsiveness of semiautonomous public ports to the intent of their enabling law or the will of their supervisory government or to the wishes of the people.

ACCOUNT PARTY Party for whom a letter of credit is opened. "Account party" and "applicant" are generally synonymous, but sometimes one party will agree with the issuing bank to make all payments under a letter of credit showing the name of another party (often two affiliated companies). Banks may refer to one of these parties as the applicant and the other as the account party, but there is no consistency among banks regarding which is which.

ACCRUAL The accounts maintained for services rendered, or the sum of the amount due.

ACEP *See* Approved Continuous Examination Program.

AC GENERATOR Generator using slip rings and brushes to connect armature to external circuit. Output is alternating current

ACH Automated Clearinghouse is a feature of U.S. Customs' Automated Broker Interface combining elements of bank lock box arrangements with electronic funds transfer services to replace cash or check for payment of estimated duties, taxes, and fees on imported merchandise.

ACID The term, as used in connection with petroleum, usually means sulfuric acid and its aqueous solutions.

ACIDITY The amount of free acid in any substance. In lubricating oils, acidity denotes the presence of acid-type constituents whose concentration is usually defined in terms of neutralization number.

ACIDIZING A method used to increase production from an oil well. Hydrochloric acid is pumped outward from the well bore into the surrounding formation to dissolve limestone or sandstone, thus making larger flow channels.

ACID TREATING A process for removing undesirable constituents of oil by contacting with sulfuric acid. The acid sludge that is formed by the action of the acid on the oil is separated from the oil and takes with it coloring

4

matter, some sulfuric compounds, and unstable bodies, leaving the oil, after finishing by neutralizing, rerunning, or clay treating, lighter colored and a more stable product than before (if not treated too far).

ACKNOWLEDGEMENT OF RECEIPT   A notification relating to the receipt of e.g., goods, messages, and documents.

ACOCKBILL   The position of the anchor when it hangs over the bow by a chain.

ACOUSTIC CLOUDS   Areas of atmosphere where sound is obstructed, deflected, or stopped.

ACP   Alternative Compliance Program.

ACQUIESCENCE   When a bill of lading is accepted or signed by a shipper or shipper's agent without protest, the shipper is said to acquiesce to the terms, giving a silent form of consent.

ACQUISITION   The selection of those targets requiring a tracking procedure and the initiation of their tracking. Used only in connection with ARPA performance standards.

ACQUITTANCE   A written receipt in full, in discharge from all claims.

ACS   U.S. Customs' master computer system, "Automated Commercial Systems."

ACTION MESSAGE   An alert that a software system generates to inform the controller of a situation requiring his or her attention

ACTIVE GLACIER   A glacier in motion.

ACTIVE LAYER   The zone, subject to annual freezing and thawing, between the surface of the ground and the permafrost. The depth of the active layer differs from one locality to another, ranging from a few inches to several feet.

ACTIVE STOCK   Goods in active pick locations and ready for order filling.

ACTIVITY-BASED COSTING   A method of cost management that identifies business activities performed, accumulates costs associated with these activities, and uses various cost drivers to trace costs of activities to the products.

ACT OF GOD   Operation of an uncontrollable natural force. An act beyond human control, such as lightning, flood, or earthquake.

ACT OF MAN   In water transportation, the deliberate sacrifice of cargo to make the vessel safe for the remaining cargo. Those sharing in the spared cargo proportionately cover the loss.

ACTUAL CASH VALUE (INS)   The sum of money required to pay for damages or lost property, computed on the basis of replacement value less its depreciation by obsolescence or general wear.

ACTUAL TOTAL LOSS (INS)   Occurs when: the insured property is completely destroyed or the Assured is irretrievably deprived of the insured property or cargo changes in character so that it is no longer the thing that was insured or a ship is posted "missing" at Lloyd's, in which case both the ship and its cargo are deemed to be an actual total loss.

ACTUAL USE   When the classification of an article is dependent upon its actual use after importation.

ACTUAL VOYAGE NUMBER   A code for identification purposes of the voyage and vessel that actually transports the container/cargo.

ACUTE   Short-term effect, usually of a temporary high-level exposure.

ACUTE TOXIC EFFECT   The effect on a person of a single exposure of short duration to high concentrations of poisonous compounds or vapors.

ADCOM   Addressee Commission.

ADD ONS (INS)   Additional coverages to your basic policy.

ADDAMS MODEL   Acronym for Automated Dredging and Disposal Alternatives Management Systems; a computerized program developed by the U.S. Army Corps of Engineers Waterways Experiment Station to model and assess the impacts of waterborne contaminants due to disposal of dredged material in open water.

ADDED VALUE   A term implying that at each production and distribution function, a product's value is increased in terms of time, place, and form.

ADDED WEIGHT METHOD   A method of solving for damage stability where the water, which enters the vessel, is considered as an added weight.

ADDENDUM   Additional clause or terms in a contract.

ADDITIONAL INSURED (INS)   A person or firm or corporation other than the named insured on a policy or mortgage company named in a mortgagee clause, who is protected against loss by the terms of the policy or mortgage company named in the mortgage clause.

ADDITIONAL SECONDARY PHASE FACTOR (ASPF)   A factor based on the variation introduced when signals travel over or near landmasses, since Loran C navigational patterns are based upon signal propagation over water, not over land. Therefore, a correction must be used by the navigator seeking a high degree of accuracy.

ADDITIVES   Chemicals that are added in minor proportion to a parent substance to create, enhance, or suppress a certain property or properties in the parent material.

ADDITIVE-TYPE OIL   Lubricating oil to which chemical agents have been added in the refining process to make it particularly suitable for its intended use.

ADEQUATELY WET   Fixing or coating with water or water to which a surfactant has been added, or with a remover-encapsulant, so as to prevent a friable condition and visible emissions.

ADF   Automatic Direction Finder.

AD HOC   For this specific case for this point only.

ADIABATIC   Applied to the changes of temperature, volume, or pressure not accompanied by gain or loss of heat.

ADJUSTER   An individual charged with the responsibility of determining if a particular loss is covered by the insurance policy and, if so, the amount that should be paid to the claimant.

ADJUSTMENT FUNCTION Selecting a point in the exchange channel to concentrate goods, make a new selection from that concentration, and form a new selection of goods to move forward in the channel.

ADJUSTMENT OF A COMPASS Term given to the compensation made to a magnetic compass.

ADJUSTMENT OF THE SEXTANT Adjustments made to the setting of index and horizon mirrors so they are perpendicular to plane or arc, setting the mirrors parallel when the index is at zero, setting line of collimation parallel to plane of arc.

ADMEASUREMENT The confirmed or official dimensions of a ship.

ADMINISTRATIVE LAW JUDGE A representative of a government commission or agency vested with power to administer oaths, examine witnesses, take testimony, and conduct hearings of cases submitted to, or initiates by, that agency. Also called Hearing Examiner.

ADMIRAL The commanding officer of a naval fleet. There are four classifications: Fleet Admiral, Admiral, Vice-Admiral, and Rear Admiral.

ADMIRALTY (ADM.) Refers to marine matters such as an Admiralty Court.

ADMIRALTY LAW Dealing with cases associated with the rights and duties of shipping. A court-exercising jurisdiction over maritime cases.

ADMIRALTY LIST OF RADIO SIGNALS A publication by the Hydrographer of the Royal Navy of the United Kingdom that contains information on the range, frequency, characteristics, and position of radio beacon transmitters.

ADR *See* Articles Dangereux de Route.

ADRIFT Afloat: loose from the moorings.

ADSORPTION The adhesion of molecules of gases or liquids to the surface of other bodies, usually solids, resulting in a relatively high concentration of the gas or solution at the point of contact.

AD VALOREM A term from Latin meaning, "according to value." Also known as ad val. A tariff calculated as a percentage of the value of goods cleared through Customs.

An additional freight charged to this type of cargo that is of high value. Usually at a rate, so much percent on the declared value of the goods.

ADVANCE (1) The distance a vessel moves in its initial direction from the point where the rudder is started over until the heading has changed more or less than 90 degrees. Also the distance between position at which a vessel commences to alter course and the position at which she has turned through 90 degrees, measured along a line parallel to the original course. To move cargo up-line to a vessel leaving sooner than the one booked. (*See* Roll.)

(2) To move forward, as to move a line of position forward, parallel to itself, along a course line to obtain a line of position at a later time. The opposite of "retire."

(3) To move cargo up line to a vessel leaving sooner than the one booked. (*See* Roll.)

ADVANCE ARRANGEMENT Agreement between the shipper and the carrier concerning contacts between those parties prior to tendering the consignment.

ADVANCE FREIGHT Partial payment of the bill of lading freight in advance; in other respects is the same as guaranteed freight.

ADVANCE MAINTENANCE A procedure whereby additional channel depth is provided to decrease the required dredging frequency. In many cases, this procedure provides significant cost savings as well as facilitating scheduling of dredging activities.

ADVANCE PAYMENT Funds given by the buyer of goods to the seller prior to shipment, often just a percentage of the value of the goods with the remainder paid after shipment.

ADVANCE PAYMENT BOND Bond, guarantee, or standby letter of credit given by a seller receiving an advance payment to the buyer to ensure that the funds will be returned if goods are never shipped.

ADVANCED AMOUNT Quantity of cash or cash equivalents expressed in a monetary amount given to a driver to cover expenses during a trip.

ADVANCED CHARGE Transportation charge advanced by one carrier to another to be collected by the later carrier from the consignor or consignee.

ADVANCED INTERLINE An interline carrier that picks up cargo from the shipper and delivers it to another carrier for shipment to the consignee.

ADVANCED SHIPMENT NOTICE (ASN) A list transmitted to a customer or consignor designating items shipped. May also include expected time of arrival.

ADVECTION A meteorological term denoting the horizontal transfer of heat by air currents.

ADVENTURE Shipment of goods on shipper's own account. A bill of adventure is a document signed by the master of the ship that carries goods at owner's risk.

ADVERSE POSSESSION Occupation of land inconsistent with the right of the true owner; if adverse possession continues, the effect at the expiration of the prescribed period is that not only the remedy but the title of the former owner is extinguished.

ADVERSE SELECTION (INS) Selection against the insurance company; the tendency of more poor risks to buy and maintain insurance than good risks.

ADVICE NOTE A written piece of information, e.g., about the status of the goods.

ADVICE OF SHIPMENT A notice sent to a local or foreign buyer advising that shipment has gone forward and containing details of packing, routing, etc. A copy of the invoice is often enclosed and, if desired, a copy of the bill of lading.

ADVISING BANK A bank operating in the seller's country that handles letters of credit on behalf of a foreign bank.

AERIAL Single wire or a set of wires, forming a radio antenna.

AEROBIC   Having the presence of oxygen.

AEROQUIP SYSTEM   Special accessories in a container consisting of among others the attachment rails on the inside walls to provide facilities for lashing and separation of the cargo.

AEROSOL   A system of solid or liquid particles dispersed in a gas.

AEV   Articles of Extraordinary Value.

AF   Audio frequency.

AFFIDAVIT   Solemn declaration made before a person legally authorized to administer an oath.

AFFILIATE   A company that controls, or is controlled by another company, or is one of two or more commonly controlled companies.

AFFREIGHTMENT   An agreement by an ocean carrier to provide cargo space on a vessel at a specified time and for a specified price to accommodate an exporter or importer. A contract for chartering a vessel for transportation of merchandise.

AFLOAT   Resting on the water.

AFORE   Forward of; before.

AFSPS   Arrival First Sea Pilot Station.

AFT   The section of the ship behind amidships; towards the stern of ship.

AFTER   Further aft or nearer the stern.

AFTER BODY   That portion of a ship's body aft of the amidships section.

AFTER FRAMES   Frames aft of amidships or frames near the stern of the ship.

AFTER GUARD   The men who worked tending the gear at the after part of a vessel, also officers who have their quarters aft.

AFTERMARKET PART   Any part of a motor vehicle emission control system sold for installation on a vehicle after the original retail sale of the vehicle.

AFTER PART   Part of a vessel, or any space in a vessel, that is nearer the stern. Part of a watch who work, or would have worked, the after sails.

AFTER PEAK   The compartment in the narrow part of the stern, aft of the last watertight bulkhead; or the aftermost tank or compartment forward of the sternpost.

AFTER PEAK BULKHEAD   Watertight bulkhead farthest aft.

AFTER PERPENDICULAR (AP)   A line perpendicular to the base line, intersecting the after edge of the sternpost at the design waterline. The aftermost frame station and is usually located at the after end of the sternpost. On submarines or ships having a similar stern, it is a vertical line passing through the point where the design waterline intersects the stern of the ship.

AFTER YARDS   Those abaft the foremast.

AGAINST   In foreign commerce, used as synonym for "upon."

AGAINST THE SUN   Term applied to a rotary motion that is opposite to the hands of a watch.

AGC   Automatic Gain Control. Circuit employed to vary gain of amplifier in proportion to input signal strength so output remains at constant level.

AGE   The stage in the ice cycle from inception to dissolution. Not to be confused with Ice Age, a subdivision of geologic time. Under standard conditions freshwater freezes at 32°F, but seawater freezes at various lower temperatures depending on its salinity. The greater the salinity (about 35 parts per thousand) the freezing point is 29°F. Ice forms first in shallow water near the coast or over shoals and banks, particularly in bays, inlets, and straits in which there is no current; also in regions with lower salinity such as those near the mouths of rivers.

AGENCY FEE   A fee charged to the ship by the ship's agent, representing payment for services while the ship was in port. Sometimes called attendance fee.

AGENCY TARIFF   A tariff published by an agent on behalf of several carriers.

AGENT (AGT.)   A person authorized to transact business for and in the name of another person or company. Types of agent are: brokers, commission merchants, resident buyers, sales agents, and manufacturer's representatives.

AGGLOMERATION   A net advantage a company gains by sharing a common location with other companies.

AGGRAVATING FACTORS   Factors that when proven to exist, increase the severity of a penalty. (19CFR171)

AGGREGATE SHIPMENT   Numerous shipments from different shippers to one consignee that are consolidated and treated as a single consignment.

AGGREGATE TENDER RATE   A reduced rate offered to a shipper who tenders two or more class-related shipments at one time and one place.

AGITATION DREDGING   This practice of mechanically lifting sediment from the bottom of a dredging site and into the upper layers of the local stream. The local currents can act on the sediment to move it from the dredging site. Agitation dredging is normally used with fine-grained sediments. Allowing the hoppers of hopper dredges to overflow is an example of agitation dredging.

AGONIC LINE   Line connecting points of zero variation as shown on a pilot chart.

AGREED VALUATION   The value of a shipment agreed upon in order to secure a specific freight rate.

AGREED WEIGHT   The weight prescribed by agreement between carrier and shipper for goods shipped in certain packages or in a certain number.

AGRICULTURE   Those practices involved with the cultivation of soil for purposes of crop production and/or the raising of livestock when such crops are produced primarily for commercial foodstuffs and such livestock are raised primarily for commercial foodstuffs or work purposes.

AGROUND   Resting on the bottom; stranded. The ship is in contact with the bottom.

AGVS   *See* Automated Guided Vehicle System.

AHOY   A term used in hailing a vessel or a boat.

AHULL Term applied to a vessel hove-to under bare poles with helm alee.

AI All Inclusive.

AID Agency for International Development.

AID TO NAVIGATION Any device external to a vessel or aircraft specifically intended to assist navigators to determine their position or safe course, or to warn them of dangers or obstructions to navigation.

AIR Atmosphere.

AIR CARGO Any property carried or to be carried in an aircraft, not including passenger baggage.

AIR CARGO AGENT An agent appointed by an airline to solicit and process international airfreight shipments.

AIR CARGO CONTAINERS Containers designed to conform to the inside of an aircraft. There are many shapes and sizes of containers. Air cargo containers fall into three categories: air cargo pallets, lower deck containers, and box-type containers.

AIR CARGO GUIDE Basic reference publication for shipping freight by air. It contains current domestic and international cargo flight schedules, including pure cargo, wide body, and combination passenger-air cargo flights. Each monthly issue contains information on air carriers' special services, labeling, airline and aircraft decodings, air carriers and freight forwarders directory, cargo charter information, U.S. and Canadian city directory small package service, interline air freight agreements, aircraft loading charts and more.

AIR CARGO, INC. (ACI) A ground service corporation established and jointly owned by the United States scheduled airlines. In addition to its airline owners, ACI also serves over 30 airfreight forwarders and international air carriers. Services include, but are not limited to: negotiating and supervising the performance of a nationwide series of contracts under which trucking companies provide both local pickup and delivery service at airport cities and over-the-road truck service to move air freight to and from points not directly served by airlines, claims inspection, terminal handling, telemarketing service, and group purchasing.

AIR CARRIER An enterprise that offers transportation service via air—airline

AIR CASING A ring-shaped plate coaming surrounding the stack and fitted at the deck just below the umbrella to protect the deck from heat and to help ventilate the fireroom.

AIR CONTAINER Any unit load device, primarily intended for transport by air, having an internal volume of 1 cubic meter or more, incorporating restraint provisions compatible with an aircraft restraint system, and an entirely flush base bottom to allow handling on roller-bed cargo handling systems.

AIR CONTAMINANT Any substance or man-made physical phenomenon in the ambient air space and includes, but is not limited to, dust, flash,

11

gas, fume, mist, odor, smoke, vapor, pollen, microorganism, radioactive material, radiation, heat, sound, any combination thereof, or any decay or reaction product thereof.

AIR CONTAMINATION SOURCE Any place at or from which any air contaminant is emitted to the ambient air space.

AIRCRAFT CARRIER A vessel designed to carry aircraft and fitted with a flying deck from which aircraft are launched and on which they land. A floating flying field that usually operates as a unit of a fleet.

AIR CUSHION VESSEL Any vessel designed to operate above the surface of the water on a cushion of air.

AIR DRAFT (DRAUGHT) The distance of the highest part of a vessel above the water.

AIR ESCAPE HOLE An aperture cut in the top of floors or in tanks to prevent air lock from inhibiting the free flow of the liquid.

AIR-FUEL RATIO The ratio of air weight to fuel weight consumed in an internal combustion engine or furnace.

AIR FUNNEL One of the air courses for ventilation between the frames, ceiling, and planking of a wooden ship.

AIR POLLUTION Gases or particulate matter in the atmosphere that affect visibility and are health concerns. It can cause a nuisance, be injurious, or be on the basis of current information, potentially injurious to human or animal life, to vegetation, or to property.

Also, unreasonably interfere with the comfortable enjoyment of life and property or the conduct of business.

AIR PORT A circular window with hinged glass in the ship's side or deckhouse. The purpose of the air port is to provide light and ventilation to and vision from the interior of the ship; also called porthole.

AIR STRAKES Ducts for ventilating the holds.

AIR TANK A metal airtight tank built into a boat to ensure flotation when the boat is swamped.

AIR TAXI An exempt for-hire air carrier that will fly anywhere on demand; air taxis are restricted to a maximum payload and passenger capacity per plane.

AIR TRANSPORTATION ASSOCIATION (ATA) The trade and service organization of the U.S. scheduled airlines. ATA acts on behalf of the airlines to serve the government and public in activities ranging from improvement in air safety to planning for the airlines' role in national defense.

AIR WAYBILL The forwarding agreement or carrying agreement between shipper and air carrier and is issued only in nonnegotiable form. Contract of carriage between shipper and air carrier.

AIS Automatic Identification System.

AISLE SPACE Space in cargo sheds or warehouses found necessary by operating experience; also usually required by fire regulation.

AISLE WAYS   Spaces between stacks of cargo used for the segregation of shipments and for passageways.

ALCOHOL-TYPE FOAM   Firefighting foam effective against many water-soluble and some nonwater-soluble cargoes.

ALEE   To the leeward side; away from the direction of the wind.

ALERT DATA   The generic term for COSPAS-SARSAT 406 MHz and 121.5 MHz data received from distress beacons.

ALIMENTATION   A combination of processes contributing to the growth and maintenance of glaciers. Accumulation of snowfall is usually the principal factor but condensation of water vapor into its various solid forms and snow slides are important agents.

ALIVE   Alert.

ALKALI   Any substance such as ammonia, hydrated lime, or caustic soda containing a reactive oxide, which forms salts when reacted with acids. In chemical circles it is often spoken of as a base.

ALKALINE   Having the properties of an alkali.

ALKALINITY   The amount of free alkali in any substance.

ALKAYLATE   Product obtained in the alkylation process. Chemically, it is a complex molecule of the paraffinic series, formed by the introduction of an alkyl radical into an organic compound.

ALKYLATION   An important synthetic process for the manufacture of components for aviation gasoline.

ALKYL RADICAL   Any radical of the saturated paraffinic series, such as methyl, ethyl, propyl, etc., having the general formula CnH_{2n+1}.

ALL CARGO CARRIER   An air carrier that transports cargo only.

ALL CLEAR   A term used in towboating to announce the boat is ready to leave the barge or is clear of an obstruction.

ALL HANDS   The entire crew.

ALL IN   The total price to move a container from origin to destination, inclusive of all charges.

ALL IN THE WIND   All sails shaking. Usually occurs when the ship passes through wind from one tack to the other. Also occurs by bad steering when close hauled.

ALLISION   The act of a moving vessel striking or colliding against a stationary object.

ALL NIGHT IN   Having no night watches.

ALLOCATION   The process of assigning activities, costs, or facilities, e.g., space to a certain organizational unit.

ALL OTHER PERILS & MISFORTUNES   Phrase in cargo policy meaning perils of the same nature as those described specifically in the perils clause.

ALLOTMENT   A share of the capacity of a means of transport assigned to a certain party, i.e., a carrier or an agent, for the purpose of the booking of cargo for a specific voyage.

ALLOWABLE OVERDEPTH DREDGING The inability of dredge operators to precisely locate the suction intake of their dredge is recognized by allowing and paying for a certain amount of overdepth dredging.

ALL PURPOSE VESSEL A ship that can handle break-bulk cargo, neo-bulk cargo, unit loads, containers, roll on/roll off vehicles, cargo, and equipment.

ALL-RISK CLAUSE An insurance provision that all loss or damage to goods is insured except those self-caused.

ALL STANDING To bring to a sudden stop; to turn in with all one's clothing on; fully equipped.

ALL WATER A shipment made exclusively by water.

ALLUVIAL STREAM Any stream whose banks are subject to attack and allows channel meander. The stream has the property of depositing material such as soil, sand, or gravel and building up land in one area while washing it away in another.

ALOFT Above the upper deck; in the top or upper rigging; on the yards or overhead.

ALONGSHOREMEN The handlers of cargoes.

ALONGSIDE A phrase referring to the side of a ship. Goods delivered "alongside" are to be placed on the dock or barge within reach of the transport ship's tackle so that they can be loaded. When a vessel is next to a berth or another vessel side to side. In towing, when a tug is made up to a unit with the two vessels next to each other. Also known as "on the hip."

ALOOF To windward.

ALOW Low; near the decks; not aloft.

ALPHABET FLAGS The International Code: Alfa, Bravo, Charlie, Delta, Echo, Foxtrot, Golf, Hotel, India, Juliet, Kilo, Lima, Mike, November, Oscar, Papa, Quebec, Romeo, Sierra, Tango, Uniform, Victor, Whiskey, X-ray, Yankee, Zulu.

ALTERNATING CURRENT (AC) Current of electrons that moves first in one direction and then in the other.

ALTERNATING LIGHT A light showing different colors alternately.

ALTERNATIVE RATES Privilege to use the rate producing the lowest charge.

ALTERNATOR An AC generator.

ALTITUDE The height of a body above the horizon. The altitude measured with a sextant is the observed altitude. In the case of the sun, this needs correction for dip, semi-diameter, refraction, parallax, and index error in order to get the true altitude.

ALTITUDE AZIMUTH Method used to obtain the bearing of the sun or a star by solving the astronomical triangle for the azimuth, or angle at the zenith. The altitude gives zenith distance; the declination gives the polar distance; the latitude by dead reckoning gives the co-latitude.

ALTO-CUMULUS Clouds that are partially shaded white or grayish composed of flattened globular, small clouds in regular layers.

ALTO-STRATUS Thick gauzelike clouds, at middle altitudes, that look like fog. The stars, sun, and moon may be easily seen through these clouds.

ALUMINUM BASE GREASE Grease composed of a mineral oil thickened with aluminum soaps.

AM Amplitude modulation.

AMBIENT AIR SPACE The unconfined space occupied by the atmosphere above the geographical area of the district, which includes the air outside a facility or structure.

AMBIENT TEMPERATURE The temperature of a surrounding body. The ambient temperature of a container is the atmospheric temperature to which it is exposed.

AMBIGUITY A situation in which a loop antenna picks up a signal when either edge of the loop is aligned with the transmitter, causing a potential 180 degree error in the user's radio bearing.

AMC American Maritime Congress.

AMERICAN BUREAU OF SHIPPING (ABS) U.S. classification society that certifies seagoing vessels for compliance to standardized rules regarding construction and maintenance. A non-profit organization that prescribes rules for building and maintaining ships, machinery, and equipment. ABS publishes a record, similar to Lloyd's Register, that lists ships alphabetically and describes their type or build, machinery tonnage, age, ownership, home port, status, and dates of surveys required to ensure that the ship is in good material condition.

AMERICAN NATIONAL STANDARDS INSTITUTE (ANSI) ANSI was founded in 1918 to coordinate national standards in the U.S. ANSI is the central body responsible for the identification of a single consistent set of voluntary standards called American National Standards. ANSI provides an open forum for the identification of standards requirements, development of plans to meet those requirements, and agreement on standards. ANSI itself does not develop standards. In 1979 ANSI chartered a new committee, which in now known as Accredited Standards Committee (ASC) X12 Electronic Data Interchange to develop uniform standards for electronic interchange of business transactions.

AMERICAN TRUCKING ASSOCIATIONS, INC. A motor carrier industry association that is made up of thirteen sub-conferences representing various sectors of the motor carrier industry.

AMERICAN WATERWAY OPERATORS A domestic water carrier industry association representing barge operators on the inland waterways.

AMIDSHIPS In the vicinity of the middle portion of a ship, as distinguished from the ends. The term is used to convey the idea of general locality but not that of definite extent. As a rudder order, when the rudder is placed in the position of fore and aft.

AMMETER Meter used to measure current.

AMPERAGE The measure of the amount of current moving through a conductor.

AMPERE This unit measures electricity "on the move" or flowing in a circuit. Moving electricity is called current. It is this movement of electrical energy that does the work. It produces heat for your electric stove and light for your home. It produces music from your stereo and pictures and sounds from television. Scientists have agreed that if a certain quantity of electricity passes a given point in a circuit in one second, it will be called one ampere. Smaller units than an ampere are milliampere, which is one thousandth of an ampere or .001 ampere and microampere, which is one millionth of an ampere or .000001 ampere.

AMPERE HOUR Capacity rating measurement of batteries. A 100 ampere-hour battery will produce 100 amperes for one hour.

AMPHIPOD TOXICITY TESTS A laboratory testing procedure using a sensitive marine crustacean to determine the potential acute toxicity of proposed dredged material intended for ocean disposal. This testing is part of the U.S. EPA and Corps of Engineers national and regional testing protocol.

AMPLIFICATION Ability to control a relatively large force by a small force. In a vacuum tube, relatively small variation in grid input signal is accompanied by relatively large variation in output signal.

AMPLIFIER CIRCUIT A component that increases the oscillator's output within a transmitter.

AMPLIFIERS Power. Electron tube used to increase power output. Sometimes it's called a current amplifier. There are several different types of amplifiers:
AF Amplifier: Used to amplify audio frequencies.
IF Amplifier: Used to amplify intermediate frequencies.
RF Amplifier: Used to amplify radio frequencies.

AMPLITUDE The height of a wave along the y-axis from its baseline. Extreme range of varying quantity. The extent of an oscillation, swing, or excursion. The angle at the zenith between the prime vertical and the vertical circle passing through the observed body. Amplitude should be observed when the sun is about one apparent diameter above the horizon. The bearing is taken by compass and compared with the calculated or true amplitude. The difference is the error of the compass. The true amplitude is found by using Tables 27 and 28 of Bowditch or by adding the secant of the latitude and the sine of the declination, which gives the sine of the true amplitude.

AMPLITUDE MODULATION (AM) A common form of voice transmission system that uses frequencies in medium and high frequency bands. These systems can be broadcast over greater distances with lower power. Modulating a transmitter by varying strength of rf carrier at audio rate.

AMS The U.S. Customs' "Automated Manifest System."

AMTRAK   The National Railroad Passenger Corporation, a federally created corporation that operates most of the nation's intercity passenger rail service.

AMVER   *See* Automated Mutual Assistance Vessel Rescue System.

ANAEROBIC BIORECLAMATION   The process of transforming an organic contaminant into another less threatening form by using biological organism (microbes) in a nonoxygenated environment.

ANADROMOUS   Pertaining to fish that ascend freshwater rivers and streams from the sea to spawn.

ANCHOR   A heavy steel device designed to secure the ship to the bottom for mooring purposes. A heavy iron or steel implement attached to a vessel by means of a rope or chain cable for holding it at rest in the water. When an anchor is lowered to the bottom, the drag on the cable causes one or more of the prongs, called flukes, to sink into or engage the ground, which provides holding power. There are many types of anchors. The largest or heaviest anchor on a vessel is called a street anchor. The parts of an anchor are: shank, arms, flukes, bill or pea, stock and ring. The "Merchant Shipping Acts" require that every anchor must be marked in two places with the name or initials of the maker and must have a serial or progressive number.

ANCHOR, BOWER   The large anchors carried in the bow of a vessel. Three are usually carried, two (the main bowers) in the hawse pipes, and a third (spare) lashed on deck or elsewhere about the vessel for use in the event either of the main bowers is lost.

ANCHOR, KEDGE   A small anchor used for warping or kedging. It is usually planted from a small boat, the vessel being hauled up toward it. The weight varies, being usually from 900 to 1,200 pounds.

ANCHOR, SEA   This is not a true anchor, as it does not sink to the bottom. It is a conical-shaped canvas bag required by the Steamboat Inspection Service to be carried in each lifeboat. When placed overboard it serves a double purpose in keeping the boat head-on into the sea and in spreading a vegetable or animal oil from a container placed inside the bag. It is sometimes called an oil spreader.

ANCHOR BAR   A bar used in prying the anchor or working the anchor chain.

ANCHOR CHAIN   Heavy stud linked chain secured to an anchor for mooring or anchoring purposes.

ANCHOR DECK   A very short forecastle for the stowing of an anchor.

ANCHOR FLAGS   Small red, green, and numeral flags used when anchoring. A red or green flag used on the bridge indicates which anchor is to be let go; the numeral flag used forward to indicate to the bridge the number of shackles that are out.

ANCHOR HOY   A lighter equipped with a derrick for the handling of heavy anchors.

ANCHOR ICE (OR BOTTOM ICE)   Ice formed on the bed of a river or shallow sea, irrespective of its nature of formation.

17

ANCHOR LIGHTS   The riding lights required to be carried by vessels at anchor.

ANCHOR POSITION   Place where a specific vessel is anchored or is to anchor.

ANCHOR SHACKLE   Used between chain and anchor and all towing connections.

ANCHOR WATCH   The detail on deck at night when at anchor to safeguard the vessel.

ANCHOR WINDLASS   A large piece of machinery designed to control the anchor, involving hydraulics, steam, or electrical power.

ANCHORAGE   An area identified for safe anchoring. A designated area, usually adjacent to the navigation channel, for temporary mooring of vessels. Site where a ship drops anchor.

ANCHOR'S AWEIGH   Said of the anchor when clear of the bottom.

ANCILLARY CHARGES   Charges that may be assessed against goods in addition to the monthly storage and handling charges.

ANCILLARY GUARANTEE   Type of guarantee where the guarantor joins with one of the parties to the contract and agrees to fulfill that party's obligations if necessary, effectively co-signing the contract. As opposed to an independent or demand guarantee, under an ancillary guarantee the guarantor also acquires rights under the contract and may resort to terms in the contract to dispute claims against the guarantee. Also called a "contract guarantee." Although banks in the Untied States are generally prohibited by law from issuing ancillary guarantees, banks in other countries are not. U.S. banks instead issue demand guarantees or standby letters of credit.

AN EASY DISTANCE OFF   To maintain a reasonably close and comfortable distance off the bank, yet, allow ample room for maneuverability. This is a relative term depending upon size of stream and size of tow. The term "easy" pertains more to ease of mind than to closeness of distance and indicates that this portion of the river has no tight spots.

ANESTHESIA   A total loss of feeling and consciousness or the loss of control of feeling over a limited area of skin.

ANESTHETICS   Chemicals that produce anesthesia.

ANGLE   Same as angle bar.

ANGLE BAR   A bar of angle-shaped section used as a stiffener and for attachment of one plate or shape to another.

ANGLE BULB   A structural shape having a bulb on one flange of the angle, used as a frame, beam, or stiffener.

ANGLE CLIP   A short piece of angle bar used for attachment to connect various parts of the structure such as floor or bracket plates to vertical keel or longitudinals. May be welded or riveted. Also called lug, lug piece, or angle lug.

ANGLE COLLAR   A collar or band made of one or more pieces of angle bar and fitted tightly around a pipe, trunk, frame, longitudinal, or stiffener intersection or projecting through a bulkhead or deck for the purposes of making a watertight or oil tight joint. *See* Stapling.

ANGLED BOW RAMP Ramp that extends from aperture in bow at an angle to the centerline of a RO/RO vessel.

ANGLED STERN RAMP A ramp that extends from the stern of a RO/RO vessel at an angle to the centerline of the vessel. Fixed stern ramps are customarily located on the starboard side.

ANHYDROUS Destitute of water, especially water of crystallization.

ANILINE POINT The minimum temperature at which equal volumes of dry, freshly distilled aniline and petroleum products are completely miscible.

ANNEAL To heat a metal and to cool it in such a fashion as to toughen and soften it. Brass or copper is annealed by heating to a cherry red and dipping suddenly into water while hot. Iron or steel is slowly cooled from the heated condition to anneal. Also done to alter ductility, toughness, and electrical, magnetic, or other physical properties. Done to relieve stress.

ANNEX A detailed segment of an operating plan based upon the summary.

ANOXEMIA A condition of deficient oxygen in the blood.

ANOXIA A deficiency of oxygen in the tissues of the body.

ANPRM Advanced Notice of Proposed Rulemaking.

ANSI *See* American National Standards Institute.

ANTE Before.

ANTENNA Device for radiating or receiving radio waves. A conductor common to both transmitters and receivers that converts high-frequency electrical current into radio waves or vice versa.

ANTENNA GAIN The ratio of output voltage or signal strength to input voltage or signal strength.

ANTENNA SYSTEM An assembly consisting of the antenna as commonly understood, the feed line to the transmitter and receiver, and any coupling devices for transferring power from the transmitter to the feed line.

ANTENNA TUNER A device that matches the antenna to the transmitted frequency by varying the capacitance and resistance that the signal will encounter as it moves to the antenna.

ANTHAM Antwerp-Hamburg Range.

ANTI Against.

ANTICLINE Folds of earth layers that are bent in such a fashion that they are convex upward.

ANTICOLLISION LOOP A logical progression of analysis that aids a mariner in determining the best actions to avoid collision.

ANTIDUMPING CLAUSE A special tariff imposed to discourage the sale of foreign goods in the United States at prices below what they sell for in the home market.

ANTIGLARE SAFETY COATING A low-gloss coating formulated to eliminate glare for safety purposes on interior surfaces of a vehicle, as specified under the U.S. Department of Transportation Motor Vehicle Safety Standards.

ANTIKNOCK   Resistance to detonation or "pinging" of spark-ignited engines.

ANTIKNOCK AGENTS   Chemical compounds that, when added in small amounts to the fuel charge of an internal-combustion engine, have the property of suppressing or at least of strongly depressing knocking. The principal antiknock agent, which has been developed for use in fuels, is tetraethyl lead.

ANTINOSEDIVE LEG   A support installed at the front end of a container chassis used to support that end during loading operations when the initial weight of the cargo is concentrated at the front and beyond the fulcrum point of balance.

ANTIOXIDANTS   Chemicals added to gasoline, lubricating oils, waxes, and other products to inhibit oxidation.

ANTIROLLING DEVICES   These include the bilge keel, or rolling chocks, anti-rolling tanks, gyrostabilizer, and stabilizing fins.

ANTITRANSMIT-RECEIVE (ATR) TUBE   A component used to block the passage of echoes to the radar transmitter.

ANTITRUST IMMUNITY   The exemption by law of an organization or firm from prosecution under part or all of the U.S. antitrust laws.

ANY-QUANTITY (AQ)   Usually refers to a rating that applies to an article regardless of weight but in any quantity.

AP   After Perpendicular.

APERTURE   The space provided between rudderpost and propeller post for the propeller.

API   American Petroleum Institute.

API GRAVITY   An arbitrary scale for measuring the density of liquid petroleum products. The standards and methodology are established by the American Petroleum Institute.

APPAREL   A vessel's outfit, such as rigging, anchor, and lifeboats. Term used in distribution/transport of clothing for a single piece of clothing, a garment.

APPARENT GOOD ORDER   Statement denoting that goods are free from damage and in good condition, as far as their external appearance is concerned.

APPENDAGES   Collectively small portions of a vessel projecting beyond its main outline, as shown by cross-sections and water-sections. The word applies to the following parts of the stern and stern post: the keel below its shell line; below its shell line, the rolling keel or fin, the rudder, rudder post, screw, bilge, keelstruts, bossing, and skeg. (Another version:) Relatively small portions of a vessel extending beyond its main outline as shown by transverse and water plane sections, including such items as shafting, struts, bossings, docking and bilge keels, propellers, rudder, and any other feature, extraneous to the hull and generally immersed.

APPLICATION (INS) A signed statement by a prospective insured client who becomes a part of the insurance contract.

APPLICATION AREA Any area where a coating is applied, including but not limited to application by dipping, rolling, spraying, or flowcoating techniques.

APPLICATION SERVICE PROVIDER (ASP) An online outsourcer or hosting service for applications, letting net market makers rent instead of buy applications and services such as auctions, exchanges and catalog aggregation. Many application vendors are moving to a hosting model, but ASPs are often application-agnostic, plugging a feature of one application into a marketplace when appropriate and using another feature from another vendor elsewhere.

APPRAISAL (INS) A survey of property made for determining its insurable value or the amount of loss sustained.

APPRAISEMENT Determination of the dutiable value of imported merchandise by a Customs official who follows procedures outlined in its country's tariff, such as the U.S. Tariff Act of 1930.

APPRAISER'S STORES The warehouse or public stores to which samples of imported goods are taken to be inspected, analyzed, weighted, etc., by examiners or appraisers. Government-owned warehouse, where examiners (appraisers) inspect and survey designated goods imported from abroad.

APPROVAL DOCUMENTS SENT ON Treatment of letter of credit documents wherein the negotiating bank does not certify that the documents meet the requirements of the L/C, but rather forwards the documents to the issuing bank with a request that it examine the documents, obtain waiver of any discrepancies, and pay, or, in the case of time drafts, accept the drafts, if drawn on them, or authorize acceptance by the drawee bank.

APPROVED Approved by the U.S. Coast Guard Commandant unless otherwise stated.

APPROVED CONTINUOUS EXAMINATION PROGRAM (ACEP) An agreement between the owners of the equipment and the responsible governmental body to allow continuous examination of the equipment (e.g., containers).

APPROVED EQUIPMENT Equipment of a design that has been tested and approved by an appropriate authority such as a government department or classification society. Such authority should have certified the particular equipment as safe for use in a specified hazardous atmosphere.

APRON The part of the pier or quay that is between the enclosed structure and the edge upon which cargo is unloaded. A reinforcing timber bolted to the after side of the stem. Also, the top surface of a pier or dock; the area along the waterfront edge of a wharf or pier; the extensive paved part of an airport adjacent to the terminal or hangers.

APRON TRACK Railroad track along the apron of a wharf or pier designed for direct transfer of cargo from rail to ship or ship to rail.

APS Arrival Pilot Station.

AQUATIC BORROW PIT A disposal site located offshore in a manmade pit; this type of disposal site is intended for containment of material.

AQUATIC SHORELINE A diked disposal site (for dredged material) located in coastal water but attached to shore.

AQUATIC SUBAQUEOUS A (dredged material) disposal site located below the intertidal zone, usually offshore.

ARAG Amsterdam-Rotterdam-Antwerp-Ghent Range.

ARBITRAGE The practice of exchanging the currency of one country from that of another or a series of countries to gain an advantage from the differences in exchange rates.

ARBITRARY A stated amount over a fixed rate to one point to make a rate to another point.

ARBITRATION An arrangement whereby two parties in dispute refer to one or more impartial persons for settlement, with formal agreement to accept the decision given.

ARBITRATION CLAUSE A clause in a sales contract outlining the method under which disputes will be settled.

ARBOR The principal axis member, or spindle, of a machine by which a motion of revolution is transmitted.

ARCH LINE Line used to scribe an arch, such as a radius line, such as templates.

ARCHED ICEBERG An iceberg eroded in such a manner that a large opening at the waterline extends horizontally through the iceberg forming an arch.

ARCHING Sometimes used in lieu of "hogging."

ARC OF VISIBILITY The portion of the horizon over which a lighted aid to navigation is visible from seaward.

ARCTIC PACK (OR POLAR ICE) Thickest and heaviest form of sea ice; more than one year old.

ARCTIC WHITEOUT A peculiar condition affecting visibility caused by a snow cover obliterating all landmarks and accompanied by an overcast sky or cirrostratus and/or altostratus clouds. No shadows are cast and the picture is one of an unrelieved expanse of white. Earth and sky blend so that the horizon is not distinguishable. This condition is extremely dangerous to low-flying aircraft, particularly those attempting to land.

AREA OFF HIRE SUBLEASE Geographical area where a subleased container becomes off hire.

AREA OF HIRE LEASE Geographical area where a leased container becomes off hire.

AREA OF REPAIR Geographical area where a container is under repair

AREA OF SECTIONS The area of any cross section of the immersed portion of a vessel, the cross section being taken at right angles to the fore and aft centerline of the vessel.

AREAS OF CRITICAL CONCERN (ACECS)   Areas within a jurisdiction that have been designated for special protection or management because of their importance; examples include coastal beaches, estuaries, barrier beach systems, salt marshes, shellfish concentration areas, and habitat for threatened, rare, or endangered species.

ARMATURE   Revolving part in a generator or motor. Vibrating or moving part of a relay or buzzer.

ARMY CORPS OF ENGINEERS   A federal agency responsible for the construction and maintenance of waterways.

AROMATIC HYDROCARBONS   Hydrocarbons derived from or characterized by the presence of the benzene ring. Many of this large class of cyclic and polycyclic organic compounds are odorous.

AROMATIZATION   Rearrangement of saturated or unsaturated straight-chain hydrocarbons, (provided they contain the necessary number of carbon atoms) into ring structures, with subsequent dehydrogenation to form aromatic hydrocarbons of excellent antiknock characteristics or dehydrogenation of naphthenes to form aromatics.

ARPA   Automatic Radar Plotting Aid.

ARRIVAL NOTICE   A notification by carrier of ship's arrival to the consignee, the "Notify Party," and when applicable, the "Also Notify Party." These parties in interest are listed in blocks 3, 4, and 10, respectively, of the bill of lading.

ARRIVAL POST   A signboard placed approximately ½ mile below the lock on the upstream and the downstream side to inform the pilot of the towboat that he has arrived at the lock and his preference is rated upon his first arrival either below or above. This term is falling into disuse because the advent of radio communications between towboats and the lock.

ARTICLES DANGEREUX DE ROUTE (ADR)   A European agreement concerning the international carriage of dangerous goods by road.

ARTICLES OF AGREEMENT   The document containing all particulars relating to the terms of agreement between the master of the vessel and the crew. Sometimes called ship's articles, shipping articles.

ARTICULATED BEACON   A lighted or unlighted floating aid to navigation consisting of a pipe attached directly to a sinker.

ARTICULATED CAR   A car consisting of two or more full-sized units free to swivel, the portions being carried on one common center truck.

ARTIFICIAL HARBOR   One in which shelter or depth or both have been provided by man.

ARTIFICIAL INTELLIGENCE (AI)   Sophisticated use of the computer on which it is programmed to "think" as a trained, skilled human in specific situations.

ARTIFICIAL REEFS   A man-made structure located in the ocean for the purpose of habitat enhancement.

A/S   After Sight. Term of sale. Payment due upon approval.

ASBA American Shipbrokers Association.

ASBESTOS All asbestiform varieties of the mineral family called silicates including: serpentinite (chrysotile), riebeckite (crocidolite), cuming-tonite-grunerite (atmosite), tremolite-actinolite, and anthophyllite.

ASBESTOS-CONTAINING MATERIAL Friable asbestos and any material containing 1% or more asbestos by weight. This term includes but is not limited to sprayed-on and troweled-on materials applied to ceilings, walls, and other surfaces, insulation on pipes, boilers, tanks, ducts, and other equipment, structural members, tiles, shingles, or asbestos-containing paper.

ASBESTOS-CONTAINING WASTE MATERIAL Any friable asbestos-containing material removed during a demolition/renovation project and anything contaminated in the course of a demolition/renovation project including asbestos waste from control devices, bags or containers that previously contained asbestos, contaminated clothing, materials used to enclose the work area during the demolition/renovation operation, and demolition/renovation debris.

ASC X12 American Standards Committee X12 responsible for developing EDI standards for the United States.

ASH Inorganic residue remaining after ignition of combustible substances, determined by definite prescribed methods.

ASH CONTENT An expression of the inorganic matter in a combustible material. It is determined by completely burning the substance and weighing the residue.

ASHORE On the shore.

ASN *See* Advanced Shipment Notice.

ASP *See* Application Service Provider.

ASPECT The angle at which radar energy hits a radar contact.

ASPF Additional Secondary Phase Factor.

ASPHALT Brown-to-black solid or semisolid bituminous substance occurring in nature or obtained as a residue from cracked stocks or from the distillation of certain crude petroleums. It consists chiefly of a mixture of comparatively nonvolatile hydrocarbons and their derivatives (e.g., sulfur compounds), but usually contains some mineral matter.

ASPHYXIA The condition arising when the blood is deprived of an adequate supply of oxygen, so that loss of consciousness or death may follow.

ASPHYXIANT A gas or vapor that when inhaled leads to asphyxia.

ASPW Any Safe Port in the World.

ASRS *See* Automated Storage & Retrieval System.

ASSAILING THIEVES Forcible taking of property but not sneak thievery.

ASSEMBLE To put together sections of the ship's structure on the skids, in advance of erection on the ways.

ASSEMBLY The stage of production in which components are put together into an end product appropriate to the process concerned.

ASSESSMENT An estimate or appraisal of the importance, size, capacity, or value of something.

ASSET A property of tangible value.

ASSHOLE A twist or knot in wire rope that will damage the lay when a strain is applied.

ASSIGNED POSITION The latitude and longitude position for an aid to navigation.

ASSIGNMENT A term commonly used in connection with a bill of lading. It involves the transfer of rights, title, and interest in order to assign goods by endorsing the bill of lading. Legal transfer of title, property, or right.

ASSIGNMENT OF PROCEEDS Legal mechanism by which the beneficiary of a letter of credit may pledge the proceeds of future drawings to a third party. Assigning proceeds involves giving the letter of credit to a bank, which will hold the L/C until drawn upon, along with irrevocable instructions to the bank to disburse proceeds, when generated, in a specified way, e.g., "pay 75% of each drawing to XYZ Company." The bank will acknowledge the assignment to the assignee but has no obligation actually to pay any funds to the assignee unless the beneficiary draws upon the L/C and payment is received from the issuing or confirming bank. An assignment of proceeds is not an assignment or transfer of the letter of credit and the assignee acquires no rights to perform under the L/C in order to generate funds.

ASSIST Technical instructions for manufacture or materials, parts, tools, dies, molds, merchandise consumed in the products, etc., supplied directly or indirectly, and free of charge or at a reduced cost by the buyer for use in connection with the production or the sale of export to the United States.

ASSISTANT ENGINEER A licensed member of the engine department, where third is the lowest, and first is the highest. First a/e are usually in charge of machinery maintenance; second a/e is in charge of fuel systems, and third a/e is in charge of electrical systems. The first a/e should be involved in all fire parties due to his or her comprehensive knowledge of shipboard systems.

ASSOCIATION OF AMERICAN RAILROADS A railroad industry association that represents the larger U.S. railroads.

ASSUMED LIABILITY (INS) Liability that would not rest upon a person except that he has accepted responsibility by contract, expressed or implied. This is also known as contractual liability.

ASTERN Signifying position, in the rear of or abaft the stern; as regards motion, the opposite of going ahead; backwards. The bearing of an object 180 degrees from ahead. Move in a reverse direction.

When moving toward the after end of a ship, or when observing something behind the ship.

ASTM American Society for Testing Materials.

ASTM DISTILLATION A distillation test made on such products as gasoline and kerosene to determine the initial and final boiling points and the boiling range.

ASTRAY Refers to cargo that becomes separated from the balance of the freight while in transit.

ATA American Trucking Association.

ATA CARNET An international customs document that is recognized as an internationally valid guarantee. It may be used in lieu of national customs documents and as security for import duties and taxes to cover the temporary admission of goods.

AT ANCHOR Any vessel attached to the ground through the use of an anchor or ground tackle.

ATD Actual Time of Departure.

ATDNSHINC Any Time Day or Night Sundays and Holidays Included.

ATFI Automated Tariff Filing Information System.

ATHWART Across, from side to side, transverse, across the line of a vessel's course.

ATHWARTSHIP Moving from side to side, at right angles to the fore and aft centerline of the ship. Refers to anything constructed, lying, or running at right angles to a vessel's fore and aft line.

ATMOSPHERE The mass of air surrounding the earth. The pressure of the air at sea level is used as a unit of measure.

ATMOSPHERIC NOISE Interference usually caused by the buildup of static electrical charges in the atmosphere. This commonly is caused by thunderstorms associated with a passage of a cold front.

ATMOSPHERIC PRESSURE The pressure of air exerted equally in all directions. The standard pressure is that at sea level under which a mercury barometer stands at 760 mm.

ATOMIZATION CHARACTERISTICS The ability of an oil to be broken up into a fine spray by some mechanical means.

ATR TUBE Antitransmit-Receive tube.

AT SEA In marine insurance this phrase applies to a ship that is free from its moorings and ready to sail.

AT SIGHT A payment term meaning that a negotiable instrument is to be paid upon presentation or demand.

ATTAINMENT AREA Any area determined by the administrator as one in which the ambient air concentration for a criteria pollutant does not exceed a primary or a secondary National Ambient Air Quality Standard.

ATTENUATION The decrease of signal strength due to the medium through which it passes.

ATTENUATOR Decrease in amplitude or intensity.

ATUTC Actual Times Used To Count.

AUCTIONS Let multiple buyers bid competitively for products from individual suppliers. Suitable for hard-to-move goods such as used capital equipment (forklifts) and surplus or excess inventory. Prices only move up, but buyers can buy below list prices while sellers sell for more than a liquidator pays. Auctions are becoming a feature of many net markets, but some use auctions as their primary market mechanism. Examples: Ad Auction, TradeOut.com (used equipment).

AUDIO AMPLIFIER The final-stage amplifier within a receiver for communications equipment. It generates input to a speaker, finally converting electrical energy into acoustic energy or sound.

AUDIO FREQUENCY (AF) The range of frequency in the electromagnetic spectrum detected by normal human hearing (15 to 15,000 hertz).

AUDIT The routine of inspecting to ensure that all functions adhere to a stated standard.

AUDIT TRAIL Various records and management controls that document the activity of a facility.

AUGUST EFFECT A substantial reduction in the amount of dissolved oxygen that occurs in certain shallow estuaries and harbors during the late summer. This change is felt to cause a corresponding depression in biological activity in the affected area.

AURAL NULL INDICATOR A type of receiver, similar to the portable recreational boat receiver, that depends on the ability of the user to listen for and, sometimes with visual assistance, locate the null of a transmitted signal to determine direction.

AUTHENTICATION Proof by means of a signature or otherwise that a certain document or certain data is of undisputed origin and genuine.

AUTHORITY TO PAY An advice from the buyer's bank to the seller's bank authorizing the seller's bank to pay the seller's draft up to a given amount. The seller has no protection against cancellation or modification of the instrument until the issuing bank makes the payment on the draft drawn on it.

AUTHORITY TO PURCHASE Similar to above except the seller's drafts are drawn directly on the buyer. The buyer's bank purchases them with or without recourse to the drawer.

AUTHORIZATION The commission to a certain person or body to act on behalf of another person or body. The person or body can be authorized, e.g., to issue Bills of Lading or to collect freight.

AUTO ACQUIRE ALARM An audible and visual warning that a contact has been acquired.

AUTO DRIFT A function that allows the operator to acquire a contact that is known to be stationary, such as a lighthouse, beacon, or small island.

AUTO-IGNITION TEMPERATURE The lowest temperature to which a solid, liquid, or gas must be raised to cause self-sustained combustion.

AUTOMATED BROKER INTERFACE (ABI) Part of U.S. Customs' Automated Commercial System, permits transmission of data pertaining to merchandise being imported into U.S. qualified participants include brokers, importers, carriers, port authorities, and independent data processing companies.

AUTOMATED CLEARINGHOUSE (ACH) Automated Clearinghouse is a feature of the Automated Broker Interface combining elements of bank lock box arrangements with electronic funds transfer services to replace cash or check for payment of estimated duties, taxes, and fees on imported merchandise.

AUTOMATED GUIDED VEHICLE SYSTEM A computer-controlled materials handling system consisting of small vehicles (carts) that move along a guideway.

AUTOMATED MUTUAL ASSISTANCE VESSEL RESCUE SYSTEM (AMVER) An international search-and-rescue system operated by the U.S. Coast Guard. Through international cooperation, ships and other vessels on the high seas report their positions and route of travel so that in case of emergency, they may be called upon to render aid to another vessel in distress.

AUTOMATED STORAGE & RETRIEVAL SYSTEM An automated, mechanized system for moving merchandise into storage locations and retrieving it when needed.

AUTOMATIC An activity that is performed wholly by a machine. Used only in connection with ARPA performance standards.

AUTOMATIC ACQUISITION A function by which an ARPA tracker is sensitized to window, or look for, hits either over the whole display or in particular areas.

AUTOMATIC DIRECTIONAL FINDER (ADF) A receiver that searches for the direction of a carrier wave and then locks onto the broadcaster signal.

AUTOMATIC GEAR An arrangement on a towing winch that allows the tow cable to pay out and heave in automatically when set at certain tensions.

AUTOMATIC IDENTIFICATION A means of identifying an item, e.g., a product, parcel, or transport unit by a machine (device) entering the data automatically into a computer. The most widely used technology at present is bar code; others include radio frequency, magnetic stripes, and optical character recognition.

AUTOMATIC PILOT An instrument designed to control automatically a vessel's steering gear so that it follows a pre-determined track through the water.

AUTOMATIC REPEAT REQUEST (ARQ) A mode used with narrow band direct printing (NBDP) used to detect errors and make corrections. In the ARQ mode, an acknowledgement signal or repeat request is provided by the receiving station for each block of data that is transmitted.

AUTOMATIC STEERING SYSTEM A system that uses input from the master gyrocompass through the repeater system to automatically keep the vessel on the course set.

AUTOMOBILE A motor vehicle capable of carrying no more than 12 passengers.

AUTOMOTIVE EXTERIOR FLEXIBLE PARTS Flexible plastic parts used in the manufacture or repair of exterior components of automobiles.

AUTOMOTIVE EXTERIOR RIGID (NONFLEXIBLE) PARTS Rigid plastic parts used in the manufacture or repair of exterior components of automobiles.

AUTOMOTIVE INTERIOR PARTS Plastic parts used in the manufacture or repair of interior components of automobiles.

AUTOMOTIVE REFINISHING FACILITY Any facility at which the interior or exterior bodies of automobiles, motorcycles, light/medium-duty trucks, or vans are painted. Refinishing of aftermarket vehicles and new vehicles damaged in transit before their initial sale are included under this definition.

AUTOMOTIVE SURFACE COATING The coating at automobile assembly plants of bodies and front-end sheet metal (hood and fenders) of passenger cars capable of seating 12 or fewer passengers or light-duty vehicles rated at 8,500 pounds gross weight or less or derivatives of such vehicles.

AUXILIARIES Various winches, pumps, motors, and other small engines required on a ship, as distinguished from main propulsive machinery (boilers and engines on a steam installation).

AUXILIARY LOCK A smaller secondary lock adjacent to the main lock.

AVAL Guarantee added by a bank to an accepted time draft by endorsing the front of the draft "per aval." The avalizing bank becomes obligated to pay the draft at maturity if the drawee/acceptor fails to do so.

AVALANCHE Masses of snow detached from great heights in the mountains and acquiring enormous bulk by fresh accumulations as they descend. When they fall into the valleys below, they often cause great destruction.

AVALIZED DRAFT Trade acceptance to which an aval has been added.

AVAST An order to stop or cease hauling.

AVERAGE Insurance term for partial loss or damage.

AVERAGE ADJUSTER An adjuster of marine losses. In general average affairs average adjusters are entrusted with the task of apportioning the loss and expenditure over the parties interested in the maritime venture and to determine which expenses are to be regarded as average or general average.

AVERAGE AGREEMENT Document signed by cargo owners by terms of which they agree to pay any general average contribution properly due so that cargo may be released after a general average loss has occurred.

AVERAGE CLAUSE (INS) A clause in a marine insurance policy whereby partial losses are subject to special conditions (e.g., a franchise or deductible is to be applied to claims).

AVERAGE CLAUSES Clauses in cargo policy that determine the amount of particular average loss recovery.

AVERAGE COST Total cost, fixed plus variable, divided by total output.

AVERAGE IRRESPECTIVE OF PERCENTAGE Broadest "with average" clause. Losses by insured perils are paid regardless of percentage.

AVERAGE SAMPLES A sample so taken as to contain parts from all sections of a container or pipe, in proportion to the volume of each part.

AVOIRDUPOIS POUND Same as 0.4535924277 kilograms.

AWB Airway Bill: Document made out by or on behalf of the carrier confirming receipt of goods by carrier and evidencing contract between shipper and carrier for the carriage of goods.

AWG American Wire Gauge used in sizing wire by numbers.

AWKWARD CARGO Cargo of irregular size that is either containerized or uncontainerized. It requires prior approval, depending on the circumstances, before confirmation of booking.

AWNING A canvas canopy secured over the ship's deck as a protection from the weather.

AWWL Always Within institute Warranties Limits (insurance purpose).

AYE AYE, SIR The reply to an officer's order signifying that it is understood and will be obeyed.

AZIMUTH STABILIZATION Own ship's compass information is fed to the display so that echoes of targets on the display will not be caused to smear by changes of own ship's heading. Used only in connection with ARPA performance standards.

Course-up: An intended course can be set to the line connecting the center with the top of the display.

Head-up: The line connecting the center with the top of the display is own ship heading.

North-up: The line connecting the center with the top of this display is north.

AZOIC PARENT MATERIAL Sediment, rock, or other material that has been in place since geologic time and presently supports no life.

B

B   Symbol for center of buoyancy.

B2B   Business to Business.

B/A   Banker's Acceptance.

BACK BAR   Used to support the pieces of angle iron but on the opposite side to the bosom bar.

BACKBOARD   A portable back support nicely designed and fitted on the after side of the stern thwart in a small motor or rowboat.

BACKBONE   The rope stitched to the back of the middle of an awning and to which the crow's foot is spliced; a central high-speed network that connects smaller, independent networks. The NSFnet is an example.

BACK CHUTE   This term designates an old channel no longer used that may be located behind an island adjacent to the present navigable channel. It is sometimes used during high-water stages to navigate without having to buck the strong currents in the main channel.

BACK END SYSTEMS   Legacy enterprise systems that handle order processing, inventory, and receivables management for both buyers and suppliers. To deploy a digital trading platform, companies must often integrate new technologies with these older systems, which can include mainframe or ERP applications.

BACK 'ER DOWN   Term meaning to stop headway of a tow.

BACK FREIGHT   The owners of a ship are entitled to payment as freight for merchandise returned through the fault of either the consignees or the consignors. Such payment, which is over and above the normal freight, is called back freight.

BACKHAUL   To haul a shipment back over part of a route that it has already traveled; a marine transportation carrier's return movement of cargo, usually opposite from the direction of its primary cargo distribution.

BACKING   Counterclockwise change in wind direction (e.g., change in direction from north to northwest to west; east to northeast to north, etc.)

BACKING ANGLE   A short piece of angle for reinforcing the butt joint or splice of two angles, placed behind the angles joined.

BACKING LINE   Term used on a tow to keep barges from running ahead.

BACKING RUDDERS   *See* Flanking Rudder.

BACKLANDS   Storage area of a marine terminal that is distant from the wharf area.

BACK LETTER   Seller or Shipper issues a "Letter of Indemnity" in favor of the carrier in exchange for a clean bill of lading. Back letters are drawn up in addition to a contract in order to lay down rights and/or obligations between both contracting parties, which, for some reason cannot be included in the original contract. This expression is sometimes used for letters of indemnity, which are drawn up if the condition of the goods loaded gives rise to remarks and, nevertheless, the shipper insists upon receiving clean Bills of Lading. Letters of indemnity are only allowed in very exceptional circumstances.

BACKLOG   The quantity of goods still to be delivered, received, produced, issued, etc., for which the planned or agreed date has expired. The total number of customer orders that have been received but not yet been shipped.

BACK ORDER   Items ordered that aren't shipped due to stockout. Scheduled for shipment as available.

BACK SCHEDULING   A method of obtaining a production schedule by working backwards from the required due date, in order to predict the latest start date to meet that due date.

BACKSTAY   A wire rope or cable that serves as a support to prevent the mast going forward and also contributes to its lateral support, thereby assisting the shrouds. A backstay extends from the upper part of the mast to the ship's side at some distance abaft the mast. They serve as additional supports to prevent the masts going forward and also contribute to the lateral support, thereby assisting the shrouds.

BACK TO BACK LETTERS OF CREDIT   Two letters of credit with identical documentary requirements, except for a difference in the price of the merchandise as shown by the invoice and draft.

BACK UP   To kill headway; to flank or twist tow at foot of crossing or head of bend.

BACKUP   Making a duplicate copy of a computer file or a program on a disk or cassette so that the material will not be lost if the original is destroyed; a spare copy.

BACKUP AREA   That portion of a marine terminal consisting of paved open storage area at the inshore or upland side of a pier or wharf terminal facility.

BACKWATER   Term used for water backed up tributary stream.

BACKWATER CURVE   The term applied to the profile of the water surface above a dam or other obstruction in a channel. This may also be stated as the effect on the natural water surface profile of either of two confluent streams upstream from their confluence due to flow conditions in the other stream.

BAF   Bunker Adjustment Factor. Used to compensate steamship lines for fluctuating fuel costs. Sometimes called Fuel Adjustment Factor or FAF.

BAFFLE   A plate or structure placed in the line of flow of fluids or gases to divert the flow in order to obtain greater contact with heating or cooling surfaces.

BAGGED CARGO   Various kinds of commodities usually packed in sacks or in bags, such as sugar, cement, milk powder, onion, grain, flour, etc.

BAI CERTIFICATE   Certificate issued by the U.S. Bureau of Animal Industry, attesting to a careful veterinary inspection of animals and the absence of communicable disease or exposure.

BAIL To throw water out of a boat. Also, a metal handle.

BAILEE (INS) A person or concern having possession of property committed in trust from the owner.

BAILEE'S CUSTOMER POLICY (INS) A policy providing for loss or damages to property of bailee's customers, payable either to bailees for their account or direct to customers.

BAILMENT Delivery of goods in trust from one party to another (the Bailee) for a purpose, such as storage, in the expectation that the goods will be returned when the purpose is accomplished. Fixing responsibility for safekeeping.

BALANCE OF PAYMENTS A statement that indicates a country's foreign economic transactions over a specified time.

BALANCED RUDDER A rudder with its axis between the forward and after edge.

BALE A large compressed, bound, and often wrapped bundle of a commodity, such as cotton or hay.

BALE CAPACITY Cubic capacity of a vessel's hold to carry packaged dry cargo such as baled or pallets.

BALE CLAMP *See* Cotton Squeezer.

BALE CUBIC The space available for cargo measured in cubic feet to the inside of the cargo battens, on the frames, and to the underside of the beams.

BALE CUBIC CAPACITY Space available for loading cargo, measured in cubic feet, to the inside of the cargo battens, on the frames, and to the underside of the deck beams; measurement of a vessel's capacity for general cargo.

BALE SPACE *See* Bale Capacity.

BALK A piece of timber from 4" to 10" square, used to support a ship in dry dock; shoring timbers for the cradle.

BALLAST Any weight, liquid, or solid added to a ship to ensure stability. Any weight or weights (usually saltwater) used to keep the ship from becoming top-heavy or to increase its draught or trim. Any weight carried solely for the purpose of making the vessel more seaworthy. Ballast may be clean or dirty, depending on whether it is contaminated with petroleum products. Ballast may be either portable or fixed, depending upon the condition of the ship. Fixed or permanent ballast in the form of sand, concrete, lead, scrap, or pig iron is usually fitted to overcome an inherent defect in stability or trim due to faulty design or changed character of service. Portable ballast, usually in the form of water, pumped into or out of the bottom, peak, or wing ballast tanks, is used to overcome a temporary defect in stability or trim due to faulty loading, damage, etc., and to submerge submarines.

BALLAST BONUS Compensation for a ballast voyage.

BALLAST MOVEMENTS A voyage or voyage leg made without any paying cargo in a vessel's tanks. To maintain proper stability, trim, or draft, seawater is usually carried during such movements.

BALLAST TANK Watertight compartment to hold liquid ballast. Tanks provided in various parts of a ship for introduction of water ballast when necessary to add weight to produce a change in trim or in stability of the ship, and for submerging submarines.

BALLAST WATER Seawater, confined to double-bottom tanks, peak tanks, and other designated compartments, for use in obtaining satisfactory draft, trim, or stability.

BALLASTED CONDITION A condition of loading in which it becomes necessary to fill all or part of the ballast tanks in order to secure proper immersion, stability, and steering qualities brought about by consumption of fuel, stores, and water or lack of part or all of the designed cargo.

BALL ICE Numerous floating spheres of sea ice having diameters of one to two inches. The balls are very soft and spongy; no internal structure can be distinguished clearly. The balls are generally in belts similar to slush which forms at the same time. Ball ice has very rarely been reported.

BALLISTIC GYRO A gyrocompass that uses a ballistic (a free-flowing heavy liquid such as mercury or silicone) within the element to apply precessive forces to the gyro.

BALLOON FREIGHT Freight taking up considerable space in comparison to weight; light, bulky articles.

BALSA A lightwood: a South American raft made of lightwood.

BALTIMORE FORM C BILL OF LADING A bill of lading form used for grain shipments, derived from the Baltimore Berth Grain Charter Party-Steamer, Form C, as adopted in 1913.

BAND FILTER A filter that passes all frequencies between a high and low cutoff frequency.

BANDING Material used to wrap around the shipment to hold it in place.

BANDS Categories having specific names and frequencies within the electromagnetic spectrum.

BANDWIDTH A measurement of the amount of data that can be transferred by a line at a time. The wider the bandwidth, the more data that can move at once.

BANK GUARANTEE Guarantee issued by a bank to a carrier to be used in lieu of lost or misplaced original negotiable bill of lading.

BANK PAYMENT PLAN A service provided by banks for shippers. Carriers send freight bills to the bank to be paid. The bank pays the carrier and subtracts the payment from the shipper's account. Also called freight payment service.

BANKER'S ACCEPTANCE A time bill of exchange, or acceptance, that has been drawn on and accepted by a bank.

BANKING SYSTEM For marine purposes the practice of always keeping more than one piece of cargo on the quay or in the vessel ready for loading or discharging in order to avoid delays and to obtain optimal use of the loading gear.

BAR Section at the entrance to ports that is shallower than the ocean or waterway and must be carefully crossed. Also, sand or gravel deposits in or near the channel.

BAR ANTENNA An antenna sometimes used by direction finders, usually a piece of soft iron with a section of wire wrapped tightly around it. Wrapping wire around soft iron eliminates the need for external antennas because of the bar antenna's efficient pickup and induction of weak RF currents.

BARBER *See* Frost Smoke.

BAR CODE A symbol consisting of a series of printed bars representing values. A system of optical character reading, scanning, and tracking of units by reading a series of printed bars.

BAR CODE SCANNER A device to read bar codes and communicate data to computer systems.

BAR CODING A method of encoding data for fast and accurate readability. Bar codes are a series of alternating bars and spaces printed or stamped on products, labels, or other media, representing encoded information that can be read by electronic readers called bar.

BARE BOAT CHARTER (BBC) Lease of a bare ship to charter where charterer is responsible for crewing, provisioning, maintenance, and all expenses incident to its use.

BARGE A long large vessel, usually flat bottomed, self-propelled, towed, or pushed by another vessel, used for transporting materials. A flat boat with no sails or engines, which is towed or pushed by another vessel, usually tugboats. Technically a barge carries her cargo below deck. A heavy craft, with or without sails, used to transport bulky cargo. The craft has no machinery for self-propulsion.

BARGE CARRIERS A class of oceangoing ship that carries cargo preloaded in barges that are off-loaded and loaded from the "mother" ship by special heavy-lift crane or elevator installed at the stern-end of the ship, and the barges are then towed or pushed from the ship to shore side terminals. *See also* Freighters.

BARGE-ON-BOARD Use of specially designed barges or lighters, in which cargo is loaded directly in the barge. The barge is then moved by river and canal networks to a port area to await arrival of an oceangoing barge-carrying ship; it is then hoisted aboard a LASH or SEABEE ship by massive cranes or elevators.

BARGE SHIP A dry cargo vessel that carries relatively large boxes of cargo called barges. Loading barges is accomplished by two methods, by traveling crane called Lighter Aboard Ship (LASH) or elevator called SeaBee. Both vessels are antiquated in modern containership times.

35

BARRATRY The willful destruction of a vessel by her master. An act committed by the master or mariners of a vessel, for some unlawful or fraudulent purpose, contrary to their duty to the owners, whereby the latter sustain injury. It may include negligence, if so gross as to evidence fraud.

BARREL (BBL) A volumetric unit of measure for liquids aboard ship; the standard unit of liquid volume in the petroleum industry. A barrel is equal to 42 U.S. gallons, or approximately 35 Imperial gallons at 60°F. The usual bunker fuel oil contains about 6.67 barrels per long ton.

BARRIER MATERIALS Materials that can withstand water, oil, vapor, and various gases.

BARS Special devices mounted on container doors to provide a watertight locking. Synonym: Door lock bars.

BARTER The direct exchange of goods for other goods without the use of money and without third-party involvement.

BAR-TIGHT Solid and rigid as a steel bar.

BASE Home depot of container or trailer. The floor of a container.

BASECOAT/CLEARBOAT SYSTEM A two-stage topcoat system composed of a colored basecoat and a transparent final coat.

BASELINE The first step of the hyperbolic navigation pattern, it is the line connecting two established points at a specific distance from each other at which transmitting stations are placed. Also, a fore and aft datum line from which vertical heights are measured. On riveted hulls it is usually parallel to the top edge of the garboard strakes. On welded hulls it is usually parallel to the top edge of the flat plate keel. However, as the location of this reference line is a designer's option, the line's plan should be checked to determine its exact location.

BASELINE PLANE (BL) Established somewhere near the base of the ship, usually running through the upper edge of the flat plate keel and parallel to the water planes.

BASE POINT PRICING A pricing system that includes a transportation cost from a particular city or town in a zone or region even though the shipment does not originate at the basing point.

BASE RATE A tariff term referring to ocean rate less accessorial charges or simply the base tariff rate.

BASIC RATE (INS) The manual rate, from which are taken discounts or to which are added charges to compensate for the individual circumstances of the risk.

BASIC STOCK Items of an inventory intended for issue against demand during the resupply lead-time.

BATCH A collection of products or data that is treated as one entity with respect to certain operations, e.g., processing and production.

BATCH LOTS   A definite quantity of some product manufactured or produced under conditions that are presumed uniform and for production control purposes passing as a unit through the same series of operations.

BATCH NUMBERS   Numbers put on products when they are manufactured for identifying when they were made and at what factory.

BATCH PICKING   The picking of items from storage for more than one order at a time.

BATCH PRODUCTION   The production process whereby products/components are produced in batches and where each separate batch consists of a number of the same products/components.

BATHYMETRIC   Measurement of water depths in order to determine sea floor topography.

BATTEN   Long, thin, strips of wood, steel, or plastic, usually of uniform rectangular section, used in securing tarpaulins in place. Cargo battens are wood planks or steel shapes that are fitted to the inside of the frames in a hold to keep the cargo away from the shell plating; sweat battens. To secure by means of battens, as to "batten down a hatch."

BATTEN DOWN   Refers to closing the hatches for sea by covering with tarpaulins and securing them.

BATTENS, CARGO   A term applied to the wood planks or steel shapes that are fitted to the inside of the frames in a hold to keep the cargo away from the shell plating; the strips of wood or steel used to prevent shifting of cargo.

BATTENS, CROSS   Strips of iron or wood placed across the square of a closed hatch to hold tarps and hatch covers.

BATTENS, HATCH   Thin steel bars fitted tight against the hatch coaming to hold the hatch cover or tarpaulin in place.

BATTENS, SEAM   Wood seam straps that connect the edges of small boats having a single thickness of planking. They give additional stiffness to the plank, are continuous, and frames are notched out to fit over them.

BATTENS, SWEAT (CARGO)   Long planks in the hold or 'tween decks, secured to the side of the ship to protect cargo from sweat and rust.

BATTLE CRUISER   A naval vessel having high speed, wide radius of action, guns of large size and range, and moderate protection; often defined as a ship with cruiser speed and battleship armament, with full protection against cruisers and smaller vessels and capable of operation in all weather.

BATTLESHIP   A naval vessel having a large displacement; good speed; large radius of action; maximum armament; maximum protection against gun fire, bombs, and torpedoes; ability to keep at sea in all weather; and to bear the brunt of sea fighting as a line-of-battle ship.

BAUD RATE   The speed at which you can transmit and receive data from one computer to another.

BAUMÉ GRAVITY   Specific gravity expressed on the Baumé scale for liquids lighter or heavier than water. However, the API scale is now used for liquids by the petroleum industry instead of the Baumé scale. Both scales are identical for liquids as dense as water, but for very light oils, there is a difference.

BAY   An area in a transit shed or warehouse between post and columns, or the area between lateral ceiling beams or trusses projected down to the pier or warehouse.

BAY ICE   Young flat ice of sufficient thickness to impede navigation.

BAY PLAN   A stowage plan that shows the locations of all the containers on the vessel.

BB   (1) Ballast Bonus. Special payment above the chartering price when the ship has to sail a long way on ballast to reach the loading port.

(2) Bareboat. Method of chartering of the ship leaving the charterer with almost all the responsibilities of the owner.

(3) Break Bulk.

BBB   Before Breaking Bulk. Refers to freight payments that must be received before discharge of a vessel commences.

BBL   Barrel.

BC CODE   Safe working practice code for solid bulk cargo.

BCO   Beneficial Cargo Owner. Refers to the importer of record, who physically takes possession of cargo at destination and does not act as a third party in the movement of such goods.

BCR   Bow Crossing Range.

BD OR B/D   Barrels per Day; Bar Draft.

BDI   Both Dates Inclusive.

B/E   Bill of Exchange.

BEACHCOMBER   A derelict seaman found unemployed on the waterfront, especially in foreign countries.

BEACH NOURISHMENT   Depositing sediment on beaches to make up for loss through erosion.

BEACON   A lighted or unlighted fixed aid to navigation attached directly to the earth's surface. Lights and day beacons both constitute "beacon."

BEAM   The breadth (width) of a ship at the widest point. The largest distance across a ship or a point of observation of objects away from the ship at right angles to the centerline requires direction port or starboard. Also, an athwartship horizontal member supporting a deck or flat.

BEAM, DECK   Athwartship support of deck. A transverse structural member that supports a vessel's deck, stiffens her frames, withstands racking stress, and generally supplies the chief requirement for lateral strength.

BEAM, HATCH   Portable beam across the hatch to support covers. The ends fit into sockets riveted to the inside face of latch coamings.

BEAM, HOLD Beams in a hold, similar to deck beams, but having no plating or planking; now obsolete. Its purpose was to supply local transverse strength and stiffening to vessel's side framing.

BEAM, PANTING The transverse beams that tie the panting frames together; increased scantling.

BEAM, PLATE ANGLE A beam made from a flat plate, with the flange bent at right angles as by an angle bending machine.

BEAM, TRANSOM A strong deck beam situated in the after end of the vessel connected at each end to the transom frame. The cant beams that support the deck plating in the overhang of the stern are attached to and radiate from it.

BEAM CLAMP A ringed fitting that can be fastened to a beam in order to drag heavy cargo to and from the hatch square.

BEAM-DRAFT RATIO Ratio of beam to draft. This ratio has an important bearing on the height and movement of M.

BEAM ENDS Said of a vessel when she is hove over or listed until her deck beams approach the vertical.

BEAM KNEE End of steel deck beam that is split, having one portion turned down and a piece of plate between the split portions, forming a bracket for riveted connection to side frame; angular fittings that connect beams and frames together.

BEAM LIGHT A colloquial term used to describe a high intensity directional light.

BEAM LINE A line showing the points of intersection between the top edge of the beam and the molded frame line, also called "molded deck line."

BEAMS Antennas with extra elements that make them more directive by changing the shape of the emission pattern of the radio waves.

BEAM SEA A sea at right angles to a vessel's course.

BEAM WIND A wind at right angles to a vessel's course.

BEAR A HAND To hurry.

BEARDING LINE A term applied to the intersection of the molded line of planking or plating and the stem, sternpost, and keel, usually in connection with wood shipbuilding.

BEAR DOWN To approach from windward. To work harder.

BEARER A term applied to foundation, particularly those having vertical web plates as principal members. The vertical web plates of foundations are also called bearers.

BEARING The horizontal direction of a line of sight between two objects on the surface of the earth. The direction of one terrestrial point from another. Expressed as an angular distance from North. Used only in connection with ARPA performance standards. A block on or in which a journal rotates; a bearing block.

BEARING REPEATER   Gyro repeaters usually located on the wings of the bridge to aid the mariner in taking true direction visual compass comparisons.

BEARING RESOLUTION   The radar's ability to distinguish between two ships on the same bearing at nearly the same range. If two ships are at equal range from a radar unit and are separated by a relatively small angle, then the narrower the beam, the more capable the unit is of discerning between the two. This principle is primarily dependent upon the horizontal beam width.

BEAR TRAP   A section of a movable dam with concrete piers in either side (generally about 100 feet wide) and provided with a gate that may be raised or lowered by compressed air. The bear trap serves as a type of safety valve; when the pool level maintained at the dam becomes too high, the type dams found on the Ohio and Illinois Rivers. The bear trap will always be located on the opposite side of the river from the lock and is very dangerous to approach when open. The bear trap is lowered to permit the excess water to run out. This pool control feature of movable wicket.

BEAT FREQUENCY OSCILLATOR (BFO)   A device that provides a locally generated signal that can be mixed with a continuous wave transmission when received, allowing the user to hear the carrier wave.

BEAUFORT SCALE   A numerical and descriptive scale of wind velocities and sea conditions.

BECALMED   Sailing vessel dead in the water due to lack of wind.

BECKET   An eye for securing one end of a line to a block. A rope eye as on a cargo net, a round reinforcement inserted into a rope eye.

BECKETS   Rope or wooden appliances used to hold hand steering wheels on small tugs.

BEHALTERTRAGWAGEN (BT WAGON)   A container wagon for the German Railways.

BELAY   To fasten, i.e., belay a line to a cleat. To stop. To cancel or cease executing an order.

BELAYING PIN   A wooden or iron pin fitting into a rail upon which to secure ropes.

BELL   In pipe fitting, the recessed or enlarged female end of a pipe into which the male end of the next pipe fits. In plumbing, the expanded female portion of a wiped joint.

BELL MOUTHED   Signifies the open end of a vessel or pipe when it expands or spreads out with an increasing diameter, thus resembling a bell; also called trumpet mouthed.

BELLINI-TOSSI ANTENNA   *See* Crossed Loop Antenna.

BELLY   Under floor area of an aircraft; the cargo carrying area.

BELLY FREIGHT   Cargo that is transported in the lower freight compartments of airplanes.

BELLY STRAP   A rope passed around a boat for hanging a kedge anchor in carrying out the anchor.

BELOW Below a deck or decks corresponding to "downstairs." Underneath the surface of the water.

BELT A relatively narrow band of fragments of floating or fast ice of any concentration.

BELT GAUGING Taking readings to determine the thickness of the plating by drilling holes in the ship's hull. Today they use sound every three years.

BELT LINE A switching railroad operating within a commercial area.

BENCHMARKING A management tool for comparing performance against an organization that is widely regarded as outstanding in one or more areas, in order to improve performance.

BEND A knot by which one rope is made fast to another, such as becket bend, double becket bend, carrick bend, and double carrick bend, Also, a bend of the river is analogous to a curve in a highway.

BENDING The first stage in the formation of pressure ice caused by the action of current, wind, and tide or air temperature changes. Bending is more characteristic of thin plastic ice than heavier forms.

BENDING MOMENT (Weight × Distance) The moment at any given point of the ship's structure that tends to produce hogging or sagging. It is the sum of the products of the forces acting to produce bending and the perpendicular distances from the lines of action of those forces to the point under consideration. The maximum bending moment is frequently expressed as a ratio of the product of the ship's length and displacement.

BENDING ROLLS A machine in which power-driven steel rollers are used to give cylindrical curvature to plates.

BENDING SLABS Heavy cast iron perforated slabs arranged to form a large floor on which frames, etc., are bent, after heating in a furnace, with square or round holes for "dogging down."

BENDS Both ends (loading and discharge ports).

BENEFICAL OWERSHIP Designates the owner who receives the benefits or profits from the operation.

BENEFICIAL USES Use of (dredged) material for an economic, environmental, or other useful purpose.

BENEFICIARIES Those ship terminals and other water-related facilities that would benefit economically by deepening a Federal channel.

BENEFICIARY Entity to whom money is payable. Also, the entity for whom a letter of credit is issued. The seller and the drawer of a draft.

BENEFICIARY COUNTRY Any country, territory, or successor political entity to which there is, in effect, a proclamation by the President designating such as a beneficiary country entitled to special tariff treatment.

BENEFIT COST RATIO Also known as Cost-Benefit Ratio—An analytical tool used in public planning; a ratio of total measurable benefits divided by the initial capital cost.

BENEFIT OF INSURANCE CLAUSE (INS) A clause by which the bailee of goods claims the benefit of any insurance policy effected by the cargo owner on the goods in care of the bailee. Such a clause in a contract of carriage, issued in accordance with the Carriage of Goods by Sea Act, is void at law.

BENTHIC INFAUNA Aquatic animals that live in the bottom sediment of a body of water.

BENTHIC ORGANISMS Aquatic animals that live on or in the sea floor substrate.

BENZENE (BENZOL) A hydrocarbon of the composition C6H6 and the initial member of the aromatic or benzene series. Its molecular structure is conceived as a ring of six carbon atoms with double linkage between each alternating pair and with hydrogen attached to each carbon atom.

BENZENE RING A six-member ring of carbon atoms, joined together by alternate single and double bonds, present in all aromatics.

BENZINE A colorless, flammable, and volatile liquid obtained from petroleum by fractional distillation and consisting of various hydrocarbons. The term has been applied to various petroleum distillates lighter than kerosene, especially when these are used as solvents. It is totally distinct from the aromatic hydrocarbon benzene. ASTM states that this term is archaic and misleading and should not be used.

BENZOL *See* Benzene.

BERG Iceberg.

BERGY BIT A medium-sized fragment of glacier or packed ice, about the size of a small house, floating in the sea or aground.

BERM The sharp definitive edge of a dredged channel such as in a rock cut.

BERNE GAUGE The most restrictive loading gauge (standard measure) or the lowest common denominator of loading gauges on the railways of continental Europe.

BERTH The water area, at the waterfront edge of a wharf, reserved for a vessel; the place where a ship is tied up when alongside a wharf. Also, a sleeping space. Berths, as a rule, are permanently built into the structure of the staterooms or compartments. They are constructed singly and also in tiers of two or three, one above the other. When single, drawers for stowing clothing are often built in underneath. Tiers of berths constructed of pipe are commonly installed in the crew space.

BERTHAGE Port charges relating to the physical size of the vessel alongside the wharf and assessable on twelve-hour periods. The charges may be based on the length of the vessel, or more commonly, classified by type of business of the vessel or on the gross registered tonnage. Revenues are intended to recover expenses such as apron wharf and berth dredging.

BERTH DECK A name applied to a lower complete deck at or near the waterline on old vessels, and used primarily for berthing purposes and not as a gun deck.

BERTHING AREA   The bed or bunk space on a ship. Also, a space at a wharf for a ship to dock.

BERTH RATES   Rate charges by scheduled liner services.

BERTH TERM   Shipped under rate that does not include cost of loading or unloading carrier.

BESET   Hemmed in or surrounded by ice from all quarters causing the loss of a vessel's control or movement.

BEST AVAILABLE CONTROL TECHNOLOGY   An emission limitation based on the maximum degree of reduction of any regulated air contaminant emitted from or results from any regulated facility that the department, on a case-by-case basis, taking into account energy, environmental, and economic impacts and other costs, determines is achievable for such facility through application of production processes and available methods, systems, and techniques for control of each such contaminant. The best available shall not allow emissions in excess of any emission standard established under the New Source Performance Standards, National Emission Standards for Hazardous Air Pollutants, or under any other applicable rules and may include a design feature, equipment specification, work practice, operating control technology determination standard, or combination thereof.

BETWEEN DECKS   The space between any two continuous decks; also called 'tween decks.

BETWIXT WIND AND WATER   That part of the vessel at or near the waterline.

BEVEL   A term for a plane having any other angle than 90 degrees to a given reference plane. The angle between the flanges of a frame or other member. (Greater than right angle, open bevel; less, closed bevel). Also, a small tool similar to a try square except that the blade is adjustable for taking bevels.

BEVEL, CLOSED   A term applied where one flange of a bar is bent to form an acute angle, less than 90 degrees, with the other flange.

BEVEL, OPEN   A term applied where one flange of a bar is bent to form an obtuse angle (greater than 90 degrees) with the other flange. Frame bars in the bow and the stern of a vessel are given an open bevel to permit access for riveting to shell and to keep the standing flange parallel to the deck beams.

BEYOND   Used with reference to charges assessed for cargo movement past a line haul terminating point.

BFO   Beat Frequency Oscillator.

BHP   Brake Horsepower. The power output of a prime mover as measured by a dynamometer expressed horsepower (1hp = 33,000 ft lb/min = 746 W).

BI   Both Inclusive.

BIBB   A cock or valve with a bent outlet; strictly, the bent outlet.

BID BOND   Bond, guarantee, or standby letter of credit that accompanies a bid, issued for an amount that will be forfeited if the bidder wins the bid but then reneges.

BIFURCATION   The point where a channel divides when proceeding from seaward. The place where two tributaries meet.

BIGHT   A loop or bend in a rope; though, strictly considered, any part between the ends may be termed the bight.

BIGHT OF A BEND   The deepest portion of a bend (not in depth of water); sharpest part of a curve.

BILATERAL AGREEMENT   A contract term meaning both parties agree to provide something for the other.

BILGE   The lowest inner part of a ship. Curved section between the bottom and the side of a ship; the recess into which all water drains. Belly of a barrel or cask.

BILGE KEEL   A fin fitted on the bottom of a ship at the turn of the bilge to reduce rolling. It commonly consists of a plate running fore and aft and attached to the shell plating by welding or by angle bars. It materially helps in steadying a ship and does not add much to the resistance to propulsion if fitted in the streamline flow. Sometimes called rolling chocks.

BILGE PLATES   The curved shell plates that fit the bilge.

BILGE PUMP   Pump for removing bilge water.

BILGE STRAKE   Course of plates at the bilge.

BILGE WATER   Water collecting in the bottom of a ship owing to leaks, sweat, etc.

BILL BOARD   An inclined platform fitted at the intersection of the forward weather deck and the shell, for stowing an anchor. It may be fitted with a tripping device for dropping the anchor overboard. Seldom fitted since the stockless anchor has come into general use.

BILL OF EXCHANGE   In the United States, commonly known as a draft. However, bill of exchange is the correct term.

BILL OF HEALTH   Is a certificate issued by local medical authorities indicating the general health conditions in the port of departure or in the ports of call. The Bill of Health must have a visa before departure by the Consul of the country of destination. When a vessel has free pratique, this means that the vessel has a clean Bill of Health certifying that there are no questions of contagious disease and that all quarantine regulations have been complied with, so that people may embark and disembark.

BILL OF LADING (B/L)   A contract between a shipper and a carrier that provides proof that the merchandise was transferred from the shipper to the consignee and that the carrier has assumed responsibility for the cargo until it is delivered. It serves as a document of title, a contract of carriage and a receipt for goods.

BILL OF LADING, AMENDED   Bill of lading requiring updates that do not change financial status; this is slightly different from corrected B/L.

BILL OF LADING, CANCELED   Bill of lading status; used to cancel a processed B/L; usually per shipper's request; different from voided bill of lading.

BILL OF LADING, CLEAN A bill of lading that bears no superimposed clause or notation that declares a defective condition of the goods and/or the packaging.

BILL OF LADING, COMBINED Bill of lading that covers cargo moving over various transports.

BILL OF LADING, CONSOLIDATED Bill of lading combined or consolidated from two or more bills of lading.

BILL OF LADING, CORRECTED Bill of lading requiring any update that results in money or other financially related changes.

BILL OF LADING, DOMESTIC Nonnegotiable bill of lading primarily containing routing details; usually used by truckers and freight forwarders.

BILL OF LADING, DUPLICATE Another original bill of lading set if first set is lost. Also known as reissued bill of lading.

BILL OF LADING, EXPRESS Non negotiable bill of lading where there are no hard copies of originals printed.

BILL OF LADING, FREIGHT A contract of carriage between a shipper and forwarder (this is usually a negotiable document, NVOCC, a nonvessel operating common carrier).

BILL OF LADING, GOVERNMENT A document issued by the U.S. government (GBL).

BILL OF LADING, HITCHMENT Bill of lading covering parts of a shipment, which are loaded at more than one location. Hitchment bill of lading usually consists of two parts, hitchment and hitchment memo. The hitchment portion usually covers the majority of a divided shipment and carries the entire revenue.

BILL OF LADING, HOUSE Bill of lading issued by a freight forwarder or consolidation covering a single shipment containing the names, addresses, and specific description of the goods shipped.

BILL OF LADING, INTERMODAL Bill of lading covering cargo moving via multimodal means. Also known as Combined Transport Bill of Lading or Multimodal Bill of Lading.

BILL OF LADING, LONG FORM Bill of lading form with terms and conditions written on the back.

BILL OF LADING, MEMO Unfreighted bill of lading with no charges listed.

BILL OF LADING, MILITARY Bill of lading issued by the U.S. military also known as GBL or Form DD1252.

BILL OF LADING, NEGOTIABLE Consignment/banking term. Bill of lading names are legal and by endorsement the shipper can transfer the title of the goods to the bank representing the buyer or directly to the buyer of the goods.

BILL OF LADING, NONNEGOTIABLE *See* Straight Consignment. Sometimes means a file copy of a bill of lading.

BILL OF LADING NUMBER A unique number shown on a bill of lading at the time the merchandise is accepted for shipment.

BILL OF LADING, NUMBERS U.S. Customs' standardized bill of lading format to facilitate electronic communications.

BILL OF LADING, ONBOARD Bill of lading validated at the time of loading to transport. Onboard air, boxcar, container, rail, truck, and vessel are the most common types.

BILL OF LADING, OPTIONAL DISCHARGE Bill of lading covering cargo with more than one discharge point option possibility.

BILL OF LADING, ORDER *See* To Order, Bill of Lading or Negotiable, Bill of Lading.

BILL OF LADING, ORIGINAL The part of the bill of lading set that has value, especially when negotiable; rest of set are only informational file copies. Abbreviated as OBL.

BILL OF LADING, PORT OF DISCHARGE Port where cargo is discharged from means of transport.

BILL OF LADING, RECEIVED FOR SHIPMENT Validated at time cargo is received by ocean carrier to commence movement but before being validated as "Onboard."

BILL OF LADING, RECONCILED Bill of lading set that has completed a prescribed number of edits between the shipper's instructions and the actual shipment received. This produces a very accurate bill of lading.

BILL OF LADING, SHORT TERM Opposite of long form B/L, a bill of lading without the terms and conditions written on the back. Also known as a short form bill of lading.

BILL OF LADING, SPLIT One of two or more bills of lading that have been split from a single bill of lading.

BILL OF LADING, STALE A late bill of lading; in banking, a B/L that has passed the time deadline of the L/C and is void.

BILL OF LADING, STATUS Represents whether the bill of lading has been input, rated, reconciled, printed, or released to the customer.

BILL OF LADING, STRAIGHT (CONSIGNMENT) Consignment issue. *See above* Nonnegotiable, Bill of Lading.

BILL OF LADING, TERMS AND CONDITIONS The fine print on back of B/L; defines what the carrier can and cannot do, including the carrier's liabilities and contractual agreements.

BILL OF LADING, TO ORDER Consignment issue. *See* Negotiable, Bill of Lading.

BILL OF LADING, TYPE Refers to the type of bill of lading being issued. Some examples are: a Memo (ME), Original (OBL), Nonnegotiable, Corrected (CBL), or Amended (AM) B/L.

BILL OF LADING, UNIQUE B/L IDENTIFIER U.S. Customs' standardization: four alpha code unique to each carrier placed in front of nine digit bill of lading number; APL's unique bill of lading identifier is "APLU." Sea land uses "SEAU." These prefixes are also used as the container identification.

BILL OF LADING, VOIDED   Related to consolidated bill of lading; those B/Ls absorbed in the combining process. Different from canceled bill of lading.

BILL OF MATERIALS   The list of materials and components necessary to support planned production runs.

BILL OF SALE   Confirms the transfer of ownership of certain goods to another person in return for money paid or loaned.

BILL TO PARTY   Customer designated as party paying for services.

BILLED WEIGHT   The weight shown in a waybill and freight bill.

BILLING   A carrier terminal activity that determines the proper rate and total charges for a shipment and issues a freight bill.

BIMCO   Baltic and International Maritime Council.

BIMODAL TRAILER   A road semitrailer with retractable running gear to allow mounting on a pair of rail boogies. Synonym: Road-Rail trailer. A trailer that is able to carry different types of standardized unit loads, (e.g., a chassis that is appropriate for the carriage of one FEU or two TEUs).

BINDER   A strip of cardboard, thin wood, burlap, or similar material placed between layers of containers to hold a stack together.

BINDER (INS)   In lines other than life and health, a binder is an acknowledgment, usually from the agent, that insurance applied for is in force whether or not premium settlement has yet been made or the policy issued. In life and health insurance, binders are not issued, but if premium settlement is made with the application, what is often erroneously referred to as a "binder" is issued. Actually this is a conditional binding receipt.

BINDING RECEIPT (INS)   *See* Binder.

BINNACLE   A stand or box for holding and illuminating a compass so that the steersman may conveniently observe it. Binnacles differ in shape and size according to where used and the size of the compass to be accommodated. A binnacle for a ship's navigating compass consists essentially of a pedestal at whose upper end is a bowl-shaped receptacle having a sliding hood-like cover. This receptacle accommodates the gimbals supporting the compass. Compensating binnacles are provided with brackets or arms on either side, starboard and port, for supporting and securing the iron cylinders or spheres used to counteract the quadrantal deviation due to the earth's magnetization of the vessel. This type of binnacle is usually placed immediately in front of the steering wheel, having its vertical axis in the vertical plane of the fore and aft centerline of the vessel.

BINNACLE HOUSING   A protective container for all the components of the master gyrocompass.

BIOACCUMULATION   The uptake of a contaminant in a living organism and the increase in concentration of a chemical of interest in an animal when exposed to proposed dredged material for a specified period of time. This testing is part of the national and regional testing protocol regulated under the Ocean Dumping Act.

BIODEGRADABLE   The property of a material to decompose naturally.

BIOTA   Environmental life forms; examples include fish, lobster, crabs, marine worms, and clams.

BIT   A single fragment of brash, not to be confused with bergy bit.

BITTER END   The last part of a rope or last link in an anchor chain. The absolute end of an unspliced line or wire cable, or the part fastened to any object.

BITTS   A pair of heavy metal posts, fastened on a deck to which mooring lines are secured. An assembly of short metal columns (usually two) mounted on a base plate attached to the deck for the purpose of securing wire ropes, hawsers and the like, which are used to tie a vessel to a pier or a tugboat. Forward bitts are any single, double, or triple arrangement for the fastening of lines on the tug's bow. Side bitts or quarter bitts are built into bulwark rails on either side of the tug about one quarter of the way from the stem, and approximately even with the after H bitts or towing winch. These are used in mooring and towing alongside. H bitts are heavy double posts joined by a cavil, forming a letter H. These are located at the tug's stern and are used for securing any heavy lines.

BITUMASTIC   A black tar-like composition largely of bitumen or asphalt and containing such other ingredients as rosin, Portland cement, slaked lime, petroleum, etc. It is used as a protective coating in ballast and trimming tanks, chain lockers, shaft alleys, etc. Bitumastic protects steel.

B/L   Bill of lading.

BLACK CARGO   Cargo banned by general cargo workers for some reason. This ban could be because the cargo is dangerous or hazardous to health. Also a general term used to describe liquid cargoes of crude oil, diesel fuel, or fuel oils.

BLACK GANG   Members of the engineers' force.

BLACK ICE   Transparent ice crust that reveals the color of seawater beneath.

BLACK OIL TANKER   A tanker of medium size that is usually carrying large consignments of heavy heating oils.

BLACK OILS   A general term applied to crude oils and the heavier and the darker colored petroleum products such as residual fuel oils.

BLANK ENDORSEMENT   Writing only one's own name on the back of a document.

BLANK FLANGE   A flat plate added to a piping system for the purpose of closing off the line. This is sometimes known as a blind flange.

BLANKET   A rubber-covered cylinder that receives the printed image from the plate cylinder and transfers the image to the substrate.

BLANKET BOND   A bond covering a group of persons, articles, or properties.

BLANKET INSURANCE INS)   Property-liability insurance that covers more than one type of property in one location in one policy or form instead of under separate items one or more types of property at more than one location; a contract of health insurance that covers all of a class of persons not individually identified.

BLANKET RATE   A rate applicable to or from a group of points. A special rate applicable to several different articles in a single shipment.

BLANKET WAYBILL   A waybill covering two or more consignments of freight.

BLEEDER   A small cock, valve, or plug to drain off small quantities of fluids from a container or system.

BLEEDER VALVE   Small valve inserted into a riser back of the flange for admitting air into hose or line or used to take samples from the line.

BLENDED FUEL OIL   A fuel oil that is a mixture of residual and distillate fuel oils.

BLENDS   Mixtures of two or more crudes, two or more products, or crudes and products.

BLIND PULLEY   A circular block of hard wood with rounded edges perforated by several holes having grooves running from them to one side of the block. One of these blocks is secured to an end of a part of the standing rigging, as a shroud, and another to the chain plate or to some part of the ship. The two are connected to one another by a lashing passing through the holes. Commonly called "dead eyes."

BLIND SHIPMENT   A bill of lading wherein the paying customer has contracted with the carrier that shipper or consignee information is not given.

BLINK   A glare on the underside of extensive cloud areas created by light reflected from snow or ice covered surfaces; also observable in a clear sky. Blink caused by ice surfaces is usually yellowish white in contrast to the whitish, brighter glare caused by snow surfaces. Also, a Loran C receiver pulse of the master station indicating a system-wide transmitter malfunction.

BLINKER LIGHTS   Two electric lanterns secured at the ends of the signal yard and operated by controllers and a telegraph key for use in night signaling by code.

BLOCK   The name given to a pulley or sheave, or a system of pulleys or sheaves, mounted in a frame or shell and used for moving objects by means of ropes run over the pulleys or sheaves. The prefixes single, double, triple, etc., indicate the number of pulleys or sheaves in the block. The principal parts of a block are (a) the shell, or outside frame; (b) the sheave, on which the rope runs; (c) the pin, on which the sheave turns; (d) the strap, by which the hook is held in position and provides bearing for the pin; and (e) the hook. The upper opening between the sheave and the shell is called the swallow; the bottom opening of the shell is called the breech; and the device attached to the bottom of the block opposite the hook for securing the standing part of the fall to the block is called the becket.

BLOCK, CHEEK   A half shell block with a single sheave bolted to a mast or other object, which serves as, the other half shell or cheek. Usually used in connection with halyards.

BLOCK, FIDDLE A block having two sheaves of different diameters placed in the same plane one above the other.

BLOCK, HEAD The block shackled into the head of the boom through which the cargo runner leads.

BLOCK, HEEL The block shackled into the heel of the boom through which the cargo runner leads.

BLOCK, RUNNING A single sheave block supported in a bight and provided at the bottom with a hook.

BLOCK, SNATCH A single sheave block having one side of the frame hinged so that it can be opened to allow the night of a rope to be placed on the sheave, thus avoiding the necessity of threading the end of the rope through the swallow of the block. Usually employed as a fair lead around obstructions.

BLOCK AND BLOCK Same as two blocks.

BLOCK AND TACKLE A mechanism used for hoisting, consisting of a system of blocks and lines rigged to increase pulling power.

BLOCK COEFFICIENT A coefficient of fineness that expresses the relationship between the volume of displacement and a block having the length, breadth, and draft of the vessel.

BLOCK STOWAGE Stowing cargo destined for a specific location close together to avoid unnecessary cargo movement.

BLOCKED TRAINS Railcars grouped in a train by destination so that segments (blocks) can be uncoupled and routed to different destinations as the train moves through various junctions. Eliminates the need to break up a train and sort individual railcars at each junction.

BLOCKING OR BRACING Wood or metal supports (dunnage) to keep shipments in place to prevent cargo shifting.

BLOW BY In internal combustion engines, leakage of combustion gases from combustion chamber, past the rings, into the crankcase.

BLOWER A mechanical device used to supply air under low pressure for artificial ventilation and forced draft, usually of the centrifugal type.

BLOW HIM DOWN To sound the danger signal in case of misunderstood passing signals: when the pilot on the other boat refuses to obey signals; or when signals are used desiring to pass information.

BLS Bales. U.S. Bureau of Labor Statistics.

BLUE ICE The oldest and hardest form of glacier ice. It is distinguished by a slightly bluish color.

BLUFF BAR A sandbar having a sharp drop off into deep water; also called a bluff reef.

BM Symbols for metacentric radius; also, distance between B and M. Board measure. A unit of measurement used in the lumber trade. One board foot is equivalent to a piece of wood 1 foot × 1 foot × 1 inch.

BMEP Brake Mean Effective Pressure.

BN Booking Note.

BO Bad Order or Buyer's Option.

BOARD To gain access to a vessel.

BOARD FEET The basic unit of measurement for lumber. One board foot is equal to a one-inch board, 12 inches wide and one foot long. Thus, a board ten feet long, 12 inches wide and one inch thick contains ten board feet.

BOARDING The act of going on board a ship.

BOAT DECK Deck on which lifeboats are kept.

BOAT FALL A purchase of two blocks and a length of rope for hoisting a boat to its davits.

BOAT HOOK A long pole with a hook attached to the end, used for catching, holding, and steadying small boats.

BOATSWAIN (BO'SN) The senior unlicensed deck rate aboard a merchant ship, generally regarded as the deck gang foreman, or a deck rate on a naval vessel.

BOATSWAIN'S CHAIR *See* Bo'sn Chair.

BOATSWAIN'S LOCKER The locker in which the boatswain keeps his deck gear.

BOATSWAIN'S PIPE A small shrill whistle used by the boatswain's mate in passing a call or in piping the side.

BOB Bunker On Board.

BOBSTAYS The chains or ropes attached underneath the outer end of the bowsprit and led aft to the stem to prevent the bowsprit from jumping up. Where two are fitted they are called the inner and the cap bobstays; when three are fitted they are called the inner, the middle, and the cap bobstays.

BOBTAIL Movement of a tractor, without trailer, over the highway.

BODILY INJURY LIABILITY (INS) The liability that may arise from injury or death of another person.

BODY PLAN A plan consisting of two half transverse elevations or end views of a ship, both having a common vertical center line, so that the right-hand side represents the ship as seen from ahead, and the left-hand side as seen from astern. On the body plan appear the forms of the various cross sections, the curvature of the deck lines at the side, and the projections, as straight lines of the waterlines, the bow and buttock lines, and the diagonal lines.

BOFFER Best Offer.

BOGIE A set of wheels built specifically as rear wheels under a container.

BOIL Turbulence in the water caused by deep holes, ends of dikes, channel changes, or other submerged obstructions. Indicates a changing channel condition. A boil is easily detected by electronic depth sounders by rapidly changing depths appearing as waves on the tracing paper.

BOIL OFF The vaporization of LNG.

BOILER Any vessel, container, or receptacle that is capable of generating steam by the internal or external application of heat. The two general classes are fire tube and water tube.

BOILER AND MACHINERY POLICY (INS) Insurance against loss due to accidents to boilers, pressure vessels, or other machinery including the equipment itself, as well as liability arising out of the accident.

BOILER CASING Walls forming a trunk leading from the boiler room to the boiler hatch, which protect the different deck spaces from the heat of the boiler room.

BOILER CHOCK Stay brace to prevent fore and aft movement of boilers; also called "ramming chock."

BOILER FUEL OIL A fuel oil that is burned in the furnaces of boilers to generate heat.

BOILER ROOM A compartment in the hold, in the middle or after section of a vessel, where the boilers are placed.

BOILER SADDLE Support for boilers.

BOILING POINT The temperature at which the vapor pressure of a liquid is equal to the pressure of the atmosphere. The temperature varies with the atmospheric pressure.

BOILING RANGE A scale of temperatures over which a substance will vaporize. The low temperature is that at which the substance starts to vaporize; the high temperature is that at which the last of the substance vaporizes.

BOLD REEF A bluff reef that acts like a weir and is plainly visible for quite some distance.

BOLD RIGHT-HAND REEF A sandbar or group of rocks that can be seen or detected by water turbulence, located on the right bank of the channel.

BOLLARD A line securing device on a wharf around which mooring and berthing lines are fastened. An upright, wooden or iron post on deck to which hawsers may be secured. A short metal column extending up from a base plate, which is attached to a wharf and used for securing the lines from a ship. Also applies to timber posts extending above the level of a wharf for the same purpose.

BOLLARD PULL Pull measured at bollard; pull by a tug at zero speed or at towing speed.

BOLSTER A device fitted on a chassis or railcar to hold and secure the container.

BOLSTER PLATE A piece of plate adjoining the hawsehole to prevent the chafing of the hawser against the cheek of a ship's bow. A plate for support like a pillow or cushion. A piece of timber used as a support. A temporary foundation.

BOLT A metal rod used as a fastening. With few exceptions, such as drift bolts, a head or shoulder is made on one end and a screw thread to carry a nut is cut on the other.

BOLTING UP Securing by means of bolts and nuts parts of a structure in proper position for permanent attachment by riveting or welding. A workman employed on this work is called a "bolter up."

BOMB   Steel cylinder with screwed on head used as testing device for conducting oil tests under high pressure. Used for test methods such as Reid Vapor Pressure and gum in gasoline.

BONA FIDE   In good faith.

BOND   An acceptable, written financial guarantee required to be given to Customs to secure a transaction specifically binding the obligatory to certain covenants for certain amounts.

An obligation of the insurance company to protect one against financial loss caused by acts of another.

BOND OF INDEMNITY   A certificate filed with the carrier for the purpose of relieving the carrier from liability to which the carrier would otherwise be subject.

BOND PORT   Port of initial Customs entry of a vessel to any country. Also known as First Port of Call.

BOND SYSTEM   Bond System is part of U.S. Customs' Automated Commercial System providing information on bond coverage.

BONDED   *See* Bond-In.

BONDED FREIGHT   Freight moving under a bond to U.S. Customs or to the Internal Revenue Service and to be delivered only under stated conditions.

BONDED GOODS   Goods in the charge of Customs officers on which bonds instead of cash have been given. The goods in question have not "cleared Customs."

BONDED STORAGE   The most common type involves the collection of excise taxes, such as those on cigarettes. Excise taxes do not have to be paid until the product leaves the bonded warehouse.

BONDED WAREHOUSE   Warehouse approved by the U.S. Treasury Department into which noncleared goods may be placed.

BOND-IN   Goods are held or transported In-Bond under Customs' control either until import duties or other charges are paid, or in order to avoid paying the duties or charges until a later date.

BONDING (ELECTRICAL)   The connecting of metal parts to ensure electrical continuity; for instance, grounding a pipe by a wire to a dock.

BONDING CABLE   An insulated heavy gauge wire designed to ground the static charge of a ship-to-shore terminal while loading or unloading.

BONJEAN CURVES   Curves of areas of transverse sections of a ship. The curves of the moments of these areas above the base line are sometimes included.

BONNET   A cover used to guide and enclose the tail end of a valve spindle.

BOOBY HATCH   A watertight covering over an opening on deck of a ship for a stairway or ladder. An access hatch from a weather deck protected by a hood from sea and weather. The hood is often fitted with a sliding cover to facilitate access.

BOOKING   Arrangements with a carrier for the acceptance and carriage of freight, i.e., a space reservation.

BOOKING NUMBER   A number assigned to a contract of affreightment used as an identifying reference on bills and correspondence.

BOOKING REFERENCE NUMBER   *See* Booking Number.

BOOM   A long pole extending upward at an angle from the mast of a derrick to support or guide objects lifted or suspended (similar to a crane). A floating barrier used to contain materials upon the surface of the water, such as oil. Tubular steel posts, hinged to the mast or deck, to which wires are run for the purpose of hoisting, lowering, or swinging cargo on or off the ship.

BOOM, CARGO   Spar extending from a mast or king post like a derrick arm to raise or lower cargo.

BOOM, HATCH   The boom spotted over the hatch, also called the inboard boom, amidship boom, or up and down boom.

BOOM, JUMBO   A heavy lift boom capable of handling weights up to 100 tons.

BOOM, MIDSHIP   The boom placed over the hatch; also called inboard boom, hatch boom.

BOOM, OUTBOARD   The boom spotted over the side of the ship, also called the burton boom or yard boom.

BOOM, STAY   The boom placed over the hatch; also called inboard boom or midship boom.

BOOM, YARD   The boom placed over the dock; also called outboard boom.

BOOM CRADLE   A rest for a cargo boom when lowered to the deck for securing.

BOOM CRUTCH   A fitting to support the boom in a vertical position against the mast, usually secured by a collar.

BOOM GUY   That part of the rigging that controls the sideways movements of the booms, called variously the port and starboard and the inboard and outboard.

BOOM PIECE   A short piece of angle riveted inside a butt joint of two angles; butt strap for angle bars; splice piece.

BOOM TABLE   An outrigger attached to a mast or a structure built up around a mast from the deck to support the heel bearings of booms and to provide proper working clearances when a number of booms are installed on or around one mast. Also called "mast table" or "tabernacle."

BOOSTER STATIONS—PUMPING STATIONS   Suitable storage tanks, motive power, and pumps for pumping oil through pipelines.

BOOSTERS   Additional pumps used in conjunction with pipeline disposal to increase the maximum transport distance between the dredging operation and the disposal area. As a rule of thumb, maximum economic transport distance, through employment of multiple boosters, is about five miles.

BOOT TOPPING   An outside area on a vessel's hull from bow to stern between certain waterlines, to which special air, water, and grease resisting paint is applied; also the paint applied to such areas.

BOP Balance of Payments.

BORDEREAU Document used in road transport, listing the cargo carried on a road vehicle, often referring to appended copies of the road consignment note.

BORING Forcing a vessel under power through ice by breaking a lead.

BORING BAR A portable, heavy duty tool used for boring, counter boring, reboring, facing, grooving, etc., where true alignment is a primary importance.

BO'SN *See* Boatswain.

BO'SN'S CHAIR A piece of plank hung in four straps forming a seat on which a person may be hoisted aloft or lowered over the ship's side.

BOSOM The inside of an angle bar.

BOSOM BAR An angle fitted inside another.

BOSOM PIECE A short piece of angle riveted inside a butt joint of two angles; butt strap for angle bars; splice piece.

BOSOM PLATE A plate bar or angle fitted in the bosoms of two angle bars to connect the end of the two angles as if by a butt strap.

BOSON Boatswain or bo'sn. The senior member of the unlicensed crew aboard a vessel.

BOSON STORES A storage location for equipment and mooring lines, usually below the fo'c'sle deck.

BOSS The curved swelling portion of the ship's hull around the propeller shaft.

BOSS FRAME Hull frame that is bent for clearing propeller shaft tube.

BOSS PLATE Shell plate covering curved portion of hull where propeller shaft passes outboard.

BOSTON BLUE CLAY Naturally occurring clay parent material commonly found in Boston Harbor.

BOTTLENECK A stage in a process that limits performance.

BOTTOM That portion of a vessel's shell between the keel and the lower turn of the bilge.

BOTTOM, DOUBLE Compartments at the bottom of a ship between inner and outer bottoms; used for ballast tanks, water, etc.

BOTTOM, INNER Plating forming the upper boundary of the double bottom. Also called "tank top."

BOTTOM, OUTER Term used to describe the bottom shell plating in a double-bottom ship.

BOTTOM AIR DELIVERY A type of air circulation in a temperature control container. Air is pulled by a fan from the top of the container, passed through the evaporator coil for cooling, and then forced through the space under the load and up through the cargo. This type of airflow provides even temperatures.

BOTTOM CARGO (WEIGHT CARGO) Cargo, which usually is, but need not be, stowed in the holds, and so is ordered delivered first at the wharf. It is cargo that is heavy in proportion to its size. Examples are tanks and machinery.

BOTTOM DUMP DOORS Doors at the bottom of a hopper dredge that allow disposal of hopper contents by simply opening them at the disposal site. Not all hopper dredges are equipped with bottom dump doors and emptying the hoppers is much more complicated and time consuming.

BOTTOM FILLING The filling of a tank truck or stationary storage tank through an opening, which is flush with the bottom of the tank.

BOTTOMFISH Abundant pelagic fish, such as cod, halibut, hake, and sole, often found in large schools near the seabed of coastal waters.

BOTTOM FITTINGS Special conical-shaped devices inserted between a container and the permanent floor on the deck of a vessel in order to avoid shifting of the container during the voyage of this vessel.

BOTTOM ICE (OR ANCHOR ICE) Ice formed on the bed of a river or shallow sea, irrespective of its nature of formation.

BOTTOM LIFT Handling of containers with equipment attached to the four bottom corner fittings (castings).

BOTTOM PLATING The part of the shell plating that is below the waterline. More specifically, the immersed shell plating from bilge to bilge.

BOTTOM RETURN MODE Depth sounder readings that indicate speed over ground.

BOTTOMS In a distilling operation, that portion of the charge remaining in the still or flask at the end of the run; in pipe stilling or distillation, the portion that does not vaporize.

BOTTOM SEDIMENT AND WATER (BS&W) A test made on fuel oils, crude oils, and used crankcase oils to show the approximate amount of sediment and water.

BOTTOM SIDE RAILS Structural members on the longitudinal sides of the base of the container.

BOTTOM TRACK *See* Bottom Return Mode.

BOUNDING BAR A bar connecting the edges of a bulkhead to tank top, shell decks or another bulkhead.

BOW The front of the vessel or boat. The sides of the vessel at and for some distance abaft the stem, designated as the right hand, or starboard bow, and the left hand, or port bow.

BOW BOAT The lead barge in an integrated tow of several barges having a square stern and rake at the bow end to assist in the steering and maneuvering of large tows.

BOW CROSSING RANGE (BCR) Distance ahead of a vessel's relative motion line at the intersection of the ship's course.

BOW LINES Curves representing vertical sections parallel to the center longitudinal vertical plane of the bow end of a ship. Similar curves in the aft part of a hull are called buttock lines. Also, a rope leading from the vessel's bow to another vessel or to a wharf for the purpose of hauling her ahead or for securing her.

BOW PUDDING   Fendering found on the forward end of a tug or vessel designed for pushing.

BOWSPRIT   A spar extending forward from the stem end carrying the load of part of the gear for the head sails.

BOW THRUSTERS   Nozzles located on both the port and starboard bow of hopper dredges that use jetted water to give greater maneuverability during the dredging operation. Tunnel through ship's bow with a small propeller used instead of a tugboat in maneuvering.

BOX   Slang term for container.

BOXCAR   A closed car used for hauling freight.

BOXING THE COMPASS   Calling names of the 32 points of the compass in order.

BOX PALLET   Pallet with at least three fixed, removable, or collapsible vertical sides.

BP B/P   Balance of Payments; Bills Payable.

BPR   *See* Business Process Reengineering.

BRACE   A rope attached to the yardarm, used to alter the position of the yardarm in a horizontal plane. The operation is known as trimming the sail.

BRACING   Act of holding anything in place, usually by supporting it laterally. Also the material used.

BRACKET   A steel plate, commonly of triangular shape with a reinforcing flange on its free edge, used to connect two parts such as deck beam to frame, frame to margin plate, etc.; also used to stiffen or tie beam angles to bulkhead, frames to longitudinals, etc.

BRACKET, BILGE   A flat plate welded or riveted to the tank top or margin plate and to the frame in the area of the bilge, sometimes called "margin bracket."

BRACKET, DECK BEAM   Athwartship member of a vessel's structure that supports deck plating and acts as a strut or tie connecting the vessel's side.

BRACKET, MARGIN   A bracket connecting the frame to the margin plates. Sometimes called bilge bracket or wing bracket. Triangular plate welded to support where frame joins floor.

BRACKET, TANGENCY   A bracket whose inner face is curved rather than straight to distribute the stress over the face of the bracket rather than concentrate it in the corners.

BRACKET, TRIPPING   A small piece of steel placed beside a plate or shape to prevent its collapsing or folding over. A more correct name would be antitripping bracket.

BRAILS   Ropes rove through blocks fastened to a spar and attached to the leech of the sail. The overhauling of these ropes gathers the sail up against the spar.

BRASH   Small fragments of sea, lake, or river ice less than 6 feet long; the wreckage of other forms of ice.

BRAZE To join certain metals by the use of a hard solder.

BREADTH Same as Beam.

BREADTH, EXTREME The maximum breadth measured over plating or planking, including beading or fenders.

BREADTH, MOLDED The greatest breadth of the vessel measured from heel of frame on one side to heel of frame on other side.

BREADTH, REGISTERED Measured amidships at its greatest breadth to outside of plating.

BREAK A surface disturbance of the water similar to a boil caused by an underwater obstruction.

BREAK BULK The splitting up of one consolidated shipment into smaller ones for ultimate delivery to various consignees. A dry cargo vessel in which the cargo can be packaged in small consignments, or bulk commodities can be loaded too. Break bulk vessels are very flexible in carrying different cargo, but are somewhat antiquated in modern containership times. Also, to unload and distribute a portion or all of the contents of a railcar, container, or trailer. Also, loose, noncontainerized cargo. Also, a method of transport. Instead of being stored in a container, pallets, and boxes of goods are stacked in the hold of a vessel.

BREAK BULK CARGO General cargo loaded package by package, unitized or not (palletized or sling), but not in containers or in bulk.

BREAK BULK TERMINAL A terminal where commodities packaged in bags, drums, cartons, creates, etc., are commonly but not always palletized and loaded and unloaded.

BREAK DOWN To put cargo in step formation. Also step-down.

BREAK GROUND Said of an anchor when it lifts clear of the bottom.

BREAK OF FORECASTLE OR POOP The point at which the partial decks known as the forecastle and poop are discontinued.

BREAK OUT To unstow. To prepare for use.

BREAK UP TOW To disassemble the tow either at the end of the voyage or inadvertently on a sandbar.

BREAKAGE *See* Waste Cube.

BREAKBULK CARGO Palletized cargo and miscellaneous items such as tanks, machinery, or bagged cargo that is not shipped in containers. Heterogeneous items of general cargo, packaged and moved as single parcels or assembled together on pallet boards and wire or rope cargo slings as a means of lifting on and off a vessel by ship's gear or by wharf cranes.

BREAK BULK DISTRIBUTION CENTER A warehouse where large shipments are sent by a shipper. Shipments are broken down by customer, and each consignee receives what was ordered.

BREAKDOWN BAR (CHEATER) A length of pipe used to increase the leverage in setting up ratchets when connecting two rigging.

BREAKER Small cask for freshwater carried in ship's boats; surf.

BREAK EVEN RATE   The weight at which it is cheaper to charge the lower rate for the next higher weight-break multiplied by the minimum weight indicated, than to charge the higher rate for the actual weight of the shipment (air cargo).

BREASTHOOK   A flanged-plate bracket joining port and starboard side stringers at their forward end. A triangular-shaped plate fitted parallel to and between decks or side stringers in the bow for the purpose of rigidly fastening together the peak frames, stem, and outside plating; also used, in conjunction with the above duties, to fasten the ends of side stringers firmly together.

BREASTING FLOAT   A raft-like float used to keep a vessel, while secured, away from the pier. Also called Camel.

BREAKWATER   A term applied to plates or timbers fitted on a forward weather deck to form a V-shaped shield against water that is shipped over the bow.

BREAST LINE   Any line that leads straight in or square. Keeps a barge from moving out from its mooring facilities. Mooring lines running perpendicular to the centerline, designed to control lateral motion alongside the dock.

BREATHER VALVE   *See* Pressure/Vacuum Valve.

BREATHING   The movement of gas (oil vapors or air) in and out of the vent lines of storage tanks due to alternate heating and cooling.

BRIDGE   The location aboard ship where the control of the vessel motions are directed, also vessel surveillance alarms. A high transverse platform, often forming the top of a bridge house, extending from side to side of the ship, and from which a good view of the weather deck may be had. An enclosed space called the pilothouse is erected on the bridge in which are installed the navigating instruments, such as the compass and binnacle, the control for the steering apparatus, and the signals to the engine room. While the pilothouse is generally extended to include a chartroom and sometimes staterooms, a clear passageway should be left around it. As the operation of the ship is directed from the bridge or flying bridge above it, there should also be a clear, open passage from one side of the vessel to the other. The term is also applied to the narrow walkways, called connecting bridges, which connect the bridge deck with the poop and forecastle decks. This type of bridge is usually found on tankers and is desirable whenever bulwarks are not fitted.

BRIDGE, NAVIGATING OR FLYING   The uppermost platform erected at the level of the top of the pilothouse. It generally consists of a narrow walkway supported by stanchions, running from one side of the ship to the other and the space over the top of the pilothouse. A duplicate set of navigating instruments and controls for the steering gear and engine room signals are installed on the flying bridge so that the ship may be navigated in good weather from this platform. Awnings erected on stanchions and weather cloths fitted to the railing give protection against sun and wind.

BRIDGE DECK   Deck at top of bridge superstructure.

BRIDGE FITTINGS/ PIECES (BP)   Locking and tensioning devices placed between containers on the top tier to secure them rigidly together, or used to secure double- or triple-stacked containers.

BRIDGE HOUSE   A term applied to an erection or superstructure fitted about amidships on the upper deck of a ship.

BRIDGE PLATE   A plate, usually of steel, used to span the space between a freight car or truck bed and the loading platform.

BRIDGE POINT   An inland location where cargo is received by the ocean carrier and then moved to a coastal port for loading.

BRIDGE PORT   A port where cargo is received by the ocean carrier and stuffed into containers then moved to another coastal port to be loaded on a vessel.

BRIDGE -TO- BRIDGE   Marine radiotelephone communication, VHF.

BRIDGE WINGS   Extension of the bridge house out to the very side edge of a ship.

BRIDLE   A Y-shaped arrangement of line, wire, or chain. Each part or leg must be of equal length. They are joined together at a fishplate or shackle, which in turn is connected to the pendant. An assembly of wire rope or chain, used as a sling.

BRIDLE LEG   A single part or leg of a bridle.

BRIGHT STOCKS   Pressure distillate bottoms, which have had petrolatum wax, removed and which have been filtered so that the stock has a low cold test and a good color (dark red by transmitted light and green by reflected light). Bright stock constitutes the body of lubricants manufactured for internal combustion engines.

BRIGHT WORK   Brass work, polished.

BRITTLE FRACTURE   A break in a material or structure with little or no deformation prior to the break.

BROADCAST NOTICE TO MARINERS   A radio broadcast designed to provide important marine information.

BROB   Bunker Remaining On Board.

BROKEN BACKED   Said of a vessel when, owing to insufficient longitudinal strength, grounding, or other accident, her sheer is reduced or lost, thereby producing a drooping effect at both ends.

BROKEN STOWAGE   The waste and loss of space caused by irregularity in the size and shape of packages. Also, any void or empty space in a container not occupied by cargo.

BROKER   Middleman between buyer and seller. A person who arranges for transportation of loads for a percentage of the revenue from the load.

BROKERAGE   Fee or commission that is paid to a broker for services performed. Freight forwarder/broker compensation as specified by ocean tariff.

BROW   A gangplank, usually fitted with rollers at the end resting on the wharf to allow for the movement of the vessel with the tide.

BROW PLATE   A plate forming a riser on the sides of a 'tween deck hatch coaming. It enables the stevedores to truck cargo on the hatch covers so that it can be hoisted from the square of the hatchway.

BRUSH AXE (BRUSH HOOK)   A tool with a curved pointed blade on the end, especially adaptable for clearing small trees and brush.

BRUSH OUT   Term used for the clearing of brush or vegetation around a light or daymark so that the structure is visible to navigation in all-necessary directions. An aid should be cleared or brushed out so as to be completely visible to navigation from the beginning of its use in a set of marks until it is no longer being used in that or another set of marks. *See* Landscaping.

BRUSSELS TARIFF NOMENCLATURE (BTN)   The old Customs Cooperation Council Nomenclature for the classification of goods. Now replaced by the Harmonized System.

BSI SPECIFICATION   British Standards Institution specification for freight containers.

BSS   Basis.

BSS 1/1   Basis 1 Port to 1 Port.

BS&W   Bottom Sediment and Water.

BS&W TEST   Standard test for the sediment (bottom settlings) and water content of an oil. Test performed by measuring the material separated from a sample of the oil by centrifuging under standard conditions.

BT   Berth Terms.

BT WAGEN   *See* Behaltertragwagen.

BTN   *See* Brussels Tariff Nomenclature.

B-TO-B   Business to Business.

BTU   British Thermal Unit. The amount of heat required to raise the temperature of 1 pound of water 1°F.

BU   Bushel.

BUBBLE   An alternative emission control strategy where several emission points are regarded as being placed under a hypothetical dome, which is then regarded as a single emission source.

BUBBLE CAP TOWER   A fractionating tower so constructed that rising vapors pass through layers of condensate on a series of plates. The vapor passes from one plate to the next above by bubbling under one or more caps and out through the liquid on the plate. In bubbling through the liquid the less volatile portions of vapor condense on the plate and overflow to the next lower plate and ultimately back into the reboiler. Fractionation is thereby effected.

BUCKET   A container for temporarily holding quantities of materials in bulk while being conveyed from one point to another. Part of equipment for moving earth or other material for excavation or filling.

BUCKET DREDGE   A dredge type that mechanically operates an endless belt of buckets that revolves around the dredge ladder. The individual buckets contact the bottom and bring dredge materials to the surface through the water and dump them into an onboard hopper or into a barge built for that purpose.

BUCKLE A distortion, such as a bulge; to become distorted; to bend out of its own plane.

BUCKLER Generally, but not exclusively, applied to various devices used to prevent water from entering turret gun ports, hawse and chain pipes, etc.

BUCKLING The departure of a plate, shape, or stanchion from its designed plane or axis when subjected to load or to strains introduced during fabrication, thereby reducing its ability to carry loads.

BUFFER STOCK A quantity of goods or articles kept in storage to safeguard against unforeseen shortages or demands.

BUILDING BLOCK CONCEPT Combining smaller packages into larger units that can be more efficiently handled at one time.

BUILDING SLIP A place where a ship is built before launching.

BUILDINGS & PERSONAL PROPERTY COVERAGE FORM (INS) A commercial property coverage form designed to insure most types of commercial property (buildings or contents or both). It is the most frequently used commercial property form and has replaced the General Property Form, Special Building Form, Special Personal Property Form, and others.

BULB ANGLE Angle shape reinforced at one toe. An angle with one edge having a bulb or swell. To increase area for welding.

BULB PLATE Narrow plate reinforced on one edge. Used for hatch coamings, built up beams, etc.

BULB TEE T-bar with toe of web reinforced.

BULBOUS BOW Protruding bow below waterline intended to reduce vessel's resistance to motion under certain circumstances. Was considered at one time to be favorable only for moderate to high-speed ships. Has, however, been found to be beneficial in relatively low speed ships such as tankers and bulk carriers. Research has shown that the bulb has a greater effect when situated some distance forward of the stem. This has led to adoption of the ram bulb.

BULK A mass of a product, unpackaged and generally homogeneous in nature.

BULK AREA The pallet load for large items which at a minimum most efficiently handles a storage area.

BULK BAGS A large polythene liner that can be fitted to a 20'GP as an alternative to bulk containers.

BULK CARGO Selected commodities that are normally shipped loose and in large quantities, which in the loading and unloading thereof are ordinarily shoveled, scooped, forked, or mechanically conveyed, and are not in packages, containers, or in units of such size to permit piece-by-piece handling, e.g., salt, gypsum, sugar, etc. Goods that are transported in large ocean going vessels; examples include salt, coal, petroleum, and grain. Petroleum carried in cargo tanks and not shipped in drums, containers, or packages.

BULK CARRIERS Ships designed to carry dry bulk cargo. Category includes: ore/bulk/oil carriers and other combination bulk/oil, and ore/oil carriers.

BULK CHEMICAL ANALYSES The laboratory testing of sediment to determine the chemical concentrations of key parameters of interest. This testing is part of the U.S. EPA/Corps Regional testing protocol.

BULK CONTAINERS These containers are designed for the carriage of dry powders and granular substances in bulk. To facilitate top loading, three circular hatches (500 mm diameter) are fitted in the roof. For discharge, a hatch is fitted in the right-hand door of the container. Full width doors are fitted to allow loading of conventional cargo.

BULK FREIGHT Not in packages or containers; shipped loose in the hold of a ship. Grain, coal and sulfur are usually bulk freight.

BULK FREIGHT CONTAINER A container with a discharge hatch in the front wall; allows bulk commodities to be grasped by loading hatches.

BULKHEAD A term applied to any one of the partition walls that subdivide the interior of a ship into compartments or rooms to protect against shifting cargo and/or to separate the load and to retard the spread of leakage or fire. A fixed pier or wall back filled to be continuous with the land. The various types of bulkheads are distinguished by location, use, kind of material or method of fabrication, such as fore peak, longitudinal, transverse, watertight, wire mesh, pilaster, etc. Bulkheads that contribute to the strength and seaworthiness of a vessel are called strength bulkheads, those that are essential to the watertight subdivision are watertight or oil tight bulkheads, and gas tight, fume tight bulkheads serve to prevent fumes from entering or leaving certain parts of a vessel.

BULKHEAD, AFTER PEAK A term applied to the first transverse bulkhead forward of the sternpost. This bulkhead forms the forward boundary of the after peak tank and should be made watertight.

BULKHEAD, COLLISION First watertight bulkhead from the bow of a ship; extending from the keel to the shelter deck. This bulkhead prevents the entire ship from being flooded in case of a bow collision. The foremost transverse watertight bulkhead in a ship, which extends from the bottom of the hold to the freeboard deck. It is designed to keep water out of the forward hold in case of collision damage. Usually, this is the fore peak bulkhead at the after end of the fore peak tank.

BULKHEAD, JOINER Wood or light metal bulkheads serving to bound staterooms, offices, etc., and not contributing to the ship's strength. Included under this head are corrugated metal, pressed panel, plaster, aluminum, stainless steel, etc.

BULKHEAD, SCREEN   A bulkhead, dust tight but not watertight, usually placed between the engine and the boiler rooms.

BULKHEAD, SHORE REVETMENT   A steel or concrete wall designed to create a flat wall between the shore and water. Commonly used to hold back deteriorating shorelines or provide structure for quick land development or dredge spoil disposal.

BULKHEAD, STIFFENER   Members attached to the plating of a bulkhead for the purpose of holding it in a plane when pressure is applied to one side. The stiffener is generally vertical, but horizontal stiffeners are used and both are found on same bulkheads. The most efficient stiffener is a T section; flat bars, angles, channels, zees, H and I sections are commonly used.

BULKHEAD, SWASH   A strongly built, nontight bulkhead placed in oil or water tanks to slow down the motion of the fluid set up by the motion of the ship.

BULKHEAD, WIRE MESH   A partition or enclosure bulkhead, used largely in storerooms, shops, etc., made of wire mesh panels.

BULKHEADING   Segregating cargo by putting up a wooden wall between packages of one item and those of another. To partition off a section of shoreline by constructing a vertical wall for containment of (dredged) material.

BULKING FACTOR   A factor that describes the tendency of a given soil to take on water when disturbed.

BULK PACKING   Packing a number of small pieces into a single larger container to facilitate movement.

BULK PLANT   Any organic material storage and/or distribution facility with an average daily throughput ($\frac{1}{30}$ of the total throughput on a rolling 30 day time period) of greater than or equal to 4,000 but less than 20,000 gallons of organic material having a true vapor pressure greater than 1.5 psia under actual storage conditions.

BULK SHIPMENTS   Shipments that are not packaged but are loaded directly into the vessel's holds. Examples of commodities that can be shipped in bulk are ores, coal, scrap, iron, grain, rice, vegetable oil, tallow, fuel oil, fertilizers, and similar commodities.

BULK STORAGE   Some warehouses have silos and/or storage tanks for the storage and dispensing of materials in bulk on a weight or liquid measure.

BULK TERMINAL   Terminal where unpackaged commodities carried in holds and tanks of cargo vessels and tankers are generally transferred by such means as conveyors, clamshell pipelines, etc, are handled.

BULK TREATMENT   Any organic material storage and/or distribution facility with an average daily throughput (1/30 of the total throughput on a rolling 30 day time period) of greater than 20,000 gallons of organic material having a true vapor pressure greater than 1.5 psia under actual storage conditions.

BULK UTILIZATION CHARGE   Charge, which applies to consignments, carried from airport of departure to airport of arrival, entirely in Unit Load devices (air cargo).

BULL CHAIN   Heavy chain used with a single topping lift to hold the boom in the desired working position.

BULLDOZER   A machine, usually hydraulic or electric, for bending bars, shapes, or plates while cold.

BULLETIN BOARD   A board located at each dam upon which is displayed information concerning the navigability of the dam such as indicating when movable dams are down and open river conditions exist. Also located elsewhere such as at gauges to publish gauge readings and river level trend.

BULL LINK   Line used to top or lower a boom rigged with a single topping lift.

BULLNOSE   The closed chock at the stem of a tug or ship. Also, a slanted riverward end of the intermediate lock wall.

BULL RINGS   Cargo securing devices mounted in the floor of containers; allow lashing and securing of cargo.

BULL ROPE   A rope used for "snaking out" cargo to the square of the hatch from the 'tween deck or lower hold, or used to work the cargo into these spaces. It is used in combination with a snatch block. Also, a rope used in connection with the topping lift. One end is secured to the topping lift and the other is wound on the drum of the winch.

BULWARK   Steel plating acting as railings on weather decks, usually near the bow. The strake of shell plating or the side planking above a weather deck. It helps to keep the deck dry and also serves as a guard against losing deck cargo or men overboard. Where bulwarks are fitted, it is customary to provide openings in them that are called freeing ports, to allow the water that breaks over to clear itself. The raised portion of the tug's hull running from the stem to the stern on either side, usually used in plural form.

BULWARK STAY   A brace extending from the deck to a point near the top of the bulwark, to keep it rigid.

BUMP   This term is usually used in the phrase "watch the bump," used on board tows when one or more barges are likely to make contact. Term may also mean a momentary grounding usually due to excess speed in shallow water.

BUMPED   A term applied to a plate that has been pressed or otherwise formed to a concave or convex shape. Used for head of tanks, boilers, etc.

BUMPERS (POSSUM)   Fenders.

BUNDLING   Assembling of pieces of cargo, secured into one manageable unit.

BUNK   A built in bed onboard ship.

BUNKER   (Noun) A compartment below deck for storing fuel or coal used for ship propulsion. (Verb) To load fuel into a vessel's bunker for its own use as distinguished from loading it as cargo.

BUNKER ADJUSTMENT FACTOR (BAF)   Adjustment applied by shipping lines or liner conferences to offset the effect of fluctuations in the cost of bunkers.

BUNKER "C"   An obsolete term used to describe a commercial fuel similar to Navy Heavy.

BUNKER CHARGE An extra charge sometimes added to steamship freight rates; justified by higher fuel costs. Also known as Fuel Adjustment Factor or FAF.

BUNKERING The loading of fuel used on board.

BUNKERING FUEL Fuel used in the boiler firing of ships.

BUNKERS Fuel for operation of a vessel's own engines or boilers. A Maritime term referring to fuel used aboard the ship. Coal stowage areas aboard a vessel in the past were in bins or bunkers.

BUNKER TANKS Storage location for bunker fuel, usually in double bottom on freighters, aft of bow and near engine room on tankers.

BUNTING Flag material or flags collectively.

BUOYANCY The tendency or capacity to remain afloat in a liquid. The upward force of a fluid upon a floating object. It is equal to the weight of the displaced liquid.

BUOYANCY, RESERVE The additional buoyancy that would result if that part of the vessel's hull, which is above the load waterline, were immersed. Usually referred to a specific condition of loading. It is usually expressed as a percentage of the total volume of the vessel or total buoyancy; and is thus a measure of the additional weight, which could be placed on the ship before it would sink through loss of buoyancy. Free board is an indicator.

BUOY LINE A line formed by two or more buoys marking a contour edge of a channel.

BUOY RANGE MARKERS Painted stakes set up on shore so placed as to form a range through the exact location of a buoy. Used only on the Tennessee River to mark buoys in dredged cuts.

BUOYS Floats that warn of hazards such as rocks or shallow ground, to help ships maneuver through unfamiliar harbors. Lighted or unlighted floating aids to navigation that is secured to the seabed or riverbed by a mooring.

BURDEN The carrying capacity of a vessel expressed in long tons.

BUREAU VERITAS French classification society

BURNER FUEL OIL A fuel oil that is used primarily in oil burning equipment for the generation of heat in furnaces for heating buildings.

BURNERS Men who operate gas torches for burning plates and shapes to proper sizes for assembly into the structure.

BURR The rough, uneven edge of a sheared or burned plate or around a punched or burned hole. Also a washer-shaped piece or metal through which the rivet is inserted and against which the rivet point is riveted over.

BUSBARS (FEEDER) Noninsulated copper bars at back of main switchboard to which feeders from main alternator or generator main breakers are attached.

BUSINESS AUTO COVERAGE FORM (INS) The latest commercial automobile insurance coverage form, which may be written as a monoline policy or as part of a commercial package. This form has largely replaced the Business Auto Policy.

BUSINESS INCOME   Business pre-tax profit type income. It includes profit, interest income, rental income, and depreciation.

BUSINESS INCOME COVERAGE FORM (INS)   A commercial property form providing coverage for "indirect losses" resulting from property damage, such as loss of business income and extra expenses incurred. It has replaced earlier Business Interruption and Extra Expense forms.

BUSINESS INTERRUPTION INSURANCE (INS)   A type of policy that pays for loss of earnings when operations are curtailed or suspended because of property loss.

BUSINESS LIABILITY (INS)   The term used to describe the liability coverages provided by the business owners Liability Coverage Form. It includes liability for bodily injury, property damage, personal injury, advertising injury, and fire damage.

BUSINESS PERSONAL PROPERTY (INS)   Traditionally known as "contents," this term actually refers to furniture, fixtures, equipment, machinery, merchandise, materials, and all other personal property owned by the insured and used in the insured's business.

BUSINESS PROCESS REENGINEERING (BPR)   The fundamental analysis and radical redesign of everything: business processes and management systems, job definitions, organizational structures and beliefs and behaviors to achieve dramatic performance improvements to meet contemporary requirements. Information technology (IT) is a key enabler in this process.

BUSINESS TO BUSINESS INTEGRATION (B2BI)   Form of Supply Chain Management—manufacturers implement integration at the business process, application, data, and network layers to accomplish tight synchronization with their supply chain partners. B2BI projects promise to "extend the enterprise" to encompass business partners in much the same way the enterprise currently encompasses internal departments.

BUTADIENE   A hydrocarbon (diolefin) used to make synthetic rubber.

BUTT   The joint formed when two parts are placed edge to edge; the end joint between two plates.

BUTT STRAP   A strip or strap that overlaps both pieces, serving as a connecting strap between the butted ends of plating. The strap connections at the edges are called seam straps.

BUTTERWORTH   A commercially developed method of cleaning and gas freeing tanker cargo tanks with hot water sprayed from a special machine.

BUTTOCK   The intersection of a fore and aft vertical plane with the molded form of the ship. The rounded in overhanging part on each side of the stern in front of the rudder, merging underneath in the run.

BUTTOCK LINES   The intersection of a fore and aft vertical plane with the molded form of the ship. The curved lines shown by taking a vertical longitudinal section of the after part of the ship's hull; parallel to the keel. Buttock lines are curved lines on the profile or sheer plan. The curves shown by taking vertical longitudinal sections of the after part of a ship's hull parallel to the ship's keel. Similar curves in forward part of hull are "bow lines."

BUTTON A heavy steel casting found mostly on lock walls, designed to hold the eye of a line or wire. It is also used as deck fittings on towboats and on barges. A short mushroom shaped bitt or a short timberhead.

BUYER An enterprise that arranges for the acquisition of goods or services and agrees to payment terms for such goods or services.

BUYER'S MARKET A "buyer's market" is considered to exist when goods can easily be secured and when the economic forces of business tend to cause goods to be priced at the purchaser's estimate of value. In other words, a state of trade favorable to the buyer, with relatively large supply and low prices.

BWAD Brackish Water Arrival Draft.

BX Box.

BY THE BOARD Overboard.

BY THE HEAD When a ship is loaded in such a way that the bow is drawing more water than the stern, often creating a situation of difficult steering; deeper forward.

BY THE RUN To let go altogether.

BY THE STERN When a ship is loaded in such a way that the stern is drawing more water than the bow, also known as "drag."

C

CABIN   The interior of a deckhouse, usually the space set aside for the use of officers and passengers.

CABLE   A rope or chain of great length, generally used in reference to chain or rope bent to the anchor.

CABLE ADDRESS   A code word of less than 10 letters, registered annually with the Central Bureau of Registered Addresses, used in lieu of the entire name and address of a firm receiving or sending cablegrams in order to reduce the number of words required in a cablegram.

CABLE CODE   System of letters, figures, or words with arbitrary meaning for shortness or secrecy.

CABLE FOR AUTHORITY   Request for permission to pay a letter of credit drawing despite discrepancies, sent electronically by the negotiating bank to the issuing bank.

CABLE LENGTH   100 fathoms or 600 feet.

CABLE SHIP   A specialty ship designed for the laying of undersea cables.

CABLE TOOL DRILLING   A method of drilling in which a steel bit is alternately raised and lowered to strike the formation.

CABOTAGE   Water transportation term applicable to shipments between two or more ports of the same nation; commonly refers to coastwide navigation or trade. Many nations, including the United States, have cabotage laws that require domestic vessels to provide domestic interport service. Coastwise and intercoastal navigation and trading.

CABOTAGE POLICIES   Reservation of a country's coastal (domestic) shipping for its own flag vessels.

C/A CODE   Course Acquisition Code

CAD   *See* Cash Against Documents.

CAF   Currency Adjustment Factor. A charge, expressed as a percentage of a base rate that is applied to compensate ocean carriers of currency fluctuations.

CAGE   A secure enclosed area for storing highly valuable items. Pallet-sized platform with sides that can be secured to the tines of a forklift to carry people for inventory.

CAISSON   A watertight structure used for raising sunken vessels by means of compressed air. Also the floating gate to close the entrance to a dry dock.

CALCIUM BASE GREASE   A grease composed of a mineral oil thickened with calcium (lime) soaps.

CALIBER   Inside diameter of a cylinder, tube, or pipe. The length of a naval gun is frequently expressed in terms of its caliber.

CALIFORNIA AIR RESOURCES BOARD   The California state agency established and empowered to regulate sources of air pollution in California, including motor vehicles, pursuant to California Health & Safety Code Sections 39500 et seq.

CALKING   The operation of jamming material into the contact area to make a joint watertight or oil tight.

CALL   The visit of a vessel to a port.

CALL SIGN   A code published by the International Telecommunication Union in its annual List of Ships' Stations to be used for the information interchange between vessels, port authorities, and other relevant participants in international trade.

CALLING IN POINT (CIP)   *See* Way Point.

CALM   A wind of force less than one knot.

CALORIE   The amount of heat required to raise the temperature of 1 gram of water 1°C at or near the maximum density.

CALORIFIC VALUE   A measure of the heating value of a fuel.

CAM   A projecting part of a wheel or other simple moving piece in a machine, shaped to give predetermined variable motion in repeating cycle to another piece against which it acts.

CAMBER   The rise or crown of a deck, athwartship. At any point is the vertical distance between the side of the deck and the deck at that point. It is the transverse slope of the deck. The purpose of the camber is to direct water on deck out to the side where it can be drained by the scuppers.

CAMEL   A wooden float, such as a large timber, placed between a vessel and a dock and acting as a fender. A decked vessel having great stability designed for use in lifting sunken vessels or structures. A submersible float used for the same purpose by submerging, attaching, and pumping out. *See also* Caisson.

CANCELABLE POLICY (INS)   A policy that may be terminated by the company or the insured by proper notification sent to the other party according to terms set forth in the policy.

CANT   A term signifying an inclination of an object from a perpendicular; to turn anything so that it does not stand perpendicularly or square to a given object.

CANT FRAME   A frame not square to the centerline, usually at the counter of the vessel.

CANTLINE   The space or groove between two fore and aft rows of casks stowed side by side. When the bilge of one cask is laid in the cantline of the tier below and rests over the heads of four other casks, it is said to be stowed "bilge and cantline."

CAORF   Computer-Assisted Operations Research Facility: A MarAd R&D facility located at U.S. Merchant Marine Academy, Kings Point, New York.

CAPACITY   The available space for, or ability to handle, freight.

CAPACITY CALCULATOR   A device that calculates quickly the capacity of a hold at any point in the loading of the hold.

CAPACITY CONTROL Process of registering and steering of capacity.

CAPITAL The resources, or money, available for investing in assets that produce output.

CAPPING The fore and aft finishing piece on top of the clamp and sheer strake at the frame heads in an open boat; called a covering board, margin plank, or plank sheer in a decked over boat. Also, use of a clean dredged material as a cover for contaminated dredged material disposal in open water as a means of isolating the contaminated sediment from the overlying aquatic environment.

CAPSIZE To "turn turtle" due to loss of transverse stability.

CAPSTAN A revolving device with axis vertical, used for heaving in mooring lines. Unlike the windlass, it is generally not set up for chain.

CAPSTAN, STEAM A vertical drum or barrel operated by a steam engine and used for handling heavy anchor chains, heavy hawsers, etc. The engine is usually nonreversing and transmits its power to the capstan shaft through a worm wheel. The drum is fitted with pawls to prevent overhauling under the strain of the hawser or chain when the power is shut off. The engine may be disconnected and the capstan operated by hand through the medium of capstan bars.

CAPSTAN BAR A wooden bar that may be shipped in the capstan head for heading around by hand.

CAPTAIN The commanding officer of a vessel, regardless of rank on naval vessel, referred to as Captain; the person designated as or acting as the watch officer in charge and maneuvering the vessel at any particular time.

CAPTAIN'S PROTEST A document prepared by the captain of a vessel on arriving at port; shows conditions encountered during voyage, generally for the purpose of relieving ship owner of any loss to cargo and shifting responsibility for reimbursement to the insurance company.

CAPTIVE CARGO Cargo whose origin or destination is so close to a port that it flows, of necessity, through that port.

CARBON BLACK A substantially pure form of finely divided carbon produced from gaseous hydrocarbons by controlled combustion with impingement of over ventilated small flames on iron surface (channel black). It is used as a filler in the rubber industry being especially valuable by virtue of the improved wearing quality that it imparts to tires. Smaller quantities are used as pigment in printing inks and paints.

CARBON RESIDUE The residue remaining after volatilizing an oil under specified conditions.

CARDINAL POINTS The four principal points of the compass: North, East, South, and West.

CARE, CUSTODY, & CONTROL Defines/clarifies who is responsible for a service to be performed such as: "These goods are insured while under the care, custody and control of . . ." NOTE: Incoterms are commonly used to define responsibilities in the movement of goods. *See* Incoterms.

CARFLOAT   A barge equipped with tracks on which up to about 12 railroad cars are moved in harbors or inland waterways. A barge used for ferrying railroad cars.

CARGO   Merchandise or goods accepted for transportation by ship. The commodities or goods that are transported in commercial enterprise, domestic trade, or international trade by a common carrier.

CARGO, DEADWEIGHT   The number of tons of cargo that a vessel can carry when loaded in saltwater to her summer freeboard marks. Also called cargo carrying capacity, net capacity, useful deadweight. (Stowage factor below 40 cubic feet.) Cargo is charged by weight.

CARGO, MEASUREMENT   Any cargo with a stowage factor above 40 cubic feet per ton. Cargo is charged by the space. Also called measurement goods or measurement freight.

CARGO, PORT   Opening in the ship's side for loading and unloading cargo into the 'tween decks. Also called side ports.

CARGO, SPECIAL   A term usually applied to goods for which special stowage, supervision and checking are considered necessary because of their desirability and value. Special cargo should not be confused with precious or valuable goods that are carried in a special room.

CARGO AD VALORUM   An additional freight charged to this type of cargo that is of high value. Usually at a rate of certain percentage on the declared value of the goods.

CARGO AGENT   An agent appointed by an airline to solicit and process international airfreight for shipments.

CARGO AIRCRAFT   Any aircraft other than a passenger aircraft or a combi (freighter).

CARGO ASSEMBLY   The separate reception of parcels or packages and the holding of them for later dispatches as one consignment (air cargo).

CARGO/BALLAST TANKS   Tanks used interchangeably for bulk cargo or ballast. *See* Permanent Ballast Tanks.

CARGO BATTEN   Strip of wood used to keep cargo away from the hull. Battens are usually about 6' × 1½", running fore and aft and bolted to the frames about one foot apart. Also held by cleats.

CARGO BOOM   Heavy boom used in loading cargo.

CARGO DEADWEIGHT TONNAGE OR CARGO CAPACITY TONNAGE   The deadweight tonnage minus items that are not part of the cargo, such as fuel, water, stores, dunnage, etc. The cargo deadweight is the maximum amount of cargo, in long tons, that the ship is able to carry: 2,240 pounds. It is the difference between the light ship weight and the displacement loaded.

CARGO DISASSEMBLY   The separation of one or more of the component parts of a consignment (from other parts of such consignment) for any purpose other than that of presenting such part or parts to customs authorities at the specific request of such authorities (air cargo).

CARGO DIVERSION *See* Absorption.

CARGO HANDLING The loading, discharging, and transferring of cargo.

CARGO HATCH Large opening in a deck to permit loading of cargo into holds.

CARGO HOLD A large open area within the hull of a ship designed to carry large objects such as containers.

CARGO HOSES Steel reinforced neoprene rubber hoses flanged on both ends and designed to provide the connection between a tanker and the facility.

CARGO INSURANCE Most of the larger customhouse brokers and foreign freight forwarders offer insurance coverage under their own blanket policy. Due to their (usually) sizable account base, brokers/forwarders can very often purchase marine insurance for an amount significantly less than one would normally pay if bought independently. Moreover, when you use a broker/forwarder insurance program, you are virtually assured of their assistance in facilitating adjustments should cargo loss or damage occur.

CARGO MANIFEST A manifest that lists only cargo, not charges.

CARGO MAT A mat, usually square and made of manila rope, used to protect the deck covering while taking stores, etc., on board.

CARGO NET A square net, made in various sizes of manila rope or chain, and used in connection with the ship's hoisting appliances to load cargo, etc., aboard the vessel.

CARGO NOS Cargo Not Otherwise Specified. Usually the first rate entry in a tariff that can apply to commodities not covered under a specific item or subitem in the applicable tariff.

CARGO PLAN Stowage plan that is prepared by the pier superintendent and carried out by the stevedore.

CARGO PORT An opening, provided with a watertight cover or door, in the side of a vessel of two or more decks, through which cargo is received and discharged.

CARGO PREFERENCE Cargo reserved by a nation's laws for transportation only on vessels registered in that nation. Typically the cargo is moving due to a direct or indirect support or activity of the government.

CARGO RESTRICTION CODE A code indicating that the use of a certain container is restricted to particular cargo.

CARGO SELECTIVITY SYSTEM The Cargo Selectivity System, a part of Customs' Automated Commercial System, specifies the type of examination (intensive or general) to be conducted for imported merchandise. The type of examination is based on database selectivity criteria such as assessments of risk by filer, consignee, tariff number, country of origin, and manufacturer/shipper. A first time consignee is always selected for an intensive examination. An alert is also generated in cargo selectivity the first time a consignee files an entry in a port with a particular tariff number, country of origin, or manufacturer/shipper.

CARGO TONNAGE Most ocean freight is billed on the basis of weight or measurement tons (W/M). Weight tons can be expressed in short tons of 2,000 pounds, long tons of 2,240 pounds or metric tons of 1,000 kilos (2,204.62 pounds). Measurement tons are usually expressed as cargo measurement of 40 cubic feet (1.12 meters) or cubic meters (35.3 cubic feet).

CARGO TRACER A document sent by the agent to all relevant parties, stating that certain cargo is either missing or over landed.

CARGO UNIT A vehicle, container, pallet, flat, portable tank or any other entity or any part thereof that belongs to the ship but is not permanently attached to that ship.

CARGO WAR RISK POLICY A separate cargo policy covering cargo while waterborne only (except at transshipping point, which may be on land or water). Insures against war risks.

CARLINGS Fore and aft member at side of hatch, extending across ends of beams where cut to form hatch, also placed between beams to stiffen areas under points of great stress such as under winches. Also called carlines. Short beams forming a portion of the framing about deck openings. Also called headers when they support the end of interrupted deck beams.

CARLOAD RATE A rate applicable to a carload of goods.

CARMACK AMENDMENT An Interstate Commerce Act amendment that delineates the liability of common carriers and the bill of lading provisions.

CARNET A Customs document permitting the holder to temporarily carry or send merchandise into certain foreign countries (for display, demonstration or similar purposes) without paying duties or posting bonds. Any of various Customs documents required for crossing some international borders.

CAROUSEL Rotating system of layers of bins and/or drawers that can store many small items using relatively little floor space.

CAR POOLING Use of individual carrier equipment through a central agency for the benefit of carriers and shippers.

CARRIAGE The process of transporting (conveying) cargo, from one point to another. Also chasis for trucks.

CARRIAGE OF GOODS BY SEA ACT (COGSA) A law enacted in 1936 covering the transportation of merchandise by sea to or from ports of the United States and in foreign trades.

CARRIAGE PAID TO (CPT) Carriage paid to CPT and carriage and insurance paid to CIP, a named place of destination. Used in place of CFR and CIF, respectively for shipment by modes other than water.

CARRIED ON/ CARRIED OFF (CO/CO) Break bulk cargo that is carried on and carried off the ship, by cargo handling equipment such as lift trucks, as opposed to LO/LO, RO/RO.

CARRIER   An individual, partnership, or corporation engaged in the business of transporting goods or passenger by rail, road, sea, air, inland waterway, or by a combination of such modes.

CARRIER FREQUENCY   A frequency continuously broadcast by a radio direction finder station that allows the operator to have a steady signal for tuning. Over this frequency, a specific identifying signal involving long dashes and Morse code designator letters is superimposed. For radar waves these frequencies range between the 3,000 and 10,000 MHz band.

CARRIER LIABILITY   The obligation to deliver merchandise to its proper destination with reasonable speed and in the same condition it was in when received from the shipper.

CARRIER WAVE   The transmitted base signal of all forms of transmitting systems.

CARRIER'S CERTIFICATE   A certificate required by U.S. Customs to release cargo properly to the correct party.

CARRIER'S LIEN   When the shipper ships goods "collect," the carrier has a possessory claim on these goods, which means that the carrier can retain possession of the goods as security for the charges due.

CARRYING CAPACITY   In ecology, the limit to the amount of life, in numbers or mass, that can be supported by a habitat.

CARRYING TEMPERATURE   Required cargo temperature during transport and storage.

CAR SEAL   Metal strip and lead fastener used for locking freight car or truck doors in such a manner that the doors cannot be opened without breaking the seals. Seals are numbered for record purposes.

CAR SUPPLY CHARGE   A railroad for a shipper's exclusive use of special equipment.

CARTAGE   The charge made for hauling freight on carts, drays or trucks.

CARTAGE AGENT   Ground service operator who provides pickup and delivery in areas not served directly by air carrier.

CARTMENT   Customs form permitting inbound cargo to be moved from one location to another under Customs control, within the same Customs district. Usually in motor carrier's possession while draying cargo.

CASE LOT PICKING   Selection of full cases of a product when the order is less than a full pallet load.

CASE-OF-NEED   Agent of the exporter located in the country of the importer who is to be notified by the presenting bank under a draft collection of any difficulties in collecting payment. The case-of-need may be given the power to change the collection instructions or even the draft amount, or may just be expected to make arrangements to store the goods and locate an alternate buyer. Whatever authority the case-of-need has should be specified in the collection instructions letter.

CASH AGAINST DOCUMENTS (CAD)   Method of payment for goods in which documents transferring title are given the buyer upon payment of cash to an intermediary acting for the seller, usually a commission house.

CASH IN ADVANCE (CIA)   A method of payment for goods in which the buyer pays the seller in advance of the shipment of goods. Usually employed when the goods, such as specialized machinery, are built to order.

CASH ON DELIVERY (COD)   Terms of payment: if the carrier collects a payment from the consignee and remits the amount to the shipper (air cargo).

CASH WITH ORDER (CWO)   A method of payment for goods in which cash is paid at the time of order and the transaction becomes binding on both buyer and seller.

CASHIER'S CHECK   Check drawn by and on the same bank, signed by its cashier.

CASING   Bulkheads enclosing portion of vessel, such as engine or boiler casing. Also, covering for parts of machinery, such as engine cylinder casing.

CASINGHEAD   A fitting at the top of the casing (or outer pipe) of an oil or gas well that permits cleaning, pumping, and the separation of oil or gas.

CASINGHEAD GASOLINE (NATURAL GASOLINE)   Gasoline recovered from the gas issuing from the casing head of oil wells and the gas from natural gas wells.

CASINGS, ENGINE AND BOILER ROOMS   The walls or partitions forming trunks above the engine and boiler spaces, providing air and ventilation and enclosing the uptakes. They extend somewhat above the weather deck, or superstructure deck if fitted, and are of sufficient size to permit installation and removal of engines and boilers. Doors are fitted at the several deck levels to permit access to the grating and ladders.

CAST OFF   To let go.

CASTING   A part made by pouring molten metal into a mold and allowing it to cool. Also, motion of turning a vessel's head away from the wind in getting underway, so as to bring it on the side desired. Design or drawing of a sail, indicating its shape and dimensions, position of reef points, bull's eyes, etc.

CASUAL LABOR   Temporary workers used to meet peak workloads.

CASUALTY INSURANCE (INS)   The type of insurance that is primarily concerned with losses caused by injuries to persons and legal liability imposed for such injury or for damage to property of others. It also includes such diverse forms as plate glass, insurance against crime, such as robbery, burglary or forgery, boiler and machinery insurance, and aviation insurance. Many casualty companies also write surety business.

CATALYST   A chemical that, without changing itself, causes a chemical reaction to proceed faster. A substance that effects, provokes, or accelerates reactions without itself being altered.

CATALYTIC CRACKING   A method of cracking in which a catalyst is employed to bring about the desired chemical reaction.

CATAMARAN   A platform used for work alongside a ship. It is secured to two hollow floats. Also a type of twin hulled ferryboat.

CATENARY   The dip in a line or tow cable when strung between two objects such as tug and tow.

CAT HEAD   An auxiliary drum usually fitted on one or both ends of a winch or windlass. Also called Drum End, Gypsy Head, Winch Head. It is used to haul rope or cable.

CATHODIC PROTECTION   A method of preventing wastage of a vessel's hull plating due to a combined chemical and electrical reaction caused by the movement of the vessel through the water. The most common method of protection is the mounting of zinc anodes on the hull that waste away instead of the ship's plating.

CATUG   Catamaran Tug. A rigid catamaran tug connected to a barge. When joined together, they form and look like a single hull of a ship; oceangoing integrated tug-barge vessels.

CAT WALK   A fore and aft raised walk connecting the fore and aft deckhouses.

CAULK (CALK)   To make a joint watertight. To drive oakum or other fiber into seams of planking of a vessel or boat to prevent leakage, which operation is completed by painting seams with pitch or some such water resisting preparation. In shipbuilding and boiler making, to drive down the faying edges of plating or other overlapping metal in order to make the work water or steam tight. (Use tar, pitch, or resin.)

CAUSES OF LOSS (INS)   Under the latest commercial property forms, this term replaces the earlier term "perils" insured against.

CAUSTIC   Describing an alkali solution chemical action that disintegrates most animal and vegetable matter and causes chemical burns on the skin.

CAVEAT EMPTOR   Let the buyer beware.

CAVIL (CAVAL AND KEVEL)   A steel cleat of special design used on barges and towboats for making fast mooring and towing lines. Also, a heavy timber fastened to the forward or after bitts about midway between the base and top to form a cleat. The bitt so built.

CAVING BANK   Caused by swift running currents along the shore and is more prevalent during periods of high water; very common occurrence on the lower Mississippi River. Can also be caused by eddies below bends or along the shoreline whether on right- or left-handed drafts. Caving banks are much more prevalent on rivers with unstable channels.

CAVITATION   In marine engineering, a partial vacuum around propeller blades caused by shaft speed exceeding that in which a screw attains its maximum effective driving effort. A source of lost propulsion efficiency, its reduction to a minimum is procured by proper number of blades consistent in pitch and surface area with normal depth of immersion and proposed revolution. Reduces thrust and efficiency. You can prevent cavitations by reducing speed.

The formation of cavities around a pump rotor or propeller blade, often in the back of the blade, these cavities being filled with air or water vapor. The effect of cavitation on a propeller is two fold: (1) the cavities formed eventually collapse resulting in a severe mechanical action that produces erosion of the blade surface, (2) with severe cavitation there is a loss in propulsion efficiency. Experiments have been devised to study the pressure distribution around the blade by operating the propeller in a closed channel or cavitation tunnel in which the fluid can be controlled.

CBFT OR CFT   Cubic Feet.

CBI   Caribbean Basin Initiative.

CBM   Cubic meter, also abbreviated CMC or m³.

CC   Current Cost.

CCC   Commodity Credit Corporation: An agency within the U.S. Department of Agriculture.

CDS   Construction Differential Subsidy: A direct subsidy paid to U.S. shipyards building U.S.-flag ships to offset high construction costs in American shipyards. An amount of subsidy (up to 50 percent) is determined by estimates of construction cost differentials between U.S. and foreign yards. Program has not been funded since 1981.

CE   Consumption Entry. The process of declaring the importation of foreign-made goods for use in the United States.

CEILING   The very bottom of a cargo hold, often wood installed over the steel deck; a term applied to the planking with which the inside of a vessel is sheathed. Also applied to the sheet metal or wood sheathing in quarters and storerooms.

CEILING, FLOOR   Planking fitted on top of the floors or double bottom in the cargo holds.

CEILING, HOLD   Thick strakes of planking fastened to the inside flanges or edges of the framing in the cargo holds.

CEILING VALUE   A maximum level. No exposure should ever exceed this level.

CELCIUS   *See* Centigrade.

CELL GUIDE   Steel bars and rails used to steer containers during loading and discharging while sliding down into the ship.

CELL POSITION   The location of a cell on board of a container vessel identified by a code for successively the bay, the row and the tier, indicating the position of a container on that vessel.

CELLS   The construction system employed in container vessels; permits below ship containers to be stowed in a vertical line with each container supporting the one above it.

CELLULAR VESSEL   Ship specially designed and arranged for the carriage of containers. Holds or cells are arranged so that the containers are lowered and stowed in a vertical line and restrained at all four corners by vertical posts or guides.

CEMS   Continuous Emissions Monitoring System.

CENTERLINE PLANE   A longitudinal plane at right angles to the base line plane and parallel to buttock planes port and starboard.

CENTER OF BUOYANCY   The point aboard a vessel in which all the upward forces of buoyancy are to be considered acting; the geometric center of gravity of the immersed volume of the displacement or of the displaced water, determined solely by the shape of the underwater body of the ship. It is calculated for both the longitudinal location, forward or aft of the middle perpendicular, and the vertical location above the base line or below the designed waterline.

The point at which the buoyant force of water on the immersed portion of the ship's hull may be considered as concentrated. The position of this point changes as the vessel is inclined.

CENTER OF FLOTATION   The geometric center of gravity of the water plane at which the vessel floats, forward or aft of the middle perpendicular. It is that point about which a vessel rotates longitudinally when actuated by an external force without change in displacement.

CENTER OF GRAVITY   The point aboard a vessel in which all the downward forces of gravity are to be considered acting upon; the point of equilibrium of the combined weight of the containership or stacktrain and its cargo.

CENTER OF LATERAL RESISTANCE   The point through which a single force could act and produce an effort equal to the lateral resistance of the vessel. It is ordinarily assumed to be coincident with the center of gravity of the immersed central longitudinal plane.

CENTER OF PRESSURE   The point in a sail or an immersed plane surface at which the resultant of the combined pressure forces acts.

CENTERLINE   An imaginary line drawn over the keel from the bow to the stern; the fore and aft middle line of the ship, from stem to stern.

CENTIGRADE   Temperature scale based on 0° for the temperature at which water freezes and 100° for the temperature at which water boils.

CENTILANE   A percentage of a lane, determined by a Decca receiver through a phase comparison measurement.

CENTIPOISE   1.01 Poise or centistokes times specific gravity at the test temperature.

CENTISTOKE   1.02 Stoke. *See* Stokes.

CENTRAL LATERAL PLANE   The immersed longitudinal vertical middle plane of a vessel.

CENTRECASTLE SPACE   The part of the midship superstructure of a tanker that is immediately over the tank deck and which does not contain accommodation.

CENTRIFUGAL PUMP High-speed cargo pumps using centrifugal force in a circular motion to throw cargo up a pipeline.

CENTRIFUGAL SEPARATOR A machine using centrifugal force to separate two phases of differing gravity, such as wax from oil or acid sludge from treated oil.

CENTRIFUGE An instrument for separating liquids of different specific gravities by use of centrifugal force produced by high speed rotation. Applied to diesel engine fuels and lubricating oils to remove moisture and other extraneous materials.

CERTIFICATE A document certifying that merchandise (such as of inspection perishable goods) was in good condition immediately prior to its shipment. The document issued by the U.S. Coast Guard certifying an American flag vessel's compliance with applicable laws and regulations.

CERTIFICATE OF ANALYSIS A document, often required by an importer or governmental authorities, attesting to the quality or purity of commodities. The origin of the certification may be a chemist or any other authorized body such as an inspection firm retained by the exporter or importer. In some cases the document may be drawn up by the manufacturer certifying that the merchandise shipped has been tested in its facility and found to conform to the specifications.

CERTIFICATE OF CLASSIFICATION A certificate issued by the classification society and stating the class under which a vessel is registered.

CERTIFICATE OF DELIVERY A certificate indicating the condition of a vessel upon delivery for a charter including ballast, available bunkers and freshwater.

CERTIFICATE OF FREE SALE A certificate, required by some countries as evidence that the goods are normally sold on the open market and approved by the regulatory authorities in the country of origin.

CERTIFICATE OF INSPECTION A document certifying that merchandise (such as perishable goods) was in good condition immediately prior to its shipment. And a document issued by the U.S. Coast Guard certifying an American flag vessel's compliance with applicable laws and regulations.

CERTIFICATE OF ORIGIN A certified document showing the origin of goods; used in international commerce.

CERTIFICATE OF PUBLIC CONVENIENCE AND NECESSITY The grant of operating authority that is given to common carriers. A carrier must prove that a public need exists and that the carrier is fit, willing, and able to provide the needed service. The certificate may specify the commodities to be hauled, the area to be served, and the routes to be used.

CERTIFICATE OF REDELIVERY A certificate indicating the condition of a vessel upon redelivery from a charter including ballast, available bunkers, and freshwater.

CERTIFICATE OF REGISTRATION   A document used to authenticate the description of the contents, the means of conveyance, and the date of departure of merchandise exported from the United States.

CERTIFICATE OF REGISTRY   A document specifying the nation registry of the vessel.

CERTIFICATED   Applied to tank vessels, refers to a vessel covered by a Certificate of Inspection issued by the Coast Guard; applied to men employed on tank vessels, refers to a certificate of ability issued by the Coast Guard.

CERTIFICATED CARRIER   A for-hire air carrier that is subject to economic regulation and requires an operating certification to provide service.

CERTIFIED GAS FREE   Verification by a document signed by an authorized person (usually a marine chemist from ashore) that states that a tank, compartment or container has been tested using an approved testing instrument and method and proved to be sufficiently free, at the time of the test, of toxic or explosive gases for a specific purpose, such as hot work or entry. If an authorized person is not available, the test should be carried out by a senior officer present, and the certificate will take the form of an entry in the vessel's logbook.

CETANE   A saturated liquid hydrocarbon used as the primary reference fuel when determining the ignition characteristics of diesel fuels.

CETANE NUMBER   Diesel fuel ignitability performance measured by the delay of combustion after injection of the fuel. It represents a comparison of a fuel with standards, which are cetaine in alpha methyl naphthalene.

CF   Cubic Foot; Customs Form.

C&F   Obsolete term of sale meaning "cargo and freight" whereby Seller pays for cost of goods and freight charges up to destination port. In July 1990 the International Chamber of Commerce Terms of Sale, or INTCOTERMS. Replaced C&F with CFR.

C&F NAMED PORT (CFR)   Cost and Freight. The seller must pay the cost and freight necessary to bring the goods to the port of destination, not including insurance. Buyer pays insurance while aboard ship up to overseas inland destination. The goods must be cleared for export.

CFR   Code of Federal Regulations.

CFS   Container Freight Station. A shipping dock where cargo is loaded ("stuffed") into or unloaded ("stripped") from containers. Generally, this involves less than container load quantities of freight, although small shipments destined to same consignee are often consolidated into full containers as well as reloading container load quantities from "foreign" rail or motor carrier equipment.

CFS/CFS   Cargo movement delivered loose at origin point, devanned by carrier at destination, and picked up loose at destination terminal.

CFS/CY   Loose cargo received at origin point, loaded in a container by carrier, then delivered intact at destination.

CFT   Cubic feet.

CGL (INS)   *See* Commercial General Liability Coverage Part.

CGS   Civil GPS service.

CHAFING GEAR   A guard of canvas or rope around spars or rigging to take the chafe. Any material used to prevent wear on lines to towing cables.

CHAFING PLATE   A plate fitted to take the wear due to dragging moving gear or to protect ropes from wearing where they rub on sharp edges. Also fitted on decks under anchor chains.

CHAIN   A group of specific stations that interact with each other in hyperbolic systems such as Loran C or Decca.

CHAIN CONVEYOR   A conveyor consisting of two or more strands of chain running in parallel tracks with the loads carried directly on the chains.

CHAIN LOCKER   Compartment in forward lower portion of ship in which anchor chain is stowed. Usually located directly below the windlass and immediately forward of the collision bulkhead in merchant vessels.

CHAIN OF SOUNDINGS   A method of navigation using water depth to determine a vessel's track with reasonable accuracy. The depth readings and the distance between them are then compared to the charted contours near the vessel's dead reckoning position. Where they match the contours is the vessel's most probable track and approximate position.

CHAIN PIPE   The iron bound opening or section of pipe leading from the chain locker to the deck, through which the chain cable passes. Also called a spill pipe.

CHAIN PLATE   A bar or plate secured to the shell of the vessel to which the standing rigging is attached.

CHAIN SHACKLE   A metal fitting, commonly U-shaped, used to connect chain to anchor or other chain.

CHAIN STOPPER   A device used to secure the chain cable when riding at anchor, thereby relieving the strain on the windlass, and also for securing the anchor in the housing position in the hawse pipe.

CHAINS   Usually refers to heavy chains attached to the anchor. Also applied to the lower parts of standing rigging that are attached to the chain plates.

CHAMFER   A bevel surface formed by cutting away the angle of two intersecting faces of a piece of material.

CHANDLER   An individual or company selling equipment and supplies for ships.

CHANGE OF TRIM   The algebraic sum of the initial trim and the trim after weight has been shifted, loaded, or discharged.

CHANNEL   The buoyed, dredged, and policed fairway through which ships proceed from the sea to their berth or from one berth to another within a harbor.

CHANNEL BOTTOM   Grade elevation or project depth.

CHANNEL MENDER An unstable river channel that changes its location after high water periods.

CHANNEL OF DISTRIBUTION A means by which a manufacturer distributes products from the plant to the ultimate user, including warehouses, brokers, wholesalers, retailers, etc.

CHANNEL PRISM The channel design dimensions, including required side slopes, width, allowable over depth, and advance maintenance.

CHANNEL REPORT A report of channel conditions, soundings, etc., found by an aid to navigation tender on routine patrol; includes report of courses steered. These reports are usually written in pilot's jargon.

CHANNOINE WEIR A section of a dam, built in the form of a spillway, lying between the anchor weir proper on the landside of a lock wall and the bear trap that is adjacent to the navigable path.

CHARACTERISTIC The audible, visual, or electronic signal displayed by an aid to navigation and assists in the identification of the aid to navigation. Characteristic refers to lights, sound signals, racons, radio beacons, and day beacons.

CHARGE An amount to be paid for carriage of goods based on the applicable rate of such carriage, or an amount to be paid for a special or incidental service in connection with the carriage of goods.

CHARGE TYPE A separate, identifiable element of charges to be used in the pricing/rating of common services rendered to customers.

CHARGEABLE WEIGHT The weight of the shipment used in determining airfreight charges. The chargeable weight may be the dimensional weight or on container shipments, the gross weight of the shipment less the tare weight of the container.

CHARGING AREA A warehouse area where a company maintains battery chargers and extra batteries to support a fleet of electrically powered materials handling equipment. The company must maintain this area in accordance with government safety regulations.

CHARLEY NOBLE The galley smoke pipe.

CHARTER The leasing or renting of an entire vessel, or part of its space, for a particular trip or period of time.

CHARTER PARTY A written contract between the owner of a vessel and the person desiring to employ the vessel (charterer) for the carriage of goods or hire of a vessel for a period of time; sets forth the terms of the arrangement such as duration of agreement, freight rate, and ports involved in the trip.

CHARTER RATES The tariff applied for chartering tonnage in a particular trade.

CHARTERER The legal person who has signed a charter party with the owner of a vessel or an aircraft and thus hires or leases a vessel or an aircraft or a part of the capacity thereof.

CHARTHOUSE Small room adjacent to steering wheel for charts and navigational instruments.

CHASSIS Special trailer or undercarriage on which containers are moved over the road.

CHEATER BAR (BREAKDOWN BAR) A length of pipe used to increase the leverage in setting up ratchets when connecting two rigging.

CHECK To ease off gradually.

CHECKING Service of counting and checking cargo against appropriated documents for the account of cargo or the vessel.

CHECK LINE A line used to help check a boat's headway when landing or entering a lock.

CHECK POST A mooring bitt on a lock wall.

CHECK VALVE Nonreturn valves that regulate flow of fluids to boilers, in piping systems and machinery.

CHEEK The side of a block.

CHELATION A chemical process involving the retention of a hydrogen or metal atom between two atoms of a single molecule.

CHEMICAL ABSORPTION INDICATOR An instrument used for discovering the presence of gases or vapor, which works on the principle of discoloring a chemical agent in the apparatus.

CHICAGO GRIPS A colloquial term used for a wire "come along"; used in hoisting wire rope.

CHICKSTAND A rigid loading arm for petroleum cargo, commonly found at marine terminals. Loading arm is equipped with universal couplings to provide flexibility for attachment to a ship or barge.

CHIEF ENGINEER The senior member of the engine department.

CHIEF MATE Crewmember whose area of responsibility is primarily cargo movement and labor relations.

CHIKSAN *See* Loading Arms.

CHIME The part of the cask or barrel at the end of the staves. Also spelled Chine.

CHINE The line formed by the intersection of side and bottom in ships having straight or slightly curved frames. The point in a tug's hull where the straight side turns inward below the water. The usual location of the bilge keel.

CHINSING The inserting of oakum or cotton between the plank edges of boats to secure water tightness. Also called caulking. *See* Caulk.

CHIP LOG The earliest type of speed log employed that was trailed astern of a vessel to measure the distance traveled through the water over a specific period of time.

CHIPPER A workman who chips, cuts, or trims the edges of plates, shapes, castings or forgings, using either hand or pneumatic tools, in order to secure a good caulking edge, fit, or finish.

CHOCK A piece of rubber, wood, or metal placed at the side of cargo to prevent rolling or moving sideways. A term applied to oval-shaped castings, either open or closed on top, and fitted with or without rollers, through which hawsers and lines are passed. Also applied to blocks of wood used as connecting or reinforcing piece, filling pieces, and supports for lifeboats. Also applied to the brackets fitted to boiler saddles to prevent fore and aft motion and to small brackets on the webs of frames, beams and stiffeners to prevent tipping of the member.

CHOCK, ROLLER A chock with a sheave to prevent chafing of rope.

CHOCK-A-BLOCK Two blocks of a tackle drawn together as close as possible; this condition is also referred to as two blocked. Also, crowded, packed full, referring to a barrel or compartment, etc.

CHOKED Fouled in the block, because of a kink or because of slipping off the sheave. Tightened up on the bight. *See* Sling.

CHOPT Charterer's Option.

CHRISTMAS TREE An assembly of pipes and valves at the top of the casing of an oil well that controls the flow of oil from the well.

CHROMOMETER An instrument used for determining the color of gasolines, kerosenes, and white oils.

CHRONIC Long-term effect. Low-level exposure over long periods gives rise to symptoms that develop over time.

CHRONIC TEST EFFECT The cumulative effect on man of prolonged exposures to low concentrations, or of intermittent exposures to higher concentrations, of a poisonous compound or vapor.

CHTRS Charterers.

CHURN The relentless cycle of acquiring new customers and losing others that characterizes consumer e-commerce and reduces lifetime customer value because switching is so easy.

CHUTE Section of river that is narrower than ordinary and through which the river current increases, often navigable from bank to bank. Also, a narrow sloping passage by which water falls or flows to a lower level (between an island and a bank).

CI Cost and Insurance. A price that includes the cost of the goods, the marine insurance, and all transportation charges except the ocean freight to the named point of destination.

CIA Cash in Advance.

CIDS Concrete Inland Drill System of platforms built for and towed to arctic waters, where they rest on the bottom.

CIF (NAMED PORT) Cost, Insurance, and Freight. Same as CFR except seller also provides insurance to named destination.

CIF&C Same as CIF, plus Commission.

CIFCI Cost, Insurance, Freight, Collection, and Interest.

CIF&E Same as CIF, plus the Exchange of currency from U.S. to foreign money.

CIFI&E Cost, Insurance, Freight, Interest, and Exchange.

CIP (CARRIAGE AND INSURANCE PAID TO)   An acronym meaning that the seller has the same obligations as under CPT but with the addition that the seller has to procure cargo insurance against the buyer's risk of loss of or damage to the goods during the carriage. The seller contracts for insurance and pay the insurance premium. The buyer should note that under the CIP term the seller is only required to obtain insurance on minimum coverage. The CIP term requires the seller to clear the goods for export. This term may be used for any mode of transport including multimodal transport.

CIRCA   About.

CITY TERMINAL SERVICE   A service provided by some airlines to accept shipments at the terminals of their cartage agents or other designated in town terminals or to deliver shipments to these terminals at lower rates than those charged for door-to-door pickup and delivery service.

CIVIL AERONAUTICS BOARD   A federal regulatory agency that implements economic regulatory controls over air carriers.

CIVIL GPS SERVICE (CGS)   A service consisting of the GPS Information Center (GPSIC) and the Precise Positioning Service Program office that provides information to and is the point of contact for civil users of the GPS system.

CKD   Completely Knocked Down. Automobile parts and subassemblies manufactured abroad and transported to a U.S. assembly plant.

CL   Carload. The minimum weight necessary to fully load a forty-foot railcar; and Container Load.

CLAIM   A demand made upon a transportation line for payment because of a loss sustained through its alleged negligence. A formal request for payment of a loss under an insurance contract or bond; the actual amount of the final settlement.

CLAIMANT (INS)   One who seeks reimbursement for loss under the terms and conditions of the insurance contract.

CLAIMS AGENT   A representative of the insuring Underwriters, usually located overseas, who has been authorized to accept the papers and documents required to prove a claim. While the claims agent does not have authority to make settlement with the claimant, he/she performs a valuable service in expediting the processing of a claim.

CLAIMS MADE COVERAGE (INS)   A policy providing liability coverage only if a written claim is made during the policy period or any applicable extended reporting period. For example, a claim made in the current reporting year could be charged against the current policy even if the injury or loss occurred many years in the past. If the policy has a retroactive date, an occurrence prior to that date is not covered. (Contrast this with Occurrence Coverage.)

CLAMP   A metal fitting used to grip and hold wire ropes. Two or more may be used to connect two ropes in lieu of a short splice or in turning in an eye. Also a device, generally operated by hand, for holding two or more pieces of material together, usually called a "C" clamp. In small boats, the main longitudinal strength member at the side and under the deck beams in decked over boats and at the gunwale in open boats.

CLAMP DOWN   To sprinkle and swab down, as a deck in hot weather.

CLAMSHELL DREDGE   A type of dredge that uses a single bucket attached to the dredge with cables. The dredge operates by lifting the bucket (the clamshell), dropping it into the bottom sediments, lifting the bucket and dredged material to the surface, and emptying the dredged material into a nearby disposal facility.

CLASS I CARRIER   A classification of regulated carriers based upon annual operating revenues: motor carriers of property—$5 million; railroads—$50 million; motor carriers of passengers—$3 million.

CLASS I HARDBOARD PANELING FINISH   A finish that meets the specifications for Class I of Voluntary Product Standard PS-59-73 as approved by the American National Standards Institute (ANSI).

CLASS II CARRIER   A classification of regulated carriers based upon annual operating revenues: motor carriers of property—$1–$5 million; railroads—$10–$50 million; motor carriers of passengers—0–$3 million.

CLASS II HARDBOARD PANELING FINISH   A finish that meets the specifications of Voluntary Product Standard PS-59-73 as approved by the American National Standards Institute (ANSI).

CLASS III CARRIER   A classification of regulated carriers based upon annual operating revenues: motor carriers of property—$1 million; railroads—$10 million.

CLASSIFICATION   A publication, such as Uniform Freight Classification (railroad) or the National Motor Freight Classification (motor carrier), that assigns ratings to various articles and provides bill of lading descriptions and rules.

CLASSIFICATION CLAUSE CARGO (INS)   A clause in a cargo insurance open cover that details the minimum classification for an overseas carrying vessel that is acceptable to the insurers for carriage of the insured goods at the premium rate/s agreed in the contract. Goods carried by lower class vessels are accepted under the open cover, subject to payment of an additional premium.

CLASSIFICATION RATING   The designation provided in a classification by which a class rate is determined.

CLASSIFICATION SOCIETY   An institution that supervises the construction of vessels under established rules, tests all materials for hulls, machinery, and boilers, proof tests all anchors and chains, and issues a certificate of classification.

CLASSIFICATION YARD   A railroad yard with many tracks used for assembling freight trains.

CLASS RATE A grouping of goods or commodities under one general heading. All the items in the group make up a class. The freight rates that apply to all items in the class are called "class rates."

CLASS RATING A single freight rate applicable to a group of commodities with similar attributes.

CLAUSE (INS) A section or paragraph in an insurance policy that explains, defines, or clarifies the conditions of coverage.

CLAYTON ACT An antitrust act of the U.S. Congress making price discrimination unlawful.

CLEAN BALLAST Ballast water that when discharged in calm water will not create a sheen upon the water nor sludge below the surface.

CLEAN BILL OF LADING A receipt for goods issued by a carrier with an indication that the goods were received in "apparent good order and condition," without damage or other irregularities.

CLEAN CARGOES Cargoes such as aviation and motor gasolines, diesel oils, jet fuels, kerosenes, and lubricating oils.

CLEAN DRAFT A draft to which there are no attachments.

CLEAN OILS Refined oils either colorless or light colored. Sometimes referred to as clean petroleum products, white oils, or white products.

CLEAN ON BOARD When goods are loaded onboard and the document issued in respect to these goods is clean.

CLEAN SHIP Refers to tankers that have their cargo tanks free of traces of dark persistent oils, which remain after carrying crudes and heavy fuel oils.

CLEANING IN TRANSIT The stopping of articles, such as peanuts, wood-chips, coal, grain, etc., for cleaning at a point between the point of origin and destination.

CLEANUP SOLUTION A solution that is used to clean any equipment and its parts.

CLEAR COAT A coating that lacks color and opacity or is transparent and uses the undercoat as a reflectant base or undertone color.

CLEARANCE LIMITS The size beyond which cars or loads cannot use bridges, tunnels, etc.

CLEARANCE OR ENTRY FEE This is a charge assessed to the importer by the customhouse broker for the service of filing an "entry" with U.S. Customs. The basic entry price encompasses all formalities required to expeditiously "clear" the shipment. The entry fee comprises some eighteen (give or take a couple) separate cost components including, e.g., "automated interface" with U.S. Customs, error and omission insurance coverage, etc. The basic entry charge normally does not cover special or unique services that may be required to expedite a shipment under unusual circumstances. Once Customs formalities have been properly satisfied, the goods are "released," and may enter the country.

CLEARANCE TERMINAL   Terminal where Customs facilities are available for the clearance of goods.

CLEARED WITHOUT EXAMINATION (CWE)   Cleared by Customs without inspection.

CLEAT (CLEVIS)   A device attached to a wharf to secure mooring lines. Piece of wood or metal of various shapes according to their uses, usually having two projecting arms or horns upon which to belay ropes. The term Cavil is sometimes applied to a cleat of extra size and strength.

CLERICAL ERROR   An error made by a clerical level employee that does not involve knowledge of Customs matters. An error by a classifier would not fall into this area. An example would be number transposition.

CLIENT   A party with which a company has a commercial relationship concerning the transport of cargo or concerning certain services of the company concerned, either directly or through an agent.

CLINCH   To spread or rivet the point of a pin or bolt upon a plate or ring to prevent it from pulling out; to turn the point of a nail back into the wood to give it greater holding power.

CLINOMETER   An instrument used for indicating the angle of roll or pitch of a vessel.

CLIP   A four to six inch angle bar welded temporarily to floors, plates, webs, etc. It is used as a hold fast; with the aid of a bolt, pulls objects up close in fitting. Also, short length of bar, generally angle, used to attach and connect the various members of the ship structure. Also called Clamp.

CLIP-ON   Refrigeration equipment attachable to an insulated container that does not have its own refrigeration unit.

CLIPPER BOW   A stem curving up and forward in graceful line.

CLM   *See* Council of Logistics Management.

CLOSE BUTT   A riveted joint in which the ends of the connected members are brought into metal-to-metal contact by grinding and pulling tight by clips or other means before the rivets are driven.

CLOSED GAUGING SYSTEM (CLOSED ULLAGING)   A method of measuring the contents of a tank by means of a device that penetrates the tank, but is part of a closed system to keep tank contents from being released. Examples are the float type, electronic probe, magnetic probe, and the protected sight glass systems.

CLOSED VENTILATED CONTAINER   A container of a closed type, similar to a general-purpose container, but specially designed for carriage of cargo where ventilation, either natural or mechanical (forced), is necessary.

CLOSEST POINT OF APPROACH (CPA)   Nearest distance a relative motion line of a target passes to a vessel.

CLOSING DAM   An earthen, sand, rock, or rock and brush structure built across a slough or back channel to stop current flow at water stages belowthe crest elevation of the structure. Low flows are thus diverted to the main channel.

CLOTHES STOP Small cotton line used for stopping clothes to the line or for securing clothes rolled up in bags or lockers.

CLOUD POINT The temperature at which paraffin wax or other solid substances begin to crystallize out or separate from solution when an oil is chilled under prescribed conditions.

CLP *See* Container Load Plan.

CLT Collect.

CLUB FOOT A fore foot in which displacement or volume is placed near the keel and close to the forward perpendicular, resulting in full waterlines below water and fine lines at and near the designed waterline, the transverse sections being bulb shaped. Also called a bulb or bulbous bow.

CM Cubic Meter (capital letters); Centimeter (small letters).

CNC *See* Compagneurs Nationales des Conteneurs.

C/O *See* Certificate of Origin.

COACP Contract of Affreightment Charter Party.

COALITION Coalitions are either buy-side or sell-side and are generally groups of buyers or sellers who agree to channel procurement through a single marketplace. They operate a marketplace without having a third party, neutral Net market as the hub. Many claim to be neutral—that anyone can join—but by the nature of their partnership their first audience is either buyers or sellers. The advantage of coalitions, particularly buy-side coalitions, is they can do a lot of transactions, which creates marketplace liquidity. However, the problem with coalitions is they have several challenges to overcome—political challenges, both from regulators and relationships between powerful companies, as well as technology challenges of integrating legacy systems. Due to the complexity of these issues, none are operational yet. If they do in fact successfully overcome these obstacles and operationalize, we expect they will conduct a large number of transactions because they can force their suppliers to go through this marketplace to conduct the transactions.

COAMING A vertical barrier designed to provide protection from openings on deck. When coamings are very close to the deck, railings are provided additionally; the vertical boundary of a hatch or skylight.

COAMING, BULKHEAD A term applied to the top and bottom strakes of bulkheads, which are usually made thicker than the remainder of the plating and act as girder web plates in helping to support the adjacent structure.

COAMING, HATCH A frame bounding a hatch for the purpose of stiffening the edges of the opening and forming the support for the covers. In a steel ship it generally consists of a strake of strong vertical plating completely bounding the edges of a deck opening.

COAMING, HOUSE A term applied to the narrow vertical plates bounding the top and bottom of a deckhouse, made somewhat thicker than the side plating and forming a frame for the base and top of the house. Also applied to the heavy timbers that form the foundation of a wood deckhouse.

COAMING, MANHOLE The frame worked around a manhole to stiffen the edges of the plating around the opening and to provide a support for the cover.

COAST EARTH STATION (CES) A land-based earth station in the INMARSAT satellite communications system that connects the space segment to ground-based telecommunication networks.

COAST GUARD U.S. government agency charged with regulating all aspects of the maritime industry.

COASTAL CARRIER Water carriers that provide service along coasts serving ports on the Atlantic or Pacific Oceans or on the Gulf of Mexico.

COASTAL CONFLUENCE SYSTEM A category within hyperbolic radio navigation systems designed to provide highly accurate position fixing information in potentially hazardous navigation areas. Its accuracy decreases the greater the distance from shore.

COASTAL REFRACTION A signal alteration caused by the passage of radio signals over or near a landmass, particularly where topographic features are prominent.

COASTING If two-tracked targets pass very close to each other, the ARPA processor looks for the contacts hit in a position farther down the relative motion line, based upon the time since it last tracked a hit using the contact's last known relative course and speed.

COASTWISE This term refers to any area within 20 miles of the shoreline and, in towing, routes that stay within such an area.

COASTWISE RECEIPTS AND SHIPMENTS Domestic traffic receiving carriage over the ocean, e.g., Boston to Puerto Rico, New Orleans to Boston.

COASTWISE TRAFFIC Domestic trade made up of traffic between ports on the same coast within natural territorial limits, as distinguished from foreign traffic, intercoastal traffic, or traffic to noncontiguous territories.

COATING A material applied onto, or impregnated into, a substrate for protective, decorative, or functional purposes. Such materials include, but are not limited to, paints, varnishes, sealants, adhesives, and temporary protective coatings.

COATING LINES One or more apparatuses or operations that apply, convey, and dry a surface coating comprised of including but not limited to the coating applicator (knife coating, roll coating, spray booths, flow coaters, dipping), conveyors, flash off areas, air dryers, drying ovens, and curing ovens. A coating line is considered to convey, apply, and dry one or more layers of surface coating including but not limited to base coat, single coat, prime coat, and top coat.

COATING MIXING TANK Any portable or stationary tank used to disperse, blend, strain, thin, or tint an ink or formulation used for surface coating.

COAXIAL CABLE (COAX) A cable consisting of a center conductor placed in the center of a nonconducting tube. Then a second conductor, called the shield, is placed around the nonconductive tube, which in turn is surrounded by thick insulation. This construction causes the fields to remain entirely inside the tube, which prevents RF energy from appearing outside the cable or other fields from mixing with the signal in the line. The shield is grounded to protect the internal fields of the cable and to dissipate any external RF energy.

COB Close of Business.

COBLDN Close of Business London.

CO-BRANDING One location where customers can purchase products from two or more name-brand retailers.

COC Carrier Owned Container.

COCK A valve that is opened or closed by giving a disc or a tapered plug a quarter turn. When a plug is used, it is slotted to correspond with the ports in the valve.

COCKBILL To hang an anchor up and down clear of the water. To incline the yards in a vertical position.

COCKPIT A term used in connection with small boats to refer to an uncovered, sunken place or pit, usually for the accommodation of passengers. The well of a sailing vessel, especially a small boat, for the wheel and steersman.

COD Cash on Delivery and Carried on Docket (pricing).

COFC Railway Service "Container On Flat Car."

COFC RAIL TERMINAL A rail terminal at which the rail carriers provide lifting facilities for the placing of containers on flatcars when the containers are being transported without chassis, as well as facilities for the placement of containers on flatcars when the containers are moving on chassis.

COFFER DAM Narrow empty space between two oil tight bulkheads to prevent leakage of oil into compartments adjoining oil tanks. Also, an enclosure from which the water can be pumped to expose the bottom of a river for the purposes of construction.

COFR Certificate of Financial Responsibility.

COGSA Carriage of Goods by Sea Act. U.S. federal codification passed in 1936, which standardizes carrier's liability under carrier's bill of lading. U.S. enactment of The Hague Rules.

COHESIVE When referring to grease or oil, good cohesive properties mean that the various particles of the lubricant hold tightly together and resist being pulled apart by mechanical action such as occurs in gears and bearings.

COI Certificate of Inspection. A document issued to U.S. flag vessels prior to oil transfer by the U.S. Coast Guard.

COINSURANCE/COINSURANCE (INS) In property insurance, a clause under which the insured shares in losses to the extent that he is underinsured at the time of loss. In health insurance, a provision that the insured and insurance company will share covered losses in agreed proportion. In health insurance, the preferred term is "percentage participation."

COKE The carbon residue left in the still after a charge of reduced crude oil has been run to dryness. Coke is largely carbon and is used mostly as a domestic fuel, but has some sale for special purposes, such as carbon electrodes.

COKING The process of distilling a charge of oil to coke. In the last part of a coking run on a shell still, the bottom of the still is red heat and most of the volatile matter is driven out, leaving the coke hard and dry.

COLD PRESSING The process of separating wax from oil by chilling and filtering under pressure.

COLD SETTLING The process used for the removal of petroleum wax from cylinder stock and high viscosity distillates. A naphtha solution of the oil is chilled and the wax crystallizes out. It is then allowed to stand until the wax settles to the bottom leaving a clear, nearly wax-free oil naphtha mixture at the top that is stripped of naphtha, after percolation through clay, to produce bright stock.

COLD WORK Work not involving the use of fire or heat.

COLLABORATION When several organizations work towards common goals.

COLLAPSIBLE CONTAINER A freight container, the major components of which can be disassembled and later reassembled for use.

COLLAR A piece of plate or a shape fitted around an opening for the passage of a continuous member through a deck, bulkhead, or other structure to secure tightness against oil, water, air, dust, etc.

COLLECT BILL OF LADING A bill of lading calling for charges to be paid by the consignee.

COLLECT FREIGHT Freight payable to the carrier at the port of discharge or ultimate destination. The consignee does not pay the freight charge if the cargo does not arrive at the destination.

COLLECTING (1) A bank that acts as an agent to the seller's bank (the presenting bank). The collecting bank assumes no responsibility for either the documents or the merchandise. (2) A draft drawn on the buyer, usually accompanied by documents, with complete instructions concerning processing for payment or acceptance. Item received by a bank subject to collection of proceeds before being credited to the depositor's account.

COLLECTION PAPERS Documents (invoices, bills of lading, or air waybill, etc.) submitted to a buyer for the purpose of receiving payment for a shipment.

COLLECTION SYSTEM Collections System, a part of Customs' Automated Commercial System, controls and accounts for the billions of dollars in payments collected by Customs each year and the millions in refunds processed each year. Daily statements are prepared for the automated brokers who select this service. The Collection System permits electronic payments of the related duties and taxes through the Automated Clearinghouse capability. Automated collections also meet the needs of the importing community through acceptance of electronic funds transfers for deferred tax bills and receipt of electronic payments from lockbox operations for Customs bills and fees.

COLLECTIVE PAPER All documents (commercial invoices, bills of lading, etc.) submitted to a buyer for the purpose of receiving payment for a shipment.

COLLECTOR OF CUSTOMS The representative of the U.S. Treasury Department acting for the government in connection with foreign traffic to specifically named inland sea ports.

COLLIER Any vessel designed for the carrying of coal.

COLLISION (INS) Physical damage protection for the insured's own automobile(s) for damage resulting from a collision with another object or upset.

COLLISION AVOIDANCE SYSTEM A synonym for automatic radar plotting aid.

COLLISION MAT A square sheet of heavy canvas roped like a sail for placing over a damaged part of a ship's shell plating in order to stop or reduce ingress of water until repairs may be affected.

CO-LOADING The loading, on the way, of cargo from another shipper, having the same final destination as the cargo loaded earlier.

COLONIZATION The establishment of a visible population of benthic animals.

COLORIMETER An apparatus used to determine the color of petroleum products.

COLORS The National Ensign.

COMBI Combination passenger/cargo vessel; a vessel specifically designed to carry both containers and conventional cargoes.

COMBINATION CARRIER A class of ship configured to carry both liquid bulk and dry bulk cargoes.

COMBINATION CHARGE An amount that is obtained by combining two or more charges.

COMBINATION CHASSIS A chassis that can carry either one forty foot or thirty foot container or a combination of shorter containers, e.g., 2 × 20 foot.

COMBINATION EXPORT MGR A firm that acts as an export sales agent for more than one U.S. manufacturer, all of which are noncompetitive with the others. Business is transacted under the names of the manufacturers and revenue is derived from sales commissions.

COMBINATION JOINT RATE A joint rate that is obtained by combining two or more published rates (air cargo).

COMBINATION RATE A rate made up of two or more factors, separately published.

COMBINATION UNIT A descriptive term for a tug and tow that are designed to work together, always in the pushing mode. The vessels are rigidly connected by mechanical means, and only separate during overhaul periods. Usually in bulk liquid carriage, composite units may look exactly like a tanker to the untrained eye.

COMBINED CYCLE COMBUSTION TURBINE Any combustion turbine, including the duct burner portion, in which heat is recovered from the exhaust gases to heat water or generate steam.

COMBINED TRANSPORT Intermodal transport where the major part of the journey is by one mode such as rail, inland waterway, or sea and any initial and/or final leg carried out by another mode such as road. *See also* Multimodal Transport or Intermodal.

COMBINED TRANSPORT BILL OF LADING (B/L) *See* Bill of Lading.

COMBINED TRANSPORT DOCUMENT (CTD) Negotiable or nonnegotiable document evidencing a contract for the performance and/or procurement of performance of combined transport of goods.

COMBINED TRANSPORT OPERATOR (CTO) A party who undertakes to carry goods with different modes of transport.

COMBUSTIBLE The general term describing any material that will burn. However, in the case of petroleum products only those that give off flammable vapors above 80°F are classed as combustible.

COMBUSTIBLE GAS INDICATOR An instrument for detecting a combustible gas/air mixture and usually measuring its composition in terms of the Lower Explosive Limit (LEL).

COMBUSTIBLE LIQUID Any liquid with a flash point from 100 to 200°F or any liquid mixture with 99% or more combustible components.

COMBUSTION The act or process of burning. Chemically, it is the process of rapid oxidation caused by the union of the oxygen of the air, which is the supporter of combustion, with any material that is capable of oxidation.

COMBUSTION DEVICE All equipment, including, but not limited to, thermal incinerators, catalytic incinerators, flares, boilers, and process heaters used for combustion of organic vapors.

COMBUSTION EFFICIENCY (CE) A measure of the completeness of combustion, expressed as a percent, determined by the measurement of carbon dioxide (CO_2) and carbon monoxide (CO) in flue gas in accordance with the following formula: $CE = (CO_2/CO + CO_2) \times 100$.

COME ABOARD A greeting when guests come on a boat.

COMMERCIAL AVIATION Transport of persons or cargo via air routes operated as a business enterprise (air cargo).

COMMERCIAL CODE A published code designed to reduce the total number of words required in a cablegram.

COMMERCIAL GENERAL LIABILITY COVERAGE PART (CGL) (INS) General liability coverage that may be written as a monoline policy or part of a commercial package. CGL now means Commercial General Liability forms, which have replaced the earlier comprehensive general liability forms.

The latest forms include all sublines, provide very broad coverage, and two variations are available, Occurrence, and Claims Made coverage.

COMMERCIAL INVOICE An invoice required to be presented to Customs representing one shipment of merchandise by one consignor to one consignee by one vessel or conveyance, which clearly identifies the product for classification and appraisement purposes. Also reports the content of the shipment and serves as the basis for all other documents about the shipment.

COMMERCIAL LETTER OF CREDIT (LOC) Letter of credit intended to act as the vehicle of payment for goods sold by one party to another.

COMMERCIAL RISKS With respect to Eximbank guarantees, commercial risks cover nonpayment for reasons other than specified political risks. Examples are insolvency or protracted default.

COMMERCIAL SET Set of four "negotiable" documents that represents and takes the place of the goods themselves in the financing of the cargo sales transaction.

COMMERCIAL ZONE The area surrounding a city or town to which rate carriers quote for the city or town also apply; the ICC defines the area.

COMMINGLING The combining of two or more petroleum products resulting from improper handling, particularly in pipeline or tanker operations.

COMMISSION An amount paid to the seller's agent or the buyer's agent. May be dutiable. Also may refer to the Federal Maritime Commission.

COMMISSIONED The action of placing a previously discontinued aid to navigation back in operations.

COMMISSIONER Commissioner of Customs (19CFT114.1).

COMMITTEE OF AMERICAN STEAMSHIP LINES An industry association representing subsidized U.S. flag steamship firms.

COMMODITIES CLAUSE A clause that prohibits railroads from hauling commodities that they produced, mined, owned, or had an interest in.

COMMODITY Any article of commerce; goods shipped. A collection of materials or items with similar characteristics. Also an article shipped. For dangerous and hazardous cargo, the correct commodity identification is critical. An element of movable commercial wealth that is bought and sold, therefore an economic good.

COMMODITY BOX RATE A rate classified by commodity and quoted per container.

COMMODITY CODE A code describing a commodity or a group of commodities pertaining to goods classification. This code can be carrier tariff or regulating in nature.

COMMODITY ITEM RATE Specific description number required in air transport to indicate that a specific freight rate applies.

COMMODITY RATE Fees applicable to a described commodity without regard to other freight classifications. Carriers typically charge commodity rates for a large movement made on a routine basis.

COMMON CARRIER   Any business enterprise performing a transportation service of moving cargo and passengers from one location to another, such as railroads, buses, trucks, steamship companies, and airlines. A transportation company operating under a Certificate of Public Convenience and Necessity; provides service to the general public at published rates.

COMMON CARRIER DUTIES   Common carriers are required to serve, deliver, charge reasonable rates, and not discriminate.

COMMON COST   A cost that cannot be directly assignable to particular segments of the business but that is incurred for the business as a whole.

COMMON LAW   Law that derives its force and authority from precedent, custom, and usage rather than from statutes, particularly with reference to the laws of England and the United States.

COMMON USER   A dock or storage facility that is used by a variety of companies, although it may have a single owner.

COMMUTER   An exempt for-hire air carrier that publishes a time schedule on specific routes; a special type of air taxi.

COMPAGNEURS NATIONALES DES CONTENEURS (CNC)   Affiliate of the French National Railways for Container traffic.

COMPANION WAY   A hatchway or opening in a deck provided with a set of steps or ladders leading from one deck level to another for the use of personnel.

COMPARATIVE ADVANTAGE   A principle based on the assumption that an area will specialize in producing goods for which it has the greatest advantage or the least comparative disadvantage.

COMPARTMENT   A subdivision of space or room in a ship.

COMPARTMENT STANDARD   The number of compartments in any location that can be flooded up to the margin line without causing the vessel to sink. Based on a certain permeability, usually 63 percent for cargo spaces and 80 percent for machinery space.

COMPASS   The compass is the most important instrument of navigation in use onboard ship, the path of a ship through the water depending on the efficient working and use of this instrument. There are two types of navigational compasses, the magnetic, which has long been in use, and the gyroscopic, which has been developed within recent years. The former is actuated by the earth's magnetism, the latter by that property of a rapidly rotating body by which, when it is free to move in different directions, it tends to place its axis parallel to the earth's axis, that is north and south.

COMPASS, GYROSCOPIC   The gyroscopic compass may have one or more gyroscopes. It is usually located as nearly at the rolling axis of the ship as possible and in a protected place. The directive force of a gyroscope, while 100 times more powerful than that of the magnetic needle, is still further amplified by an auxiliary electric motor sufficiently powerful to operate the compass card in azimuth. Repeater compasses, installed wherever desired about the ship, are operated by the master compass containing the gyroscopes by a simple electric follow-up system. The gyroscopic compass is not affected by magnetism from any source. It points to the true north, not the magnetic pole, and hence requires no calculations for corrections. It is not affected by cargo or any type of magnetic field, which may surround it, and it is not disturbed by jarring. It has become standard equipment in navies and is coming into more general use on commercial vessels.

COMPASS, MAGNETIC There are two kinds of magnetic compasses, the Dry Card Compass and the Liquid Compass. The dry compass consists essentially of a number of magnetic needles, suspended parallel to each other, and fastened to the rim of a circular disc that has a paper cover upon which are marked the points of the compass and the degrees. This card rests upon a pivot centered in the compass bowl, which in its turn is suspended by gimbals in the binnacle or stand, the latter having means for lighting the card at night and for adjustment of compass errors due to the magnetism of the ship. In the liquid compass, the bowl is filled with alcohol and water or with oil. The needles are sealed in parallel tubes and form a framework that connects the central boss with the outer rim, the whole resting upon a pivot in the compass bowl. Upon the rim are printed the points and degrees. The liquid compass is less susceptible to vibration and shock. The "Standard Compass" on board ship is a magnetic compass.

COMPASS, RADIO This apparatus is used to determine the direction from which a radio wave is sent and the location of the sending station. It consists of a coil of wire wound around a frame and mounted on a vertical shaft, which can be rotated. The radio wave is received by the operator, being loudest when the coil is at right angles to the wave and ceasing when the coil is parallel to the wave. Positions are determined by plotting the bearings to two known sending stations. The apparatus is especially valuable when a vessel is sufficiently close to the shore to contact two sending stations.

COMPATIBILITY A measure of the degree to which structural materials, contaminants, and other cargoes react with a particular chemical cargo.

COMPENSATORY MITIGATION In environmental management, the practice of creating additional fish and wildlife habitat to replace unavoidable habitat losses, so that the legal requirement of no net loss of habitat can be fulfilled.

COMPLETELY (CKD) Parts of a vehicle or machine shipped unassembled to a plant for assembly.

COMPLEX LOW A large area often more than 1,000 nm across in which two or more low centers exist.

COMPONENT A uniquely identifiable product that is considered indivisible for a particular planning or control purpose, and/or that cannot be decomposed without destroying it. A component for one organization group may be the final assembly of another group (e.g., electric motor).

COMPOSITE SAMPLE   A sample that is a mixture of samples taken from the upper, middle, and lower thirds of a container.

COMPOSITE UNIT   A tug and barge unit attached together through rigid means; such as the integrated tug barged unit.

COMPOSITE VESSEL   A vessel with a metal frame and a wooden shell and decks.

COMPOSITION   The basic electrical properties of the radar contact's surface. Steel offers an excellent composition, whereas wood or fiberglass offers very little reflective composition.

COMPOUND   A substance formed by the union of two or more chemical elements in definite proportions by weight.

COMPOUND OIL   A mineral oil to which animal or vegetable fat has been added. Later usage has included the addition of other additives.

COMPOUNDING   The dissolving of animal or vegetable fats or waxes such as sperm oil in petroleum oils in order to impart special properties. For example, steam cylinder oils usually contain 5–10% animal fat in order to make them emulsify readily with water and maintain a lubricating film on wet cylinder walls of a steam-operated compressor.

COMPRADORE   A local advisor or agent employed by a foreign party or company who acts as an intermediary in transactions with local inhabitants.

COMPREHENSIVE (INS)   Traditional name for physical damage coverage for losses by fire, theft, vandalism, falling objects, and various other perils. On Personal Auto Policies this is now called "other than collision" coverage. On commercial forms, it continues to be called "comprehensive coverage."

COMPREHENSIVE GENERAL LIABILITY POLICY (CGL) (INS)   A policy covering a variety of general liability exposures, including Premises and Operations (OL&T, Owner's Liability and Theft; M&C, Machinery and Cargo), Completed Operations, Products Liability, and Owners and Contractors Protective. Contractual Liability and Broad Form coverages could be added. In most jurisdictions the Comprehensive General Liability Policy has been replaced by the newer Commercial General Liability (CGL) forms that include all the standard and optional coverages of the earlier forms.

COMPREHENSIVE PERSONAL LIABILITY POLICY (CPL) (INS)   A personal liability contract. It provides personal liability coverage for the individual and family needs arising out of numerous personal activities and situations, such as the ownership of residential property, ownership of pets, sports activities, and many other everyday activities.

COMPRESSED GAS   Any material or mixture having in the container pressure exceeding 40 psi at 70°F or, having an absolute pressure exceeding 104 psi at 130°F. A chemical that has a boiling point below atmospheric pressure. Such a gas may be carried either at normal temperatures in pressurized tanks or under refrigeration at atmospheric pressure.

COMPRESSION Stress caused by pushing. Compressive stress is the result of two forces acting in opposite directions on the same line. Here, however, the forces tend to compress or push the material together.

COMPRESSION PIN Hardware used between top corner casting fittings when joining two 20-foot containers to create a 40-foot unit.

COMPULSORY SHIP A ship that is required to comply with global marine distress and safety system regulations.

COMPUTED VALUE Approved additions of dutiable amounts accumulated to reach a value of merchandise for purposes of appraisement by Customs.

COMPUTER RADAR A synonym for automatic radar plotting aid.

COMSAT Communications Satellite Corporation. The U.S. provider of satellite communication services under the IMARSAT global satellite system agreement.

CONAIR CONTAINER Thermal container served by an external cooling system (e.g., a vessel's cooling system or a Clip-On Unit), which regulates the temperature of the cargo. Conair is a brand name.

CONCEALED DAMAGE Damage to merchandise that is not discovered until the shipment is unpacked.

CONCENTRATION Volume of solute per volume of solution of a substance. Measured in parts per million (PPM) or milligrams per cubic meter (Mg/M3).

CONCENTRATIONS PPM and M/M 3:PPM Parts per million is a volume per volume relation of concentration. Mg/M3

CONDENSATE The liquid product coming from a condenser.

CONDITIONAL SALES CONTRACT Merchandise that is sold under the condition that the title to the goods will not be transferred until full payment is received.

CONDITIONALLY RENEWABLE (INS) A contract of health insurance that provides that the insured may renew the contract to a stated date or an advanced age, subject to the right of the insurance company to decline renewal only under conditions defined in the contract.

CONDITIONS Anything called for as required before the performance or completion of something else. Contractual stipulations that are printed on a document or provided separately.

CONDITIONS OF CONTRACT The terms and conditions established for a contract. These conditions are usually printed on the back of a waybill and include such items as limits of liability, claim limitation, indemnity, and dimensional weight rules.

CONDUCTOR A medium that allows current to flow within it.

CONES Devices for stacking containers on deck or one upon the other in order to restrain any lateral movement of the container. The cones fit into a deck socket or the top corner casting at each corner of the container. The container that is placed on top of each bottom corner casting resting on the upper part of the container. Cones come in a variety of types.

CONFEDERATION OF INDEPENDENT STATES' (CIS) INTERGROVERNMENTAL RADIONAVIGATION PROGRAM   The program that now operates GLONASS, the Russian satellite positioning system.

CONFERENCE   Steamship lines organization that fixes rates and sailings for the purpose of limiting competition between members and "outsiders." This may include a common tariff, but does not include joint service, consortium, pooling, sailing, or transshipment arrangement.

CONFERENCE AGREEMENT   An agreement among liner operators serving the same trade to fix rates, coordinate sailings, and cooperate in various other areas related to the production and marketing of services.

CONFERENCE CARRIER   An ocean carrier who is a member of an association known as a "conference." The purpose of the conference is to standardize shipping practices, eliminate freight rate competition and provide regularly scheduled service between specific ports.

CONFERENCE RATE   Rates arrived at by conference of carriers applicable to transportation, generally water transportation.

CONFERENCES   Associations of Ocean Carriers that regulate and set tariff rates, charges, and conditions for the transport of goods by water by member carriers.

CONFIRMED LETTER OF CREDIT   A letter of credit, issued by a foreign bank, whose validity has been confirmed by a domestic bank. An exporter with a confirmed letter of credit is assured of payment even if the foreign buyer or the foreign bank defaults.

CONFIRMING BANK   The bank that adds its confirmation to another bank's (the issuing bank's) letter of credit and promises to pay the beneficiary upon presentation of documents specified in the letter of credit.

CONGESTION   Port or berth delays. Accumulation of vessels at a port to the extent that vessels arriving to load or discharge are obliged to wait for a vacant berth.

CONNECTING CARRIER   A carrier that has a direct physical connection with or forms a link between two or more carriers.

CONNECTING ROAD HAULAGE   *See* Drayage.

CONNECTING UP   The act of connecting the tow cable and other necessary parts to a unit to be towed, whether accomplished at sea or in sheltered waters.

CONRADSON TEST   A carbon residue test method for determining the amount of carbon deposited after oil has burned. In this method, a sample of oil is tested by driving off volatile portions, weighing the residue, and calculating the percentage of original oil.

CONS   Consumption.

CONSEQUENTIAL LOSS (INS)   A loss arising indirectly from an insured peril.

CONSIGNED STOCK Finished goods. Inventories in the hands of agents or dealers that are still the property of the supplier.

CONSIGNEE Receiver of goods. A person or company to whom commodities are shipped. Officially, the legal owner of the cargo.

CONSIGNEE MARK A symbol placed on packages for identification purposes—generally a triangle, square, circle, diamond, cross, etc., with letters and/or numbers as well as port of discharge.

CONSIGNMENT A shipment (by a consignor to a consignee). A stock of merchandise advanced to a dealer and located at his place of business, but with title remaining in the source of supply. A shipment of goods to a consignee. A movement in which the title to goods remains with the shipper until the buyer sells the goods.

CONSIGNMENT INSTRUCTIONS Instructions from either the seller/consignor or the buyer/consignee to a freight forwarder, carrier or his agent, or other provider of a service, enabling the movement of goods and associated activities. The following functions can be covered: movement and handling of goods (shipping, forwarding, and stowage).

CONSIGNMENT NOTE A document prepared by the shipper that comprises a transport contract. It contains details of the consignment to be carried to the port of loading and it is signed by the inland carrier as proof of receipt.

CONSIGNMENT STOCK The stock of goods with an external party (customer) that is still the property of the supplier. Payment for these goods is made to the supplier at the moment when they are sold (used) by the customer.

CONSIGNOR Shipper of goods. A person or company shown on the bill of lading as the shipper.

CONSISTENCY A measure of the solidity or fluidity of semisolid products such as grease, petrolatum, and asphalt.

CONSOL A navigation system that was designed to provide long-range navigation from shore stations and was considered a radio directional system. It has been shut down virtually all over the world.

CONSOLIDATE To group and stuff several shipments together in one container.

CONSOLIDATED CONTAINER Container carrying goods of more than one shipper or goods for one shipper from more than one origin.

CONSOLIDATION Cargo container shipments of two or more shippers or suppliers. Container load shipments may be consolidated for one or more consignees.

CONSOLIDATION POINT The location where consolidation takes place.

CONSOLIDATOR The gathering together of diverse lots into one combined shipment. A person or firm performing a consolidation service for others. The consolidator takes advantage of lower full carload (FCL) rates and savings are passed on to shippers.

CONSOLIDATOR'S BILL OF LADING   A bill of lading issued by a consolidator as a receipt for merchandise that will be grouped with cargo obtained from other shippers. *See also* House Air Waybill.

CONSORTIUM   Group of carriers pooling resources in a trade lane to maximize their resources efficiently.

CONSTRUCTION DIFFERENTIAL SUBSIDY   A program whereby the U.S. government attempted to offset the higher shipbuilding cost in the U.S. by paying up to 50% of the difference between cost of U.S. and non-U.S. construction. The difference went to the U.S. shipyard. It has been unfunded since 1982.

CONSTRUCTIVE TOTAL LOSS (INS)   A partial loss of sufficient degree to make the cost of repairing as much or more than the property is worth or is insured for.

CONSTRUCTIVE TRANSFER   A legal function that permits acceptance of a Customs entry for merchandise in a zone before its physical transfer to the Customs territory.

CONSUL   A government official residing in a foreign country who represents the interests of her or his country and its nationals.

CONSULAR DECLARATION   A formal statement describing goods to be shipped; filed with and approved by the consul of the country of destination prior to shipment.

CONSULAR DOCUMENTS   Special forms signed by the consul of a country to which cargo is destined.

CONSULAR INVOICE   An invoice for merchandise shipped from one country to another, prepared by the shipper and certified at the shipping point by a consul of the country of destination. The consul's certification applies to the value of the merchandise, the port of the shipment, the destination, and the place of actual origin of the merchandise.

CONSULAR VISA   An official signature or seal affixed to certain documents by the consul of the country of destination.

CONSULATE   The jurisdiction, terms of office, or official premises of a consul.

CONSULTATION   Consular fees.

CONSUMPTION ENTRY (CE)   The process of declaring the importation of foreign made goods into the United States for use in the United States along with the duty due on such transportation.

CONTAINER   A large standard size protective box into which cargo may be packed for shipment aboard specially configured oceangoing containerships and designed to be easily interchangeable between the three basic modes of transportation: ship, truck, and rail. The transfer unit is the container rather than the cargo contained therein. Container dimensions are usually (in feet) 8 × 8 × 40 or 8 × 8 × 20. 40 footers are called forty-foot equivalent units (FEU), 20 footers are twenty-foot equivalent units (TEU). Also, a truck trailer body that can be detached from the chassis for loading into a vessel, a railcar, or stacked in a container depot. Containers may be ventilated, insulated, refrigerated, flat rack, vehicle rack, and open top, bulk liquid or equipped with interior devices. A container may be 20 feet, 40 feet, 45 feet, 48 feet, or 53 feet in length, 8'0" or 8'6" in width, and 8'6" or 9'6" in height. Also, there are generally 5 types of containers (1) General Dry Cargo Container, (2) "Reefer" Refrigerator or Temperature Controlled Container, (3) Half High Container or Bin (flat with removable sides), (4) Tank Container, and (5) Collapsible Steel Flat. Containers can be transported intermodaly by road and rail carriers and certain sizes by air carriers.

CONTAINER BOLSTER A container floor without sides or end walls that does not have the ISO corner fittings and is generally used for RO/RO operations.

CONTAINER BOOKING Arrangements with a steamship line to transport containerized cargo.

CONTAINER CARGO Cargo packed in a container twenty-foot equivalent unit (TEU) or forty foot equivalent unit (FEU) and moved in a unitized form. Containerized cargo volumes are measured in metric tons.

CONTAINER CHASSIS A piece of equipment specifically designed for the movement of containers by highway transport to and from container terminals, used both by the railway's own cartage division and independent cartage companies. Some container lines have their own chassis and the cartage company has to provide only the tractor to haul the container.

CONTAINER CHECK DIGIT The 7th digit of the serial number of a container used to check whether prefix and serial number are correct.

CONTAINER CRANE Usually, a rail-mounted gantry crane located on a wharf for the purpose of loading and unloading containers on vessels. Crane back-reach is the dimension from the centerline of the landside crane rail to the centerline of the farthest landside position of the spreader. Crane outreach is the dimension from the centerline of the waterside crane rail to the centerline of the farthest waterside position of the trolley spreader.

CONTAINER DEPOT Storage yard for containers.

CONTAINER FREIGHT STATION *See* CFS.

CONTAINER FREIGHT STATION CHARGE The charge assessed for services performed at the loading or discharge location.

CONTAINER ID *See* Container Number.

CONTAINERIZATION The practice or technique of using a boxlike device in which a number of packages are stored, protected, and handled as a single unit in transit. Stowage of general or special cargoes in a container for transport in the various modes.

CONTAINERIZED Indication that goods have been stowed in a container.

CONTAINERIZED CARGO Dry bulk goods that are transported on large ocean-going vessels in steel containers. Cargo that will fit into a container and result in an economical shipment.

CONTAINER LEASE The contract by which the owner of containers (lessor) gives the use of containers to a lessee for a specified period of time and for fixed payments.

CONTAINER LOAD A load sufficient in size to fill a container either by cubic measurement or by weight.

CONTAINER LOAD CENTER A port at which containerized cargo movement is concentrated in order to reduce the number of port calls the container-ship makes and to take advantage of land transport connections.

CONTAINER LOAD PLAN A document prepared to show all details of cargo loaded in a container, e.g., weight (individual and total), measurement, markings, shipper, the origin of goods and destination, as well as location of the cargo within the container.

CONTAINER MANIFEST Document showing contents and loading sequence of a container.

CONTAINER MOVES The number of actions performed by one container crane during a certain period.

CONTAINER NUMBER Identification number of a container consisting of prefix and serial number and check digit.

CONTAINER PLATFORM A container floor without sides or end walls that can be loaded by spreader directly and is generally used for Lo-Lo operations.

CONTAINER POOL An agreement between parties that allows the efficient use and supply of containers. A common supply of containers available to the shipper as required.

CONTAINER PREFIX A four-letter code that forms the first part of a container identification number indicating the owner of a container.

CONTAINERS (TYPES): Dry cargo containers—End loading, fully enclosed: basic container, equipped with end doors suitable for general cargo not requiring environmental control when en route. Side loading, fully enclosed: equipped with side doors for use in stowing and discharge of cargo where it is not practical to use end doors. Open top: used for carriage of heavy, bulky, or awkward items where loading or discharging of the cargo through end or side doors is not practical. Ventilated: equipped with ventilating ports on ends or sides and used for heat generating cargoes or cargoes requiring protection from condensation damage.

Insulated: For cargo that should not be exposed to rapid or sudden temperature changes.

Special purpose containers: Refrigerated: insulated and equipped with a built-in refrigeration system. Dry bulk: designed for carriage of dry bulk cargoes, such as dry chemicals and grains. Flat-rack: used for lumber, mill products, large or bulky items, machinery, or vehicles. Automotive: for carriage of vehicles. Livestock: configured for the nature of livestock carried. Collapsible: configured for stowage when not in use.

CONTAINER SERVICE CHARGES   Charges at a destination to be paid by cargo interests as per tariff. Charge considered accessorial and added to base ocean rate. Often covers crane lift off vessel, drayage within terminal, and gate fees of port.

CONTAINERSHIP   A class of oceangoing vessel that is specially designed to carry standard size containers nested in vertical container cells within the hull of the ship as well as stacked on deck and lifted on and off by means of specialized container cranes operating at high speed along the wharf apron. Full containerships are fully cellular and carry only container cargo whereas partial containerships carry a combination of containerized and break bulk general cargo.

CONTAINER SIZE CODE   An indication of 2 digits of the nominal length and nominal height. *See also* Size/Type ISO6346.

CONTAINER SIZE/TYPE   Description of the size and type of a freight container or similar unit load device as specified in ISO6346.

CONTAINER STACK   Two or more containers, one placed above the other forming a vertical column.

CONTAINER STATION   A building, or part of a building, designated by the district director to serve as a receiving area for containerized cargo moved from the place of unlading for the purpose of breaking bulk and redelivering the cargo.

CONTAINER TERMINAL   A specialized facility where ocean container vessels dock to discharge and load containers, equipped with cranes with a safe lifting capacity of 3,540 tons, with booms having an outreach of up to 160 feet in order to reach the outside cells of the vessels, and back-reach of 60 feet to lift cargo from dockside. Most such cranes operate on rail tracks and have articulating rail trucks on each of their four legs, single vessel enabling them to traverse along the terminal and work various bays on the vessel and for more than one crane to work simultaneously. Most terminals have direct rail access and container storage areas and are served by highway carriers.

CONTAINER TYPE CODE   Two digits, the first of which indicates the category and the second of which indicates certain physical characteristics or other attributes

CONTAINER VESSEL   *See* Containership.

CONTAINER YARD (CY)   A materials handling/storage facility used for completely unitized loads in containers and/or empty containers. Commonly referred to as CY.

CONTAMINATION   The addition to a petroleum product of some material not normally present such as dirt, rust, water, or another petroleum product.

CONTIGUOUS ZONE   The bands of water outside or beyond the territorial sea in which the coastal national may exercise custom control and enforce public health regulations, etc. It is measured from the same base line as the territorial sea and may extend no more than 12 miles seaward from it.

CONTINENTAL UNITED STATES (CONUS) U.S. coastal navigation zone that is covered by the more powerful coastal radio beacons extending out to 50 nautical miles.

CONTINUOUS REPLENISHMENT (CRP) A system used to reduce customer inventories and improve service usually to large customers.

CONTINUOUS SEALS A term denoting that seals on a vehicle remained intact during the movement from origin to destination; or if broken in transit, by the right authority and without opportunity for loss to occur before new seals are applied.

CONTINUOUS WAVE (CW) The most basic form of RF energy, dispersed into the atmosphere at a specific frequency.

CONTRA Against.

CONTRABAND Goods smuggled into a country to avoid duty; cargo that is prohibited.

CONTRACT A legally binding agreement between two or more persons/organizations to carry out reciprocal obligations or value.

CONTRACT CARRIER Any person not a common carrier who, under special and individual contracts or agreements, transports passengers or property for compensation.

CONTRACT LOGISTICS The contracting out of all the warehousing, transport, and distribution activities or a part thereof by manufacturing companies.

CONTRACT OF AFFREIGHTMENT An agreement whereby the shipowner agrees to carry goods by water or furnishes a vessel for the purpose of carrying goods by water, in return for a sum of money called freight. There are two forms: the charter party and the contract contained in the bill of lading.

CONTRACTUAL LIABILITY (INS) Liability assumed under any contract or agreement. Coverage is generally limited in liability policies, but in most cases may be provided for an additional premium.

CONTRACT WAREHOUSING A type of contract logistics that focuses on providing unique and specially tailored warehousing services to particular clients.

CONTRIBUTION (INS) The term relates to circumstances where more than one party covers the risk. Each party is deemed to be liable for his proportion of the loss. If the Assured recovers in full from one insurer, that insurer is entitled to recover from the other insurer for that part of the loss, which should have been paid by the latter. The term is used in marine insurance, also, in relation to contributions paid by the Assured in connection with salvage and/or general average.

CONTRIBUTORY VALUE (INS) The value on which a contribution to a general average loss or salvage award is calculated.

CONTROL LIGHT Red, green, and yellow signal lights located on SEABEE mother vessel's stern, starboard side, which advises towboats of elevator well conditions.

CONTROL POINT The point in the navigation pool, the elevation of which is controlled within predetermined limits for the operation of that pool.

CONTROL SEGMENT A component of satellite navigation systems that uses earth-based tracking stations to monitor the satellite's orbit and provide corrective information to the system.

CONTROLLED ATMOSPHERE Sophisticated, computer-controlled systems that manage the mixtures of gases within a container throughout an intermodal journey reducing decay.

CONTROLLED CARRIER An ocean common carrier that is, or whose assets are, directly owned or controlled by a government. The government controls the ship in this fleet if: the government appoints the company's directors, CEO, or COO or if the government owns or controls a majority of the interest in the company through an agency or public/private group.

CONTROLLING DEPTH The least available water in a navigable channel, which limits the draft that may be carried.

CONTROLLING ELEMENT The portion of the gyrocompass that contains the ballistic or pendulous weight. Application of this weight creates the precessive forces toward a particular direction.

CONUS *See* Continental United States.

CONVENTIONAL GENERAL CARGO Synonymous with the term "break bulk cargo."

CONVERSION ANGLE TABLE Data used to establish the appropriate correction to apply prior to plotting radio bearings from a station more than 50 miles away.

CONVERTIBILITY The ability of a currency to be exchanged for another.

CONVEYANCE The application used to describe the function of a vehicle of transfer.

CONVEYOR A transfer or handling mechanism that affords continuous movement through application of power or by gravity.

CONVEYOR BELT A conveyor consisting of a wide belt, rope, or chain to carry bulk or packaged material.

COOPER Originally one who makes or repairs casks or barrels, but now applies to anyone who repairs cargo containers of any description.

COOPERATIVE ASSOCIATIONS Agricultural cooperative associations may haul up to 25 percent of their total interstate tonnage in nonfarm, nonmember goods in the movements incidental and necessary to their primary business.

CO-OPETITION Recognizes that companies can be competitors in some situations and associates in other situations.

COORDINATED TRANSPORT Two or more carriers of different modes transporting a shipment.

COORDINATED UNIVERSAL TIME (UTC) Universal Time, Coordinated. The coordinated time kept by a uniformly operating clock, corrected for seasonal variations in the earth's rotation.

COP Custom of Port.

CO-PRINCIPALS When two individual people (e.g., partnership, corporation) join together with the same legal status to become the entity accepting primary liability for all government debts secured by a bond.

COPT Captain of the Port. U.S. Coast Guard officer in charge of commercial port safety and vessel safety.

CORDAGE A comprehensive term for all ropes of whatever size or kind.

CORK FENDER A fender made of granulated cork and covered with woven tarred stuff.

CORNER CASTING (CORNER FITTING) Hardware located on top and bottom of container corner post used for handling, supporting, and securing a container in the transport mode. Must conform to standard dimensions.

CORNER CONES Pyramid shaped locking units to connect containers to the deck or to each other vertically.

CORNER POSTS Vertical frame components fitted at the corners of the container, integral to the corner fittings and connecting the roof and floor structures. Containers are lifted and secured in a stack using the castings at the ends.

CORRECTION An error has been made in this transmission, the corrected version is _____.

CORRECTION CAM Once RDF correction factors are calculated, a means installed to correct the unit.

CORRECTION FACTOR Factors applied to the user's radio bearings to compensate for quadrantal error.

CORRESPONDENT BANK A bank that, in its own country, handles the business of a foreign bank.

CORROSION Detrimental change in the size or characteristics of material under conditions of exposure or use. It usually results from chemical action either regularly and slowly as in rusting, or rapidly as in metal picking.

CORROSIVE MATERIAL Any liquid or solid that causes destruction of human skin tissue or a liquid that has a severe corrosion rate on steel or aluminum.

COS Cash on Shipment.

COSION SIGNALS Colored fireworks sometimes used for signaling purposes.

COST AND FREIGHT (C&F) The seller undertakes to pay the freight to the port of destination in addition to placing the goods onboard.

COST-BENEFIT RATIO Also known as "Benefit-Cost Ratio." An analytical tool used in public planning; a ratio of total measurable benefits divided by the initial capital cost.

COST, INSURANCE, AND FREIGHT (CIF) Cost of goods, marine insurance, and all transportation (freight) charges are paid to the foreign point of delivery by the seller.

COST OF LOST SALES The forgone profit companies associate with a stock out.

COST-SHARING   The requirement that part of the costs of federal water resources projects be borne by nonfederal participants and beneficiaries; the percentages vary widely depending on the size and purpose of the project.

COST TRADE-OFF   The interrelationship among system variables in which a change in one variable affects other variables' costs. A cost reduction in one variable may increase costs for other variables, and vice versa.

COT   *See* Customer Own Transport.

COTTER, KEY   A solid key or wedge used to secure a wheel on a shaft or the like.

COTTER, SPRING   A round split pin used to lock a nut on a bolt. The pin is passed through a hole in the bolt outside of the nut and the ends of the pin opposite its head are forced apart by a chisel or similar tool, thus preventing the cotter from slipping out.

COTTON SQUEEZER   A unit used to squeeze bales of cotton to increase their density and reduce their storage volume.

COU   *See* Clip-On Unit.

COUNCIL OF LOGISTICS MANAGEMENT   A professional organization in the logistics field that provides leadership in understanding the logistics process, awareness of career opportunities in logistics, and research that enhances customer value and supply chain performance.

COUNTER   That portion of any vessel with a rounded spoon-like stern. Overhang of stern of a ship.

COUNTERSINK   The taper of a rivet hole for a flush rivet. A term applied to the operation of cutting the sides of a drilled or punched hole into the shape of the frustum of a cone. Also applied to the tool with which countersinking is done.

COUNTERSUNK HOLE   A hole tapered or beveled around its edge to allow a rivet or bolt head or a rivet point to seat flush with or below the surface of the riveted or bolted object.

COUNTERSUNK RIVET   A rivet driven flush on one or both sides.

COUNTERVAILING DUTY   An additional duty imposed to offset export grants, bounties or subsidies paid to foreign suppliers in certain countries by the government of that country for the purpose of promoting export.

COUNTRY DAMAGE   Damage to cotton in bales caused by poor methods of bailing, discoloration, etc. This term is used in Marine Cargo insurance of cotton.

COUNTRY DAMAGE (INS)   Marine term referring to damage to baled or bagged goods (e.g., cotton) caused by excessive moisture from damp ground or exposure to weather, or by grit, dust, or sand forced into the insured property by windstorm or inclement weather.

COUNTRY OF EXPORTATION   Usually but not necessarily the country in which merchandise was manufactured or produced and from which it was first exported.

COUNTRY OF ORIGIN The country where the goods are considered to have originated for Customs purposes. The factors besides the cost of the materials involved are the cost of freight, insurance, packing, and all other costs of transferring the materials to the plant, waste, taxes and duty, etc.

COUNTRY OF PROVENANCE The country from which goods or cargo are sent to the importing country.

COUPLE MOMENT Created by two equal forces exerted in opposite directions and along parallel lines. In stability, the forces through G and B.

COUPLING A device for securing together the adjoining ends of piping, shafting, etc., in such a manner as will permit disassembly whenever necessary. Flanges connected by bolts and pipe unions are probably the most common forms of couplings.

COURIER Attendant who accompanies a shipment. Also, some courier companies provide a full transportation function, without accompanying attendants, offering door-to-door service for time sensitive documents or small packages on a same day delivery basis.

COURIER SERVICE A fast door-to-door service for high-valued goods and documents; firms usually limit service to shipments of 50 pounds or less.

COURSE ALARM An alarm that activates when the vessel varies beyond a set parameter for the intended course.

COVER (INS) A contract of insurance; to effect insurance; to include within the coverage of a contract of insurance.

COVER BARGE A barge having hatch covers over its compartments and used for various dry bulk cargoes that need weather protection such as grain, tin plate, paper, etc.

COVER CASTING Base for setting container securely on deck. One for each corner of each container.

COVERAGE (INS) The scope of protection provided under the contract of insurance.

COVERAGE PART (INS) Any one of the individual commercial coverage parts that may be attached to a commercial policy.

COVERAGE TRIGGER (INS) A mechanism that determines whether a policy covers a particular claim for loss. For example, the difference between the coverage triggers of liability "occurrence" forms and "claims made" forms is that the loss must occur during the policy period in the first case and the claim must be made during the policy period in the second case.

COWL Hood shaped top of ventilator pipe.

COW'S TAIL The frayed end of a rope; also called fag.

COXSWAIN (COX'N) The person in charge of a boat and usually serving as steersman.

CP Charter Party.

CPA *See* Closest Point of Approach.

CPD Charterers Pay Dues.

CPT (CARRIAGE PAID TO) An acronym meaning that the seller pays the freight for the carriage of the goods to the named destination. The risk of loss of or damage to the goods, as well as any additional costs due to events occurring after the time the goods have been delivered to the carrier, is transferred from the seller to the buyer when the goods have been delivered into the custody of the carrier. "Carrier" means any person who, in a contract of carriage, undertakes to perform or to procure the performance of carriage, by rail, road, sea, air, inland waterway, or by a combination of such modes. If subsequent carriers are used for the carriage to the agreed destination, the risk passes when the goods have been delivered to the first carrier. The CPT term requires the seller to clear the goods for export.

CPU The part of the computer that executes the instructions of a program.

CR Carrier's Risk.

CRACKING A sound that may arise from faulty parts in a receiver, poor contacts, or improper grounding and that allows static electricity to build up in the electrical components.

CRADLE A form on which furnaced plates are shaped. The support in which a ship lies during launching, called launching cradle.

CRADLE, LAUNCHING The structure of wood, or wood and steel, that is built up from the sliding ways, closely fitting the shell plating, which supports the weight of the ship and distributes it to the sliding ways when a ship is being launched. The extent of the cradle and the number of sections into which it may be divided depends on the weight and length of the ship.

CRADLE, MARINE RAILWAY The carriage on which the ship rests when being docked on a marine railway.

CRANE A machine used for hoisting and moving pieces of material or portions of structure or machines that are either too heavy to be handled by hand or cannot be handled economically by hand. Bridge, gantry, jib, locomotive, and special purpose cranes are used in shipyards.

CRANK SHIP A vessel with small metacentric height; top heavy.

CREDIT INSURANCE Insurance against losses due to inability or failure of the insured's customers to pay for goods sold by the insured. The insurance normally covers a specified percentage of each loss beyond a deductible indicated in the policy. Insurance is available covering a variety of risks, e.g., political and transfer risks ("country risks") and financial risks (called "commercial risks"). Even comprehensive insurance, however, will not cover nonpayment for contract disputes.

CREDIT RISK Risk incurred by a seller of goods that the buyer cannot or will not pay for them.

CREDIT RISK INSURANCE A form of insurance that protects the seller against loss due to default on the part of the buyer.

CREDIT TERMS The agreement between two or more enterprises concerning the amount and timing of payment for goods or services.

CREST OF DAM   The top of the water barrier or the dam.

CREST OF FLOOD   When the rise of a river has reached its peak.

CREW   The unlicensed personnel aboard a vessel.

CRIB   A box-like timber structure, possibly rock filled, used as a fender type of protection for bridge piers or other marine structures, or for mooring purposes. Also, a temporary wooden structure to isolate and protect cargo.

CRIBBING   Foundations of heavy blocks and timbers for supporting a vessel during the period of construction.

CRITERION OF SERVICE NUMERAL   A number (usually between 23 and 123) based on the dimensions and service in which the vessel is engaged, which is used to obtain the subdivision requirements for a vessel.

CRITICAL MASS   When enough buyers and sellers participate in a net market so goods or services change hands efficiently. Also, the time when a market gains momentum, achieves liquidity, and becomes a more efficient way to buy or sell than the traditional physical market or channel.

CRITICAL VALUE ANALYSIS   A modified ABC analysis in which a company assigns a subjective critical value to each item in an inventory.

CROSS BEAMS   Beams that support the hatch covers. Also called Hatch Beams.

CROSSBOARD   A simple type of day mark in the shape of an "X" formerly used extensively on the Missouri River only.

CROSSCURRENT   Stream flow across navigable portion of river.

CROSS CURVES OF STABILITY   Curves for various angles of inclination up to 90°. The ordinates are displacements. Intersection of ordinates with curves produce the abscissas (righting arms).

CROSS-DOCK   An enterprise that provides services to transfer goods from one piece of transportation equipment to another.

CROSS-DOCKING   The movement of goods directly from receiving dock to shipping dock to eliminate storage expense.

CROSSED LOOP ANTENNA   An antenna that focuses radiated energy into a relatively narrow beam. It also picks up signals at varying levels at different points on the antenna. These levels are analyzed by the receiver to determine transmitter direction.

CROSSING   Where a channel moves from along one bank of the river over to the other bank of the river.

CROSSING DAYMARK   A diamond-shaped day mark erected at the head and foot of crossings and used by pilots to steer on.

CROSSING THE LINE   Crossing the equator.

CROSS MEMBER   Transverse members fitted to the bottom side rails of a container that support the floor.

CROSSOVERS   Main cargo lines and stripper lines running athwartship from tank to tank; also sections of pipe containing main lines that connect separate cargo systems.

CROSS SPALL   A temporary horizontal timber brace to hold a frame in position. Cross spalls are replaced later by the deck beams.

CROSS SPRING   A second spring line that crosses over and works in the opposite direction from a primary spring line.

CROSS-SUBSIDIZATION   A practice within an organization where the costs of one activity are partly or wholly covered by the revenue generated by another activity.

CROSS-TRADERS   Ships that transport cargo between two countries, neither of which is the nationality of the vessel. A U.S.-registered ship carrying products from Mexico to Spain would be engaged in cross trading.

CROSS TRACK ERROR (XTE)   The Loran C term for a vessel's ability to navigate on a straight rhumb line from point A to point B.

CROSS TRADE   Foreign-to-foreign trade carried by ships from a nation other than the two trading nations.

CROSS TREE   Athwartship pieces fitted on a mast. They serve as a foundation for a platform and also are used to secure the blocks used in connection with the topping lift.

CROWN   Term sometimes used denoting the round up or camber of a deck. The crown of an anchor is located where the arms are welded to the shank.

CROW'S NEST   An elevated lookout station on a ship, usually attached to forward side of foremast.

CRP   Continuous Replenishment. A system used to reduce customer inventories and improve service usually to large customers.

CRT (CATHODE RAY TUBE)   A component of the radar used to form the video display. The CRT screen is coated with a film of phosphorescent material that reacts when excited by the narrow beam formed as the cathode draws electrons from a filament. The beam also passes by a series of coils that focus and deflect the beam to create images on the screen.

CRUDE OIL   Unrefined petroleum. A liquid occurring naturally and consisting principally of many different types of hydrocarbons, but also containing varying proportions of other substances.

CRUDE OIL WASHING   To wash a cargo tank with crude oil. A system using fixed washing machines to deliver high velocity crude oil against tank surfaces to remove sludge, requires IGS. Used to reduce clingage and sedimentation of cargo in cargo tanks.

CRUDE PETROLEUM   A naturally occurring mixture consisting predominantly of hydrocarbons and/or sulfur, nitrogen and/or oxygen, derivatives of hydrocarbons, which is removed from the earth in liquid state or is capable of being so removed. Crude petroleum is commonly accompanied by varying quantities of extraneous substances such as water, inorganic matter, and gas.

CRUISE SHIP   A passenger vessel that offers carriage for recreation only, usually returning passengers to the point of departure.

CRUISER A high-speed vessel designed to keep at sea for extended periods and in which protection against gunfire is subordinated to speed and long radius of action. Light cruisers and heavy cruisers are so designated in accordance with the caliber of the guns carried. Used largely for scouting and convoy work.

CRUISER STERN Rounded stern that is hydrodynamically efficient and improves water flow into and away from the propeller.

CRUTCH A term applied to a support for a boom. Also applied to the jaw of a boom or gaff.

CRYOGENIC Relating to the production of very low temperatures as in the case of carriage of liquefied natural gas in special tanker vessels.

CRYOGENIC MATERIAL Extremely low temperature gaseous material transported as a liquid. Maintained in liquid form by low temperature rather than pressure.

C/SNEE Consignee.

CSO Combined Sewer Outfalls. There are many CSOs that discharge into Boston Harbor.

CSR Continuous Synopsis Record. An onboard record of the history of a ship.

CST Centistoke Commodity Specialist Team.

CTD *See* Combined Transport Document.

CTL An instance in which the cost of recovering and/or repairing damaged goods would, when recovered or repaired, exceed the insured value.

CTLO Constructive Total Loss Only.

CTO *See* Combined Transport Operator.

CTR Container or Container Fitted.

CU Cubic. A unit of volume measurement.

CUBE OUT When a container has reached its volumetric capacity before its permitted weight limit.

CUBIC CAPACITY The carrying capacity within a conveyance or container according to the measure in cubic feet. Bale cubic capacity is the space available for cargo, in cubic feet, to the inside of the cargo battens, on the frames, and to the underside of the beams, in other words, the space that can be occupied by general cargo.

CUBIC FOOT 1,728 cubic inches.

CUDDY A galley structure on deck; a small cabin.

CULPABILITY The degree to which an individual is responsible for a wrongdoing. The various degrees are Negligence, Gross Negligence, and Fraud.

CUMULATIVE REVOLVING LETTER OF CREDIT (LOC) Revolving letter of credit that permits the seller to carry over any amounts not drawn into successive periods.

CUNTLINE A small paper strip woven into the lay of a fiber line containing information on the date of manufacture.

CUP GREASE   Originally used to indicate a grease for use in compression cups, but usage now indicates a grease having a calcium fatty acid soap base.

CURRENCY   A medium of exchange of value defined by a reference to the geographic location of the authorities for it (ISO 4217). In general, the monetary unit, involved in a transaction and represented by a name or symbol.

CURRENCY ADJUSTMENT FACTOR   A percentage charge applied against the freight that adjusts the rate to account for a change in the valuation of the currency.

CURVES OF FORM   *See* Hydrostatic Curves.

CURVES OF STATICAL STABILITY   *See* Statical Stability Curves.

CUSHION   Repulsion of the bow away from bank due to buildup in water level at the inshore bow.

CUSTODIAL BOND   A basic covenant entered into by the obligators on a surety bond taken to secure the lawful activities of a custodian of any bonded articles, which describes the requirements of conveyance, protection, and general compliance in the handling of bonded merchandise.

CUSTOMER ORDER   The seller's internal translation of their buyer's purchase order. The document contains much of the same information as the purchase order but may use different product IDs for some or all of the line items. It will also determine inventory availability.

CUSTOMER OWN TRANSPORT (COT)   The customer arranges his own transport of the container to and from the terminal or depot but agrees to restitute the container back to the terminal or depot.

CUSTOMER PICK-UP   Cargo picked up by a customer at a warehouse.

CUSTOMHOUSE   A government office where duties are paid, import documents filed, etc., on foreign shipments and are paid on vehicles or vessels entered or cleared.

CUSTOMHOUSE BROKER   A person or firm, licensed by the Treasury Department of their country when required, engaged in entering and clearing goods through Customs for a client (importer). The duties of the broker include preparing the entry blank and filing it; advising the importer on duties to be paid; advancing duties and other costs; and arranging for delivery to his client, his trucking firm, or other carrier.

CUSTOMS   A government authority designated to regulate the flow of goods to and from a country and to collect duties levied by a country on imports and/or exports. The term also applies to the procedures involved in such collection.

CUSTOMS BOND FEE   U.S. Customs regulations require that a "Surety Bond" be posted with each entry. A Custom House Broker can file (on behalf of an importer who does not have one), a "Single Transaction Bond" (STB), for an amount equal to the value of the goods, plus the duty. The STB costs around $3.50 per $1,000.00 Ad Valorem, (minimum charge $35.00/$40.00). Imports anticipating more than eight/ten entries within any given year should consider purchasing an annual "Continuous Bond" (CB), (CF301). The price of the CB starts at approximately $350.00 and could represent significant savings to an importer planning multiple annual Customs transactions.

CUSTOMS BONDED WAREHOUSE   A warehouse authorized by Customs to receive duty-free merchandise.

CUSTOMS BROKER   *See* Customhouse Broker.

CUSTOMS BROKERS   Individuals or organizations that assist shippers in complying with Customs laws and regulations and other requirements affecting the import and export of goods.

CUSTOMS CLEARANCE   The procedures involved in getting cargo released by Customs through designated formalities such as presenting import license/permit, payment of import duties, and other required documentations by the nature of the cargo such as FCC or FDA approval.

CUSTOMS COLLECTION   Tax payments collected by a government when foreign products enter its country.

CUSTOMS COURT   A U.S. Customs Services court based in New York, NY, consisting of three third-party divisions to which importers may appeal or "protest" classification and value decisions and certain other actions taken by the U.S. Customs Service.

CUSTOMS DECLARATION   A statement, oral or written, attesting to the correctness of description, quantity, value, use, etc., of merchandise offered for importation into the United States.

CUSTOMS ENTRY   All countries require that the importer make a declaration of incoming foreign goods. The importer then normally pays a duty on the imported merchandise. The importer's statement is compared against the carrier's vessel manifest to ensure that all foreign goods are properly declared. Consumption Entry—A form required by U.S. Customs for entering goods into the United States. The form contains information as to the origin of the cargo, a description of the merchandise, and estimated duties applicable to the particular commodity. Estimated duties must be paid when the entry is filed. Immediate Delivery Entry (I.D. Entry)—Procedure used to expedite the clearance of cargo. It allows up to ten days for the payment of estimated duty and processing of the consumption entry. In addition, it permits delivery of the cargo prior to payment of the estimated duty and then allows subsequent filing of the consumption entry and duty. Immediate Transportation Entry (I.T. Entry)—Allows the cargo to be moved from the pier to an inland destination by a bonded carrier without the payment of duties or finalization of the entry at the port of arrival. Cargo must clear Customs at the inland destination point. Transportation and Exportation Entry (T&E Entry)—Allows goods coming from or going to a third country (such as Canada or Mexico) to enter the United States for the purpose of transshipments.

CUSTOMS IMPORT VALUE This is the U.S. Customs Service appraisal value of merchandise. Methodologically, the Customs value is similar to f.a.s. (free alongside ship) value since it is based on the value of the product in the foreign country of origin and excludes charges incurred in bringing the merchandise to the United States (import duties, ocean freight, insurance, and so forth); but it differs in that the U.S. Customs Service, not the importer or exporter, has the final authority to determine the value of the good.

CUSTOMS INVOICE A form requiring all data in a commercial invoice along with a certificate of value and/or a certificate of origin. Required in a few countries (usually former British territories) and usually serves as a seller's commercial invoice.

CUSTOMS OF THE PORT A phrase often included in charter parties and freight contracts referring to local rules and practices that may impact the costs borne by the various parties.

CUSTOMS TARIFF A schedule of charges assessed by the federal government on imported and/or exported goods.

CUSTOMS VALUE The value of the imported goods on which duties will be assessed.

CUT Same as fraction. Also, a straight channel that is the result of dredging through a winding watercourse.

CUTBACK To reduce the viscosity of a heavy product by adding and blending a lighter product with it.

CUT HER LOOSE Untie all lines.

CUT OF THE JIB General appearance of a vessel, sometimes applied to a person.

CUTOFF Any man-made cut by dredging that eliminates a bend in the river or curve. Usually referring to a new channel made by entering at the head of a bend, passing through the cut, and emerging at the end of the bend on the downstream side. *See also* Cut-Off Time.

CUT-OFF TIME The latest time cargo may be delivered to a terminal for loading to a scheduled train or ship.

CUTTER A double-banked, square-sterned ship's boat, used for general ship duty. A sloop.

CUTTERHEAD A device for mechanically cutting stiff clays and compacted sands. The device is located at the end of the dredge ladder, is driven by a motor and shaft assembly, and is designed to feed the dredged material into the dredge suction.

CUTTING OIL Oil used to lubricate and cool metal cutting tools. It may be water-soluble or water insoluble. Usually mineral oils are blended with lard oil or other oils or extreme pressure agents to produce water insoluble cutting oils, or with sulfonated products and other emulsifying agents to produce soluble cutting oils.

CUT WATER The forward edge of the stem at or near the waterline.

CW *See* Continuous Wave.

CWE *See* Cleared Without Examination.

CWO Cash with Order.

CWT Hundredweight (United States, 100 pounds; U.K., 112).

CY Cubic yards. Approximately 1 cubic yard of dredged material weighs about 1.5 tons. Also an abbreviation for Container Yard, the designation for full-container receipt/delivery.

CYC Container Yard Charges

CY/CFS Cargo loaded in a full container by a shipper at origin, delivered to pier facility at destination, and then devanned by carrier for loose pickup.

CY/CY Cargo loaded by shipper in a full container at origin and delivered to carrier's terminal at destination for pickup intact by consignee.

CYCLE One complete oscillation or one complete wave, beginning when the wave passes zero in one direction until it passes zero in the same direction.

CYCLE ALARM A Loran C receiver alarm that appears when initializing the receiver or when the signal is lost. It indicates that the receiver is not reading the transmission pattern correctly because it has not picked up the performance pulse.

CYCLE TIME The elapsed time between commencement and completion of a process.

CYCLIZATION Rearrangement of saturated or unsaturated straight chain hydrocarbons into a cyclic structure.

CYLINDER OILS Oils used to lubricate the cylinders and valves of steam engines.

CYLINDER STOCK A class of high viscous oils so called because originally their main use was in the preparation of products to be used for steam cylinder lubrication. Cylinder stocks are usually produced as bottom oils but may also be distilled under suitable conditions. They may be high or low cold test according to whether they have been cold settled or not.

CZMA (COASTAL ZONE MANAGEMENT ACT) A federal law, originally passed in 1972, giving state and local governments incentives to upgrade the regulation of land and water resources in the coastal zone.

D

D A penny or pence.

DA Documents for Acceptance; Disbursement Account.

D/A Discharge Afloat. When prefixed to the work "clause" vessel must discharge afloat.

Documents Against Acceptance. Instructions given by a shipper to a bank indicating that documents transferring title to goods should be delivered to the buyer only upon the buyer's acceptance of the attached draft.

DAF (DELIVERED AT FRONTIER) The seller fulfills his obligation to deliver when the goods have been made available, cleared for export, at the named point and place at the frontier, but before the Customs border of the adjoining country. The term "frontier" may be used for any frontier including that of the country of export. Therefore, it is of vital importance that the frontier in question be defined precisely by always naming the point and place in the term. The term is primarily intended to be used when goods are to be carried by rail or road, but it may be used for any mode of transport.

DAGGER A piece of timber that is fastened to the poppets of the bilge-way and crosses them diagonally to keep them together. Dagger applies to anything that stands in a diagonal position in a fore and aft plane.

DAGGER PLANK One of the planks that unite the heads of the poppet or stepping up pieces of the cradle on which the vessel rests in launching.

DAM BULLETIN BOARD Located at certain dams and gives stage readings and indicates as to whether to use lock or go over the dam. "NP" means use the lock. "Pass" means to go over the dam. Largely obsolete in use since the advent of radio communications.

DAM OPEN A term used when the gates are open so as to pass water unimpeded.

DAM WARNING BUOY Buoys placed above the face of a dam to warn traffic of danger. These buoys may be of peculiar shape and generally have the word "danger" posted on them.

DAM WICKET Movable hinged carriers in certain dams on the Ohio and Illinois Rivers that can be raised or lowered to control the depth of water in the pool behind the dam.

DAMAGE CONTROL LOCKER (EMERGENCY GEAR LOCKER) A locker or compartment used for storage of emergency equipment such as firefighting gear.

DAMAGE REPORT Form on which physical damage is recorded (e.g., containers).

DAMAGE STABILITY The analysis of vessel's stability when in a damaged condition such as grounded, holed, or flooded; stability of a vessel after flooding.

DAMAGED CARGO REPORT   Written statement concerning established damages to cargo and/or equipment.

DAMFORDET   Damages For Detention. Penalty charged if cargo is not ready on the first day the ship is ready to load that cargo. This is different than detention, which simply measures ship's time lost.

DAMOS   Disposal Area Monitoring System. Open water disposal of dredged material monitoring program conducted by the U.S. Army Corps of Engineers.

DAMPING   A ship has six degrees of freedom: heaving, swaying, surging, rolling, pitching, and yawing. The first are linear motions. Rolling is rotation about a vertical axis. It is necessary to damp these motions, and many devices have been suggested for damping the rolling of ships such as passive water tanks and activated fins. Damping units are fitted to control systems to avoid surging and excessive oscillation in machinery systems; friction and viscosity have the same effect.

DANGEROUS GOODS   Articles or substances that are capable of posing a significant risk to health, safety, or property when transported and that are classified according to the most current editions of the ICAO Technical Instructions for the Safe Transport of Dangerous Goods and the IATA Dangerous Goods Regulations. Legally, dangerous goods are products classified as dangerous by government, being substances that can harm the public, workers, property, or the environment if they escape from the container or vehicle in which they are being sorted or transported.

DANGEROUS GOODS DECLARATION   Document issued by consignor in accordance with applicable conventions or regulations describing hazardous goods (*see also* HAZMAT) or materials for transport purposes and stating that latter have been packed and labeled in accordance with the provisions of relevant conventions and regulations.

DANGEROUS GOODS PACKING CERTIFICATE   Document as part of dangerous goods declaration in which responsible party declares cargo has been stowed in accordance with rules in compliance with regulations and properly secured.

DAPS   Days All Purposes. Total days for loading and unloading.

D/A SIGHT DRAFT   Documents Against Acceptance Sight Draft. A method of payment for goods in which documents transferring title are delivered to the buyer as soon as he signs an acceptance, stamped on a draft, guaranteeing payment of the draft.

DATABASE   Data stored in a form that allows for flexible sorting and report generation.

DATA MINING   Uses sophisticated quantitative techniques to find hidden patterns in large volumes of data.

DATA PLATE   Plate affixed to a container giving details of gross and tare weights and external dimensions.

DATA TERMINAL Point for the sending and receiving of information by computer.

DAVIT A crane arm for handling anchors, lifeboats, stores, etc. A device used to lower and raise ship's boats and sometimes for other purposes. The rotary, or most common type, consists of a vertical pillar, generally circular in section, with the upper portion bent in a fair curve and having sufficient outreach to clear the side of the ship plus a clearance. Each ship's boat has two davits, one near its bow and one near its stern; they both rotate, lifting the boat by means of blocks and falls suspended from the overhanging end, from its stowage position on deck, and swinging it clear of the ship's side.

DAYBEACON An unlighted fixed structure that is equipped with a day mark for daytime identification.

DAYMARK The daytime identifier of an aid to navigation presenting one of several standard shapes (square, triangle, diamond, or rectangle) and colors (red, green, white, orange, yellow, or black.)

DAY'S DUTY Tour of duty on shipboard lasting 24 hours.

DBA Doing Business As. A legal term for conducting business under a registered name.

DB&B Deals, battens, and brands.

DC Distribution Center; Direct Current.

DD Double Deck; Demand Draft.

D/D Date Draft; Date Drafted.

DDC Destination Delivery Charge. A charge based on container size that is applied in many tariffs to cargo. This charge is considered accessorial and is added to the base ocean freight. This charge covers crane lifts off the vessel, drayage of the container within the terminal, and gate fees at the terminal operation.

DDP (DELIVERED DUTY PAID) The seller fulfills his obligation to deliver when the goods have been made available at the named place in the country of importation. The seller has to bear the risks and costs, including duties, taxes, and other charges of delivering the goods thereto, cleared for importation. While the EXW term represents the minimum obligation for the seller, DDP represents the maximum obligation. This term should not be used if seller is unable directly or indirectly to obtain the import license. If the parties wish the buyer to clear the goods for the importation and to pay the duty, the term DDU should be used. If the parties wish to exclude from the seller's obligations some of the costs payable upon importation of the goods (such as value added tax (VAT), this should be made clear by adding words to this effect: "Delivered duty paid, VAT unpaid (. . . named place of destination)." This term may be used irrespective of the mode of transport.

DDU (DELIVERED DUTY UNPAID) The seller fulfills his obligation to deliver when the goods have been made available at the named place in the country of importation. The seller has to bear the costs and risks involved in bringing the goods thereto (excluding duties, taxes, and other official charges payable upon importation formalities). The buyer has to pay any additional costs and to bear any risks caused by his failure to clear the goods for import in time. If the parties wish the seller to carry out Customs formalities and bear the costs and risks resulting there from, this has to be made clear by adding words to this effect. If the parties wish to include in the seller's obligations some of the costs payable upon importation of the goods (such as value added tax (VAT)), this should be made clear by adding words to this effect: "Delivered unpaid, VAT paid, (. . . named place of destination)." This term may be used irrespective of the mode of transport.

DEACTIVATION CONTROL If the steering system is installed as a secondary system to a hydraulic system, a control on the telemotor steering stand is there to cause the system to automatically shut down the electric steering if the telemotor is engaged.

DEAD AHEAD Directly ahead on the extension of the ship's fore and aft line.

DEAD END An offshoot in a vessel's piping that ends in a blank. A petroleum product in a dead end can contaminate a cargo or produce explosive vapors if not flushed out.

DEADEN THE WAY To impede a vessel's progress.

DEAD EYE *See* Blind Pulley.

DEAD FLAT The portion of a ship's form or structure that has the same transverse shape as the midship section.

DEADHEAD Any water-soaked wooden pile, tree, or log that is floating just awash in a nearly vertical position. A menace to small boats and to the propellers of vessels. A term to mean a tow returning from a trip without barges. Also, one leg of a move with either a bobtail tractor alone or a tractor pulling an empty container.

DEAD IN THE WATER Referring to a vessel with no way on.

DEADLIGHT Thick glass in the deck of a vessel for lighting purposes below; metal cover for a porthole. Also, a port light that does not open and also with strong shutters that screw down upon airport holes and keeps out water in heavy weather.

DEADLOAD The difference between the actual and calculated ship's draft.

DEADMAN A block or object usually buried in solid ground to serve as an anchor to restrain some object or structure from movement.

DEAD RISE Rise or slant up athwartship of the bottom of a ship from the keel to the bilge. At any point is the vertical distance between the bottoms at the centerline and the bottom at that point. Dead rise causes a shift upwards of the center of buoyancy and is, therefore, principally concerned with the stability aspect of hull design.

DEAD SHIP A ship that has no power or is not using its propeller during towage.

DEAD STOCK   Product for which there is no demand.

DEAD STORAGE   Product that does not move in or out of its storage location once it has been received.

DEADWEIGHT CARGO   The number of tons remaining after deducting from the deadweight the weight of fuel, water, stores, dunnage, and crew and their effects necessary for use on a voyage. Also called "useful" or "paying" deadweight, "dead load," and "burden." A long ton of cargo that can be stowed in less than 70 cubic feet.

DEADWEIGHT SCALE   A scale of values of TPI, MT1, displacement, and deadweight, for all drafts.

DEADWEIGHT TONNAGE   The displacement loaded minus the displacement light. In other words, it is the carrying capacity of the ship (long tons).

DEADWEIGHT TONS (DWT)   The ship's payload, in long tons, by draft. The total lifting capacity of a ship, expressed in tons of 2,240 pounds. It is the difference between the displacement light and the displacement loaded. Cargo deadweight capacity is determined by deducting from total deadweight the weight of fuel, water, stores, dunnage, crew, passengers, and other items necessary for use on a voyage.

DEADWOOD   The reinforcing structure built in between the keel and keelson in the after body of a ship or back of the joint between the stem and the keel in the fore body.

DEASPHALTING   A process for removing asphalt from reduced crude that uses the widely different solubility's of nonasphaltic hydrocarbons and asphaltic compounds in liquid propane.

DECCA   A phase comparison hyperbolic system first developed by the British. It is considered to be a relatively accurate, short-to-medium range radio navigation system designed for use in coastal confluence areas. Decca operates in the low frequency band, 70 to 130 kHz.

DECCA LANE   The distance or interval between each successive zero phase point for the Decca system.

DECENTRALIZED AUTHORITY   A situation in which a company management gives decision-making authority to managers at many organizational levels.

DECISION SUPPORT SYSTEM (DSS)   A set of computer-oriented tools designed to assist managers in making decisions.

DECK   A horizontal carrier or support level, commonly called a floor ashore. Deck may be named aboard some vessels, numbered on others. U.S. Naval vessels number decks consecutively below the main deck down starting at 1, and consecutively up from the main deck using zero as a prefix. Ex. 02 deck is the second deck above the main deck. Ex 2.3 deck is the second deck below the main deck. Although merchant vessels number below the main, they may use descriptive words for upper decks, such as promenade deck, sun deck, or boat deck. Only familiarity with a vessel will ensure full understanding. The deck on a ship corresponds to the floor in a building. It is the plating, planking, or covering of any tier of beams above the inner bottom forming a floor, either in the hull of superstructure of a ship. Decks are designated by their location as upper deck, main deck, etc., and forward lower deck, after superstructure deck, etc. The after portion of a weather deck was formerly known as the quarterdeck and on warships is allotted to the use of the officers.

DECK, BULKHEAD The uppermost continuous deck to which all the main transverse watertight bulkheads are carried. This deck should be watertight in order to prevent any compartment that is open to the sea from flooding the one adjacent to it.

DECK, FREEBOARD The deck to which the classification societies require the vessel's freeboard to be measured. Usually the upper strength deck.

DECK, MAIN *See* Main Deck.

DECK, ORLOP A partial deck in hold.

DECK, SHELTER Full deck, lightly constructed, above regular weather deck, forming complete superstructures, normally not closed in, but actually available for cargo.

DECK, TURTLE A term applied to a weather deck that is rounded over from the shell of the ship so that it has a shape similar to the back of a turtle. Used on ships of the whaleback type and on the forward weather deck of torpedo boats.

DECK, WEATHER Uppermost continuous deck with no overhead protection having watertight openings except in case of a shelter deck, which has tonnage openings.

DECK BEAM Athwartship support of deck.

DECKBOARDS The planks of a pallet deck.

DECK BOLT A special type of bolt used to secure the planks of a wood deck to the frames or deck plating.

DECK CARGO Cargo carried outside rather than within the enclosed cargo spaces of a vessel.

DECK HEIGHTS The vertical distance between the molded lines of two adjacent decks.

DECK HOUSE Shelter built on deck or a partial superstructure that does not extend from side to side. It is used for storage of deck machinery.

DECK LINE *See* Beam Line.

DECK LOAD Cargo carried on deck.

DECK MACHINERY Steering gear, capstans, windlasses, winches, and miscellaneous machinery located on the decks of a ship.

DECK OPENING The space between the deckboards of a pallet.

DECK PLANKS OR PLANKING A term applied to the wood sheathing or covering on a deck. Oregon pine, yellow pine, and teak are most commonly used. The seams between the planks should be thoroughly caulked.

DECK PLANS Overview of all the horizontal levels of a vessel, inclusive of vertical separation. Difference deck plans exist for different purposes. *See* Fire Plan Control.

DECK PLATING A term applied to the steel plating of a deck.

DECK SPRINKLER Used for cooling decks when carrying inflammable cargoes in hot climates and it is connected to the fire main.

DECK STRINGER The strake of plating that runs along the outer edge of a deck.

DECLARATION Form filled out by Assured and sent to the insurance company when reporting individual shipments coming within the terms of an open policy.

DECLARATION BY FOREIGN SHIPPER The U.S. Customs Service defines this term as a statement by the shipper in the foreign country attesting to certain facts. For example, articles shipped from the United States to an insular possession and then returned must be accompanied by a declaration by the shipper in the insular possession, indicating that, to the best of his or her knowledge, the articles were exported directly from the United States to the insular possession and remained there until the moment of their return to the United States.

DECLARATION OF DANGEROUS GOODS *See* Dangerous Goods Declaration.

DECLARATION OF INSPECTION (DOI) Cargo form determining the safety condition of the vessel prior to cargo transfer.

DECLARATION OF ORIGIN Appropriate statement as to the origin of the goods, made in connection with their exportation by the manufacturer, producer, supplier, exporter, or other competent person on the commercial invoice or any document relating to goods.

DECLARATION PAGE (INS) That page of the insurance policy that lists the insurance company, its address, name of the policyholder, starting and ending dates of coverage, and the actual coverages given in the contract, including the locations and amounts.

DECLARED VALUE (CARTAGE) The value of goods declared to the carrier by the shipper for the purposes of determining charges or of establishing the limit of carrier liability for loss, damage, or delay.

DECLARED VALUE FOR CARRIAGE The value of the goods, declared by the shipper on a bill of lading, for the purpose of determining a freight rate or the limit of the carrier's liability.

DECOMETER The Decca digital readout that simultaneously indicates the phase comparisons between the master and each of the slave stations.

DECONSOLIDATION POINT Place where loose or other noncontainerized cargo is ungrouped for delivery.

DECONSOLIDATOR An enterprise that provides services to ungroup shipments, orders, goods, etc., to facilitate distribution.

DECOUPLING INVENTORY A stock retained to make the independent control of two successive operations possible.

DECOUPLING POINT   The point in the supply chain that provides a buffer between differing input and output rates.

DEDICATED EQUIPMENT   In railroading, cars assigned for use by a specific customer.

DEDICATED TRUCK   Truck assigned exclusively to one shipment for security or other reasons.

DEDUCTIBLE   The amount of loss paid by the policyholder before the insurance policy benefits become payable. Also known as excess, or franchise.

DEDUCTIVE VALUE   A method of determining value for appraisement purposes if transaction value doesn't apply. From the "sale price" various things are deducted to arrive at the appraised value.

DEEP DRAFT PORT   A seaport that is accessible to seagoing ship, i.e., it has water depths in harbor channels and at marine terminal facilities capable of accommodating deep draft ships.

DEEPENING LOW   A low in which the central pressure is decreasing with time. Winds would be expected to increase as the low deepens.

DEEP FLOORS   Floors at the ends of a ship that are deeper than the standard depth of floor at amidships.

DEEP LOW   A rather subjective term used to describe the central pressure of a low center (usually when it is about 975 mb or less). Winds are strong gale force to storm force around the low.

DEEP SCATTERING LAYER   *See* Thermocline.

DEEP STOWAGE   Any bulk, bagged or other type of cargo stowed in single hold ships.

DEEP TANKS   Tanks extending from the bottom or inner bottom up to or higher than the lowest deck. They are often fitted with hatches so that they also may be used for dry cargo in lieu of fuel oil, ballast water, or liquid cargo.

DEEP WATERLINE   The waterline at which the vessel floats when carrying the maximum allowable load.

DEEPWATER OIL PORT   Associated with special offshore or onshore terminal berthing facilities for handling the unloading of the very large crude oil carriers (VLCCs) and ultra large crude oil carriers (ULCCs) requiring a 100 feet and more of water depths.

DEEP WATER ROUTE   A route in a designated area within definite limits that has been accurately surveyed for clearance of sea bottom and submerged obstacles to a minimum indicated depth of water.

DEEPWELL SYSTEM   Water runs aft and is pumped by deep well pumps (Roe Box); dunnage placed towards rose box.

DEFAULT CHARGE   A (standard) charge applicable for a trade, stretch, or location. In the absence of specifics (not otherwise specified/enumerated), a general amount has been set.

DEFECTIVE GOODS INVENTORY (DGI)   Those items that have been returned, have been delivered damaged and have a freight claim outstanding, or have been damaged in some way during warehouse handling.

DEFERRED FREIGHT   Freight requiring dependable, reliable service, but at a less time sensitive nature, with delivery provided over a period of days.

DEFERRED PAYMENT L.C.   A letter of credit under which payment is deferred to a determinable future date.

DEFERRED REIMBURSEMENT   Arrangement under a letter of credit where the issuing bank agrees up front with its customer, the applicant, to pay the beneficiary upon presentation of the documents required in the L/C but to defer charging the applicant until a later date, thereby financing the purchase of goods under the L/C, usually for the expected amount of time the applicant needs in order to re-sell the goods.

DEFICIT WEIGHT   The weight by which a shipment is less than the minimum weight.

DEFLECTION   The amount of bending.

DEGASSING   Quite often, gasses created by organic substances or that are trapped in dredged materials come out during the dredging process and significantly decrease the performance of the dredge pump. When gasses are a chronic problem on a dredging project, a degassing system is used that removes the gasses prior to the dredged mixture reaching the dredge pump.

DEGRADIBILITY   The process of spilled oil to convert to simpler or other compounds.

DEGREE OF SUBDIVISION   A relative term expressing the relation of actual subdivision to required compartment standard.

DEGROUPAGE   Splitting up shipments into small consignments.

DEHYDROGENATION   The process of removing hydrogen from adjacent carbon atoms of an organic compound with resultant formation of a double bond.

DELAY   The amount of time in excess of the scheduled time for a movement.

DELCREDERE   Shifting of risk to someone else or acceptance by a party other than the original creditor.

DELIVERED AT FRONTIER (DAF)   Delivered at Frontier means that the seller's obligations are fulfilled when the goods have arrived at the frontier—but before the Customs Border of the country named in the sales contract. The term is primarily intended to apply to goods by rail or road but is also used irrespective of the mode of transport.

DELIVERED PRICE   A price for the merchandise that includes transportation charges to a delivery point agreed upon by the seller and buyer.

DELIVERED-PRICING SYSTEMS   A price that includes delivery to the buyer.

DELIVERING CARRIER   The carrier who delivers the consignment to the consignee or his agent (air cargo).

DELIVERY   The act of transferring possession, such as the transfer of property from consignor to carrier, one carrier to another, or carrier to consignee.

DELIVERY APPOINTMENT   The time agreed upon between two enterprises for goods or transportation equipment to arrive at a selected location.

DELIVERY CYCLE   The time from receipt of an order to the time of customer receipt of the product.

DELIVERY DUTY PAID   This term designates the maximum obligation to the seller who must bear all costs, risk, and duty to the buyer's specified premises.

DELIVERY INSTRUCTIONS   Order to pick up goods at an in transit (temporary) terminal and deliver them to a pier. Usually issued by exporter to trucker but may apply to a railroad, which completes delivery by land. Use is limited to a few major U.S. ports. Also known as shipping delivery order.

DELIVERY NOTE   A document recording the delivery of products to a consignee (customer).

DELIVERY ORDER (DO)   Issued by the consignee or his Customs broker to the ocean carrier as authority to release the cargo to the inland carrier. Includes all data necessary for the pier delivery clerk to determine that the cargo can be released to the domestic carrier.

DELIVERY PARTY   The party to which goods are to be delivered.

DELIVERY RECEIPT   A carrier-prepared form that is signed by the consignee at the time of delivery.

DELIVERY RELIABILITY   The proportion of total delivery occasions in which the time, place, quality, and quantity of products delivered accords with the order.

DELIVERY SCHEDULE   The required and/or agreed time of delivery of goods or services, purchased for a future period.

DELIVERY TIME   The time between order and delivery.

DELIVERY VERIFICATION CERTIFICATE (DVC)   The U.S. Customs Service defines a DVC as a form used to track imported merchandise from the custody of the importer to the custody of a manufacturer and is used to substantiate a manufacturing drawback claim. The DVC is also known as a Certificate of Delivery.

DELIVERY WINDOW   The time span within which a scheduled delivery must be made.

DEM   Demurrage. Money paid to shipper for occupying port space beyond a specified "free time."

DEMAND   The quantity of goods required by the market to be delivered in a particular period or at a specific date.

DEMAND CAPACITY ANALYSIS   The comparison of waterborne commerce demand forecasts with marine terminal cargo handling capability estimates in order to discover any shortfalls or deficits in port terminal capacity and hence assess future facility requirements.

DEMAND GUARANTEE   Type of guarantee that is payable immediately upon presentation of documents specified, without inquiry as to the validity of the documents or into compliance with the underlying contract, as opposed to an "ancillary guarantee." Also called an "independent guarantee." Although there are separate rules of practice for demand guarantees and letters of credit, they are both considered letters of credit under U.S. law.

DEMDES Demurrage/Despatch money. Under vessel chartering terms, the amount to be paid if the ship is loading/discharging slower/faster than foreseen.

DEMERSAL Living at or near the bottom of the sea.

DEMISE CHARTER *See* Bareboat Charter. A contract whereby the shipowner leases his vessel to the charterer for a period of time during which the whole use and management of the vessel passes to the charterer, which involves that the charterer is to pay all expenses for the operation and maintenance of the vessel. Officers and crew will become servants of the charterer. A demise charter whereby the charterer has the right to place his own master and crew onboard of the vessel is also called bareboat charter.

DEMOGRAPHIC Relates to size, density, and distribution of population, as in the case of a port city.

DEMULSIBILITY The ability of an oil to separate from any water with which it is mixed.

DEMURRAGE In Domestic U.S. Transportation: Excess time taken for loading or unloading of a vessel not caused by the vessel operator, but due to the acts of a charterer or shipper. A penalty charge against shippers or consignees for delaying the carrier's equipment beyond the allowed free time provision of the tariff at the rail ramp. In International Transportation: A storage charge to shippers that starts accruing after a container is discharged from a vessel. The charge varies according to rules of the appropriate tariff. *See also* Detention; Per Diem.

DENSE FOG Fog in which visibility is less than ¼ mile.

DENSITY The mass of a unit volume. Its numerical expression varies with the units selected. The weight of water displaced by a floating object. The weight of freight per cubic foot or other unit.

DENSITY METER A device that detects the specific gravity of the mixture in the discharge pipe of the dredge system.

DENSITY RATE A rate based upon the density and shipment weight.

DEPENDANT DEMAND A demand directly related to or derived from the demand for other items or end products. Dependent demands are, therefore, calculated and need not and should not be forecast.

DEPOSIT OF ESTIMATED DUTIES This refers to antidumping duties, which must be deposited upon entry of merchandise, which is the subject of an antidumping duty order for each manufacturer, producer, or exporter equal to the amount by which the foreign market value exceeds the United States price of the merchandise.

DEPOT The place designated by the carrier where empty containers are kept in stock and received from or delivered to the container operators or merchants.

DEPOT, CONTAINER Container freight station or a designated area where empty containers can be picked up or dropped off.

DEPRECIATION An accounting term that signifies the process of allocating the costs of plant and equipment to the accounting periods in which they are used. Loss in value of a capital asset due to wear that cannot be compensated for by ordinary repairs, or to allowance for the asset becoming obsolete before it wears out. D.E.Q. (Delivered Ex Quay duty paid) An acronym that means the seller fulfills his obligation to deliver when he has made the goods available to the buyer on the quay (wharf) at the named port of destination goods for importation and pay the duty the words "duty unpaid" should be used instead of "duty paid." If the parties wish to exclude from the seller's obligations cleared for importation. The seller has to bear all risks and costs including duties, taxes and other charges of delivering the goods. This term should not be used if the seller is unable directly or indirectly to obtain the import license. If the parties wish the buyer to clear the goods, the sum of the costs payable upon importation of the goods such as value added tax (VAT) should be made clear by adding words to this effect: "Delivered ex quay, VAT unpaid (. . . named port of destination)." This term can only be used for sea or inland waterway transport.

DEPTH The vertical distance from the lowest point of the hull to the side of the deck to which it is referred.

DEPTH, MOLDED The vertical distance from the molded base line to the top of the uppermost strength deck beam at side, measured at mid-length of the vessel.

DEPTH SOUNDER A hydrosonic system specifically designed to generate sonic pulses that are directed toward the ocean floor. The system then measures the amount of time it takes for the echo to be received and, based on an average velocity of sound through water, calculates depth.

DEQ Delivered Ex Quay.

DERANGEMENT (MECHANICAL) (INS) Mechanical and/or electrical derangement is an insurance industry term to describe malfunction or nonfunction of an appliance for reasons other than obvious external damage. From time to time, an electronic or mechanically operated item will prove to be inoperable upon arriving at its destination. *See* Mechanical Derangement.

DEREGULATION Revisions or complete elimination of economic regulations controlling transportation. The Motor Carrier Act of 1980 and the Staggers Act of 1980 revised the economic controls over motor carriers and railroads, and the Airline Deregulation Act of 1978 eliminated economic controls over air carriers.

DERELICT An abandoned vessel at sea.

DERIVED DEMAND   The demand for a product's transportation is derived from the product's demand at some location.

DERRICK   A device consisting of a kingpost boom with variable topping lift, and necessary rigging for hoisting heavy weights, cargo, etc.

DES (DELIVERED EX SHIP)   The seller fulfills his obligation to deliver when the goods have been made available to the buyer onboard the ship uncleared for import at the named port of destination. The seller has to bear the costs and risks involved in bringing the goods to the named port of destination. This term can only be used for sea or inland waterway transport.

DESICCANT   A chemical substance capable of absorbing moisture from the atmosphere.

DESPATCH ADVICE   Information sent by shippers to the recipient of goods informing that specified goods are sent or ready to be sent advising the detailed contents of the consignment.

DESPATCH DAYS   The days gained if the free time included in the rate and allowed for the use of certain equipment is not fully used.

DESPATCH/DISPATCH   An incentive payment paid to a carrier to load and unload the cargo faster than agreed. Usually negotiated only in charter parties.

DESP/DISP   Despatch/Dispatch.

DESTINATION   The place to which a shipment is consigned. Also, the place where goods are to be delivered.

DESTINATION CONTROL STATEMENTS   Various statements that the U.S. government requires to be displayed on export shipments. The statements specify the authorized destinations.

DESTROYER   A naval vessel of small displacement and high speed, armed with light, rapid-fire guns and deck torpedo tubes, used for convoy and scouting work and as a protection to capital ships.

DET   *See* Detention.

DETECTION   The recognition of the presence of a target. Used only in connection with ARPA performance standards.

DETECTOR   Through the use of a tuning control, frequencies of desired radio signals are located and passed on to this second stage of a receiver.

DETENTION   A penalty charge against shippers or consignees for delaying carrier's equipment beyond allowed time. Demurrage applies to cargo; detention applies to equipment. *See* Per Diem.

DETENTION CHARGE   Charges levied on usage of equipment exceeding free time period as stipulated in the pertinent inland rules and conditions.

DETERGENT OIL   A lubricating oil possessing special sludge dispersing properties for use in internal combustion engines. These properties are usually conferred on the oil by the incorporation of special additives. A detergent oil has the ability to hold sludge particles in suspension and thus to promote engine cleanliness.

DETERGENTS Compounds (typically alkyl sulfonates, fatty alcohol sulfates, etc.), which act to wet, disperse, and deflocculate solid particles. The respective functions, in turn, are assumed to be dependent upon surface tensions, interfacial tension, viscosity, and perhaps even sudsing of the solution.

DETERIORATION The downgrading of a product due to long storage, damage to packing or other external influences.

DET NORSKE VERITAS Norwegian Classification Society.

DETONATION Sharp explosion. The term is applied to the knock producing type of combustion in spark ignition internal combustion engines that may be induced by low octane rating of fuel, high air/fuel ratio, advanced spark, or excessive engine or mixture temperature.

DETRIMENTAL RELIANCE A "reasonable reliance" upon either a ruling letter or "treatment previously accorded by Customs to substantially identical transaction" over a period of at least two years. As a direct consequence of that "reasonable reliance," the party must have suffered to their detriment.

DEV *See* Deviation.

DEVALUATION A government decision to lower the trade value of a nation's currency with respect to other currencies by reducing the gold content or by revising the ratio to a new standard.

DEVANNING The unloading of a container to cargo van.

DEVELOPING COUNTRIES A broad range of countries that lack a high degree of industrialization, infrastructure, other capital investment, sophisticated technology, widespread literacy, and advanced living standards.

DEVELOPING HIGH A change in the weather pattern in which higher pressure is building up over an area.

DEVELOPING LOW A change in the weather pattern in which lower pressure is forming over an area that is likely to result in a definite low center.

DEVIATION A vessel's going to some other point or taking some course other than that described in the bill of lading.

DEVIATION FROM ROUTE A divergence from the agreed or customary route.

DEVIL'S CLAW A turnbuckle device having two heavy claws designed to fit over a link in the anchor chain for the purpose of securing the anchor hard up in stowed position in the hawse pipe.

DEVISEN (GERMAN) Foreign currencies.

DEWATERING The process of removing excess water from (dredged) material; dewatering includes removal of ponded or surface water and could also include removal of water bound into the sediment. Use of trenches and other engineering techniques to expedite removal of water from a confined disposal facility after dredging. Used in conjunction with other site management techniques to increase the life expectancy of the site as well as to improve foundation properties.

DEWAXING   Removal of wax. In one method, propane is used as a refrigerant and wax antisolvent for removing wax from wax bearing distillates.

DF CAR   Damage Free Car. Boxcars equipped with special bracing material.

DFRT   Dead freight. Unused space aboard carrier.

DFZ   *See* Duty Free Zone.

DGI   *See* Defective Goods Inventory.

DGPS   *See* Differential Global Positioning System.

D&H   Dangerous and Hazardous cargo.

DHDATSBE   Despatch Half Demurrage on All Time Saved Both Ends.

DHDWTSBE   Despatch Half Demurrage on Working Time Saved Both Ends.

DIAGONAL LINE   A line cutting the body plan diagonally from the frames to the middle line in the loft lay out and usually a mean normal to a group of frames of similar curvature, representing a plane introduced for line fairing purposes.

DIE   A tool, having several cutting edges, used for cutting threads. In drop forging work, a template tool used to stamp out a piece of work in one operation.

DIELECTRIC STRENGTH   The rating of the insulating power of insulating oils. Thus, oils with the highest dielectric strength (expressed in kilovolts) are the best electrical insulators.

DIESEL INDEX   The product of aniline point in degrees Fahrenheit and the API gravity at 60°F divided by 100. The diesel index increases with the increase in cetane number.

DIFFERENTIAL   An amount added or deducted from base rate to make a rate to or from some other point or via another route.

DIFFERENTIAL GLOBAL POSITIONING SYSTEM (DGPS)   A system designed to provide the same information as the regular global positioning system, except that an additional correction, or differential signal, was added to improve accuracy. This correction signal is broadcast over a specific frequency that covers particular geographic areas.

DIFFERENTIAL GLOBAL POSITIONING SYSTEM (DGPS) NAVIGATION SERVICE   A U.S. Coast Guard service designed to provide coverage at the specified levels for all harbors and harbor approach areas and other critical waterways for which the Coast Guard provides aids to navigation.

DIFFERENTIATION   The strategy of producing a unique product that is clearly distinct from, and superior in performance from competing products.

DIFFRACTION   The bending of waves around a solid object and filling in behind it. This can be seen when radio waves pass around an object or can be picked up from over the horizon.

DIFFUSE REFLECTION   When waves reflect back at various angles caused by contours and the variability of the reflective surface.

DIFFUSER   A device placed on the end of a discharge pipeline to slow the velocity of discharged material, thereby providing better control over point disposal and reducing turbidity and water column impacts.

DIGESTION   The process of breaking down a material or chemical compound into an absorbable and/or simpler chemical form.

DIGITAL SELECTIVE CALLING (DSC)   A system used for the transmission of critical information such as distress calls, navigational alerts, automatic position reporting, communication relays and reporting, routine communications, and reception acknowledgments between ships and coastal radio stations.

DIKE   Usually constructed of piling or stone, usually at right angles to the current for the purpose of diverting the river current away from the banks and toward the channel. A dike serves the same purpose as a WING DAM. Dike pilings are usually visible at normal water stages but are often submerged in high water and constitute a navigation hazard.

DIKE LIGHT   A light installed on the end of a dike, normally a portable 90 mm battery-operated light.

DILIGENCE   A requirement of a broker to handle all financial settlements, correspondence, or the filing of documents relating to their brokerage business with due diligence.

DILUTION OF CRANKCASE OILS   The percentage of fuel used in internal combustion engine oil.

DIM WEIGHT   Dimensional weight. When the shipment's dimensions (length, height, etc.) are sufficiently extreme that they determine the rate charged by the carrier.

DIMENSION   A measured distance between two ends of a scrap or bulk piece of wood that is to be remanufactured into a piece of pallet.

DIMENSIONAL WEIGHT   Refers to weight per cubic foot, etc. The weight of a shipment per cubic foot is one of the most important transportation characteristics, directly involving such factors as the efficient loading and economy of freight traffic. Some commodities have a high density, such as machinery, while others have a low density, such as ladies hats. Hence, the dimensional weight rule was developed as a practice applicable to low density shipments under which the transportation charges are based on a cubic dimensional weight rather than upon the actual weight.

DIMENSIONS   Measurements in length, width, and height, regarding cargo.

DIN   Deutsche Industrie Norm (German Standards Institute).

DINGHY   A small handy boat issued to certain vessels of the U.S. Navy, signal banked, with four oars, fitted with sail of sprit rig and either 18 feet or 20 feet in length.

DINNER BUCKET BOAT   A boat operating without benefit of a cookhouse.

DIOLEFINS   Open chain hydrocarbons having two double bonds per molecule.

DIP   A position of a flag when hoisted part way of the hoist; to lower a flag part way and then hoist it again; the vertical angle, at the eye of an observer, between the horizon and the horizontal. This is also an expression referring to passing one line under another.

DIPPER DREDGE A type of dredge that uses a single bucket that is rigidly attached to the dredge by a mechanical arm. The dipper dredge works by gouging material from the bottom with the dipper and emptying the dredged material into a nearby disposal area.

DIP ROPE A length of open link chain or wire fitted with an eye and shackle and tailed with a manila rope; used in clearing hawse and in mooring, and in rigging a collision mat.

DIRECIONAL LIGHT A light illuminating a sector or very narrow angle and intended to mark a direction to be followed.

DIRECT COLLECTION Service for handling export draft collections in which the exporter's bank provides him with forms that bear the bank's own letterhead for mailing documents to the buyer's bank for collection. To the buyer's bank, it will appear that the documents were sent from the exporter's bank, but time and expense are saved by bypassing unnecessary processing at the exporter's bank.

DIRECT CURRENT (DC) The continuous flow of electrons in the same direction.

DIRECT DELIVERY The conveyance of goods directly from the vendor to the buyer. Frequently used if a third party acts as intermediary agent between vendor and buyer.

DIRECT DRIVE The coupling of a propulsion engine to a propeller by a shaft without intermediate gearing.

DIRECT EXPORTING Sale by an exporter directly to a buyer located in a foreign country.

DIRECT IMPACTS This represents impacts associated with the initial round of spending and employment generated by a maritime activity. The direct impact of the port industry is comprised of transportation activities (pilotage, bunkering, freight forwarding, cargo handling, and inland transportation).

DIRECT INTERCHANGE Transfer of leased equipment from one lessee to another (container).

DIRECT OR HELD COVERED (INS) A condition requiring that the insured voyage be direct from one place to another. If the voyage is delayed en route or there is a deviation from the direct route, the insurance coverage continues subject to payment of an additional premium, but only if the Assured gives prompt notice of such delay or deviation immediately on receipt of advices, unless the policy provides otherwise.

DIRECT PRODUCT PROFITABILITY (DPP) Calculation of the net profit contribution attributable to a specific product or product line.

DIRECT ROUTE The shortest operated route between two points.

DIRECT STORE DELIVERY (DSD) A logistics strategy to improve services and lower warehouse inventories.

DIRECT WAVES Radar waves traveling outward in a straight manner.

DIRECTION OF RELATIVE MOTION (DRM) The vectorial sum of the motions of the own ship and the contact vessel shown in the plot as the RM line.

DIRECTIONAL LOOP ANTENNA   *See* Crossed Loop Antenna.

DIRTY BALLAST   Ballast water that has been contaminated by oil and will produce a sheen upon the water or a sludge below the surface if discharged into calm waters.

DIRTY CARGOES   *See* Black Cargoes.

DISBURSEMENTS   Sums paid out by a ship's agent at a port and recovered from the carrier.

DISCH   Discharge.

DISCHARGE LOAD AND RELOAD   Cargo discharged from a vessel and reloaded aboard same vessel or another for transshipment.

DISCHARGE PIPE   A device placed at the end of the discharge pipe to distribute the outflow of dredged material over a larger area in the disposal facility and thereby minimize undesirable effects of direct impact.

DISCHARGE PORT   The name of the port where the cargo is unloaded from the export vessel. This is the port reported to the U.S. Census on the Shipper's Export Declaration, Schedule K, which is used by U.S. companies when exporting. This can also be considered the first discharge port.

DISCLOSURE (INS)   The duty of the Assured and his broker to tell the Underwriter every material circumstance before acceptance of the risk.

DISCONTINUED   To remove from operation (permanently or temporarily) a previously authorized aid to navigation.

DISCONTINUOUS HINTERLAND   The area to which a port's exports are destined or where its imports originate.

DISCOVERY PERIOD (INS)   The time allowed the insured after termination of certain bond and policy provisions to discover that he has sustained a loss that occurred during the period covered by the contract.

DISCREPANCIES   In the context of letters of credit, term used to describe deviations between documents presented and requirements set in the letter of credit or inconsistencies among the documents themselves.

DISCREPANCY   Failure of an aid to navigation to maintain its position or function as described in the light list.

DISCREPANCY BUOY   An easily transportable buoy used to temporarily replace an aid to navigation not operating properly.

DISCREPANCY LETTER OF CREDIT   When documents presented do not conform to the requirements of the letter of credit (L/C), it is referred to as a "discrepancy." Banks will not process L/Cs that have discrepancies. They will refer the situation back to the buyer and/or seller and await further instructions.

DISECONOMY   An activity within a business organization where revenues do not cover costs, requiring internal or cross-subsidization.

DISHED PLATES   Plates, generally of circular shape, that have been furnaced or pressed into a concave form.

DISHONOR   Failure or refusal by the drawee to accept a draft presented for acceptance or to pay a draft presented for payment.

DISINTERMEDIATION   When a net market bypasses a traditional channel, more directly linking buyers with suppliers.

DISMANTLE   To strip a vessel of her spars and upper masts.

DISP   Dispatch (Despatch)—Displacement.

DISPATCH   An amount paid to a charterer by the vessel operator if loading or unloading is accomplished in less time than provided for in the charter party.

DISPATCHING   Carrier activities involved with controlling equipment; involves arranging for fuel, drivers, crews, equipment, and terminal space.

DISPERSABILITY   The ability of oil products to break up or scatter.

DISPLACEMENT   (1) The weight, in tons of 2,240 pounds, of the vessel and its contents. Calculated by dividing the volume of water displaced in cubic feet by 35, the average density of seawater. Displacement may be expressed either in cubic feet or long tons. A cubic foot of seawater weighs 64 pounds, and one of freshwater 62.5 pounds; consequently, one long ton is equal to 35 cubic feet of seawater or 35.9 cubic feet of freshwater. One long ton equals 2,240 pounds.

(2) The weight of a ship, excluding cargo, passengers, Tonnage lightship fuel, water, stores, dunnage, and other items necessary for voyage.

(3) In harbor management, the removal of working maritime industry by an urban use (residence, office, retail) that can pay higher rent.

DISPLACEMENT, DESIGNED   The displacement of a vessel when floating at her designed draft.

DISPLACEMENT, FULL LOAD   The displacement of a vessel when floating at her greatest allowable draft as established by the classification societies. In warships an arbitrary full-load condition is established.

DISPLACEMENT, LIGHT   The weight of the ship with all items of outfit, equipment, and machinery onboard but excluding cargo, fuel, ballast, stores, passengers, dunnage, and the crew and their effects. Naval and merchant practice differs in that the naval ships, the machinery weights are dry, while the merchant light condition includes the water and oil in the machinery with boilers at steaming level.

DISPLACEMENT, LOADED   The weight of the ship including cargo, passengers, fuel, water, stores, dunnage, and other such items necessary for use on a voyage, which brings the ship down to her load draft.

DISPLACEMENT CURVES   Curves drawn to give the displacement of the vessel at varying drafts. Usually these curves are drawn to show the displacement in either salt or freshwater, or in both, the saltwater curves being based on 35 cubic feet to a ton and fresh water curves on 36 cubic feet to a ton. Corrections are made from these basic standards for variable density of the water.

DISPLACEMENT TONNAGE   The amount of water a ship is pushing out of the way to float, computed as 35 pounds per cubic foot for saltwater. The actual weight of a vessel by calculation of the weight of volume of water displaced.

DISPLAY   The plan position presentation of ARPA data with radar data. Used only in connection with ARPA performance standards.

DISPLAY TYPE   The way the radar image presents changes in the vessel's surroundings.

DISPOSABLE PALLET   Pallet intended to be discarded after a single cycle of use. Also known as: one-way pallet, expendable pallet.

DISPOSAL AREA   A specific location, usually specified through required procedures of the Clean Water Act or Ocean Dumping Act, that represents the least costly, environmentally acceptable site for a specific dredged material.

DISPOSITIONING   All activities relating to the inland movement of empty and/or full containers.

DISSEMINATE   To remove cargo from a container containing more than one shipment for separate deliveries.

DISSIPATING LOW   A low center that is becoming weaker as the central pressure increases with time. Winds, in most cases, decrease; low expected to vanish.

DISTANCE RATE   A rate that is applicable according to distance.

DISTILLATE   The portion of oil that is removed as a vapor and condensed during a distillation process.

DISTILLATE FUEL OILS   Fuel oils that are distillates derived directly or indirectly from crude petroleum (chiefly from the gas oil fraction).

DISTILLATION   Distillation generally refers to vaporization processes in which the vapor evolved is recovered, usually by condensation, and a separation effected between those fractions that vaporize and those that remain in the bottoms.

DISTILLATION RANGE   Initial boiling point, final boiling point, and temperatures at which various fractions are distilled, as determined under specified test conditions.

DISTRESS SIGNAL   A flag display or a sound, light, or radio signal calling for assistance.

DISTRIBUTION   The physical path and legal title that goods and services take between production and consumption.

DISTRIBUTION CENTER   A warehouse for the receipt, the storage, and the dispersal of goods among customers.

DISTRIBUTION CHANNEL   The route by which a company distributes goods.

DISTRIBUTION CHANNEL MANAGEMENT   The organizational and pipeline strategy for getting products to customers. Direct channels involve company sales forces, facilities, and/or direct shipments to customers; indirect channels involve the use of wholesalers, distributors, and/or other parties to supply the products to customers. Many companies use both strategies, depending on markets and effectiveness.

DISTRIBUTION LICENSE (DL)   The DL is a special license that allows the holder to make multiple exports of authorized commodities to foreign consignees who are approved in advance by the Bureau of Export Administration. The procedure also authorizes approved foreign consignees to re-export among themselves and to other approved countries. Applicants and consignees must establish Internal Control Programs to ensure the proper distribution of items under the DL. Each program must include comprehensive procedures for ensuring that the items exported will be used only for legitimate end-uses.

DISTRIBUTION RESOURCE PLANNING   A computer system that uses MRP techniques to manage the entire distribution network and to link it with manufacturing planning and control.

DISTRIBUTION WAREHOUSE   A finished goods warehouse from which a company assembles customer orders.

DISTRIBUTOR   A foreign agent who sells directly for a manufacturer and maintains an inventory on hand.

DITTY BAG   A small bag used to hold twine, marline, sewing palm, needles, and marlinespikes, such as is required to be carried in ships' lifeboats; any small bag used by seamen for sewing gear, personal trinkets, etc.

DIVERSION   A change made either in the route of a shipment in transit (*see* Reconsignment) or of the entire ship, or any change in the billing after shipment has been received by the carrier at point of origin and prior to delivery at destination.

DIVESTITURE   The transfer of title or disposal of interests. Corporate holdings that do not require government ownership to fulfill their public mandate are considered for divestiture to the private sector.

DIVIDER   A vertically mounted partition in a compartment onboard.

DIVISION   Carriers' practice of dividing revenue received from through rates where joint hauls are involved. This is usually according to agreed formulae.

DK   Deck.

DL   *See* Distribution License.

DLO   Dispatch Loading Only.

DM   Decimeter (one tenth of a meter long).

DNRCAOSLONL   Discountless and Nonreturnable Cargo and/or Ship Lost or Not Lost.

DNV   Der Norske Veritas, Norwegian ship classification society.

DO   Diesel Oil.

DOCK   A shore side facility designed to moor vessels, technically one in which the water may flow below the apron area. A cargo handling area parallel to the shoreline. Wet docks are used for the loading and unloading of ships. Dry docks are used for the construction or repair of ships. Also, a place such as a wharf or platform, for the loading and unloading of materials from ships. The part of a carrier's building where freight is sorted, loaded, and unloaded from vehicles.

DOCK BUMPERS   Cushioning devices (rubber, plastic, wood, etc.) mounted at the extreme rear of a chassis or trailer to take the impact when it backs into a loading dock or platform (road cargo).

DOCK RECEIPT A form used to acknowledge receipt of cargo and often serves as basis for preparation of the ocean bill of lading. A receipt given for a shipment received or delivered at a shipment pier. When delivery of a foreign shipment is completed, the dock receipt is surrendered to the vessel operator or his agent and serves as basis for preparation of the ocean bill of lading.

DOCKAGE Charge levied against the vessel for berthing space.

DOCKET Present a rate proposal to a conference meeting for adoption as a conference group rate.

DOCKING KEEL Keel on each side, and in plane of regular keel, used to distribute the weight in dry dock in the case of large ships. (Seldom used except on largest naval ships.)

DOCKING PLAN The ship's plan furnishing all necessary information concerning the underwater hull for dry docking purposes.

DOCKING PLANS Gives essential information required by dock master. Consists of outboard profile and midship section. Frame spacing, extent of double bottoms, decks, watertight bulkheads, and machinery spaces are shown. Positions of all openings in shell below waterline, rise of floor, bilge radius, and bottom longitudinals are indicated.

DOCKYARD A shipyard or plant where ships are constructed for repaired.

DOCTOR TEST A qualitative method of detecting undesirable sulfur compounds in petroleum distillates, that is, determining whether an oil is sour or sweet.

DOCUMENT Anything printed, written, relied upon to record or prove something.

DOCUMENTARY CREDIT *See* Letter of Credit.

DOCUMENTARY DRAFT COLLECTION Process for collecting payment in a sale of goods wherein a legal demand for payment from the buyer is made by a bank acting as collecting agent for the seller. Demand is made by presenting a draft. The collecting bank is also entrusted with documents to deliver in accordance with accompanying instructions, usually once the draft is either paid or accepted. These documents are generally needed by the buyer to show title to the goods and/or to clear customs.

DOCUMENTARY LETTER OF CREDIT Term sometimes used (incorrectly) to refer to commercial letters of credit. The term is redundant in that all letters of credit are documentary. *See* Letter of Credit; Commercial Letter of Credit.

DOCUMENTATION The papers attached or pertaining to goods requiring transportation and/or transfer of ownership.

DOCUMENT HOLDER Usually fastened to the door on the front of a container. May contain, e.g., a certificate of approval of the container.

DOCUMENT OF TITLE A term to mean that possession of the specified document entitles the holder to control of the goods listed in that document.

DOCUMENTS AGAINST ACCEPTANCE (D/A) Instructions given by a shipper to a bank indicating that documents transferring title to goods should be delivered to the buyer only upon the buyer's acceptance of the attached draft.

DOCUMENTS AGAINST PAYMENT (D/P) A type of payment for goods in which the documents transferring title to the goods are not given to the buyer until he has paid the value of a draft issued against him.

DOG Mechanical device that holds watertight doors securely in the closed position. A small bent metal fitting used to hold doors, hatch covers, manhole covers, etc., closed. A bent bar of round iron used for holding shapes on bending slab.

DOG SHORES Diagonal braces placed to prevent the sliding ways from moving when the shores and keel blocks are removed before launching. Dog shores are the last timbers to be knocked away at a launching. Also called daggers or dagger shores.

DOGWATCH One of the two-hour watches from 1600 to 2000. From 1600 to 1800 is the first dogwatch; from 1800 to 2000 is the second dogwatch.

DOLDRUMS The belt on each side of the equator in which little or no wind ordinarily blows.

DOLLY A set of wheels that support the front of a container; used when the tractor unit is disconnected.

DOLLY BAR A heavy steel bar used to hold against the heads of rivets while the points are being clinched when the space is not sufficient to permit the use of a regular holding-on tool.

DOLPHIN An isolated cluster of piles used as a support for mooring devices or marker lights. A minor aid to navigation structure consisting of a number of piles driven into the seabed or riverbed in a circular pattern and drawn together with wire rope.

DOMESTIC Refers to traffic beginning and terminating in the provinces and territories of a single national jurisdiction.

DOMESTIC CARRIAGE Carriage whereby the place of departure and the place of destination are situated within one country (air cargo).

DOMESTIC RATE Rate applicable within a country, and in most cases subject to special conditions other than those of IATA (air cargo).

DOMESTIC TRADE This includes only the domestic ocean movements of coastwise, lakewise, noncontiguous, and intraterritory cargo receipts and shipments.

DOMESTIC TRUNK-LINE CARRIERS An air carrier classification for carriers that operate between major population centers. These carriers are not classified as major carriers.

DONKEY ENGINE A small gas, steam, or electric auxiliary engine set on the deck and used for lifting, etc.

DOOR, AIRTIGHT A door so constructed that when closed it will prevent the passage of air under a small pressure. Used on air locks to boiler rooms under force draft and in similar locations.

DOOR, JOINER A light door fitted to staterooms and quarters where air and water tightness is not required. Made of wood, light metal, and metal-covered wood. Metal joiner doors with pressed panels are extensively used.

DOOR, WATERTIGHT A door so constructed that, when closed, it will prevent water under pressure from passing through.

DOOR, WEATHERTIGHT A term applied to outside doors on the upper decks, which are designed to keep out the rain and spray.

DOOR LOCK BARS *See* Bar.

DOOR-TO-DOOR Through transportation of a container and its contents from consignor to consignee. Also known as house-to-house. Not necessarily a through rate.

DOOR-TO-PIER/DOOR-TO-DOOR (D/P) Combination of door-to-door and pier-to-pier services, depending upon the desires of the shipper, capabilities of the carrier, and facilities available to the shipper and consignee.

DOOR-TO-PORT The through transport service from consignor to port of importation.

DOPPLER EFFECT The frequency Doppler shift of an approaching signal due to the signal's velocity/distance relationship.

DORMANT ROUTE A route over which a carrier failed to provide service 5 days a week for 13 weeks out of a 26-week period.

DOT Department of Transport or Transportation.

DOUBLE (DOUBLE LOCKAGE) The maneuver whereby a towboat with barges in tow must break the tow and push half of it into the lock chamber, lock that part through and then enter the remaining barges with the towboat. In other words, two distinct lockages must be made to pass the entire tow of barges and towboat.

DOUBLE BANKING Two vessels moored alongside each other on a certain berth.

DOUBLE BOTTOM The area between the hull and the inner bottom of a ship, its top usually level with the top of the keelson, used to store fuel, water or ballast. Compartments at bottom of ship between inner and outer bottoms used for ballast tanks, oil, water, fuel, etc.

DOUBLE-DECK PALLET Flat pallet with a top and bottom deck.

DOUBLE HULL On tankers, a void area encompassing the sides and bottom of cargo tanks. Double hulls need only be built within the cargo tank length, excluding ship's fuel tanks.

DOUBLE PALLET JACK A mechanized device for transporting two standard pallets simultaneously.

DOUBLE SKIN The use of two separated material layers for containment or construction purposes. A double skin construction is used on the sides and bottom of containerships.

DOUBLE STACK   A special articulated railcar to haul containers one on top of another. The typical car consists of five articulated rail "platforms" each capable of holding two 40 foot containers.

DOUBLE STACKER CONE   A double set of cones mounted on a steel plate used to stack one container on another and bridge between two adjacent containers.

DOUBLE TRIP   When a towboat has more barges in tow than the power of the boat can handle in certain areas of swift current or conditions at the lock will permit, double tripping is necessary. A tow will tie off below the swift water a portion of his tow, pushing the others above the questionable area, tying them off to the bank, and going back for the remainder of the tow. This is also a necessary maneuver at times in ice.

DOUBLE UP   To double a vessel's securing lines.

DOUBLING PLATE   A plate fitted outside or inside of and faying against another to give extra strength or stiffness.

DOVETAILING   When vendors (suppliers) locate their plants in close proximity to customers. The idea is growing rapidly because of JIT inventory systems.

DOWEL   A pin of wood or metal inserted in the edge or face of two boards or pieces to secure them together.

DOWN BY THE HEAD   When any vessel's draft is greater forward than aft.

DOWN DRAFT   The natural tendency for the river current to pull downstream while making a river crossing.

DOWNGRADING   Assigning a petroleum product for use where a lower grade of product would normally be employed, provided it meets the requirements for the lower grade.

DOWN SHAPE OF (REVETMENT SHORE, ETC.)   Means to run the shape of shore, staying approximately the same distance off the shore at all times.

DOWN TIME   The period when equipment is not operating or productive.

DOWSE   To take in, or lower, a sail; to put out a light; to cover with water.

DP   Direct Port.

D/P   *See* Documents Against Payment. Instructions a shipper gives to his bank that the documents attached to a draft for collection are deliverable to the drawee only against his payment of the draft.

DPP   *See* Direct Product Profitability.

DRAFT   The number of feet that the hull of a ship is beneath the surface of the water. When measured at the bow it is called the forward draft; when measured at the stern, the draft aft; the average of the draft forward and the draft aft is the mean draft. The term draft is used when referring to a sling load of cargo. Also, an unconditional order in writing, addressed by one party (drawer) to another party (drawee), requiring the drawee to pay at a fixed or determinable future date a specified sum in lawful currency to the order of a specified person. Also, the vertical distance from the waterline to the keel of a vessel. The depth of water necessary for the dredge to enter an area or to operate. Crosscurrent; tows will drift to the right or left depending on the draft. (Usually qualified as outdraft, or left- or right-handed draft).

DRAFT, BANK An order issued by a seller against a purchaser; directs payment, usually through an intermediary bank. Typical bank drafts are negotiable instruments and are similar in many ways to checks on checking accounts in a bank.

DRAFT, CLEAN A draft to which no documents are attached.

DRAFT, DATE A draft that matures on a fixed date, regardless of the time of acceptance.

DRAFT, DISCOUNTED A time draft under a letter of credit that has been accepted and purchased by a bank at a discount.

DRAFT, DRAUGHT The depth of the vessel below the waterline measured vertically to the lowest part of the hull, propellers, or other reference point. When measured to the lowest projecting portion of the vessel, it is called the "draft, extreme"; when measured at the bow, it is called "draft, forward"; and when measured at the stern, the "draft, aft."

DRAFT, SIGHT A draft payable on demand upon presentation.

DRAFT, TIME A draft that matures at a fixed or determinable time after presentation or acceptance.

DRAFT COLLECTION Process for collecting payment in a sale of goods wherein a legal demand for payment from the buyer is made by a bank acting as collecting agent for the seller. Demand is made by presenting a draft.

DRAFT GAUGE The device for determining the current draft for the dredge.

DRAFT MARKS The numbers that are placed on each side of a vessel near the bow and stern, and sometimes amidships, to indicate the distance from the number to the bottom of the keel or a fixed reference point. These numbers are six inches high, and spaced twelve inches bottom to bottom vertically, and are located as close to the bow and stern as possible. U.S. ships use feet, some foreign ships use meters.

DRAFTING The act of acquiring water for fire pumps from a static water supply by creating a negative pressure on the vacuum side of the fire pumps.

DRAG A heavy frame dragged along the bottom as in oyster dredging; a semisubmerged contrivance for keeping a vessel's head to wind and sea. The difference in the amount of a vessel's draft when it is greater aft than forward.

DRAG ARM Extendable suction pipes associated with hopper dredges, usually located both port and starboard, that are lowered to the bottom during dredging to convey sediment from the bottom into the hopper bins.

DRAG HEAD The device placed at the terminus of the drag arm and contacts the bottom. There are several designs available and the specific design used depends on the type material to be dredged at the project site.

DRAG LINE Used to pull cargo out of the wings into the square of the hatch for convenience of hoisting.

DRAGGING (OF ANCHOR)   An anchor moving over the sea bottom involuntarily because it is no longer preventing the movement of the vessel.

DRAUGHT   Depth of water at which a ship floats. Simply the distance from the bottom of the ship to the waterline. If the waterline is parallel to the keel, the ship is said to be "on the keel." If not parallel, the ship is said to be trimmed. If draught at after end is greater than at the fore end, the ship is trimmed by the stern. If the converse applies, the ship is trimmed by bow or by the head. Draught marks are cut in the stern, which give the distance from the bottom of the ship, and the figures are 10 cm high with a 10 cm spacing.

DRAUGHT (U.S. "DRAFT")   The vertical distance of the lowest point of the ship below the surface of the water when she is afloat. Also, the depth of a loaded vessel in the water taken from the level of the waterline to the lowest point of the hull of the vessel; depth of water or distance between the bottom of the ship and the waterline.

DRAUGHT MARKS   The numbers painted at the bow and stern of a vessel to indicate how much water she draws. These marks are 6 inches high and spaced 12 inches apart vertically.

DRAWBACK   A partial refund of duties paid on importation of goods, which are further processed, and then reexported.

DRAWBACK SYSTEM   A part of U.S. Customs' Automated Commercial System provides the means for processing and tracking of drawback claims.

DRAWBRIDGE   A bridge that pivots or lifts so as to let a boat through.

DRAW DOWN   The procedure of spilling water through one dam prior to the arrival of excessive water from the upper reaches of the river. This maneuver is used when flash floods are expected or have occurred or where tributary streams are emptying excessive amounts of water into the main streams.

DRAWEE   The individual or firm that issues a draft and thus stands to receive payment. Party to whom a draft is addressed and from whom payment is demanded, or, in a documentary collection with no draft, party from whom payment is requested in exchange for delivery of documents.

DRAW WORKS   The hoisting equipment on a rotary drilling rig, used to lift and lower the pipe into the hole.

DRAYAGE   Charge made for local hauling by dray or truck. Same as Cartage.

DREDGE   A specialty ship designed to dig bottom sediment from harbor channels. Dredges are often self-propelled and store dredgings in hoppers for disposal elsewhere. The mechanical device that is used to remove sediment from a channel, berth or other portion of a water body. The three basic types of dredges are mechanical, hydraulic, and hopper. Also, a device used in dredging. Normally, this device is hydraulic in that hydraulic forces are generated to entrain bottom materials into the pumping system. Sometimes a combination of hydraulic and mechanical systems are used to fragment or dislodge bottom materials.

DREDGE LADDER The structural assembly that supports the dredge suction pipe, the cutter head (if installed), and other flow augmentation devices such as jet assists. Occasionally, the dredge pump will be placed on the dredge ladder to improve dredge production.

DREDGE TENDER A support vessel that is responsible for moving nonself-propelled dredges from one dredging site to another. The tender provides other services such as placing anchors and assisting in deployment of floating discharge line.

DREDGED MATERIAL Marine sediment that has been removed by dredging activity; dredged material was historically referred to as "spoil."

DREDGED OUT One pass made by a dredge in a channel within the confines of the riverbed for the purpose of maintaining the proper depth of water. Also, a term to mean a dredged channel.

DREDGING The practice of removing material from underwater locations.

DREDGING ANCHOR Vessel moving, under control, with anchor moving along the sea bottom.

DREDGING CYCLE Length of time required by a hopper dredge to fill the hopper bins to specified capacity, transport the material to a disposal site, and return to the point of dredging activity.

DREDGING FREQUENCY Time interval between required project mainte-nance dredging requirements. Ranges from two or more times per year to intervals of 10 to 15 years.

DREDGING SPOIL A term meaning the discharge from a dredge.

DRESSING SHIP A display of national colors at all mastheads and the flag-staff. Full dressing ship requires, in addition, a rainbow of flags from bow to stern over the mastheads.

DRFS Destination Rail Freight Station. Same as CFS at destination, except a DRFS is operated by the rail carrier participating in the shipment.

DRIFT The motion of a boat floating with no mechanical aid. Also, debris floating in the river or lodged along shore in a drift pile. Also, colloquially used as a synonym for currents: "How does the drift set around this bridge pier?" Also, when erecting the structure of a ship and rivet holes in the pieces to be connected are not concentric, the distance that they are out of line is called the drift. This should be corrected by reaming the holes, but common practice, which is prohibited in naval work, is to drive tapered pins, called "drift pins," into the unfair holes to force them into line.

DRIFT PIN A small tapered tool driven through rivet holes and used to draw adjoining plates or bars into alignment with each other.

DRILL SHIP Used for drilling oil in water depth down to about 500 m. *See also* Dynamic Positioning.

DRILLING RIG A structure erected over a well to carry the drill and machin-ery for boring the well.

DRIVE To use full power ahead.

DRIVE HER THROUGH Full speed ahead.

DRIVING TIME REGULATIONS Rules administered by the U.S. Department of Transportation that limit the maximum time a driver may drive in commerce; both daily and weekly maximums are prescribed.

DRK Derrick.

DRM *See* Direction of Relative Motion.

DROP A situation in which an equipment operator deposits a trailer or box-car at a facility at which it is to be loaded or unloaded.

DROP-OFF CHARGE Charge made by container owner and/or terminal operators for delivery of a leased or pool container into depot stock. The drop-off charge may be a combination of actual handling and storage charges with surcharges.

DROP SHIPMENT A request for the goods to go to the retailer directly from the manufacturer when the invoice comes from another party in the transaction, typically the distributor from whom the retailer would normally receive the goods.

DROP STRAKE A strake that is terminated before it reaches the bow or stern. The number of strakes dropped depends on the reduction of girth between the midship section and the ends.

DROPPING OUT LINE A line used in dropping a barge out of a tow.

DROPPING POINT OF GREASE The temperature at which grease passes from semisolid to liquid state under specified test conditions.

DROPS Piping to bring cargo down from the ship's deck piping to the ship's bottom piping or the ship's tanks.

DRP *See* Distribution Resource Planning.

DRUM, WINCH Cylinder or barrel on winch around which is wound cable or rope used in raising loads or drafts or in other hoisting or hauling.

DRUM END A large steel spool on the extension of the axle of a winch drum. Sometimes called "gypsy head" or "gypsy."

DRY BULK CARGO Cargo that may be either loose, grained, free flowing, or solid but is not shipped in packaged form and is usually handled by specialized mechanical handling equipment as specially designed dry bulk terminals such as grain, coal, ore, and the like.

DRY BULK CONTAINER A container constructed to carry grain, powder, and other free flowing solids in bulk. Used in conjunction with a tilt chassis or platform.

DRY BULK SELF UNLOADER SHIP A self-unloading vessel highly automated with a built-in cargo discharging system.

DRY BULK SHIP A vessel with holds suitable for the accommodation and transportation of dry bulk cargoes such as coal, iron ore, and grain.

DRY BULK TERMINAL Terminal equipped to handle dry goods that are stored in tanks and holds about the vessel.

DRY CARGO Cargo that does not require temperature control.

DRY CARGO CONTAINER   Shipping container that is designed for the carriage of goods other than liquids.

DRY CARGO SHIP   Vessel that carriers all merchandise, excluding liquid in bulk.

DRY DOCK   A dock in which a ship's hull may be kept out of water during construction or repair. Three types are used: (1) the GRAVING dock, a basin excavated near a waterway, with a gate to exclude the water after pumping out; (2) the FLOATING dock, a hollow structure of wood or steel, which is sunk to receive the ship to be docked and is pumped out to lift it from the water; (3) the MARINE RAILWAY, a cradle of wood or steel on which the ship may be hauled out of water along inclined tracks leading up the bank of a waterway.

DRYING OIL   An oil that possesses the property of readily absorbing oxygen from the air and of changing to a relatively hard, tough, and elastic film when exposed in thin layers to the atmosphere.

D/S   Days After Sight.

DSD   *See* Direct Store Delivery.

DSS   *See* Decision Support System.

DST   Double Stack Train or Daylight Savings Time.

DSU   Delay in Start-up insurance is a policy to protect the seller of a construction project from penalties if the project is not completed on time. *See* Liquidated Damages.

DUAL FUEL ENGINES   Engines designed to burn either oil or gas or a mixture of the two with simple, frequently automatic means of changing from one fuel to the other. Normally the gas is ignited by injection of 210% of full load oil, but some engines have been designed to use spark ignition when running on gas.

DUAL OPERATION   A motor carrier that has both common and contract carrier operating authority.

DUAL-RATE SYSTEM   An international water carrier pricing system in which a shipper signing an exclusive use agreement with the conference pays a rate 10 to 15 percent lower than nonsigning shippers do for an identical shipment.

DUCK WATER   Slack water. Smooth water generally found on the inside shore of a river bend, under a point, under a bar, etc.

DUCTILITY   The property of a material that permits its being drawn out into a thread of wire.

DUCTING   An extreme condition of reflection when a radio wave is rebounded off the surface of two separate layers of different densities, such as an atmospheric layer and the earth's surface, and can travel great distances within these two layers.

DUE BILL PRIVILEGES   Credit for freight charges extended to the shipper or consignee, usually for a specified period after the sailing or arrival of a vessel. Due bill privileges are defined in the applicable tariff and may be extended either at the discretion of the carrier or by the filing of a surety bond, usually in the amount of $25,000 or more.

DUMP BOTTOMS   Truck or railcar bodies with bottom doors to permit the dumping of bulk products through the bottom.

DUMPING   Sending goods for sale at low prices abroad with the intent to maintain home prices and capture foreign markets. Attempting to import merchandise into a country at a price less than the fair market value, usually through subsidy by exporting country.

DUNGAREES   Blue working overalls.

DUNNAGE   Any material, such as blocks, boards, paper, burlap, etc., necessary for the protection of cargo; also used in reference to staging used by workmen during building and repair operations.

DUPLICATING PIPE   A piece of tubing, generally brass, used with paint to transfer rivet hole layout from template to plate. The end of the pipe is dipped in paint, and while still wet is pushed through each template hole, leaving an impression on the plate. Also called a marker.

DUSTPAN DREDGE   The dustpan dredge is so named because the suction looks like a large vacuum cleaner or dustpan. The dustpan is outfitted with high velocity water jets for agitating and mixing the material. The dustpan is not suited for hard compacted materials, but works well in soft, free flowing materials.

DUTCH COURAGE   False courage due to liquor.

DUTCHMAN   A piece of wood or steel fitted into an opening to cover up poor joints or crevices caused by poor workmanship.

DUTY   A tax levied by a government on the import, export, or use and consumption of goods. A Customs Ad Valorem fee levied against the importer. Duty is based upon the value of any import property that is dutiable, irrespective of quality, weight, or other considerations. Ad Valorem rates are expressed in percentages of the value of the goods, which is usually ascertained from the invoice.

DUTY DRAWBACK   A refund of duty paid on imported merchandise when it is exported later, whether in the same or a different form.

DUTY-FREE ZONE (DFZ)   An area where goods or cargo can be stored without paying import Customs duties while awaiting manufacturing or future transport.

DUTY OF ASSURED CLAUSE (INS)   This appears in the Institute Cargo Clauses published for use with the MAR form of policy. It directs the attention of the Assured, his agents, etc., to the duty (as required by the MIA, 1906) to take reasonable measures to avert or minimize any loss, which is recoverable under the policy; also to ensure that all rights against carriers and others are properly preserved and exercised. Underwriters agree to reimburse the Assured for any reasonable expenditure incurred by his compliance with the clause; in practice, these expenses are termed "sue and labor" charges. *See* Sue & Labor Clause.

DUTY RATES Tax imposed by U.S. Customs on imported merchandise. There are three basic types: ad valorem—based on the entered value, specific—an amount per unit of quantity, and compound—combination of ad valorem and specific rates.

DW Deadweight (ton 2,240 pounds).

DWAT OR DWT Deadweight. Weight of cargo, stores, and water, i.e., the difference between lightship and loaded displacement.

DWC Deadweight for Cargo.

DYNAMIC Referring to movement.

DYNAMIC POSITIONING Highly sophisticated drilling ships today are generally fitted with fully automated dynamic positioning systems. A computer-controlled system enables vessel to operate independently of anchors or any other mechanical mooring system. System can control bow thrusters, stern thrusters, and main propulsion propellers.

DYNAMICAL STABILITY The energy that a vessel possesses to right herself due to the work performed in inclining her.

E

EAON Except As Otherwise Noted.

EARNED PREMIUM (INS) The portion of a premium for which the policy protection has already been given during the now-expired portion of the policy term.

EASEMENT A right enjoyed by the owner of land over the lands of another. An easement must exist for the accommodation and better enjoyment of the land to which it is annexed.

EASTERLY WINDS True wind direction from the northeast to southeast sector; used when the forecaster is uncertain about the exact wind direction, but is confident that it will come somewhere between NE and SE.

EASY Carefully.

EB Eastbound.

EBB Receding current.

EBL *See* Electronic Bearing Line.

EC East Coast or European Community.

ECCENTRIC A form of crank in which a circular disk set upon a shaft forms both the crank web and the crank pin and converts circular to rectilinear motion. This rectilinear travel is usually short relative to the diameter of the shaft so that an ordinary form of crank is impractical.

ECDIS *See* Electronic Chart Display and Information System.

ECHO A reflection of a radar wave.

ECHO SOUNDER *See* Depth Sounder.

ECLIPSE A phase of the characteristic of a lighted aid to navigation during which the light is not exhibited.

ECMCA Eastern Central Motor Carriers Association.

ECONOMIC IMPACT This is a measure of economic activity performed by or closely related to a specified region.

ECONOMIC IMPACT STUDIES Studies done by ports that describe the positive benefits on port business on the regional economy through the generation of employment, income, and business on the regional economy through the generation of employment, income, and demand for additional goods and services produced in the region.

ECONOMIC ORDER QUALITY (EOC) An inventory model that determines how much to order by determining the amount that will minimize total ordering and holding costs.

ECONOMY OF SCALE The lowering of costs with added output due to allocation of fixed costs over more units.

ECR *See* Efficient Consumer Response.

ECS *See* Electronic Chart Systems.

ECSI *See* Export Cargo Shipping Instructions/Preadvice.

EDD *See* Estimated Delivery Date.

EDDY Indicated turbulence of the water, for example, below the bridge pier where a swift current is passing through, or below a bar or point.

EDDY ABOVE AND BELOW Means that you can expect eddies, i.e., tricky water, both above and below the object mentioned in the marks such as dikes, top and bottom of crossings, sunken obstructions.

EDDY EXTENDS WELL OUT Means that an eddy extends from the shore or the dike into or across the range formed by this set of marks, or where extends one third or more across the river.

EDGE An abrupt border or margin, a bounding or dividing line, the part along the boundary.

EDGE, SIGHT That edge of a strake of plating that laps outside another strake and is, therefore, in plain sight.

EDGE PROTECTOR An angle piece fitted over the edge of boxes, crates, bundles and other packages to prevent the pressure from metal bands or other types from cutting into the package.

EDI Electronic Data Interface. Generic term for transmission of transactional data between computer systems. EDI is typically via a batched transmission, usually conforming to consistent standards.

EDIFACT International data interchange standards sponsored by the United Nations. *See* UN/EDIFACT.

EDI INTERCHANGE Communication between partners in the form of a structured set of messages and service segments starting with an interchange control header and ending with an interchange control trailer.

EDP *See* Electronic Data Processing.

EDR *See* Equipment Damage Report.

EDUCTOR Another name for an ejector or jet pump.

EE Errors Excepted.

EFFECTIVE DATE (INS) The date on which an insurance policy or bond goes into effect, and from which protection is furnished.

EFFECTIVE HOPPER CAPACITY The volume of dredged material that can be placed and retained in the hoppers of a hopper dredge.

EFFECTIVE POWER GAIN The signal leaving a transmitting antenna that is powerful enough to induce a current in a receiving antenna. It is expressed as the ratio of power required to produce a certain signal strength at a receiving comparison antenna to the power needed to have as strong a signal with another specific antenna.

EFFECTIVE WORKING CAPACITY Refers to the average annual practical cargo handling capability estimated for a major cargo movement category in a specific coastal region and expressed in long tons on a per berth per year basis (in this study).

EFFICIENT CONSUMER RESPONSE (ECR) A customer-driven system where distributors and suppliers work together as business allies to maximize consumer satisfaction and minimize cost.

EFT Electronic Fund Transfer. Movement of money between two entities by electronic means.

EFTA European Free Trade Association. Comprises Iceland, Norway, and Switzerland.

E-FULFILLMENT Coordinated inbound and outbound logistics functions that facilitate the management and delivery of customer orders placed online.

EGC *See* Enhanced Group Call.

EHA *See* Equipment Handover Agreement.

EHF *See* Extremely High Frequency.

EIN *See* Export Identification Number.

EIR *See* Equipment Interchange Receipt.

EIU Even If Used.

EJECTOR A type of pumping device used for discharging or expelling a liquid or gas from a space or tank. A jet of water, steam, or air is forced under pressure from a nozzle and creates a partial vacuum or low-pressure area, which acts on the suction pipe from the space to draw from it. No moving parts exist in this device.

ELASTIC LIMIT The amount of stress that can be applied to a material whereupon within this limit the material will return to its original length.

ELBOW ELL A pipe fitting that makes an angle between adjacent pipes, always 90 degrees unless another angle is stated.

ELBOWS Curved pieces of pipe, a different diameter, and with different angles of curvature; also fitted with a flange at each end.

ELECTRIC CURRENT The rate of flow of electrons through a conductor.

ELECTRIC STYLUS A pen used in conjunction with an electronically driven clock mechanism in newer course recorders.

ELECTRICAL DERANGEMENT (INS) Mechanical and/or electrical derangement is an insurance industry term to describe malfunction, or nonfunction, of an appliance for reasons other than obvious external damage. From time to time, an electronic or mechanically operated item will prove to be inoperable upon arriving at its destination. *See* Mechanical Derangement Exclusion.

ELECTRICITY A physical phenomenon, it is the existence of moving electrons by means of a conducting element such as air, water, or solid material.

ELECTRODE Either a positive or negative pole or terminal in an electric circuit.

ELECTROMAGNETIC RADIATION Radio signals or the radiated radio signal energy that travels in open space.

ELECTROMAGNETIC SPECTRUM (EMS) The classification structure of all radio frequencies based on frequency value.

ELECTROMAGNETIC SPEED LOG A system that uses a flow probe or rod meter that extends out beyond the ship's hull. The probe contains a coil through which an electric current passes, producing a magnetic field around the probe. As water moves past the probe, the magnetic field becomes altered, producing a variation in the signal voltage. The measurement of this variation can be used to indicate the vessel's speed through the water.

ELECTROMECHANICAL Both electronic and mechanical.

ELECTRONIC BEARING LINE (EBL) A line showing on the radar screen that allows an approximate bearing of an object to be taken.

ELECTRONIC CHART DISPLAY AND INFORMATION SYSTEM (ECDIS) Data equivalent to the latest edition of material originated by a government authorized hydrographic office and in conformance with International Hydrographic Organization standards. ECDIS data should be capable of accepting official updates to correct changes in the chart's database.

ELECTRONIC CHART SYSTEMS (ECS) A system that comprises all types of electronic charts that do not comply with the International Maritime Organization and International Hydrographic Organization ECDIS specifications. These systems are not yet regarded by IMO as acceptable equivalents to paper charts.

ELECTRONIC COMMERCE Economic activity that can be conducted via electronic connections such as EDI and the Internet.

ELECTRONIC DATA INTERCHANGE (EDI) A process that allows any computer to communicate with another computer, in order to pass information that would otherwise be exchanged in writing or verbally. This type of "electronic commerce" has been under intensive development in the transportation industry driven by both business and government to achieve a competitive advantage in international markets. The technology of EDI is the result of the marriage of the communication and computer industries.

ELECTRONIC DATA PROCESSING (EDP) The computerized handling of information (e.g., business data).

ELECTRONIC FUNDS TRANSFER (EFT) Movement of money between two entities by electronic means.

ELECTRONIC INTERFERENCE A situation in which your own ship's radar is operating near another ship with the same, or nearly the same, carrier frequency. The display will show segmented spirals emitting from the sweep center. These are temporary and there is little the operator can do about them.

ELECTRONIC NAVIGATIONAL CHART (ENC) A database with a specified electronic format that meets International Maritime Organization and International Hydrographic Organization ECDIS specifications and must be provided by official government sources.

ELECTRONICS Motion of electrons in which the conduction is controlled within the component, such as a vacuum tube or a semiconductor.

ELECTROSTRICTIVE A type of transducer used in depth sounders to convert electrical signals to sound vibrations by passing a current through two plates that sandwich a nonconductive material. The electrically induced magnetic field causes the plates to vibrate, creating the sound vibrations.

ELEVATING   A charge for services performed in connection with floating elevators. Also, charges assessed for handling of grain through grain elevators.

ELEVATOR   Equipment used to discharge some bulk cargoes such as grain, which is removed from the hold by a continuous line of buckets or by suction and carried on a conveyor belt to store.

ELIMINATION PERIOD (INS)   A loosely used term sometimes designating the waiting period and sometimes the probationary period.

ELKINS ACT   An act of Congress (1903) prohibiting rebates, concession, misbilling, etc., and providing specific penalties for such violations.

ELVENT   Electric Ventilation.

EMBANKMENT   A man-made levee or fill located on a bank of a river.

EMBARGO   An order restricting the acceptance or hauling of shipments.

EMBARK   To go onboard.

EMBAYMENT   An area built by the U.S. Corps of Engineers for flood control, generally covering a large area, that can be flooded during high water or to ease pressure on a levee.

EMC   *See* Export Management Consultant.

EMERGENCY GENERATOR   An alternate source of power on larger vessels used in case of a loss of power from the main engineering system.

EMERGENCY RATE   A rate established to meet an immediate and pressing need without regard to normal rate factors.

EMERGENCY SHUTDOWN DEVICE   A device installed near a tanker's manifolds that can stop the flow of liquid onto the ship from shore.

EMINENT DOMAIN   The right of government to take private property for a necessary public use, with reasonable compensation.

EMPLOYER'S LIABILITY (INS)   Coverage against common law liability of an employer for accidents to employees, as distinguished from liability imposed by workers compensation law.

EMPLOYER'S NONOWNERSHIP AUTO LIABILITY (INS)   Liability arising out of the operation of an automobile not owned by the insured. This frequently results when an employee uses his own personal car in the business activities of the insured; insurance coverage for the liability exposure mentioned above.

EMPLOYMENT   This is measured in year round jobs, both full and part time. No distinction is made between these two categories. All jobs generated at businesses in the region are included as regional employment, even though the associated wages of commuters may be expended by households in other regions.

EMPTY REPO   Contraction for empty repositioning. The movement of empty containers.

EMS   *See* Electromagnetic Spectrum.

EMULSIBILITY   The ability of an oil to mix readily with water. Oils of good emulsibility make emulsions readily with water.

EMULSIFYING AGENTS Surface-active substances that help to promote an emulsion and to keep it stable after formation.

EMULSION Intimate mixture of two immiscible liquids, one of them being dispersed in the other in the form of fine droplets.

ENC *See* Electronic Navigational Chart.

ENCROACHMENT A trespass or intrusion on the rights or property of another.

END FOR END Reversing the position of an object.

END ON Head on.

ENDORSE Sign one's name on back of document (checks, B/L).

ENDORSED IN BLANK Not endorsed.

ENDORSEMENT A legal signature usually placed on the reverse of a draft; signifies transfer of rights from the holder to another party.

ENDORSEMENT (INS) A form attached to the policy bearing the language necessary to change the terms of the policy to fit special circumstances.

END POINT (FINAL BOILING POINT) The highest temperature indicated on the thermometer inserted in the flask during a standard laboratory distillation test. This is generally the temperature at which no more vapor can be driven over into the condensing apparatus.

END USER The final buyer of the product who purchases the product for immediate use.

ENGINE CASING Plating surrounding deck opening to engine room.

ENGINE ORDER TELEGRAPH, ANNUNCIATOR An electrically or mechanically controlled signal or indicator for transmitting and receiving orders between two stations in a ship.

ENGINE ROOM Common term for the vessel's machinery space, or the location of the main propulsion system and auxiliary systems such as power generators and air compressors. Space where the main engines of a ship are located.

ENGLISH JURISDICTION CLAUSE (INS) A condition, printed in the MAR form of policy, whereby Underwriters agree to recognize judgments only from courts convened within English jurisdiction. Subscribing Underwriters may agree to replace this clause with a foreign jurisdiction clause. Please note this is not applicable to business emanating from the United States, which is subject to the Service of Suit Clause (USA) appearing in the standard conditions.

ENGLISH LAW & PRACTICE (INS) This clause appears in institute clauses published for use with the MAR form or policy. It applies where a foreign jurisdiction clause attaches to the policy and requires that the foreign court shall base its decisions on English law and practice.

ENHANCED GROUP CALL (EGC) Used by a GMDSS coordination center to contact vessels, it allows broadcast messages to be made to selected groups of stations located anywhere within a satellite's coverage area. Information regarding vessels in need of assistance can be put out to vessels in a specified geographical area that may be able to render aid.

ENHANCEMENT   In environmental management, providing additional environmental resources as part of a public works project beyond those that would compensate for unavoidable environmental losses.

ENQUIRY/INQUIRY   Document issued by a party interested in the purchase of goods specified therein and indicating particular, desirable conditions regarding delivery terms, etc., addressed to a prospective supplier with a view to obtaining an offer.

ENROUTE   On the way.

ENSIGN   The National Flag; a junior officer in the Navy.

ENTERPRISE RESOURCE PLANNING (ERP)   A cross-functional/regional planning process supporting regional forecasting, distribution planning, operations centers planning, and other planning activities. ERP provides the means to plan, analyze, and monitor the flow of demand/supply alignment and to allocate critical resources to support the business plan.

ENTRANCE   The portion of a vessel that lies forward of the middle body and under the load waterline.

ENTREPOT   An intermediary storage facility where goods are kept temporarily for distribution within a country or for re-export.

ENTRY (CUSTOMS)   A statement of the kinds, quantities, and values of goods imported together with duties, if any, declared before a Customs official.

ENTRY FORM   The document that must be filed with Customs to obtain the release of imported goods and to allow collection of duties and statistics. Also called a Customs Entry Form or Entry. Generic term for any form for which input is needed.

ENTRY PAPERS   Those documents that must be filed with the Customs official describing goods imported, such as consumption entry, Ocean Bill of Lading or Carrier Release, and U.S. Consular Invoice.

ENTRY SUMMARY SELECTIVITY SYSTEM   The Entry Summary Selectivity System, a part of Customs' Automated Commercial System, provides an automated review of entry data to determine whether team or routine review is required. Selectivity criteria include an assessment of risk by importer, tariff number, country of origin, manufacturer, and value. Summaries with census warnings, as well as quota, antidumping and countervailing duty entry summaries are selected for team review. A random sample of routine review summaries is also automatically selected for team review.

ENTRY SUMMARY SYSTEM   An entry is the minimum amount of documentation needed to secure the release of imported merchandise. The Entry Summary System, a part of Customs' Automated Commercial System, contains data on release, summary, rejection, collection, liquidation, and extension or suspension.

ENTRY VALUE   U.S. Customs Service defines entry value (or entered value) as the value reflected on the entry documentation submitted by the importer.

EOC   *See* Economic Order Quality.

E&OE   Errors and Omissions Excepted.

EPIDEMIOLOGY   The study of epidemics, such as contagious diseases, that spread rapidly.

EP LUBRICANT   Extreme Pressure Lubricant.

EQUALIZATION   A monetary allowance to the customer for picking up or delivering at a point other than the destination shown on the bill of lading. This provision is covered by tariff publication.

EQUILIBRIUM   Vessel is in a state where there is no movement; G must be in the same vertical line with B.

EQUILIBRIUM, NEUTRAL   The state of equilibrium in which a vessel inclined from its original position of rest by an external force tends to maintain the inclined position assumed after that force has ceased to act.

EQUILIBRIUM, STABLE   The state of equilibrium in which a vessel inclined from its original position of rest by an external force tends to return to the original noninclined position after that force has ceased to act.

EQUILIBRIUM, UNSTABLE   The state of equilibrium in which a vessel inclined from its original position of rest by an external force tends to depart farther from the inclined position assumed after that force has ceased to act.

EQUIPMENT   The rolling stock of a railroad or motor carrier; the ships of a steamship line and the planes of an airline.

EQUIPMENT BOND   A bond secured by carriers' equipment.

EQUIPMENT DAMAGE REPORT (EDR)   Written statement concerning damage to equipment, based on a physical inspection.

EQUIPMENT HANDOVER AGREEMENT (EHA)   *See* Interchange Agreement.

EQUIPMENT ID   An identifier assigned by the carrier to a piece of equipment. *See also* Container Number.

EQUIPMENT INTERCHANGE REPORT (EIR)   A document executed by a truck carrier and a terminal transferring possession of a container or chassis from one to the other and showing equipment condition at time of transfer.

EQUIPMENT MONITORING AND ALARMS   Audible and visual alarms, generated by a radio navigation system processor following a self-test and detection of a failure, that alert the operator that the unit is not functioning properly.

EQUIPMENT POSITIONING   The process of placing equipment at a selected location.

ERECT   To hoist into place and bolt up on the ways fabricated and assembled parts of a ship's hull, preparatory to riveting or welding.

ERP   Effective Radiated Power. A measure of a radio transmitter's power. *See also* Enterprise Resource Planning and Extended Reporting Period (INS).

ESCAPE HOLE OR ESCAPE HATCH   Small manhole in the deck.

ESCAPE TRUNK   A vertical trunk or shaft fitted with a ladder to permit personnel to escape if trapped. Usually provided from the after end of the shaft tunnel to topside spaces.

EST Estimated.

ESTABLISHED To place an authorized aid to navigation in operation for the first time placed in position.

ESTER A compound formed by the action of an alcohol and an acid.

ESTIMATED DELIVERY DATE (EDD) The date and time a package or shipment is expected to be delivered to a given destination.

ESTUARIES A semi-isolated portion of the ocean that is diluted by freshwater drainage from land.

EST WT Estimated weight.

ETA Estimated Time of Arrival. Also, Estimated Time of Availability. That time when a tractor/partner carrier is available for dispatch.

ET AL And other.

ETC Estimated Time of Completion. *See also* Export Trading Company.

ETD Estimated Time of Departure.

ETHERNET A specialized local area network that allows each piece of integrated equipment to exchange specific information.

ETHYLENE A gas produced by many fruits and vegetables that accelerates the ripening and aging processes.

ETIOLOGIC AGENT An etiologic agent means a viable microorganism, or its toxin, that causes or may cause human disease.

ETS Estimated Time of Sailing.

EU European Union.

EUROPEAN FREE TRADE ASSOCIATION (EFTA) Free trading area comprising Iceland, Norway, and Switzerland.

EUROPEAN PALLET POOL Pool for the exchange of standard size pallets (the so-called Euro pallets) in European cargo traffic, formed in 1961 by a number of European rail administrators.

EUROPEAN ZONE CHARGE (EZC) A charge for inland haulage transport in case of carrier haulage in Europe.

EUSC Effective U.S. Control.

EVAPORATION LOSS The loss of petroleum products particularly gasoline through the evaporation of the most volatile fractions.

EVAPORATION RATE The time it takes a given amount of material to completely dry up, compared with an equal amount of a reference material.

EVAPORATOR An auxiliary for supplying fresh water, consisting of a saltwater chamber heated by coils or nests of tubing through which live steam is circulated, converting the water into steam, which is passed to a condenser or distiller to make up loss of boiler feed water or for other purposed requiring freshwater.

EVEN KEEL A ship is said to be on an even keel when the keel is level or parallel to the surface of the water and the hull is not listed or tipped sideways.

EVERGREEN LETTER OF CREDIT Letter of credit with an initial expiration date but containing a clause that states that it will be automatically extended for additional periods unless the issuing bank provides notice to the beneficiary stating otherwise.

EVIDENCE OF INSURABILITY (INS)   Any statement of a person's physical condition, occupation, etc., affecting his acceptance for insurance.

EWIB   Eastern Weighing and Inspection Bureau.

EX   From.

EX (POINT OF ORIGIN)   From the point where the shipment begins movement, e.g., Ex Factory, Ex Mine, or Ex Warehouse. *See* Terms of Sale.

EXAQUATUR   Government's authorization of another country's consul.

EXCEPTION   Notations made when the cargo is received at the carrier's terminal or loaded aboard a vessel. They show any irregularities in packaging or actual or suspected damage to the cargo. Exceptions are then noted on the bill of lading.

EXCEPTION CLAUSE   Contract wordings detailing how variations from a specified parameter will be handled.

EXCEPTION RATE   A deviation from the class rate; changes (exceptions) made to the classification.

EXCESS   An English insurance term. A deductible, or franchise, after which losses will be paid. Going over the prescribed amount or degree, e.g.. excess baggage is luggage when weight is over the weight for free carriage.

EXCHANGE RATE   The rate at which one currency can be exchanged for another, usually expressed as the value of the one in terms of the other.

EXCLUSIONS (INS)   Specified hazards for which a policy will not provide benefit payments (often called Exceptions).

EXCLUSION ZONE   An option that offers the ARPA operator a means to limit the automatic acquire function in areas where no unwanted plotting is desired.

EXCLUSIVE ECONOMIC ZONE (EEZ)   Area extending out 200 miles from the coast of a country. Granting exclusive mineral and fishing rights.

EXCLUSIVE PATRONAGE AGREEMENT   A shipper agrees to use only a conference's member liner firms in return for a 10 to 15 percent rate reduction.

EXCLUSIVE USE   Vehicles that a carrier assigns to a specific shipper for its exclusive use.

EX-DEC   *See* Shippers' Export Declaration.

EX DOCK (IMPORT USAGE ONLY)   The seller is obligated to place the specified goods at the specified price on the import dock clear of all customs and duty requirements. The buyer must do nothing further than pick up the goods within a prescribed time limit.

EXEMPT CARRIER   A for-hire carrier that is exempt from economic regulations.

EXEMPTION CLAUSE   A clause in a contract, which relieves the carrier's responsibility for certain events. *See* Exceptions Clause.

EX FACTORY   Seller owns goods until they are picked up at his factory; selling price is the cost of the goods.

EX-FACTORY *See* Ex Works and Incoterms.

EX "FROM" When used inpricing terms such as "Ex Factory" or "Ex Dock," it signifies that the price quoted applies only at the point of origin indicated.

EX GRATIA As a matter of favor.

EXIM BANK Export-Import Bank of the United States. An independent U.S. government agency that facilitates exports of U.S. goods by providing loan guarantees and insurance for repayment of bank-provided export credit.

EXISTENT GUM Under specified test conditions, the amount of nonvolatile residue (expressed as milligrams per 100 milliliters of sample) present in gasoline as received for the test.

EX MILL (EX WAREHOUSE, EX MINE, EX FACTORY) The seller is obligated to place the specified quantity of goods at the specified price at his mill loaded on trucks, railroad cars, or any other specified means of transport. The buyer must accept the goods in this manner and make all arrangements for transportation.

EX OFFICIO By virtue of one position or office in the incumbent automatically fills another.

EXPANSION JOINT A term applied to a joint that permits linear movement to take up the expansion and contraction due to changing temperature or ship movement.

EXPANSION TANK A tank extending above a space, which is used for the stowage of liquid cargo. The surface of the cargo liquid is kept sufficiently high in the tank to permit expansion without risk of excessive strain on the hull or of overflowing, and to allow contraction of the liquid without increase of free surface.

EXPANSION TRUNK Upper portion of tank on an oil tanker, used to allow for the expansion of oil when temperature rises.

EXPANSION VALVE An auxiliary valve fitted on some reciprocating steam engines to provide an independent control of the point of cut off. A valve in refrigeration and air-conditioning systems used to regulate the amount of refrigerant flowing around the circuit. When the liquid from the condenser is reduced in pressure by the valve, some liquid vaporizes cooling the rest down. This mixture, mainly liquid, then passes to the evaporator as the cooling medium. The amount of refrigerant passing through the valve is automatically controlled by the conditions at the evaporator.

EX PARTE On the one side; where only one side is heard.

EXPATRIATE WORKERS Employees who are sent to work in other countries for extended periods of time.

EXPEDITED SHIPMENT A shipment that a carrier moves more quickly than usual.

EXPEDITING Determining where an in-transit shipment is and attempting to speed up its delivery.

EXPENDABLE PALLET *See* Disposable Pallet.

EXPENSES   Costs paid out in connection with booking of cargo and arranging transport (e.g., commission).

EXPERIENCE (INS)   The loss record of an insured, class of coverage, or of an insurance company.

EXPERIENCE RATING (INS)   Determination of the premium rate for an individual risk, made partially or wholly on the basis of that risk's own past claim experience.

EXPIRATION   Termination of a certain period.

EXPIRY DATE   Issued in connection with documents such as letters of credit, tariffs, etc., to advise that states provisions will expire at a certain time.

EXPLOSION PROOF   Unable to sustain instantaneous combustion. Electrical equipment or apparatus is defined and certified as explosion proof or flameproof when enclosed in a case that is capable of withstanding an explosion of a flammable hydrocarbon vapor/air mixture or other specified flammable vapor, which may occur within it and of preventing the ignition of hydrocarbon or other specified vapor surrounding the enclosure by sparks, flashes, or explosions of the vapor within.

EXPLOSIVE LIMITS (EXPLOSIVE RANGE)   The limits of percentage composition of mixtures of gases and air within which an explosion takes place when the mixture is ignited.

EXPLOSIVES   Any chemical compound, mixture, or device the primary or common purpose of which is to function by explosion, i.e., with substantially instantaneous release of gas or heat, unless such compound, mixture, or device is otherwise specifically classified.

CLASS A: Detonating or otherwise of maximum hazard. There are nine types of Class A explosives.

CLASS B: Generally function by rapid combustion rather than detonation and include some explosive devices, such as special fireworks, flash powder, etc. Flammable hazard.

CLASS C: Certain types of manufactured articles containing Class A or Class B explosives, or both, as components but in restricted quantities, and certain types of fireworks. Minimum hazard.

EXPORT   Shipment of goods to a foreign country.

EXPORT BROKER   One who brings together the buyer and seller for a fee and then withdraws from the transaction.

EXPORT CARGO SHIPPING INSTRUCTIONS - PREADVICE   Instructions from shipper with details of all parties involved and description of goods.

EXPORT COMMISSION HOUSE   An organization that for a commission acts as a purchase agent for a foreign buyer.

EXPORT CONTROL CLASSIFICATION NUMBER   Every product has an export control classification number (formerly: Export Control Commodity Number) within the Commerce Control List. Each ECCN consists of five characters that identify the category, product group, type of control, and country group level of control.

EXPORT DECLARATION A formal statement made to the collector of customs at a port of exit declaring full particulars about goods being shipped out of the country.

EXPORTER The party responsible for the export of goods.

EXPORT IDENTIFICATION NUMBER (EIN) Number required for the exporter on the Shipper's Export Declaration. A corporation may use their Federal Employer Identification Number as issued by the IRS; individuals can use their Social Security Numbers.

EXPORT LICENSE A government document that permits the "licensee" to engage in the export of designated goods to certain destinations. List of such goods are found in the comprehensive Export Schedule issued by the Bureau of Foreign Commerce.

EXPORT MANAGEMENT CONSULTANT Individual or company that assists other companies in identifying potential foreign markets for their goods, often named as a sales agent or representative of the company being served and paid a commission for each sale.

EXPORT MERCHANT A producer or merchant who sells directly to a foreign purchaser without going through an intermediate such as an export broker.

EXPORT PACKERS Companies that prepare the protective packing for shipments transported overseas.

EXPORT RATE A freight rate specially established for application on export traffic and generally lower than the domestic rate.

EXPORT REQUEST FORM Document showing shipping instructions advising details of cargo, routing, and payment terms.

EXPORT SALES CONTRACT The initial document in any international transaction; it details the specifics of the sales agreement between the buyer and seller.

EXPORT TRADING COMPANY Company that buys and sells goods with the objective of taking advantage of market opportunities around the world.

EX POST FACTO After the fact.

EXPOSURE (INS) State of being subject to the possibility of loss; extent of risk as measured by payroll, gate receipts, area, or otherwise; possibility of loss to a risk being caused by its surroundings.

EXPUNGE To delete or obliterate a resolution or comment from the minutes.

EXQ Ex Quay. The seller makes the goods available to the buyer on the quay (wharf) at the destination named in the sales contract. The seller has to bear the full cost and risk involved in bringing the goods there. There are two "Ex Quay" contracts in use: (a) Ex Quay "duty paid" and (b) Ex Quay "duties on buyer's account" in which the liability to clear goods for import is to be met by the buyer instead of by the seller.

EXS   Ex Ship. The seller makes the goods available to the buyer onboard the ship at the destination named in the sales contract. The seller has to bear full cost and risk involved in bringing the goods to this destination. Price includes all charges to the port of destination but the buyer must pay the cost of taking the goods from the ship.

EXTENDED PRODUCER RESPONSIBILITY   A program that shifts responsibility for the end-of-life products to the manufacturer.

EXTENDED REPORTING PERIOD (ERP) (INS)   A period allowed for making claims after expiration of a "claims made" liability policy. Also known as a "tail."

EXTINGUISHED   A lighted aid to navigation that fails to show a light characteristic.

EXTRACTION PUMP   This pump draws the condensate directly from the condenser of a steam plant and pumps it to the deaerator, usually against the considerable static head of the deaerator.

EXTREME BREADTH   The linear distance from the most outboard point on either side of a vessel's hull to the other side.

EXTREME PRESSURE LUBRICANT   Lubricating oil or grease that contains a substance or substances specifically introduced to prevent metal-to-metal contact in the operation of highly loaded gears.

EXTREMELY HIGH FREQUENCY (EHF)   The range within the electromagnetic spectrum (beginning at 3 gHz) that includes the heat and infrared ranges, invisible light, ultraviolet light, X-rays, gamma rays, and cosmic rays.

EXW, EX-WORKS   The seller fulfills his obligation to deliver when he has made the goods available at his premises (i.e., works, factory, warehouse, etc.) to the buyer. In particular, he is not responsible for loading the goods on the vehicle provided by the buyer or clearing the goods for export, unless otherwise agreed. The buyer bears all costs and risks involved in taking the goods from the seller's premises to the desired destination. This term thus represents the minimum obligation for the seller. This term should not be used when the buyer cannot carry out directly or indirectly the export formalities. In such circumstances, the FCA term should be used.

EYE   A hole through the head of a needle, pin, bolt, etc., or a loop forming a hole or opening through which something is intended to pass, such as a hook, pin, shaft, or rope. A "worked eye" is one having its edges rounded off like a ring, while a "shackle eye" is drilled straight through, permitting an inserted bolt or pin to bear along its entire length.

EYE BOLT   A bolt having either a head looped to form a worked eye or a solid head with a hole drilled through it forming a shackle eye.

EYE BROW   The metal lip over a port to carry the water to the side of the port.

EYES   The forward end of the space below the upper deck of a ship that lies next abaft the stem where the sides of the ship approach very near to each other. The hawse pipes are usually run down through the eyes of a ship.

EZC   *See* European Zone Charge.

F

F/A Free Astray.

FAA *See* Federal Aviation Administration.

FABRICATE To process hull material in the shops prior to assembly or erection. In hull work fabrication consists in shearing, shaping, punching, drilling, countersinking, scarfing, rabbeting, beveling, etc.

FABRICATION Distinguish manufacturing operations for components as opposed to assembly operations.

FAC Fast As Can.

FACE LINE A line used from head of your boat to the tow.

FACE PLATE A flat plate fitted perpendicular to the web and welded to the web plate, or welded or riveted to the flange or flanges of a frame, beam stiffener, or girder to balance the continuous plating attached to the opposite flange of the member.

FACE UP To make up the towboat to the tow (i.e., maneuvering barges into position and securing for towing behind the tow).

FACE VALUE Nominal value on coin, paper currency, or other negotiable instrument; may be lower or higher than the market value.

FACE WIRES Heavy cables securing boat to tow (pusher to barge).

FACTOR A factor is an agent who will, at a discount (usually five to eight percent of the gross), buy receivables.

FACTOR OF SAFETY The ratio between either the ultimate strength or the elastic limit of the material and the allowed working stress. The former is usually referred to as the "nominal factor of safety" and the latter as the "real factor of safety." Elastic materials may have both nominal and real factors of safety, while for those materials having approximately the same values for ultimate strength and elastic limit; the distinction between real and nominal factors of safety is nonexistent.

FACTOR OF SUBDIVISION A number less than one obtained from curves of factor of subdivision that, when multiplied by floodable length, produces permissible length of compartment. It is the reciprocal of the compartment standard.

FACTORING Service of assuming the credit risk of another party's sales, generally including collecting payment when due. Factors often provide or arrange limited-recourse financing against the accounts receivable they are guaranteeing, referred to as "purchasing receivables."

FACTORY DELIVERY The delivery of goods by a factory whereby the goods are put at the disposal of another (internal) party such as a commercial department.

FACTORY TRAWLER A vessel that harvests fish by dragging a trawl net through the water and that processes the fish at sea into a saleable product.

FADING The variation in the strength of signals received by a transmitter.

FAG The end of a rope eyed or untwisted; British slang for a cigarette.

FAIR (FAIR UP) To correct or fair up a ship's lines on mold loft floor, to assemble the parts of a ship so that they will be fair, i.e., without kinks, bumps, or waves; to bring the rivet holes in alignment.

FAIR CURRENT When tug and tow are favored by a current running in the direction they are proceeding.

FAIR CURVES Curves, which do not in any portions of their entire lengths, show such changes of direction as to mark those portions as out of harmony in any respect with the curves as a whole or with the other portions of the curves.

FAIRLEAD OR FAIRLEADER A fitting or device used to preserve or to change the direction of a rope, chain, or wire so that it will be delivered fairly or on a straight lead to a sheave or drum without the introduction of extensive friction. Fairleaders, or fairleads, are fixtures as distinguished from temporary block rigs.

FAIRLY CLOSE This means to run as close to the shore, dike, or light as practicable (approximately 150 feet off).

FAIR MARKET VALUE (INS) Value on open market of goods of similar age and condition.

FAIR RETURN A profit level that enables a carrier to realize a rate of return on investment or property value that the regulatory agencies deem acceptable for that level of risk.

FAIR VALUE The value of the carrier's property; the calculation basis has included original cost minus depreciation, replacement cost, and market value.

FAIRWATER A term applied to plating fitted to form a shape similar to a frustum of a cone around the ends of shaft tubes and strut barrels to prevent an abrupt change in the streamlines. Also applied to any casting or plating fitted to the hull of a vessel for the purpose of preserving a smooth flow of water.

FAIRWAY Navigable part of a waterway.

FAIRWAY SPEED Mandatory speed in a fairway.

FAK Freight All Kinds. Usually refers to full container loads of mixed shipments.

FAKE To lay a rope down in long bights side by side in order that it will run out clear or can be easily and rapidly paid out. Chain can also be faked. Also, one complete circle of a coil of rope.

FAKE DOWN To coil down a rope so that each fake of rope overlaps the next one underneath, and hence the rope is clear for running.

FALL (1) The entire length of rope used in a tackle. (a) The end secured to the block is called the standing part. (b) The opposite end, the hauling part. (2) The cargo fall is the cargo hoisting wire or rope used through blocks on booms for working cargo. (a) The Burton Fall, also called outboard fall, is the cargo fall suspended over the side of the ship. (b) The hatch fall, also called the up and down fall, or inboard fall is the fall suspended over the hatch.

FALLING RIVER   When gauge readings are decreasing day by day.

FALSE BILLING   Misrepresenting freight or weight on shipping documents.

FALSE ECHO   Interference on radar caused by the ship's superstructure appendages, such as masts, kingposts, or stacks.

FANNING THE WILLOWS   Boat running close to the bank.

FANTAIL   The overhanging stern section of vessels that have round or elliptical after endings to uppermost decks and that extend well abaft the after perpendicular. Plates forming overhang at stern.

FANTAINER   The fantainer is identical to a general purpose container. Located high in the left-hand door is a special hatch. This hatch can be fitted with an electric extraction fan. Fantainer proves valuable for the carriage of many cargoes that are prone to condensation when carried in a general-purpose unit.

FAQ   Frequently Asked Questions. A document about a given topic in a question/answer form.

FARM   Open storage area near the pier entrances.

FAS (FREE ALONGSIDE SHIP)   *See* Free Alongside Ship.

FASCIA   A strip of wood used in covering openings in joiner work.

FASHION TRANSPORT   Transport of clothing and/or garments including shoes, belts, and handbags in dedicated means of transport. Often in a "garment container."

FAST   A rope or chain used to moor a vessel to a wharf, designated in accordance with the end of the boat with which it is used as bow fast or stern fast. *See* Painter.

FAST TIME CONSTANT (FTC)   A switch on a radar that reduces receiver sensitivity and reduces amplified signals transmitted to the CRT to reduce rain clutter.

FAT   A naturally occurring mixture of triglycerides.

FATHOM   A measure of length, equivalent to 6 linear feet, used for depths of water and lengths of rope or chain.

FATHOMETER   *See* Depth Sounder.

FATIGUE STRENGTH   A property relating to the ability of a metal to withstand continuing changes in direction of approximate location of stress.

FATTY OIL   A fat, which is liquid at room temperature.

FAULT   Geologically, a structural closure caused by the fracturing of the crustal rocks during earth movements.

FAX   Facsimile, electronic transmission of a document. Flame-on offensive newsgroup posting or piece of e-mail.

FAYING SURFACE   The surface between two adjoining parts.

FB   Freight Bill.

FBM Foot Board Measure. The normal measurement unit for lumber and logs (1 square foot × 1 inch thick).

FCA (FREE CARRIER) The seller fulfills his obligation to deliver when he has handed over the goods, cleared for export, into the charge of the carrier named by the buyer at the named place or point. If no precise point is indicated by the buyer, the seller may choose within the place or range stipulated where the carrier shall take the goods into his charge. When, according to commercial practice, the seller's assistance is required in making the contract with the carrier (such as in rail or air transport) the seller may act at the buyer's risk and expense. This term may be used for any mode of transport; terminal means a railway terminal, a freight station, a container terminal or yard, a multipurpose cargo terminal or any similar receiving point. "Container" includes any equipment used to unitize cargo, e.g., all types of containers and/or flats whether ISO accepted or not, trailers, swap bodies, including multicarriage, undertakes to perform or to procure the performance of carriage by rail, road, sea, air, inland waterway, or by a combination of such modes. If the buyer instructs the seller to deliver the cargo to a person, e.g., a freight forwarder who is not a "carrier," the seller is deemed to have fulfilled his obligation to deliver the goods when they are in the custody of that person. Transport or equipment, igloos, and applies to all modes of transport.

FCC Federal Communications Commission. Fully Cellular Containership.

FCL Full Container Load.

FCR Forwarder's Cargo Receipt.

FCS Free Capture and Seizure.

FD Free Discharge.

FDA Food and Drug Administration.

FDD Freight Demurrage Dead freight.

FDEDANRSAOCLONL Freight Deemed Earned, Discountless And Non-Returnable (Refundable) Ship And Or Cargo Lost Or Not Lost.

FDESP Free Despatch.

FEDERAL AVIATION ADMINISTRATION The U.S. federal agency that administers federal safety regulations governing air transportation.

FEDERAL COMMUNICATIONS COMMISSION (FCC) The government agency charged with control of all forms of communications within the United States; it classifies radio wave emissions according to their characteristics.

FEDERAL MARITIME COMMISSION U.S. regulatory agency responsible for rates and practices of ocean carriers shipping to and from the United States.

FEDERAL NAVIGABLE WATERWAY Non-U.S. waterbodies developed and maintained in large part by U.S. COE, designed to serve interstate and foreign waterborne commerce and national defense needs.

FEDERAL TAXES This consists of corporate and personal income, social security, and excise taxes estimated from the changes in value added and wages that are generated in the model run.

FED FUNDS RATE Interest rate at which banks in the United States lend each other dollars for next-day repayment ("overnight loans").

FEEDBACK The flow of information back into the control system so that actual performance can be compared with planned performance.

FEEDER A grain container or reservoir constructed around the hatchway between two decks of a ship that when filled with grain automatically feeds or fills in the vacant areas in the lower holds.

FEEDER BARGES Barges that are stacked with containers for short coastal passages, to eventually be loaded aboard larger ships for ocean crossings.

FEEDER PORTS Ports from which locally produced goods, destined to be international cargo, are transshipped to or from a load center.

FEEDER RAILROAD DEVELOPMENT PROGRAM Any financially responsible person (except Class I and Class II carriers) with ICC approval can acquire a rail line having a density of less than 3 million gross ton-miles per year.

FEEDER SERVICE A connecting ship service between ports. Also, loaded or empty containers in a regional area are transferred to a "mother ship" for a long haul ocean voyage.

FEEDER VESSEL A vessel that transfers containers to a "mother ship" for an ocean voyage.

FEED HORN Antenna component at end of wave-guide that radiates energy in a highly directional pattern from the focal point of the directional reflector of a radar antenna.

FEED WATER Water supplied to boiler to compensate for water that vaporized.

FELLOES Pieces of wood that form the rim of a wheel.

FENDER A device or framed system placed against the edge of a dock to take the impact from vessel berthing. Also, a heavy strip of wood or steel attached to the side of the vessel, running fore and aft, above the waterline, for the purpose of preventing rubbing or chafing of the hull.

The term applied to devices built into or hung over the sides to prevent the shell plating from rubbing or chafing against other ships or piers; a permanent hardwood or steel structure that runs fore and aft on the outside above the waterline and is firmly secured to the hull; wood spares, bundles of rope, used automobile tires, woven cane, or covered cork hung over the sides by lines when permanent fenders are not fitted.

FENDER PILE A pile driven close to a structure to prevent contact between vessel and structure.

FEND OFF To push off when making a landing.

FERRY A ship that carries passengers or motor vehicles, or both. Ramps are provided for vehicles. Ferries are usually small coastal vessels, sometime double ended, but in some locations these vessels are quite large, oceangoing ships. Construction arrangement offers little longitudinal separations.

FEU Forty-foot Equivalent Unit. A term used to indicate container vessel or terminal capacity. Two 20 foot containers (TEUs) equals one FEU.

FEW SHOWERS Low probability of precipitation in which a small number of showers will occur.

FFA Free From Average.

FFU *See* Full Follow Up Control System.

FGMDSS Future Global Maritime Distress and Safety System developed by IMO.

FHEX Fridays/Holidays Excluded.

FHINC Fridays/Holidays Included.

FIA Full Interest Admitted.

FID A hardwood tapering pin or tool, used by sail makers and riggers to open the strands of a rope, eye, grommet, etc. A "hand fid" is rounded at the ends; a "standing or cringle fid" is larger than a hand fid and has a flat base. Also a wood or metal bar used to support the weight or a topmost or a top gallant mast when in position, being passed through a hole or mortise at its heel and resting on the trestle trees or other support.

FIDELITY The degree of clarity and completeness with which a receiver can reproduce the original characteristics of a received signal.

FIDELITY BOND (INS) A bond that will reimburse an employer for loss up to, the amount of the bond, sustained by an employer (the insured) by reason of any dishonest act of an employee (or employees) covered by the bond.

FIDLEY Framework built around a weather deck hatch through which the smoke pipe passes. Top of engine room casing around the smokestack.

FIDLEY DECK A partially raised deck over the engine and boiler rooms, usually around the smokestack.

FIDLEY HATCH Hatch around smokestack and uptake for ventilation of boiler room.

FIDUCIARY A person who holds assets in trust for a beneficiary; "it is illegal for a fiduciary to misappropriate money for personal gain." Relating to or of the nature of a legal trust (i.e., the holding of something in trust for another).

FIELD DAY A day for general ship cleaning.

FIELD STRENGTH The strength of a signal measured as the distance between peaks of a wave.

FIFE RAIL; PIN RAIL Rail worked around a mast and fitted with holes to take belaying pins for securing the running gears.

FIFTH WHEEL The semicircular steel-coupling device mounted on a tractor that engages and locks with a chassis semitrailer.

FIGHTING SHIPS A vessel used in a particular trade by an ocean common carrier group of carriers for the purpose of excluding, preventing or reducing competition by driving others out of a trade.

FIGURE HEAD A carved wooden figure carried on old sailing vessels under the bowsprit.

FILED RATE DOCTRINE The legal rate the common carrier may charge; it is the rate published in the carrier's tariff on file with the ICC.

FILIALE Branch office (German).

FILLERS Any substance such as talc, mica, or various powders that may be added to greases to make them heavier in weight or in consistency, but form no useful function in making the grease a better lubricant.

FILLET A term applied to the metal filling in the bosom or concave corners where abrupt changes in direction occur in the surface of a casting, forging, or weldment.

FILLING LOW Low center in which the central pressure is increasing with time; not the same as dissipating low because the low may not necessarily vanish.

FILL RATE Percentage of order items that the picking operation actually found.

FILM STRENGTH The ability of a lubricant to form a film that separates bearing surfaces, without breaking down and causing metal-to-metal contact. The higher the film strength, the greater the load the lubricant can carry.

FILO *See* Free In Liner Out. Sea freight with which the shipper pays load costs and the carrier pays for discharge costs.

FILS French for "Sons" at the end of a business firm's name.

FILTER A component in a power supply that cleans the electrical power that flows through it.

FIN A projecting keel. A thin plane of metal projecting from hull.

FINAL BOILING POINT *See* End Point.

FINAL DESTINATION The last stopping point for a shipment.

FINANCE LEASE An equipment-leasing arrangement that provides the lessee with a means of financing for the leased equipment; a common method for leasing motor carrier trailers.

FINANCIAL RESPONSIBILITY Motor carriers must have bodily injury and property damage (not cargo) insurance of not less than $500,000 per incident per vehicle; higher financial responsibility limits apply for motor carriers transporting oil or hazardous materials.

FINANCING RISK The increasing uncertainty that the buyer of goods will have the capacity to pay when payment is due the longer the time period he is given to make payment.

FINE ON THE BOW Near to fore and aft line of a ship.

FINES The small pieces and particles of a bulk commodity.

FINGER PIER *See* Pier.

FIO *See* Free In and Out.

FIOS Free In Out Stowed freight rates quoted FIOS exclude all aspects related to cargo handling. The ship is responsible only for expenses related to the ship calling the port.

FIOST Free In/Out Stowed and Trimmed. Charterer pays for cost of loading/discharging cargo, including stowage and trimming.

FIOT Free In/Out and Trimmed. As per FIOS but includes trimming, e.g., the leveling of bulk cargoes. FIOS includes sea freight, but excludes loading/discharging and stowage costs.

FIPS   Federal Information Processing Standards.

FIRE CONTROL   A deck plan of a vessel that fully describes the firefighting systems aboard a vessel, strategically placed to be available to shore side firefighters responding to shipboard fire.

FIRE CONTROL PLAN   A set of general arrangement plans showing for each deck the fire control stations, fire resisting and fire retarding bulkheads, together with particulars of the fire detection, manual alarm, and fire extinguishing systems, fire doors, means of access to different compartments, and ventilating systems including locations of dampers and fan controls. It is required to be stored in a prominently marked weather tight enclosure outside the deckhouse for the assistance of shore side firefighting personnel.

FIRE DAMPER   A device installed in ventilation ductwork that inhibits passage of gases. Dampers are automatic or manual.

FIRE MAIN SYSTEM   The ship's primary firefighting equipment includes pumps, piping, valves, and stations (hydrants) with hoses and nozzles.

FIRE POINT   The lowest temperature at which, under specified test conditions, a petroleum product vaporizes sufficiently rapidly to form above its surface an air vapor mixture, which burns continuously when ignited by a small flame.

FIRESCREEN DOORS   Hinged doors that are constructed of such fire retardant material as to resist the spread of fire by convection. Firescreen doors must open temporarily only unless equipped with hold back mechanism, which can be remotely released.

FIRE STATION   A location for the firefighting water supply outlet, hose, and equipment onboard ship.

FIRE WARPS (FIRE WIRES)   A wire rope or other fireproof materials of sufficient strength extended out off the side of a tanker as insurance that the ship could be towed free from a dock during emergency. A line or wire rope run out to a buoy by a vessel handling dangerous goods alongside a wharf so that the vessel can be moved away rapidly in the event of a fire.

FIRKIN   A capacity measurement equal to one fourth of a barrel.

FIRST CARRIER   The carrier who actually performs the first part of the air transport (air cargo).

FIRST IN–FIRST OUT (FIFO)   The method whereby the goods that have been longest in stock (first in) are used, delivered (sold) and/or consumed first (first out).

FIRST NAMED INSURED (INS)   The first named insured appearing on a commercial policy. The latest forms permit the insurer to satisfy contractual duties by giving notice to the "first" named insured rather than requiring notice to all named insureds.

FISHERIES CONSERVATION ZONE   A band of ocean area adjacent to U.S. territory that extends from the seaward limit of the 3-mile territorial sea to a distance 200 miles from the coastline.

FISHING VESSEL A specialty vessel of varying size designed to harvest fish from below the surface. Special reference is made in the Rules of the Road to these vessels. *See* Trawler.

FISH PLATE The extension above the deck line on weather decks designed to trap liquids on deck. Freeing ports and scuppers clear the trapped liquid. The existence of fishplates in modern times is to retain spilled oil on deck to prevent pollution. *See* Flounder Plate.

FISHPORT A homeport for fishing fleets that provides a wide range of services, such as fish processing and handling, and boat repair and provisioning.

FIT Free In Trimmed.

FITTINGS, PIPE A term applied to the connections and outlets, with the exception of valves and couplings that are attached to pipes.

FIW Free in Wagon.

FIXED COSTS Costs that do not vary with the level of activity. Some fixed costs continue even if no cargo is carried. Terminal leases, rent, and property taxes are fixed costs.

FIXED CRANE A crane of which the principal structure is mounted on permanent or semipermanent foundations.

FIXED CROSSED LOOP ANTENNA Used on newer RDF/ADF receivers, an antenna that is placed higher for better reception and that does not require adjustment, as did those placed on top of the receiver.

FIXED DAM A dam that does not permit the passage of marine traffic and requires the use of a lock in contrast to movable dams that during periods of high water are lowered allowing traffic to pass directly over the dam. Also, any dam that has a fixed height without adjustment such as a concrete spillway throughout the length of the dam exclusive of the lock chamber. All excessive water must be spilled over the top.

FIXED ERRORS Those errors in the Decca system that are relatively constant and are caused by the path that the ground waves travel, particularly over or near land. This type of travel introduces diversions in the signal path because of the terrain and can cause the speed of the signal to vary from its point of transmission until the time it is received.

FIXED FIREFIGHTING SYSTEM A system permanently installed aboard a vessel to provide fire protection. Systems include carbon dioxide, halon, and water systems.

FIXED HEIGHT LOAD CARRYING TRUCK Fixed platform truck. Truck carrying its load on a nonelevating platform.

FIXED LIGHT A thick glass, usually circular in shape, fitted in a frame fixed in an opening in a ship's side, deckhouse, or bulkhead to provide access for light. The fixed light is not hinged. Often incorrectly called a dead light.

FIXED ORDER INTERVAL SYSTEM Inventory is replenished on a constant, set schedule and is always ordered at a specific time; the quantity ordered varies depending on forecasted sales before the next order date.

FIXED ORDER QUANTITY SYSTEM   Inventory is replenished with a set quantity every time it is ordered; the time interval between orders may vary.

FIXED PLATFORM TRUCK   *See* Fixed Height Load Carrying Truck.

FIXED WAREHOUSE SLOT LOCATION   Each product is assigned a specific location and is always stored there.

FIXING   Chartering a vessel or setting a time.

FIXTURE   Conclusion of shipbrokers negotiations to charter a ship—an agreement.

FJORDS   A narrow inlet or arm of the sea bordered by steep cliffs, especially in Norway and Alaska. Also spelled fiords.

FLAG OF CONVENIENCE   The registration of ships in a country whose tax on the profits of trading ships is low or whose requirements concerning manning or maintenance are not stringent. Sometimes referred to as flags of necessity; denotes registration of vessels in foreign nations that offer favorable tax structures and regulations; also the flag representing the nation under whose jurisdiction a ship is registered. Ships are always registered under the laws of one nation but are not always required to establish their home location in that country.

FLAGSTAFF   Flag pole, usually at the stern of a ship; carries the ensign.

FLAM   A term often used to express the same meaning as flare, but more properly used to denote the maximum curl or roll given to the flare at the upper part, just below the weather deck.

FLAME ARRESTER   A device or assembly of a cellular, tubular, pressure, or other type used for preventing the passage of flames into enclosed spaces. It is at the top of the mast to allow for the flow of the vapors into the atmosphere.

FLAMEPROOF   Unable to sustain combustion.

FLAME SCREEN   A small mesh wire screen designed to restrict the entry of fire to a cargo or fuel tank. A portable or fitted device incorporating one or more corrosion resistant wire woven fabrics of a very small mesh used for preventing sparks from entering a tank opening or for a short period of time preventing the passage of a flame, yet permitting the passage of gas. According to regulation, fitted single screen's mesh is at least 30 by 30; for two fitted screens the mesh is at least 20 by 20, spaced not less than ½ inch or more than 1½ inches apart. It is fitted in the ullage hole when cover is open.

FLAMMABLE   Term describing any combustible material that can be ignited easily and will burn rapidly. Petroleum products, which have a flash point of 80°F or lower, are classed as flammable.

FLAMMABLE (EXPLOSIVE) LIMITS   LEL and UEL. A flammable material will burn in air when ignited. These materials are referred to as flammable, combustible, or explosive. The range of concentration in which these materials will burn is limited by the Lower Explosive Limit (LEL). When the gas or vapor is below this concentration, the mixture is to lean to burn.

The Upper Explosive Limit (UEL) above this concentration is too rich for the mixture to burn.

FLAMMABLE COMPRESSED GAS Any flammable material or mixture having in the container a pressure exceeding 40 psi at 100°F.

FLAMMABLE LIQUID Any liquid with a flash point less than 100°F as measured by the tests specified in 33CFR173.115.

FLAMMABLE RANGE The limits between the minimum and maximum concentrations of vapor in air that form explosive or burnable mixtures. Usually abbreviated LEL (Lower Explosive Limit) and UEL (Upper Explosive Limit).

FLAMMABLE SOLID Any sold material, other than an explosive, that is liable to cause fires through friction, absorption of moisture, spontaneous chemical changes, retained heat from manufacturing or processing, or that can be ignited readily and when ignited burns so vigorously and persistently as to create a serious transportation hazard.

FLANGE A piece of metal attached to a riser, a hose, or the end of a pipe that has a flat edge 90 degrees to the unit it is attached to. Sections of units are attached to each other at flanges that may contain boltholes or other means of connecting. To flange is to bend over to form such an angle.

FLANK *See* Flanking Maneuver.

FLANKING BUOY Buoy tied to the corner of a tow so the pilot can tell when the tow has been checked.

FLANKING MANEUVER Maneuvering action of a tow (when down bound) approaching at an angle (usually 30 to 45 degrees) at bridges or locks or in sharp bends. The current only is used for headway and the engines and rudders are used to maintain the angle until just before the lead barges reach the bridge span, at which time the engines are backed down and the head of the tow is swung gently in line with the opening. Then full power is applied to drive through the opening. This is the safest way that a heavy tow can make tight passages.

FLANKING RUDDER (BACKING RUDDER) A rudder installed forward of the screw, used for maneuvering when the propellers are turning astern, regardless of the direction of actual movement of the towboat.

FLAP VALVE A device in the dredge discharge line that is designed to maintain a certain minimum resistance to flow in the discharge line. This is a safety device that provides protection to the prime mover by preventing overloading.

FLARE The spreading out from the central vertical plane of the body of a ship with increasing rapidity as the section rises from the waterline to the rail. Also a night distress signal.

FLARE STACK An isolated chimney or pipe at the end of which waste or unwanted gases are burnt off. Oil production platforms have special nozzles, which are designed to prevent the flame being extinguished in high winds.

FLASH FLOOD   A rapid rise in the river that inundates land and usually disappears as rapidly as it arose.

FLASH POINT   The lowest temperature at which, under specified test conditions, a petroleum product vaporizes rapidly enough to form above its surface an air vapor mixture that gives a flash or slight explosion when ignited by a small flame. The temperature at which a flammable liquid produces enough vapor to burn.

FLASH TUBE   An electronically controlled high-intensity discharge lamp with a very brief flash duration.

FLAT   A small barge with a flat top used for transporting fuel or other miscellaneous cargo.

FLAT CAR   An open car without sides, ends, or top, used principally for hauling lumber, stone, heavy machinery, etc.

FLAT CANCELLATION (INS)   Cancellation of an insurance policy as of the date of its start with no premium charge.

FLATPACKING   Cargo to present stacked and secured as an integral unit.

FLAT POOL   The normal stage of water in the area between two dams that is to be maintained by design when little or no water is flowing, consequently, the pool flattens out.

FLAT RACK/FLAT BED CONTAINER   A container with no sides and frame members at the front and rear. Container can be loaded from the sides and top. There are 20' and 40' versions of this container type. It should be noted that no tarpaulin cover is supplied, therefore, cargo should be suitably weather protected.

FLAT-RATE LEASE   One type of container terminal lease in which the operator (tenant) pays a stipulated yearly rate regardless of the amount of cargo passing through the terminal.

FLEET   A grouping of ships.

FLEETING AREA   Mooring area where LASH barges are held (where no cargo operations are performed), awaiting either shifting to cargo decks or towing to another location.

FLEMISH DOWN   To coil flat down on deck, each fake outside the other, beginning in the middle and all close together.

FLEXIBLE COUPLINGS   In some situations where shafts have to be coupled, there are complications that necessitate the use of a flexible coupling, for example, temperature differences can produce lateral and axial misalignment. Vibration and shock loading can occur. The types vary from the ordinary flange couplings to bushing the boltholes with rubber. The rubber disc type can accommodate severe misalignment. Some flexible couplings use springs to give the resilience required. Other designs involve hydraulic and electromagnetic couplings.

FLEXIBLE PATH EQUIPMENT   Materials handling devices that include hand trucks and forklifts.

FLEXITANKS   A large polythene liner that can be fitted inside a 20'GP for the transportation of nonhazardous liquids.

FLIGHT NUMBER   An identifier associated with the air equipment (plane). Typically a combination of two letters, indicating the airline, and three or four digits indicating the number of the voyage.

FLOAT LIGHT   A 10-foot wooden platform mounted on pontoons supporting a battery-operated light. These are used exclusively on the Upper Mississippi River in a certain area.

FLOATER POLICY (INS)   A policy under the terms of which protection follows moveable property, covering it wherever it may be.

FLOATING AID TO NAVIGATION   A buoy secured in its assigned position by a mooring.

FLOATING CRANE   A crane mounted on a barge or pontoon that can be towed or is self-propelled

FLOATING DECK   A floating structure that can be partially submerged to enable vessels to enter and to leave and can be raised for use as a dry dock.

FLOATING DOCK   A moveable dock, which is not grounded from below.

FLOATING ICE   Any form of ice found floating in water. The principal kinds of floating ice are lake ice, river ice, and sea ice, which form by the freezing of water at the surface and glacier ice (ice of land origin) formed on land or in an ice shelf. The concept includes ice that is stranded or grounded.

FLOATING PIN   A mooring pin or timberhead attached to a floating tank in a lock chamber set in a guided recess in the lock walls for mooring tows within the lock chamber whereby a short mooring line suffices without an attendant.

FLOATING PIPELINE   In most cases, the discharge line from a nonhopper dredge must span some open water between the dredge and the disposal site. This discharge pipe is normally attached to floating pontoons between the dredge and the disposal site.

FLOATING POWER   The sum of the used and the reserve buoyancy of a vessel, or the displacement of the completely watertight portion of the vessel when fully submerged. The used buoyancy is that buoyancy required to support the weight of the vessel.

FLOATING STOCK   *See* Pipeline Inventory.

FLOODABLE LENGTH   The length of the ship that may be flooded without sinking below her safety or margin line. The floodable length of a vessel varies from point to point throughout her length and is usually greatest amidships and least near the quarter length.

FLOOD STAGE   When the river rises above a stage predetermined by the Corps of Engineers to be designated as flood stage. Also, the stage at which some part of the main bank may be overflowed, not necessarily all of it.

FLOOR   A vertical structural member within a double-bottom tank that runs perpendicular to the centerline. A plate placed vertically in the bottom of a ship, usually on every frame and running athwartship from bilge to bilge.

FLOOR PLATE   Vertical plate in double bottoms. *See* Floor.

FLOORING OFF   Laying a floor with dunnage.

FLOTSAM   Cargo swept from a vessel and found floating in the water. Since ownership of such property is not lost, flotsam is liable for salvage.

FLOUNDER PLATE   A heavy triangular steel plate with a bushed hole in each corner that accepts the shackle pin from each leg of a towing bridle and that of the towing pendant. It is also known as a fishplate, union plate, or spider.

FLOW CHART   A diagram, using symbols and depicting the sequence of events that should take place in a complex set of tasks.

FLOW METER   A device that detects the amount of mixture produced by the dredge system in a given time.

FLOW PROBE   A component of an electromagnetic speed log. The probe contains a coil through which an electric current passes, producing a magnetic field around the probe. As water moves past the probe, the magnetic field becomes altered, producing a variation in the signal voltage.

FLOW RACK   A storage method where product is presented to picking operations at one end of a rack and replenished from the opposite end.

FLT   Full Liner Terms.

FLUE GASES   Mixture of air and burnt and unburnt fuel leaving a boiler combustion chamber. The principal constituents are oxygen, nitrogen, and carbon dioxide, but some carbon monoxide may be present if insufficient air is available for combustion. Information about the combustion of fuel in boilers is obtained by the analysis of the flue gases. For general control work, an apparatus is used in which 100 ml of gas is taken into a water-jacketed, graduated burette and the constituents of the gas removed separately by absorption.

FLUKE   The palm or broad holding portion at the arm extremities of an anchor that penetrate the ground.

FLUSHING OIL   Oil or a compound designed for the purpose of removing used oil, decomposition products, and dirt from lubrication passages, crankcase surfaces, and moving parts of automotive engines accessible to the lubrication system.

FLUX   A fusible material or gas used to dissolve or prevent the formation of oxides, nitrides, or other undesirable inclusions formed in welding and brazing.

FLYING A NATION'S FLAG   A ship that is registered in a particular country (e.g., a ship registered in France flies a French flag).

FM   Fine Measurement.

FM   *See* Frequency Modulation.

FMC   Federal Maritime Commission. The U.S. governmental regulatory body responsible for administering maritime affairs including the tariff system, Freight Forwarder Licensing, enforcing the conditions of the Shipping Act, and approving conference or other carrier agreements.

FME   Force Majeure Excepted.

FMS   Fathoms (each fathom is 6 feet or approximately 2 meters).

FO   For Orders. Fuel oil/intermediate—free out.

FOAM   A froth used for firefighting.

FOAM COMPOUND   Foam compound is the full strength foam making liquid as received from the supplier.

FOAM SOLUTION   Mixture of water with foam compound before agitation and aeration.

FOAMED BUOY   A buoy whose interior is filled with styrofoam for the purpose of improving floatation when in a damaged condition.

FOB   *See* Free On Board. *See also* Terms of Sale, FOB.

FOB (FREE ONBOARD)   The seller fulfills his obligation to deliver when the goods have passed over the ship's rail at the named port of shipment. This means that the buyer has to bear all costs and risks of loss of or damage to the goods from this point. The FOB term requires the seller to clear the goods for export. This term can only be used for sea or inland waterway transport. When the ship's rail serves no practical purpose, such as in the case of roll on/roll off of container traffic, the FCA term is more appropriate to use. *See also* Terms of Sale.

FOB FREIGHT ALLOWED   The same as F.O.B. named inland carrier, except the buyer pays the transportation charge and the seller reduces his invoice by like amount.

FOB FREIGHT PREPAID   The same as F.O.B. named inland carrier, except the seller pays the freight charges of the inland carrier.

FOB NAMED INLAND CARRIER   Seller must place the goods on the named carrier at the specified inland point and obtain a bill of lading. The buyer pays for the transportation.

FOB NAMED POINT OF EXPORTATION   Seller is responsible for placing the goods at a named point of exportation at the seller's expense. Some European buyers use this vessel form when they actually mean F.O.B. vessel.

FOB VESSEL   Seller is responsible for goods and preparation of export documentation until actually placed aboard the vessel.

FOC   *See* Flag Of Convenience.

FOG   *See* Water Fog.

FOG DETECTOR   An electronic device used to automatically determine conditions of visibility that warrant the turning on and off of a sound signal or additional light signals.

FOG HORN   A sound signal device operated by the mouth or by mechanical appliance.

FOG SIGNAL   A sound signal used in thick weather. *See also* Sound Signal.

FOG SOUND   Said of a vessel when forced to lie at anchor due to fog.

FOOTINGS   Bottom boards of walking flats attached to the inside of the frames of small boats where deep floors are not fitted.

FOOTS Sample of cargo taken from ship's cargo tanks usually after only a foot or so of cargo is in the space.

FOR *See* Free On Rail.

FORCE MEJEURE A concept of International Customary Law that provides that a vessel in distress may enter a port and may claim "as a right an entire immunity" from local jurisdiction. Admiralty courts have upheld this concept as long as the distress was real and valid. The title of a common clause in contracts, exempting the parties for nonfulfillment of their obligations as a result of conditions beyond their control, such as earthquakes, floods, or war.

FORE A term used in indicating portions or that part of a ship at or adjacent to the bow. Also applied to that portion and parts of the ship lying between the midship section and stem, as fore body, fore hold, and foremast.

FORE & AFT In line with the length of the ship; at bow and stern, all over ship; longitudinal. The direction on a vessel parallel to the centerline.

FORE & AFT LINE A line used to secure two barges end to end.

FORE & AFT STOWAGE Stowage from the bow to the stern (lengthwise), as opposed to stowage athwartships.

FORE BAY An enclosure of the river usually above a dam.

FORECASTLE (FO'C'SLE) The elevated deck at the bow of a seagoing vessel, designed to increase a vessel's reverse buoyancy. The forward upper portion of the hull, usually used for the crew's quarters. Also, the section of the upper deck of a ship located at the bow, forward of the foremast. A superstructure at the bow of a ship where maintenance shops, rope lockers, and paint lockers may be located.

FORECASTLE HEAD (FO'C'SLEHEAD) The enclosed deck below the elevated bow deck.

FOREFOOT The lower end of a vessel's stem that is stepped on the keel. That point in the forward end of the keel about which the boat pivots in an endwise launching.

FOREHOOK *See* Breasthook.

FOREIGN BRANCH OFFICE A sales (or other) office maintained in a foreign country and staffed by direct employees of the exporter.

FOREIGN EXPORTS Exports of foreign merchandise (re-exports) consist of commodities of foreign origin, which have entered the United States for consumption or into Customs bonded warehouses or U.S. Foreign Trade Zones, and which, at the time of exportation, are in substantially the same condition as when imported.

FOREIGN FREIGHT FORWARDER A corporation carrying on the business of forwarding who is not a shipper or consignee. The foreign freight forwarder receives compensation from the shipper for preparing documents and arranging various transactions related to the international distribution of goods. Also, a brokerage fee may be paid to the "forwarder" from steamship lines if the forwarder performs at least two of the following services:

181

(1) Coordination of the movement of the cargo to shipside.

(2) Preparation and processing of Ocean Bill of Lading.

(3) Preparation and processing of dock receipts or delivery orders.

(4) Preparation and processing of consular documents or export declarations.

(5) Payment of the ocean freight charges on shipments.

FOREIGN SALES AGENT An agent residing in a foreign country who acts as a salesman for a domestic manufacturer.

FOREIGN SALES CORPORATION Takes the place of the Domestic International Sales Corporation (DISC). Studies the legal aspects of importing goods produced or assembled in more than one country. Under U.S. tax law, a corporation created to obtain tax exemption on part of the earnings of U.S. products in foreign markets. Must be set-up as a foreign corporation with an office outside the U.S.

FOREIGN TRADE The exchange of waterborne commodity movements imports and exports between the United States and foreign countries and between Puerto Rico and the U.S. Virgin Islands and foreign countries.

FOREIGN TRADE ZONE A free port in a country divorced from Customs authority but under government control. Merchandise, except that which is prohibited, may be stored in the zone without being subject to import duty regulations.

FOREIGN TRADE ZONE ENTRY A form declaring goods that are brought duty free into a Foreign Trade Zone for further processing or storage and subsequent exportation.

FORELAND *See* Discontinuous Hinterland.

FOREMAST The first mast of a ship abaft the bow.

FORE PEAK A watertight compartment at the extreme forward end of a ship; the forward trimming tank.

FORESHORE A strip of land lying along tidal water. *See* Shore.

FOREST PRODUCTS In an unfinished or semifinished state that require special handling moving in lot sizes too large for a container, including, but not limited to, lumber in bundles, rough timber, ties, poles, piling, laminated beams, bundled siding, bundled plywood, bundled core stock or veneers, bundled particle or fiberboards, bundled hardwood, wood pulp in rolls or unitized bales, paper board in rolls, and paper in rolls.

FORFAIT Purchase of negotiable instruments, most often avalized drafts, without recourse. The forfaiter assumes the credit risk of being able to collect payment when due.

FORGING A piece of metal hammered, bent, or pressed to shape while white-hot.

FOR-HIRE CARRIER A carrier that provides transportation service to the public on a fee basis.

FORK BEAM A half beam to support a deck where hatchways occur.

FORKLIFT   A machine used to pick up and move goods loaded on pallets or skids.

FORKLIFT POCKETS   Openings in the bottom supports of containers for the entry of the forks of lift trucks.

FORK TRUCK   A gasoline- or electric-powered industrial machine equipped with two extended forks used to pick up, carry, and stack cargo.

FORTY FOOT EQUIVALENT UNIT (FEU)   Unit of measurement equivalent to one forty-foot shipping container.

FORWARD   The section of the ship that is in front of midship. To move toward the bow of the ship.

FORWARD AND AFT   Terms used to describe locations with reference in line with the length of a ship. *See also* Fore & Aft.

FORWARD ERROR CORRECTION (FEC)   A method of reducing error and poorly received characters used with narrow band direct printings.

FORWARD PERPENDICULAR (FP)   A line perpendicular to the base line; intersection of the forward edge of the stem at the designed waterline. The forward most frame station and is usually located at the intersection of the designer's load waterline (DLWL) and the forward part of the stem.

FORWARDER   Freight Forwarder. The party arranging the carriage of goods including connected services and/or associated formalities on behalf of a shipper or consignee.

FORWARDER COMPENSATION   *See* Brokerage.

FORWARDER'S CARGO RECEIPT   Document issued by a freight forwarder or freight consolidator indicating goods have been received from the seller and are being held at the disposal of the buyer. Goods are generally received in the seller's country and the forwarder/consolidator will arrange for their transport.

FORWARDER'S CERTIFICATE OF RECEIPT (FCR)   The forwarding agent's own through document for goods, negotiable worldwide.

FORWARDING INSTRUCTION   Document issued to a freight forwarder, giving instructions to the forwarder for the forwarding of goods described therein.

FOT   Free On Truck.

FOUL   A term applied to the underwater portion of the outside of a vessel's shell when it is more or less covered with sea growth or foreign matter. It has been found that even an oily film over the vessel's bottom will retard the speed, while sea growth will reduce a vessel's propulsive efficiency to a large extent. Also, obstructed or impeded by an interference.

FOUL ANCHOR   Said of an anchor when the cable is twisted about it or has fouled an obstruction.

FOUL BILL OF LADING   A receipt for goods issued by a carrier with an indication that the outward containers or the goods have been damaged when received. Compare Clean Bill of Lading.

FOUL HAWSE   Said of the hawse when moored and the chain does not lead clear of the other chain.

FOUL PROPELLER   A line, wire, net, etc., is wound around the propeller.

FOUND   To fit and bed firmly. Also, equipped.

FOUNDATIONS, AUXILIARY   Supports for small machinery such as winches and also for condensers, heaters, etc.

FOUNDATIONS, MAIN   The structural supports for the boilers, main engines or turbines and reduction gears are called main foundations.

FOUNDATIONS, STEERING ENGINE   Supports for deck machinery.

FOUNDER   To sink due to loss of reserve buoyancy.

FOUR-WAY PALLET   A pallet designed so that the forks of a forklift truck can be inserted from all four sides. *See* Forklift.

FOW   First Open Water.

FP   Free Pratique. Clearance by the Health Authorities.

FPA   *See* Free of Particular Average.

FPAAC (FREE OF PARTICULAR AVERAGE, AMERICAN CONDITIONS)   Average clause that limits recovery of partial losses under the perils clause to those losses directly resulting from fire, stranding, sinking, or collision of the vessel.

FPAEC (FREE OF PARTICULAR AVERAGE, ENGLISH CONDITIONS)   Same as FPAAC except that partial losses under the perils clause are fully recoverable if the vessel has been stranded, sunk, burned, been on fire, or in collision, without requiring that the damage actually be caused by one of these perils.

FR   First Refusal. First attempt at best offer that can be matched.

FRACTION   A portion of distillate (having a particular boiling range) separated from other portions in the fractional distillation of petroleum products.

FRACTIONAL DISTILLATION   Fractional distillation implies the use of equipment for effecting a more complete separation between the low and high boiling components in a mixture being distilled than does the general term distillation. It is usually accomplished by the use of a bubble tower or its equivalent. *See also* Distillation.

FRACTIONATION   As used in petroleum, generally means fractional distillation.

FRAGILE   Easily breakable. Term denoting that goods should be handled with care.

FRAGILITY FACTOR (GM)   The vibration and shock limit that must not be exceeded to avoid malfunctioning of the equipment; usually expressed in Gs (force of gravity) for shock and in Gs (force of gravity) and cycles per second for vibration.

FRAME   Structural member extending up from the floors in the ship's side, running perpendicular to the centerline, number consecutively from bow to stern usually, but may reverse on some tankers. One of the ribs forming the skeleton of a ship.

FRAME, BOSS   A frame that is bent to fit around the boss in the way of a stern tube or shaft.

FRAME, WEB   Heavy side or continuous frame, made with web plate between its members.

FRAME LINES   Molded lines of a vessel as laid out on the mold loft floor for each frame, showing the form and position of the frames.

FRAME SPACING   The fore and aft distance between heel and heel of adjacent transverse frames along the centerline.

FRANCHISE (INS)   A provision in some policies stating that the insurance company shall not be responsible for any loss that is less than a certain amount. If the loss equals or exceeds that amount, however, it will be paid in full. A provision in freight insurance conditions that exempts the insurer from particular average losses, in any one accident, under 3%. The provision is varied if the loss is caused by fire, or ship stranding, sinking, or being in a collision.

FR&CC   Free of Riot and Civil Commotion.

FREE ALONGSIDE SHIP (FAS)   The seller fulfills his obligation to deliver when the goods have been placed alongside the vessel on the quay or in lighters at the named port of shipment. This means that the buyer has to bear all costs and risks of loss of or damage to the goods from that moment. The FAS term requires the buyer to clear the goods for export. It should not be used when the buyer cannot carry out directly or indirectly the export formalities. This term can only be used for sea or inland waterway transport

FREE ASTRAY   Any astray shipment (a lost shipment that is found) sent to its proper destination without additional charge.

FREEBOARD   The distance measured vertically downward at the side of a vessel, amidships, from the upper edge of the deck line to the upper edge of the load line. The vertical distance between the waterline and the main deck.

FREE CARRIER   This term has been designed to meet the requirements of modern transport, particularly such multimodal transport as container or roll on/roll off traffic by trailers and ferries. It is based on the same main principle as FOB except that the seller fulfills his obligations when he delivers the goods into the custody of the carrier at a named point. If no precise point can be named at the time of the contract of sale, the parties should refer to name a contract of carriage by road, rail, air, sea, or a combination of modes that has been made. When the seller has to furnish a bill of lading, waybill, or carrier's receipt, he duly fulfills his obligation by producing such a document issued by a person so defined, place, or range where the carrier should take the goods into his charge. The risk of loss or damage to the goods is transferred from seller to buyer at that point.

FREE CIRCULATION   The movement of goods within the European Community without the need to pay any duty.

FREE DESPATCH   If loading/discharging achieved sooner than agreed, there will be no freight money returned.

FREE EXINS   Free of any extra insurance.

FREE HOUSE UNCLEAR   Delivered at a certain destination without payment of certain duties or incurred costs.

FREE IN   Pricing terms indicating charterer of vessel is responsible for cost of loading goods onto vessel.

FREE IN AND OUT (FIO)   Cost of loading and unloading a vessel is borne by the charterer.

FREEING PORT   A large opening in the bulwark just above the deck so that when seas break over the deck, the ship can clear itself of rain and seawater quickly. Rods or bars are generally fitted across freeing ports to prevent men from being washed overboard through these openings.

FREE IN LINER OUT (FILO)   Transport condition denoting that the freight rate is inclusive of the sea carriage and the cost of discharging, the latter as per the custom of the port. It excludes the cost of loading and, if appropriate, stowage and lashing.

FREE IN OUT STOWED (FIOS)   Freight rates quoted FIOS exclude all aspects related to cargo handling. The ship is responsible only for expenses related to the ship calling the port.

FREE LIFT   The maximum elevation of the forks of a forklift truck.

FREELY NEGOTIABLE LETTER OF CREDIT   Letter of credit that indicates it is "available with any bank by negotiation." By including this wording, the issuing bank authorizes the beneficiary to present documents to the bank of his choice for examination and collection of payment.

FREE MOISTURE   Water present in a cargo hold due to a leak in the hull plating. Free moisture is most notable because it can damage cargo.

FREE OF CAPTURE AND SEIZURE (FC&S)   An insurance clause providing that the loss is not insured if due to capture, seizure, confiscation, and like actions, whether legal or not, or from such acts as piracy, civil war, rebellion, and civil strife.

FREE OF PARTICULAR AVERAGE (FPA)   A marine insurance clause providing that partial loss or damage is not insured. American condition (FPAAC)—Partial loss not insured unless caused by the vessel sinking, stranded, burned, on fire, or in collision. English conditions (FPAEC)—Partial loss not insured unless a result of the vessel sinking, stranded, burned, on fire, or in collision.

FREE ON RAIL/FREE ON TRUCK   These terms are synonymous because the word "truck" relates to the railway wagons. The terms should only be used then the goods are to be carried by rail. Free on railroad defines seller's responsible for the cost of goods is to the point of loading it to the train's loading deck. FOR normally comes with loading railroad station where the goods are to be loaded.

FREE OUT (F.O.)   Cost of unloading a vessel is borne by the charterer.

FREE PORT   A restricted area at a seaport for airport for the handling of duty exempted import goods. Also called a Foreign Trade Zone.

FREE POUR   Pouring grain from a spout at full capacity without the use of a trimmer.

FREE PRACTIQUE   Permission granted by local medical authorities, denoting that the vessel has a clean Bill of Health so that people may embark and disembark.

FREE SALE CERTIFICATE   The U.S. government does not issue certificates of free sale. However, the Food and Drug Administration, Silver Spring, Maryland, will issue, upon request, a letter of comment to the U.S. manufacturers whose products are subject to the Federal Food, Drug, and Cosmetic Act or other acts administered by the agency. The letter can take the place of the certificate.

FREE SURFACE   A condition in stability analysis when liquids partially fill a tank or space aboard ship. Because of the fluid nature, weight is allowed to shift and affect stability. Free surface is considered a dangerous condition because it reduces a vessel's stability.

The effect that occurs when liquid is free to move transversely in a tank. Free surface effect shortens the vessel's GM. The most important factor in determining the effect is the breadth of the tank. It only occurs in slack tanks.

FREE SURFACE EFFECT   Liquid in a partially filled tank or vessel that can move freely and without restriction, causing the vessel to list or roll.

FREE TIME   The amount of time allowed by the carriers for the loading or unloading of freight at the expiration of which demurrage or detention charges will accrue.

FREE TRADE ZONE   An area to which goods may be imported for processing and subsequent export on a duty free basis. A port designated by the government of a country for duty-free entry of any nonprohibited goods. Merchandise may be stored, displayed, used for manufacturing, etc., within the zone and re-exported without duty.

FREEZING POINT   The temperature at which the liquid state of a substance is in equilibrium with the solid state; at lower temperatures the liquid will solidify. The temperature at which a substance freezes.

FREIGHT   Refers to either the merchandise hauled by transportation or the charges assessed for transporting the cargo.

FREIGHT, ALL KINDS (FAK)   A uniform rate or tariff applicable irrespective of commodity. Most FAK rates are charged per unit, i.e., per container of a given kind and not on the weight or volume of its contents.

FREIGHT ABSORPTION   Buyer pays a lower freight charge than the shipper incurs in shipping the product.

FREIGHT BILL   A document issued by the carrier based on the bill of lading and other information; used to account for a shipment operationally, statistically, and financially.

FREIGHT BROKERAGE A commission paid to a licensed Freight Forwarder or Custom House Broker by the steamship line concerning export transactions. Commission is paid either as a percentage of the freight charges or as a lump sum amount per container, depending on the carrier and/or trade lane.

FREIGHT CARRIAGE AND INSURANCE PAID TO ... *See* CIF.

FREIGHT CARRIAGE PAID TO. *See* C&F.

FREIGHT COLLECT Freight charges to be paid by consignee at destination.

FREIGHT CONSOLIDATION Putting cargoes from different sources into one shipping unit, usually a container or truck trailer, to reduce transportation costs.

FREIGHT CONTAINER *See* Container.

FREIGHT CORRECTION NOTICE (FCN) A document used to record any and all changes to the freight manifest involving charges. These changes may be additions, deletions, or corrections of information on the manifest that will affect charges.

FREIGHT COSTS Costs incurred by the merchant in moving goods, by whatever means, from one place to another under the terms of the contract of carriage. In addition to transport costs this may include such elements as packing, documentation, loading, unloading, and transport insurance.

FREIGHTERS General cargo carriers, full containerships, partial containerships, roll on/roll off (RO/RO) ships, and barge carriers.

General Cargo Carriers: Include refrigerated and unrefrigerated breakbulk carriers, car carriers, cattle carriers, pallet carriers, and timber carriers.

Full Containerships: Ships equipped with permanent container cells with little or no space for other types of cargo.

Partial Containerships: Multipurpose containerships where one or more but not all compartments are fitted with permanent container cells, and the remaining compartments are used for other types of cargo. Also includes container/car carriers, container/railcar carriers, and container/roll on/roll off ships.

Roll On/Roll Off: Ships that are especially designed to carry wheeled containers or trailers and only use the roll on/roll off method for loading and unloading. Containers and trailers are usually stowed onboard on their transport wheels.

Barge Carriers: Ships designed to carry either barges or some variable number of barges and containers simultaneously. Currently this class includes two types of vessels, the LASH and the SEABEE.

FREIGHT FORWARDER A person engaged in the business of assembling, collecting, consolidating, shipping, and distributing less than carload or less than truckload freight. Also a person acting as agent in a transshipping of freight. To or from foreign countries and their clearing through Customs.

FREIGHT FORWARDING   A function performed on behalf of a shipper or cargo owner where goods completing one transport mode are reshipped by another mode to their destination.

FREIGHT HANDLING AREA   Square feet or surface floor space between the waterfront edge of the wharf and the line where freight is customarily piled, plus the area of lanes or roadways reserved for the trucking or handling of cargo to and from shipside.

FREIGHT INVOICE   An itemized list of goods shipped and services rendered stating fees and charges.

FREIGHT MANIFEST   A (cargo) manifest including all freight particulars.

FREIGHT PAYMENT SERVICES   *See* Bank Payment Plan.

FREIGHT PREPAID   Freight charges to be paid by shipper/exporter prior to shipment.

FREIGHT QUOTATION   A quotation from a carrier or forwarder covering the cost of transport between two specified locations.

FREIGHT RATE   The charge made for the transportation of freight.

FREIGHT RELEASE   Evidence that the freight charges for the cargo have been paid. If in writing, it may be presented at the pier to obtain release of the cargo. (Normally, once the freight is paid, releases are usually arranged without additional documentation.)

FREIGHT TON   A unit for freighting cargo according to weight and/or cubic measurement.

FREQUENCY   The number of cycles a wave completes in a specific period of time.

FREQUENCY CONTROL   The ability of a tuner (which can be variable, crystal controlled, or synthesized) within a receiver to receive one or more frequencies.

FREQUENCY MODULATION (FM)   A type of voice transmission system that uses the VHF band. The transmission and reception ranges for this system are determined by antenna height.

FREQUENCY RANGE   The spectrum of frequencies within an upper and lower limit of a receiver that determines what specific signals can be tuned and reproduced. A unit may cover a broad group of frequencies, such as on a multiband communications receiver or a single frequency, as in a radio navigation receiver like Loran C.

FRESHEN THE NIP   To shift the rope to take the wear in another place.

FRESHWATER ALLOWANCE (FWA)   Amount that load line mark may be submerged when loading in water of less density than that of seawater.

FROM A LITTLE OPEN   To depart on a new course from a point 50 yards or less from a defined object.

FROM END OF DIKE   From the outward or channel end of a dike.

FROM FOOT TO DIKE   From the end of the dike where it is attached to the shore.

FROM LOWER END OF DIKE From the outward or channel end of a dike.

FRONT Boundary zone separating two masses of air, one of which is colder than the other. Types of front: (1) warm front (warmer air overtaking colder air); (2) cold front (colder air overtaking warmer air); (3) occluded front (cold front overtaking warm front); (4) arctic front (special case of cold front in which air behind front is very cold, say less than 10°F); (5) stationary front (a front that is not moving).

FRONT-END TOP PICK LOADER A forklift truck or similar unit equipped with a top lift container bridle for the handling of containers.

FROST SMOKE Deposition that occurs when very cold air passes over relatively cold water. This occurs in the polar regions.

FRP Fiberglass Reinforced Plywood. Used in container construction.

FRT Freight.

FRUSTRATION Charterers when canceling agreement sometimes quote "doctrine of frustration," i.e., vessel is lost, extensive delays.

FT Foot.

FTC *See* Fast Time Constant.

FTL Full Truck Load.

FUEL DEPOT (STORAGE TERMINAL, TANK FARM) Bulk storage installation composed of storage tanks and related facilities such as docks, loading racks, and pumping units.

FUEL OIL Any liquid petroleum product used for the generation of heat in a furnace or firebox.

FULL AND DOWN A ship is said to be "full and down" when its cargo spaces are full and it is down to its marks. With an extremely light cargo, the vessel would be full but not down to its marks. With a heavy cargo, such as ore, it will be down to its marks, but its total cargo spaces will not be filled.

FULL CONTAINER LOAD (FCL) The load carried in a container equals one of the two operating maximum, weight or volume.

FULL CONTAINERSHIPS *See* Freighters.

FULL-COST PRICING The carrier prices the transportation service to each customer so that the full cost of providing the service is charged to each customer.

FULL DOUBLE The maximum tow that can be locked.

FULL FOLLOW-UP CONTROL SYSTEM (FFU) A joystick or control lever that allows direct control of the rudder without use of the wheel. This unit is designed as the primary steering station or as a remote station that can be placed anywhere on the vessel. This system will automatically return the rudder to amidships when the control lever is released.

FULL LINER TERMS Freight amount includes both shore-based and on-board stevedoring, lashing, unlashing, dunnage materials, securing, unsecuring, and all costs for receiving the cargo.

FULL SERVICE LEASING An equipment-leasing arrangement that includes a variety of services to support the leased equipment; a common method for leasing motor carrier tractors.

FULL SET All signed originals of a document. For example, bills of lading are often issued in three originals, all having the same validity for claiming goods at the place of delivery.

FULL TRAILER A truck trailer constructed in such way that its own weight and that of the cargo rest upon its own wheels, instead of being supported by e.g., a tractor.

FULLER'S EARTH Any of a class of naturally occurring absorbent clays, so called from their original use in fulling cloth, but now used more extensively as a filter medium for refining oils, fats.

FULLY ALLOCATED COST The variable cost associated with a particular unit of output plus an allocation of common cost.

FULLY CELLULAR CONTAINERSHIP (FCC) A vessel specially designed to carry containers, with cell-guides under deck and necessary fittings and equipment on deck.

FUMIGATION Treating of cargoes with gases to exterminate unwanted life forms.

FUNNEL Smokestack of a vessel.

FURNACE Heater or large forge for heating plates or shapes for bending. To furnace is to bend by heating in furnace.

FURNACE OIL A distillate fuel intended primarily for domestic heating.

FURNACED PLATE A plate that requires heating in order to shape it as required.

FURRINGS Strips of timber, metal, or boards fastened to frames, joists, etc., in order to bring their faces to the required shape or level, for attachment of sheathing, ceiling, flooring.

FWDD Fresh Water Departure Draft.

FWPCA Federal Water Pollution Control Act. 33 USC 1251-1387.

G

G   Symbol for center of gravity.

GA   General Average.

GAFF   A spar to which the top of a fore and aft sail is attached. It is usually fitted with a jaw at the mast end to clasp the mast.

GAUGE   A scale graduated in tenths of a foot that indicates the water level or river stage.

GAUGE, DRAFT   An installation comprising a graduated glass tube, connected at the bottom end with the sea and with the top end open to the air, on which the draft of the vessel is shown by the level of the water in the tube.

GAIN CONTROL   *See* Volume.

GALE   Sustained wind speed of 34 through 47 knots.

GALE WARNING   Special alert to mariners for sustained winds of 34 through 47 knots.

GALLEY   The ship's kitchen.

GALLOWS   The framework sometimes fitted above the main or superstructure deck for boat stowage and for the purpose of stowage of spare parts.

GALVANIZING   The process of coating metal parts with zinc for protection from rust.

GANG BOARD, GANGPLANK   A term applied to boards or a movable platform used in transferring passengers or cargo from a vessel to or from a dock.

GANGWAY   A temporarily affixed access ladder to a ship running perpendicular to the centerline, common on tankers. Often provided by the port. A term applied to a place of exit from a ship. A passageway, a ladder, or other means of boarding a ship.

GANTLINE   A line passed through a single block aloft, used for hoisting or lowering rigging, a boatswain's chair.

GANTLING (GIRTLINE)   A line rove through a single block secured aloft; e.g., hammock gantline.

GANTRY CRANE   A crane or hoisting machine mounted on a frame or structure spanning an intervening space and designed to hoist containers into or out of a ship. *See also* Container Crane.

GARBOARD STRAKE   The strake next to the keel.

GAS   Hydrocarbon and other vapors from petroleum as well as their mixture with air; a term used to cover all vapor/air mixtures.

GAS ABSORPTION DETECTOR   An instrument used for finding the presence of gases that works on the principle of discoloring a chemical agent in the apparatus.

GAS FREE   Gas free means that a tank, compartment, or container has been tested using an appropriate gas indicator and found to be sufficiently free, at the time of the test, of toxic or explosive gases for a specified purpose.

GAS INDICATOR (COMBUSTIBLE GAS INDICATOR) An instrument used to detect the presence of flammable gases or vapors in the atmosphere. (Also known by various trade names as explosimeter, vapor-tester.)

GASKET Packing materials, by which air, water, oil, or steam tightness is secured in such places as on door, hatches, steam cylinders, manhole covers, or in valves, between the flanges of pipes. Such materials as rubber, canvas, asbestos, paper, sheet lead and copper, soft iron, and commercial products are extensively used.

GAS OIL Term originally used to mean oil suitable for cracking to make illuminating gas. Now used to designate an overhead product, intermediate between refined oils and low viscosity lubricating oils, used primarily as thermal or catalytic cracking feed stock, diesel fuel, furnace oil, and the like.

GASOLINE Volatile petroleum liquid principally used as a fuel in internal combustion engines with spark ignition.

GAS TURBINE Rotary heat engine that converts some of the energy of fuel into energy by using the combustion gas as the working medium. There are various types.

GAS VENT LINES The piping system fitted in a tanker to relieve pressure or vacuum in cargo tanks.

GATE DAM A type of opening in a dam whereby the water passes over the top.

GATEHOUSE A building, usually with associated check in/check out booths, for processing entering and exiting trucks with their loads.

GATE VALVE Valve fitted to the end of a pipe leading to a tank and admitting or shutting off liquid by means of a vertically sliding plate.

GATEWAY Industry related: A point at which freight moving from one territory to another is interchanged between transportation lines.

GATHER WAY To attain headway.

GATHERING LINES Oil pipelines that bring oil from the oil well to storage areas.

GATT General Agreement on Tariffs and Trade. A multilateral treaty to help reduce trade barriers between the signatory countries and to promote trade through tariff concessions.

GAUGE The distance between the rails of a railroad track. Also, the measurement of a gantry crane's rail width, i.e., 34-foot gauge, 100-foot gauge.

GBL Government Bill of Lading.

GCR *See* General Cargo Rate.

GDOP *See* Geometric Dilution of Precision.

GDSM General Department Store Merchandise. A classification of commodities that includes goods generally shipped by mass.

GEAR A comprehensive term in general use on shipboard signifying the total of all implements, apparatus, mechanical, machinery, etc., appertaining to and employed in the performance of any given operation as "cleaning gear," "steering gear," "anchor gear."

GEARED Vessel/conveyance carries its own means of loading/unloading cargo.

GEARING A term applied to wheels provided with teeth that mesh, engage, or gear with similar teeth on other wheels in such manner that motion given one wheel will be imparted to the other.

GENERAL *See* Insurance General.

GENERAL AGGREGATE LIMIT (INS) A commercial general liability limit that applies to all damages paid for bodily injury, property damage, personal injury, advertising injury, and medical expenses, except damages included in the products-completed operations hazard.

GENERAL ARRANGEMENT Plan showing general layout of ship design equipment in each compartment A drawing showing the compartment parts of an engine, or unit, in their correct assembled relationship. Such a drawing may consist of three views, a plan and two elevations, and may include also one or more sectional arrangements showing internal construction.

GENERAL AVERAGE A deliberate loss or damage to goods in the face of peril, which sacrifice is made for the preservation of the vessel and other goods. The cost of the loss is shared by the owners of the saved goods.

GENERAL AVERAGE ACT (YORK-ANTWERP RULES) There is a general average act when, and only when any extraordinary sacrifice or expenditure is intentionally and reasonably made or incurred for the common safety for the purpose of preserving from peril the property involved in a common maritime adventure.

GENERAL AVERAGE CONTRIBUTION (INS) The proportionate shares of the vessel owner and each of the cargo owners in order to make up the expenditure or sacrifice incurred for the common good.

GENERAL AVERAGE DEPOSIT (INS) Paid by a consignee to obtain release of the cargo from the carrier following a general average act. This may be replaced by an Underwriter's guarantee.

GENERAL AVERAGE GUARANTEE (INS) Paid by a consignee to obtain release of the cargo from the carrier following a general average act. This may be replaced by an Underwriter's guarantee.

GENERAL AVERAGE IN FULL (INS) An agreement in a cargo insurance whereby Underwriters do not reduce a claim for general average contribution in event of underinsurance.

GENERAL AVERAGE SACRIFICE The voluntary destruction of part of the vessel or the cargo, or the deliberate expenditure of funds in time of grave peril, which is successful in avoiding total disaster.

GENERAL AVERAGE SECURITY Documents the cargo owner presents to the General Average Adjuster to replace the vessel owner's maritime lien on cargo for its share of general average and to obtain release of the goods by the Steamship Company. GA security consists of a GA bond and either a cash deposit or an Underwriter's Guarantee.

GENERAL AVERAGE STATEMENT This shows in detail all general average costs and expenses and the contribution of each interest in the general average in proportion to its value.

GENERAL CARGO Commodities that are usually unitized, boxed, bagged, crated, etc., and normally require handling by piece, unit load or in separate drafts. Also, miscellaneous commodities shipped in various types of packaging of irregular size and weight, or of regular uniform size and weight. The shipping and handling techniques can be as break bulk, containerized, or neobulk general cargo.

GENERAL CARGO CARRIERS Include refrigerated and unrefrigerated break bulk carriers, car carriers, cattle carriers, pallet carriers, and timber carriers. *See also* Freighters.

GENERAL CARGO RATE (GCR) The rate for the carriage of cargo other than a class rate or specific commodity rate.

GENERAL COMMODITIES CARRIER A common motor carrier that has operating authority to transport general commodities, or all commodities not listed as special commodities.

GENERAL COMMODITY RATE (GCR) *See* General Cargo Rate.

GENERAL EXCLUSION CLAUSE (INS) A clause in the Institute Cargo Clauses 1982 that specifies risks that are excluded, irrespective of the risks covered elsewhere in the wording.

GENERAL LICENSE (EXPORT) Authorization to export without specific documentary approval.

GENERAL LICENSE, LIMITED VALUE (GLV) Authorization to export a limited value amount of a good without specific documentary authorization.

GENERAL OBLIGATION FUNDS A debt instrument that pledges the full faith and credit of the issuing government entities, including tax revenue.

GENERAL ORDER (GO) When U.S. Customs orders shipments without entries to be kept in their custody in a bonded warehouse.

GENERAL ORDER WAREHOUSE A bonded warehouse to which goods that are not claimed within five days after arrival are sent at the owner's expense.

GENERAL PERMIT Authorization in advance by the U.S. Corps of Engineers for a class of activities in navigable waters that are minor and that have minimal environmental impact. General permits can be either "nationwide" or "regional."

GENERAL PURPOSE CONTAINER A closed container suitable for the carriage of all types of general cargo, and with suitable temporary modification for the carriage of bulk cargoes, both solid and liquid. The tare weights of containers vary, therefore, no absolute figure is quoted for payload, but it should be mentioned that the P&O Containers fleet of 20' general purpose containers have a maximum gross weight of between 22,860 and 30,480 kilograms. All 40' GP containers have a maximum gross weight of 30,480 kilograms.

GENERAL QUARTERS Battle station.

GENERATOR SET (GEN SET) A portable generator that can be attached to a refrigerated container to power the refrigeration unit during transit.

GEOGRAPHIC RANGE The greatest distance the curvature of the earth permits an object of a given height to be seen from a particular height of eye without regard to luminous intensity or visibility conditions.

GEOMETRIC DILUTION OF PRECISION (GDOP) Based on the geometric relationship of the GPS satellites to the receiver, a measurement of the spacing or spread of the satellites, with the best situation being one satellite nearly overhead and the others equally spaced around the horizon.

GERMANISCHER LLOYD German Classification Society.

GETTING WAY OFF Slowing a tug or tow to stop.

GETTING WAY ON Moving a tug or tow ahead after being stopped.

GG' Distance that the center of gravity moves due to weight movement or free surface of liquid.

GIB A metal fitting to hold a member in place or press two members together, to afford a wearing or bearing surface, or to provide a means of taking up water.

GIGA Metric prefix for one billion.

GILGUY (OR GADGET) A term used to designate an object for which the correct name is forgotten.

GILL NETTING Fishing with the use of a type of net that is designed to float in the water from the surface to a depth of 80 feet. The top of the net consists of a rope with corks attached every 3 to 5 feet. The bottom of the net is also a rope, but it is filled with lead so that it will sink. The fish are caught in the diamond shapes of the netting.

GIMBALS A device by which a ship's compass, chronometer, etc., is suspended so as to remain in a constant horizontal position irrespective of the rolling or pitching of the vessel. It consists of two concentric brass hoops or rings whose diameters are pivoted at right angles to each other on knife-edge bearings.

GIN BLOCK A steel block consisting of a sheave supported by a skeleton frame, that is, without solid sides.

GINGERLY Cautiously.

GIN POLE A portable pole rigged with tackles that is used to handle loads where a boom is not available.

GIPSEY (GYPSY) A drum of a windlass for heaving in a line.

GIRDED A situation in which a tug capsizes due to the strain from a line at an angle of 90 degrees or more, which was not released. Girding is also incorrectly referred to as being caught in irons. Sometimes also referred to as tripping.

GIRDER A continuous member running in a fore and aft direction under the deck for the purpose of supporting the deck beams and deck. The girder is generally supported by widely spaced pillars.

GIRTH Distance around a vessel's frame from gunwale to gunwale. The linear distance from the intersection of the upper deck with the side, around the hull of the vessel to the corresponding point on the opposite side.

GIT *See* Goods In Transit.

GIVE WAY VESSEL A ship that is directed by the Rules to keep out of the way of another vessel.

GLASS Term used by mariners for a barometer.

GLOBAL COVERAGE SYSTEM A category within hyperbolic radio navigation systems that was designed to provide position-fixing information in all areas with the same average accuracy throughout the system. There was only one global hyperbolic system and it has been terminated.

GLOBAL MARINE DISTRESS SAFETY SYSTEM (GMDSS) International agreed radio safety system.

GLOBAL NAVIGATION SATELLITE SYSTEM (GLONASS) The Russian equivalent of the U.S.-operated global positioning system. Designed to function in a similar manner, the system may ultimately use more satellites, resulting in greater accuracy than the Western system.

GLOBAL POSITIONING SYSTEM (GPS) A satellite-based radio navigation system designed to provide continuous worldwide coverage of navigation, position, and timing information to marine-, air-, and land-based users.

GLOBAL SOURCING Willingness to buy anywhere in the world.

GLONASS *See* Global Navigation Satellite System.

GLORY HOLD OR HOLE Space forward or aft used for storage of nondescript material. Also space used for sleeping quarters.

GLOW PLUG: A heater installed in the combustion chamber of some diesel engines to assist in the starting of the engine from cold. The heater is switched off once the engine is running. An igniter for relighting the fuel to a gas turbine in the event of the flame becoming unstable such as under cold conditions.

GLS/GLSS Gearless.

GM Gram. This is a measure of stability related to the tug's draft, loading, and weight distribution and is closely related to the metacenter. Its position indicates the stability or lack of it and it may be figured from tables established for this purpose.

Metacentric height: distance from the center of gravity to the metacenter.

GMDSS *See* Global Marine Distress and Safety System.

GMDSS RADIO MAINTAINER'S LICENSE The accepted certification for a GMDSS radio maintainer (separate from the GMDSS Radio Operator's license). The maintainer is responsible for preventive and corrective maintenance to equipment to ensure it is available in case of emergency.

GMDSS RADIO OPERATOR'S LICENSE The accepted certification for a GMDSS radio operator. This license is approved in the United States by the FCC, which did not permit existing licenses to cover GMDSS requirements. This license is issued separately, by authorized agents, and is not an endorsement attached to existing FCC or U.S. Coast Guard licenses.

GN Grain.

GNCN GenCon General Conditions.

GO Gas Oil. *See also* General Order.

GO ADRIFT Break loose.

GOBLINE (GOBROPE) A line used on many European tugs to regulate the lead of a short towline. One end is usually fastened on deck and the other leg through a shackle or closed fairlead to a gypsy so that its tension can be adjusted. Occasionally, it refers to the hold down arrangement of towing hawsers on ocean tugs.

GO DEVIL A scraping device that is forced through pipelines to ensure that there are no obstructions.

GODOWN In the Far East, a warehouse where goods are stored and delivered.

GOING-CONCERN VALUE The value that a firm has as an entity, as opposed to the sum of the values of each of its parts taken separately, particularly important in determining a reasonable railroad rate.

GONDOLA A railcar with a flat platform and sides three to five feet high, used for top loading long, heavy items.

GONIOMETER A device in the RDF (radio direction finder) receiver that separates the incoming signals by their varying strengths.

GOOD FAITH (INS) A basic principle of insurance. The Assured and his broker must disclose and truly represent every material circumstance to the Underwriter before acceptance of the risk. A breach of good faith entitles the Underwriter to avoid the contract. (Proposed changes in law may affect this definition.)

GOODS Common term indicating moveable property, merchandise, or wares. All materials that are used to satisfy demands. Whole or part of the cargo received from the shipper, including any equipment supplied by the shipper.

GOODS CONTROL CERTIFICATE Document issued by a competent body evidencing the quality of goods described therein, in accordance with national or international standards, or conforming to legislation in the importing country, or as specified in the contract.

GOODS IN TRANSIT (GIT) The goods that have departed from the initial loading point and have not yet arrived at the final unloading point.

GOODS RECEIPT Document issued by a port, warehouse, shed, or terminal operator acknowledging receipt of goods specified therein on conditions stated or referred to in the document.

GOOSENECK A swivel fitting that connects the heel of the boom with the mast table. Also, the front rails of the chassis that raise above the plane of the chassis and engage in the tunnel of a container.

GOOSENECK VENTS Natural vents from double-bottom tanks, equipped with flame screens if fuel tanks, which extend up to the main deck and are curved back towards the deck to avoid sea and rain water from entering.

GOVERNMENT IMPELLED Cargo owned by or subsidized by the federal government.

GOVERNMENT LIGHT A colloquial term applied to an aid to navigation maintained by the Coast Guard.

GOVERNOR The centrifugal governor conical pendulum is one in which the rising of a rotating ball with increase of speed, controls the speed of an engine by operating levers to check the supply of fuel.

GO WELL OVER A term applied in making a crossing; go well over near the shore on the opposite side before turning out to either shape the shore or pass an easy distance off before coming up on the next set of marks.

GP Grain Capacity (cubic capacity in grain).

GPS *See* Global Positioning System.

GPS CONSTELLATION The layout and spacing of the satellites used by the global positioning system.

GPS INFORMATION CENTER (GPSIC) A U.S. Coast Guard center providing information to and that is the point if contact for civil users of the GPS system. Unplanned system outages resulting from system malfunctions or unscheduled maintenance are announced by the GPSIC system as they become known.

GPSIC *See* GPS Information Center.

GR Geographical Rotation (ports of call).

GRAB, HAND A metal bar fastened to a bulkhead, house side, or elsewhere to provide means of steadying a person when the ship rolls or pitches.

GRAB ROPE A line used for steadying oneself. *See also* Man Ropes.

GRABS Large buckets that open like clamshell buckets. Used for handling bulk commodities.

GRACE, DAYS OF A certain number of days allowed by law for payment of due bill.

GRACE PERIOD *See* Grace, Days of.

GRADIENT The difference between each hyperbolic line within a hyperbolic pattern on a chart, represented as a specific distance in nautical miles.

GRADUALLY PULL DOWN To swing slowly to a new course on a mark further downstream.

GRADUALLY PULL DOWN SHORE Used in crossings, when well over gradually swing the vessel's head downstream along the shore.

GRADUALLY PULLING DOWN SHAPE OF BEND Used in crossings, keeping well out until tow is well down then altering the course to follow the shore shape of the bend.

GRAIN CUBIC The maximum space available for cargo measured in cubic feet, the measurements being taken to the inside of the shell plating of the ship or to the outside of the frames and to the top of the beams or underside of deck plating.

GRANDFATHER CLAUSE A provision that enabled motor carriers engaged in lawful trucking operations before the passage of the Motor Carrier Act of 1935 to secure common carrier authority w/o proving public convenience and necessity; a similar provision exists for other modes.

GRAPNEL An implement having from four to six hooks or prongs, usually four arranged in a circular manner around one end of a shank having a ring at its other end. Used as an anchor for small boats, for recovering small articles dropped overboard, to hook on to lines, and for similar purposes; also known as grappling hook; a small anchor with several arms used for dragging.

GRAPPLING IRON Same as grapnel.

GRASS LINE A Manila or fiber rope of any description as distinguished from a wire cable.

GRATING A structure built out of wooden strips or metal bars, to for a walkway above a deck or opening without interference with light, drainage, or ventilation.

GRAVEYARD WATCH The middle watch.

GRAVITATION To let oil flow by itself from one tank to another or to fill the ship with ballast water by use of the Sea Suction without pumps.

GRAVITY *See* API Gravity.

GRD Geared.

GREASE A combination of a petroleum product and a soap, or a mixture of soaps, suitable for certain types of lubrication.

GREAT GUNS A violent wind.

GREEN SEA A large body of water taken aboard.

GRI General Rate Increase. Used to describe an across-the-board tariff rate increase implemented by conference members and applied to base rates. *See also* Group Repetition Interval.

GRID SYSTEMS A location technique using a map or grid, with specific locations marked on the north-south and east-west axes. Its purpose is to find a location that minimizes transportation costs.

GRIPE The sharp forward end of the dished keel on which the stem is fixed. A curved piece of timber joining the forward end of the keel and the lower end of the cutwater. A lashing, chain, or the like used to secure small boats in the chocks and in sea position in the davits.

GROMMET A ring of rope used as an eye or as a gasket. Fiber, usually soaked in red lead or some such substance, and used under the heads and nuts of bolts to secure tightness. A worked eye in canvas.

GROSS REGISTERED TONS (GRT) Total vessel volume in 100 feet equals 1 ton.

GROSS FREIGHT Freight money collected or to be collected without calculating the expenses relating to the running cost of the ship for the voyage undertaken.

GROSS MANIFEST   A manifest containing freight details without any appropriate disbursements.

GROSS TARE WEIGHT   Total weight of a container or chassis or any combination of transportation equipment without weight of cargo.

GROSS TON   2,240 pounds. One ton equals 100 cubic feet. *See also* Short Ton.

GROSS TONNAGE   Applies to vessels, not to cargo. A figure obtained by dividing the total volume of the ship, in cubic feet, by 100, after the omission of all spaces exempted from measurement by law. The entire internal cubic capacity of the ship expressed in tons of 100 cubic feet to the ton, except certain spaces that are exempted, such as: (1) peak and other tanks for water ballast; (2) spaces above the uppermost continuous deck, such as: open forecastle, bridge and poop, certain light and air spaces, domes of skylights, condenser, anchor gear, steering gear, wheel house, galley and cabins for passengers.

GROSS WEIGHT   Entire weight of goods, packaging and freight car or container, ready for shipment. Generally, 80,000 pounds maximum container, cargo and tractor for highway transportation.

GROUND LOCK   *See* Auto Drift.

GROUND SEGMENT   Portion of the COSPAS- SARSAT system composed of local user terminals and mission control centers.

GROUND TACKLE   Used for all anchors, cables, ropes, etc., used in anchoring a ship to the bottom.

GROUND WAVES   Waves that travel parallel to the earth's surface due to the refractory tendency of RF energy in the atmosphere.

GROUND WAYS   Timbers fixed to the ground and extending fore and aft under the hull on each side of the keel, to form a broad surface track on which the ship is end launched.

GROUNDING   Running ashore.

GROUP REPETITION INTERVAL (GRI)   Used in the Loran system, the amount of time it takes for a chain to broadcast all of its signals in sequence from the beginning of the first pulse of the master to the beginning of the first pulse of the master station transmission in the next cycle. Group repetition intervals are established between 40,000 and 99,000 microseconds.

GROUPAGE   A consolidation service, putting small shipments into containers for shipment.

GROUPAGE AGENT   One who consolidates LCL consignments to offer to a carrier as an FCL.

GROUPEUR   *See* Groupage Agent.

GRT   Gross Registered Tonnage.

GSB   Good Safe Berth.

GSP   Good Safe Port.

GT   Gross ton (2,240 pounds).

GTDI   European Guidelines for Trade Data Interchange.

GTEE Guarantee.

GUARANTEED FREIGHT Freight payable whether the goods are delivered or not, provided the failure to deliver the goods resulted from causes beyond the carrier's control.

GUARANTEED LOANS The federal government cosigned and guaranteed repayment of loans made to railroads.

GUARANTEED RENEWABLE POLICY (INS) A policy that the insured has the right to continue in force by the timely payment of premiums to a specified age, (usually age 50) during which period the insurer has no right to make unilaterally any change in any provision of the policy while the policy is in force but make changes in premium rates for the entire policyholder classification. *See also* Noncancelable Policy.

GUARD WALL River wall of a lock that prevents boats from being drawn into the dam.

GUARD ZONE ARPA targets that pass through the outer guard zone are automatically plotted; those that are not displayed until inside the outer guard zones, are intended to be auto acquired at the inner guard zone.

GUDGEONS Lugs cast or forged on the sternpost for the purpose of hanging and hinging the rudder. Each is bored to form a bearing for a rudder pintle and is usually bushed with lignum vitae or white bearing metal.

GUI Graphical User Interface.

GUIDE WALL The extension of the inner lock wall on the upper and lower side of the lock chamber to assist navigators in guiding vessels or tows into the lock chamber. It is usually 600 feet in length although some are now 1,200 feet long.

GUM Resin like, naphtha insoluble deposits formed by the oxidation and polymerization of certain petroleum products, particularly gasoline.

GUNWALE The upper edge of a side of a vessel or boat designed to prevent items from being washed overboard. The upper edge of the side of an open boat. Pronounced Gun' el.

GUNWALE BAR Angle bar that connects deck stringer plate and shell plates at weather deck.

GUSSET PLATE Triangular plate that connects members or braces.

GUTTER LEDGE A bar laid across a hatchway to support the hatch cover.

GUY Wire or hemp ropes or chains to support booms, davit, etc., laterally, employed in pairs. Guys to booms that carry sails are also known as back ropes.

GUY, AMIDSHIP A single guy secured to the heads of two booms to swing them both inboard.

GUY, INBOARD A guy that pulls a boom inboard.

GUY, LAZY A guy with little or no strain.

GUY, OUTBOARD A guy that pulls the boom outboard.

GUY, PENDANT The rope or wire attached to the guy block and the link band of the boom. Used to save rope.

GUY, SCHOONER   Same as amidship guy. Another name for it.

GVW   Gross Vehicle Weight. The combined total weight of a vehicle and its container, inclusive of prime mover.

GYPSY   A small auxiliary drum usually fitted on one or both ends of a winch or windlass. The usual method of hauling in or slacking off on ropes with the aid of a gypsy is to take one or more turns with the bight of the rope around the drum and to take in or pay out the slack of the free end.

GYPSY HEAD   A cylinder-like fitting on the end of winch or windlass shafts. Fiber line or wire rope is hauled or slacked by winding a few turns around it; the free end being held taunt manually as it rotates.

GYRO   Anything that spins rapidly enough to render stability of motion.

GYROCOMPASS   An electromechanical compass that uses the properties of gyroscopic inertia, precession, gravity, and the rotation of the earth to line up with the geographical meridians of the earth and assist the mariner in discerning true north.

GYROPILOT   *See* Automatic Steering System.

GYROREPEATER   An element within the repeater system for the master gyrocompass, designed to give indication of ship's heading.

GYROSCOPIC INERTIA   The property that causes a gyro to remain in the same plane of rotation or rigidity in space. It causes the spinning element of the object to remain stale and in its initial lane of rotation.

GZ   Righting arm or lever. Distance between lines of force through G and B.

H

HABITAT CREATION A form of environmental mitigation in which natural resources such as soils, plants, and water flow are installed for the purpose of increasing the amount of wildlife and environmental values produced.

HABITAT SUITABILITY INDEX The ratio of existing habitat conditions in a study area to the optimal habitat conditions of the area where "habitat conditions" is the capacity of the habitat environment to support indicator species.

HABITAT UNITS A value derived from multiplying the habitat suitability index for an evaluation species by the size of the study area. The habitat unit provides a standardized basis for comparing habitat changes over time and space.

HAGUE PROTOCOL Amendment of the Warsaw Convention at The Hague, September 28, 1955 (air cargo).

HAGUE RULES, THE A multilateral maritime treaty among adopted 1921 (at The Hague, Netherlands). Standardizes liability of an international carrier under the Ocean B/L. Establishes a legal "floor" for B/L. *See* COGSA.

HAGUE VISBY RULES A set of rules, amending the Hague Rules published in 1968 and subsequently given the force of law by many maritime nations.

HAIL To address a vessel to come from, as to hail from some port.

HALF-BREADTH PLAN A plan or top view of one half of a ship divided by the middle vertical plane. It shows the waterlines, cross section lines, bow and buttock lines, and diagonal lines of the ship's form projected on the horizontal base plane of the ship.

HALF-HEIGHT Identical to the open top, but with 4' 3" ends and not the standard 8' 6". Suitable for the carriage of heavy cargo as the box weight is considerably less, 20' only.

HALF-MAST The position of a flag when hoisted half way.

HALF MODEL A model of one half of a ship divided along the middle vertical plane.

HALF POWER POINTS Predetermined points along the radar beam where power has decreased by 50 percent.

HALF WAVE ANTENNA The most fundamental antenna type, where the total length of the antenna is equal to half of the wavelength of the transmitted frequency.

HALF WAVE DIPOLE ANTENNA A common variation of the whip antenna that, when mounted over earth, is bidirectional and radiates equally well in both horizontal directions perpendicular to it. In order for a half wave dipole to take on unidirectional characteristics, it needs additional elements. It has excellent directive capabilities and is very efficient when placed at least a half wavelength above the ground.

HALYARDS   Ropes used for hoisting gaffs and sails. Also light lines used in hoisting signals, flags.

HAMBURG RULES   Rules governing the rights and responsibilities of carrier and cargo interests that may be incorporated into a contract for the carriage of goods by sea either by agreement of the parties or statutorily. These rules were adopted by the United National Convention on the Carriage of Goods by Sea in 1978.

HAMMOCK   A sailor's bed made of canvas and swung at each end to the deck beams.

HAMMOCK NETTINGS   The bins for stowage of hammocks.

HAMPER, TOP HAMPER   Articles of outfit, especially spars, rigging, etc., above the deck that while ordinarily indispensable, may become in certain emergencies both a source of danger and an inconvenience.

HAMPERED VESSEL   A vessel restricted in her ability to maneuver by the nature of her work.

HAND   A member of the ship's company; to furl a sail.

HAND-BILLY   A light, handy tackle for general work about the deck. Also called a jigger.

HAND LEAD   A lead of from 7 to 14 pounds, used with the hand lead line for ascertaining the depth of water in entering or leaving port.

HANDLING   Loading, discharging, or transferring bulk cargo, package cargo or ballast.

HANDLING INSTRUCTIONS   Indication how cargo is to be handled.

HANDLING SERVICE   Service concerning the physical handling of cargo.

HAND RAIL   A steadying rail of a ladder.

HAND ROPE   Same as Grab Rope.

HANDSOMELY   Carefully, not necessarily slow.

HAND TAUT   As tight as can be pulled by hand.

HANDY LINE   A small line used to throw between separated barges or boat and shore, i.e., heaving line.

HARBOR   An area of water affording a natural or artificial haven for ships. A harbor is a port only when used for cargo transfer or other business between ship and shore.

HARBOR DUES   Various local charges against all seagoing vessels entering a harbor to cover maintenance of channel depths, buoys, lights, etc. All harbors do not necessarily have this charge.

HARBORFRONT   That part of a city's downtown waterfront that faces the main commercial harbor; often synonymous with "central waterfront."

HARBOR MAINTENANCE TAX (HMT)   Payment of the HMT is mandated by the Water Resources Development Act of 1986. It's assessed at 0.125 percent ad valorem, which translates to $1.25 per each $1,000.00 of cargo value. HMT monies are used by the U.S. Army Corps of Engineers to improve and maintain U.S. ports and harbors.

HARBOR MASTER   An officer who attends to the berthing, etc., of ships in a harbor.

HARD AGROUND   A vessel that has gone aground and is incapable of refloating under her own power.

HARD COPY   Computer output printed on paper.

HARDNESS   Property of a metal that enables it to resist plastic deformation.

HARD OVER   Full rudder in either direction.

HARD PATCH   A plate riveted over another plate to cover a hole or break.

HARD RIGGING   When wire slings, chain, and ratchets are used for making up a tow.

HARMONIZED SYSTEM OF CODES (HS)   An international goods classification system for describing cargo in international trade under a single commodity-coding scheme. Developed under the auspices of the Customs Cooperations Council (CCC), an international Customs organization in Brussels, this code is a hierarchically structured product nomenclature containing approximately 5,000 headings and subheadings. It is organized into 99 chapters arranged in 22 sections. Sections encompass an industry (e.g.: Section XI, Textiles and Textile Articles); chapters encompass the various materials and products of the industry (e.g.: Chapter 50, Silk) The basic code contains four digit headings and six digit subheadings. Many countries add digits for Customs tariff and statistical purposes. In the United States duty rates will be the eight digit level; statistical suffixes will be at the tenth.

HARPINGS; HARPINS   The fore parts of the wales of a vessel that encompass her bows and are fastened to the stem, thickened to withstand plunging. The ribbands bent around a vessel under construction to which the cant frames are temporarily secured to hold them in their proper position.

HARTER ACT   A law passed by Congress in 1893. The Harter Act provides that a vessel owner is not responsible for loss or damage caused by faults or errors in navigation, provided the ship owner has taken proper care to see that his/her ship is in all respects seaworthy and properly manned and equipped.

HASH MARK   A slang expression for a diagonal strip on an enlisted man's sleeve to denote a previous enlistment.

HATCH   A large opening in the main deck of a ship, covered by mechanical means, to which cargo is loaded and discharged from below deck.

HATCH, BOOBY   An access hatchway leading from the weather deck to the quarters. A small companionway that is readily removable in one piece. A wooden, hood-like covering for a hatchway, fitted with a sliding top.

HATCH BAR   Flat bars used for securing and locking hatch covers. A bar over the hatch for rigging a tackle.

HATCH BATTENS   Flat bars used to fasten and make tight the edges of the tarpaulins that are placed over hatches. The batten and the edge of the tarpaulin are wedged tightly in closely spaced cleats.

HATCH BEAM   Portable beam across the hatch to support covers; also, strong beam at ends of hatch.

HATCH CARRIER   The supports that are attached to the inside of the coaming to take the ends of the hatch beams.

HATCH CLEATS   Clips attached to the outside of the hatch coaming for the purpose of holding the hatch battens and wedges that fasten the edges of the tarpaulin covers.

HATCH COVERS   Boards fitted to rest on top of hatch beams to cover the hatch opening. Also called hatch boards or fore and afters. These covers are often powered by hydraulic of electrical motors. Pontoon hatch covers are large hollow metal covers, and only a few are needed to cover an entire hatch.

HATCH LIST   A list showing the various commodities and quality of cargo stowed in one particular hatch.

HATCH RESTS   Shelf fitted inside and just below the top of the coaming for the purpose of supporting the hatch covers.

HATCH TENDER   Signalman; a person stationed at the top of a hatch to supervise raising or lowering drafts.

HATCHWAY   Opening in the deck of a vessel through which cargo is loaded into, or discharged from the hold and is closed by means of a hatch cover.

HATCHWAY TRUNK   Space between a lower deck hatchway and the hatchway or hatchways immediately above it when enclosed by a casing. A trunk may be either watertight or nonwatertight.

HATCH WEDGES   Small wedges of wood or steel. Driven between cleats and battens to secure tarps.

HATCH WHIPS   Runner, cargo fall; the runner on the boom spotted over the hatch running to the winch.

HAUL   To pull; a change of wind in the direction of the hands of a clock.

HAULAGE   The inland transport service that is offered by the carrier under the terms and conditions of the tariff and of the relative transport document.

HAUL DISTANCE   The one-way distance the hopper dredge must travel to a disposal area after filling its hopper at the dredging site.

HAULIER   Road carrier.

HAULING PART   The part of the rope making up a tackle, which is hauled upon. Part made fast is the standing part.

HAWAIIAN CARRIER   A for-hire air carrier that operates within the state of Hawaii.

HAWB   House Airway Bill of Lading.

HAWSE   The horizontal distance between the stem of a vessel at anchor and a point in the water directly over her anchor.

HAWSE BAG   A conical-shaped canvas bag, stuffed with sawdust, oakum, or similar material and fitted with a lanyard at apex and base, used for closing the hawse pipes around the chain to prevent shipping water through the pipes; also called a "jackass," "hawse plug," or "hawse block."

HAWSE BOLSTER   A timber or metal bossing at the ends of a hawse pipe to ease the cable over the edges and to take the wear.

HAWSE BUCKLER   An iron plate covering a hawse pipe.

HAWSE HOLE   A hole in the bow through which a cable or chain passes.

HAWSE PIPE   Casting extending through deck and side of ship for passage of anchor chain and for stowage of anchor in most cases.

HAWSER   A large rope, 5 inches or more in circumference, used for heavy work such as towing other vessels. When used for securing a vessel to a pier, it is called a mooring line.

HAWSER BOARD   A wooden, steel, or aluminum plate or beam placed under the tug's hawser to prevent chafing on the stern rail when towing at sea.

HAZARD (INS)   A specific situation that increases the probability of the occurrence of loss arising from a peril, or that may influence the extent of the loss. For example, accident, sickness, fire, flood, liability, explosion are perils. Slippery floors, unsanitary conditions, shingled roofs, congested traffic, unguarded premises, and uninspected boilers are hazards.

HAZARDOUS AREA   A hazardous area is one in which an explosive (flammable) atmosphere may be present continuously or intermittently in sufficient concentrations to create a dangerous (flammable and/or toxic) atmosphere.

HAZARDOUS MATERIALS   Cargo or goods deemed dangerous because of their nature, such as caustic substances, radioactive materials, explosives, and combustibles.

HAZMAT   An industry abbreviation for "Hazardous Material."

HBF   Harmless Bulk Fertilizer.

H/C   *See* High Cube.

HDLTSBENDS   Half Despatch Lay Time Saved Both Ends.

HDWTS   Half Despatch Working (or Weather) Time Saved.

HEAD   The ship's toilet, so named because of its origins of being located in the bow or head of a ship, so as to keep the odor downwind. The upper edge of a quadrilateral sail.

HEAD AND TAIL   When two vessels are side by side with their bows and sterns in opposite directions.

HEADBOARD   The end wall of a vehicle's platform body.

HEAD CURRENT   When tug or tow are heading into the current. Also known as bucking the current.

HEADER   Longshoreman who works in a hold and at the same time directs several others. Another name for the valve at the cargo manifold.

HEADER BOARD   *See* Bulkhead (road cargo).

HEADER TANK   Container connected to an engine cooling system, generally at the highest point, partly filled with water. The air or other gas above the water allows for expansion and contraction due to temperature change and may be vented to atmosphere or allowed to reach a higher pressure limited by a relief valve.

HEADING   The direction in which the bow of a vessel is pointing. Expressed as an angular distance from north. Used only in connection with ARPA performance standards.

HEADING UP   An unstabilized display that will always be available on relative motion radars since the unit is acting independently of all other sources, notwithstanding electricity.

HEAD LEDGE   Forward or after end coaming of a hatch, more frequently used in connection with wood coamings.

HEADLINE   Mooring line used in combination to hold fleet or barge "in."

HEAD LINES   Mooring lines running from the bow at 45 degree angles from the centerline, AKA bow lines.

HEAD LOG   The heavily reinforced section at each end of the barges and at the bow of the towboat to take the pressure of pushing the entire tow.

HEADMARK   Identifying mark placed on a package by the shipper.

HEAD OF A SHIP   The fore end of a ship, which was formerly fitted up for the accommodation of the crew. A term applied to a toilet on board of a ship. A ship is trimmed by the head when drawing more water forward and less aft than contemplated in her design.

HEAD OF BEND   The top or upstream beginning of a bend.

HEAD ON LANDING   The bow of the boat only is made fast.

HEAD REACH   The distance a vessel will run before she is stopped in the water after the telegraph has been rung to "stop."

HEADROOM   The height of the decks, below deck.

HEADWAY   A vessel's motion forward or ahead.

HEART   The inside center strand of a rope.

HEAT   A factor caused by resistance within an electrical component.

HEAT EXCHANGER   A unit for cooling engine lube oil and steam drains, etc., the cooling medium being sea, fresh or feed water. To avoid the deposition of salt in marine engines, the direct seawater cooling temperature should not exceed 57°C. A better procedure is to use a closed circuit with freshwater in association with a heat exchanger to transfer the heat to the seawater. By this method corrosion difficulties are avoided.

HEATED CONTAINER   Thermal container served by a heat producing appliance.

HEAVE   To throw. The rise and fall of a vessel in a seaway.

HEAVE AROUND   To revolve the drum of a capstan, winch, or windlass.

HEAVE AWAY   An order to haul away or to heave around a capstan.

HEAVE IN   To haul in; to pull by hand or power any line, wire, or cable.

HEAVE SHORT   To heave in until the vessel is riding nearly over anchor.

HEAVE TAUT   To haul in until the line has a strain upon it.

HEAVE THE LEAD   The operation of taking a sounding with hand lead.

HEAVE THE LOG   The operation of taking speed measurement by use of the ship log.

HEAVE TO   To bring a vessel's head to the wind or sea and hold her there by the use of sails or engines. To hold a vessel or tow heading into the wind and sea at very slow speed and still maintain control while minimizing the effect during rough weather or during other conditions that may prevent progress on a desired course.

HEAVING LINE   A small line secured to a hawser and thrown to an approaching vessel or to a dock, usually to allow a larger line to be hauled over to a ship, dock, or tug.

HEAVY DUTY OILS   Lubricating oils that were originally developed for use in certain types of high-speed diesel engines and spark ignition engines subject to high piston and crankcase temperatures. They combine the properties of detergency, resistance to oxidation, and relative freedom from corrosive action on alloy-type bearings. Normally they contain special additives, which confer these properties.

HEAVY ENDS   Oils where the distillation range is of importance, meaning the highest boiling portion present. The maximum or end point as obtained in the 100-milliliter distillation of a sample of gasoline is determined largely by the amount and character of the heavy ends present in the gasoline.

HEAVY LIFT   Single commodities exceeding normal loading equipment design capacities and requiring special equipment or rigging techniques for handling containers exceeding the average design.

HEAVY LIFT CHARGE   A charge made for lifting articles too heavy to be lifted by a ship's tackle.

HEAVY-LIFT VESSEL   A vessel specially designed and equipped for the carriage of heavy cargo.

HEDGING   Buying or selling earlier and more than really needed in order to protect the company against price increases or shortages of commodities or components to realize profits when prices fluctuate.

HEEL   A small amount of liquid left in a tank; a transverse angle of inclination of a vessel. The convex intersecting point or corner of the web and flange of a bar. The inclination of a ship to one side, caused by wind or wave action or by shifting weights onboard.

HEELING   Tipping of a vessel to one side; also called listing.

HEEL PIECE, HEEL BAR   A bar that serves as a connecting piece between two bars that butt end to end. The flange of the heel bar is reversed from those of the bars it connects.

HEIGHT   Height of highest point of vessel's structure above waterline, e.g., radar, funnel, cranes, masthead.

HELD COVERED (INS)   A provisional acceptance of risk, subject to confirmation at a later date that the agreed cover is needed. Where applicable to an existing insurance, cover is conditional, in practice, on prompt advice to the Underwriter as soon as the Assured is aware of the circumstances to be held covered coming into effect, and a reasonable additional premium is payable if the risk held covered comes into effect.

HELM   Designate the rudder's position as controlled by the tiller, wheel, or steering gear. To "port the helm" means to put the tiller to port, the vessel's head and the rudder both turning the opposite way, or to starboard.

HEP (HABITAT EVALUATION PROCEDURE)   A standardized procedure for conducting environmental impact assessments that was developed by the U.S. Fish and Wildlife Service. Using this procedure, the project site and mitigation site can be compared by the determining respective habitat value.

HERE SHE COMES   When another boat appears around a bend.

HERTZ   One cycle per second.

HETEROGENEOUS CARGO   Cargo of a varied nature; general cargo.

HEURISTIC   The process of solving problems by evaluating each step in the process, searching for satisfactory solutions rather than optimal solutions. It comprises a form of problem solving where the results are determined by experience or intuition instead of by optimization.

HF   *See* High Frequency.

H/H   House to House (same as CY/CY); Hold Harmless.

HH/GOODS   Household Goods.

HHD   Hogshead.

HHDW   Handy Heave Dead Weight (scrap).

HHGPE   Household Goods & Personal Effects.

HIGH   An anticyclone, a weather pattern in which isobars at the center of the pattern are higher than those farther from the center. Winds are clockwise in the Northern Hemisphere.

HIGH CAP   Tarpaulin for unit where cargo is above a height, used with RO/RO vessels.

HIGH CUBE   Any container that exceeds 8'6" (102") in height. Usually refers to a container, which is 9'6" in height.

HIGH DENSITY COMPRESSION   Compression of a flat or standard bale of cotton to approximately 32 pounds per cubic foot. Usually applies to cotton exported or shipped coastwise.

HIGH FREQUENCY (HF)   The range in the electromagnetic spectrum (3 to 30MHz) where shortwave broadcast and single sideband ship-to-shore communications occur. Many nations broadcast radio time signals, or time ticks, in this range, as well as shortwave programming

HIGH PASS FILTER   A type of filter that allows all frequencies above a certain specified frequency to pass through into an electrical system.

HIGH WATER STATION   The location to which lights or buoys are moved when the river is at or near flood stage. The purpose being (1) to guide navigation in the high water and (2) to locate the light in a position of security against loss.

HIGHWAY TRUST FUND   Federal highway use tax revenues are paid into this fund and the federal government's share of the highway construction is paid from the fund.

HIGHWAY USE TAX   Taxes assessed by federal and state governments against users of the highway (the fuel tax is an example). The use tax money is used to pay for the construction, maintenance, and policing of highways.

HIJACKING   Theft that typically involves stealing both the transport vehicle and the cargo inside it.

HINTERLAND   The area served by a tributary to a port, where a port's exports are produced and its imports are marketed.

HIRED AUTOMOBILE (INS)   Autos the insured leases, hires, rents, or borrows but not autos owned by employees or members of their households.

HIT   A term meaning the ARPA has not stopped the tracking of the contact due to poor return or inconsistent display.

HITCH   Method of securing a line to a hook, ring, spar on another line.

HITCHMENT   The marrying of two or more portions of one shipment that originate at different locations, moving under one bill of lading, from one shipper to one consignee. Authority for this service must be granted by tariff publication. *See* Bill of Lading.

HITCHMENT CARGO   An amount of goods that is added to an original consignment as the owner and the destination are the same as those of the original consignment

HM   Hazardous Materials. *See* Hazardous Materials.

HMS   Heavy Metal Scraps.

HMT   Harbor Maintenance Tax.

HO   *See* Hold.

HOG   The upward deflection of a vessel's midbody above its bow and stern caused by excessive loading fore and aft; when the mean draft is deeper than the midship draft. A scrub broom for scraping a ship's bottom underwater.

HOG FRAME   A fore and aft frame, forming a truss for the main frames of a vessel to prevent bending.

HOGGED   Loading condition of a vessel in such a way that the center of the vessel is slightly raised (arched in the center).

HOGGING   Straining of the ship that tends to make the bow and stern lower than the middle portion.

HOG SHEER   The sheer curve of the deck on a vessel, constructed so that the middle is higher than the ends.

HOIST   To raise or elevate by manpower or by the employment of mechanical appliances; any device employed for lifting weights.

HOIST AWAY   An order to haul up.

HOISTING ROPE   Special flexible wire rope for lifting purposes, generally being of six strands with 19 wires in each strand and in most cases having a hemp rope at the center.

HOLD   The spaces below deck allotted for the storage of cargo; the lowermost cargo compartments.

HOLD BEAMS   Beams in a hold, similar to deck beams, but having no plating or planking on them.

HOLD DOWN   Shackle or hook used to hold towline close to the deck at the after rail. In this way, a turning vessel will not move the towline off center and cause the vessel to trip.

HOLD HARMLESS AGREEMENT (INS)   A contractual arrangement whereby one party assumes the liability inherent in a situation, thereby relieving the other party of responsibility. Such agreements are typically found in contracts like leases. A typical lease may provide that the lessee must "hold harmless" the lessor for any liability from accidents arising out of the premises.

HOLD OPEN   Hold below or above an object (i.e., wide of the mark) being steered on, depending on direction. Upstream tows normally hold above; downstream tows normally hold below the object.

HOLDING MARK   An object, usually an aid to navigation, on which the pilot of a tow will steer.

HOLDING ON   To steer steadily on a mark or object.

HOLIDAY   An imperfection; spots left unfinished.

HOLYSTONE   A large flat stone used to clean and whiten a vessel's wooden decks.

HOME   To tune a signal and allow the bearing to be used as the vessel's course. Also, to the limit; an anchor comes home when it fails to hold and is dragged towards the vessel; close up; snugly in place.

HOME PORT   The port of registration of a vessel.

HOMOGENEOUS CARGO   Cargo of the same density throughout.

HOOD   A covering of wood or canvas over a hatch, companionway or skylight.

HOODING END   The end most plate of a complete strake. The hooding ends fit into the stem or sternpost.

HOODS   A term applied to those plates placed at the extreme forward or after ends of a ship.

HOOK HER UP!   Used by captains and pilots as an order to go full speed.

HOOKING UP   An expression used in referring to connecting up to a tow.

HOOKS

Bale Hook: A hook something like an ice tong, used in handling bales.

Barrel or Cant Hook: Used in pairs to grip the ends of a drum or cask when hoisting. Also called chime hook.

Box Hook: A pair of pronged hooks clamped on opposite sides of a box and drawn together by the rope that lifts the box.

Bridle Hook: A type of hook used in connection with wire rope bridles to secure a grip on the cargo.

Burton Hook: A hook used to connect one cargo fall with another in one of the methods of cargo handling.

Cargo Hook: The general name for hooks used to hoist cargo.

Lip or Safety Hook: A cargo hook used for added safety.

Liverpool or New York Hook: A cargo hook with a single swivel.

Longshoreman's Hand Hook or Cotton Hook: The hook carried by most longshoremen to facilitate the handling of boxes, bales, etc.

Pelican Hook: A quick releasing hook device.

Plate Hook: A hook used in pairs to grip and lift metal plates. The weight of the plate causes the hook to grip tightly.

Portland Hook: A cargo hook with no swivel.

Seattle Hook: A cargo hook on a swivel, mounted on a ring, which in turn is suspended by two swivels.

Sister Hook: A hook made in two parts, set facing each other in such a manner that when combined they form a link.

Western or West Coast Hook: A cargo hook set on a ring, which is suspended by two swivels.

Wire Sling or Pedro Hook: A simple form of hook used to secure a wire rope sling to a draft of cargo, such as a box.

HOOK TO HOOK   Given that this is a notional point in chartering terms, this is best described as the shipper/receiver arranging for delivery/receival of cargo to/from directly under ships hook and the ship paying for the labor to stow the cargo in the vessels' cargo holds, as well as onboard lashing and securing and provision of dunnage materials, and to discharge again over the ship's side. Shore-based stevedoring aspects remain the responsibility of the shipper/receiver; however, there are some owners who may incorporate these costs into their LTHH rate. Once again, ask owners to clearly define this aspect. Wharfage charges/dues/taxes can be a contentious issue but are usually considered to be for the shippers/receivers account, and there may also be many other statutory levies on cargo or freight that may apply. Many shippers/receivers are unaware of these additional costs and do not include them into their costing and consequently may be left with an unexpected considerable expense at the completion of a project.

HOP   The bouncing back of a sky wave.

HOPPER   A temporary container for bulk material, shaped like a funnel, but with four flat, tapered sides arranged like an inverted truncated pyramid, with the large end up and generally open, and the small end down and generally closed by a gate or valve.

HOPPER BARGE   One of the most basic and versatile of barge types, consisting of a simple double skinned, open top box with the inner hull shell forming a long hopper or cargo hold. A variant of the open hopper barge is a covered hopper barge with rolling weathertight hatch covers.

HOPPER CAPACITY   The maximum volume of the hoppers of a hopper dredge.

HOPPER CAR Railcar that permits top loading and bottom unloading of bulk commodities; some hopper cars have permanent tops with hatches to provide protection against the elements.

HOPPER OVERFLOW Overfilling of hoppers to remove excess water and suspended sediments to increase total hopper sediment concentration and thus increase the effective capacity of the dredge.

HOPPER PUMPOUT Alternative to bottom gravity disposal from hopper dredges; ability designed into all Federal hopper dredges for direct pump out from the hopper for the purposes of beach nourishment when such use of dredged material is needed or for direct disposal into a confined disposal facility.

HORIZONTAL BEAM WIDTH The angular distance, parallel to the earth's surface, of a radar beam. It is relatively narrow, measuring between 0.65 and 2 degrees.

HORIZONTAL POSITIONING Line of site triangulation with defined shore stations to provide accurate position of the dredging or disposal activity. Available technology includes Loran and microwave transmitters.

HORIZONTAL WHIP ANTENNA The most commonly used antenna by radio-telegraph aboard ship. Horizontal receiving antennas work best with horizontal transmitting antennas.

HORNING Setting the frames of a vessel square to the keel after the proper inclination to the vertical due to the declivity of the keel has been given.

HORSE LATITUDES The latitudes on the outer margins of the trades where the prevailing winds are light and variable.

HORSESHOE PLATE Small horseshoe-shaped plate around rudderstock on shell of ship for the purpose of preventing water from backing up into the rudder trunk.

HORSE TIMBER The after longitudinal strength member (often called counter timer) fastening the shaft log or keel and the transom knee together. A small boat term.

HORSING (In naval architecture). Calking planking with oakum with a large maul or beetle and a wedge-shaped iron.

HOSTLER/HUSTLER A tractor, usually unlicensed, for moving containers within a yard. An employee who drives a tractor for the purpose of moving cargo within a container yard.

HOT WORK Work involving flames or temperatures likely to be sufficiently high to cause ignition of flammable gas. This includes any work involving the use of welding, burning or soldering equipment, blow torches, some power-driven tools, nonexplosion proof portable electrical equipment, sand blasting and equipment with internal and external combustion engines, and like fire producing operations.

HOT WORK PERMIT A document issued by an authorized person permitting specific work for a specified time to be done in a defined area employing tools and equipment that could cause ignition of flammable gas. *See* Hot Work.

HOURGLASS EFFECT   An expansion or constriction near the center of the radar screen because of time base problems. It can be detected in narrow rivers or canals.

HOUSE   The upper structure of a vessel accommodating passengers and crews. To stow or secure in a safe place; a topmast is housed by lowering it and securing it to a lower mast; an awning is housed by hauling the stops down and securing them to the rail.

HOUSE AIRWAY BILL   A bill of lading issued by a forwarder to a shipper as a receipt for goods that the forwarder will consolidate with cargo from other shippers for transport.

HOUSEFALL   The system of cargo handling whereby a fall is passed through a block attached high on a pier structure and used in conjunction with the fall from a boom spotted over the ship's hatch. The fall passing through the block may lead either to the winch on the ship or to a winch on the pier.

HOUSE FLAG   The distinguishing flag of a merchant marine company flown on the mainmast of merchant ships.

HOUSEMAST   The structure on the pier to which a block is attached when using the housefall system.

HOUSE TO HOUSE   *See* Door to Door.

HOUSE TO PIER   Cargo loaded into a container by the shipper under shipper's supervision. When the cargo is exported, it is unloaded at the foreign pier destination.

HOUSING   Enclosure partially or wholly worked around fittings or equipment. That portion of the mast below the surface of the weather deck. Applied to topmasts, that portion overlapping the mast below.

HOVERCRAFT   A specialty ship of high power, skirt, blowers and above-water propellers that rides on a pillow of air. Known technically as a nondisplacement vessel, when operating they no longer float in the water. Special reference to these vessels is made in the Rules of the Road. An air cushion vessel that lifts up and travels just above the water at high speeds.

H/P   House to Pier (same as CY/CFS).

HT   Height.

HUB   The central transshipment point in a transport structure, serving a number of consignees and/or consignors by means of spokes. The stretches between hubs mutually are referred to as trunks.

HUB AND SPOKE   A carrier's route system with many routes (spokes) radiating out from a single center (hub).

HUCKEPACK CARRIAGE.   *See* Piggyback.

HUG   To keep close.

HULK   A worn out and stopped vessel.

HULL The portion of the ship that lies below the main deck, inclusive of structural members of shell plating. The body of a ship, together with all decks, including shell plating, framing, decks, and bulkheads but exclusive of masts, yards, rigging, and all outfit or equipment.

HULL DOWN Said of a vessel when due to its distance only the spurs are visible.

HULL INSPECTOR Any large piece of drift or submerged piling, log, rock, etc.

HUM A common type of equipment noise caused by antenna lines picking up the magnetic fields of power lines when they are located too close to each other.

HUMPING The process of connecting a moving railcar with a motionless railcar within a rail classification yard in order to make up a train. The cars move by gravity from an incline or "hump" onto the appropriate track.

HUNDREDWEIGHT (CWT) The pricing unit used in transportation; a hundredweight is equal to 100 pounds.

HURDLE A colloquial term for a dike.

HURRICANE Severe tropical cyclone with winds higher than 65 knots. Winds are counterclockwise in the Northern Hemisphere and have been estimated at over 200 knots in the severest of hurricanes.

HUSBANDING Taking care of a vessel's noncargo-related operations as instructed by the master or owner of such vessel.

HUSTLER *See* Yard Tractor.

HW High Water.

HYDRAULIC FLUID Fluids, which may be of petroleum or nonpetroleum origin intended for use in hydraulic systems. Low viscosity, low rate of change of viscosity with temperature, and low pour point are desirable characteristics.

HYDROCARBON Any of the compounds made up exclusively of hydrogen and carbon in various ratios.

HYDRODYNAMIC A measurement of the velocity of the flow of water.

HYDROFAC In oil well drilling, a method developed to create highly permeable flow channels through the formation radiating out from the well bore.

HYDROFOIL A specialty ship of high power and below surface foils (wings) that lift the vessel out of the water upon the application of power. Mistakenly confused with hovercraft, the hydrofoil is not an air cushion vessel. A wing-like structure that lifts and carries a watercraft just above the water at high speed.

HYDROFORMING A special catalytic reforming process employed for upgrading straight run gasolines.

HYDROGENATION The process of adding hydrogen to the hydrocarbon molecule.

HYDROGRAPHIC A measurement of the velocity of the flow of water.

HYDROLYSIS The decomposition of a compound by water into two parts, one part then combining with the hydrogen ion from the water and the other part with the hydroxyl ion.

HYDROMETER An instrument for determining the specific gravity of a liquid.

HYDROPHOBIC Image areas of the plate are on the same geometric plane. The image area is oil receptive (hydrophobic) the nonimage area is water receptive (hydrophilic).

HYDROSONIC Systems designed to generate sound waves that are directed through the water medium and reflected off the seabed to provide required information, such as water depth or speed over ground.

HYDROSTATIC CURVES Curves based on the form of the immersed portions of a vessel. They include: coefficients of fineness, TPI, displacement in salt and freshwater, MT1, height of B and M above the keel, increase of displacement for one foot trim by the stern.

HYDROSTATIC HEAD That portion of existing pressure at a point that is attributable to the weight of the superimposed column of fluid.

HYDROUS Containing water chemically combined, as in hydrates or hydroxide.

HYDROXIDE A compound consisting of an element and the radical or ion, OH, as sodium hydroxide (NaOH).

HYGROSCOPIC TENDENCY The readiness of a substance to absorb moisture from the air.

HYPERBOLA The locus of all points in a flat plane that have a constant difference of distance from two fixed points.

HYPERBOLIC RADIONAVIGATION SYSTEM An electronic navigation system created by establishing a specific hyperbolic radio pattern over a geographical area. This pattern is established through a series of mathematical calculations that define the exact coordinates of each point. To use this as a navigation system, transmitting antennas are placed at separate points and broadcast signals in a specific sequence on a specific time base. The system receiver can measure the difference in time or the variance in the phase of the two received signals. This information is used to determine where the vessel is within the hyperbolic pattern.

I

I　Symbol for moment of inertia.

I/A　Independent Action. The right of a conference member to publish a rate of tariff rule that departs from the agreement's common rate or rule.

IACS　*See* International Association of Classification Societies.

IALA　International Association of Lighthouse Authorities.

IATA　*See* International Air Transport Association.

IATA CARGO AGENT　An agent approved by IATA and registered in the IATA Cargo Agency List. This enables the agent, upon authorization of the IATA carrier, to receive shipments, to execute Air Waybills, and to collect charges (air cargo).

IATA MEMBER　An airline that is a member of IATA (air cargo).

ICAO　International Civil Aviation Organization.

ICC　Interstate Commerce Commission; International Chamber of Commerce.

ICC CLAUSES (INS)　*See* Institute Cargo Clauses.

ICD　*See* Inland Clearance Depot.

ICE BOUND　Caught in the ice.

ICE CLAUSE　An ice clause is a standard clause in the chartering of ocean vessels. It dictates the course a vessel master may take if the ship is prevented from entering the loading or discharge port because of ice, or if the vessel is threatened by ice while in the port. The clause establishes rights and obligations of both vessel owner and charterer if these events occur.

ICE GORGE　A conglomeration of ice solidly packed from bank to bank that is obstructing the flow of the river and marine traffic.

ICE PIER　A heavily constructed cluster of piling or concrete behind which towboats moor or shelter from running ice.

ICHCA　International Cargo Handling Coordinating Association.

ICING　Accumulation of freezing water droplets on a vessel. Light (0.4 to 1.4 inches accretion in 24 hours); moderate (1.4 to 2.6 inches accretion in 24 hours); heavy (2.6 to 5.7 inches accretion in 24 hours); very heavy (5.7 inches accretion or more in 24 hours).

ICS　*See* International Chamber of Shipping.

ICTF　Intermodal Container Transfer Facility.

ICW　Intracoastal Waterway. Series of waterways along a coast connected so that vessels may travel without venturing into open sea.

IDLERS　Member of a ship's company with no night watches.

IDLE TIME　The amount of ineffective time whereby the available resources are not used, e.g., a container in a yard.

IE　Immediate Exit. In the U.S., Customs IE form is used when goods are brought into the U.S. and are to be immediately reexported without being transported within the U.S.

IFM Inward Foreign Manifest.

IGS Inert Gas System.

IGLOOS Pallets and containers used in air transportation; the igloo shape fits the internal wall contours of a narrow-body airplane.

IGNITION Setting on fire or catching fire.

IGNITION POINT The temperature to which a liquid must be raised before its surface layers will catch fire.

IGNITION QUALITY The ability of a fuel to ignite upon injection into the cylinder.

IGNITION TEMPERATURE The temperature required of a solid, liquid, or gaseous substance to cause sustained oxidation when the heating agent is removed.

IHP The indicated horsepower of the engine is the brake horsepower (b.h.p.) divided by the mechanical efficiency. So termed because it is usually obtained by calculation from the measured or estimated indicator diagram of the pressure cycle in the cylinder.

ILA International Longshoremen's Association (East Coast).

ILLUMINATING OIL A petroleum product, heavier than gasoline, used for lighting purposes.

ILO *See* International Labour Organization.

ILWU International Longshoremen's and Warehousemen's Union (West Coast).

IMB International Maritime Bureau.

IMBALANCE *See* Deadhead.

IMC *See* Intermodal Marketing Company.

IMCO International Maritime Consultative Organization. A form in which most major maritime nations participate and through which recommendations for the carriage of dangerous goods, bulk commodities, and maritime regulations become internationally acceptable. Now IMO.

IMDG CODE International Maritime Dangerous Goods Code. The regulations published by the IMO for transporting hazardous materials internationally.

IMMEDIATE (IT) Allows foreign merchandise arriving at one port to be transported in bond to another port, where a superseding entry is filed.

IMMEDIATE DELIVERY ENTRY *See* Customs Entry.

IMMEDIATE EXPORTATION An entry that allows foreign merchandise arriving at one port to be exported from the same port without the payment of duty.

IMMEDIATE TRANSPORTATION ENTRY A Customs form declaring goods for transportation by a bonded carrier from a port of entry to a bonded warehouse at an inland port.

IMO *See* International Maritime Organization.

IMPELLER The rotating component of a centrifugal pump or blower that imparts kinetic energy by centrifugal force to the fluid. Fluid enters at the shaft or eye of the impeller and passes via radial vanes out at the radius or perimeter.

IMPINGING   Releasing a liquid or vapor under pressure in the form of a spray or stream, which is directed against a surface.

IMPLIED WARRANTY   A warranty is a representation by the policyholder that certain conditions exist or will be met. Even if the warranty is not in writing, it may exist as an "implied" warranty, e.g., that a building is not on fire when insured or that a vessel is seaworthy.

IMPORT   To receive goods from a foreign country.

IMPORT CERTIFICATE   The import certificate is a means by which the government of the country of ultimate destination exercises legal control over the internal channeling of the commodities covered by the import certificate.

IMPORTER DISTRIBUTOR   A merchant who imports goods, usually on an exclusive territory arrangement, maintains an inventory and, through sales staff, sells to retailers.

IMPORTER OF RECORD   U.S. Customs Service defines the importer of record as the owner or purchaser of the goods; or, when designated by the owner, purchaser, or consignee, a licensed Customs broker.

IMPORT LETTER OF CREDIT   Term used by an importer to describe a commercial letter of credit he has asked a bank to issue or by a bank to describe a letter of credit it has issued. The same L/C will be called an "export letter of credit" by the exporter and all other banks.

IMPORT LICENSE   A document required and issued by some national governments authorizing the importation of goods.

IMPORT MERCHANT   A merchant who buys overseas for his own account for the purpose of later resale, handling all details of import documentation and transportation. Usually the merchant is specialized in one or two commodities.

IMPORT QUOTAS   Absolute limits to the quantity of a product that can be imported into a country during a particular time period.

IMPORT RATE   A rate established specifically for application on import traffic and generally less, when so published, than a domestic rate.

INBOARD   Inside the ship, toward the centerline and below the weather deck.

INBOARD PROFILE   A plan representing a longitudinal section through the center of the ship; showing deck heights, transverse bulkheads, assignment of space, machinery, etc., located on the center plane or between the center and the shell on the far side.

IN BOND   Cargo moving under Customs control where duty has not yet been paid. The transportation of a shipment to an inland point for Customs clearance rather than filing an entry to clear the goods at the port of arrival.

INBOUND CARGO   Cargo that is being imported into a country engaged in international trade.

INBOUND LOGISTICS   Movement and storage of the materials into a firm.

INCENDIVE SPARK   A spark of sufficient temperature and energy to ignite a flammable gas.

INCENTIVE RATE   A lower than usual tariff rate assessed because a shipper offers a greater volume than specified in the tariff. The incentive rate is assessed for that portion exceeding the normal volume.

INCHMAREE CLAUSE   (So-called for a famous legal decision involving a vessel of that name.) Covers losses resulting from a latent defect in the vessel's hull or machinery and losses resulting from errors in navigation or management of the vessel by the master or crew.

INCLINATION   The motion of a ship as it reacts to an external force such as the wind and sea, temporary condition dependent upon stability.

INCLINING EXPERIMENT   Experiment that by inclining a vessel a few degrees produces with the aid of a formula the metacentric height (GM) and the position of the center of gravity of a vessel. An analysis of a vessel's initial stability (static) conducted by a naval architect. Sometimes called a stability test.

INCLINOMETER   A device installed, usually on the bridge, on the centerline to determine list or the amount of roll.

INCOTERMS   The recognized abbreviation for the International Chamber of Commerce Terms of Sale. These terms were last amended, effective July 1, 1990.

IND (INS)   In insurance terms an offer of a premium rate that is not binding on either party.

INDEMNIFICATION   Compensation for a loss and/or the expenses incurred.

INDEMNIFY   To relieve a party from the liability to which it would otherwise be subject.

INDEMNIFY (INS)   To restore the victim of a loss, in whole or in part, by payment, repair, or replacement.

INDEMNITY BOND   An agreement to hold a carrier harmless with regard to a liability.

INDENT   A requistion for goods, enumerating conditions of the sale. Acceptance of an indent by a seller constitutes his agreement to the conditions of the sale.

INDEPENDENT ACTION   The right of a steamship company that is a member of a conference that has agreed jointly on rates and service to alter rates and services unilaterally without need of conference approval.

INDEPENDENT ADJUSTER (INS)   An adjuster who works as an independent contractor, hiring himself out to insurance companies or other organizations for the investigation and settlement of claims.

INDEPENDENT GUARANTEE   *See* Demand Guarantee.

INDEPENDENT TARIFF   Any body of rate tariffs that are not part of an agreement or conference system.

INDIRECT EXPORTING   Sale by the exporter to the buyer through a domestically located intermediary.

INDIRECT IMPACTS   These include the effects of other industrial and service sectors caused by the direct activity. This includes the inter-industry economic activity supported by the purchases of supplies, services, labor, and other inputs.

INDIRECT ROUTE   Any route other than the direct route (air cargo).

INDIVIDUAL VALIDATED LICENSE (IVL)   An IVL is written approval by which the U.S. Department of Commerce grants permission, which is valid for 2 years, for the export of a specified quantity of products or technical data to a single recipient. IVLs also are required, under certain circumstances, as authorization for the reexport of U.S. origin commodities to new destinations abroad.

IN DRAFT   Current moving across the lock entrance toward the shore.

INDUCED IMPACTS   These include the economic activity that comes from household purchases of goods and services made possible because of the wages generated by the direct and indirect economic activities.

INDUCEMENT   Placing a port on a vessel's itinerary because the volume of cargo offered by that port justifies the cost of routing the vessel.

INDUSTRIAL LEAD   A railroad track serving an industrial area, with numerous branch tracks.

INERT GAS   A gas or mixture of gases incapable of supporting combustion, such as nitrogen, carbon dioxide, or flue gas containing less than 11% oxygen.

INERT GAS SYSTEM   A fire prevention system installed aboard tankers that prevents the spread of fire into cargo tanks. Inert gas is produced onboard by burning diesel fuel or by drawing uptake gases off boilers.

INERTIA   Reluctance of a body to change its position or rate and direction of motion.

INERTING   Filling and maintaining the cargo tanks and associated piping systems with an inert gas.

INFLAMMABLE   Same as flammable, but flammable is the preferred term. Opposite of nonflammable.

INFLAMMABLE LIQUIDS   Liquids liable to spontaneous combustion that give off inflammable vapors at or below 80°F. For example, ether, ethyl, benzene, gasoline, paints, enamels, carbon disulfide, etc.

INFRASTRUCTURE   System of roads, waterways, airfields, ports, and/or telecommunication networks in a certain area.

IN GATE   The transaction or interchange that occurs at the time a container is received by a rail terminal or water port from another carrier.

INGESTION   Taking a material by mouth; the act of introducing a substance into the body via the digestive system.

INHALATION   Breathing in a material either through the nose or the mouth.

INHERENT ADVANTAGE   The cost and service benefits of one mode compared with other modes.

INHERENT VICE (INS)   An insurance term referring to any defect or other characteristic of a product that could result in damage to the product without external cause (for example, instability in a chemical that could cause it to explode spontaneously). Insurance policies may exclude inherent vice losses.

INHIBITING CHEMICAL   A chemical to which an inhibitor has been added.

INHIBITOR   Substance used to prevent any chemical reaction.

INHIBITORS   Chemical compounds that, when added in small amounts, reduce rates of chemical reactions.

IN IRONS   The situation of a vessel having missed stays and when she refused to fall off from the wind or when a vessel is encumbered by a tow wire so that she can not properly maneuver.

INITIAL BOILING POINT   The temperature at which the first drop of distillate falls from the condenser into the receiver in a standard laboratory distillation procedure.

INITIAL STABILITY   Stability of a vessel for small angles of inclination (up to 15 degrees). It is usually represented by the metacentric height.

INLAND BILL OF LADING   A bill of lading used in transporting goods overland to the exporter's international carrier. Although a through bill of lading can sometimes be used, it is usually necessary to prepare both an inland bill of lading and an ocean bill of lading for export shipments. *See also* Bill of Lading.

INLAND CARRIER   A transportation line that hauls export or import traffic between ports and inland points.

INLAND CLEARANCE DEPOT (ICD)   Inland location where cargo, particularly containerized, may be cleared by customs.

INLAND MARINE INSURANCE (INS)   A branch of the insurance business that developed from the insuring of shipments, which did not involve ocean voyages. Exposures eligible for this form of protection are described in the nationwide definition of marine insurance. Such diverse properties as bridges, tunnels, jewelry, and furs can now be written under Inland Marine forms.

INLAND PORTS INTERMODAL (IDP)   *See* Micro Bridge.

INLAND RIVERPORT   Usually associated with port terminal facilities served by towboats and barges moving over shallow draft, inland river navigation channels.

INMARSAT   International Maritime Satellite system.

INNAGE   Actual amount of oil in the compartment measured from the bottom of the tank to the surface of the oil.

INNER BOTTOM   Plating forming the upper boundary of the double bottom; also called tank top.

INOPERATIVE   Sound signal or radio navigation aid to navigation out of service due to a malfunction; not functioning.

INORGANIC ACID   An acid of nonorganic origin, hence containing no carbon.

INORGANIC COMPOUND   A compound containing no carbon, hence composed of matter other than animal or vegetable, such as clay or glass.

IN &/OR OVER   Goods carried below and/or on deck.

INPUT OUTPUT ANALYSIS   This is a type of economic analysis that identifies inter-industry purchases of goods and services. For every dollar spent on a purchase in one industry, input output analysis would indicate how much is respent in all other industries.

IN SHAPE   When a tow is properly aligned for entering a lock or passing through a narrow channel or opening between bridge piers.

INSHORE TRAFFIC ZONE   A designated area between the landward boundary of a traffic separation scheme and the adjacent coast intended for coastal traffic.

IN SITU DENSITY   The density or specific gravity of bottom materials in their undisturbed state.

INSOLUBLE   Incapable of being dissolved in a liquid.

INSOLUBLE OILS   Oils that do not form stable emulsions or colloidal solutions with water.

INSPECTION CERTIFICATE   A certificate issued by an independent agent or firm attesting to the quality and/or quantity of the merchandise being shipped. Such a certificate is usually required in a letter of credit for commodity shipments.

INSTABILITY LINE   Band of unstable air usually found ahead of a cold front that may develop into a squall line of thunderstorms. Usually 10 to 50 miles wide and several hundred miles long. Not all cold fronts have instability lines.

INSTALLMENT LETTER OF CREDIT   Letter of credit calling for multiple shipments within specified date ranges.

INSTALLMENT SHIPMENTS   Successive shipments are permitted under letters of credit. Usually they must take place within a given period of time.

INSTITUTE CARGO CLAUSES (INS)   Treaty wordings developed by the International Chamber of Commerce. There are three basic sets of these clauses (A, B, and C). The A clauses cover "all risks," subject to specified exclusions. The B and C clauses cover specified "risks," subject to specified exclusions.

INSULATED CONTAINER   These containers are insulated against heat loss or gain and are used in conjunction with a blown air refrigeration system to convey perishable or other cargo that needs to be carried under temperature control.

INSULATED CONTAINER TANK   The frame of a container constructed to hold one or more thermally insulated tanks for liquids.

INSULATED TANK   The frame of a container constructed to hold one or more thermally insulated tanks for liquids.

INSULATING FLANGE   An insulating device placed between metallic flanges, bolts, and washers to prevent electrical continuity between pipelines, sections of pipelines, hose strings and loading arms, or equipment/apparatus.

INSULATING OILS   Oil, such as transformer oil, used to insulate and cool the core and windings of transformers.

INSURABLE INTEREST (INS)   A direct monetary interest in the insured property sufficient to result in monetary loss should the property be damaged or destroyed.

INSURABLE RISK (INS)   A risk that meets most of the following requisites: the loss insured against must be defined; it must be accidental; it must be large enough to cause hardship to the insured; it must belong to a homogenous group of risks large enough to make losses predictable; it must not be subject to the same loss at the same time as a large number of other risks; the insurance company must be able to determine a reasonable cost for the insurance; the insurance company must be able to calculate the chance of loss.

INSURANCE   A system of protection against loss under which a number of parties agree to pay certain sums (premiums) for a guarantee that they will be compensated under certain conditions for specified loss and damage.

INSURANCE, ALL RISK   This type of insurance offers the shipper the broadest coverage available, covering against all losses that may occur in transit.

INSURANCE, GENERAL AVERAGE   This clause covers damages or losses arising from maritime ventures or losses arising for all parties shipping or owning.

INSURANCE, PARTICULAR AVERAGE   A marine insurance term to refer to partial loss on an individual shipment from one of the parties insured against, regardless of the balance of the cargo. Particular average insurance can usually be obtained, but the loss must be in excess of a certain percentage of the insured value of the shipment, usually three to five percent, before a claim will be allowed by the company.

INSURANCE CERTIFICATE   Certificate used to assure the consignee that insurance is provided to cover loss of or damage to the cargo while in transit.

INSURANCE COMPANY   The party covering the risks of the issued goods and/or services that are insured.

INSURANCE RIDER   Additional clause, amending or supplementing the insurance policy.

INSURANCE WITH AVERAGE-CLAUSE   This type of clause covers merchandise if the damage amounts to three percent or more of the insured value of the package or cargo. If the vessel burns, collides, or sinks, all losses are fully covered. In marine insurance, the word average describes partial damage or partial loss.

INSURED (INS)   The person whose risk is transferred and shared; the party to an insurance agreement whom the insurer agrees to indemnify for losses, provide benefits for, or render services to.

INSURED VALUE   Usually computed by adding the invoice cost, guaranteed freight, other costs, and insurance premium plus a percentage, commonly 10%. This usually represents landed value.

INSURER (INS)   The company or group offering protection through the sale of an insurance policy to an insured; the party to an insurance agreement who undertakes to indemnify for losses, provide pecuniary benefits, or render services.

INTACT BUOYANCY   Intact space below the surface of a flooded area.

INTEGRATED CARRIER   Carriers that have both air and ground fleets, or other combinations, such as sea, rail, and truck. Since they usually handle thousands of small parcels an hour, they are less expensive and offer more diverse services than regular carriers.

INTEGRATED TOW   Consists of specially designed barges such that they fit to each other and to the towboat as one unit. They are not intended to be pushed separately.

INTEGRATED TUG BARGE (ITB)   Consists of a propelling unit that is rigidly connected to a barge and is designed to remain so for the duration of the voyage; a composite unit.

INTENSIFYING HIGH   Anticyclone in which the central pressure is increasing.

INTERACTION   The forces of attraction and repulsion experienced by two ships passing close to one another on parallel courses.

INTER BOX CONNECTOR (IBC)   A manual or automatic device for connecting stacked containers onboard ship or on double-stacked trains. Also called stacking cone, stacking shore, or twist lock.

INTERCEPTOR TANK   An online tank used to remove undesirable solids or liquids from the normal fluid in the system.

INTERCHANGE   Transfer of a container from one party to another.

INTERCHANGE AGREEMENT   Formal agreement whereby participants agree to exchange equipment in intermodal movements.

INTERCHANGE POINT   A location where one carrier delivers freight to another carrier.

INTERCOASTAL   Water service between two coasts; in the U.S., this usually refers to water service between the Atlantic and Pacific Coasts.

INTERCORPORATE HAULING   A private carrier hauling the goods of a subsidiary and charging the subsidiary a fee; this is legal of the subsidiary if wholly owned (100 percent) or the private carrier has common carrier authority.

INTERIM RECEIPT   A receipt given by a carrier pending execution of an air waybill (air cargo).

INTERLINE   Two or more motor carriers working together to haul a shipment to a destination. Carriers may interchange equipment but usually they rehandle the shipment without transferring the equipment.

INTERLINE AGREEMENT   The cooperation between two or more airlines for the carriage over particular routes (air cargo).

INTERLINE CARRIAGE   The carriage over the routes of two or more parties of an interline agreement (air cargo).

INTERLINE FREIGHT Freight moving from origin to destination over the lines of two or more transportation carriers.

INTERLOCKING An arrangement of signals and special track work where rail routes meet, including turnouts and crossovers (as the case may be) and connected such that movements from one track to another can only be made safely and in the proper sequence, preventing opposing or conflicting train movements. Interlockings occur at the crossing of two railroads, at junctions or upon entering or leaving terminals or yards.

INTERMEDIATE CONSIGNEE An intermediate consignee is the bank, forwarding agent, or other intermediary (if any) that acts in a foreign country as an agent for the exporter, the purchaser, or the ultimate consignee for the purpose of effecting delivery of the export to the ultimate consignee.

INTERMEDIATE POINT A point located en route between two other points.

INTERMODAL Used to describe the capability of marine containers to be moved, transported, or interchanged between rail, truck, and ship in any order and where the equipment is compatible within the multiple systems.

INTERMODAL CONTAINER A reusable cargo container of a rigid construction and rectangular configuration; fitted with devices permitting its ready handling, particularly its transfer from one mode of transport to another. It is designed to be readily filled and emptied; intended to contain one or more articles of cargo or bulk commodities for transportation by water and one or more other transport modes.

INTERMODAL CONTAINER TRANSFER FACILITY A facility where cargo is transferred from one mode of transportation to another, usually from ship or truck to rail.

INTERMODAL MARKETING COMPANY An intermediary that sells intermodal services to shippers.

INTERMODAL RATES A single financial charge for transportation of goods where two or more modes of transport are used.

INTERMODAL TRANSPORTATION This enables cargoes to be consolidated into economically large units (containers) optimizing use of specialized intermodal handling equipment to effect high speed cargo transfer between ships, barges, railcars, and truck chassis using a minimum of labor to increase logistic flexibility, reduce consignment delivery times, and minimize operating costs.

INTERMODAL YARD *See* COFC Rail Terminal.

INTERNAL MOVEMENTS Domestic traffic consisting primarily of receipts and shipments between two ports or landings within the same region wherein the entire movement takes place on inland waterways.

INTERNAL RECEIPTS Movements of marine products, and gravel taken directly from beds of the ocean.

INTERNAL TERMINAL VEHICLE *See* Yard Tractor.

INTERNATIONAL AIR TRANSPORT ASSOCIATION (IATA) An international organization of airlines, founded in 1945, with the aim of promoting the commercial air traffic. This should be achieved by cooperation between parties concerned and by performance of certain rules, procedures and tariffs, regarding both cargo and passengers, by those parties.

INTERNATIONAL AND TERRITORIAL OPERATIONS In general operations outside the territory of the United States, including operations between U.S. points separated by foreign territory or major expanses of international waters.

INTERNATIONAL ASSOCIATION OF CLASSIFICATION SOCIETIES (IACS) An organization in which the major classification societies, among others American Bureau of Shipping, Lloyd's Register of Shipping, and Germanischer Lloyd, are joined, whose principal aim is the improvement of standards concerning safety at sea.

INTERNATIONAL CARRIAGE Carriage whereby the place of departure and any place of landing are situated in more than one country (air cargo).

INTERNATIONAL CHAMBER OF COMMERCE (ICC) International standards and practices organization.

INTERNATIONAL CHAMBER OF SHIPPING A United Nations sponsored boy established to define terms used in international trade to facilitate trade among nations.

INTERNATIONAL IMPORT CERTIFICATE A document required by the importing country indicating that the importing country recognizes that a controlled shipment is entering their country. The importing country pledges to monitor the shipment and prevent its re-export, except in accordance with its own export control regulations.

INTERNATIONAL LABOUR ORGANIZATION (ILO) A United Nations agency, dealing with employment rights and working conditions, covering work at sea and in ports.

INTERNATIONAL LOAD LINE CERTIFICATE A certificate giving details of a ship's freeboards and states that the ship has been surveyed and the appropriate load lines marked on her sides. A classification society or the Coast Guard issues this certificate.

INTERNATIONAL MARITIME BUREAU A special division of the International Chamber of Commerce.

INTERNATIONAL MARITIME DANGEROUS GOODS CODE (IMDG) A code, representing the classification of dangerous goods as defined by the International Maritime Organization (IMO) in compliance with international legal requirements.

INTERNATIONAL MARITIME ORGANIZATION The IMO was established as a specialized agency of the United Nations in 1948. The IMO facilitates cooperation on technical matters affecting merchant shipping and traffic, including improved maritime safety and prevention of marine pollution. Headquarters are in London, England.

INTERNATIONAL PASSENGERS Passengers that arrive in a port at the end of or during an international voyage, from either a foreign or domestic port, aboard a foreign or U.S. flag cruise ship, ferry, or passenger vessel.

INTERNATIONAL SHORE CONNECTION A universal connection to the vessel's fire main to which shoreside firefighting water may be connected. This allows use of the vessel's fire stations and associated hoses. Required on all vessels over 500 gross tons subject to SOLAS, and on U.S. Inspected vessels over 1,000 gross tons. A slotted flange with the ship's appropriate fire hose threads designed to allow universal water connection to the ship's fire main system.

INTERNATIONAL STANDARDS ORGANIZATION (ISO) ISO deals in standards of all sorts, ranging from documentation to equipment packaging and labeling.

INTERNATIONAL TONNAGE CERTIFICATE A certificate issued to a shipowner by a government department in the case of a ship whose gross and net tonnages have been determined in accordance with the International Convention of Tonnage Measurement of Ships. The certificate states the gross and net tonnages together with details of the spaces attributed to each.

INTERNATIONAL WATERWAYS Consist of international straits, inland, and interocean canals and rivers where they separate the territories of two or more nations. Provided no treaty is enforced, both merchant ships and warships have the right of free and unrestricted navigation through these waterways.

INTERSTATE COMMERCE The transportation of persons or property between states; in the course of the movement, the shipment crosses a state boundary.

INTERSTATE COMMERCE COMMISSION (ICC) The U.S. federal body charged with enforcing acts of the U.S. Congress that affect common carriers in interstate commerce.

INTERTANKO An association of independent tanker owners whose aims are to represent the views of its members internationally.

IN THE MARKS Being in the marks means that you are proceeding along the channel line as described in the channel report. When in the marks you are well on the line (imaginary) running from one mark to the other or from one light to the other.

IN TRANSIT In passage.

INTRANSIT ENTRY (IT) Allows foreign merchandise arriving at one port to be transported in bond to another port, where a superseding entry is filed.

IN TRANSPORT (IT) Cargo moves under bond from port of entry to designated point within the continental United States.

INTRAPORT Vessel or freight movements within the confines of a port.

INTRASTATE COMMERCE The transportation of persons or property within a state; in the course of the movement, the shipment does not cross a state boundary.

INTRATERRITORY TRAFFIC   Refers to traffic consisting of domestic receipts and shipments between ports in Puerto Rico and the U.S. Virgin Islands, which are considered a single unit.

INTRINSICALLY SAFE   A device with electric components certified as not being able to produce any type of spark or other similar manner of ignition when utilized in a flammable atmosphere.

INV   Invoice.

INVENTORY   The number of units and/or value of the stock of goods a company holds.

INVENTORY COST   The cost of holding goods, usually expressed as a percentage of the inventory value, includes the cost of capital, warehousing, taxes, insurance, depreciation, and obsolescence.

INVENTORY IN TRANSIT   Inventory in a carrier's possession, being transported to the buyer.

INVOICE   An itemized list of goods shipped to a buyer, stating quantities, prices, shipping charges, etc.

INWARD FOREIGN MANIFEST (IFM)   A complete listing of all cargo entering the country of discharge. Required at all world ports and is the primary source of cargo control, against which duty is assessed by the receiving country.

IPI   Inland Point Intermodal. Refers to inland points (nonports) that can be served by carriers on a through bill of lading.

IRISH PENNANT   An untidy loose end of a rope.

IRREGULAR ROUTE CARRIER   A motor carrier that is permitted to provide service using any route.

IRRESPECTIVE OF PERCENTAGE   Letter of Credit wordings requiring no deductible/excess.

IRREVOCABLE LETTER OF CREDIT   Letter of credit in which the specified payment is guaranteed by the bank if all terms and conditions are met by the drawee and that cannot be revoked without joint agreement of both the buyer and the seller.

IRRITATING MATERIAL (FORMERLY CLASS C POISON)   A liquid or solid substance that upon contact with fire or when exposed to air gives off dangerous or intensely irritating fumes, but not including any poisonous material, Class A.

ISHERWOOD SYSTEM   A system of building ships that employs close spaced, relatively light, longitudinal main framing supported on widespread transverse members of comparatively great strength instead of transverse main framing.

ISM CODE   The International Maritime Organization Assembly adopted the International Safety Management Code (ISM Code) in 1993. On July 1, 1998, the ISM Code became mandatory for passenger vessels, passenger high-speed craft, oil tankers, chemical tankers, bulk carriers, and cargo high-speed craft of 500 gross tons or more. On July 1, 2002, the ISM Code became applicable to other cargo ships and to self-propelled mobile off-shore drilling units of 500 gross tons or more.

ISO International Standards Organization that deals in standards of all sorts, ranging from documentation to equipment packaging and labeling.

ISOLATING VALVE A valve in a piping system, normally fully open, that can be closed to separate one part of the system from another for use in an emergency or during maintenance of part of the plant.

ISOMERIZATION Process for altering the fundamental arrangement of the atoms in a molecule without adding or removing anything from the original materials. In petroleum refining, straight chain hydrocarbons are chain hydrocarbons of substantially higher octane rating, in the presence of a catalyst, usually at moderate temperature and converted to branched pressures.

ISO OCTANE A hydrocarbon showing 100-octane value, used primarily as a reference fuel in determining the octane rating of gasolines. It is isomeric with normal octane and, therefore, has the same chemical formula, C_8H_{18}.

ISOPENTANE A saturated branched chain hydrocarbon having 5 carbon atoms and 12 hydrogen atoms, obtained by fractionation of natural gasoline or isomerization of normal pentane. It is used extensively as a component of aviation gasoline.

ISPF CODE The International Ship and Port Facility code adopted by an IMO Diplomatic Conference in December 2002. Measure is designed to strengthen maritime security.

ISSUING BANK Bank that opens a straight or negotiable letter of credit and assumes the obligation to pay the bank or beneficiary if the documents presented are in accordance with the terms of the letter of credit.

ISSUING CARRIER The carrier issuing transportation documents or publishing a tariff.

IT Immediate Transport. The document (prepared by the carrier) allows shipment to proceed from the port of entry in the U.S. to Customs clearing at the destination. The shipment clears Customs at its final destination.

ITB Integrated Tug Barge. Consists of a propelling unit that is rigidly connected to a barge and is designed to remain so for the duration of the voyage; a composite unit.

ITF International Transport Workers Federation.

ITF (ICTF) Intermodal Transfer Facility. A facility used for the transfer of cargo from ship to truck to rail in any order.

ITINERARY Route scheduled.

ITOPF International Tanker Owners Pollution Federation.

IU If Used.

IUHTAUTC If Used, Half Time Actually Count.

IVL *See* Individual Validated License.

IWL Institute Warranty Limits.

J

JACK The flag similar to the union of the national flag.

JACKASS A conical canvas stopper stuffed with tarred oakum and hove tight into a between deck hawse pipe as a watertight stopper.

JACKET A wood or fiber cover placed around containers such as cans and bottles.

JACK LADDER A ladder with wooden steps and side ropes.

JACK ROD Pipe or rod to which the edges of awnings or weather cloths are secured.

JACK STAFF A vertical pole erected on the lead barge of a tow used by the pilot for aligning the heading of the tow.

JACKSTAY A general term for any rope or rod used for hanging up sea bags, awnings, or miscellaneous gear.

JACOB'S LADDER A rope of chain ladder lowered over the ship's side to allow access from small boats or shore, in lieu of an accommodation ladder. A ladder having either fiber or wire rope or chain sides with wood or metal rungs attached at regular intervals. One end is usually fitted with sister hooks or shackles for hooking on.

JET DOWN To sink an object, generally a buoy sinker, deep into the mud below the river bottom by the use of high-pressure water jet.

JETSAM Goods that sink when thrown overboard.

JET SUCTION ASSIST A device for improving the suction characteristics of a dredge pump by injecting high energy jets of water into the dredge suction pipe.

JETTISON Act of throwing cargo or equipment (jetsam) overboard when a ship is in danger.

JETTY A landing wharf or pier; also, a breakwater.

JEW'S HARP A lyre-shaped shackle for joining the chain cable to the anchor so that another cable may be fastened in addition to the ordinary chain.

JIB Projecting arm of a crane.

JIT Just In Time. In this method of inventory control, warehousing is minimal or nonexistent; the container is the movable warehouse and must arrive "just in time"; not too early nor too late.

JIT DELIVERY Planned delivery of cargo to minimize storage for direct just on time distribution.

JOC Journal of Commerce.

JOCKEY LINE Lashing used to prevent lateral movement between barges connected in tandem.

JO DOG Set of wheels that converts a two-axle trailer to a three-axle trailer. Slang word for dolly.

JOG   Short distance movement of a LASH vessel barge crane in the fore and aft direction.

JOGGLE   To offset a plate or shape to save the use of liners.

JOHNBOAT   Flat-bottomed skiff-type boat with square bow and stern.

JOINT, BUTT   A term applied where a connection between two pieces of material is made by bringing their ends or edges together (no overlap) and by welding alone, or by welding, riveting, or bolting each to a strip or strap that overlaps both pieces.

JOINT, LAPPED   A connection between two pieces of material is made by overlapping the end or edge of one over the end or edge of the other and by fastening the same by bolts, rivets, or welding.

JOINT CHARGE   A charge that applies to the carriage over the lines of two or more carriers and is published as a single amount (air cargo).

JOINT COST   A type of common cost where products are produced in fixed proportions, and the cost incurred to produce one product necessarily entails the production of another; the back-haul is an example.

JOINT RATE   A rate applicable from a point on one transportation line to a point on another line, made by agreement and published in a single tariff by all transportation lines over which the rate applies.

JOINT SERVICES   A single type of transportation service that two or more carriers agree to provide, in which the equipment of both is used, and marketing, scheduling, and pricing are done jointly.

JOINT VENTURE   In fisheries, an arrangement whereby fish harvested by U.S. fishermen are sold and delivered to foreign processing vessels operating within the Fisheries Conservation Zone of the United States.

JOLLY ROGER   A pirate's flag carrying the skull and cross bones.

JONES ACT   A law to protect U.S. domestic ocean-borne commerce and U.S. flag vessels engaged in coastwise trade by prohibiting the transportation of cargoes in foreign flag vessels between points in the United States, either directly or via a foreign port, in any other vessel than a vessel built in and documented under the laws of the United States, and owned by persons who are U.S. citizens.

JOURNAL   The part of a shaft or axle that rotates in or against a bearing.

JUMBO BARGE   A barge that is 35 feet wide by 195 to 200 feet long and may also be either a hopper or covered-type barge.

JUMBO BOOM   A heavy lift capable of handling from 10–75 tons.

JUMP SHIP   To leave a ship without authority.

JUNCTION   The point where a channel divides when proceeding seaward. The place where a tributary departs from the main stream.

JUNK   Old rope. A Chinese or Japanese lateen rigged sailing vessel of heavy construction.

JURISDICTION   Legal authority exercised by a nation over its adjacent waters or coastal confluence zone.

JURISPRUDENCE   Juridical decisions used for explanation and meaning of law.

JURY   Temporary structures, such as masts, rudders, etc., used in an emergency.

JURY RIG   A makeshift arrangement of cargo handling gear, rigged when regular gear is not available.

JUST-IN-TIME   An inventory control system that attempts to reduce inventory levels by coordinating demand and supply to the point where the desired item arrives just-in-time for use.

K

K Symbol for keel.

KANAWHA RIVER RATCHET Placing toothpick or bar between doubled up line to bring two barges together by twisting bar around and around. Very dangerous to use.

KANBAN A just-in-time inventory system used by Japanese manufacturers.

KB Linear distance from the keel to the center of buoyancy (when vessel is upright).

KD Knocked down; also kiln dried, when used in reference to lumber.

KDF Knocked down flat.

KEDGE ANCHOR One or more anchors carried in addition to the main, or bower, anchors usually stowed aft. A kedge may be dropped while the ship is under way or carried out in a suitable direction by a tender or ship's boat, to enable the ship to be winched off if aground, or swung into a particular heading, or even to be held steady against a tidal or other stream.

KEEL The bottom structural member of a ship running on the centerline; on smaller vessels this member extends out of the hull and on ships it usually does not in modern construction. The backbone of the ship's frame. *See* Keelson.

KEEL, BAR A keel that protrudes through the bottom.

KEEL, BILGE A fin fitted on the bottom of a ship at the turn of the bilge to reduce rolling. It commonly consists of a plate running fore and aft and attached to the shell plating by angle bars. It materially helps in steadying a ship and does not add much to the resistance to propulsion when properly located.

KEEL, BLOCKS Heavy blocks on which ship rests during construction.

KEEL, DOCKING In dry-docking, the weight of a ship is carried almost entirely on the keel and bilge blocks. The keel and keelson provide the means of distributing the pressure on the centerline, and docking keels composed of doubling strips of plate or a heavier plate or built up girders are sometimes fitted on the bottom at a distance from the centerline corresponding to the best position for the bilge block. The docking keels are fitted in the fore and aft direction, generally parallel or nearly so to the keel.

KEEL, FLAT A fore and aft row of flat plates end to end on the centerline, running along the bottom of the ship from stem to stern, the forward and after plates being dished up into a U shape to fit the stem and stern castings.

KEEL HAUL An ancient punishment, consisting of hauling a person under the keel by whips from the yardarms.

KEELSON, SIDE The bottom structural member running on the centerline; on larger vessels this member extends into the hull. Fore and aft member placed on each side of, and similarly to, the center vertical keel.

KEELSON, VERTICAL CENTER   The lower middle line girder, which, in conjunction with a flat plate keel on the bottom and a rider plat on top, forms the principal fore and aft strength member in the bottom of a ship. In addition to its importance as a "backbone" or longitudinal strength member, it serves to distribute and equalize the pressure on the transverse frames and bottom of the ship when grounding or docking occurs. In steel ships this keelson usually consists of a vertical plate with two angles running along the top and two along the bottom, The girder, however, may be made up of various combinations of plates and shapes. This member should continue as far forward and aft as possible. Usually called the Vertical Keel.

KENTLEDGE   Pig iron used as ballast, or as a weight for inclining a vessel.

KERF   The slit made by the cut of a saw. Also the channel burned out by a cutting torch.

KEROSENE   A refined petroleum distillate of volatility between Gasoline and Gas Oil. A general term covering the class of refined oils boiling between 370 degrees F and 515 degrees F, used primarily in domestic oil lamps and cooling stoves.

KEVEL   Colloquial term used for a large cleat secured to the deck of a boat or a barge, used for securing mooring lines. It is provided with two prongs called "horns." Also spelled cavil, cavel, caval.

KG   Height of center of gravity above keel; kilogram.

KI YI   A scrubbing brush.

KICK LINE   A line used to hold towboat while stern is being backed in so that head will swing out into the stream.

KILL OUT TOW (KILL HER OUT)   To back until headway is checked.

KILOGRAM   1,000 grams or 2.2046 pounds.

KIND OF PACKING   Description of the packaging material used for goods to be transported.

KINEMATIC VISCOSITY   The ratio of viscosity of a liquid to its specific gravity at the temperature at which the viscosity is measured.

KING PIN   A coupling pin centered on the front underside of a chassis; couples to the tractor.

KING POST   A strong vertical post used instead of a mast to support a boom and rigging to form a derrick; also called samson post.

KING SPOKE   The upper stoke of a wheel when the rudder in amidships, usually marked in some fashion.

KIP   Kilo pound (1,000 pounds of force).

KM   Height of metacenter above keel.

KNEE   A block of wood having a natural angular shape or one cut to a bracket shape and used to fasten and strengthen the corners of deck openings and the intersections of timers, and to connect deck beams to the frames of wood vessels. The term is also applied to the ends of steel deck beams that are split, having one leg turned down and a piece of plate fitted between the split portion, thus forming a bracket of knee.

KNEE COATING The application of any coating to a substrate by means of drawing the substrate beneath a thin blade that spreads the coating evenly over the full width of the substrate.

KNOCK In gasoline engines, detonation caused by sudden burning of the last remaining portion of the fuel in the combustion chamber.

KNOCK CHARACTERISTICS Tendency of a gasoline to knock. *See* Octane Number and Performance Number.

KNOCKED DOWN The situation of a vessel when listed over by the wind to such an extent that she does not recover. Also, articles that are taken apart to reduce the cubic footage displaced or to make a better shipping unit and are to be reassembled.

KNOCK OFF To stop, especially to stop work.

KNOCKOUT To release towboat from tow.

KNOCKOUT SINGLE To uncouple the towboat and lay along side the barges for single lockage. Also called single set over.

KNOT A speed measurement of 1 nautical mile per hour, a nautical mile being about 11/7 land miles (6,082.66 feet or 1/60 degree at the equator). The international nautical mile is 1,852 meters or 6,076.1 feet. In the days of sail, speed was measured by tossing overboard a log that was secured by a line. A knot was tied into the line at approximately 6 foot intervals. The number of knots measured was then compared against time required to travel the distance of 1,000 knots in the line. Also, a line tied to/on itself.

KNOWN LOSS A loss discovered before or at the time of delivery of a shipment.

KNUCKLE An abrupt change in direction of plating, frames, keel, deck, or other structure of a vessel.

KNUCKLE PLATE A plate bent to form a knuckle.

KORT NOZZLE A cylindrical ring encompassing the propeller(s) on many tugs. Tugs with fixed propeller(s) have the rudder directly behind the nozzle. Rudder propeller tugs have the nozzle arranged to turn 360 degrees. Nozzles increase propulsion efficiency up to 30 percent as the water leaves the propeller(s) as a jet stream.

KT Kilo or metric ton. 1,000 kilos or 2,204.6 pounds.

L

LA   Letter of authority.

LABEL   A slip of, e.g., paper or metal attached to an object to indicate the nature, ownership destination, contents, and/or other particulars of the object.

LABOR   A vessel is said to labor when she works heavily in a seaway.

LABORING   The effect of shallow water on the sound or performance of the boat's engine.

LACQUER (VARNISH)   A coating similar to a natural varnish, left on engine parts as a result of high temperature of oil and gasoline.

LADDER   Inclined steps aboard ship, taking the place of stairs. A device, which allows motion vertically aboard ship, usually steeply inclined and may be vertical in confined spaces.

LADDER, ACCOMMODATION   A staircase suspended over the side of a vessel from a gangway to a point near the water to provide easy access to the deck from a small boat alongside.

LADDER, COMPANION   A staircase fitted as a means of access from a deck to the quarters.

LADDER, SEA   Rungs secured to the side of a vessel to form a ladder from the weather deck to the water.

LADDER-MOUNTED DREDGE PUMP   Positioning the dredge pump on the dredge ladder near the point of the suction intake. This design offers considerable dredging efficiency advantage over the on dredge location for the pump. Disadvantages are cost and increased size of plant required.

LADDER TRACK   A track with numerous turnouts leading to parallel yard or body tracks. Often, a yard will have ladder tracks at both ends for improved access.

LADDERWELLS   An enclosed staircase that allows vertical motion between decks. Ladder wells below the main deck must have firescreen door mechanisms.

LADEN   Loaded aboard a vessel.

LADING   Freight shipped; the contents of a shipment.

LAGGING   Insulating material that is fitted on the outside of boilers, piping, etc.

LAID-DOWN COST   The total cost of a product delivered at a given location; the cost of production plus the transportation cost to the customer's location.

LAID UP TONNAGE   Ships not in active service; a ship that is out of commission for fitting out, awaiting better markets, needing work for classification, etc.

LAKE ICE   Ice formed on a lake, regardless of observed location.

LAKER   Type of ship that trades only in the Great Lakes of North America. They usually carry grain and ore cargoes.

LAKEWISE TRAFFIC Pertains to domestic receipts and shipments or traffic between U.S. ports on the Great Lakes system.

LAMPBLACK A solid product, consisting largely of carbon, obtained by the incomplete combustion of hydrocarbon materials. It is substantially different from carbon black and channel black, being grayish in color.

LAMPLIGHTER A part-time federal employee who tends battery-operated lights in isolated areas to provide greater reliability of the light and to protect equipment from loss due to high water.

LAND The act of mooring or bringing a boat to the riverbank.

LANDBRIDGE Movement of cargo by water from one country through the port of another country, therefore, using rail or truck, to an inland point in that country or to a third country. Example: A through movement of Asian cargo to Europe across North America.

LANDED COST The total cost of a good to a buyer, including the cost of transportation.

LANDED VALUE Wholesale market value at destination on final day of discharge.

LANDING CERTIFICATE Certificate issued by consular officials of some importing countries at the point or place of export when the subject goods are exported under bond.

LANDING EDGE That portion of the edge or end of a plate over which another plate laps. The covered-up edge.

LANDING GEAR Support legs on the front part of a chassis or trailer that can be cranked up or down and used to support the front of a semitrailer when the tractive unit has been removed.

LANDING SIGNAL Some companies have prearranged signals that their towboats sound when approaching their dock.

LANDLORD PORT A public port agency that leases the majority of its facilities to others for operations.

LANDLUBBER The seaman's term for one who does not go to sea.

LANDSCAPING Colloquial term meaning to clear shore structure of brush and vegetation in order to obtain optimum range of visibility (brush out).

LAND WALL The concrete wall that forms part of the lock and is nearest to the land on the shore on which the lock chamber is constructed.

LANE METER A method of measuring the space capacity of RO/RO ships whereby each unit of space (linear meter) is represented by an area of deck 1.0 meter in length x 2.0 meters in width.

LANYARD A piece of rope or line having one end free and the other attached to any object for the purpose of either near or remote control.

LAP A joint in which one part overlaps the other, the use of a butt strap being thus avoided.

LAPSTRAKE Boats built on the clinker system in which the strakes overlap each other. The top strake always laps on the outside of the strake beneath.

LARD OILS Animal oils prepared from chilled lard or from the fat of swine. They are compounded with mineral oils to yield lubricants of special properties.

LARGE APPLIANCE SURFACE COATING The coating of doors, cases, lids, panels, and interior support parts of residential and commercial washers, dryers, ranges, refrigerators, freezers, water heaters, dishwashers, trash compactors, air-conditioners, and other associated products.

LARGE NAVIGATION BUOY (LNB) A 40 feet diameter, automated disc-shaped buoy used to replace lightships. All LNBs are equipped with emergency lights.

LASH A maritime industry abbreviation for "Lighter Aboard Ship" or a type of oceangoing barge carrying vessel with the cargo being loaded in sealed floatable boxes or barges that are handled on and off the "mother" ship by ship-mounted cranes and are then pushed or towed to a shoreside terminal.

LASH (AND CARRY) The order to lash up the hammocks and stow them in the nettings.

LASHING Rope, wire, chain, or steel strapping usually used with turnbuckles to secure cargo or gear. A comparatively short manila line with an eye spliced in one end used to moor barges and tows when passing through locks. Its average length is about 60 feet with sizes varying from 1 3/4 to 3 inches in circumference. The line is thrown somewhat in the manner of a lasso (the eye spliced) to catch a wall pin or bollard so as to snub the movement of barges and then moor them in the lock chamber. Also, any short length of line used to secure two barges end-to-end or side-by-side.

LASHING POINT Point on a means of transport to which wires, chains, ropes, or straps that are used to hold goods in position are attached.

LASHING RODS Wires for securing from the top of the container to the deck (locking wires).

LASHING TURNBUCKLE Adjustable turnbuckle for tightening lashing rods and wires.

LASH UP A slang expression referring to the manner in which tugs or other vessels are secured to each other.

LAST CARRIER The participating airline over which air routes the last section of carriage under the waybill is undertaken or performed (air cargo).

LAST IN - FIRST OUT (LIFO) A method of which the assumption is that the most recently received (last in) is the first to be used or sold (first out).

LAT Latitude.

LATENT DEFECT A defect not immediately apparent.

LATENT HEAT The latent heat of fusion of a substance is the amount of heat required to convert unit mass of the substance from solid to liquid without change of temperature. The latent heat of vaporization is the amount of heat required to convert a unit mass of a substance from liquid to vapor without change of temperature.

LATERAL DAM   Usually a rock and brush structure constructed parallel with normal stream flow to train or confine the current to a definite channel.

LATERAL & FRONT-STACKING TRUCK   High-lift stacking truck capable of stacking and retrieving loads ahead and on either sides of the driving direction.

LATERAL SYSTEM   A system of aids to navigation in which characteristics of buoys and beacons indicate the sides of the channel or route relative to a conventional direction (usually upstream).

LATITUDE   The angular distance of a position on its meridian north or south from the equator, measured in degrees (a vessel at 25 degrees north latitude).

LAUNCH   Small power or motorboat. *See* Launching.

LAUNCHING   The operation of placing the hull in the water by allowing it to slide down the launching ways. During launching the weight of the hull is borne by the cradle and sliding ways that are temporarily attached to the hull and slide with it down the ground ways.

LAY   Direction of twist in a rope, such as left lay, right lay.

LAY ALOFT   The order to go aloft.

LAYCAN   Laydays/Canceling (date): Range of dates within which the hire contract must start.

LAY DAYS   The dates between which a chartered vessel is to be available in port for loading or cargo.

LAYING OFF   Marking plates, shapes, etc., for fabrication.

LAYING ON   To make additions.

LAYING OUT   Placing the necessary instructions on plates and shapes for shearing, planning, punching, bending, flanging, beveling, rolling, etc., from templates made in the mold loft or taken from the ship.

LAYTIME   Time at charterer's disposal for purpose of loading/unloading.

LAY UP   Temporary cessation of trading of a ship by a ship owner during a period when there is a surplus of ships in relation to the level of available cargoes. This surplus, known as overtonnaging, has the effect of depressing freight rates to the extent that some ship owners no long find it economical to trade their ship, preferring to lay them up until there is a reversal in the trend.

LAZARETTE   A storage room, usually for mooring lines, usually aft below the main deck, having access through a watertight hatch or manhole. A space between decks used as a storeroom.

LAZY GUY   A guy that carries very little strain.

L/C   Letter of credit.

LCD   Liquid Crystal Display. Used on electronic equipment.

LCL   Less Than Container Load. The quantity of freight, which is less than that, required for the application of a container load rate. Loose freight.

LCR   Lowest Current Rate

L&D   Loss and damage.

LDG Loading.

LEAD BARGE The head or first barge of a tow generally a barge with a long rake.

LEADING EDGE That edge of a propeller blade that cuts the water when the screw is revolving in the ahead direction. That edge of a rudder, diving plane, or strut arm that faces toward the bow of the ship.

LEAD SUSCEPTIBILITY The ability of gasoline to respond to the addition of tetraethyl lead, as reflected in the increase in octane number per increment of lead added.

LEAD TIME The total time that elapses between an order's placement and its receipt. It includes the time required for order transmittal, order processing, order preparation, and transit.

LEAD WALL The long wall of a lock also known as a guide wall outside the confine or the lock chamber, usually the land wall in the case of older locks.

LEAK (BY REGULATION) The emission of a volatile organic compound concentration greater than or equal to 10,000 parts per million by volume (ppmv) as shown by monitoring or dripping of process fluid.

LEAKING COMPONENT Any component that has a leak.

LEAN BURN ENGINE A stationary reciprocating internal combustion engine in which the amount of O_2 in the engine exhaust gases is 1.0% or more.

LEASE A contract by which one party gives to another party the use of property or equipment, e.g., containers, for a specified time against fixed payments.

LEASE CUSTODY TRANSFER The transfer of produced crude oil and/or condensate, after processing and/or treating in the producing operations, from storage tanks or automatic transfer facilities to pipelines or any other form of transportation.

LEASEHOLD INSURANCE (INS) Insurance for the tenant of a property leased against the loss of value of the lease or of profit from a sub-lease through termination of the lease by fire or other peril insured against.

LEASING COMPANY The company from which property or equipment is taken on lease.

LEASING CONTRACT A contract for the leasing of property or equipment.

LEATHER SURFACE COATING The coating of a leather substrate to impart properties that are not initially present, such as strength, stability, water or chemical repellency, or appearance.

LEAVE Special permission to be absent from ship or station for a longer period than the usual liberty.

LED Light emitting diode used to illuminate dials on electronic equipment.

LEE Side away from wind or protected from wind.

LEE SHORE The land to leeward of the vessel.

LEE SIDE The side of the ship away from the wind.

LEEWARD The direction away from the wind.

LEEWAY   Sideways movement of ship caused by wind or current.

LEFT BANK   The left descending bank of a river. The side of the river marked by red buoys, white or red lights, and red reflectors.

LEFT-HAND DRAFT   Where current pulls tow to the left.

LEFT-HAND DRAFT IN THIS SET OF MARKS   You can expect the tow to drift to the left while running this course.

LEFT-HAND REEF MAKES WELL IN TOWARD CHANNEL   An underwater sandbar is building in toward the channel. A condition requiring extra caution on the part of the pilot for the possible need of a flanking maneuver; the channel is considerably constricted.

LEG   A leg has an origin, destination, and carrier and is composed of all consecutive segments of a route booked through the same carrier. Also called Bookable Leg.

LEGAL WEIGHT   The weight of the goods plus any immediate wrappings that are sold along with the goods, e.g., the weight of a tin can as well as its contents. *See* Net Weight.

LEG OF MUTTON   A triangular lower sail.

LEND A HAND   To assist.

LENGTH BETWEEN PERPENDICULARS (LBP)   The length of a ship measured from the forward perpendicular to the after perpendicular. The linear distance from the most forward point of the stem to the aftermost point of the stern, measured parallel to the baseline. The forward perpendicular is a vertical line at the intersection of the fore side of the stem and the summer load waterline. The after perpendicular is a vertical line at the intersection of the summer load line and the after side of the rudder post or sternpost, or the centerline of the rudder stock if there is no rudder post or stem post.

LENGTH ON THE LOAD WATERLINE (LWL)   The linear distance from the most forward point of the LWL to the aftermost point of the LWL.

LENGTH OVER ALL (LOA)   The length of a ship from the extreme end of the bow to the aftermost point of the stern. The linear distance from the most forward point of the stem to the aftermost point of the stern, measured parallel to the baseline.

LESS THAN CONTAINER LOAD (LCL)   For operational purposes container is considered a container in which multiple consignments or parts thereof are shipped. *See* Consolidation.

LESS THAN TRUCKLOAD   Also known as LTL or LCL.

LESSOR   A person or firm that grants a lease.

LET FALL   An order to let the oars fall from position, "toss" into the rowlocks.

LET GO   To release and take in lines from a tug or towed unit as directed.

LETTER OF CREDIT (LC)   A method of payment for the goods in which the buyer establishes his credit with a local bank, clearly describing the goods to be purchased, the price, the documentation required, and a time limit for completion of the transaction. Upon receipt of the documentation, the bank is either paid by the buyer or takes title to the goods themselves and proceeds to transfer funds to the seller. The banks insist upon exact compliance with terms of sale and will not pay if there are discrepancies. A letter of credit is a document, issued by a bank per instructions by a buyer of goods, authorizing the seller to draw a specified sum of money under specified terms, usually the receipt by the bank of certain documents within a given time. Some of the specific descriptions are:

Back-to-Back: A secondary letter of credit issued to a beneficiary on the strength of a primary credit.

Clean: A letter of credit that requires the beneficiary to present only a draft or a receipt for specified funds before receiving payment.

Confirmed: A revolving letter of credit that permits any amount not used during any of the specified periods to be carried over and added to amounts available in later periods.

Deferred Payment: A letter of credit issued for the purchase and financing of merchandise, similar to acceptance type letter of credit, except that it requires presentation of sight drafts payable on an installment basis.

Irrevocable: An instrument that, once established, cannot be modified or canceled without the agreement of all parties concerned.

Noncumulative: A revolving letter of credit that prohibits the amount not used during the specific period to be available afterwards.

Restricted—A condition within the letter of credit that restricts its negotiation to a named bank.

Revocable: An instrument that can be modified or canceled at any moment without notice to and agreement of the beneficiary, but customarily includes a clause in the credit to the effect that any draft negotiated by a bank prior to the receipt of a notice of revocation or amendment will be honored by the issuing bank.

Revolving: An irrevocable letter issued for a specific amount; renews itself for the same amount over a given period.

Straight: A letter of credit that contains a limited engagement clause that states that the issuing bank promises to pay the beneficiary upon presentation of the required documents at its counters or the counters of the named bank.

Transferable: A letter of credit that allows the beneficiary to transfer in whole or in part any amount which, in aggregate, of such transfers does not exceed the amount of the credit.

Unconfirmed: A letter of credit forwarded to the beneficiary by the advising bank without engagement on the part of the advising bank.

LEVEE   A built-up embankment on or back from the riverbank for the purpose of containing floodwater.

LF   Load Factor.

LIABILITY   Legal responsibility for the consequences of certain acts or omissions.

LIABILITY (INS)   Broadly, any legally enforceable obligation; a responsibility of one person to another, enforceable in law.

LIABILITY INSURANCE (INS)   Insurance that pays and renders service on behalf of an insured for loss arising out of his responsibility, due to negligence, to others imposed by law or assumed by contract.

LIABILITY LIMITS (INS)   The sum or sums beyond which a liability insurance company does not protect the insured on a liability policy.

LIBERTY   Permission to be absent from the ship or station for a short period.

LIBERTY SHIPS   Liberty ships were the product of a number of shipyards in the U.S. during the years 1942–45; 2,700 Liberty ships were built on mass production lines.

LIBOR   London Interbank Offered Rate. The interest rate at which banks in London place Eurocurrency/Eurodollar deposits with each other for specified, fixed periods of time, most commonly six months.

LICENSES   Some governments require certain commodities to be licensed prior to exportation or importation. Clauses attesting to compliance are often required on the bill of lading. Various types issued for export (general, validated) and import as mandated by governments.

LIEN   A legal claim upon goods for the satisfaction of some debt or duty.

LIFEBOAT   A small boat carried on ships for use in emergency.

LIFE LINE   A line secured along the deck to lay hold of in heavy weather; a line thrown onboard a wreck by lifesaving crew; a knotted line secured to the span of a lifeboat davits for the use of the crew when hoisting and lowering.

LIFO   *See* Last In/First Out; Liner In Free Out.

LIFT   To "lift" a template is to make it from measurements taken from the job.

LIFT A TEMPLATE   To construct a template to the same size and shape as the part of the ship involved, from either the mold loft lines or from the ship itself, from which laying out of material for fabrication may be performed.

LIFTING   Transferring marks and measurements from a drawing model, etc., to a plate or other object, by templates or other means.

LIFTING EYE (SECURING EYE)   Rings or loops attached to a container or unit of cargo for lifting or securing.

LIFT ON/LIFT OFF (LO/LO)   Cargo loaded or unloaded by either ship or shore cranes.

LIFT VAN (LV)   A wooden or metal container used for packing household goods and personal effects. The van must have a capacity of at least 100 cubic feet and be suitable for lifting by mechanical device.

LIGHT   The signal emitted by a lighted aid to navigation. The illuminating apparatus used to emit the light signal. A lighted aid to navigation on a fixed structure.

LIGHT, PORT   An opening in a ship's side, provided with a glazed lid over it.

LIGHT BOAT   A towboat without a tow.

LIGHT DISPLACEMENT   Weight in long tons of vessel in a light condition.

LIGHT DRAFT   The draft of the dredge at its lightest load, which includes empty hoppers, fuel and stores low, and no extra equipment or personnel.

LIGHT DUTY TRUCK   Any motor vehicle rated at 8,500 pounds gross vehicle weight or less that is designed primarily for the transportation of property. As used in regulations, light duty truck means any motor vehicle, rated at 6,000 pounds gross vehicle weight or less that is designed primarily for purposes of transportation of property or is a derivative of such a vehicle, or is available with special features enabling off street or off highway operation and use.

LIGHTED ICE BUOY (LIB)   A lighted buoy without a sound signal and designed to withstand the forces of shifting and flowing ice. Used to replace a conventional buoy when that aid to navigation is endangered by ice.

LIGHT ENDS   In any given batch of oil, that portion of lowest boiling point. In gasoline, it is the portion distilling off up to about 158°F. In making lubricating oils, the light ends must be removed in order to produce finished oils of high flash point.

LIGHTENING   A vessel discharges part of its cargo at anchor into a lighter to reduce the vessel's draft so it can then get alongside a pier.

LIGHTENING HOLE   A large hole cut in a structural member, as in the web, where very little loss of strength will occur. These holes reduce the weight and in many cases serve as access holes. This condition is particularly true in floor plates and longitudinals in double bottom.

LIGHTER   A barge, boat, or small ship used to discharge or load a larger vessel while at anchor. Also, the act of discharging or loading cargo while at anchor from another vessel. Usually a large ship will lighter to a smaller ship to reduce her draft enough to fit in a berth.

LIGHTERAGE   Refers to carriage of goods by lighter and the charge assessed therefore.

LIGHTERING OR LIGHTERING OPERATION   Offshore transfer of a bulk liquid cargo from one marine tank vessel to another vessel.

LIGHT LIQUID   A fluid with a vapor pressure greater than 0.3 kilopascals (0.044 psi) at 20°C.

LIGHT SECTOR   The arc over which a light is visible, described in degrees true, as observed from seaward toward the light. May be used to define distinctive color difference of two adjoining sectors, or an obscured sector.

LIGHT STAND   Colloquial term meaning the position or location of a shore lighted aid to navigation.

LIGHT TUG   A tug or towboat running without a tow, also known as running lightheaded.

LIGHTWEIGHT   Weight of an empty vessel including equipment and outfit, spare parts required by regulatory bodies, machinery in working condition and liquids in the systems, but excluding liquids in the storage tanks, stores, and crew.

LIGHTWEIGHT TONS (LWT)   Actual weight of the empty ship (might have some water and fuel, AKA Light Ship).

LIMBER CHAINS   Chains passing through the limber holes of a vessel, by which they may be cleaned of dirt.

LIMBER HOLE   A hole of a few inches in diameter cut in a floor plate to allow water to drain through it near the bottom. Most frequently found in floor plates just above the frames and near the centerline of the ship.

LINE   Fibrous material twisted or braided together for securing purposes, called rope ashore. Rope cut from its coil used for various purposes; small cords such as log line, lead line, or small stuff as marlin, ratline, houseline, etc.

LINE DISPLACEMENT   Usually done after loading to clean shoreside piping and loading arms of cargo. Cargo is pushed into the ship's tanks.

LINE FUNCTIONS   The decision-making areas companies associate with daily operations. Logistics line functions include traffic management, inventory control, order processing, warehousing, and packaging.

LINE HAUL SHIPMENT   A shipment that moves between cities and over distances more than 100 to 150 miles in length.

LINE ITEM   A specific and unique identifier assigned to a product by the responsible enterprise.

LINE OF CONVERGENCE   Area in the trade wind zone found between about 10 degrees to 15 degrees latitude north or south of the equator where the NE winds meet the SE trade winds from the Southern Hemisphere. Often called the Intertropical Convergence Zone or ITCZ. May also be used to denote any area in the tropics where winds from different directions meet. Weather often consists of heavy rain and thunderstorms.

LINE OF DIVERGENCE   Zone in the tropics where winds flow away from each other. Area should be free of rain or extensive cloudiness.

LINER   A cargo ship that is operated between scheduled advertised ports on a regular basis. A flat or tapered metal strip placed under a plate or shape to bring it in line with another part that it overlaps.

LINER CONFERENCE   A group of two or more vessel-operating carriers that provides international liner services for the carriage of cargo on a particular trade route and that has an agreement or arrangement to operate under uniform or common freight rates and any other agreed conditions (e.g., FEFC = Far Eastern Freight Conference).

LINER IN FREE OUT (LIFO)   Transport condition denoting that the freight rate is inclusive of the sea carriage and the cost of loading, the latter as per the custom of the port. It excludes the cost of discharging.

LINER SERVICE   Type of service offered by regular line operators of vessels. The itineraries and sailing schedules are predetermined and fixed. Most of the cargo is containerized general cargo.

LINER SHIPPING COMPANY   A company transporting goods over sea in a regular service.

LINER TERMS   General statement of undefined terms of contract that tend to vary from port to port around the world.

LINER TERMS HOOK TO HOOK   Given that this is a notional point in chartering terms, this is best described as the shipper/receiver arranging for delivery/receival of cargo to/from directly under ship's hook and the ship paying for the labor to stow the cargo in the vessel's cargo holds, as well as onboard lashing and securing and provision of dunnage materials, and to discharge again over the ship's side. Shore-based stevedoring aspects remain the responsibility of the shipper/receiver; however, there are some owners that may incorporate these costs into their LTHH rate. Once again, ask owners to clearly define this aspect. Wharfage charges/dues/taxes can be a contentious issue but are usually considered to be for the shippers/receivers account and there may also be many other statutory levies on cargo or freight that may apply. Many shippers/receivers are unaware of these additional costs and do not include them into their costing and consequently may be left with an unexpected considerable expense at the completion of a project.

LINES   These are the names of the lines used in towing:

Back Line	Handy Line	Quarter Line
Backing Line	Head Line	Side Line
Breast Line	Jockey Line	Spar Line
Check Line	Lashing Line	Stern Line
Dropping Out Line	Lead Line	Tow Line
Face Line	Lock Line	Spring Line
Fore and Aft Line	Monkey Line	Peg Line

LINES   The plans of a ship that shows its form. From the lines drawn full size on the mold loft floor are made templates for the various parts of the hull.

LINE THROUGH   Lines placed on the bank and the boats would pull themselves through swift shallow channels. (A seldom-used term today.)

LINK   The transportation method used to connect the nodes (plants, warehouses) in a logistics system.

LINKBAND   A band fitted around the head of a cargo boom into which is shackled the topping lift, headblock, and boom guys.

LIQUEFIED GAS   A chemical that, being a vapor at all normal ambient temperatures and pressures, is liquefied for transportation either by cooling and refrigeration to a temperature below its boiling point or by pressuration at ambient temperatures. Also, a category of waterborne cargo movement that includes primarily liquefied natural gas (LNG) and liquefied petroleum gas (LPG), and other manufactured gases, coal gases, and natural gas products.

LIQUEFIED NATURAL GAS (LNG) Liquefied methane or ethane and mixtures in which methane and ethane predominate. Liquefied C1 and C2 hydrocarbons that can be only liquefied either by refrigeration or by pressurization at ambient temperatures. The liquid methane is carried at about 270°F and under less than 2 pounds of pressure.

LIQUEFIED PETROLEUM GAS (LPG) Liquefied propane or butane and mixtures of these or similar gases derived from petroleum. Gaseous forms of petroleum that have been converted into liquids by changes in temperature and pressure. C3 and C4 hydrocarbons that can be liquefied at moderate pressure. LPG is carried at about 50°F and under slightly more pressure than LNG.

LIQUIDATED DAMAGES The penalty a seller must pay if the construction project does not meet contractual standards or deadlines.

LIQUID BULK CARGO Liquid cargo shipped in large enough quantities to make it practical to employ tankers or tank barges rather than containers consisting of barrels, casks, or drums to be handled separately as breakbulk.

LIQUID FUEL Any liquid used as fuel that can be poured or pumped.

LIQUID MOUNTED SEAL A primary seal mounted in continuous contact with the liquid between the tank wall and the floating roof around the circumference of the tank.

LIST An inclination to one side; a tilt. Refers to a condition in which a vessel is deeper on one side than the other due to loading, wind, or icing. The amount in degrees that a vessel tilts from the vertical.

LITER 1.06 liquid U.S. quarts or 33.9 fluid ounces.

LITHIUM BASE GREASE A grease composed of a mineral oil thickened with lithium soaps.

LITHOGRAPHIC PRINTING A printing process in which the image and nonimage areas of the plate are on the same geometric plane. The image area is oil receptive (hydrophobic) and the nonimage area is water receptive (hydrophilic).

LITTORAL CURRENT A measurable drift of water running parallel and adjacent to the shore; synonymous with "longshore current."

LIVE LOAD A nonpermanent vertical load to which a structure is subjected, such as movable equipment or stored materials.

LIVESTOCK OR LIVE STOCK Cargo consisting of live animals, such as horses, cows, sheep, and chickens.

LLOYD'S OPEN FORM A form for continuous or "open" coverage based on standards and forms set by Lloyd's of London.

LLOYD'S REGISTRY An organization maintained for the surveying and classing of ships so that insurance Underwriters and others may know the quality and condition of the vessels offered for insurance or employment.

LLOYD'S SYNDICATE A group of Underwriters at London Lloyd's who entrust the underwriting of their business to one Underwriter.

LNG   Liquefied Natural Gas. One of the major types of liquefied gas cargoes transported in special cryogenic or LNG tanker vessels. The natural gas is liquefied at the source by cooling to –259°F and pumped via pipeline into LNG tankers special cargo tanks designed to maintain cryogenic temperatures during the voyage.

LOA   Length Overall.

LOAD CENTER   Railroad and marine transportation term for concentrating cargo in one location for distribution to other locations. Similar to airline "hubs."

LOAD DISPLACEMENT   Weight of vessel in long tons when fully loaded.

LOAD FACTOR   Percentage of capacity used. A measure of operating efficiently used by air carriers to determine the percentage of a plane's capacity that is used, or number of passengers/total number of seats.

LOAD FRAME   Hydraulic.

LOAD LINE   The line on a vessel defining the maximum mean draft to which the vessel may lawfully be submerged.

LOAD ON TOP   The practice of loading a fresh cargo of oil on top of oil recovered after tank cleaning operations. Systems now widely used in tankers engaged in the crude oil trade. The main object is to collect and settle onboard water and oil mixture resulting from ballasting and cleaning of tanks. The oil/water mixture can be pumped ashore at loading terminals that have special reception facilities and thus reduce risk of oil pollution at sea. If the mixture cannot be pumped ashore, the new cargo can be loaded on top and pumped ashore at the discharge port. Effective control of this system requires quantitative monitoring of the ballast prior to discharge.

LOAD RATIO   The ratio of loaded miles to empty miles per tractor.

LOAD TENDER   Pick-Up Request. An offer of cargo for transport by a shipper. Load tender terminology is primarily used in the motor industry.

LOADED DISPLACEMENT   The most a vessel can weigh or the deepest it can be immersed.

LOADED DRAFT   The draft of the dredge at its heaviest load, which includes full hoppers, full, stores, and fuel.

LOADED LEG   Subdivision of a ship's voyage during which the ship is carrying cargo.

LOADEN VESSEL   Vessel where cargo has been put onboard.

LOADING ALLOWANCE   A reduced rate that carriers offer to shippers and/or consignees who load and/or unload LTL or AQ shipments.

LOADING ARMS   Rigid steel pipes, hinged in three locations, and designed to allow the transfer of liquid cargo from ship to facility. Loading arms are permanently installed to shore piping and allow very little surging motion on the part of the ship.

LOADING DOCK   A warehouse or factory door where trucks are loaded or unloaded.

LOADING EVENT   An occurrence beginning with the connecting of marine terminal storage tanks to a marine tank vessel by means of pipes or hoses followed by the transferring of organic liquid cargo from the storage tank into the tank vessel and ending with the disconnecting of the pipes or hoses; or any other means of admitting any other organic liquid into marine vessel cargo tanks.

LOADING OVERALL   Loading through hatches or other deck openings by means of portable open-ended pipes or hoses.

LOADING PLAN   Cargo plan; stowage plan; a diagram of the placement of cargo in ship.

LOADING PORT   The port where the cargo is loaded onto the exporting vessel. This port must be reported on the Shipper's Export Declaration.

LOADING SEQUENCE   The rotation in which containers are to be loaded to or discharged from the vessel. The rotation in which barges are to be discharged from a lash or seabee vessel and delivered to the fleeting area or taken from the fleeting area and loaded onboard the vessel.

LOADING TRAMWAY   A pair of rails running down the river bank upon which a cart rides for the purpose of loading buoys and other equipment aboard a tender.

LOAD LINE   A predetermined distance below the main deck that a ship can be loaded, or the maximum draft it can load to. Load lines are issued for tropical, summer, and winter zones on the oceans of the world.

LOAN RECEIPT   Document signed by the Assured where he acknowledges receipt of money advanced by the insurance company as an interest-free loan (instead of payment of a loss) repayable to the insurance company only if the loss is recovered from a third party and then only to the extent of the recovery.

LOCAL   Movements of freight within the confines of the port.

LOCAL CARGO   Cargo delivered to/from the carrier and carrier's West Coast terminal where origin/destination of the cargo is in one of the states lying west of the Rocky Mountains.

LOCALIZED RAW MATERIAL   A raw material found in certain locations only.

LOCALLY STRONGER WINDS   Conditions in which winds over many small areas too numerous to mention are expected to be higher than the general wind in the area covered by the forecast (e.g., locally stronger winds may occur in fjords and channels as compared to winds over the open water).

LOCAL MOVEMENTS   Domestic traffic shipments and receipts between terminal berths in the same port or harbor area.

LOCAL NOTICE TO MARINERS   A written document issued by each Coast Guard District that is used to disseminate important information affecting aids to navigation, dredging, marine construction, special marine activities, and bridge construction, on the waterways within the district.

LOCAL RATE   A rate published between two points served by one carrier.

LOCAL SERVICE CARRIERS An air carrier classification of carriers that operate between areas of lesser and major population centers. These carriers feed passengers into the major cities to connect with trunk (major) carriers. Local service carriers are now classified as national carriers.

LOCAL TAXES Revenues that accrue to local governments (countries, municipalities, special districts, and school districts) through property tax, local sales taxes, and other revenues (i.e., local license fees).

LOCATING PIN *See* Cone.

LOCATING SYSTEM Military vessels use a system of numbers to provide location reference for the purpose of certain equipment on board, but is a useful tool when confused as to your whereabouts during emergencies. Three separated numbers are used, the first being the deck, the second the frame, and the third centerline, starboard or port designations (0 = centerline, 1 = starboard, 2 = port, 3 = second location away from centerline to starboard, etc. For example, 21420 could be placed on a fire station on the second deck (first below main), frame 142 (from forward) and on the centerline.

LOCATION Any named geographical place, recognized by a competent national body, with permanent facilities used for goods movements associated with international trade, and used frequently for these purposes: geographical place such as a port, an airport, an inland freight terminal, a container freight station, a container yard, a container depot, a terminal or any other place where customs clearance and/or regular receipt or delivery of goods can take place. an area (e.g., in a warehouse) marked off or designated for a specific purpose.

LOCATION CLAUSE (INS) Used in cargo open covers this limits Underwriters' liability in any one location.

LOCK A chamber built at one side of a river dam for the purpose of raising or lowering the floating traffic, which wishes to pass the dam.

LOCK CELL The chamber of a lock.

LOCKER A storage compartment on a ship.

LOCK GATE A movable structural barrier to hold back the water in a lock chamber.

LOCKING PAD Devices for securing containers to a ship's deck, chassis, etc.

LOCK LINE A long line led from the bow and the stern of the tow to the lock wall.

LOCK NUT A thin nut that is turned down over the regular nut on a bolt to lock the regular nut against turning off. Also applied to a thin nut placed on a pipe to hold packing at a joint or used on both sides of a bulkhead through which a pipe passes to secure tightness.

LOCK TRAFFIC LIGHTS Red, yellow, and green lights displayed at the entrances of the lock, both up and downbound, for the purpose of controlling traffic.

LOFTSMAN A man who lays off the ship's lines to full size in the mold loft to make templates from.

LOG This is the vessel's official record. It may be written "in the rough" when on watch or may be "smooth," as prepared from the rough log.

LOG BOOK A book containing the official record of a ship's activities together with remarks concerning the state of the weather.

LOG DECK Large, high storage pile of logs at a sawmill or loading terminal.

LOGISTICS The planning and organization of supplies, stores, and accommodations required for the support of large personnel movements and expenditures.

LOGISTICS CHANNEL The network of intermediaries engaged in transfer, storage, handling, and communications functions that contribute to the efficient flow of goods.

LOGISTICS COSTS The factors associated with the acquisition, storage, movement, and disposition of goods.

LOGISTICS EXCHANGES Online portals that offer logistics services in several different categories.

LOGISTICS INFORMATION SYSTEM (LIS) People, equipment, and procedures to gather, sort, analyze, evaluate, and distribute needed, timely, and accurate information to logistics decision makers.

LOGISTICS SERVICE PROVIDER (LSP) Companies that specialize in providing various types of logistics services.

LOG PICKER A front-end loader with large jaws for handling logs.

LOI Letter of Indemnity.

LOLL, ANGLE OF A dangerous condition of unstable equilibrium when a vessel flops from an apparent list of one side, to another list the opposite direction, usually caused due to free surface.

LO/LO Lift On/Lift Off. A type of vessel that allows cargo to be loaded or unloaded by either ship or shore cranes.

LONDON INTERBANK OFFERED RATE (LIBOR) The interest rate at which banks in London place Eurocurrency/Eurodollar deposits with each other for specified, fixed periods of time, most commonly six months.

LONGITUDE The angular distance of a position on the equator east or west of the standard Greenwich meridian up to 180 east or west.

LONGITUDINAL A structural member, usually in a double-bottom tank, that runs parallel to the centerline.

LONGITUDINAL CONSTRUCTION AKA Isherwood Construction. A system of building a ship offering larger weight carrying capacity due to long, full longitudinal bulkheads and large web frames. Usually used in tanker construction.

LONGITUDINAL STABILITY Tendency of a vessel to return to its original longitudinal position. Longitudinal stability terms: longitudinal metacenter, GML, BML, center of buoyancy, center of gravity.

LONG LENGTH   A charge assessed against cargo that is longer than specified lengths.

LONGSHORE LABOR   Workers hired to move cargo between the terminal and the vessel and to manage vessel stowage and cargo marshaling.

LONGSHOREMAN   Individual employed locally in a port to load and unload ships.

LONG TON   Equivalent to a measure of 2,240 pounds avoirdupois weight per ton.

LOOKOUT   The man stationed aloft or in the bows for observing and reporting objects seen.

LOOM   The part of an oar between the blade and handle; the reflection of a light that is below the horizon due to certain atmospheric conditions.

LOOP   Louisiana Offshore Oil Port. Corporate name of some 10 major oil companies who organized to construct and operate a deepwater oil port off the coast of the State of Louisiana capable of accommodating very large crude oil carriers with drafts of 90 feet and over.

LOOSE   To unfurl a sail. Also, without packing.

LOOSE HEADED   Light boat underway.

LORRY (BRIT)   Motor truck used for transport of goods.

LOSS AND DAMAGE   Loss or damage of shipments while in transit or in a warehouse.

LOSS OF USE INSURANCE (INS)   Insurance against loss due to the inability to use property because of its damage or destruction.

LOSS PAYABLE CLAUSE (INS)   Clause in an insurance policy to specifically identify interested parties (the insured, mortgagees, trustees, lienholders, etc.).

LOST OR NOT LOST   A clause used in ocean marine insurance under which the company will pay even if the loss insured against has occurred prior to the effective date of the insurance. The company would, of course, not be liable if the policyholder knew that the loss had occurred when he/she bought the insurance. In days past, a ship could easily be lost or damaged and the owner would not find out about it until later, during which time he might want to insure it.

LOUVER   A small opening to permit the passage of air for the purpose of ventilation, which may be partially or completely closed by the operation of overlapping shutters.

LOW   Cyclone or depression. Weather pattern in which closed isobars at the center of the pattern are of lower pressure than those farther from the center. Also Last Open Water.

LOW BOY   A trailer or semitrailer with no sides and with the floor of the unit close to the ground.

LOW CAP   Tarpaulin for unit where cargo is below gate height.

LOWER EXPLOSIVE LIMIT (LEL)   The minimum concentration of a vapor in air, which forms an explosive mixture.

LOWER GAUGE   A gauge located in the tail water of a dam (downstream side); colloquially called tail gate.

LOWER TOXIC LIMIT   The maximum permissible content of petroleum vapor (0.1 percent by volume) in a tank or compartment that is to be entered by persons.

LOW LOADING   A freight vehicle (usually a semitrailer) with a large well between the rear wheels and the king pin on which heavy loads can be carried.

LOW PROFILE CARRIER (MOONWALKER, TRADE NAME)   Handles low 16 feet 6 inches units on crane deck of RO/RO vessels.

LOW WATER DAM   A low lever dam designed to hold back a head of water so as to maintain project depth in a certain area. The dam may be visible at the low water stage. Also, a dam that is more effective at low water. At high water, the dam becomes a weir.

LOW WATER DATUM   A term used by the Corps of Engineers to define their originating point of elevation in determining stages of water when erecting various gauges along the river.

LOYALTY CONTRACT   A contract with an ocean common carrier or conference, other than a service contract or contract based on time volume rates; by which a shipper obtains lower rates by committing all or a fixed portion of its cargo to the carrier or conference and the contract provides for a deferred rebate agreement.

LPG   Refers to "liquefied petroleum gas"; another one of the principal types of liquefied gas cargoes transported in LPG tanker vessels.

L&R   Lake and rail.

LS (LUMPS)   Lump Sum freight. Money paid to shipper for a charter of a ship (or portion) up to stated limit irrespective of quantity of cargo.

LSA   Liner Shipping Agreements.

LSD   Lashed Secured Dunnage.

LSW 1130   London "War On Land" insurance clauses. (ICC war clauses end coverage once goods are offloaded from the ship or aircraft.)

LT   Liner Terms; Long Ton.

LTGE   Lighterage.

LTHH   Liner Terms - Hook-to-Hook.

LTL (LESS-THAN-TRUCKLOAD)   A load that is too small to qualify as a "truckload" under motor freight classification rules. As such, it pays a higher rate per pound.

LUBBER POINT (LINE)   The vertical blank line marked on the inner surface of the bowl of a compass indicating the compass direction of the ship's head.

LUBRICANT   Material, especially oils, greases, and solids such as graphite, used to decrease friction.

LUBRICATING GREASE   A solid or semisolid material consisting of fluid lubricant(s) and soap and/or thickening agent(s), with or without additives or fillers, suitable for reducing friction between mechanical moving parts.

LUFF BAR Colloquial term describing a steep bank on the lower Mississippi River. A bold reef that has become dry at low water.

LUFFING CRANE A crane with which the load can be moved to or from the crane horizontally.

LUMINOUS RANGE The greatest distance a light can be expected to be seen given its nominal range and the prevailing meteorological visibility.

LUMPING The act of assisting a motor carrier owner-operator in the loading and unloading of property; quite commonly used in the food industry.

LUMPS *See* LS (Lumps).

LUMP SUM An agreed sum of money that is paid in full settlement at one time. This term is often used in connection with charter parties.

LUMP SUM CHARTER A voyage charter whereby the ship owner agrees to place the whole or a part of the vessel's capacity at the charterer's disposal for which a lump-sum freight is being paid.

LURCH The sudden roll of a vessel.

LW Low Water.

LYCN Laycan. Layday canceling date.

LYSLE GUN A gun used in the lifesaving service to throw a lifeline to a ship in distress.

M

M   Symbol for metacenter.

MACHINERY SPACE   *See* Engine Room.

MAFI (GER)   German brand name of a roll trailer used for RO/RO purposes.

MAF/TRAILER   A low bed trailer used to transport cargo on RO/RO vessels.

MAGAZINE   Compartment used for stowage of ammunition and explosives. Often specifically applied to compartments for the stowage of powder as a distinction from shell stowage spaces.

MAGNET WIRE INSULATION SURFACE COATING   The application of electrically insulating varnish or enamel to aluminum or copper wire for use in electrical machinery.

MAIL OUT   A widely distributed general correspondence issued by the California Air Resources Board whenever said board needs information from the public or when it wishes to inform the public of new information.

MAIN BODY   The hull proper, without the deckhouses, etc.

MAIN CARGO PUMP   Pumps used for discharging main body of cargo.

MAIN DECK   The uppermost deck extending continuously throughout the length of the vessel; the principle deck, usually immediately below weather deck. The deck from which the freeboard is determined

MAIN LINE OPERATOR (MLO)   A carrier employing vessel(s) in the main or principal routes in a trade but not participating within a consortium.

MAIN LOADING AND DISCHARGE LINES   Those lines running fore and aft from pump room and connected by crossovers.

MAIN MAST   Mast, second from the bow.

MAIN STEM   The main portion of navigable channel of a river where more than one channel exists.

MAIN SUCTION FOOT   Bell mouthed casting attached to foot of main suction valve 2 or 3 inches from the bottom.

MAIN SUCTION VALVE   Master suction valve in each tank through which the main body of oil is drawn.

MAINTENANCE CHAIN   A sequence of events in a goods flow that preserves and/or restores the value of a specific good. This may include repair.

MAJOR CARRIER   A for-hire certificated air carrier that has annual operating revenues of $1 billion or more; the carrier usually operates between major population centers.

MAKE COLORS   Hoisting the ensign at 8:00 a.m.

MAKE SAIL   An order to set the sail.

MAKE THE COURSE GOOD   Steering and turning on required lights at sundown.

MAKE THE LAND   Landfall.

MAKEUP SOLVENT   Any solvent(s) that is(are) added to printing inks to reduce viscosity or otherwise modify properties.

MAKE UP TOW   Assemble barges into a tow.

MAKE WATER   To leak, to ship water on deck, to distill freshwater from saltwater.

MAKING UP   The placing and securing of lines from a tug or towboat in order to tow.

MAKING WAY   Moving through the water under propulsion.

MALICIOUS DAMAGE CLAUSE (INS)   A clause published by the Institute of London Underwriters for use in a cargo policy that is subject to the Institute Cargo Clauses (1982) B or C. It adds the risks of malicious acts, vandalism, and sabotage to the cargo policy.

MALPRACTICE   A carrier giving a customer special preference to attract cargo. This can take the form of a money refund (rebate); using lower figures than actual for the assessment of freight charges (undercubing); mis-declaration of the commodity shipped to allow the assessment of a lower tariff rate; waiving published tariff charges for demurrage, CFS handling, or equalization; providing specialized equipment to a shipper to the detriment of other shippers, etc.

MANDAMUS   A writ issued by a court; requires that specific things be done.

MANDATED COSTS   Refers to added development costs incurred by ports brought about by Federal legislation in the areas of environmental protection, employee health and safety, and cargo security regulations.

MANEUVER BOAT   Boat used by the Corps of Engineers in raising and lowering movable wickets of dams on the Ohio River.

MANGER   Space created by a low coaming running athwartships abaft the hawse pipes in an internal space or shelter deck. A grating in the chain locker that holds the anchor chain to allow for drainage.

MANHOLE   An opening through a deck to allow access, usually to a vertical ladder into a tank, with a watertight fit. A round- or oval-shaped hole cut in a ship's divisional plating, large enough for a man to pass through.

MANIFEST   A document that lists in detail all the bills of lading issued by a carrier or its agent or master, i.e., a detailed summary of the total cargo of a vessel. Used principally for Customs purposes.

MANIFOLD   Deck piping onboard a tanker that runs athwartship, from which liquid cargo is directed to tanks throughout the vessel. A box casting containing several valves to which pipelines are led from various compartments and pumps on a ship, so as to allow any tank to be connected to one or more pumps.

MANIFOLD VALVES   In a tanker's plumbing system, the valves immediately adjacent to the ship/shore connecting flanges. Generally, a convenient grouping of valves in a piping system or common pipe.

MANILA   Rope made from the fibers of the abaca plant.

MANNING SCALES   The minimum number of officers and crew members that can be engaged on a ship to be considered as sufficient hands with practical ability to meet every possible eventuality at sea.

MAN ROPES   Ropes hung over the ship's side and used for assistance in ascending or descending.

MANTLET PLATE   A thin plate for the protection of personnel, fitted over bolt or rivet heads to act as a screen to prevent the heads flying about when the structure is subjected to impact.

MANUAL   An activity that a radar observer performs, possibly with assistance from a machine. Used only in connection with ARPA performance standards.

MANUAL RATES (INS)   Usually the published rate for some unit of insurance. An example is the Workers' Compensation Manual where the rates shown apply to each $100 of the payroll of the insured, $100 being the unit.

MANUFACTURER'S EXPORT AGENT   A firm that acts as an export sales agent for several noncompeting manufacturers. Business is transacted under the name of the agent firm.

MANUFACTURER'S ADVISORY CORRESPONDENCE   A document issued by the California Air Resources Board that is a policy interpretation for further clarification of the California Code of Regulations applicable to motor vehicles.

MANUFACTURER'S PLATE   A plate indicating the name and address of the container manufacturer and particulars of the container.

MANUFACTURING PLANT   A stationary source where automobile or light duty truck bodies are manufactured and/or finished.

MAQUILADORA   Manufacturing plants that exist just south of the U.S.-Mexican border.

MAR POLICY (INS)   A market term for the form of marine policy used by Lloyd's and the London company market. It is a basic contract form to which the conditions agreed by the insurers subscribing a marine insurance contract are attached.

MARAD   The U.S. Maritime Administration.

MARCONI RIG   A sloop rig with a high leg of mutton sail.

MARGIN ANGLE   Angle bar connecting margin plates to shell.

MARGIN BRACKET   A bracket connecting the frame to the margin plates.

MARGIN PLANK   A plank forming the boundary or margin of the deck planking.

MARGIN PLATE   Any one of the outer row of plates of the inner bottom, connecting with the shell plating at the bilge.

MARGINAL COST   The cost to produce one additional unit of output; the change in total variable cost resulting from a one-unit change in output.

MARINE CARGO INSURANCE   Insurance protection for goods in transit whether moving via ocean, air, rail, or truck. Broadly, insurance covering loss of, or damage to, goods at sea. Marine insurance typically compensates the owner of merchandise for losses in excess of those that can be legally recovered from the carrier that are sustained from fire, shipwreck, piracy, and various other causes. Three of the most common types of marine insurance coverage are "free of particular average" (f.p.a.), "with average" (w.a.), and "all risks coverage."

MARINE DEFINITION In the past, marine Underwriters, fire Underwriters, and casualty Underwriters had different ideas about what constituted "marine" insurance. To resolve the resulting confusion, committees were formed to work with state insurance departments in creating a standard definition of marine insurance. A "Joint Committee of Interpretation and Complaint" was formed for the purpose of interpreting this definition as it applied to specific cases that were submitted from time to time by interested parties. Insurance departments have, in general, adopted the findings of this committee as their own rules.

MARINE EXTENSION CLAUSE Cargo policy clause that continues coverage on goods during deviation, delay, re-shipment, transshipment, or any other variation in normal transit beyond the Assured's control.

MARINE INSURANCE Broadly, insurance covering loss or damage of goods at sea. Marine insurance typically compensates the owner of merchandise for losses sustained from fire, shipwreck, etc., but excludes losses that can be recovered from the carrier.

MARINE PERILS The perils that are insured against in an ocean marine insurance policy.

MARINE RAILWAY *See* Dry-dock.

MARINE SURVEYOR Specialist who determines the nature, extent, and cause of loss and/or damage.

MARINE SYNDICATES Groups of companies acting in common to insure certain ocean marine classes. Also, a term used to describe groups that make inspections and surveys and institute standards for the construction of vessels.

MARINE TANK VESSEL Any marine vessel that is capable of carrying liquid bulk cargo in tanks.

MARINE TERMINAL Consists of a pier or wharf structure located in a harbor used for transferring cargo between ship and shore, and includes one or more ship berths together with cargo handling equipment, railroad and truck accommodations, covered and open storage space, and other facilities. Also, wharves, bulkheads, quays, piers, docks, and other berthing locations and adjacent storage or adjacent areas and structures associated with the primary movement of cargo or materials from vessel to shore or shore to vessel including structures that are devoted to receiving, handling, holding, consolidating and loading or delivery of waterborne shipments or passengers, including areas devoted to the maintenance of the terminal or equipment. The term does not include production or manufacturing areas nor does it include storage facilities directly associated with those production or manufacturing areas.

MARINE VESSEL Any tugboat, tanker, freighter, barge, passenger ship, or any other boat, ship, or watercraft except those used primarily for recreation.

MARITIME Business pertaining to commerce or navigation transacted upon the sea or in seaports in such matters as the court of admiralty has jurisdiction.

MARITIME ADMINISTRATION U.S. governmental agency that oversees subsidy programs to the United States Merchant Marine. Assigns routes to subsidized liners.

MARK General term for a navigational mark, e.g., buoy, structure, or topographical feature that may be used to fix a vessel's position.

MARK TWAIN Colloquial term for 12-foot depth or mark 2 on the lead line.

MARKED CHANNEL Channel marked by buoys.

MARKER/CLEARENCE LIGHTS Lights located on the front, side, and rear of chassis in accordance with over-the-road regulations.

MARKET VALUE CLAUSE (INS) A provision that may be used in property damage insurance form covering some risks that obligates the insurance company, in the event of loss, to pay the established cash selling price of the destroyed or damaged stock, rather than the actual case value as provided in the standard fire policy.

MARKING Letters, numbers, and other symbols placed on cargo packages to facilitate identification. Also known as marks.

MARKS *See* Marks and Numbers; Shipping Marks.

MARKS AND NUMBERS Marks and numbers placed on goods used to identify a shipment or parts of a shipment.

MARLIN A double-threaded, left-handed tarred cord, about $\frac{1}{8}$" diameter, made of a good grade of American hemp used for seizing.

MARLINE HAMMER *See* Serving Mallet.

MARLINSPIKE A pointed iron or steel instrument used to separate the strands in splicing wire rope and as a lever in marling or putting on seizings. The wire rope spike has a flat, rounded end and the manila rope spike has a sharp point.

MAROON To put a person ashore with no means of returning.

MARPOL The International Convention for the Prevention of Pollution from Ships, adopted in 1973 and amended in 1978. It constitutes the basic international law for limiting all ship source pollution, including structural and operational provisions for tank vessel pollution control; the term is used in this study to describe the current standard for vessel design.

MARRY To join any two objects, usually falls. The Married Fall system consists of handling cargo by two connected falls. Also called Yard and Stay method or Union Purchase method.

MARSHALLING Accumulating products or materials needed for a project.

MARSHALLING YARD Open space adjacent to containership berthing facilities at marine container handling terminals designed for parking and stacking inbound and outbound containers moving between ship and terminal storage and between the hinterland and terminal storage.

MAST   A long pole of steel or wood, usually circular in section, one or more of which are usually located, in an upright position, on the center-line of a ship. Originally intended for carrying sails, they are now used more as supports for the rigging, cargo, and boat handling gear and wireless equipment. Along with supporting booms or antenna, it provides ventilation.

MAST COLLAR   A piece of wood or a steel shape formed into a ring and fitted around the mast hole in a deck.

MASTER   Senior officer aboard a merchant vessel, referred to as captain.

MASTER AIRWAY BILL (MAWB)   The bill of lading issued by air carriers to their customers.

MASTER INBOND   U.S. Customs' automated program under AMS. It allows for electronic reporting of inbound (foreign) cargoes in the United States.

MASTER OR BLOCK VALVES   Those valves used to block off one tank from another and block off tanks from pumps. These are on the main cargo lines.

MASTER'S PROTEST   Sworn statement by captain describing any unusual happening during the voyage.

MAST HEAD   The top of a mast.

MAST HOUNDS   The upper portion of the mast at which the outrigger or trestletrees are fitted. Also applied to that portion at which the hound band for attaching the shrouds is fitted on masts without outrigger or trestletrees.

MAST PARTNERS   Wood planking or steel plating worked around a mast hole to give side support to the mast.

MAST STEP   The frame on the keels into which the keel of a mast is fitted.

MAST TABLE   Same as Boom Table and Tabernacle.

MASTHEAD LIGHT   The white running light carried by steam vessels underway on the foremast or in the fore part of the vessel.

MATE   A deck officer on a merchant ship ranking below the master.

MATERIAL BREACH   A breach serious enough to destroy the value of the contract and to give a basis for an action for breach of contract. Breach of contract—a breach of a legal duty; failure to do something that is required in a contract.

MATERIAL FACT (INS)   Anything affecting an insurance contract significant enough to change the agreement between the insurance company and the policyholder.

MATERIAL HANDLING EQUIPMENT   Forklift trucks, platform tracks, ware-housing industrial cranes, straddle carriers, pallet trucks, platform trucks, warehouse trailers, conveyer systems and other equipment used in storage and handling operations.

MATERIAL RECOVERY SECTION   A vacuum devolatilizer system, styrene recovery system, or other system of equipment that separates styrene monomer and/or reaction by products from polystyrene, or separates styrene monomer from reaction by products.

MATERIALS MANAGEMENT The inbound phase of business logistics concerned with the movement and storage of raw materials.

MATE'S RECEIPT An archaic practice. An acknowledgment of cargo receipt signed by a mate of the vessel. The possessor of the mate's receipt is entitled to the bill of lading, in exchange for that receipt.

MAWB *See* Master Airway Bill.

MAXIMUM GROSS WEIGHT Maximum total weight of a container, including its payload and any internal fittings. This is also called the rating.

MAXIMUM HIGH WATER ELEVATION The highest water level reached during the past 200 years of record keeping.

MAXIMUM PAYLOAD Maximum allowable weight of a payload, i.e., maximum gross weight less tare weight.

MB Merchant Broker.

MBM One thousand board feet. One MBM equals 2,265 cm.

MBS One thousand board feet, Brereton Scale. Used in log loading only.

MCFS Master Container Freight Station. *See* CFS.

MCO *See* Miscellaneous Charge Order.

MDO Marine Diesel Oil.

MDSE. Merchandise.

MEAN DRAFT Draft midway between the draft forward and draft aft.

MEAN LOW WATER (MLW) The average height of the low water determined from records taken in some predetermined period.

MEAN SEA LEVEL (MSL) The average height of the sea, determined by averaging the hourly heights of the tide for a period of time.

MEASUREMENT CARGO Freight on which transportation charges are calculated on the basis of volume measurement.

MEASUREMENT TON Bale cubic in units of 40 cubic feet to the ton. A capacity of 10,000 M/T is the same as 400,000 bale cubic.

MECHANICAL DERANGEMENT EXCLUSION (INS) Typical mechanical derangement clauses: "Excluding loss or damage due to mechanical, electrical, or electronic breakdown or derangement unless caused by a peril insured against under the terms of this policy and there is evidence of an external damage."

MECHANICALLY VENTILATED CONTAINER A container fitted with a means of forced air ventilation.

MECHANIC'S LIEN The legal enforceable claim that a person who has performed work or provided materials is permitted to make against title to the property or as a preferential person in the event the estate or business is liquidated.

MEDICINAL OIL A highly refined, colorless, tasteless, and odorless petroleum lubricating oil of low viscosity used as a medicine in the nature of an internal lubricant.

MEET A DRAFT To pay or honor a draft falling due.

MELTING POINT   The temperature at which the liquid state of a substance is in equilibrium with the solid state; at a high temperature the solid will melt.

MEMORANDUM BILL OF LADING (MEMO BILL)   An in-house bill of lading. A duplicate copy.

MERCAPTANS   Organic compounds having the general formula R-SH, meaning that the thiol group (SH) is attached to a radical such as CH_3 or C_2H_5. The simpler mercaptans have a strong, repulsive, garlic-like odor that becomes less pronounced with increasing molecular weight and higher boiling points.

MERCHANDISE PROCESSING FEE (MPF)   MPF was first implemented on December 1, 1986, and it's assessed at the rate of 0.17 percent ad valorem on all formal merchandise entries. MPF collections are used to partially offset the cost of U.S. Customs' commercial operations. 0.17% translates into $1.70 per each $1,000.00 of commercial cargo value.

MERCHANT HAULAGE   Inland transport of cargo in shipping containers arranged by the merchant. It includes empty container-moves to and from hand-over points in respect of containers released by the carrier to merchants.

MERCHANT-INSPIRED CARRIER HAULAGE   Carrier haulage by a carrier, which is nominated by the shipper or receiver of the goods, but paid by the carrier.

MESSENGER   A term used for a light line made fast to a heavier line or hawse and used to take the heavier line across an intervening space. The messenger line is thrown and then the heavier line is hauled in. It is larger and stronger than a heaving line.

MESS GEAR   Equipment for serving meals.

MESS ROOM (MESS DECK)   A space or compartment where members of the crew eat their meals; a dining room. A dining room in which officers eat their meals is called a wardroom mess (military) or saloon mess or salon (merchant marine).

METACENTER   A point above the center of buoyancy that is the center of a circle to which the center of buoyancy rotates. M—The highest point to which G may rise and still permit the vessel to have positive stability. Found at the intersection of the line of action of B when the ship is erect with the line of action of B when the ship is given a small inclination.

METACENTRIC HEIGHT   A measure of a ship's initial stability, it is the distance between the metacenter and the center of gravity. If the center of gravity is below the metacenter, the vessel is stable. The center of gravity of the vessel. Used as a measure of initial stability.

   The distance between the center of gravity (G) and the metacenter (M), usually called (GM). The greater this distance, the greater is the tendency of the vessel to right itself from any position of heel.

METACENTRIC RADIUS   Distance between B and M.

METAL CAN SURFACE COATING   The coating of two or three piece metal cans.

METAL COIL SURFACE COATING   The coating of any flat metal sheet or strip that comes in rolls or coils.

METAL DEACTIVATORS   Organic compounds that suppress the catalytic action of heavy metal compounds sometimes contained in hydrocarbon distillates. (Metal compounds tend to promote the formation of gum.)

METAL FURNITURE SURFACE COATING   The coating of any metal parts that will be assembled with other metal, wood, fabric, plastic, or glass parts to form a furniture piece.

METEOROLOGICAL VISIBILITY   The greatest distance at which a black object of suitable dimension could be seen and recognized against the horizon sky by day or in the case of night observations, could be seen and recognized if the general illumination were raised to the normal daylight level.

METER   Approximately 39.37 inches.

METRIC TON   2,204.6 pounds or 1,000 kilograms.

MHW   Mean High Water.

MIB   Marine Index Bureau.

MICROBRIDGE   Cargo movement in which the water carrier provides a through service between an inland point and the port of load/discharge. The carrier is responsible for cargo and costs from origin on to destination. Also known as IPI or Thru Service.

MICRO LANDBRIDGE   A through movement in which cargo moves between an inland U.S. point and a port via rail or truck, connecting with a ship for movement to or from a foreign port. (The ocean carrier accepts full responsibility for the entire movement on a single through bill of lading).

MICRO OR MINI BRIDGE   A joint water, rail, or truck movement of containers offered by ocean carriers from a foreign port to an inland U.S. city through an intermediate U.S. port or the reverse.

MIDCONTINENT OILS   Petroleum oils obtained from the central regions of the United States, usually having characteristics between those of Pennsylvania and Coastal oils.

MIDDLE BAR   Bar in the middle of the river.

MIDDLE BODY   The midships portion of a vessel throughout the length of which a constant cross-sectional shape is maintained.

MIDSHIP   At or near the middle point of a ship's length.

MIDSHIP BEAM   A deck beam of the transverse frame located at the midpoint between the forward and after perpendiculars. Also applicable to the transverse dimension of the hull at the same point.

MIDSHIP FRAME   The frame located at the midpoint between the perpendiculars.

MIDSHIP GUY   The guy between the heads of the booms on a married fall, or yard and stay, cargo system. Also called schooner guy or spanner guy. A tackle connecting the heads of the outboard and hatch booms, also called schooner guy. The inboard guys for the booms, where these are used in place of a single midship guy connecting the heads of the booms. Also called lazy guy.

MIDSHIP SECTION   A plan showing a cross section of the ship through the middle or amidships. This plan shows sizes of frames, beams, brackets, etc., and thicknesses of plating. That frame section halfway between the forward and after perpendiculars.

MIDSHIPS   Same as amidships.

MILE   5,280 feet.

MILEAGE ALLOWANCE   An allowance, based upon distance, that railroads give to shippers using private railcars.

MILEAGE NUMBER   A number assigned to aids to navigation that gives the distance in sailing miles along the river from a reference point to the aid to navigation. Used principally in the Mississippi River system.

MILEAGE PRORATION   Proration on the basis of the applicable local mileage (air cargo).

MILEAGE RATE   A rate based upon the number of miles the commodity is shipped.

MILE BOARD   A 12" × 36" board mounted horizontally above a shore aid to navigation and labeled with the river mileage at that point.

MILL SCALE   A magnetic product formed on iron and some steel surfaces during the manufacturing process.

MINERAL OIL   A wide range of products derived from petroleum and within the viscosity ranges of products spoken of as oils.

MINERAL SEAL OIL   A light lubricating oil that is chemically refined.

MINI LANDBRIDGE   A through movement of cargo between Europe and the Pacific Coast of the U.S., or between the Far East and the Atlantic or Gulf Coast of the U.S. Also, a unit train movement across the U.S. that substitutes for the all water route through the Panama Canal. (The ocean carrier accepts full responsibility for the entire movement on a single through bill of lading).

MINIMUM BILL OF LADING   A clause in a bill of lading that specifies the least charge that the carrier will make for issuing a lading. The charge may be a definite sum or the current charge per ton for any specified quantity.

MINIMUM CHARGE   The lowest charge that can be assessed to transport a shipment.

MINIMUM POOL ELEVATION   The least depth to which a pool is permitted to go and still maintain project channel depth.

MINIMUM PREMIUM (INS)   The smallest premium that an insurance company will accept for writing a particular policy or bond for a designated period.

MINIMUM WEIGHT   The shipment weight the carrier's tariff specifies as the minimum weight required to use the TL or CL rate; the rate discount volume.

MIN/MAX   Minimum/Maximum (cargo quantity).

MIN-MAX LEASE In container port management, a lease arrangement whereby the landlord port is guaranteed a minimum compensation from the steamship tenant, but earns more as cargo volumes increase up to a maximum. After the maximum is reached, the steamship tenant pays no additional compensation

MISCELLANEOUS CHARGE ORDER (MCO) A document issued by a carrier or his agent requesting the issue of an appropriate passenger ticket and baggage check or revision of services to the person named in such document

MISCELLANEOUS METAL PARTS AND PRODUCTS Farm machinery (harvesting, fertilizing, and plant machines, tractors, combines, lawn mowers, roto-tillers, etc.); small appliances; commercial and office equipment (computers and auxiliary equipment, typewriters, calculators, vending machines, etc.); fabricated metal products (metal doors, frames, etc.); industrial machinery (pumps, compressors, conveyor components, fans, blowers, transformers, etc.); and any other metal parts or products that are coated under Standard Industrial Classification Codes of Major Groups 33, 34, 35, 36, 37, 38, and 39. The use of auto body antichip coatings and underbody plastisols in automobile and light duty truck surface coating is considered coating of miscellaneous parts and products. In addition, this definition includes exterior coating of assembled entire aircraft and assembled entire metal marine vessels. This definition does not include metal cans, flat metal sheets, and strips in the form of rolls or coils; magnet wire for use in electrical machinery; metal furniture; large appliances; automobile and light duty trucks, automobile refinishing; or customized top coating of automobiles and trucks, if production is less than 35 vehicles per day.

MISREPRESENTATION (INS) An incorrect statement made about a material fact that, if made deliberately and with intent to deceive, could cause the insurance contract to become null and void.

MISSION STATEMENT In port management, a statement adopted by the governing body of the port organization that outlines its "reason-for-being."

MIST Any liquid aerosol formed by the condensation of vapor or by the atomization of liquids.

MITER SILL The concrete sill across the openings in the upper and lower lock chamber underwater that the movable lock gates close on. The depth over these sills exceeds project depth and is registered on the several gauges within the lock chamber.

MITIGATE (INS) To make less severe; steps to eliminate further damage after a loss occurs.

MITIGATION In environmental management, avoiding, minimizing, rectifying, reducing, and compensating for project-induced resource losses.

MITIGATION BANK In environmental management, the process whereby habitat is created, restored, or enhanced in advance of a specific mitigation requirement and is used to fulfill that requirement.

MITRED   Cut to an angle of 45 degrees on two pieces joined to make a right angle.

MIXED BASED GREASE   A grease composed of a mineral oil thickened by soaps made from two alkalis.

MIXED CONSIGNMENT   A consignment of different commodities, articles, or goods, packed or tied together or contained in separate packages (air cargo).

MIXED CONTAINER LOAD   A container load of different articles in a single consignment.

MIXED LOADS   The movement of both regulated and exempt commodities in the same vehicle at the same time.

MIXED SHIPMENT   A shipment consisting of more than one commodity, articles described under more than one class, or commodity rate item in a tariff.

MIXTURES   The combination of two or more substances united in such a way that each retains its original properties.

MLB   Mini Land Bridge.

MLLW   Mean Lower Low Water. The average height of the lower of the daily low tide over a 19-year period.

MLO   *See* Main Line Operator.

MLW   Mean Low Water.

MMFB   Middlewest Motor Freight Bureau.

MOA   Memorandum of Agreement.

MOCK UP   To build up of wood or light material to scale or full size a portion of the ship before actual fabrication of the steel work. Used to study arrangement, methods of fabrication, workability, etc.

MODAL SPLIT   The relative use made of the modes of transportation; the statistics used include ton-miles, passenger-miles, and revenue.

MODEL BOW   A shaped pointed bow.

MODEL YEAR   A motor vehicle manufacturer's annual production period that includes January 1 of a calendar year or, if the manufacturer has no annual production period, the calendar year. In the case of any vehicle manufactured in two or more stages, the time of manufacture shall be the date of completion of the chassis.

MODERATE LOW   A rather subjective term used to describe the intensity of a low; used when the central pressure is about 975 to 1,000 mb. Winds generally less than about 40 knots.

MODE OF TRANSPORT   Method of transport used for the conveyance of goods, (e.g., by rail, by road, by sea).

MODIFIED ATMOSPHERE   A blend of gases tailored to a specific load of cargo that replaces the normal atmosphere within a container.

MODULAR CONTAINER   A lightweight, reusable container complying with the basic specification MIL-C-22443. Produced by using the "tinkertoy" concept of standard components joined together, and having sheet aluminum alloy panels epoxy bonded into an extruded aluminum framework.

MOLCHOPT   More or Less Charterers Option.

MOLD   A light pattern of a part of a ship. Usually made of thin wood or paper. Also called a template.

MOLDED BREADTH   The linear distance from the molded surface on one side to the molded surface on the other side measured at the widest portion of a vessel hull parallel to the waterlines.

MOLDED EDGE   The edge of a ship's frame that comes in contact with the skin and is represented in the drawings.

MOLDED LINE   A datum line from which is determined the exact location of the various parts of a ship. It may be horizontal and straight as the molded baseline, or curved as a molded deck line or a molded frame line. These lines are determined in the design of a vessel and adhered to throughout the construction. Molded lines are those laid down in the mold loft.

MOLD LOFT   Usually the second floor of a building with a large smooth floor for laying down the lines of a vessel to actual size and making templates from them for the structural work entering into a hull.

MOLE   A breakwater used as a loading pier.

MOLLY GOGGER   A line, chain, or short wire connected to a shackle on the towing cable that restricts its lead and arc at the stern.

MOLOO   More or Less Owners Option.

MOMENT   Created by a force or weight moved through a distance.

MOMENTUM   The resultant of weight multiplied by speed.

MONITOR   Checking or regulating the performance of machines. Usually used to refer to the checking of refrigerated containers.

MONKEY FIST   A heavy knot with a weight placed on the end of a heaving line. It is made of three interwoven strands of cordage.

MONKEY GAFF   The light gaff fitted on some vessels on the after masthead for the display of the colors when underway.

MONKEY LINE   Small hand line used by a lockman; to throw down or bring up a lock line.

MOORED   The vessel is securely fastened to the shore.

MOORING   Equipment, such as anchors, chains or lines, for holding fast a vessel. Securing a ship at a dock or elsewhere by several lines or cable so as to limit her movement. A place at which a vessel can be moored. Any place where a boat is wet stored or berthed.

MOORING CELL (DOLPHIN)   A riverfront structure generally comprised of steel piling or a cluster of wooden piles used for securing barges along the bank at loading facilities.

MOORING DOLPHIN   An isolated cluster of piles used as a support for mooring devices.

MOORING LINES   Large lines used to hold a ship in position at a berth and may be constructed of natural fibers, synthetic fibers, steel wires, or combinations of any of the three types.

MOORING PIPE   An opening through which mooring lines pass.

MOORING RING   A round or oval casting inserted in the bulwark plating of a ship, through which the mooring lines, or hawsers, are passed.

MOORING WINCH   A piece of machinery designed to control the mooring lines.

MORTISE   A hole cut in any material to receive the end or tenon of another piece. *See also* Score.

MOTOR TRUCK CARGO OWNER'S FORM (INS)   This form insures the owner of a truck against loss to his own property while being transported. It pays for the loss or damage of cargo for the perils insured against, regardless of the legal liability.

MOTOR TRUCK CARGO TRUCKER'S FORM (INS)   This form indemnifies the policyholder, a trucker, for loss or damage resulting from his legal liability as a carrier while transporting the property of others. It does not insure against any loss for which he is not legally liable.

MOTOR VEHICLE FUEL   Any petroleum distillate having a Reid Vapor Pressure of more than four pounds per square inch as determined by ASTM Method D323 and which is used primarily to power motor vehicles. This definition includes, but is not limited to, gasoline and mixtures of simple alcohols and gasoline.

MOTOR VEHICLE FUEL DISPENSING FACILITY   Any facility where motor vehicle fuel is dispensed into motor vehicle fuel tanks or portable containers from a storage tank with a capacity of 250 gallons or more.

MOTOR VEHICLE POLLUTION CONTROL SYSTEM   The combination of emission-related parts that controls air pollutant emissions from a motor vehicle or motor vehicle engine.

MOTORSHIP   A ship driven by some form of internal combustion engine. Not generally applied to small boats driven by gasoline engines, which are usually called motorboats.

MOUSING   Closing the end of a hook with seizing to prevent the sling from slipping off.

MOVABLE DAM   A dam that is predominantly constructed of a series of wickets that may be raised or lowered as water stage dictate for passing water through the dam. These wickets may all be lowered to the bed of the river and vessels may pass over the dam during periods of high water. The dam and/or river is then said to be "open."

MPC   *See* Multipurpose Vessel.

M&R   Maintenance and Repair. Facility used to maintain container yard equipment and containers.

MRO ITEMS   Maintenance, repair, and operating items—office supplies, for example.

MSC   Maritime Safety Committee. A major committee within the International Maritime Organization.

MT   Metric Ton (1,000 kilos or 2,204.6 pounds) or cubic meter, whichever produces the greater revenue. Most often used in reference to shipping charges.

MT1   The moment necessary to change the trim of the vessel one inch.

MTO CARRIER   *See* Multimodal Operator/Carrier.

MUCKING   The emptying of sludge and debris out of a cargo or ballast tank. Usually done with shovels and pails by crewmembers.

MUCOUS MEMBRANE   Lining surfaces of the body; for example, the inside of the nose, throat, windpipe, lungs, and eyes.

MUD BALLS   An upwelling of clay that does not break the surface. These occur frequently in the various passes of the Mississippi River Delta.

MUD SCOW   A large, flat-bottomed boat used to carry the mud from a dredge.

MULE   East Coast designation for hostler or yard tractor.

MULE TRAIN   The maneuver of towboats in ice choked channels whereby the tow is strung out single file and the barges fitted with loose couplings or lashings and the tow pulled behind the towboats.

MULLION   The vertical bar dividing the lights in a window.

MULTIMODAL   Synonymous for all practical purposes with intermodal.

MULTIMODAL BILL OF LADING   Bill of lading covering shipment of goods by more than one means of transportation but including an ocean leg. The two major forms of multimodal bill of lading are the combined transport bill of lading and the through bill of lading. Under the former, the carrier signing the bill of lading (the contractual carrier) frequently subcontracts the various legs to other carriers (the actual carriers), but still takes responsibility for delivery of the goods to the "place of delivery" and for any damage that might occur during carriage. Under the latter, the carrier takes responsibility for the goods only up to a specified point (still called the place of delivery) and then passes responsibility to a second carrier for "on-carriage" to the "final destination."

MULTIMODAL TRANSPORT   Shipment of goods by more than one means of transportation but including an ocean leg.

MULTIMODAL TRANSPORT OPERATOR/CARRIER (MTO)   The person on whose behalf the transport document or any document evidencing a contract of multimodal carriage of goods is issued and who is responsible for the carriage of goods pursuant to the contract of carriage.

MULTIPLE CAR RATE   A railroad rate that is lower for shipping more than one carload at a time.

MULTIPLE CONSIGNEE CONTAINER   A container loaded with cargo for two or more consignees.

MULTIPLIER EFFECT   A measure of the indirect impact of port-related wage payments and purchases on the local economy; the regeneration of production as the original wage payments and purchases spread through the economy.

MULTIPORT BILL OF LADING   A bill of lading issued for cargo shipped from two or more ports by one shipper to one consignee. Formerly known as a consolidated bill of lading.

MULTIPURPOSE TUG   A tug built for all types of general towing rather than specifically to fit into a barge notch or for any other special type of towing.

MULTIPURPOSE VESSEL   Any ship capable of carrying different types of cargo that require different methods of handling. There are several types of ships falling into this category, for example, ships that can carry roll on/roll off cargo together with containers.

MULTITANK CONTAINER   A container frame fitted to accommodate two or more separate tanks for liquids.

MUSHROOM ANCHOR   An anchor without a stock and shaped like a mushroom.

MUSHROOM VENTILATOR   A ventilator whose top is shaped like a mushroom and fitted with baffle plates so as to permit the passage of air and prevent the entrance of rain or spray. Located on or above a weather deck to furnish ventilation to compartments below deck.

MUTINY   The forcible seizure of a vessel over the authority of the Master and officers by the crew.

M/V   Motor Vessel.

N

NAKED LIGHTS Open flames or fires, exposed incandescent material, any other unconfined source of ignition.

NAMED PERILS POLICY Any marine policy limiting coverage to perils specifically listed in the policy; opposed to All Risks policy. Institute Clauses C is a "Named Perils" cover. *See* All-Risk Clause.

NAPALM Gasoline that has been chemically thickened so that it spreads over the ground while burning instead of going up instantaneously.

NAPHTHALENE A hydrocarbon (polynuclear aromatic) that forms plate-like crystals, has the odor of mothballs, and is always present to a considerable extent in coal tar and coal gas.

NAPHTHAS Oils of low boiling range (80°F–440°F), usually of good color and odor when finished. Sometimes refers to gasoline components and sometimes to special products, solvents, etc.

NAPHTHENES Saturated hydrocarbon series, characterized by the closed chain arrangement of carbon atoms.

NAPHTHENIC CRUDES Crude oils containing large proportions of naphthenic compounds.

NARCOSIS A condition of profound insensibility, sometimes resembling sleep, in which the unconscious person can only be roused with great difficulty but it is not entirely indifferent to sensory stimuli. Sometimes manifested by laughter, giddiness, or dizziness.

NARCOTICS Substance that produces narcosis.

NARROW BODY An airliner with a single aisle such as the A319 or B737.

NARROW CHANNEL Very little room to spare.

NATIONAL CARRIER A for-hire certificated air carrier that has annual operating revenues of $75 million to $1 billion; the carrier usually operates between major population centers and areas of lesser population.

NATIONAL EMISSION STANDARD FOR HAZARDOUS AIR POLLUTANTS (NESHAPS) Those standards adopted by the U.S. Environmental Protection Agency and contained in the Code of Federal Regulations, Title 40, Part 61, and subsequent revisions as specified in the Regulations. Any emission testing to be compared with NESHAPS must be conducted in accordance with applicable procedures as specified in said Code of Federal Regulations, Title 40, Part 61, or amendments thereto, or by another method that has been demonstrated to the satisfaction of the department as being equivalent.

NATIONAL FLAG The flag carried by a ship to show her nationality.

NATIONAL INDUSTRIAL TRANSPORTATION LEAGUE (NITL) An association representing shippers' and receivers' interests in matters of transportation policy and regulation.

NATIONWIDE PERMITS   A form of general permit issued by the Corps of Engineers authorizing in advance certain classes of minor work in U.S. navigable waters, e.g., maintenance activities, installation of aids to navigation.

NATURAL GASOLINE   *See* Casinghead Gasoline.

NATURALLY TRIBUTARY   A term used in reference to cargo when a port claims that certain cargo is inherently dependent on their port because of historic transportation routing proximity, economics, or other factors; a technical term used by the FMC in some of its decisions.

NAUTICAL MILE   *See* Knot.

NAVIGABLE PASS   The water pass through which vessels may pass over a movable dam during periods of high water. The wickets of the dam are lowered to the riverbed and the water flows with little or no obstruction. Navigable passes are usually from 600 feet to 900 feet in width when the dam is lowered. These are found only in the Ohio and Illinois Rivers.

NAVIGABLE WATERS   Sufficient depth of water to permit the passage of vessels.

NAVIGATION   The act of determining position, location, and course to the destination of an aircraft or a vessel.

NAVIGATION BULLETIN   A public notice issued by the Corps of Engineers containing marine information.

NAVIGATOR   The officer charged with planning the safe navigation of the vessel, generally the second mate on a merchant ship.

NCB   National Cargo Bureau.

NCITD   National Committee on International Trade Documentation.

ND   Nondelivery.

NEC   Not Elsewhere Classified.

NEEDLE   A long stick of timber placed between the wickets of a movable dam to stop the leakage of water between the gates.

NEEDLE FLAT   A small barge used in transporting the above-mentioned timbers.

NEGATIVE SPEED   Engine speed less than observed speed or when the propeller operates at more than 100% efficiency

NEGATIVE STABILITY   Exists when G is above M, that is, when there exists a negative GM or GZ.

NEGLIGENCE   Imprudent action or omission that may cause injury, damage, or loss. Failure to use the degree of care, expected from a reasonable and prudent person.

NEGOTIABLE   Quality belonging to a document of being able to transfer ownership of money, goods, or other items of value specified in the document by endorsement and/or delivery of the document. Checks, drafts, promissory notes, bonds, stock certificates, bills of lading, and warehouse receipts are examples of documents often issued in negotiable form.

NEGOTIABLE B/L   Original bill of lading endorsed by shipper that is used for negotiating documents with bank.

NEGOTIABLE INSTRUMENTS   A document of title (such as a draft, promissory note, check, or bill of lading) transferable from one person to another in good faith for a consideration. Nonnegotiable bills of lading are known as "straight consignment." Negotiable bills are known as "order bills of lading."

NEGOTIATE   To "buy" documents representing ownership of money, goods, or other items of value. The seller is also said to "negotiate to" the buyer. Unless otherwise agreed between the buyer and seller (e.g., by negotiating "without recourse"), the seller continues to be fully responsible for the enforceability of the documents. A bank that negotiates documents under a letter of credit advances funds to the presenter before submitting the documents to the issuing bank for payment.

NEGOTIATING BANK   The name derives from the fact that the negotiating bank is normally authorized by the issuing bank to negotiate documents, but it may or may not choose actually to do so. Furthermore, recognizing that this bank may be authorized to pay or accept drafts, rather than negotiate them, UCP500 now uses the term "nominated bank" rather than "negotiating bank." Unless otherwise instructed, negotiating banks in North America generally examine the documents for discrepancies before forwarding them to the issuing bank, but this is properly viewed as a service separate from negotiating and is not even necessary when negotiating with recourse.

NEOBULK   Cargoes carried on specialized vessels that are not carried in containerized, bulk, or breakbulk form. Typical neobulk cargoes include automobiles, steel, logs, lumber, or scrap carried on wood products carriers and steel cargoes.

NEPA (NATIONAL ENVIRONMENTAL POLICY ACT)   The 1970 federal law that required all federal agencies to consider environmental impacts in their decision-making, to avoid them whenever possible, and to prepare environmental impact statements in certain circumstances.

NEPTUNE   The mythical god of the sea.

NES   Not Elsewhere Specified.

NESTED   Articles packed so that one rests partially or entirely within another, thereby reducing the cubic foot displacement.

NESTING   Packaging tapered articles inside each other to reduce the cubic volume of the entire shipment.

NET MANIFEST   A manifest containing all freight details including negotiated disbursements.

NET REGISTERED TONS   Vessel's volume available for cargo.

NET SHORT TON   2,000 pounds.

NET TARE WEIGHT   The weight of an empty cargo-carrying piece of equipment plus any fixtures permanently attached.

NETTING   A rope network.

NET TONNAGE   A figure obtained by making deduction from the gross tonnage for space not available for carrying cargo or passengers. The tonnage most frequently used for the calculation of tonnage taxes and the assessment of charges for wharfage and other port dues. Net tonnage is obtained by deducting from the gross tonnage, crew and navigating spaces and an allowance for the space occupied by the propelling machinery. A vessel's net tonnage expresses the space available for passengers and cargo.

NET TONS   A measure of a vessel's true volumetric carrying capacity, computed by deducting "noncargo" spaces from gross tons.

NET WEIGHT (ACTUAL NET WEIGHT)   Weight of the goods alone without any immediate wrappings. (Example: the weight of the contents of a tin can without the weight of the can.)

NEUTRAL BODY   An organization established by the members of an ocean conference acts as a self-policing force with broad authority to investigate tariff violations, including authority to scrutinize all documents kept by the carriers and their personnel. Violations are reported to the membership and significant penalties are assessed.

NEUTRAL EQUILIBRIUM   Exists when G coincides with M. The vessel does not tend to return to an upright position if inclined, nor to continue its inclination if the inclining force is removed.

NEUTRAL OILS   Term used quite generally to mean a lubricating oil of medium viscosity made from a wax bearing crude.

NEUTRALIZATION NUMBER   The number is the weight in milligrams of an alkali (potassium hydroxide) needed to neutralize the acidic material in one gram of oil. The neutralization number of an oil is an indication of its acidity.

NEW ICE   A general term for recently formed ice that includes frazil ice, grease ice, slush, and shuga. These types of ice are composed of ice crystals that are only weakly frozen together (if at all) and have a definite form only while they are afloat.

NEW SOURCE PERFORMANCE STANDARDS (NSPS)   Standards of Performance for New Stationary Sources adopted by the U.S. Environmental Protection Agency and contained in 40 CFR 60, and subsequent revisions as specified in the Regulations. Any emission testing to be compared with NSPS must be conducted in accordance with applicable procedures as specified in 40 CFR 60, or amendments thereto, or by another method that has been demonstrated to the satisfaction of the department as being equivalent.

NEW VEHICLE   Any passenger car or light duty truck with 7,500 miles or less on its odometer.

NIBBING PLANK   A margin plank that is notched to take the ends of regular deck planks and ensure good calking of the joint.

NIGGER HEADS   A small auxiliary drum on a winch for heaving in lines.

NILAS   An elastic crust of ice, easily bending on waves and swell and under pressure, thrusting in a pattern of interlocking "fingers." Has a matt surface and is up to 10 cm in thickness. May be subdivided into dark nilas and light nilas. Dark nilas is nilas that is under 5 cm in thickness and very dark in color. Light nilas is nilas that are more than 5 cm in thickness and rather lighter in color.

NINE-FOOT CONTOUR LINE   A meandering line not necessarily on the channel edge at which a depth of 9 feet is obtained at river stage low water reference plane.

NIP   A sharp bend or turn in a rope or wire.

NIPPLE   A piece of pipe having an outside thread at both ends for use in making pipe connections. Various names are applied to different lengths, as close, short, long, etc.

NITL   *See* National Industrial Transportation League.

N/M   No marks.

NMFC   National Motor Freight Classification.

NMU   National Maritime Union.

N/N   No marks, no numbers.

NOE   Not Otherwise Enumerated.

NOHP   Not Otherwise Herein Provided.

NOI   Not Otherwise Indexed.

NOIBN   Not Otherwise Indexed By Name; Not Otherwise Indexed By Number.

NO LOCATION (NO LOC)   A received item for which the warehouse has no previously established storage slot.

NODE   A fixed point in a firm's logistics system where goods come to rest; includes plants, warehouses, supply sources, and markets.

NOISE   Sound of sufficient intensity and/or duration as to cause or contribute to a condition of air pollution.

NOMENCLATURE OF THE CUSTOMS COOPERATION COUNSIL   The Customs tariff used by most countries worldwide. It was formerly known as the Brussels Tariff Nomenclature and is the basis of the commodity coding system known as the Harmonized System.

NOMINAL RANGE   The maximum distance a light can be seen in clear weather (meteorological visibility of 10 nautical miles). Listed for all lighted aids to navigation except range lights, directional lights, and private aids to navigation.

NONATTAINMENT AREA   An area classified by the EPA as not meeting or exceeding the National Ambient Air Quality Standard for a criteria pollutant published at 40 CFR 81.

NONCANCELABLE POLICY (INS)   A policy that the insured has the right to continue in force by the timely payment of premiums set forth in the policy, during which period the insurer has no right to make unilaterally any change in any provision of the policy while the policy is in force. *See also* Guaranteed Renewable Policy.

NONCARGO FUNCTIONS Those activities carried out by the public port that are intended to generate revenues and/or employment, but are not directly related to the cargo-handling mandate of the port authority.

NONCERTIFICATED CARRIER A for-hire air carrier that is exempt from economic regulation.

NONCOMBUSTION ENERGY SOURCE A facility that does not rely on the burning of fossil or alternative fuel to produce electricity, such as wind, solar, or geothermal. Sources regulated by the NRC or using nuclear fuel are not included in this definition.

NONCONFERENCE LINE (CARRIER) A shipping line, which operates on a route, served by a liner conference but is not a member of that conference.

NONCONTIGUOUS TRADE Trade between the continental United States and Alaska, Hawaii, Puerto Rico, and the U.S. Virgin Islands.

NONCUMULATIVE REVOLVING LETTER OF CREDIT Revolving letter of credit that does not permit the seller to carry over any amounts not drawn upon in previous periods.

NONDELIVERY (ND) Failure to deliver all or part of a shipment.

NONDISPLACEMENT CRAFT Includes air cushion vessels and hovercraft; this means that there is not any portion of the vessel below the waterline.

NONDUMPING CERTIFICATE Required by some countries for protection against the dumping of certain types of merchandise or products.

NONFEDERAL SPONSOR A party to a federal navigation improvements project who initiates the review and approval process, pays part of the costs, and who may undertake planning, design, and construction subject to federal approval and subsequent reimbursement.

NONIMPINGING The outflow at atmosphere of a liquid or vapor to form a puddle.

NONINCENDIVE Nonincendive equipment is approved equipment that will not release sufficient energy in its normal working condition to ignite a specific hazardous atmospheric mixture. An ignition source is therefore not normally present. The probability is low that the equipment will fail and become ignition capable.

NONNEGOTIABLE B/L Copy of original bill of lading that cannot be negotiated with bank.

NONREVERSIBLE (Detention). If loading completed sooner than expected, then saved days will not be added to discharge time allowed.

NONSPARKING TOOLS Tools made of a metal alloy that, when struck against other objects, will not usually cause sparks of sufficient temperature to ignite flammable vapors.

NONVESSEL OPERATING COMMON CARRIER (NVOCC) (1) A cargo consolidator in ocean trades who will buy space from a carrier and resell it to smaller shippers. The NVOCC issues bills of lading, publishes tariffs, and otherwise conducts itself as an ocean common carrier, except that it will not provide the actual ocean or intermodal service. (2) A carrier defined by maritime law, offering an international cargo transport service through the use of underlying carriers and under one's own rate structure, in accordance with tariffs filled with the Federal Maritime Commission.

NONVISCOUS NEUTRALS The lighter weight oils distilled overhead and used for manufacture of oils for extremely light lubricating purposes.

NOR Notice of Readiness. (When the ship is ready to load.)

NORMAL CHARGE The specified general cargo rate without any quantity discount (air cargo).

NORMAL GENERAL CARGO RATE The under 45 kilograms rate or, if no under 45 kilograms rate exists, the under 100 kilograms rate (air cargo).

NORMAL POOL ELEVATION Height in feet above sea level at which a section of the river is to be maintained behind the dam.

NORMAL POOL STAGE (NP) That level of the river maintained by the desired dam operations.

NORMALIZE To heat steel to a temperature slightly above the critical point and then allow it to cool slowly in air.

NORMAN PIN A pin passing through the head of a bollard to prevent hawsers from slipping off. Round steel pins that are operated hydraulically at the stern of large ocean tugs or inserted by hand into the rail on either quarter to keep the hawser leading to the tow winch and clear of the propeller(s).

NORSKE VERITAS Norwegian classification society.

NORTHEAST STATES Maine, New Hampshire, Vermont, Massachusetts, New York, Connecticut, Rhode Island, and New Jersey.

NORTHERLY WIND True wind direction from the NE to NW sector.

NOS Not Otherwise Specified.

NOSE Front of a container or trailer; opposite the tail. A vessel's cut water.

NOSE 'ER IN A method of landing by putting the bow of the boat into the bank.

NO-SHOW Cargo that has been booked but does not arrive in time to be loaded before the vessel sails. *See also* Windy Booking.

NOSING The part of a stairtread that projects beyond the face of the riser.

NOT MAKING WAY A vessel not moving due to her own power or propulsion.

NOT OTHERWISE SPECIFIED/NOT ELSEWHERE SPECIFIED NOS/NES This term often appears in ocean or airfreight tariffs respectively. If no rate for the specific commodity shipped appears in the tariff, then a general class rate (for example, printed matter NES) will apply. Such rates usually are higher than rates for specific commodities.

NOT UNDER COMMAND Said of a vessel when disabled from any cause.

NOT UNDER CONTROL Same as Not Under Command.

NOTCH A void or opening or any place where barge headlogs do not meet . . . or when they are not even with each other. Where no other barge is faced to barge. The indentation built into the stern of a barge designed as part of a combination unit, the notch can be shallow or deep, where deep provides the best control.

NOTICE OF LOSS (INS)   Written notice of a loss to the insurance company as outlined in the conditions of the insurance policy.

NOTICE OF READINESS (NOR)   Written document or telex issued by the master of A vessel to the charterers advising them the moment when A vessel is ready to load or discharge. Document advising A consignee or his agent that cargo has arrived and is ready for delivery.

NOTICE TO MARINERS   A bulletin or information to mariners issued by the Coast Guard.

NOTIFY ADDRESSEE   Address of the party other than the consignee to be advised of the arrival of the goods.

NOTIFY PARTY   Party to be notified on arrival of goods. Addressee of party other than consignee to be advised of arrival of goods.

NPCFB   North Pacific Coast Freight Bureau.

NRT   Net Restricted Tonnage. Net Registered Tonnage. This tonnage is frequently shown on ship registration papers; it represents the volumetric area available for cargo at 100 cubic feet = 1 ton. It often is used by port and canal authorities as a basis for determining tolls or fees.

NSPF   Not Specifically Provided For.

NUMEROUS SHOWERS   Frequent number of showers are likely over more than half the area covered by the forecast.

NVO   *See* Nonvessel Operating Common Carrier.

NYPE   New York Produce Exchange.

O

O/A Open Account.

OAKUM A substance made from soft vegetable fiber such as hemp and jute impregnated with pine tar. It is principally used for calking the planking on wood decks of steel vessels and for calking all the planking on wood ships where water tightness is desired. It is also used for calking around pipes.

OBL Original Bill of Lading. A document that requires proper signatures for consummating carriage of contract. Must be marked as "original" by the issuing carrier.

OBLIGEE (INS) Broadly, anyone in whose favor an obligation runs. This term is most frequently used in surety bonds, where it refers to the person, firm, or corporation protected by the bond.

OBLIGOR (INS) Commonly called principal; one bound by an obligation. Under a bond, strictly speaking, both the principal and the surety are obligors.

OBNOXIOUS CARGO Cargo that by its nature can contaminate its container, the vessel, or other cargo, e.g., hides, fishmeal.

OBO Or Best Offer. Ore/Bulk/Ore vessel. A multipurpose ship that can carry ore, heavy dry bulk goods, and oil. Although more expensive to build, they ultimately are more economical because they can make return journeys with cargo rather than empty as single-purpose ships often must do.

OCCUPATIONAL SAFETY AND HEALTH ACT (OSHA) A 1970 federal law regulating workplaces to ensure the safety of workers.

OCCURRENCE COVERAGE (INS) A policy providing liability coverage only for injury or loss that occurs during the policy period, regardless of when the claim is actually made. *See also* Claims Made Coverage.

OCEAN BILL OF LADING (OCEAN B/L) Document indicating that the exporter will consign a shipment to an international carrier for transportation to a specified foreign market and indicates the terms of the contract of carriage. The ocean B/L serves as a collection document. If it is a straight B/L the foreign buyer can obtain the shipment from the carrier by simply showing proof of the identity. If a negotiable B/L is used, the buyer must first pay for the goods, post a bond, surrender the original B/L, or meet other conditions agreeable to the seller.

OCEAN DATA AQUISITION SYSTEM (ODAS) Certain very large buoys in deep water for the collection of oceanographic and meteorological information. All ODAS buoys are yellow in color and display a yellow light.

OCEAN GREYHOUND A fast merchant ship.

OCEAN LINERS Ships in regularly scheduled operations that specialize in less-than-shipload quantity shipments.

OCEAN TRANSPORTATION INTERMEDIARY An ocean freight forwarder or a nonvessel operating common carrier.

OCIMF   Oil Companies International Marine Forum.

OCP   Overland Common Point. A term used on the U.S. West Coast for destinations east of the Rockies, i.e., the states of Montana, Wyoming, Utah, and Arizona.

OCS REFERENCE NUMBER (OCS REF)   OCS Reference Number. Number assigned to certain shipping/booking by Overseas Container Services.

OCTANE   The eighth member of the paraffin or saturated series of hydrocarbons, having a boiling point of 258°F, and the chemical formula C_8H_{18}.

OCTANE NUMBER   Term used to indicate numerically the relative antiknock value of automotive gasolines, and of aviation gasolines having a rating below 100. It is based on a comparison with the reference fuels, iso octane (100 octane number) and normal heptane (0 octane number). The octane number of an unknown fuel is the volume percent of iso octane with normal heptane, which matches the unknown fuel in knocking tendencies under a specified set of conditions. Either the Motor Method or the Research Method may be used in determining octane rating of automotive gasolines; either the Aviation Method or Supercharge Method may be used in determining the octane rating of aviation gasoline. The test method employed MUST be reported with the octane rating. *See* Performance Number.

OCTANE NUMBER, AVIATION METHOD   Octane number of aviation gasolines, determined by a method of testing that indicates the knock characteristics at a lean fuel air ratio (lean or cruise rating).

OCTANE NUMBER, CRUISE RATING   *See* Octane Number; Aviation Method.

OCTANE NUMBER, LEAN RATING   *See* Octane Number; Aviation Method.

OCTANE NUMBER, MOTOR METHOD   Octane number of automotive gasolines, determined by a method of testing that indicates the knock characteristics under severe conditions (high temperatures and speed).

OCTANE NUMBER, RESEARCH METHOD   Octane number of automotive gasolines, determined by a method of testing that indicates the knock characteristics under mild conditions (temperatures and speed approximating ordinary driving conditions).

OCTANE NUMBER, SUPERCHARGE METHOD   Octane number of aviation gasoline, determined by a method that indicates the knock characteristics under supercharge rich mixture conditions.

ODD BARGE   Seabee barge specially designed to conform to the contour of the mother vessel's hull at the foremost position in the lower hull. Odd barges are designed for both port and starboard use.

ODOR   Property of gaseous, liquid, or solid materials that elicits a physiologic response by the human sense of smell.

ODOR THRESHOLD   The smallest concentration of gas or vapor, expressed in parts per million (ppm) by volume in air, that can be detected by smell.

ODS   Operating Differential Subsidy. An amount of money the U.S. government will pay U.S. shipping companies that apply and qualify for this subsidy. The intent is to help offset the higher cost, if shown, of operating a U.S. flag vessel. The ODS program is administered by the U.S. Maritime Administration and is under review.

OECD Organization of Economic Cooperation and Development. Headquartered in Paris with membership consisting of the world's developed nations.

OFF AND ON Standing towards the land and off again alternately.

OFF DOCK Operations taking place at a distance from the wharf area.

OFFER *See* Tender.

OFFICER OF THE DECK The officer in charge of the ship and on deck as the captain's representative.

OFFICER OF THE WATCH The officer in charge of the engine room watch.

OFFLOAD Discharge of cargo from a ship.

OFFSETS Used by draftsmen and loftsmen for the coordinates in ship curves. Also applied to joggles in plates and shapes of structural shapes.

OFFSHORE Contracting work carried out at sea (e.g., drilling for oil).

OFFSHORE INSTALLATION Any offshore structure (e.g., a drilling rig, production platform, etc.) that may present a hazard to navigation.

OFFSHORE TOWER Manned or monitored light stations built on exposed marine sites to replace lightships.

OFFSPECIFICATION Describes a product that fails to meet the requirements of the applicable specification.

OFF STATION A floating aid to navigation not on its assigned position.

OGEE A molding with a concave and convex outline like an S.

OIL Petroleum, in crude or refined liquid form.

OIL BAG A bag filled with oil and triced over the side for making a slick in rough seas.

OIL BULK ORE VESSEL A multipurpose ship that can carry ore, heavy dry bulk goods, and oil. Although more expensive to build, they ultimately are more economical because they can make return journeys with cargo rather than empty as single-purpose ships often must do. *See also* OBO.

OILINESS Under certain conditions of lubrication, one lubricant may reduce the friction in a bearing more than a similar oil of the same viscosity and applied in the same way. The oil that reduces friction the most is oilier and is said to have a higher degree of oiliness.

OILSKINS Waterproof clothing.

OIL TANKER A ship designed for the carriage of oil in bulk, her cargo space consisting of several or many tanks. Tankers load their cargo by gravity from the shore or by shore pumps and discharge using their own pumps.

OILTIGHT Riveted, caulked, or welded to prevent oil leakage.

OLD MAN The captain of the ship. Also, a heavy bar of iron or steel bent in the form of a Z used to hold a portable drill. One leg is bolted or clamped to the work to be drilled and the drill head is placed under the other leg that holds down the drill to its work.

OLEFIN Any open chain hydrocarbon having one or more double bonds per molecule.

OMSA Offshore Marine Service Administration.

O/N Order Notify.

ON A STAND River stationary as to rise or fall.

ONBOARD On or in a ship, aboard. The cargo has been loaded onboard a combined transport mode of conveyance. Used to satisfy the requirements of a letter of credit, in the absence of an express requirement to the contrary.

ONCARRIAGE Carriage of goods by any mode of transport to place of delivery after discharge from ocean vessel at port of discharge.

ONCARRIER All of the various modes of surface transportation that handle the inbound and outbound movement of cargoes between a marine terminal and the port hinterland via rail, truck, or barge.

ON DECK On the weather deck, in the open air.

ON DOCK Operations taking place at or adjacent to the wharf area.

ONE BY FOUR A standard U.S. Pacific Coast barge used for deck or liquid cargo. Its dimensions are 100 feet in beam by 400 feet in length.

ONE-WAY PALLET *See* Disposable Pallet.

ONLINE RECEIVING A system in which computer terminals are available at each receiving bay and operators enter items into the system as they are unloaded.

ON SOUNDINGS Vessel when the depth of water can be measured by the lead with the 100-fathom curve.

ONSTREAM When a refinery-processing unit is in operation.

OO (OWNER OPTION) At discretion or choice of owner. *See also* Owner Operator.

OPACITY Characteristic of matter that renders it capable of interfering with the transmission of rays of light and causes a degree of obscuration of an observer's view.

OPAQUE STAIN All stains that contain pigments but are not classified as semitransparent stains and includes stains, glazes, and other opaque material applied to wood surfaces.

OPEN ACCOUNT A trade arrangement in which goods are shipped to a foreign buyer without guarantee of payment.

OPEN BURNING Burning under such conditions that the products of combustion are emitted directly to the ambient air space and are not conducted thereto through a stack, chimney, duct, or pipe. Open burning includes above and underground smoldering fires.

OPEN CHANNEL That portion of the river above the pool water.

OPEN COVER (INS) An agreement whereby the Assured undertakes to declare every item (e.g., shipment, vessel, etc., as appropriate) that comes within the scope of the cover in the order in which the risk attaches. The insurer agrees, at the time of concluding the contract, to accept all valid declarations up to the agreed limit for each declaration. An open cover may be for a fixed period or always open; subject to a cancellation clause.

OPEN GAUGING A system that does nothing to minimize or prevent the escape of vapor from tanks when the contents are being measured.

OPEN INSURANCE POLICY A marine insurance policy that applies to all shipments made by an exporter over a period of time rather than to one shipment only.

OPEN RATES Pricing systems that are flexible and not subject to conference approval. Usually applied to products in which tramps are substituted for liners.

OPEN REGISTRY Used in place of "flag of convenience" or "flag of necessity" to denote registry in a country that offers favorable tax, regulatory, and other incentives to ship owners from other nations.

OPEN RIVER Any river having no obstructions such as dams; also, when the stage of a pooled river running through movable dams is high enough for traffic to clear the dam. At this point, the river is said to be "open."

OPEN-SIDED CONTAINER This type of container is designed to accommodate the carriage of special commodities, e.g., plywood from the Far East and certain perishable commodities. The steel containers have a fixed roof, open sides and end opening doors, the sides being "closed" by full height gates in 1.37m wide sections and nylon-reinforced PVC curtains.

OPEN TOP CONTAINER A container fitted with a solid removable roof, or with a tarpaulin roof that can be loaded or unloaded from the top. This container is designed for the carriage of heavy and awkward cargoes and those cargoes with height in excess of what can be stowed in a standard general purpose container. The floor of the container is of hardwood timber plank or plywood.

OPERATING DIFFERENTIAL SUBSIDY A payment to an American-flag carrier by the U.S. government to offset the difference in operating costs between U.S. and foreign vessels.

OPERATING PORT A public port that manages the day-to-day activities on its terminal by scheduling vessel calls, arranging stevedoring services, employing longshore labor, and other similar functions.

OPERATING RATIO A comparison of a carrier's operating expense with its gross receipts.

OPERATOR The party responsible for the day-to-day operational management of certain premises such as warehouses, terminals, and vessels.

OPIC Overseas Private Investment Corporation.

OPPORTUNITY COSTS The cost of giving up an alternative opportunity.

OPTIMUM CUBE The highest level of cube use that can be achieved when loading cargo into a container.

OPTIONAL CARGO Cargo of which the final destination is not known at the moment of booking but will be indicated during the transport.

OPTIONAL PORT   A port of which it is not known whether or not it will be called by a vessel during a voyage.

O&R   Ocean and Rail.

ORDER   A type of request for goods or services.

ORDER BILL OF LADING   A bill of lading on which cargo is consigned to the "order" of a specific party, usually the shipper or a bank, whose endorsement is required to effect its negotiation.

ORDER CYCLE   The time spent and the activities performed from the time an order is received to the actual delivery of the order to a customer.

ORDER CYCLE TIME   The time that elapses from placement of order until receipt of order. This includes time for order transmittal, processing, preparation, and shipping.

ORDER-DEDICATED INVENTORY   Inventory pledged to a customer that will soon be shipped to the customer involved.

ORDER FILL   A measure of the number of orders processed without stock outs, or the need to back order, expressed as a percentage of all orders processed in the distribution center or warehouse.

ORDERING COST   The cost of placing an inventory order with a supplier.

ORDER NOTIFY (O/N)   A bill of lading term to provide surrender of the original bill of lading before freight is released; usually associated with a shipment covered under a letter of credit.

ORDER PICKING   Assembling a customer's order from items in storage.

ORDER PICKING AND ASSEMBLY   In a warehouse, the selection of specific items to fill or assemble a complete order.

ORDER PROCESSING   The activities associated with filling customer orders.

ORDER TRANSMITTAL   The time from when the customer places or sends the order to when the seller receives it.

ORDINARY HIGH WATERLINE   In nature, that water elevation below which aquatic vegetation will not grow. In practice, a water surface elevation arbitrarily fixed from past experience or the establishment of navigation pools.

ORFS   Origin Rail Freight Station. Same as CFS at origin except an ORFS is operated by the rail carrier participating in the shipment.

ORGANIC   Pertaining to compounds produced in plants and animals or carbon compounds of artificial origin.

ORGANIC LIQUID   Any liquid organic material having a vapor pressure of equal to, or greater than 1.5 pounds per square inch absolute under actual storage conditions.

ORGANIC MATERIAL   Any chemical compound of carbon excluding carbon monoxide, carbon dioxide, carbonic acid, metallic carbonates, metallic carbides, and ammonium carbonates.

ORIGIN   Location where shipment begins its movement.

ORIGIN SERVICE CHARGES (OSC)   *See* Container Service Charges.

ORIGINAL BILL OF LADING (OBL)   A document that requires proper signatures for consummating carriage of contract.

ORLOP DECK   The term formerly applied to the lowest deck in a ship; now practically obsolete.

OS&D   Over, Short, or Damaged. Usually discovered at cargo unloading.

OSD   Open Shelter Deck.

OSMOSIS   The passing of a solvent through a semipermeable membrane separating two solutions of different solute concentration. The phenomenon can be observed by immersing in water a tube partially filled with an aqueous sugar solution and closed at the end with parchment. An increase in the level of the liquid in the solution results from a flow of water through the parchment into the solution.

OT   On truck or railway.

OUTAGE   Space left in a product container to allow for expansion during temperature changes it may undergo during shipment and use. Measurement of space not occupied.

OUTBOARD   Away from the centerline, toward the side of a ship.

OUTBOARD BOOM   The boom over the side of the ship.

OUTBOARD FALL   The fall leading from the outboard boom.

OUTBOARD PROFILE   A plan showing the longitudinal exterior of the starboard side of a vessel, together with all deck erections, stacks, masts, yards, rigging, rails, etc.

OUTBOUND CARGO   Cargo that is being exported from a country engaged in international trade.

OUT DRAFT   Current moving across the lock entrance toward the river or toward the dam.

OUTER LOCK WALL   The wall of the lock on the river or channel side away from the shore.

OUT GATE   Transaction or interchange that occurs at the time a container leaves a rail or water terminal.

OUT-OF-GAUGE CARGO   Cargo whose dimensions are exceeding the normal dimensions of a 20 or 40 feet container, e.g., over length, over width, over height, or combinations thereof.

OUT-OF-POCKET COST   The cost directly assignable to a particular unit of traffic that a company would not have incurred if it had not performed the movement.

OUT OF SHAPE (CONVERSELY IN SHAPE)   Used to indicate when a tug, towboat, or tow is not in the proper position to negotiate the channel or to shove into or come out of a lock.

OUT OF TRIM   Not properly trimmed or ballasted.

OUTREACH   The horizontal distance from the end of the boom to the mast.

OUTSIDE OF A BEND   The side of the river channel with the largest projected circumference.

OUTSIDER   A carrier that operates on a route served by a liner conference but is not a member of that conference.

OUTSOURCING   Purchasing a logistics service from an outside firm, as opposed to performing it in-house.

OUTTURN REPORT   Written statement by a stevedoring company in which the condition of cargo discharged from a vessel is noted along with any discrepancies in the quantity compared with the vessel's manifest.

OUTWARD HANDLING   The operations to be performed on outgoing goods from a production unit, both administrative and physical, starting at the moment forwarding orders can be executed to the moment of actual departure of the goods.

OUT WIDE, JUST BELOW   A channel report term meaning that after passing the mark, you swing out wide away from the bank.

OVERAGE (INS)   An additional premium charged on a cargo open cover declaration because the carrying vessel is outside the scope of the classification clause.

OVER ALL   The extreme deck fore and aft measurement of a vessel.

OVERBOARD   Outside, over the side of a ship, in the water.

OVERCAPACITY   The ability of a marine terminal, or a set of terminals in a port range, to handle considerably more cargo throughput than is available.

OVERCHARGE   To charge more than the proper amount according to the published rates.

OVERHANG   Portion of the hull over and unsupported by the water.

OVERHAUL   To separate the blocks of a tackle.

OVERHAULING WEIGHT   A weight used to keep the rope taut when a load is not hooked on to a tackle. Also used on cargo falls to prevent slack from developing.

OVERHEAD   The term used for ceiling aboard ship. Also, in a distilling operation, that portion of the cargo that is vaporized, led off through suitable lines, and condensed to liquid in cooling coils, thus separating it from the portion of the cargo withdrawn from the condenser as gas or vapor.

OVERHEIGHT CARGO   Cargo stowed in an open top container; projects above the uppermost level of the roof struts.

OVERLAND CARGO   Commodities originating from or destined for OCP territory. *See also* Overland Common Point.

OVERLAND COMMON POINT (OCP)   A term stated on the bills of lading offering lower shipping rates to importers east of the Rockies, provided merchandise from the Far East comes in through the West Coast ports. OCP rates were established by U.S. West Coast steamship companies in conjunction with western railroads so that cargo originating or water rates via the U.S. Atlantic and Gulf ports. Applied to Eastern Canada destined for the American Midwest and East would be competitive with all.

OVERLAP The situation where an overtaking vessel has forged ahead so as no longer to have the choice on which side to pass.

OVERLENGTH CARGO Cargo, exceeding the standard length.

OVERLOAD Use all available power.

OVERNIGHT DELIVERY Goods shipped on one day and delivered the next morning.

OVERPACK A unit used by a single shipper to contain one or more packages and to form one handling unit for convenience of handling and stowage. Dangerous goods packages contained in the overpack must be properly packed, marked, labeled, and in proper condition as required by the Regulations regarding dangerous goods (air cargo).

OVER PIVOT RATE The rate per kilogram to be charged for the over pivot weight (air cargo).

OVERSTOW CARGO Cargo that must be discharged prior to commencing regular unloading operations. Normally reloaded to same vessel prior to departure.

OVERTAKING Said of a vessel when she is overhauling or overtaking another vessel.

OVER-THE-ROAD A motor carrier operation that reflects long distance, intercity moves; the opposite of local operations.

OVERTONNAGING A situation where there are too many ships generally or in a particular trade for the level of available cargoes.

OVERVARNISH A coating applied directly over ink to reduce the coefficient of friction, to provide glass and/or to protect the finish against abrasion and corrosion.

OVERWIDTH CARGO Cargo exceeding the standard width.

OWNER The legal owner of cargo, equipment, or means of transport.

OWNER CODE (SCAC) Standard Carrier Abbreviation Code. Identifies that individual common carrier. A three-letter carrier code followed by a suffix identifies the carrier's equipment. A suffix of "U" is a container and "C" is a chassis.

OWNER OPERATOR (OO) A trucking operation in which the truck's owner is also the driver.

OWS Owners.

OXIDATION In general, the process in which oxygen is added to a compound. The oxidation reaction in petroleum may lead to gum or resin formation, which is of importance in the use of gasolines, particularly those that contain unsaturated compounds.

OXIDATION INHIBITORS Chemical compounds added to petroleum products in small quantities to reduce the rate of oxidation.

OXIDIZING AGENT An element or compound that is capable of adding oxygen or removing hydrogen, or one that is capable of removing one or more electrons from an atom or group of atoms.

OXIDIZING MATERIAL   A substance that yields oxygen readily to stimulate the combustion of organic matter.

OXTER PLATE   A bent shell plate that fits around upper part of sternpost; also called tuck plate.

P

PA (INS) Particular Average.

PACKAGE Any physical piece of cargo in relation to transport consisting of the contents and its packing for the purpose of ease of handling by manual or mechanical means. The final product of the packing operation consisting of the packing and its contents to facilitate manual or mechanical handling.

PACKAGE POLICY (INS) An insurance policy including two or more lines or types of coverages in the same contract.

PACKAGING Materials used for the containment, protection, handling, delivery, and presentation of goods and the activities of placing and securing goods in those materials.

PACKED CARGO All general cargo in containers, including petroleum in drums or other packages and liquefied petroleum gas in cylinders.

PACKING Material put between plates or shapes to make them watertight. Wooden blocks and wedges supporting ship on sliding ways.

PACKING LIST Itemized list of commodities with marks/numbers but no cost values indicated.

PACKING INSTRUCTION Document issued within an enterprise giving instructions on how goods are to be packed.

PACKING UNIT A type of package where a standard quantity of products of a specific product type can be packed and that requires no additional packaging for storage and shipment.

PADAG Please Authorize Delivery Against Guarantee. A request from the consignee to the shipper to allow the carrier or agent to release cargo against a guarantee, either bank or personal. Made when the consignee is unable to produce original bills of lading.

PADDING Filling and maintaining the cargo tank and associated piping system with an inert gas, other gas or liquid, which separates the cargo from the air.

PAD EYE A metal eye attached to a deck or bulkhead through which a hook, ring, or line may be passed. It usually receives a shackle attached to a chain, wire, or block. A securing point found on deck, usually associated with lifting gear. Sometimes found in overheads of machinery spaces or pump rooms.

PAINTER A short piece of rope secured in the bow of a small boat used for making her fast.

PAIRED PORTS A U.S. Customs program wherein at least two designated Customs ports will enter cargo that arrives at either port without the necessity of an inbound document.

PAIR MASTS *See* King Posts.

PALE OIL Lubricating oils of light color (not darker than about 4 NPA) and of comparatively low viscosity, usually obtained as overhead products.

PALLET   A wooden platform with or without sides, on which material can be stacked to facilitate handling by a lift truck.

PALLET CONVERTER   Superstructure that can be applied to a pallet to convert it into either a box or post pallet.

PALLETIZATION   *See* Unitization.

PALLET RACK   A skeleton framework, of fixed or adjustable design, to support a number of individual pallet loads.

PALLET TRUCK   Pedestrian or rider-controlled nonstacking lift truck fitted with forks.

PALLET WRAPPING MACHINE   A machine that wraps a pallet's contents in stretch-wrap to ensure safe shipment.

PALM   The fluke, or more exactly, the flat inner surface of the fluke of an anchor; a sailmaker's protector for the hand, used when sewing canvas; a flat surface at the end of a strut or stanchion for attachment to plating, beams, or other structural member.

PALM AND NEEDLE   A seaman's sewing outfit for heavy work.

PALM WHIPPING   A short length of sail twine sewn into the end of a rope to prevent its unlaying.

PANAMA CHOCKS   Steel casting with oval opening. Chocks must be fitted at each end of ship passing through the Panama Canal, for use in the locks.

PANAMAX   The maximum size of ships allowed to transit the Panama Canal: length 948 feet, beam 106 feet, draft 34.8 feet.

PANTING   The pulsating in and out of the bow and stern plating as the ship alternately rises and plunges deep into the water. Most noticeable in the bow and stern.

PANTING BEAMS   The transverse beams that tie the panting frames together.

PANTING FRAMES   The frames in the forepeak, usually extra heavy to withstand the panting action of the shell plating.

PAPER RAMP   A technical rail ramp, used for equalization of points not actually served.

PAPER RATE   A published rate that is never assessed because no freight moves under it.

PARAFFIN WAX   The wax removed by chilling and pressing paraffin distillates from wax bearing crudes such as Mid Continent and Pennsylvania crudes. It is an overhead product. Paraffin wax has a very definite crystalline structure and the crystals are much larger than those obtained from petroleum wax.

PARALLEL SINKAGE   Vessel increases her draft so that the drafts forward and aft are increased by the same amount; increase of draft without change of trim.

PARAVANE   The paravane is a special type of water kite that, when towed with wire rope from a fitting on the forefoot of a vessel, operates to ride out from the ship's side and deflect mines that are moored in the path of the vessel, and to cut them adrift so that they will rise to the surface where they may be seen and destroyed.

PARBUCKLE   A method of rolling an object, such as a drum, up an incline by means of a rope. Also pulling a set of bitts out of the deck.

PARCEL   *See* Package.

PARCEL RECEIPT   An arrangement whereby a steamship company, under rules and regulations established in the freight tariff of a given trade, accepts small packages at rates below the minimum bill of lading and issues a parcel receipt instead of a bill of lading.

PARCELLING   Wrapping a rope spirally with long strips of tarred canvas, overlapped, in order to protect it from water.

PARENTAL GOVERNMENTS   In port governance, the governmental unit that creates and empowers the port agency and to whom it is in part accountable.

PARK (TRAILER PARK)   *See* Container Yard.

PARTED   Any line or cable that has broken.

PARTIAL CONTAINERSHIPS   Multipurpose containerships where one or more but not all compartments are fitted with permanent container cells, and the remaining compartments are used for other types of cargo. Also includes container/car carriers, container/railcar carriers, and container/roll on/roll off ships. *See also* Freighters.

PARTIAL LOSS (INS)   A loss under an insurance policy that does not either completely destroy or render worthless the insured property or exhaust the insurance applying thereto.

PARTIAL SHIPMENTS   Under letters of credit, one or more shipments are allowed by the phrase "partial shipments permitted."

PARTICIPATING CARRIER   A carrier participating in a tariff and who therefore applies the rates, charges, routing and regulations of the tariff (air cargo). A carrier over whose air routes one or more sections of carriage under the air waybill is undertaken or performed (air cargo).

PARTICULAR AVERAGE   Partial loss or damage to goods. *See* Insurance, Particular Average.

PARTICULAR AVERAGE (INS)   *See* Insurance, Particular Average. A fortuitous partial loss to the subject matter insured, proximately caused by an insured peril but is not a general average loss. Particular average only relates to damage and/or expenses that are exclusively borne by the owners of a vessel that has sustained damage as a result of, e.g., heavy weather or by the owners of the cargo that has been damaged in transit.

PARTITION   *See* Divider.

PARTNERS   Similar pieces of steel plate, angles, or wood timbers used to strengthen and support the mast where it passes through a deck, or placed between deck beams under machinery bedplates for added support.

PASSAGEWAY   A corridor or hallway within the superstructure of a vessel used to facilitate horizontal movement between compartments onboard a ship.

PASS A LINE   To reeve and secure a line.

PASS A STOPPER   To reeve and secure a stopper.

PASS DOWN THE LINE   A signal repeated from each ship to the next astern in column.

PASSENGER/COMBINATION SHIPS   Ships with a capacity for 13 or more passengers.

PASSENGER-MILE   A measure of output for passenger transportation that reflects the number of passengers transported and the distance traveled; a multiplication of passengers hauled and distance traveled. (Also Revenue Passenger Mile or RPM.)

PASSENGER VESSEL   A ship designed to accommodate passengers on ocean passages. Cruise ships have overtaken this type of ship, although essentially the same, traditional passenger vessels would provide a more comfortable ride in rough ocean conditions than modern cruise ships.

PASSING LIGHT   A low intensity light that may be mounted on the structure of another light to enable the mariner to keep the latter light in sight when they pass out of its beam during transit.

PATCHY FOG   Fog occurring in less than half the area covered by the forecast.

PATENT BLOCK   Block having roller bearings for the pin bearings.

PATENT EYE   A metal eye or socket secured to the end of a wire rope in place of a spliced eye.

PAULIN   Pliable canvas hatch cover; also to pieces of canvas used as a shelter for workmen or as a cover for deck equipment.

PAWL   Short-hinged piece of metal used to engage the teeth of gear-like mechanisms so that recoil will be prevented.

PAY   To fill the seams of a vessel with pitch.

PAYEE   A party named in an instrument as the beneficiary of the funds. Under letters of credit the payee is either the drawer of the draft or a bank.

PAYER   A party responsible for the payment as evidenced by the given instrument. Under letters of credit, the payer is the party on whom the draft is drawn, usually the drawee bank.

PAYING   The operation of filling the seams of a wood deck, after the calking has been inserted with pitch, marine glue, etc. Also applied to the operation of slackening away on a rope or chain.

PAYLOAD   The carrying capacity of a container. The revenue-producing load carried by a means of transport.

PAYMENT   The transfer of money, or other agreed upon medium, for provision of goods or services.

PAYMENT AGAINST DOCUMENTS   Instructions given by a seller to a bank to the effect that the buyer may collect the documents necessary to obtain delivery of the goods only upon actual payment of the invoice.

PAYMENT COLLECTION   Obtaining money, or other agreed upon medium, for provision of goods or services.

PAY OFF   To turn the bow away from the wind; to pay the crew.

PAY OUT   To let run or slack out from the vessel any line or hawser.

PAY QUANTITIES   Normally, pay quantities are computed by comparing pre- and post-dredge surveys. The computations are correct for such actions as dredging outside the channel limits, dredging deeper than authorized, and leaving undredged areas within the project.

PC   Piece. Period of Charter.

PCC   Pure Car Carrier. A type of vessel configured to carry only automobiles.

PCGO   Part Cargo.

PCT   Percent.

PD   Per Diem.

P&D   Pickup & Delivery.

PDPR   Per Day Pro Rata.

PEACOAT   A blue jacket's reefer.

PEAK   The space at the extreme lower bow or stern.

PEAK, FORE AND AFTER   The space at the extreme bow or stern of a vessel below the decks.

PEAK DEMAND   Time period during which customers demand the greatest quantity.

PEAK SEASON /PEAK SHIPPING SEASON   Usually associated with the pre-holiday shipping season—the months of July through November as merchants move goods for the holiday shopping season.

PEAK TANK   Compartments at the extreme fore (bow) and aft (stern) ends of the ship either left void or used for water ballast.

PEDESTAL   The fitting that takes the gooseneck of the jumbo boom.

PEEN   To round off or shape an object, smoothing out burrs and rough edges. The lesser head of a hammer and is termed ball when it is spherical, cross when in the form of a rounded edge ridge at right angles to the axis of the handles, and straight when like a ridge in the plane of the handle.

PELICAN HOOK   A quick release hook used on boat gripes, cargo gear, or wherever rapid release is desired. Consists of a hinged hook held together by a ring or bridge-piece. When the ring is knocked off, the hook swings open.

PELORUS   A navigational instrument, similar to a binnacle and mariner's compass but without a magnetic needle, used in taking bearings, especially when the object to be sighted is not visible from the ship's compass. Also known as a dumb compass.

PENDANT   A length of wire rope with a socket or an eye splice at each end. Also known as pennant.

PENETRATION NUMBER   The depth, in tenths of a millimeter, that a standard cone penetrates a sample of grease under prescribed condition. *See* Unworked Penetration; Worked Penetration.

PENETRATIONS   Opening in horizontal and vertical surfaces onboard a vessel.

PENETROMETER   Apparatus for measuring penetration of grease.

PENGUIN PIECES/PENGUINS   Fittings for lashing containers on RO/RO vessels.

PENNANT   Fittings for lashing containers on RO/RO vessels. *See* Pendant.

PENSKY MARTENS   A closed cup test method for determining flash and fire points of oils.

PER CONTAINER RATE   Rates and/or changes on shipments transported in containers or trailers and rated on the basis of the category of the container or trailer.

PER DIEM   A charge, based on a fixed daily rate, made by one transportation line against another for the use of its equipment.

PERFORMANCE BOND   Bond issued at the request of one party to a contract in favor of the other party to the contract to protect the other party against loss in the event of default on the contract by the requesting party. The bonding agent may undertake to fulfill the contract or may simply undertake to pay a specific amount in monetary damages. A standby letter of credit or demand guarantee is often used as a performance bond with the latter characteristics.

PERFORMANCE INDICATOR   A variable indicating the effectiveness and/or efficiency of a process.

PERFORMANCE MEASUREMENT   The comparison of the results of business processes with each other or with standards in order to know the effectiveness of these processes and/or the supportive actions.

PERFORMANCE NUMBER   An arbitrary scale, normally used to denote knock characteristics of aviation gasolines having an octane rating above 100. The reference fuel is iso octane with additions of tetraethyl lead. Both lean and rich mixture ratings are reported. *See* Octane Number.

PERIL (INS)   A term used in the Marine Insurance Act (1906) to denote a hazard. The principle of proximate cause is applied to an insured peril to determine whether or not a loss is recoverable. In modern practice the term "risk" often replaces "peril."

PERILS OF THE SEA   Those causes of loss for which the carrier is not legally liable. The elemental risks of ocean transport.

PERIOD   Time (in seconds) it takes for successive wave crests (or troughs) to pass a fixed point. The interval of time between the commencement of two identical successive cycles of the characteristic of a light or sound signal.

PERIOD OF ROLL   The time occupied in performing one double oscillation or roll of a vessel as from port to starboard and back to port.

PERISCOPE   An instrument used for observing objects from a point below the object lens. It consists of a tube fitted with an object lens at the top, an eyepiece at the bottom, and a pair of prisms or mirrors that change the direction of the line of sight. Mounted in such a manner that it may be rotated to cover all or a part of the horizon or sky and fitted with a scale graduated to permit the taking of bearings, it is used by submarines to take observations when submerged.

PERISHABLE COMMODITY   A commodity that is subject to spoilage while en route.

PERISHABLES   Cargo that spoils quickly and requires special attention.

PERMANENT BALLAST TANKS   Those tanks having no connection with the cargo system and are used for the carriage of the carriage of ballast only.

PERMANENT SET   A material will become permanently distorted when stressed beyond its elastic limit.

PERMEABILITY   A measure of the ease with which a fluid can flow through a porous medium. The easier the flow, the greater the permeability of the medium. Also, the percentage of the volume of a compartment that can be occupied by water if flooded.

PERMEABILITY OF SURFACE   The percentage of the surface of a flooded compartment, which is occupied by water.

PERMISSIBLE LENGTH   Maximum length permitted between main, transverse bulkheads. Found by multiplying factor of subdivision by floodable length.

PERMIT   A grant of authority to operate as a contract carrier.

PERPENDICULARS   Forward perpendicular is a vertical line through the intersection of the load waterline and the stern contour. After perpendicular is where the aft side of the sternpost meets the load waterline or if no post, at the center of the rudderstock. Length between perpendiculars is horizontal distance between the perpendicular and forward perpendicular.

PER SE   By itself.

PERSISTENCE   Ability of a substance to have an effect over a period of time.

PERSONAL DISCRIMINATION   Charging different rates to shippers with similar transportation characteristics, or, charging similar rates to shippers with differing transportation characteristics.

PETROCHEMICALS   Organic chemicals manufactured from petroleum.

PETROL   Used, particularly in England, to designate petroleum or its derivatives.

PETROLEUM   Crude oil and its products. A compound consisting of mixed hydrocarbons.

PETROLEUM CARGO   A cargo consisting of crude oil or its products shipped generally in bulk form aboard tank ships or tank barges, or in barrels or similar containers.

PETROLEUM WAX   A high boiling wax product obtained from cylinder stocks by the cold settling process. To the human eye, the wax appears to be amorphous, but under the microscope it consists of a network of needle crystals. Petrolatum wax, as obtained from the cylinder stock, has a reddish brown color similar to that of the oil but by further refining may be produced in any shade up to pure white. Petrolatum wax is seldom sold as such but is mixed with oils of proper color to make commercial petroleums.

PH The degree of acidity or alkalinity of aqueous solutions; values above 7 up to 14 indicate alkaline solutions, and values of 0 up to 7 indicate acid solutions.

P/H Pier to House (same as CFS/CY).

PHANTOM FREIGHT Occurs in delivered pricing when a buyer pays an excessive freight charge calculated into the price of goods.

PHPD Per Hatch Per Day.

PHYSICAL DISTRIBUTION Those activities related to the flow of goods from the end of conversion to the customer.

PHYSICAL DISTRIBUTION MANAGEMENT The planning execution and control of those activities that are related to the flow of goods from the end of conversion to the customer.

PHYTOSANITARY INSPECTION CERTIFICATE A certificate issued by the U.S. Department of Agriculture to satisfy import regulations of foreign countries; indicates that a U.S. shipment has been inspected and found free from harmful pests and plant diseases.

P&I Protection and Indemnity; an insurance term.

PIANC Permanent International Association of Navigational Congresses.

PICKING Taking products or components out of a stock.

PICKING LIST A list used to collect items from stores needed to fulfill an order.

PICK ORDER An order to pick certain quantities of goods out of a stock.

PICK & PACK Picking and packing immediately into shipment containers.

PICKUP The act of calling for freight by truck at the consignor's shipping platform.

PICK UP & DELIVERY A service concerning the collection of cargo from the premises of the consignor and the delivery to the premises of the consignee.

PICKUP SERVICE The carriage of outbound consignments from the point of pickup to the airport of departure (air cargo).

PIER The location in a seaport where cargo arrives or departs. A shoreside facility to which a ship is secured. A structure used for loading and unloading vessels that projects into the water. Piers extending at right angles to the shoreline are called finger piers.

PIERHEAD LEAP A jump to a deck made by a deserter as soon as a vessel approaches a dock.

PIERHEAD LINE Line set by the U.S. Army Corps of Engineers, or other competent authority, beyond which the pier may not normally extend.

PIER RELEASE *See* Delivery Order. Issued by the consignee or his Customs broker to the ocean carrier as authority to release the cargo to the inland carrier. Includes all data necessary for the pier delivery clerk to determine that the cargo can be released to the domestic carrier.

PIER TO HOUSE A shipment loaded into a container at the pier or terminal, then to the consignee's facility.

PIER TO PIER   Containers loaded at port of loading and discharged at port of destination.

PIG   Railroad term. Wheeled vehicle, usually a trailer or container on a chassis, loaded on a railroad flatcar.

PIGGYBACK   A transportation arrangement in which truck trailers with their loads are moved by train to a destination. Also known as rail pigs.

PIGGY PACKER   Trade name for a Raygo Wagner front-end toppick forklift vehicle that is used to lift containers and trailers on or off rail flatcars.

PIGTAIL   A term applied to the chain pendant that is connected to the bridles used on tugs on the U.S. West Coast.

PILE   A timber driven into the bottom and projecting above water; those driven at the corners of a dock are called fender piles.

PILE TAG   The tag affixed to the pile or shipment of cargo in the transit shed identifying it and indicating what ship it is to be loaded on. The original copy usually acts as a dock receipt and one copy serves as a mate's receipt.

PILFERAGE   When cargo is broached and part or all of the content is stolen.

PILING HEIGHTS   Limit set for stacking cargo to ensure that supports will not be loaded beyond stated capacity.

PILLAR   Vertical member or column giving support to a deck girder. Also called stanchion.

PILOT   A person experienced in local navigation, tested by the U.S. Coast Guard, and employed to navigate a vessel. Some smaller vessels use the term "pilot" to describe a mate who possess the proper qualifications for navigation, but ocean going ships employ "harbor pilots" to assist bringing the ship into port. Pilots access the ship via Jacob's Ladders, therefore the nickname "pilot ladder."

Bar Pilot: A general term used in the U.S. Gulf and West Coast referring to a pilot who takes a vessel into the entrance of a harbor from the sea. He may also have to dock the vessel, anchor it, or turn it over to another pilot for transit up a river or bay.

Docking Pilot: A person, either independent or a member of a tug crew, who goes aboard another vessel or ship to take charge in the docking operation. His legal status is that of an independent contractor.

Harbor Pilot: A pilot used in a harbor for shifting berths or taking the vessel over from the bar pilot.

Riding Pilot: An independent operator, frequently a tug captain, who rides ships or tows being assisted by tugs.

River Pilot: Usually a pilot who takes over from the bar pilot in long rivers, such as the Mississippi or Columbia.

Sea Pilot: The pilot who takes a vessel or tow outside of jetties and over the bar when bound for sea.

Tug Pilot: A watch officer on a tug or towboat.

PILOT BOAT   A power or sailing boat used by pilots.

PILOTHOUSE   Deckhouse containing steering wheel, compass, charts, etc., used for navigation of a ship; generally placed forward, near navigating bridge.

PILOT VALVE   Small valve used to admit fluid to one side of a piston operating a large valve.

PILOT VESSEL   A small boat used by the pilots to go to and from a vessel employing his services.

PIN, BELAYING   A small iron or rough wood pin, made with a head, shoulder, and shank. It is fitted in holes in a rail and is used in belaying or making fast the hauling parts of light running gear, signal halyards, etc.

PIN LOCK   A hard piece of iron, formed to fit on a trailer's pin, that locks in place with a key to prevent an unauthorized person from moving the trailer.

PINTLES   The pins or bolts that hinge the rudder to the gudgeons on the sternpost.

PIPELINE INVENTORY   The amount of goods in a pipeline: the sum of loading stock, goods in transit, and receiving stock.

PIRACY   Any illegal acts of violence, detention or any act of depredation, committed for private ends by the crew or the passengers of a private ship and directed on the high seas, against another ship or against persons or property onboard such ship, or against a ship, persons or property in a place outside of the jurisdiction of any state.

PITCH   For a ship to rotate about the midship horizontal axis, or the bow dipping and rising into the seas. The distance a vessel will travel in one revolution of the propeller if it worked in a solid, tar used to pay seams, lengthwise measurement of a chain link.

PITCHING   The alternate rising and falling motion of a vessel's bow in a nearly vertical plane as she meets the crests and troughs of the waves.

PITTING   The localized corrosion of iron and steel in spots, usually caused by irregularities in surface finish, and resulting in small indentations or pits.

PIVOT WEIGHT   Minimum chargeable weight of a unit load device (air cargo).

PIVOTING POINT   Point during the progress of a launching at which the moment of buoyancy about the fore poppet equals the moment of the vessel's weight. At this point the stern begins to lift and the vessel pivots about the fore poppet.

PLACE OF DELIVERY   Place where cargo leaves the care and custody of carrier.

PLACE OF ORIGIN   Location where goods are received by a carrier or agent from the consignor or agent.

PLACE OF RECEIPT   Location where cargo enters the care and custody of the carrier.

PLAIN SUCTION DREDGE   A dredge with no special device on the suction pipe for dislodging or agitating the material.

PLAIT   To braid; used with small stuff.

PLAN   A drawing prepared for use in building a ship.

PLANAMETRICS   A measurement of a flat or level surface by means of an instrument that measures the area by tracing its boundary line.

PLANKING   Broad planks used to cover a wooden vessel's sides or deck beams.

PLASTICIZER   A compound added to a lacquer to counteract the tendency of the finished surface to become brittle.

PLATEN   Skids on which structural parts are assembled.

PLATFORM   Any flattop vessel, such as a barge, capable of providing a working area for personnel or vehicles. A partial deck in the machinery space. A partial deck usually without camber or sheer; also called a flat.

PLATFORM BODY   A truck or trailer without ends, sides or top but with only a floor.

PLATFORMING   A special reforming process, employing platinum as a catalyst, for upgrading straight run gasolines.

PLATING   Steel plates welded to the structural members to afford the hull rigidity and water tightness. *See* Scantlings.

PLATING, SHELL   The plating forming the outer skin of a vessel. In addition to constituting a watertight envelope to the hull, it contributes largely to the strength of the vessel.

PLAY   Freedom of movement.

PLIMSOLL LINE   Statutory load line.

PLIMSOLL MARK   A series of horizontal lines painted on the outside of a ship marking the level that must remain above the surface of the water for the vessel's stability.

PLUG   A wooden wedge fitting into a plug hole in the bottom of a boat; the hole is for draining water from the boat.

PLUME   A cloud of LNG vapor above a spill.

PMA   Pacific Maritime Association.

PO   *See* Purchase Order.

POA   Port of Arrival. Location where imported merchandise is off-loaded from the importing aircraft or vessel.

POCKET   When a free surface liquid is trapped against the upper tank or compartment overhead, thereby reducing the effect of free surface. A cylindrical tank would have no pocketing.

POD   Port of Discharge. Port of Destination. Proof of Delivery. A document required from the carrier or driver for proper payment.

POINT   To taper the end of a rope; one of the 32 divisions of the compass card; to head close to the wind.

POINT OF ORIGIN   The location at which a shipment is received by a carrier from the shipper.

POINT OF REST   Trace the movements of a container in the container terminal from arrival to departure. It is used to determine intraterminal movements by type of moving equipment and it also indicates a functional interchange point.

POISE Unit of absolute viscosity.

POISON A toxic substance that when absorbed into the human body, such as by ingestion, skin absorption, or inhalation, can kill, injure, or impair an organism. Notwithstanding the above, corrosive liquids, such as acids which due solely to their corrosive nature can be fatal if ingested, should not be classed as poisons. The four classes of poison are: Class A, Extremely dangerous; Class B, Less dangerous; Class C, Tear gases or irritating substances; Class D, Radioactive materials.

POISON CONTROL CENTER Usually a hospital that can be telephoned for emergency remedy advice for poison victims.

POL Port of Lading; Petroleum, Oil, and Lubricants.

POLAR ICE (OR ARCTIC PACK) Thickest and heaviest form of sea ice more than one year old.

POLARITY The property possessed by electrified bodies by which they exert forces in opposite directions. The current in an electrical circuit passes from the positive to the negative poles.

POLE MAST A complete mast constructed from a single spar.

POLICY (INS) The written statement of a contract effecting insurance, or certificates thereof, by whatever name called and including all clauses, riders, endorsements, and papers attached thereto and made part thereof.

POLICY PERIOD (INS) The period during which the policy contract affords protection.

POLITICAL RISK In export financing, the risk of loss due to currency inconvertibility, foreign government action preventing the delivery of goods, revolution, war, expropriation, confiscation, etc.

POLYMERIZATION A process for uniting light olefins to form hydrocarbons of higher molecular weight. The phenomenon whereby the molecules of a particular compound link together to form extended chains containing from two to thousands of molecules; the new unit is called a polymer. A compound may change from a free flowing liquid to a viscous one or even to a solid thereby giving off a great deal of heat. Polymerization may occur automatically with no external influence; it may occur if the compound is heated or if a catalyst or impurity is added. It may under some circumstances be dangerous.

POMERENE ACT, THE Also known as (U.S.) Federal Bill of Lading Act of 1916. U.S. Federal law enacting conditions by which a B/L may be issued. Penalties for issuing B/L's containing false data include monetary fines and/or imprisonment.

PONTOON A type of boat in which buoyancy is secured by a watertight subdivision of the hull, and not by the addition of air tanks. Also applied to cylindrical air and watertight tanks or floats used in salvage operations. The floatation devices that support most pipeline dredges. There are also pontoons that support the floating portion of the discharge line. These are also the removable hatch covers on containerships.

POOL The shared use of equipment by a number of companies that make together the investments in the equipment mentioned.

POOLING The sharing of cargo or the profit or loss from freight by member lines of a liner conference. Pooling arrangements do not exist in all conferences.

POOLING OF CARGO The practice of a group of cargo shippers to combine cargo into larger lots to achieve economies in transportation costs.

POOLING OF TRANSPORTATION SERVICES The practice of a group of carriers to jointly market their services in order to achieve fuller capacity.

POOP A superstructure fitted at the after end of the upper deck. Aft part of a vessel where the steering engine is located.

POOP DECK The after upper portion of the hull, usually containing the steering gear.

POOPED Said of a vessel when a sea breaks over the stern.

POPPETS Those pieces of timber that are fixed perpendicularly between the ship's bottom and the bilge ways at the foremost and aftermost parts of the ship, to support it when being launched. They are parts of the cradle.

POR Port of Origin.

PORT A harbor area located at marine terminal facilities for transferring cargo between ships and land transportation. Left side of a ship when facing forward. Opening in a ship's side for handling freight.

PORT ACTIVITIES The concerns of individual owners, operators, or agents, the sum of which comprises the port industry.

PORT AREA Any zone contiguous to or associated in the traffic network of a seaport, within which exists facilities for the transshipment of persons and/or property between domestic carriers and carriers engaged in coastwise, intercoastal, or overseas transportation.

PORT AUTHORITY A state or local government that owns, operates, or otherwise provides wharf, dock, and other terminal investments as ports.

PORT CAPACITY In terms of tons per year, the total capability of a port to move cargoes through terminal facilities located within the port precincts.

PORT CARGO An opening in the side plating provided with a watertight cover or door and used for loading and unloading.

PORT EMERGENCY OPERATING BOARD A board that may be comprised of the same membership as a Planning Committee. The board may be activated during periods of emergency to implement the provisions of a Port Emergency Operating Plan.

PORT EMERGENCY PLANNING COMMITTEE A committee comprised of representatives of port industries whose function is to develop, and maintain current, a plan for the continuity of port operations to be implemented during periods of emergency.

PORT EQUIPMENT Barges, lighters, and floating equipment, all stevedoring gear, other handling equipment on piers, docks, wharves and marine terminals, and in warehouses (which warehouses are entirely or principally engaged with traffic through ports), and all other loading and unloading equipment and service watercraft normally used in the transfer or interchange of cargo and/or passengers between oceangoing watercraft and other media of transportation or in connection therewith.

PORT FACILITIES   Piers, docks, wharves, marine terminals, transit sheds, warehouses (which warehouses are entirely or principally engaged with traffic through ports), and other land and water facilities at ports or contiguous thereto, within the local traffic network, incident to or effecting the transfer or interchange of cargo and/or passengers between oceangoing watercraft and other media of transportation.

PORT FLANGE   *See* Watershed.

PORT GANGWAY   An opening in the side plating, planking, or bulwark for the purpose of providing access through which people may board or leave the ship or through which cargo may be handled.

PORT HOLE   *See* Air Port.

PORT INDUSTRY   Any economic activity that is directly needed in the movement of waterborne cargo. This not only includes the loading and discharge of ships but also the many port activities that take place beyond the piers and wharves on the waterfront. The sum of the individual activities, municipal and private, parent or subdivision, located within the port area, engaged in operations incident to or effecting the transfer of cargo and/or passengers between oceangoing watercraft and other media of water or land transportation, and all other operations beneficial to or in support of the port's normal and/or emergency operations. Also, any economic activity that is needed for the movement of waterborne cargo. Specifically, it includes the economic activities required for the total handling of both domestic and foreign waterborne cargo tonnages (not passengers). The port industry impact is estimated by entering cargo tonnage handled for each kind of vessel type (container, breakbulk, neobulk, dry bulk, liquid bulk, coastwise and inland barge).

PORT MARKS   An identifying set of letters, numbers, and/or geometric symbols followed by the name of the port of destination that are placed on export shipments. Foreign government requirements may be exceedingly strict in the manner of port marks.

PORT OF ARRIVAL   Location where imported merchandise is off-loaded from the importing aircraft or vessel.

PORT OF CALL   Port where a ship discharges or receives cargo.

PORT OF DISCHARGE   Port where cargo is discharged/unloaded from seagoing vessel.

PORT OF ENTRY   A port at which foreign goods are admitted into the receiving country.

PORT OF EXIT   Place where cargo is loaded and leaves a country.

PORT OF LOADING   Port where cargo is loaded on board seagoing vessel.

PORT PAIRING   A balanced load of inbound containers, so that a vessel will load the same number of containers it has discharged.

PORT PERSONNEL   All personnel primarily used or engaged in the administration, operation, and maintenance of a port and the port facilities located in the port area, and in the furnishing of port services in the port area.

PORT- PORT   Can also be CY/CY, CY/CFS, CS/CY, CFS/CFS.

PORT SERVICES   Activities of stevedores, terminal operators, contractors furnishing railroad car and truck loaders and unloaders and other waterfront labor, and all other services normally used or performed in the transfer or interchange of cargo and/or passengers between oceangoing watercraft and other media of transportation or in connection therewith.

PORT SIDE   The left side of a vessel when looking forward. Opposite to starboard.

PORT SIDE TO   Refers to a vessel docked with its left side adjacent to the wharf.

PORT STATE CONTROL   The inspection of foreign ships in national ports for the purpose of verifying that the condition of a ship and its equipment comply with the requirements of international conventions and that the vessel is manned and operated in compliance with applicable international law.

PORT TO PORT BILL OF LADING   Bill of lading covering shipment by ocean only. The shipper/seller is responsible for transporting the goods to the port of loading and the buyer for picking the goods up at the port of discharge. Multimodal, rather than port-to-port, bills of lading should generally be used for containerized shipments and other shipments where the place of receipt and/or the place of delivery is inland.

PORT USERS   Industries that make use of a port to receive inputs or ship outputs. The extent of port usage is defined by the proportion of inputs to the output received or shipped via a port. The dollar value of U.S. exports provides an indication of the extent that manufacturers, distributors, and shippers depend on the maritime industry.

PORTABLE DREDGES   A class of smaller dredges that are designed to be easily disassembled for overland transporting to the next dredge site.

PORTABLE FIREFIGHTING SYSTEM   Basically a system of strategically located fire extinguishers.

PORTAINER   The registered trade name for low profile container gantry cranes manufactured by Pacific Coast Engineering Company (PACECO).

PORTAL CRANE   A type of gantry crane with vertical legs of sufficient height and width to permit vehicles or railroad equipment to pass between the legs.

PORTHOLE   A circular opening in the ship's side. *See* Air Port.

PORTLAND HOOK   *See* Hooks.

PORTPACKER/TOP PICK   Trade name for a front-end forklift made by Raygo Wagner Corporation that lifts a container by securing the lift mechanism on the top of the container.

PORTUGUESE MAN OF WAR   A jelly fish with a sail-like protuberance above the water.

POSITIONING   The transport of empty equipment from a depot to shipper's premises or from consignee's premises back to a depot as the empty leg of a carrier haulage transport.

POSITIONING RINGS   Winch-operated spotting device on vessel, used to hold and align barges in elevator well.

POSITIVE SLIP   Engine speed is more than observed speed or when the propeller operates at less than 100% efficiency.

POST DREDGE HYDROGRAPHIC SURVEY   A survey taken of the channel bottom following completion of maintenance dredging. This survey is compared with both the predredge survey and the channel project dimensions to ensure that all necessary maintenance material has been removed, but that excessive material has not been removed, by the dredge without authorization.

POSTAL CODE   A national code maintained by the Postal Authorities designed to indicate areas and accumulated addresses to facilitate sorting and the delivery of mail and other goods. Note: The coding system is different in the various countries throughout the world.

POSTPONEMENT   The delay of value-added activities such as assembly, production, and packaging to the latest possible time.

POTENTIAL GUM   Gum that may be formed and deposited by a gasoline during storage or under accelerated aging conditions.

POUR POINT   The lowest temperature at which an oil will flow or can be poured under specified conditions of test. By ASTM instruction, it is taken as the temperature 15°F above the solid point.

POUR POINT DEPRESSANT   A compound that when added to a wax containing product (a diesel fuel, lubricant, etc.) reduces the solid point of the product. The additive apparently functions by modifying the crystal structure of wax, which separates at low temperatures.

POV   Privately Owned Vehicle.

POWER OF ATTORNEY   The legal ability or authority given by one individual or firm to another individual or firm to act on behalf of the first in certain specific matters.

POWER PACK   An auxiliary power unit (generator) that provides electricity for a refrigerated container or specially adapted, temperature-controlled containers.

P/P   Pier to Pier (same as CFS/CFS).

PPD.   Prepaid.

PRACTICAL HANDLING CAPACITY   The estimated practical total cargo that can be processed or moved across a pier or wharf apron and through a marine terminal during normal working hours in the period of one effective cargo working year.

PRACTICE   What has become customary as a result of repeated acts.

PRATIQUE   A limited quarantine; a permit by the port doctor for an incoming vessel being clear of contagious disease, to have the liberty of the port.

PRATIQUE CERTIFICATE   Lifts temporary quarantine of a vessel; granted pratique by the Health Officer.

PRAYER BOOK   A small holystone.

PREBLOCKED RUN THROUGH TRAIN   A through train made up of blocks or cuts of cars that are not separated until reaching a destination yard, where the blocks may be sent off on separate branch lines or to individual consignees.

PRECARRIAGE   Carriage of goods by any mode of transit from place of receipt to port of loading.

PRECARRIER   The carrier by which the goods are moved prior to the main transport.

PRECHECK   A system of collecting portions of check in data from a vehicle prior to its reaching the gatehouse, using remote cameras, scales, intercoms, etc.

PRECIPITATE   Material, formed during the accelerated oxidation of loaded fuel, which is insoluble in both the fuel and the gum solvent.

PRECIPITATION NUMBER   The number of milliliters of solid matter precipitated in a mixture of oil and solvent under prescribed conditions.

PRECOOLING   A process employed in the shipment of citrus fruits and other perishable commodities. The fruit is packed and placed in a cold room from which the heat is gradually extracted. The boxes of fruit are packed in containers that have been thoroughly cooled and transported through to destination without opening the doors.

PREDREDGE HYDROGRAPHIC SURVEY   A condition survey of the channel bottom taken prior to initiation of dredging. This survey is compared to channel project dimensions to determine the amount and extent of maintenance dredging required.

PREEXPORT FINANCING   Specific form of working capital lending in which the borrower is given funds needed to obtain or manufacture goods that have been ordered by a buyer in another country. As such financing is normally earmarked to individual sales, documentation of each sale must be provided to the lender, often in the form of a letter of credit with proceeds assigned to the lender. Generally only a percentage of the sale value is lent.

PREMISES (INS)   The particular location of a property or a portion thereof as designated in a policy.

PREMIUM (INS)   The payment for an insurance policy, usually paid periodically (annually, semiannually, quarterly, or monthly).

PREPAID (PPD)   Freight charges paid by the consignor (shipper) prior to the release of the bills of lading by the carrier.

PREPAID B/L   Freight paid prior to movement; money to be paid prior to issuance of bill of lading.

PRESENTING BANK   In a draft collection transaction, the bank that contacts the drawee, generally the buyer of goods, for acceptance and/or payment.

PRESHIPMENT INSPECTION (PSI)   The checking of goods before shipment for the purpose of determining the quantity and/or quality of said goods by an independent surveyor (inspection company) for phytosanitary, sanitary and veterinary controls. Presently there is a tendency by developing countries to use the inspection also for the purpose of determining whether the price charged for certain goods is correct.

PRESLINGING   The act of placing goods in slings that are left in position and used for loading into and discharging from a conventional vessel.

PRESSURE DISTILLATE   The light, gasoline bearing distillate product from the pressure stills that has been produced by cracking, as contrasted with virgin or straight run stock.

PRESSURE DISTILLATE BOTTOMS   Residue from distillation of topped crude.

PRESSURE GRADIENT   Difference in pressure between two points divided by the distance between them. The greater the difference in pressure between the same two points, the greater the wind. The closer the isobars are together on a weather map, the greater the pressure gradient.

PRESSURE RELIEF VALVE (PV VALVE)   A spring-loaded valve installed on discharge side of pump to protect pump against excess pressure. A dual-purpose valve incorporated in the cargo tank venting system of tank vessels, the operation of which, when appropriately set, automatically prevents excessive pressure or vacuum in the tank or tanks concerned.

PRESSURE/VACUUM VALVE (SOMETIMES REFERRED TO AS P/V VALVE OR BREATHER VALVE)   A dual-purpose valve commonly incorporated in the cargo tank venting system of tankers the operation of which, when appropriately set, automatically prevents excessive pressure or vacuum in the tank or tanks concerned. On a tanker such a valve may be manually jacked open or bypassed when the vent system must handle large gas flows during loading or gas freeing.

PRETRIP   Preparation and cleaning of a reefer or container prior to a trip.

PRETRIP INSPECTION (PTI)   A technical inspection of reefer containers prior to positioning for stuffing.

PREVENTER   A rope or wire used for additional support or safety, as a preventer guy.

PRICE TRANSPARENCY   When both buyer and seller know pricing. Net markets can eliminate arbitrage situations when only a broker knows the price. Net markets can result in sellers making more money and buyers paying a lower price, since broker margins are reduced.

PRICKER   A small marlinspike.

PRIMARY AID TO NAVIGATION   An aid to navigation established for the purpose of making landfalls and coastwise passages from headland to headland.

PRIME   To physically displace the air within a pump with liquid to prevent loss of suction.

PRIME MOVER   The engine and gear train that drives the dredge pump. Drive machinery including the diesel engine, electric motor, steam turbine and the like.

PRINCIPAL   Party entrusting a draft and/or documents to a bank for collection of payment, generally the seller of goods.

PRIOR DAMAGE (INS)   Preexisting damage that occurred prior to the loss in question.

PRIORITY ORDER   An order, which is, identified as taking precedence over other orders to ensure its completion in the minimum time.

PRIVATE AIDS TO NAVIGATION   Aids to navigation other than those operated by the federal government.

PRIVATE CARRIER   Business that operates trucks primarily for the purpose of transporting its own products and raw materials. The principle business activity of a private carrier is not transportation.

PRIVATE CODE   A secret code system devised to conceal the contents of a message and to reduce the number of words required in a cablegram.

PRIVATE WAREHOUSE   A warehouse operated by the owner of the goods stored there.

PRIVATE WAREHOUSING   Owning or leasing storage space for one's exclusive use.

PRIVILEGE VESSEL   One that has the right of way.

PROBE   Any electrically conductive object or piece of apparatus introduced into a tank which may increase the electrical field strength in its vicinity, for example, metal ullage tapes or metal sampling equipment.

PROCUREMENT   The activities that ensure the availability of the material and or services in the desired quantity, quality, place, and time from the supplier.

PRODUCT CARRIER   A tanker that is generally below 70,000 deadweight tons and used to carry refined oil products from the refinery to the consumer. In many cases, four different grades of oil can be handled simultaneously.

PRODUCT TANKER   A smaller tanker usually carrying smaller consignments of refined petroleum goods, usually no larger than 70,000 deadweight tons.

PRODUCTION   Raising crude oil from underground geological formations to the earth's surface.

PRODUCTION METER   A device that combines the signals from a flow meter and a density meter and reports dredge production in terms of volume of dredged material pumped per unit time.

PROFESSIONAL LIABILITY INSURANCE (INS)   Liability insurance to indemnify professionals, doctors, lawyers, architects, etc., for the loss or expense resulting from claim on account of bodily injuries because of any malpractice, error, or mistake committed or alleged to have been committed by the insured in his profession.

PROFILE   Side elevation or fore and aft centerline section of a ship's form or structure.

PRO FORMA   A Latin term meaning "For the sake of form."

PRO FORMA INVOICE   An invoice provided by a supplier prior to the shipment of merchandise, informing the buyer of the kinds and quantities of goods to be sent, the value and specifications such as weight, size, etc.

PROGRESS PAYMENT   One in a series of payments made at stages in the performance of a contract of sale, e.g., up front to obtain materials, after completion of manufacturing, upon shipment, upon installation, and upon final inspection.

PROJECT CARGO   Quantity of goods connected to the same project and often carried on different movements and from various places.

PROJECT DEPTH   The depth at which a project is maintained to ensure safe navigation by user traffic. Project depth may be equal to or less than authorized depth, depending on user traffic trends since date of project authorization.

PROJECT RATE   Single tariff item, established to move multiple commodities needed for a specified project, usually construction.

PROOF OF DELIVERY   The receipt signed by the consignee upon delivery.

PROOF OF LOSS (INS)   A statement made to the insurance company under oath setting out the basis of an insured's claim under the insurance policy.

PROOF STRAIN   The test load applied to anchors, chains, or other parts, fittings, or structure to demonstrate proper design and construction and satisfactory material.

PROOF STRENGTH   The proof strength of a material, part, or structure is the strength, which it has been proved by tests to possess.

PROPELLER   A revolving device that drives the ship through the water, consisting of three or four blades, resembling in shape those of an electric fan. Sometimes called a screw or wheel.

PROPELLER ARCH   The arched section of the stern frame above the propeller.

PROPELLER GUARD   A framework fitted somewhat below the deck line on narrow, high-speed vessels with large screws, so designed as to overhang and thus protect the tips of the propeller blades.

PROPELLER POST   Forward post of stern frame, through which propeller shaft passes.

PROPELLER SHAFT   The short aftermost section of the main shafting to which the propeller is attached; also called a tail shaft.

PROPELLER SLIP   The difference between propeller speed (or engine speed) and the vessel's actual speed.

PROPELLER THRUST   The effort delivered by a propeller in pushing a vessel ahead.

PROPERTY DAMAGE INSURANCE (INS)   Protection against liability for damage to the property of another not in the care, custody, and control of the insured, as distinguished from liability for bodily injury.

PROPERTY INSURANCE (INS) Insurance that indemnifies a person with an interest in physical property for its loss or the loss of its income-producing ability.

PROPORTIONAL LIMIT The stress within which stresses and deformations are directly proportional. Within this limit, on removing stress, there is no permanent set.

PROPORTIONAL RATE A rate that is used in combination with other rates to establish a through rate (air cargo).

PRO RATA A Latin term meaning "In proportion."

PRORATE A portion of a joint rate or charge obtained by proration (air cargo).

PRO RATE (INS) Cancellation of an insurance contract by the insurance company, allowing a policyholder a share of the premium relating to the remainder of the time under the contract that bears to the total contract premium.

PRORATION Division of a joint rate or charge between the carriers concerned on an agreed basis (air cargo).

PROTECTION & INDEMNITY CLUB (P&I) A mutual association of shipowners who provide protection against liabilities by means of contributions.

PROTECTIVE DECK The deck fitted with the heaviest protective plating.

PROTEST A sworn statement by the master describing any unusual event during A voyage. In A draft collection transaction, the formal legal process of registering that payment or acceptance of the draft has been demanded but the drawee has refused to pay or accept the draft.

PROW The part of the bow above the water.

PROXIMATE CLAUSE (INS) The immediate and effective cause of loss or damage. It is an unbroken chain of cause and effect between the occurrence of an insured peril or a negligent act and resulting injury or damage.

PRY BAR A bar located under the wildcat to force the anchor chain off the wildcat and into the chain pipe.

PSI Pressure expressed in pounds per square inch. *See also* Preshipment Inspection.

PSIG Pounds per square inch gauge, referring to pressure read from a gauge, where 0 psig indicates atmospheric pressure, which is approximately 14.7 psi.

PTI *See* Pretrip Inspection.

PUBLIC ACCESS In coastal management, pathways, parks, viewpoints, view corridors that allow the general public to reach the water's edge for recreation or to see the water from different vantage points.

PUBLIC ENTERPRISE A form of governmental unit that combines features of a traditional governmental agency (e.g., public ownership and statutorily assigned powers) with features of private enterprise (for example, reliance on private capital and autonomy in decision-making).

PUBLIC SERVICE COMMISSION A name usually given to a state body having control or regulation of public utilities.

PUBLIC WAREHOUSE   A warehouse that is available to all companies and persons who wish to make use of the services offered.

PUBLISHING AGENT   Person authorized by transportation lines to publish tariffs or rates, rule and regulations for their account.

PUDDENING, PUDDING   Pads constructed of old rope, canvas, oakum, etc., sometimes leather covered, in any desired shape and size and used to prevent chafing of boats, rigging, etc., and on the stem of a boat to lessen the force of a shock.

PULL ORDER SYSTEM   A system to provide warehouses with new stock on request of the warehouse management.

PULP TEMPERATURE   Procedure where carrier tests the temperature of the internal flesh of refrigerated commodities to ensure that the temperature at time of shipment conforms to prescribed temperature ranges.

PUMP CASTING   The external covering of the dredge pump. The casing, like the impeller, is specially designed to handle the highly abrasive dredged material with high efficiency and minimum wear.

PUMP CAVITATION   Pump cavitation occurs when local pressures in the interior of the pump are lowered below that of the vapor pressure of water. Cavitation causes decreased performance of the pump and, if neglected, can cause extensive pump damage.

PUMP EFFICIENCY   Pump efficiency is the ratio of the output of the pump in terms of work produced by the pump to the input to the pump in terms of work required to operate the pump.

PUMP IMPELLER   The internal part of the dredge pump that creates the suction that brings the mixture of water and dredged materials into the pump and pushes them through the discharge pipe to the disposal facility.

PUMPING STATION   *See* Booster Stations.

PUMPMAN   A member of the engine department in charge of running cargo pumps aboard a tanker.

PUMPROOM   A space, usually just forward of the machinery space, on a tanker where the cargo pumps are located for discharging the ship. Pump rooms are justifiably considered one of the most dangerous locations aboard a tanker due to the high quantities of liquids passing through miles of pipelines.

PUNCH   A machine for punching holes in plates and shapes.

PUNCH, PRICK   A small punch used to transfer the holes from the template to the plate. Also called a "center punch."

PUNT   A rectangular flat-bottomed boat issued to vessels in the U.S. Navy for painting the ship's side and general use around the ship's waterline, fitted with oarlocks on each side and usually propelled by sculling.

PUP   A short semitrailer used jointly with a dolly and another semitrailer to create a twin trailer.

PURCHASE   A tackle with an even number of sheaves. The mechanical advantage secured by the use of a tackle. Any mechanical advantage, which increases the power, applied.

PURCHASE ORDER (PO) A document created by a buyer to officially request a product or service from a seller. It contains, among other things, the name and address of the buyer, the ship-to address, the quantity, product code (and expected price), requested ship or receipt date, sales and shipping terms, and other appropriate information.

PURGING The pumping of fresh air into cargo spaces to force the inert gas out. This is done prior to entry into a space (gas freeing).

PURSE SEINING Fishing with the use of a large net, which is floated vertically by floats and towed around a school of fish by boats. When the school is surrounded the bottom is drawn together pursed and the vessel comes alongside the seine hoisted and fish spilled on the deck.

PUS Plus Us.

PUSH BOAT A squared off house on a squared flush deck with vertical push knees forward on a shaped bow.

PUSH KNEES Upright padded steel beam devices on bow of tugboats that fit up against barges being pushed.

PUSH ORDER SYSTEM A situation in which a firm makes inventory deployment decisions at the central distribution center and ships to its individual warehouses accordingly.

PUT OUT The act of paying out.

PUT TO SEA To leave port.

P/V VALVE *See* Pressure/Vacuum Valve.

PW Packed Weight.

PWWD Per Weather Working Day.

PYROFORIC LIQUID Any liquid that ignites spontaneously in dry or moist air at or below 130°F.

PYROTECHNICS Flares, rockets, powder, etc., used for giving signals or for illumination, more generally used as distress signals.

Q

QC Quality Control.

QUADRANT A reflecting hand navigational instrument constructed on the same principle as the sextant but measuring angles up to 90 degrees only. Also known as an octant. One fourth of the circumference of a circle. A fitting in the shape of a sector of a circle secured to the rudderstock and through which the steering leads turn the rudder. The rim is provided with two grooves to take the steering chains or ropes and is of sufficient length of arc so that the leads are tangential to the rim at all rudder angles. A casting, forging, or builtup frame, on the rudder head, to which the steering chains are attached.

QUALIFIED PETROLEUM PRODUCTS Products that have passed successfully certain tests, required to determine whether or not they conform to all qualification test requirements of applicable specifications.

QUALIFIER A data element whose value shall be expressed as a code that gives specific meaning to the function of another data element or a segment.

QUALITY ASSURANCE All those planned and systematic actions necessary to provide adequate confidence that a product or service will satisfy given requirements for quality.

QUALITY CONTROL The management function that attempts to ensure that the goods or services a firm manufactures or purchases meet the product or service specifications.

QUANTITY CHARGE The unit rate that is lower than the normal rate and applies to shipments meeting specific weight requirements (air cargo).

QUANTITY DISCOUNT A proportional reduction of a rate based on quantity (air cargo).

QUARANTINE A restraint placed on an operation to protect the public against a health hazard. A ship may be quarantined so that it cannot leave a protected point. During the quarantine period, the Q flag is hoisted.

QUARTER The upper part of a vessel's sides near the stern; also portions of the vessel's sides about midway between the stem and midlength and between midlength and the stern. The part of a yard just outside the slings.

QUARTER DECK That portion of the weather deck nearest the stern.

QUARTER RAMP Ramp on RO/RO vessels, extending on an angle to the centerline on each or both quarters.

QUARTERING SEA A sea on the quarter.

QUARTERMAN An under foreman, a term generally restricted to navy yards.

QUARTERS Living or sleeping rooms for passengers and personnel. It includes staterooms, dining salons, mess rooms, lounging places, passages connected with the foregoing, etc.; individual stations for personnel for fire or boat drill, etc.

QUARTERS BILL   A vessel's station bill showing duties of the crew.

QUAY   A wharf used for the loading and unloading of cargo, which is parallel to the shore, having water on only one side.

QUEUE   A waiting line at the entrance to a terminal or other operation for vehicles picking up or delivering cargo.

QUEUING LANE   Lane set aside at the entrance to a terminal for vehicles delivering or picking up cargo.

QUICK RESPONSE   A method of maximizing the efficiency of the supply chain by reducing inventory investment.

QUOIN   A wedge-shaped piece of timber used to secure barrels against movement.

QUOTA   The quantity of goods that may be imported without restriction or additional duties or taxes.

QUOTATION   An offer to sell goods at a stated price and under stated terms.

QUOTATION EXPIRATION DATE   The date a quotation price is no longer valid.

R

RABBET   A depression or offset of parallel depth designed to take some other adjoining part, as, for example, the rabbet in the stem to take the shell plating.

RACKING   Deformation of the section of a ship, generally applied to a transverse section, so that one set of diagonals in the plane of action is shortened while those at right angles thereto are lengthened.

RACON   A radar beacon that produces a coded response, or radar paint, when triggered by a radar signal.

RADAR   An electronic system designed to transmit radio signals and receive reflected images of those signals from a "target" in order to determine the bearing and distance to the "target."

RADAR PLOTTING   The whole process of target detection, tracking, calculation of parameters, and display of information. Used only in connection with ARPA performance standards.

RADAR REFLECTOR   A special fixture fitted to or incorporated into the design of certain aids to navigation, to enhance their ability to reflect radar energy. In general, this fixture will materially improve the aids to navigation for use by vessels with radar.

RADIOACTIVE MATERIAL   Any material, or combination of materials, that spontaneously emits ionizing radiation and having a specific activity greater than 0.002 micro curies per gram.

RADIOBEACON   Electronic apparatus that transmits a radio signal for use in providing a mariner a line of position.

RADIO ROOM   A room, usually soundproofed used for sending and receiving radio messages.

RAFFINATE   Solvent refining practice to that portion of the oil, which remains undissolved and is not removed by the selective solvent used.

RAFT, LIFE   A framework fitted with air chambers to support a number of people in case of accidents. Carried on deck and light enough to be handled without mechanical means.

RAG TOP   A slang term for an open top trailer with a tarpaulin cover.

RAIL   The steel tubing surrounding the weather deck to keep persons from falling over the side. The rounded section at the upper edge of the bulwarks, or a horizontal pipe forming part of a railing fitted instead of a bulwark.

RAILCAR   A wheeled wagon used for the carriage of cargo by rail.

RAIL CONSIGNMENT NOTE   A document evidencing a contract for the transport of goods by rail.

RAIL DIVISION   The amount of money an ocean carrier pays to the railroad for overland carriage.

RAIL GROUNDING   The time that the container was discharged (grounded) from the train.

RAILHEAD End of the railroad line or point in the area of operations at which cargo is loaded and unloaded.

RAIL SIDING A short rail track leading from a main line to a customer's plant or warehouse.

RAILYARD A rail terminal where traditional railroad activities for sorting and redistribution of railcars and cargo occur.

RAIN LOCKER Shower aboard a vessel.

RAKE Inclination from the vertical of the mast, smokestack, stem post or the like. To fire lengthwise of the target vessel's decks. The angular underbody at the bow and stern of square-ended barges.

RAKED Fore and aft inclination of the masts, funnels, etc.

RAKE TANK A tank at the extreme, shaped portion of the bow or stern of a barge.

RALLY The action of gangs of men uniting in driving wedges between the cradle and the sliding ways preparatory to launching or similar activities.

RALSTON STABILITY AND TRIM INDICATOR A device for calculating the stability and trim of a vessel by adding or removing representative weights on a metal profile of the vessel.

RAMP Railroad terminal where containers are received or delivered and trains loaded or discharged. Originally, trailers moved on to the rearmost flatcar via a ramp and driven into position in a technique known as "circus loading." Most modern rail facilities use lifting equipment to position containers onto the flatcars.

RAMP TO DOOR A movement where the load initiates at an origin rail ramp and terminates at a consignee's door.

RAMP TO RAMP A movement of equipment from an origin rail ramp to a destination rail ramp only.

RANGE A pair of beacons, lighted or unlighted, commonly located to define a line down the center of a channel.

RANGE, GALLEY The stove, situated in the galley, which is used to cook the food. The heat may be generated by coal, fuel oil, or electricity.

RANGE OF CABLE A length of cable overhauled on deck out of the locker, so as to pay out when the anchor is dropped.

RANGE OF STABILITY The end of the range of stability is reached at an angle of inclination when the righting arm is equal to zero. Practically, the range of stability is ended shortly after deck edge immersion in most vessels.

RATCHET Toothed wheel or rack capable of movement in one direction only. Movement in the other direction prevented by a pawl.

RATE Quantity, amount or degree measured or applied.

RATE AGREEMENT/SERVICE AGREEMENT A contract between a shipper and carrier that guarantees a certain volume of cargo within a stipulated time in exchange for discounted rates. "Rate agreement" is used primarily in regard to railroads; "service agreements" with ocean carriers.

RATE BASIS   A formula of the specific factors or elements that control the making of a rate. A rate can be based on any number of factors (i.e., weight, measure, equipment type, pkg, box, etc.).

RATE BASIS NUMBER   The distance between two rate basis points.

RATE BASIS POINT   The major shipping point in a local area; all points in the local area are considered to be the rate basis point.

RATE BUREAU   A carrier group that assembles to establish joint rates, to divide joint revenues and claim liabilities, and to publish tariffs. Rate bureaus have published single line rates, which were prohibited in 1984.

RATE NEGOTIATION   Negotiation between the shipper and the carrier on the rate to be charged by the carrier.

RATES   Established charges for the transport of goods.

RAT GUARD   A circular piece of metal fitted closely on hawsers and lines to prevent rats from boarding or leaving the ship while at the wharf. The concave side is placed toward the shore to prevent boarding the guard is reversed to prevent rats leaving the ship.

RATING   A class to which an article is assigned.

RATING BUREAU (INS)   An organization that classifies and promulgates and in some cases compiles data and measures hazards of individual risks in terms of rates in a given territory.

RATLINE   Light rope used as rungs between shrouds parallel to the waterline for the crew to ascend or descend.

RATTLE DOWN   To close hitch ratlines across the rigging.

RAW GASOLINE   *See* Straight Run Gasoline.

RC&L   Rail, Canal, and Lake.

RCVR   Receiver.

REACTIVATION   The restoration of a used catalyst to a chemically or physically active state.

REAL TIME   The description for an operating system that responds to an external event within a short and predictable time frame. Unlike a batch or time-sharing operating system, a real-time operating system provides services or control to independent ongoing physical processes

REAMING   Enlarging a rivet hole by means of a revolving, cylindrical, slightly tapered tool with cutting edges running along its sides.

REASONABLE & CUSTOMARY   Phrase often relating to rates, charges, or policies that, over time, have become accepted as a normal course or process of business.

REASONABLE RATE   A rate that is high enough to cover the carrier's cost but not high enough to enable the carrier to realize monopolistic profits.

REASONABLENESS   Under ICC and common law, the requirement that a rate not be higher than is necessary to reimburse the carrier for the actual cost of transporting the traffic and allow a fair profit.

REBATE   Part of a transport charge that the carrier agrees to return; an illegal form of discounting or refunding that has the net effect of lowering the tariff price. *See also* Malpractice.

REBATE (INS)   A reduction of a premium.

REBUILT   A fixed aid to navigation, previously destroyed, that has been restored as an aid to navigation.

RECAP   Recapitulation or restating.

RECAPTURE CLAUSE   A provision of the 1920 Transportation Act that provided for self-help financing for railroads. Railroads that earned more than prescribed return contributed one-half of the excess to the fund from which the ICC made loans to the less profitable railroads. The Recapture Clause was repealed in 1933.

RECEIPT   A written acknowledgment that something has been received.

RECEIPT LOCATION   A location that will receive goods.

RECEIPT POINT   The place where cargo enters the care and custody of the carrier.

RECEIPTS   Commodities received by a port from another domestic port outside the region.

RECEIVER   An enterprise that receives goods/services.

RECEIVING CARRIER   The carrier receiving a consignment on behalf of a carrier, agent, or shipper for onward transport (air cargo).

RECEIVING POINT   A mark or place at which a vessel comes under obligatory entry, transit, or escort procedure (such as for port entry, canal transit, or ice breaker escort).

RECEIVING STOCK   The stock comprising all the goods that have arrived at the door of the receiving organization and is not yet available in the stock of that organization.

RECEPTION FACILITY   A term to describe an oil terminal that has the shore tank capacity to receive dirty ballast water.

RECIPROCATING PUMPS   Pumps of the positive displacement type. A piston working in a cylinder displaces a given volume of fluid for each stroke. The amount delivered depends on the piston area and piston speed. They are used for small quantity high-pressure duties, have an efficiency of about 85%, and are self-priming.

RECIPROCITY   The practice by which governments extend similar concessions to each other.

RECLAMATION   Procedure required to restore or change the quality of contaminated petroleum products to meet desired specifications.

RECONDITIONING   All activities connected with restoring and or adjusting the packaging of a product so that it can be presented to the customer in the requested form.

RECONDITIONING OF GARMENTS   The act or process of bringing garments after transport in shop's condition.

RECONSIGNMENT Changing the consignee or destination on a bill of lading while shipment is still in transit. Diversion has substantially the same meaning.

RECOURSE An obligation, if not net, goes back to the original drawer. "Without Recourse" drawing relieves the drawer of liability.

RECOVERY (INS) Amount recovered from a third party responsible for a loss on which a claim has been paid.

RECOVERY DEVICE An individual unit of equipment, including, but not limited to, an absorber, carbon absorber, or condenser, capable of and used for the purpose of removing vapors and recovering liquids or chemicals.

REDELIVERY Return of a shipment to the party who originally delivered it to the carrier (air cargo).

RED LABEL Label required on flammable cargo.

RED OILS Lubricating oils of a red color, usually produced as bottom oils in reducing stills.

REDUCED CRUDE The bottoms remaining from a distillation of crude oil.

REDUCER A short section of pipe, one end being smaller than the other, having flanges on both ends. Used to connect a larger or smaller hose to a pipe of constant size. Also, a solvent added to dilute a coating, usually for the purpose of lowering its viscosity.

REDUCING AGENT An element or compound that is capable of removing oxygen or adding hydrogen; or one that is capable of giving electrons to an atom or group of atoms.

REDUCTION A distillation where the oil remaining in the still (the bottom) is an important product of the operation, this bottom being concentrated (reduced) to viscosity or other required test by distilling off the lighter portions of the charge.

REDUCTION GEAR An arrangement of shafts and gears such that the number of revolutions of the output shaft is less than of the input shaft, generally used between a motor or a steam turbine shaft and the propeller shaft.

REDUNDANCY In regard to port facilities, the existence of similar cargo-handling terminals at competing ports with insufficient cargo business to allow either to run profitably.

REEF To reduce the area of a sail by making fast reef points and earrings.

REEFER A ship hatch or compartment designed for carrying refrigerated cargo. Slang for refrigerated containers.

REEFER CARGO Cargo requiring temperature control.

REEFER CONTAINER A thermal container with refrigerating appliances (mechanical compressor unit, absorption unit, etc.) to control the temperature of cargo.

REEVE To pass the end of a rope through a block.

RE-EXPORT For export control purposes: the shipment of U.S. origin products from one foreign destination to another.

REFG Refrigerating, refrigeration.

REFLUX The liquid that flows down a fractionating tower to serve as a cooling and material transfer medium in the fractionation process.

REFORMING A cracking process for converting low octane number naphthas or gasolines into high octane number products.

REFORWARDING CHARGE Charges paid or to be paid for subsequent surface or air transport from the airport of destination by a forwarder, but not by a carrier under the air waybill (air cargo).

REFRIGERATED CONTAINERS These containers are designed to operate independently of a blown air refrigerated system and are fitted with their own refrigeration units that require an electrical power supply for operation. These units will operate on either 200 to 220 volts or 380 to 440 volts both at 50/60 Hz, 3 phase at 32 amps. Cargo should not be stowed to the full height of the container. An air gap of approximately 75 mm should be left at the top.

REFRIGERATED WAREHOUSE A warehouse that is used to store perishable items requiring controlled temperatures.

REFUND The repayment to the purchaser of the total charge or a portion of that charge for unused carriage.

REGENERATION In catalytic cracking, removal of carbon from the catalyst in order to make it fit for reuse.

REGIONAL CARRIER A for-hire air carrier, usually certificated, that has annual operating revenues of less than $75 million; the carrier usually operated within a particular region of the country.

REGIONAL ECONOMIC MULTIPLIER The total economic effect that occurs in a region per unit of the direct economic change that caused the effect.

REGIONAL PORT STUDIES A collaborative study by a number of independent port agencies within a region identifying projected cargo flows, existing terminal and berth capacity of the region, and the shortfall in capacity (if any), thus suggesting what new port facilities are needed within the region.

REGIONAL PURCHASE COEFFICIENT A term used in Input Output analysis to refer to a share of total purchases typically made locally.

REGIONALISM In port management, the concept of greater cooperation among competing ports, including such actions as joint promotion and marketing, collaborative studies, regional planning, and merger of port entities.

REGISTER Register tonnage is applicable to both gross and net tonnage weight. In other words, it can be expressed as gross register tons or as net register tons.

REGISTERED TONNAGE A commercial ship is measured by its cargo capacity in "tons," with each ton occupying 100 cubic feet. The cubic capacity of all enclosed spaces is thus measured and the ship's "tonnage" determined.

REGISTRY The ship's certificate determining the ownership and nationality of the vessel.

REGROUPAGE   The process of splitting up shipments into various consignments (degroupage) and combining these small consignments into other shipments (groupage).

REGULAR ROUTE CARRIER   A motor carrier that is authorized to provide service over designated routes.

REGULATORY MARKS   A white and orange aid to navigation with no lateral significance used to indicate a special meaning to the mariner, such as danger.

REID VAPOR PRESSURE (RVP)   The vapor pressure of a liquid determined by laboratory testing in a standard manner in the Reid apparatus at a standard temperature of 100°F (37.7°C) expressed in pounds force per square inch absolute or kilograms force per square centimeter absolute.

REIMBURSEMENT (INS)   Payment of an amount of money related to the amount of loss to or on behalf of the insured upon the occurrence of a defined loss.

REIMBURSING BANK   In a letter of credit transaction, the bank with which the issuing bank maintains an account and which is authorized by the issuing bank to charge that account to pay claims received from the negotiating bank for documents that have been presented.

REINSTATEMENT (INS)   Putting a lapsed policy back in force. The payment of a claim under some forms of insurance reduces the principal amount of the policy by the amount of the claim. Provision is usually made for a method of reinstating the policy to its original amount.

REINSURANCE (INS)   A contract of indemnity against liability by which the insurance company procures another insurance to insure against loss or liability by reason of the original insurance. Insurance by one insurance company of all or part of a risk accepted by it with another insurance company.

REINVOICING   The procedure whereby goods shipped directly from a supplier to the customer are invoiced in two stages: at first by the supplier to an intermediary and subsequently by the intermediary to the customer.

REJECTION   Nonacceptance of, e.g., cargo.

RELATED POINTS   A group of points to which rates are made the same in relation to rates to other points in a group.

RELATIVE COURSE   The direction of motion of a target related to own ship as deduced from a number of measurements of its range and bearing on the radar. Expressed as an angular distance from north. Used only in connection with ARPA performance standards.

RELATIVE MOTION DISPLAY   The position of own ship on such a display remains fixed. Used only in connection with ARPA performance standards.

RELATIVE SPEED   The speed of a target related to own ship, as deduced from a number of measurements of its range and being on the radar. Used only in connection with ARPA performance standards.

RELAY   Common practice in the less-than-truckload industry, in which one driver takes a truck for 8 to 10 hours, then turns the truck over to another driver, pony express style.

RELAY RESTRICTED ARTICLES   To transfer containers from one ship to another. Articles handled only under certain conditions.

RELAY TERMINAL   A motor carrier terminal that facilitates the substitution of one driver for another who has driven the maximum hours permitted.

RELEASE APPROVAL   A document to advise that goods are available for further movement or action.

RELEASED-VALUE RATES   Rates based upon the shipment's value. The maximum carrier liability for damage is less than the full value, and in return the carrier offers a lower rate.

RELIABILITY   A carrier selection criterion that considers the carrier transit time variation; the consistency of the transit time the carrier provides.

RELIEF VALE   Valve loaded by spring or other means to release fluid from a system when the pressure in the system reaches a preset level.

RELIEVING TACKLE   A tackle of double and single blocks rove with an endless fall and used to relieve the regular tiller tackles.

RELIGHTED   An extinguished aid to navigation returned to its advertised light characteristic.

REMITTANCE   Funds sent by one person to another as payment.

REMITTING BANK   In a draft collection transaction, the first bank in the chain of collection, i.e., the principal's or seller's bank.

RENUMERATION   Payment or compensation for services rendered.

REORDER POINT   A predetermined inventory level that triggers the need to place an order. This minimum level provides inventory to meet the demand a firm anticipates during the time it takes to receive the order.

REPARATION   A situation in which the ICC requires a railroad to repay users the difference between the rate the railroad charges and the maximum rate the ICC permits when the ICC finds a rate to be unreasonable or too high.

REPLACED   An aid to navigation previously off station, adrift, or missing, restored by another aid to navigation of the same type and characteristics.

REPLACEMENT   Indicating that a subject is interchangeable with another subject, but differs physically from the original subject in that the installation of the replacement subject requires extra machining or provisions in addition to the normal application and methods of attachment.

REPLACEMENT CLAUSE (INS)   A clause limiting Underwriter's liability for damage to machinery cargo.

REPLACEMENT COST (INS)   The cash value representing what it would cost to replace the specific property without deduction for depreciation.

REPLENISHMENT   Completion of stock.

REPORTING FORM (INS)   Fire or other direct damage insurance written under a form of policy that covers fluctuating values of stocks of merchandise, furniture and fixtures, and improvements by means of periodic reports submitted to the insurance company by the insured, with an annual adjustment of premium on the average value.

REPORTING POINT   *See* Way Point.

REQUEST FOR PROPOSALS (RFP)   Invitation to suppliers to bid on supplying products or services that are difficult to describe for a company or public agency.

REQUEST FOR QUOTATION (RFQ)   Invitation to suppliers to bid on supplying easily described products or services needed by a company or public agency.

REQUISITION   A request that a procurement office supply or acquire some good.

REROUTING   The route to be followed as altered from the one originally specified in the air waybill (air cargo).

RESERVATION   Allotment in advance of space or weight capacity. Also referred to as "booking."

RESERVE BUOYANCY   The volume of all intact space above the waterline.

RESERVOIR   A geological structure of rocks so formed as to trap oil or gas.

RESERVOIR TANK   A tank that stores liquid until needed.

RESET   A floating aid to navigation previously off station, adrift, or missing, returned to its assigned position (station).

RESIDUAL FUEL OILS   Fuel oils that are either topped crude petroleum or viscous cracked residuum.

RESIDUUM   The dark colored, highly viscous oil remaining from crude oil, after the more volatile portion of the charge has been distilled off.

RESIN   Originally, any of the various solid or semisolid natural organic substances, chiefly of a vegetable origin; amorphous; usually yellowish to brown in color; transparent or translucent; soluble in ether, alcohol etc., but not in water; specifically pine resin, or rosin. More recently the term has been used to include synthetic resins, such as Bakelite, built up by chemical reaction, condensation, or polymerization.

RESPIRATORY TRACT   The air passage from nose to lungs, inclusive.

RESPONSIBLE CARRIER   The carrier liable under the terms of a consortium bill of lading. Carrier responsible for the transport of goods as indicated in the transport document (air cargo).

RESPONSIBLE OFFICER   The Master or any officer to whom the Master may delegate responsibility for any operation or duty.

RESTRICTED AREA   An area immediately outside the boundaries of a hazardous area; to facilitate control of entry into a hazardous area of unauthorized persons, motor vehicles, or craft; control the movement of nonapproved equipment into a hazardous area; exclude smoking from a hazardous area. Control naked lights.

RESTRICTED ARTICLES   Articles handled only under certain conditions.

RETENTION OF TITLE   Legal arrangement under which a seller of goods delivers these goods "on consignment" into someone's custody but ownership remains with the seller until he is paid. Retention of title allows the seller to repossess the goods whenever desired and to establish a claim against the custodian if the goods are sold or used without being paid for.

RETROACTIVE DATE (INS) Date on a "claims made" liability policy that triggers the beginning of insurance coverage. A retroactive date is not required. If one is shown on a policy, any claim made during the policy period will not be covered if the loss occurred before the retroactive date.

RETURN CARGO A cargo that enables a ship to return loaded to the port or area where her previous cargo was loaded.

REVENUE Amounts of income stemming from the provision of transport services.

REVENUE BONDS A debt instrument issued by a public port agency that is secured by a pledge of the revenue due to the port from its ongoing business activity.

REVENUE FREIGHT TONNE KILOMETER (RFTK) Air cargo measure of total freight moved by metric ton (tonne).

REVENUE SHARING LEASE A lease between the landlord port and marine terminal operator in which the port receives a minimum payment up to a set level of cargo throughput, after which the port receives a percentage of the tariff revenue received for additional cargo with no maximum and often on a sliding scale.

REVENUE TON A ton on which the shipment is freighted. If cargo is rated as weight or measure (W/M), whichever produces the highest revenue will be considered the revenue ton.

REVERSE AUCTION Buyers post their need for a product or service, then suppliers bid to fulfill that need. Unlike an auction, prices only move down. Since buyer power is key to reverse auctions, they work either for large enterprises or when practiced by intermediaries that aggregate demand of many small buyers. Reverse auctions also are becoming common features of many Net markets.

REVERSE DISTRIBUTION The collection of used, damaged, or outdated products and/or packaging from end users.

REVERSE FRAME An angle bar or other shape riveted to the inner edge of a transverse frame to reinforce it.

REVERSE IPI An inland point provided by an all water carrier's through bill of lading in the U.S. by first discharging the container in an East Coast port.

REVERSE LOGISTICS The process of collecting, moving, and storing used, damaged, or outdated products and/or packaging from end users.

REVERSIBLE (Detention). If loading completed sooner than expected at load port, then days saved can be added to discharge operations.

REVOCABLE LETTER OF CREDIT (LOC) A letter of credit that can be cancelled or altered by the drawee (buyer) after it has been issued by the drawee's bank. *See also* Letter of Credit.

REVOLVING LETTER OF CREDIT Letter of credit that reverts to its original amount at specified intervals, e.g., monthly, thereby preventing drawing too much in any one period.

RFID Radio-Frequency Identification.

RFP *See* Request for Proposal.

RFQ *See* Request for Quotation.

RF TAG Radio Frequency Tag. Used to identify a container through automated container identification.

RFTK *See* Revenue Freight Tonne Kilometer.

RIB A frame of a vessel.

RIBBAND A fore and aft wooden strip or heavy batten used to support the transverse frames temporarily after erection and to keep them in a fair line; also, any similar batten for fairing a ship's structure.

RIDE To lie at anchor; to ride out; to safely weather a storm whether at anchor or underway.

RIDER (INS) An endorsement to an insurance policy that modifies clauses and provisions of the policy, adding or excluding coverage(s).

RIDER PLATE A continuous flat plate attached to the top of a centerline vertical keel in a horizontal position. Its underside is attached to the floors, and when an inner bottom is fitted, it forms the center strake.

RIDGE Area of high pressure in which the isobars are elongated instead of circular or nearly circular. Flat ridge: elongation of isobars is not great enough to prevent penetration of weather fronts through the ridge. Strong ridge: elongation of isobars is great enough to prevent weather fronts from penetrating the ridge. The concept of a ridge also applies to upper air weather maps that are made for heights over 5,000 feet.

RIDING PAWL Device used to guide anchor chain on deck from the wildcat to the hawse pipe; when engaged will also prevent the anchor chain from running free if the brake fails.

RIG A general description of a vessel's upper works; to fit out. A drill rig is a floating structure used to drill for oil. It is usually supported by legs that rest on pads on the ocean floor or it is semisubmersible.

RIGGING The lines and or wires of a ship; collective term for all the stays, shrouds, halyards, and the lines that support a vessel's masts and booms and operate its movable parts. Rigging is known as standing or running rigging. Standing rigging is rigging that is fixed in place to support masts, king posts, etc. Running rigging is rigging that is moveable within its fairleads and blocks such as cargo runners and boat falls.

RIGHT To return to a normal position, such as a vessel righting after keeling over.

RIGHTING ARM The distance between the line of force through B and the line of force through G, when there is positive stability.

RIGHTING MOMENT   The product of the weight of the vessel (displacement) and the righting arm (GZ). Also, the numerical measure of the ship's tendency to right itself from a given angle of heel. This varies with the angle of heel.

RIGHT OF EMINENT DOMAIN   Permits the purchase of land needed for transportation right-of-way in a court of law; used by railroads and pipelines.

RIGHT TO CARGO   Claims by some ports that U.S. law guarantees them a right to cargo handling business when that cargo is "naturally tributary" to the port.

RIGHT-TO-WORK LAWS   State laws that specify that a worker at a unionized plant does not have to join the union to work permanently at the facility.

RINA CERTIFICATE (IT)   Certificate issued by the Italian government for carrying dangerous goods in Italian waters.

RING   Same as Jew's Harp.

RINGBOLT   A bolt fitted with a ring through its eye, used for leading running rigging.

RIPRAP   A layer, facing, or protective mound of stones placed to prevent erosion, scour, or sloughing of a structure or embankment; also, the stone so used.

RIPS   A disturbance of surface water by conflicting current either by winds or tides.

RISE AND SHINE   A call to turn out of bunks or hammocks.

RISE OF BOTTOM   *See* Deadrise.

RISER   A vertical pipe where a hose is connected on the dock or a vertical pipe in a vessel's various piping systems for conveying liquids to various horizontal branches.

RISINGS   The fore and aft stringers inside a small boat, secured to the frames, and on which the thwarts rest.

RISK (INS)   A fortuity. A term used to designate an insured of a peril insured against. It does not embrace inevitable loss. The term is used to define causes of loss covered by a policy.

RIT   Refining in Transit.

RITF   Regional Intermodal Transfer Facility. An intermodal facility serving several marine terminals within a given region. *See* ITF.

RIVERS AND CANAL HARBORS   A type of harbor that physically is located on rivers or canals.

RIVET   A metal pin used for connecting two or more pieces of material by inserting it into holes punched or drilled in the pieces and upsetting one or both ends. The end that bears a finished shape is called the head and the end upon which some operation is performed after its insertion is called the point. Small rivets are "driven cold," i.e., without heating, and large ones are heated so that points may be formed by hammering.

RIVETING   The art of fastening two pieces of material together by means of rivets.

RIVETING, CHAIN   An arrangement of the rivets in adjoining rows where the center of the rivets are opposite each other and on a line perpendicular to the joint.

RIVETING, STAGGERED OR ZIG ZAG   An arrangement of the rivets in adjoining rows where the rivets in alternate rows are one half the pitch or spacing ahead of those in the other rows.

RIVETS, LINE OF   A term applied to a continuous line of rivets whose centers fall on a line perpendicular to the joint.

RIVETS, ROW OF   A term applied to a continuous row of rivets whose centers fall on a line parallel to the joint. Joints made by one row of rivets are known as single riveted joints; by two rows, as double riveted joints; by three rows, as treble riveted joints; by four rows, as quadruple.

R&L   Rail and Lake.

R&O   Rail and Ocean.

ROADABILITY CANOPY   Canopy over the area where vehicles are inspected for roadworthiness.

ROAD CARRIER   Party undertaking transport by road of goods from one point to another such as indicated in the contract.

ROAD ENGINE   A locomotive used by the railroads to haul cargo long distances over the main line trackage.

ROADRAILER   A specialized road chassis that has retractable rail wheels that allow it to operate directly on a rail system.

ROADSTEADS   An area of water where the shoreline configuration offers only minimal protection from wind and wave.

ROAD SWITCHER   A locomotive used for through or main line movements, often in multiple with other similar units. Road switchers may also be used to do work along branch lines.

ROAD TRAVEL ACCIDENT (RTA)   Damage to cargo caused by an accident while on a highway or motorway.

ROAD VEHICLE   A means of transport capable and allowed to move over public roads and other land ways.

ROARING FORTIES   That geographical belt approximately located in 40 degrees south latitude in which are encountered the prevailing or stormy westerlies.

ROB   Remaining On Board. It is the cargo a vessel has left onboard after discharge. Can be classified as liquid, sludge, pumpable, or unpumpable. If a vessel has a high ROB, a charterer may deduct freight or in other words, not pay all the money to the owner.

ROD   *See* Rust Oxidation and Discoloration.

ROLL   Motion of the ship from side to side, alternately raising and lowering each side of the deck.

ROLLING   The side to side (athwartship) motion of a vessel.

ROLLING CARGO   Cargo that is on wheels, such as truck or trailers, and that can be driven or towed onto a ship.

ROLLING CHOCKS   Same as keel, bilge.

ROLLING PERIOD   The time it takes a vessel to make a complete roll, that is, from port to starboard and back to port again.

ROLLING RESISTANCE   The total frictional force that a tire, a set of tires or all the tires on a vehicle is developing with the road.

ROLL ON/ROLL OFF   *See* RO/RO; Ferry.

ROLL ON/ROLL OFF SHIPS   Ships that are especially designed to carry wheeled containers or trailers and only use the roll on/roll off method for loading and unloading. Containers and trailers are usually stowed onboard on their transport wheels.

ROLLOVER   To rebook cargo to a later vessel.

ROLL TRAILER   Special trailer for terminal haulage and stowage onboard of roll on/roll off vessels. Also referred to as Mafi Trailer.

ROND   *See* Rust Oxidation and Discoloration.

ROOF LOAD   External static and dynamic loads imposed on the roof of a container.

ROOF RAIL   Longitudinal structural member situated at the top edge on either side of the container.

ROPE   The product resulting from twisting a fibrous material, such as Manila, hemp, flax, cotton, coir, etc., into yarns or threads that in turn are twisted into strands and several of these are laid up together. Fiber rope is designated as to size by its circumference. Wire rope is made of iron, steel, or bronze wires, with and without a fiber core or heart, twisted like yarns to form strands that are laid up to form the rope. Wire rope is designated as to size both by its diameter and by its circumference.

ROPE, RIDGE   A rope running through the eyes at the heads of the awning stanchions to which the edge of an awning is hauled out and stopped. The term center ridge rope is applied to the rope supporting the center of an awning.

ROPE LAY   The direction in which a rope is twisted up.

ROPE STOPPER   Made of soft line and used to temporarily hold larger lines when shifting from bitts to capstan, etc.

ROPE WORMING   Filling in the cantlines of a rope with marline. The marline should run with the lay of the rope.

RO/RO   A shortening of the term, roll on/roll off. A method of ocean cargo service using a vessel with ramps, which allow wheeled vehicles to be loaded and discharged without cranes. A cargo vessel constructed to allow containerized or unitized cargo loading without vessel's gear or wharf cranes, but by wheeled trailers driven on and off the vessel by tractor power via ramps at the cargo terminal RO/RO berth.

ROSE BOX   A galvanized iron box with the sides perforated by small holes, the combined area of which equals at least twice the area of the bilge suction pipe. The object is to collect bilge water for pumping out and to prevent refuse from clogging the pumps.

ROSES   Perforated metal plates, fitted over the outside of injection seacocks to prevent entrance of foreign substances to the ship's pumps and piping system.

ROTARY DRILLING   Drilling by rotating a drill bit on the end of a string of pipe.

ROTATE   Pivotal movement of container crane on LASH vessel.

ROTATION   Sequence in which a vessel calls at the ports on her itinerary.

ROUGH BOLT   To bolt a plate or frame to a ship until it can be faired for reaming.

ROUGH LOG   The ship's log as written up in pencil by the quartermaster and the Officer to the Deck.

ROUNDABOUT   A circular area within definite limits in which traffic moves in a counterclockwise direction around a specified point or zone.

ROUND IN   To bring the blocks of a tackle closer together.

ROUND LINE   Three-stranded rope used for fine seizings.

ROUND THE WORLD SERVICE   A one directional liner service that generally includes transatlantic, transpacific, and Europe

ROUND TO   To bring a vessel head to wind.

ROUND-TRIP   A voyage, a journey, etc., to a certain place, port, or country and back again.

ROUSE OUT   To haul or to get out for use something that is stowed such as spare hawsers, push cables, etc.

ROUTE   The manner in which a shipment moves, i.e., the carriers handling it and the points at which the carriers interchange.

ROUTING   The determination of the most efficient route(s) that people, goods, materials, and or means of transport have to follow. The process of determining how a shipment will be moved between consignor and consignee or between place of acceptance and place of delivery. This includes traffic separation schemes.

ROW   A vertical division of a vessel from starboard to portside, used as a part of the indication of a stowage place for containers. The numbers run from midships to both sides.

ROWLOCK   A U-shaped fitting with a shank or a socket that is attached to the gunwale of a boat and used as a fulcrum for oars in rowing, sculling, or steering.

RT   Revenue Ton.

RTA   *See* Road Travel Accident.

RTG   Rubber Tired Gantry Crane. *See* Gantry Crane; Transtainer.

RUBBING STRIP   A plate riveted to the bottom of the keel to afford protection in docking and grounding. A strip fastened to the face of a fender or to the shell plating where contact is likely to occur.

RUDDER   A steel mechanically operated device aft of the propeller used for steering the ship. The most common type consists of a flat slab of metal or wood, hinged at the forward end to the stern or rudderpost. When made of metal, it may be built up from plates, shapes, and castings, with or without wood filling, or it may be a casting. The rudder is attached to a vertical shaft called the rudderstock, by which it is turned from side to side.

RUDDER, BALANCED A rudder having the leading edge of a whole or a part of its area forward of the centerline of the rudderstock thus advancing the center of pressure of the water on the rudder and reducing the torque.

RUDDER, UNDERHUNG A rudder that is not hinged to or stepped on the sternpost but is supported entirely by the rudderstock and the rudder stock bearings.

RUDDER BANDS The bands that are placed on each side of a rudder to help brace it and tie it into the pintles.

RUDDER CHAINS The chains whereby a rudder is sometimes fastened to the stern. They are shackled to the rudder by bolts just above the waterline, and hang slack enough to permit free motion of the rudder. They are used as a precaution against losing a rudder at sea. These chains are also called "rudder pendants."

RUDDER FRAME Vertical main piece and the arms that project from it which form the frame of the rudder. It may be a casting, a forging, or a weldment.

RUDDER LOG A projection cast or fitted to the forward edge of the rudder frame for the purpose of taking the pintle.

RUDDER PINTLES *See* Pintles.

RUDDER POST After post of stern frame to which rudder is hung. *See also* Sternpost.

RUDDER STOCK A vertical shaft having a rudder attached to its lower end and having a yoke, quadrant, or tiller fitted to its upper portion by which it may be turned.

RUDDER STOPS Fittings attached to the ship structure or to shoulders on the rudderpost to limit the swing of the rudder.

RUDDER TRUNK A watertight casing fitted around a rudderstock between the counter shell plating and a platform or deck, usually fitted with a stuffing box at the upper end.

RULE OF RATE-MAKING A regulatory provision directing the regulatory agencies to consider the earnings necessary for a carrier to provide adequate transportation.

RUN Underwater portion of the after body that is fined off to the stern. Portion of the after hull that tapers to the sternpost.

RUNAROUND TRACK A running track kept clear to allow the movement of equipment from one end of a rail yard or ITF to the other.

RUN DOWN To collide with a vessel head on; to sail north or south to a given parallel of latitude; to stand along a coast.

RUNNER Same as Fall.

RUNNING GEAR Complementary equipment for terminal and over-the-road handling containers.

RUNNING RIGGING Ropes that are hauled upon at times in order to handle and adjust sails, yards, cargo, etc., as distinguished from standing rigging that is fixed in place.

RUST OXIDATION AND DISCOLORATION Damage to metal caused by exposure to ocean air. An insurance exclusion applied to steel and other metal shipments.

RVNX Released Value Not Exceeding. Usually used to limit the value of goods transported. The limitation refers to carrier liability when paying a claim for lost or damaged goods.

S

SACRIFICE An act accomplished for the welfare of all interests, such as throwing part of a cargo overboard to keep a ship from sinking.

SACRIFICIAL ANODE A piece of metal, usually an alloy or zinc or aluminum, several of which may be installed either to the interior surface of a cargo tank or to the exterior hull surface for the purpose of reducing their deterioration through electrical chemical reaction.

SAD *See* Single Administrative Document.

SADDLE TANKS Tanks, usually for water ballast, that "saddle" or are fitted over the upper sides of the main cargo tanks. They are triangular in longitudinal cross sections and increase in depth towards the ship's side. They are fitted principally on bulk carriers and provide a means of increasing the ship's center of gravity when a light cargo is being carried.

SAE Society of Automotive Engineers.

SAE VISCOSITY An arbitrary system for classifying motor oils according to their viscosities, established by the Society of Automotive Engineers.

SAFE WORKING LOAD (SWL) The maximum weight, which a boom, fall, tackle, hook, etc., will safely support. The breaking strength divided by the SWL is known as the safety factor.

SAFETY SHACKLE Always used as a prudent connector in all towing arrangements.

SAFETY STOCK The inventory a company holds beyond normal needs as a buffer against delays in receipt of orders or changes in customer buying patterns.

SAFETY TREADS A special nonslipping metal plate fitted to the deck at the foot of a ladder or stairway and often fitted on the upper surface of the steps of ladders and stairs. Steps made of safety treads are called safety steps.

SAFETY VALVE A valve that opens automatically in the event of excess pressure in a container, e.g., a boiler stream drum. When fitted to high-pressure systems, the valve is designed to open quickly and snap shut to avoid wire drawing and damage to the valve seat. A safety valve is normally fitted with easing gear. There are statutory as well as insurance company requirements that must be strictly observed. These demand that every boiler has two safety valves and that they may be mounted directly on the shell or steam drum.

SAG A condition when the ship is being bent down in the middle due to higher concentration of weights in the midbody area, or when the midship draft is deeper than the mean draft. The downward deflection of a vessel's midbody below its bow and stern caused by excessive loading of the midbody.

SAGGING The deformation or yielding caused when the middle portion of a structure or ship settles or sinks lower than the bow or stern. The reverse is hogging.

SAID TO CONTAIN (STC)   Term in a bill of lading signifying that the master and the carrier are unaware of the nature or quantity of the contents of, e.g., a carton, crate, container, or bundle and are relying on the description furnished by the shipper.

SAIL AREA   The area of the ship that is above the waterline and that is subject to the effects of wind, particularly a crosswind on the broad side of a ship.

SAIL HO   The hail from a lookout to notify that a vessel has been sighted.

SAIL TRACKS   A device fitted on the after side of a mast in which slides, secured to the forward edge of a fore and aft sail, travel up and down the mast as the sail is hoisted or lowered; used in lieu of mast hoops.

SAILING FREE   Sailing other than close-hauled or into the wind.

SALES (OUTPUT)   This is equal to the value of production and sales. The term is used to describe the transaction when money is exchanged for the provision of goods and services. A sales impact is typically a measure of economic impact (also referred to as output). It is intended to represent the total volume of economic activity related to the impact.

SALMON BOARD   The platform of a platform sling.

SALON   A large public space aboard a ship.

SALOON   The officers' dining room; in the U.S. Navy it is called the wardroom.

SALT DOME   Geological formation resulting from intrusion of rock salt into overlying sedimentary beds.

SALTWATER HEATERS   These are in the engine room and are used to raise the temperature of the water for discharging into the Butterworth machine.

SALVAGE   To save a vessel or cargo from dangers; recompense for having saved a ship or cargo from danger.

SALVAGE CHARGES (INS)   The award due to a salvor for services rendered in saving the insured property.

SALVAGE LOSS (INS)   Occurs when the Underwriter agrees to settle a cargo claim by paying the difference between the insured value and the proceeds realized by selling the damaged goods.

SALVAGE STOCK   Unused material that has a market value and can be sold.

SAMP (SPECIAL AREA MANAGEMENT PLANNING)   A form of harbor management in which public agency representatives work collaboratively, through consensus decision-making, to develop a long-term growth and conservation plan for the harbor, where implementation rests with existing agencies.

SAMSON POST   A short heavy vertical mast that supports cargo booms; also called king post. A single bitt in a smaller vessel.

SANCTION   An embargo imposed by a government against another country.

SAND SHOE   The pad on the foot of a chassis or trailer's landing legs.

SAPONIFICATION   The process of soap making that is the result of a chemical reaction of fat or fatty acid and an alkali.

SAPONIFICATION NUMBER   Number of milligrams of potassium hydroxide required to saponify one gram of compounded oil.

SATURATED HYDROCARBONS   Hydrocarbons in which all the valency bonds of the carbon atom have been fulfilled.

SAVE ALL   A net spread from the ship's rail to the wharf to catch any cargo falling from slings during loading and unloading operations.

SAYBOLT FUROL VISCOSITY   The viscosity of a material as measured on a Saybolt Furol viscosimeter, used primarily for high-viscosity materials. The results are approximately one tenth those obtained on a Saybolt Universal viscosimeter.

SAYBOLT UNIVERSAL VISCOSITY   The time in seconds for 60 cc of liquid to flow through the capillary tube in a Saybolt viscosimeter.

SCAC CODE   *See* Owner Code.

SCALE   Deposit or encrustation that may form on metal as a result of electrolytic or chemical action. To climb up; a formation of rust over iron or steel plating.

SCALE TON   Freighting measurement used in certain trades for various commodities.

SCANTLINGS   The dimensions of the frames, girders, plating, etc., that go into a ship's structure. For merchant ships these dimensions are taken from the classification society rules. A top classed ship would be referred to as a full scantling vessel.

SCARF   A connection made between two pieces by tapering their ends so that they will mortise together in a joint of the same breadth and depth as the pieces connected. It is used on bar keels, stem and stern frames, and other parts.

SCATTERED (SCT) SHOWERS   Precipitation is expected to fall within about 30% to 45% of the area covered by the forecast.

SCAVENGING AGENT   A gasoline soluble bromine compound added with tetraethyl lead in order to prevent the formation and deposition of lead oxide in cylinders.

SCEND   The upward heaving of the bow of a ship that is underway that is a factor in calculating the depth needed in a channel.

SCHEDULE   A timetable including arrival/departure times of ocean and feeder vessels and also inland transportation. It refers to named ports in a specific voyage (journey) within a certain trade indicating the voyage number(s). In general: the plan of times for starting and/or finishing activities. A list of specified amounts payable for ancillary services.

SCHEDULE B   The Statistical Classification of Domestic and Foreign Commodities Exported from the United States.

SCHEDULE (INS)   A list of specified amounts payable for, usually, surgical procedures, dismemberments, ancillary expenses, or the like in health insurance policies; the list of individual items covered under one policy as the various buildings or animals and other property.

SCHEDULE OF LOSS (INS)   Notice completed by the insured documenting loss or damage to contents, personal property, and/or stock.

SCHOOL   A large body of fish.

SCHOONER GUY   The guy between the heads of the booms on a married fall, or yard and stay, cargo system. Also called midship guy or spanner guy.

SCM   *See* Supply Chain Management.

SCOFF   To eat.

SCORE   Groove in the cheek of some types of blocks, to take the strap.

SCOTCHMAN   Chafing gear on backstays; a ring on a piece of metal seized to stay or a shroud.

SCOW   A large open flat-bottomed boat for transporting merchandise or sand, gravel or mud.

SCR   *See* Specific Commodity Rate.

SCRAP MATERIAL   Unusable material that has no market value.

SCREEN BULKHEAD   A bulkhead, dust tight but not watertight, usually placed between engine and boiler rooms.

SCREW   *See* Propeller.

SCREW PIN SHACKLES   A handy type of shackle for onboard use.

SCRIEVE BOARD   A large board made of soft, clear, planed lumber, sometimes a section of the mold loft floor, on which a full-sized body plan of a ship is drawn. The lines were formerly cut in by the use of a scriving knife that made a small U-shaped groove, to prevent them from being obliterated. Pencil lines have taken the place of cutting to a large extent. It is used in making templates of frames, beams, floors, etc., and in taking off dimensions. It is sanded smooth after it has served its purpose.

SCRUBBER   Cleaning tower in an inert gas system. Seawater is sprayed into the gas path to remove soot and other contaminants before the inert gas is led to the cargo tanks or holds.

SC&S   Strapped, Corded, and Sealed.

SCUPPER PIPE   A pipe conducting the water from a deck scupper to a position where it is discharged overboard.

SCUPPER PLUGS   Plugs of various types, tightly fitted or cemented in all scupper holes on the weather deck of tankers while loading, discharging, or shifting cargo in port. In the case of a spill of oil, the plugs usually prevent harbor pollution by retaining the spill on decks.

SCUPPERS   Openings or drains in the side of a ship to carry off rain water or seawater from the waterways or from the drains. The scuppers are placed in the gutters or waterways on open decks and in corners of enclosed decks and are connected to pipes usually leading overboard.

SCUTTLE   A small opening, usually circular in shape, and generally fitted in decks to provide access or to serve as a manhole or opening for stowing fuel, water, and small stores.

SCUTTLE BUTT   A drinking fountain aboard ship. Also the Navy term for rumors aboard ship.

SD   Single Decker.

S/D Sight Draft; Sea Damage.

SDD Store Door Delivery.

SDR *See* Special Drawing Rights.

SEA ANCHOR A drag (drogue) thrown over to keep a vessel to the wind and sea.

SEABEE A type of barge carrier ship, similar to the LASH (lighter aboard ship) vessel except it employs a heavy lift elevator at the stern.

SEABEE VESSELS Ocean vessels constructed with heavy-duty submersible hydraulic lift or elevator system at the stern of the vessel. The Seabee system facilitates forward transfer and positioning of barges.

SEA CHEST An opening for supplying seawater to condensers and pumps, and for discharging wastewater from the ship's water system to the sea. It is a cast fitting or a built-up structure located below the waterline of the vessel and having means for attachment of the piping. Suction sea chests are fitted with strainers or gratings.

SEA COCK, SEA CONNECTION A sea valve secured to the plating of the vessel below the waterline for use in flooding tanks, magazines, etc., to supply water to pumps, and for similar purposes.

SEA DOG An old sailor.

SEAFREIGHT Costs charged for transporting goods over the sea. This does not cover haulage or loading/discharging costs but the sea transport only.

SEA GOING Capable of putting to sea.

SEA ICE Any form of ice found at sea that has originated from the freezing of seawater.

SEAL An individually number metal, plastic, or wire strip used to seal the doors of a container for security or Customs purposes.

SEA LAWYER A seaman who is prone to argue, especially against recognized authority.

SEAL LOG A document used to record seal numbers.

SEAL NUMBER The identifier assigned to the tag used to secure or mark the locking mechanism on closed containers.

SEALS ON CONTAINERS Attached to locking device on container to prevent pilferage and to certify no tampering; made of steel by Customs or carrier.

SEAM Fore and aft joint of shell plating, deck and tank top plating, or lengthwise side joint of any plating.

SEAMLESS DISTRIBUTION A logistics organization strategy that removes impediments to the flow of information and goods.

SEAM STRAP A term applied to a strip of plate serving as a connecting strap between the butted edges of plating. Strap connections at the ends are called butt straps.

SEA PAINTER A line leading from forward and secured to a forward inboard thwart in such a way as to permit quick releasing; used to keep the boat alongside.

SEAPORT   A transshipment point on a seacoast or river where oceangoing vessels customarily call for the purpose of discharging or loading articles of commerce moving in the foreign or domestic oceanborne trade.

SEARCHLIGHT   A powerful electric lamp placed at the focus of a mirror that projects the light in a beam of parallel rays.

SEAS   Combination of wind waves and swell making up the irregular surface of the sea.

SEASONAL INVENTORY   Inventory built up in anticipation of a seasonal peak of demand in order to smooth production.

SEAWALL   A structure that is built along and parallel to a shoreline for the purpose of protecting and stabilizing the shore against erosion resulting from wave action.

SEA WAYBILL   Document indicating the goods were loaded onboard when a document of title (B/L) is not needed. Typically used when a company is shipping goods to itself.

SEAWORTHINESS WARRANTY (INS)   There is an implied warranty in every voyage policy that the ship must be seaworthy at the commencement of the insured voyage or, if the voyage is carried out in stages, at the commencement of each stage of the voyage. To be seaworthy, the ship must be reasonably fit in all respects to encounter the ordinary perils of the contemplated voyage, property crewed, fueled and provisioned, and with all her equipment in proper working order. Cargo policies waive breach of the warranty, except where the Assured or their servants are privy to the unseaworthiness. Breach of the warranty is not excused in a hull voyage policy, literal compliance therewith being required. Although there is no warranty of seaworthiness in a hull time policy, claims arising from unseaworthiness may be prejudiced if the ship sails in an unseaworthy condition with the knowledge of the Assured.

SEAWORTHY   Capable of putting to sea and able to meet usual sea conditions.

SECONDARY RECOVERY   In drilling, a method of forcing oil to flow into the well bore after natural forces fail. Water, gas, or air is usually employed.

SECTION 10   That part of the U.S. Rivers and Harbors Act of 1899 that gives the U.S. Army Corps of Engineers its primary authority to regulate the use of the navigable waters of the United States.

SECTION 404   Part of the U.S. Clean Water Act of 1977 that gives the U.S. Army Corps of Engineers and the U.S. Environmental Protection Agency authority to regulate the discharge of dredged or fill material into the waters of the United States.

SECTIONAL RATE   The rate established by scheduled air carrier(s) for a section of a through route (air cargo).

SECTOR   *See* Light Sector.

SECURE   To make fast or safe. A signal to stop the engines. An order given on the completion of an operation.

SECURE FOR SEA   Extra lashings on all movable articles.

SECURITY (INS)   The Underwriters subscribing a risk. The insurers.

SED   U.S. Commerce Department document, "Shipper's Export Declaration."

SEDIMENT   Solid matter that settles from such liquids as water and petroleum, in cargo tanks.

SEDIMENT AND WATER   Solids and aqueous solutions that may be present in an oil and either settle out on standing or may be separated more rapidly by a centrifuge.

SEGMENT OF PORT INDUSTRY   One of the various types of operations conducted by one or more activities.

SEGREGATED BALLAST   Ballast water that has been carried in tanks that by design have no cargo in them and can therefore be assumed to be clean ballast. Contamination is possible, however, through bulkhead leaks, so surveillance of the water's quality is dictated.

SEGREGATION   Distance required by the rules of IMDG or BC codes between the various commodities of dangerous and or bulk cargoes.

SEIZING   Light cordage or seizing wire used to bind together two ropes or cable. Also used to make an eye without splicing. Seized end of wire rope to prevent unlaying.

SELFIGNITION TEMPERATURE   *See* Auto-Ignition Temperature.

SELFPRIMING   To automatically expel the air from a pump and replace it with liquid via a Venturi or vacuum pump.

SELFSTORING MOORING WINCH   A mooring winch fitted with a reel on which a wire or rope is made fast and permanently stowed.

SELFSUSTAINED VESSEL   Vessel that carries its own handling equipment (crane or ramps) for the loading/discharge of containers and barges or other specialized cargoes.

SELFD   Self-Discharging.

SELLERS' MARKET   A seller's market is considered to exist when goods cannot easily be secured and when the economic forces of business tend to be priced at the vendor's estimate of value. In other words, a state of trade favorable to the seller, with relatively great demand and high prices of something for sale.

SEMAPHORE   A code indicated by the position of the arms while sometimes holding flags.

SEMI   Seabee barge: Designed with rake on one end and square bow on the other end.

Containership: A conventional freighter carrying break bulk cargo and a limited number of containers on deck, in hatch squared or in hatches fitted with cell guides.

Trailer: A trailer without front wheels. The front portion is superimposed on and is towed by a tractive unit. The link is maintained by a kingpin.

SEMITRAILERS   Containers or flatbed freight trailers pulled behind "tractors" or "lorries."

SENDER   *See* Shipper.

SEPARATION ZONE OR LINE   A zone or lines separating traffic proceeding in one direction from traffic proceeding in another direction. A separation zone may also be used to separate a traffic lane from the adjacent inshore traffic zone.

SEPARATOR TANK   A tank used to statically separate dissimilar cargo.

SEQUENCE LIST   A list or plan that provides the numerical rotation in which containers or barges are to be loaded to or discharged from a vessel.

SERVE   To wrap any small stuff tightly around a rope that has been previously wormed and parceled. Very small ropes are not wormed.

SERVICE   A string of vessels that makes a particular voyage and serves a particular market.

SERVICE BILL   A service bill (of lading) is a contract of carriage issued by one carrier to another for documentary and internal control purposes. A participating agent in a consortium uses some kind of document that, depending on the trade, is referred to as "Memo bill" that will among others state the Name of the Carrier on whose behalf the original document (Way Bill, Bill of Lading, etc.) was issued; the original document number; the agent who issued the original document and his opponent at the discharging side; the number of packages, weight and measurement, marks and numbers, and goods description; further mandatory details in case of special cargo. No freight details will be mentioned and the Memo Bill is not a contract of carriage. *See* Bill of Lading.

SERVICE CONTRACT   As provided in the Shipping Act of 1984, a contract between a shipper (or a shippers association) and an ocean common carrier (or conference) in which the shipper makes a commitment to provide a certain minimum quantity of cargo or freight revenue over a fixed time period, and the ocean common carrier or conference commits to a certain rate or rate schedule as well as a defined service level (such as assured space, transit time, port rotation or similar service features). The contract may also specify provisions in the event of nonperformance on the part of either party.

SERVICE LEVEL   A measure for the extent to which the customer orders can be executed at delivery conditions normally accepted in the market.

SERVING   Rigging that is to be exposed to the weather is protected by worming with small stuff or marlin, parceling with canvas, and serving with marlin.

SERVING MALLET   Hammer used to serve marlin. Same as marline hammer.

SET, PERMANENT SET   The permanent deformation resulting from the stressing of an elastic material beyond its elastic limit.

SET IRON   A bar of soft iron used on the bending slab as a form to which to bend frames into the desired shapes.

SETSCREW A machine screw with either a slotted or a square head used to hold a part in place.

SET THE COURSE To give the helmsman the desired course to be steered.

SET THE WATCH Strictly speaking, to divide the ship's company into watches, the order at 8:00 P.M. on a man of war to station the first watch.

SETTING A BUOY The act of placing a buoy on assigned position in the water.

SETTING/AIR DELIVERY TEMPERATURE An indication in the documents (B/L) stating the air supply temperature to the container. Note: No other details than this temperature shall be included in the Bill of Lading.

SETTLE To lower; sink deeper.

SETTLERS Tanks used for "settling" fuel oil before using.

SETTLING AGENT An Underwriter's overseas representative authorized to investigate and pay claims.

SETTLING TANKS Oil fuel must be provided to the service tank in an uncontaminated state. As oil and water separate naturally, the foregoing is achieved by providing deep settling tanks, which permit this to occur in time.

SET UP To tighten the nut on a bolt or stud; to bring the shrouds of a mast to a uniform and proper tension by adjusting the rigging screws or the lanyards through the dead eyes.

SET UP RIGGING To take in the slack and secure the standing rigging.

SF Stowage Factor. Cubic space (measurement tonne) occupied by one tonne (2,240 lb/1,000 kg) of cargo.

SHACKLE A U-shaped piece of iron or steel with eyes in the ends closed by a shackle pin. Used as a connector for wire rope and such parts and fittings as hooks, blocks, pad eyes, etc., and as a connector for chain.

SHACKLE BOLT A pin or bolt that passes through both eyes of a shackle and completes the link. The bolt may be secured by a pin through each end, or a pin through one end and through the eyes, or by having one end and one eye threaded, or one end headed and a pin through the other.

SHAFT Long, round, heavy forging connecting engine and propeller.

SHAFT ALLEY (SHAFT TUNNEL) A narrow watertight compartment through which the propeller shaft passes from the aft engine room bulkhead to the propeller, large enough to walk in, to provide access and protection. Stem-winders do not have shaft alleys.

SHAFT ANGLE The angle between the centerline of the shaft and the centerline of the ship is the horizontal angle and the angle between the centerline of the shaft and either the base line or the designed waterline is the vertical angle.

SHAFT COUPLING The means of joining together two sections of a shaft, usually by means of bolts through flanges on the ends of the sections of the shafts.

SHAFT HORSEPOWER This is the net power delivered to the shafting of an engine after passing through gearboxes, thrust blocks, etc. It is measured on the shaft, usually by a torsion meter.

SHAFT PIPE   *See* Stern Tube.

SHAFT STRUT   Bracket supporting the outboard after end of the propeller shaft and the propeller in twin or multiple screwed vessels having propeller shafts fitted off the centerline. It usually consists of a hub or boss, fitted with a bushing, to form a bearing for the shaft, and two streamlined arms connecting it to the side of the ship. The inboard ends of the arms are fitted with palms for attachment to the shell or to interior framing.

SHAFTWAY   A tunnel or alleyway through which the drive shaft or rudder shaft passes.

SHAKEDOWN CRUISE   A cruise of a newly commissioned ship for the purpose of training the crew and testing out all machinery.

SHAKES   Splits or checks in timbers that usually cause a separation of the wood between annular rings. A ring shake is an opening between annular rings; a through shake is an opening that extends between two faces of a timer.

SHAKINGS   Waste rope, canvas, etc.

SHALE   A sedimentary rock, formed by the consolidation of mud or clay.

SHALE OIL   Crude oil derived from shale.

SHANK   The main piece of the anchor having the arms at the bottom and the Jew's Harp at the top.

SHANK'S MOUTY   The opening in an awning around a mast.

SHAPE   Bar of constant cross section throughout its entire length, such as a channel, T bar, or angle bar.

SHAPE A COURSE   To ascertain the proper course to be steering to make the desired point or port.

SHAPING   Cutting, bending, and forming a structural member.

SHEAR   A stress that tends to cause the adjacent parts of a body to slide over each other. A result of two forces acting in opposite directions and along parallel lines. The tendency of shearing stress is to tear the material between the two forces.

SHEAR LEGS   A rig for handling heavy weights, consisting of an A frame of timber or steel.

SHEAR LINE   Narrow zone across which the wind direction changes rapidly.

SHEARS   Large machine for cutting plates and shapes.

SHEATHING   A term applied to the wood planking fitted over a steel deck, to the planking fitted over the underwater portion of a steel hull, and to the copper or alloy sheets with which the bottom of a wood ship, or a steel ship sheathed with wood, is covered.

SHEAVE   The wheel of a block over which the fall of the block reeves.

SHEAVE HOLES   A term applied to apertures in masts, booms, and spars in which sheaves are installed.

SHEEPSHANK   A knot used to shorten a rope or take the strain off a weakened section of line.

SHEER   Any point is the vertical distance between the ship's side amidships and the ship's side at that point. It is the longitudinal curvature of a vessel's deck. Its purpose is to increase buoyancy at the ends.

SHEER FORCES   Forces that cause a vessel to turn aside from a course.

SHEER PLAN   A side elevation of a ship's form; a profile.

SHEER STRAKE   Top full course of shell plates at strength deck level, usually made thicker than the side plating below it.

SHEET   The rope used to spread the claw of headsails and to control the boom of boom sails, forward or aftermost thwart in a lifeboat.

SHELF   A wood ship term applied to the fore and aft timber that is fastened to the frames to form a support for the ends of the beams. *See* Clamp.

SHELL   The casing of a block or the hull of a ship.

SHELL CAPACITY   The amount of oil a tank car or tank truck will hold when the oil just touches the underside of the top of the tank shell.

SHELL EXPANSION   A plan showing the shapes, sizes, and weights of all plates comprising the shell plating, and details of their connections.

SHELL LANDINGS   Points marked on the frames to show where the edges of the shell plates are to be located.

SHELL PLATING   The plates forming the outer side and bottom skin of the hull.

SHELTER DECK   Usually the first deck below the main deck. In some ships, the shelter deck may be divided by movable bulkheads.

SHEX   Saturday and Holidays Excluded.

SHIFT OF BUTTS   An arrangement of butts in longitudinal or transverse structural members where the butts of adjacent members are located a specified distance from one another, measured in the line of the members.

SHIFTING   The direct transfer of a container or a barge from one stowage location to another on the vessel or from one mooring position to another within a fleeting area. This is in contrast to restowing, whereby a unit is discharged from the vessel and later restowed to another location. This can easily endanger the seaworthiness or cargo worthiness of the ship.

SHIFTING BOARD   A temporary bulkhead in a hold to prevent the shifting of bulk cargo.

SHIM   (In naval architecture) A piece of wood or iron let into a slack place in a frame, plank, or plate to fill out a fair surface or line. Also applied to thin layers of metal or other material used to true up a bedplate or machine or inserted in bearings to permit adjustment after wear of the bearing.

SHINC   Saturday and Holidays Included.

SHIP   To enlist; to send onboard cargo; to put in place; to take onboard. *See also* Vessel.

SHIP AGENT   A liner company or tramp ship operator representative who facilitates ship arrival, clearance, loading and unloading, and fee payment while at a specific port.

SHIP ASSIST   A tug used for docking, undocking, or otherwise assisting a ship in a harbor.

SHIP BROKER   A firm that serves as a go-between for the tramp ship owner and the chartering consignor or consignee.

SHIP CHANDLER   An individual or company selling equipment and supplies for ships.

SHIP DEMURRAGE   A charge for delaying a vessel beyond a stipulated period.

SHIPLOADING CONTAINER GANTRY CRANE   *See* Container Crane; Gantry Crane.

SHIPMENT   Commodities shipped by a port to another domestic port outside the region. Also the tender of one lot of cargo at one time from one shipper to one consignee on one bill of lading.

SHIPMENT CONSOLIDATION   Freight rates are less expensive per pound shipped when large shipments are given to the carrier at one time. Therefore, shippers try to group shipments bound for the same general area.

SHIP OPERATOR   A ship operator is either the ship owner or the (legal) person responsible for the actual management of the vessel and its crew.

SHIP OWNER   The (legal) person officially registered as such in the certificate of registry where the following particulars are contained. Name of vessel and port of registry. Details contained in surveyors certificate. The particulars respecting the origin stated in the declaration of ownership. The name and description of the registered owner; if more than one owner, the proportionate share of each.

SHIPPED ONBOARD (SOB)   An endorsement on a B/L confirming loading of goods on the vessel. *See also* Cell Position.

SHIPPER   The person or company who is usually the supplier or owner of commodities shipped. Also called Consignor or Sender.

SHIPPER'S AGENT   A firm that primarily matches up small shipments, especially single-traffic piggyback loads, to permit shippers to use twin-trailer piggyback rates.

SHIPPER'S ASSOCIATION   A nonprofit entity that represents the interests of a number of shippers. The main focus of shippers associations is to pool the cargo volumes of members to leverage the most favorable service contract rate levels.

SHIPPERS' COOPERATIVES   Nonprofit groups of shippers that join to consolidate shipments.

SHIPPER'S EXPORT DECLARATION (SED, "EX DEC")   A joint Bureau of the Census International Trade Administration form used for compiling U.S. export control laws. This form is issued by the Treasury Department. It is completed by a shipper and shows the value, weight, consignee, destination, etc., of export shipments as well as Schedule B commodity code or identification number.

SHIPPER'S INDEMNITY   Indemnity given by the beneficiary of a letter of credit to the negotiating bank to induce payment despite any discrepancies that may exist in the documents.

SHIPPER'S INSTRUCTIONS   Shipper's communication(s) to agent and/or directly to the international water carrier. Instructions may be varied, e.g., specific details/clauses to be printed on the bill of lading, and directions for cargo pickup and delivery.

SHIPPER'S LETTER OF INSTRUCTIONS FOR ISSUING AN AIR WAYBILL   The document required by the carrier or freight forwarders to obtain (besides the data needed) authorization to issue and sign the air waybill in the name of the shipper.

SHIPPER'S LOAD & COUNT (SL&C)   Shipments loaded and sealed by shippers and not checked or verified by the carriers.

SHIPPER'S RISK   Cargo is carried aboard vessel under unusual circumstances, whereby shipper accepts liability.

SHIPPING ACT OF 1916   The act of the U.S. Congress (1916) that created the U.S. Shipping Board to develop water transportation, operate the merchant ships owned by the government, and regulate the water carriers engaged in commerce under the flag of the United States. As of June 18, 1984, applies only to domestic offshore ocean transport.

SHIPPING ACT OF 1984   Effective June 18, 1984, describes the law covering water transportation in the U.S. foreign trade.

SHIPPING ACT OF 1998   Amends the Act of 1984 to provide for confidential service contracts and other items.

SHIPPING CONTAINER   Standard-sized rectangular box used to transport freight by ship, rail, and highway. International shipping containers are 20 or 40 feet long, conform to International Standards Organization (ISO) standards, and are designed to fit in ships' holds. Containers are transported on public roads atop a container chassis towed by a tractor.

SHIPPING DOCUMENTS   Documents required for the carriage of goods.

SHIPPING INSTRUCTIONS   A document detailing the cargo and the requirements of its physical movement.

SHIPPING LABEL   A label attached to a shipping unit, containing certain data.

SHIPPING MARK   The letters, numbers, or other symbols placed on the outside of cargo to facilitate identification.

SHIPPING NOTE   Document provided by the shipper or his agent to the carrier, multimodal transport operator, terminal or other receiving authority, giving information about export consignments offered for transport, and providing for the necessary receipts and declarations of liability.

SHIPPING ORDER   Shipper's instructions to carrier for forwarding goods; usually the triplicate copy of the bill of lading.

SHIPPING PALLETS   Disposable pallets shipped as part of the consignment.

SHIPPING TERMS   Part of a contract of sale that specifies who, between the buyer and the seller, is responsible for each aspect of shipping the goods, e.g., for packing, arranging, and paying for transportation and insurance, clearing customs, etc.

SHIPPING WEIGHT   Shipping weight represents the gross weight in kilograms of shipments, including the weight of moisture content, wrappings, crates, boxes, and containers (other than cargo vans and similar substantial outer containers).

SHIPPING "WIND"   Declaring that a shipment weighs more than it actually does in order to pay a lower total transport charge, when the rate per pound is less for larger shipments.

SHIP PLAN   The full stowage plan of a vessel showing the location of all cargo, containers, barges, and rolling stock on board. *See also* Stowage Plan.

SHIPS   Barge Carriers: Ships designed to carry barges; some are fitted to act as full container ships and can carry a varying number of barges and containers at the same time. At present this class includes two types of vessels: LASH and Seabee.

Bulk Carriers: All vessels designed to carry bulk cargo such as grain, fertilizers, ore, and oil.

Combination Passenger and Cargo Ships: Ships with a capacity for 13 or more passengers.

Freighters: Breakbulk vessels both refrigerated and unrefrigerated, containerships, partial containerships, roll on/roll off vessels, and barge carriers.

Full Containerships: Ships equipped with permanent container cells, with little or no space for other types of cargo.

General Cargo Carriers: Breakbulk freighters, car carriers, cattle carriers, pallet carriers, and timber carriers.

Partial Containerships: Multipurpose containerships where one or more but not all compartments are fitted with permanent container cells. Remaining compartments are used for other types of cargo.

Roll On/Roll Off Vessels: Ships specially designed to carry wheeled containers or trailers using interior ramps.

Tankers: Ships fitted with tanks to carry liquid cargo such as crude petroleum and petroleum products, chemicals, liquefied gasses (LNG and LPG), wine, molasses, and similar product tankers.

SHIP'S AGENT   A person or firm who transacts all business in a port on behalf of ship owners or charterers. Also called shipping agent

SHIP'S ARTICLES   A written agreement between the master of a ship and the crew concerning their employment. It includes rates of pay and capacity of each crewman, the date of commencement of the voyage and its duration.

SHIP'S BELLS   Measure time onboard ship. One bell sounds for each half hour. One bell means 12:30, two bells mean 1:00, three bells mean

1:30, and so on until 4:00 (eight bells). At 4:30 the cycle begins again with one bell.

SHIPSHAPE A nautical term used to signify that the whole vessel, or the portion under discussion, is neat in appearance and in good order.

SHIP'S MANIFEST A statement listing the particulars of all shipments loaded for a specified voyage.

SHIP'S PROTEST Statement of the Master of a vessel before (in the presence of) competent authorities, concerning exceptional events that occurred during a voyage.

SHIP'S TACKLE All rigging, cranes, etc., used on a ship to load or unload cargo.

SHOCK LINE A piece of nylon or similar line of 10 to 12 inches or more in diameter and from 200 to 250 feet long, used between barge pendant and tug's hawser. Its elasticity absorbs some of the shock of the sea when towing. Used mainly in U.S. Gulf towing.

SHOLE A small piece of timber or plank placed under the heel of a shore.

SHOOTING A method of increasing production from an oil well. (Jellied nitroglycerin is used to enlarge the area at the bottom of the hole and to create fractures through the formation, thus increasing the flow of oil.)

SHORE A temporary wooden brace or prop placed in a vertical or inclined position used to support some part of a ship, or the ship itself, during construction or while in dry dock. A prop or support placed against or beneath anything to prevent sinking or sagging.

SHORE, SPUR OR SIDE A piece of timber placed in a nearly horizontal position with one end against the side of the ship and the other against the side of a dry dock or dock to keep the vessel at a desired distance from the face of the dock.

SHORE CLAUSE A marine cargo policy clause covering an ocean shipment against named perils while on land—necessary because the policy provides protection from warehouse to warehouse.

SHORE GANG Refers to workers who service tugs and their fittings at a tug company's tie-up yard and pier.

SHORELAND BANKING In harbor management, the purchase, use, or resale of a parcel of waterfront property by a public entity such as a port in order to reserve it for a certain class of use, for example, water-dependent industry.

SHORE PERSONNEL Personnel who are operating a shore installation or shore equipment associated with the handling of petroleum.

SHORTFALL Describes a deficit in terminal cargo throughput capacity when compared to the commerce demand forecast.

SHORTHANDED Without sufficient crew.

SHORT HAUL DISCRIMINATION Charging more for a shorter haul than for a longer haul over the same route, in the same direction, and for the same commodity.

SHORT-INTERVAL SCHEDULING An analysis of workers' productivity over short periods of time. Each worker is assigned specific duties that he or she should be able to complete during the time period provided.

SHORT RATE (INS) Cancellation of an insurance contract at the request of the policyholder with a refund of premiums to the policyholder less than would be given under pro-rata consideration.

SHORT SHIPPED Cargo manifested but not loaded.

SHORT STAY When the scope of chain is slightly greater than the depth of water. When the anchor is hove in and the cable out is a little more than the depth of water. Also known as straight up and down.

SHORT TON (ST) 2,000 pounds avoirdupois weight per ton.

SHORT WAVE Term occasionally used in forecasts that may be considered to be a moving low, weather front, or high.

SHOT Fifteen fathoms (90 feet) of cable or anchor chain.

SHOVE IN YOUR OAR To break into a conversation.

SHOW A LEG An order to make haste.

SHRINKAGE Losses in inventory that are difficult to account for.

SHRINK WRAP Polyethylene or similar substance heat treated and shrunk into an envelope around several units, thereby securing them as a single pack for presentation or to secure units on a pallet.

SHROUD A wire rope of cable extending from a masthead to the vessel's side to afford lateral support for the mast.

SHUGA An accumulation of spongy white ice lumps, a few centimeters across; they are formed from grease ice or slush and sometimes from anchor ice rising to the surface.

SHUT OUT Containers not carried on intended vessel.

SHUTTLE SERVICE The carriage back and forth over an often-short route between two points.

SIC *See* Standard Industrial Classification.

SICK BAY A name applied to the space onboard a ship where members of the crew and passengers are given medical service and includes the dispensary, operating room, wards, etc. The ship's hospital.

SID Single Decker.

SIDE BILGE Gutter or trough, dunnage placed fore and aft over side bilge.

SIDECASTER DREDGE A self-propelled dredge, normally a hopper dredge, equipped with a boom on which the discharge is located. As the dredge operates, the dredged material is discharged to the side of the channel, allowing natural currents and processes to move the dredged material from the site.

SIDE DOOR CONTAINER A container fitted with a rear door and a minimum of one side door.

SIDE FORCE (OR TRANSVERSE THRUST) The force that tends to cant the bow to port when going ahead and to starboard when going astern, on a right-handed propeller.

SIDE FRAME   Fitting used to lift containers by forklift from side.

SIDE LIGHTS   The red and green running lights carried on the port and starboard bows, respectively, of vessels underway.

SIDE LOADER   A lift truck fitted with lifting attachments operating to one side for handling containers.

SIDEPICK   A lift truck with forks situated in such a manner as to lift the container from the side by inserting the forks under the container; also called side loader.

SIDE PLATING   A term applied to the plating above the bilge in the main body of a vessel. Also to the sides of deckhouses or to the vertical sides of enclosed plated structures.

SIDE RAMP   RO/RO ramp extending into or protruding from openings in vessel's side at right angles to vessel's centerline.

SIDE SHIFTER   An attachment placed on forklifts and front-end loaders to allow the operator to make small adjustments to one side or the other so as to position a load without repositioning the forklift.

SIDING   An auxiliary to the main railroad track to allow the meeting or passing of trains.

SIDING OF A FRAME   The fore and aft dimension of a frame.

SIGHT   Time of presentation, as in a draft payable "at sight" or "90 days after sight."

SIGHT DRAFT   A draft payable upon presentation to the drawee.

SIGNAGE   Refers to the total of all signs with writing and symbols denoting directions and destinations within a container terminal or ITF.

SIGNIFICANT WAVE HEIGHT   Average of the highest one third of the waves.

SILENT CONFIRMATION   A bank's commitment to negotiate (i.e., purchase) documents under a letter of credit without recourse at a future date. A silent confirmation is not a confirmation in the true sense and will not use the word "confirm," but is rather an equivalent form of protection for the beneficiary. The bank will require that the letter of credit be negotiable or payable by itself in order to be able to establish holder-in-due-course rights equivalent to those of a confirming bank.

SIMPLIFIED CLEARANCE PROCEDURE (SCP)   A procedure covering nonrestricted goods that enables approved exporters or agents to export goods on presentation of minimum information. The full statistical information is supplied within 14 days of shipment.

SIMULATION   A terminal management assistance tool, which makes use of a computer model, that mimics, in real time, the operations of a terminal. Simulation is used to predict cargo throughput and areas of conflict under differing operating scenarios.

SINGLE ADMINISTRATIVE DOCUMENT (SAD)   A set of documents, replacing the various (national) forms for Customs declaration within European Community, implemented on January 1, 1988. The introduction of the

SAD constitutes an intermediate stage in the abolition of all administrative documentation in intra European community trade in goods between member states.

SINGLE AXLE SHIFTABLE BOGIE   Single axle bogie that can be shifted to predetermine locations on the chassis

SINGLE BILL OF LADING   One contract issued to a shipper by a transportation company promising the transport of goods between two points even though more than one mode of transport is involved.

SINGLE SOURCE LEASING   Leasing both the truck and driver form one source.

SING OUT   To call out.

SINKAGE   The lowering of a ship with respect to the mean surface of the water due to speed of ship through the water.

SISAL   Rope made of fiber of the agave plant. More lustrous than Manila, 25% less tensile strength.

SISTER BLOCKS   A shell with two sheaves, each of which holds a line, and these lines lead in opposite directions.

SISTER HOOKS   Two iron flat-sided hooks reversed to one another, suspended from a thimble with the flat sides together when in place.

SISTER SHIPS   Ships built on the same design.

SITE   In harbor management, those physical characteristics of the local area that affect port development, for example, topography, weather, water depth.

SITUATION   In harbor management, the relationship a harbor or port has with respect to existing or potential cargo/people traffic, for example, ease of transportation with hinterland, proximity to sea.

SKAG   A heavy chain used when necessary in close waters as a drag for steadying a towed barge.

SKEG   The extreme after part of the keel of a vessel, the portion that supports the rudderpost and sternpost. A fixed underwater fin used to promote directional stability.

SKELETAL CHASSIS   *See* Chassis.

SKELETON TOWER   A tower, usually of steel, constructed of heavy corner members and various horizontal and diagonal bracing members.

SKID   *See* Pallet.

SKIDS   Timbers on which structural parts are assembled. Battens, or a series of parallel runners, fitted beneath boxes or packages to raise them clear of the floor to permit easy access of forklift blades or other handling equipment.

SKIN   The term usually applied to the outside planking or plating forming the watertight envelope over the framework. It is also applied to the inner bottom plating when it is called an inner skin.

SKIP BOX   Type of sling. Also called ammunition scow.

SKIPPER   The captain.

SKU   *See* Stock Keeping Unit.

SKYLIGHT An opening in a deck to give light and air to the compartment below it usually fitted with hinged covers having fixed lights in them.

SKY PILOT The chaplain.

SLACK Part of a rope hanging loosely. The opposite of taut. Also, to pay out a line to ease off.

SLACK TANK Tank that is not completely filled or empty.

SLACK WATER The condition of the tide when there is no horizontal motion.

SLAMMING In severe pitching, the bow of the ship may leave the water, and when it plunges back again "slamming" occurs. A large instantaneous force is generated near the bow that can damage the hull unless the ship's speed is quickly reduced.

SL&C Shipper's Load and Count.

SLD Sailed.

SLED A pallet on runners so that the load can be drawn along the ground.

SLEEPER Sleeping compartment mounted behind a truck cab, sometimes attached to the cab or even designed to be an integral part of it.

SLEEPER TEAM Two drivers who operate a truck equipped with a sleeper berth; while one driver sleeps in the berth to accumulate mandatory off-duty time, the other driver operates the vehicle.

SLEEPERS Timbers placed upon the ground or on top of piling to support the cribbing, keel, and bilge blocks. Also, loaded containers moving within the railroad system that are not clearly identified on any internally generated reports.

SLEEVE A casing, usually of brass, fitted over line or other shafting for protection against wear or corrosion, or as a bearing surface.

SLI *See* Shipper's Letter of Instruction.

SLIDING TANDEM *See* Single Axle Shiftable Bogie; Tandem Axle.

SLIDING WAYS *See* Launching.

SLIGH OXIDATION TEST A test method for determining oxidation resistance of various types of oils.

SLING Rope, chain, or other gear used to suspend a draft of cargo with a crane or davit. The rods, chains, or ropes attached near the bow and stern of a small boat into which the davit or crane tackle is hooked. The chain or rope supporting the yard at the masthead.

SLIP The space between two piers for berthing a vessel; to let go by unshackling, as a cable; the lost motion of the propeller.

SLIP SEAT OPERATION A term used to describe a motor carrier relay terminal operation where one driver is substituted for another who has accumulated the maximum driving time hours.

SLIP SHEET Similar to a pallet, the slipsheet, which is made of cardboard or plastic, is used to facilitate movement of unitized loads.

SLIPWAY OR BERTH The space in a shipyard where a foundation for launching ways and keel blocks exits and is occupied by a ship while under construction. The term berth is more properly applied to the space a ship occupies at a pier or at an anchorage.

SLOP CHUTE   Chute for dumping garbage overboard.

SLOPS   A mixture of petroleum, water, and sediment.

SLOP TANKS   A tank designated to store oily waste for subsequent ecologically approved disposal.

SLOT   The space onboard a vessel, required by one TEU, mainly used for administrative purposes.

SLOT CHARTER   A voyage charter whereby the ship owner agrees to place a certain number of container slots (TEU and/or FEU) at the charterer's disposal.

SL&T   Shipper's Load and Tally.

SLUDGE   Deposits in cargo tanks that may contain petroleum and wax and also sand and scale or other foreign matter.

SLUDGE DEPOSITS   These may be hard and lumpy, grainy, and/or pasty in a lubricating system. These deposits, which are insoluble in the oil, may be the result of contamination of the oil, or from deterioration of the oil itself.

SLUGGING   In airplanes, loss of liquid fuel from tank vents owing to the pulling action of escaping vapors.

SLUICE   An opening in the lower part of a bulkhead fitted with a sliding watertight gate, or small door, having an operating rod extending to the upper deck or decks. It is used to permit liquid in one compartment to flow into the adjoining compartment.

SLURRY   A thin mixture of liquid and finely divided solids that can be handled as a fluid cargo through pipelines and transported by special tankers. Ore, coal, and several other commodities may be handled as slurry cargo.

SLUSH   Snow that is saturated and mixed with water on land or ice surfaces, or as a viscous floating mass in water after a heavy snowfall. The grease from salt pork or boiled beef, used for making a mast slippery.

SLUSHING OIL   An oil- or grease-like material used as a temporary protective coating against corrosion.

SL/W   Shippers load and count. All three clauses are used as needed on the bill of lading to exclude the carrier from liability when the cargo is loaded by the shipper.

SMALL STUFF   Small cordage.

SMART   Snappy, seamanlike. A smart ship is an efficient one.

SMELLING THE BOTTOM   Said of a ship when her keel is very close to but not touching the bottom.

SMOKE CHART   The Ringlemann Scale for grading the density of smoke, as published by the United States Bureau of Mines and as referred to in the Bureau of Mines Information Circular No. 8333, or any smoke inspection guide approved by the Department.

SMOKESTACK A metal chimney or passage through which the smoke and combustion gases are led from the boiler uptakes to the open air; also called a funnel.

SMOKE TEST A test made on kerosene that shows the highest point to which the flame can be turned before it will smoke.

SMOTHERING LINES Lines to a compartment for smothering a fire by steam or by chemical.

SN Satellite Navigation.

SNAKE OUT To unstow specific items of cargo, particularly by dragging to the square of the hatch.

SNATCH BLOCK A single block fitted so that the shell or hook hinges, so that the bight of a rope may be passed through.

SNORTER OR SNOTTER Length of rope with eye splices at each end, used as a cargo sling.

SNOTTER A short piece of chain, wire, or rope used between the hold down point and the tow hawser to restrict its movement near the stern of tugs.

SNUB To check suddenly, as a line from running out.

SNUBBING Drawing in the waterlines and diagonals of a vessel abruptly at their ends. The checking of a vessel's headway by means of an anchor and a short cable. The checking of a line or cable from running out by taking a turn about a cleat, bitts, or similar fitting.

SNY A small toggle on a flag. To twist a plate into an uneven warped shape on a mold.

SO Ship's Option; Shipping Order; Seller's Option.

SOAP A compound made by the action of an alkali on a fat or fixed oil.

SOB *See* Shipped Onboard.

SOC Shipper Owned Container.

SOCIETE ANONYME French name for corporation.

SOCKET Wire rope fitting attached to the end of the rope and secured by molten metal that has hardened. Also called speltered socket.

SODA BASE GREASE A grease composed of a mineral oil thickened with sodium soaps.

SOF Statement of Facts.

SOFT LINE Manila, hemp, sisal, all the polyesters, nylon, or other synthetic fiber blends of cordage.

SOFT OR SYNTHETIC FIBER ROPE Rope that is usually of three strands, spliceable and easy to handle when used as deck lines and ship towlines.

SOFT PATCH A temporary plate put on over a break or hole and secured with tap bolts. It is made watertight with a gasket such as canvas saturated in red lead.

SOFT RIGGING Term used when Manila or poly line is used for making up a tow. Mostly used for short movements within the harbor only.

SOJER One who dodges work.

SOLAS The International Convention for the Safety of Life At Sea, 1974.

SOLE PLATE A plate fitted to the top of a foundation to which the base of a machine is bolted. Also a small plate fitted at the end of a stanchion.

SOLID TRAIN A train transporting a single commodity from one source to one destination, in which the integrity of the loaded train is maintained. However, unlike unit trains, the empty cars may then be deadheaded separately back to the original or to other sources. *See also* Unit Train.

SOLIDS HANDLING PUMP A pump specially designed with hardened surfaces, larger internal clearances, and special lubrication facilities that allow pumping of granular, abrasive, solid materials. A dredge pump is a type of solids handling pump.

SOLUBLE OILS Oils that readily form stable emulsions or colloidal solutions with water. They usually contain metallic or ammonium soaps or sulfonated oils and may be used for cutting oils, detergents, insecticides, etc.

SOLVENCY (INS) Sufficient assets and income. The primary responsibility of a state's insurance department is to monitor insurance companies licensed to transact business within their state and make certain that they remain solvent and have the ability to pay the claims of their policyholders.

SOLVENT EXTRACTION A process for separating compounds of approximately the same boiling points, but of different chemical types by employing solvents in which the solubilities of these compounds are widely different.

SOUND To measure the depth of the water with a lead. Also said of a whale when it dives for bottom.

SOUND PIPE OR TUBE A pipe leading to the bottom of an oil or water tank, used to guide a sounding tape or jointed rod when measuring the depth of liquid in the tanks; also called a sounding tube.

SOUND SIGNAL A device that transmits sound, intended to provide information to mariners during periods of restricted visibility and foul weather.

SOUNDING PIPE Pipe in oil or water tank used to measure depth of liquid in tank.

SOUNDNESS OF STEEL CASTINGS Absence in a casting of cavities or blowholes formed by air bubbles.

SOUR CRUDE OIL Crude oil containing at least 0.05 cubic feet of dissolved hydrogen sulfide per 100 gallons with dangerously toxic vapors. Characterized by objectionable pungent odor.

SOUTHERLY WIND True wind direction from the SE to SW sector.

SOUTHWESTER An oilskin hat with broad rear brim.

SOVEREIGNTY Supreme and independent political authority.

SP Safe Port.

SPA Subject to Particular Average. *See also* Particular Average.

SPACE & EQUIPMENT REQUEST A business transaction between two enterprises. An enterprise that has goods to be moved will contact an entity that provides transport services to request space and equipment for an upcoming shipment. The request serves as the first action to launch a set of negotiations between the two enterprises.

SPACE & EQUIPMENT RESERVATION A business transaction between two enterprises to arrange for services to facilitate the movement of goods via a carrier.

SPACE CHARTER A voyage charter whereby the shipowner agrees to place part of the vessel's capacity at the charterer's disposal.

SPAN The distance between any two similar members, as the span of the frames. The length of a member between its supports, as the span of a girder. A rope whose ends are both made fast some distance apart, the bight having attached to it a topping lift, tackle, etc. A line connecting two davit heads so that when one davit is turned the other follows. A rope with both ends secured and a purchase attached to the bight.

SPANISH WINDLASS A wooden revolving roller turned by marlinespike into turns of rope wound around it.

SPANNER A form of open head wrench for use with special fittings whose character is such as to preclude the use of the ordinary type of wrench. A tool for coupling hoses.

SPANNER GUY The guy between the heads of the booms on a married fall, or yard and stay, cargo system. Also called schooner guy or midship guy.

SPANNER STAY A wire stay connecting two kingposts.

SPAR A term applied to a pole serving as a mast, boom, gaff, yard, bowsprit, etc. Spars are made of both steel and wood.

SPAR DECK Upper deck.

SPARK ARRESTOR Any device, assembly, or method of a mechanical, centrifugal, cooling, or other type and size suitable for the retrenching or quenching of sparks in exhaust pipes from internal combustion engines.

SPD Speed.

SPEAK To communicate with a vessel in sight.

SPECIAL COMMODITIES CARRIER A common carrier trucking company that has authority to haul a special commodity; the sixteen special commodities include household goods, petroleum products, and hazardous materials.

SPECIAL COMMODITY WAREHOUSE A warehouse that is used to store products requiring unique facilities, such as grain (elevator), liquid (tank), and tobacco (barn).

SPECIAL CUSTOMS INVOICE An official form usually required by U.S. Customs if the rate of duty is based upon the value and the value of the shipment exceeds $500. This document is usually prepared by the foreign exporter or his forwarder and is used by Customs in determining the value of the shipment. The exporter or his agent must attest to the authenticity of the data furnished. Prescribed form lists name of shipper, name of consignee, selling price of commodity, its character, quantity to by shipped, etc.

SPECIAL DRAWING RIGHTS (SDR) Unit of account from the International Monetary Fund (IMF), i.e., used to express the amount of the limitations of a carrier's liability.

SPECIALIZED GENERAL CARGO FACILITIES General cargo terminals that provide berthing facilities for accommodating container, RO/RO, and barge carrier ships.

SPECIAL MARINE POLICY Issued under an open policy when the buyer wants evidence of insurance for the specific merchandise and voyage involved.

SPECIAL PURPOSE BUOY A buoy having no lateral significance used to indicate a special meaning to the mariner, such as one used to mark a quarantine or anchorage area.

SPECIAL RATE A rate other than a normal rate (air cargo).

SPECIFIC COMMODITY RATE (SCR) A rate applicable to carriage of specifically designated commodities (air cargo).

SPECIFIC GRAVITY The ratio of the weight of a given volume of the material at 60°F to the weight of an equal volume of distilled water at the same temperature, both weights being corrected for the buoyancy of air. Any substance of greater weight per cubic foot has a specific gravity of more than one and will sink. Specific gravity of gases is based in a like manner on the weight of air.

SPECIFIED RATE A rate specified in an IATA Cargo Tariff Coordination Conference resolution (air cargo).

SPECTACLE FRAME A single casting containing the bearings for and furnishing support for the ends of the propeller shafts in a twin screw vessel. The shell plating is worked outboard so as to enclose the shafts and is attached at the after end to the spectacle frame. Used in place of shaft struts.

SPEEDABILITY Top speed a vehicle can attain as determined by engine power, engine governed speed, gross weight, driveline efficiency, air resistance, grade, and load.

SPIDER *See* Flounder Plate.

SPIDER BAND *See* Linkband.

SPIDERING Strengthening of circular tanks for transport, this prevents the tanks from becoming warped. The tanks are strengthened with steel or wood crossbeams giving a "spider" appearance.

SPIKE A stout metal pin headed on one end and pointed at the other, made of either square or round bar, and used for securing heavy planks and timbers together.

SPIKED CARGO One in which a certain amount of liquefied natural gas has been injected during loading. Should not be loaded into a normal tanker as due to boiling, the gas will raise the pressure in the cargo tank.

SPILE A pile.

SPILING The curve of a plate or strake as it narrows to a point.

SPILL To empty the wind out of a sail.

SPINE CAR   An articulated five-platform railcar. Used where height and weight restrictions limit the use of stack cars. It holds five forty-foot containers or combinations of forty and twenty foot containers. Also, a lightweight, low-cut multiplatform articulated railcar designed for efficient transfer of intermodal container cargo.

SPLICE   A method of uniting the ends of two ropes by first unlaying the strands, then interweaving them so as to form a continuous rope.

SPLICE THE MAIN BRACE   To have a drink.

SPLIT FRAME   A channel or Z bar frame split at the bilge so that one flange may connect to the shell plating and the other to the tank top.

SPLIT HULL HOPPER BARGE   A barge designed to augment the disposal of dredge material produced by a nonhopper dredge. The barge is filled with dredged material, moved to the disposal site, and empties by opening the hull along the axis of the barge.

SPOIL   In harbor management, the material dredged to make a channel, basin, or dock that must be disposed of in an environmentally acceptable location.

SPOKE   The stretch between a hub and one of the groups of consignees and/or consignors being served by the hub.

SPONSONS   Bulges on the upper sides of canoes and other small boats that add breadth when the boat inclines.

SPONSOR   One who christens a ship at a launching.

SPONTANEOUS COMBUSTION   Ignition of a combustible material is termed "spontaneous" if the inherent characteristics of the material cause a heat producing (exothermic) chemical action thus ignition without exposure to external fire, spark, or abnormal heat.

SPONTANEOUS IGNITION TEMPERATURE   The lowest temperature at which a substance will start burning spontaneously without an external source of ignition.

SPOOL   A short or long length of pipe flanged on both ends for extending risers.

SPORT FISHING   Fishing without use of nets, usually done for entertainment or sport.

SPOT   To swing a boom to any desired position by means of the boom guys and topping lift. Also called trimming.

SPOT (VOYAGE)   A charter for a particular vessel to move a single cargo between specified loading port(s) and discharge port(s) in the immediate future. Contract rate ("spot" rate) covers total operating expenses, i.e., bunkers, port charges, canal tolls, crew's wages and food, insurance and repairs. Cargo owner absorbs, in addition, any expenses specifically levied against the cargo.

SPOT FACE   To finish off the surface around a bolthole in a plane normal to the axis of the hole to provide a neat seat for the nut or washer.

SPOT MARKET   A market for unplanned purchases not made under contract terms. Transactions usually made on a one-time basis.

SPOTTING   The placement of a railroad car where required, so that it is accessible for loading or unloading.

SPREADER   A piece of equipment designed to lift containers by their corner castings. A horizontal iron or wooden bar used to spread the legs of a sling or bridle and to keep them that way while the cargo is suspended. The bridle is thus prevented from cutting into the upper containers in the draft.

SPRING   A deviation from a straight line or the amount of curvature of a sheer line, deck line, beam camber, etc.; an elastic body or device that recovers its original shape when released after being distorted. A mooring or docking line leading at an angle of about 45 degrees with the fore and aft lines of the vessel. To turn a vessel with a line. *See also* Crosspring.

SPROCKET, SPROCKET WHEEL   A wheel on whose periphery are teeth or cogs designed to engage with the links of a pitch or sprocket chain through which motion is transmitted to a second sprocket.

SPUD HOISTS   A device located at the rear of the dredge that lifts, repositions, and supports the spuds.

SPUD WRENCH   Open-end wrench with a tapered spike handle used for lining up flange bold holes.

SPUDS   The long, round or square poles used as legs that reach to the bottom and hold dredges, drill boats, and other work craft in place. Such poles run through a well in the vessel's hull and may be raised or lowered mechanically. Also, the devices for holding the dredge in position and about which the dredge pivots while making its cut. There are normally two, and they are cylindrical in cross section and are located at the rear of the dredge.

SPUR   A section of track connected only at one end to a main track, i.e., a stub ending siding.

SPUR LINE   A railroad track that connects a company's plant or warehouse with the railroad's track; the user bears the cost of the spur track and its maintenance.

SPUR SHORE   A wooden spar used to hold a vessel clear of a dock, fitted at the dock end with a truck and heel chains, and at the ship end with ringbolts for securing.

SQUALL   A sudden and violent gust of wind.

SQUARE OF THE HATCH   The space directly under the hatch opening, extending from the opening itself down to the bottom of the hold.

SQUARE RIGGER   A vessel having square sails suspended from yards that run crosswise rather than lengthwise of a ship.

SQUAT   The tendency of the stern of a ship underway to press lower into the water, which is a factor in calculating the depth needed in a channel.

SQUATTING   The increase in trim by the stern assumed by a vessel when running at high speed over that existing when she is at rest.

SQUEEGEE   A deck dryer composed of a flat piece of wood shed with rubber and a handle.

SRBL   Shipping & Releasing Bill of Lading

SR&CC   Strikes, Riots, and Civil Commotion perils excluded in the basic marine cargo policy, but coverable by endorsement.

SS   Shipside.

S/S   Steamship.

SSHEX   Saturdays, Sundays, Holidays Excluded

SSHINC   Saturdays, Sundays, Holidays Included

SSR   Self-sustaining reefer unit. An insulated container with its own refrigeration unit.

ST   Short Ton (2,000 pounds).

STABILITY   The tendency of a ship to remain upright or the ability to return her to normal upright position when listed by the action of waves, wind, etc. Weight in the lower hold increase stability. A vessel is stiff if it has high stability, tender if it has low stability. To have stability, a vessel must be in a state of stable equilibrium.

STABILITY, RANGE OF   The number of degrees through which a vessel rolls or lists before losing stability.

STABILITY TABLES   Tables that show the proper and improper distribution of weights and their effect on the GM and rolling period of a vessel.

STABILIZER   A fractionating column and heat exchanger system operating under pressure of 200–300 pound gauge, which is used to remove the very volatile light hydrocarbons (propane and lighter) present in raw cracking still distillate, absorption plant naphtha, and casing-head gasoline.

STABILOGAUGE   A device that automatically calculates GM when actuators indicating weights loaded or discharged are tuned.

STABLE EQUILIBRIUM   Exist when M is above G. A vessel will tend to return to an erect position if inclined to a small angle.

STACK   The exhaust pipe from the vessel's main engines, usually quite high on the superstructure. An identifiable amount of containers stowed in an orderly way in one specified place on an (ocean) terminal, container freight station, container yard, or depot (*see* Container Stack).

STACK CAR   An articulated five-platform railcar that allows containers to be double stacked. A typical stack car holds ten forty-foot equivalent units (FEUs).

STACKING   To pile boxes, bags, containers, etc., on top of each other.

STACKING CONES   Fittings used to stack containers, on the other, so as to prevent lateral movement. Locking pipe cones will also prevent vertical movement.

STACKING PIECES   Fittings for double and triple stacking of containers.

STACKTRAIN   A rail service whereby railcars carry containers stacked two high on specially operated unit trains. Each train includes up to 35 articulated multiplatform cars. Each car is comprised of five wells.

STACK WEIGHT   The total weight of the containers and cargo in a certain row.

STAGE   A floor or platform of planks supporting workmen during the construction or the cleaning and painting of a vessel, located either inside or outside the vessel.

STAGGER   To zigzag rivet holes in adjacent rows.

STAGING   Upright supports fastened together with horizontal and diagonal braces forming supports for planks that form a working platform or stage.

STANCHIONS   Vertical columns supporting decks, flats, girders, handrails, etc.; also called a pillar. Stanchions are made of pipe, steel shapes, or rods, according to the location and purpose they serve. Rail stanchions are vertical metal columns on which fence like rails are mounted.

STAND BY   A preparatory order.

STAND ON VESSEL   A ship that is directed by the Rules to keep her course and speed.

STANDARD   Efforts to create wide use of specific protocols so software from different vendors can interoperate more easily, particularly within a vertical industry. Standards bodies or efforts often work more slowly than entrepreneurial companies in setting up interoperable terms of trade. Many e-commerce standards today are based on XML (Extensible Markup Language) that provides a flexible way to describe product specifications or business terms.

STANDARD COMPASS   The compass used by the navigator as a standard.

STANDARD INDUSTRIAL CLASSIFICATION (SIC)   A standard numerical code used by the U.S. government to classify products and services.

STANDARD INTERNATIONAL TRADE CLASSIFICATION (SITC)   A standard numeric code developed by the United Nations to classify commodities used in international trade, based on a hierarchy.

STANDARD PRODUCT MODULE (SPM)   The building blocks used by business management to define services (shipment products) that can be offered to customers. They describe a more or less isolated set of activities with a standard cost attached to it. For operations management each module defines a combination of standard operations that needs to be carried out for a customer. Note: SPMs can be regarded as the interface between business and operations management.

STANDARD TEMPERATURE   This is 60°F used for figuring number of barrels to be entered on the bill of lading.

STANDBY LETTER OF CREDIT   As opposed to a commercial letter of credit, a letter of credit that does not cover the direct purchase of merchandise, so called because it is often intended to be drawn on only when the applicant for whom it is issued fails to perform an obligation. There is, nonetheless, a type of standby letter of credit that is intended to be drawn on, referred to as a "direct pay letter of credit." Standby letters of credit are based on the underlying principle of letters of credit that payment is made against presentation of documents whatever documents the applicant, beneficiary, and issuing bank may agree to, not necessarily documents showing shipment of goods.

STANDING PART   Part of a line or fall that is secured. The middle section of a rope.

STANDING RIGGING   Rigging that is permanently secured and that is not hauled upon, as shrouds, stays, etc., *See also* Running Rigging.

STAPLE ANGLE   A piece of angle bent in the shape of a staple or other irregular shape.

STAPLING   Collars forged of angle bars, to fit around continuous members passing through bulkheads, for water tightness; now obsolete.

STARBOARD   Right side of a ship looking forward. Opposite of port.

STARBOARD SIDE   The right-hand side of a ship as one faces forward.

STATE OF ORIGIN   The state in the territory in which the cargo was first loaded onboard of an aircraft (air cargo).

STATEROOM   A private room or cabin for the accommodation of passengers or officers.

STATE TAXES   This is equal to revenues that accrue to state governments through personal and corporate income, state property, excise sales, and other state taxes generated by changes in output, wages, or tourist expenditures.

STATIC ACCUMULATOR   Certain petroleum cargo has the ability to store up static electricity due to agitation in pipelines while under pressure.

STATIC ELECTRICITY   The electrification of dissimilar materials through physical contact and separation.

STATIC STABILITY   The analysis of a vessel's stability while not in motion, involving angles of inclination of less than ten degrees.

STATICAL STABILITY CURVES   Curves for various displacements to and past load displacement. The ordinates are angles of inclination. Intersection of ordinates with curves produces the abscissas (righting arms).

STATION BILL   The posted bill showing stations of the crew at maneuvers and emergency drills.

STATION BUOY   An unlighted buoy set near an important buoy, as a reference point should the primary aid to navigation be moved from its assigned position.

STATIONARY (STNRY)   Less than five-knot movement of high, low, tide, or front.

STATUS   Information concerning the state or location of a defined item.

STATUTE OF LIMITATION   A law limiting the time in which claims or suits may be instituted.

STAUNCH   Stiff, seaworthy, able.

STAYS   The ropes, whether hemp or wire, that support the lower masts, topmasts, top gallant masts, etc., in a fore and aft direction. Guy lines used to support masts or king posts.

STB Surface Transportation Board. An independent ad judicatory body administratively housed in the Department of Transportation responsible for the economic regulation of interstate surface transportation, primarily railroads. Also said to be.

STC Said to contain.

STCC Standard Transportation Commodity Code.

STD Standards.

STEADY An order to hold a vessel on the course she is maintaining.

STEALER A plate extending into an adjoining strake in the case of a drop strake. Stealer plates are located in the bow and stern, where the narrowing girth compels a reduction in the number of strakes.

STEAMBOAT RATCHET Used on river towboats and other types to tighten barge connectors and the push cables on some tugs.

STEAM CYLINDER OIL An oil that is used to lubricate the cylinder walls, pistons, and valves of a steam engine.

STEAM DRUM That part of a water tube boiler that receives the steam from the generator tubes.

STEAM EMULSION NUMBER The time in seconds for a given amount of oil to separate from condensed steam under prescribed test conditions.

STEAM HEATING COILS Placed at the bottom of tanks to heat cargo for discharging in cold weather.

STEAMSHIP AGENTS A representative of a vessel's owner or charterer that arranges port services for the vessel while it is in port, and books cargo onto the vessel.

STEAMSHIP CONFERENCE A group of vessel operators joined together for the purpose of establishing freight rates. A shipper may receive reduced rates if the shipper enters into a contract to ship on vessels of conference members only.

STEAMSHIP GUARANTEE An indemnity issued to the carrier by a bank; protects the carrier against any possible losses or damages arising from release of the merchandise to the receiving party. This instrument is usually issued when the bill of lading is lost or is not available.

STEEL TOW HAWSER 6×37 or 6×41 means 6 strands with 37 or 41 wires per strand.

STEERAGE WAY The slowest speed at which a vessel steers.

STEERING GEAR Steering wheels, leads, steering engine, and fitted by which the rudder is turned. Usually applied to the steering engines.

STEERING OF CONTAINERS The function, with the aid of specific software for tracking and forecasting (IRMA, MINKA), to direct empty containers to demanding areas at minimum costs.

STEERING WHEEL Wooden or metal wheel having its spokes extended through the rim for handholds and used to control rudder by rope leads or through steering engine.

STEM   The bow frame forming the apex of the intersection of the forward sides of a ship. It is rigidly connected at its lower end to the keel and may be a heavy flat bar or a rounded plate construction.

STEMWINDER   A nickname for a ship with the house and machinery at the stern.

STEP   To set in place, as applied to a mast.

STERLING BLOC   The British Commonwealth countries that fixed the price of sterling used in foreign exchange. With a fixed price, sterling was not readily convertible to other currencies. This resulted in trade with the Bloc being favored.

STERN   The section of the ship at the very back end; the farthest distant part from the bow. Opposite of bow.

STERN ANCHOR   An anchor carried at the stern.

STERN BOARD   Progress backwards.

STERN DISCHARGE LINE   A cargo pipeline over the deck to a point terminating at or near the stern of the tanker.

STERN FRAME   Large casting or forging attached to after end of keel to form ship's stern. Includes rudderpost, propeller post, and aperture for propeller.

STERN LINES   Mooring lines running from the stern at 45 degree angles to the centerline.

STERN PIPES   A round or oval casting, or frame, inserted in the bulwark plating at the stern of the vessel through which the mooring hawser or warping lines are passed. Also called stern chock.

STERN POST   The main vertical post in the stern frame upon which the rudder is hung. *See also* Rudder Post.

STERN RAMP – RO/RO   Vessel ramp entering into or protruding from stern aperture along centerline of vessel.

STERN TUBE   The watertight tube enclosing and supporting the propeller shaft where it emerges from the ship. It consists of a hollow cast iron or steel cylinder fitted with brass bushings, which in turn are lined with lignum vitae, white metal, etc., bearing surfaces upon which the propeller shaft, enclosed in a sleeve, rotates.

STERNWAY   The backward motion of a boat; the movement of a vessel being carried or impelled backward.

STEVEDORE   Individual or firm employing longshoremen (or other labor) for the purpose of loading and unloading a vessel.

STICK OUT   Usually refers to paying out more line or hawser; also to the original connecting of the hawser.

STICKY   The ability to retain participants.

STIFF   A vessel is stiff when its center of gravity is low, making it careen with difficulty. It returns rapidly to the upright position, with great force. *See also* Tender.

STIFFENER   An angle bar, T bar, channel, built-up section, etc., used to stiffen plating of a bulkhead, etc.

STIFF SHIP   A ship that possess a great deal of stability or metacentric height, offering a relatively uncomfortable ride due to its rapid return to the vertical. Single hull tankers are renown for this condition.

STILL   An apparatus in which a substance is changed by heat, with or without chemical decomposition, into vapor. Vapor is then liquefied in a condenser and collected in another part of the apparatus.

STOCK   In general, any oil that is to receive further treatment before going into finished products. Also the materials in a supply chain or in a segment of a supply chain, expressed in quantities, locations and or values.

STOCK ANCHOR   Has a straight shank with arms forged or cast as an integral part. Now replaced by stockless anchor.

STOCK KEEPING UNIT   A method of identifying a product without using a full description.

STOCKLESS PURCHASING   A practice whereby the buyer negotiates a purchase price for annual requirements of MRO items and the seller holds inventory until the buyer orders individual items.

STOCK LOCATER SYSTEM   A system in which all places within a warehouse are named or numbered.

STOCKOUT   A situation in which the items a customer orders are currently unavailable.

STOCKOUT COST   The opportunity cost that companies associate with not having supply sufficient to meet demand.

STOCK RECORD   A record of the quantity of stock of a single item, often containing a history of recent transactions and information for controlling the replenishment of stock.

STOCKS   A general term applied to the keel blocks, bilge blocks, and timbers upon which a vessel is constructed.

STOKES   A unit of kinematic viscosity and is equal to the viscosity divided by the density.

STOOL   A platform in the hold, on which cargo is landed. It may consist of planking, a heap of sacks, etc.

STOP CHECK STRIPPING VALVE   A gate so constructed as to become a gravity check when open 1½ to 2 turns. Valve moves up and down stem about 1 inch.

STOP CHECK VALVE   A valve designed to permit flow of liquid in only one direction.

STOP LOSS (INS)   Any provision in a policy designed to cut off the insurance company's loss at a given point. Aggregate benefits and maximum benefits are an example. A type of reinsurance designed to transfer the loss from the ceding company to the reinsurer at a given value.

STOP OFF   To tie tightly but lightly so that an object can be easily released.

STOPPER A piece of rope or chain used to hold rope under load while being transferred from drum end of the winch to a cleat or vice versa.

STOP WATER Canvas and red lead, or other suitable material, placed between the faying surfaces of plates and shapes to stop the passage of oil or water. Also applied to a wooden plug driven through a scarph joint between timbers to ensure water tightness.

STORAGE The activity of placing goods into a store or the state of being in store (e.g., a warehouse).

STORAGE CAPACITY The number of tons of a particular class of cargo that can be adequately stored at a marine terminal.

STORAGE CHARGE Fee for keeping goods in warehouse/terminal after "free time" runs out.

STORAGE TRACK A track on which railroad cars are placed when not in service.

STORE DOOR PICK UP DELIVERY A complete package of pick up or delivery services performed by a carrier from origin to final consumption point. A distribution facility.

STOREROOM The space provided for stowage of provisions or other material.

STORES Provisions and supplies onboard required for running a vessel.

STORING ANCHOR An anchor stowed on deck other than on the billboard.

STORM Low pressure system in which winds are 48 knots or higher.

STORM BALLAST Ballast water that was added to cargo tanks due to heavy weather. It may be clean if cleaning was accomplished but must still be responsibly discharged.

STORM CANVAS Small heavy sails used in heavy weather to replace the regular sails.

STORM VALVE A check valve in a pipe opening above waterline on a ship.

STORM WARNING Highest level of marine warning for storms that are not hurricanes or typhoons. Issued when winds are expected to be 48 knots or higher.

STOVE Broken in.

STOW To put in place. To stow cargo in a hold.

STOWAGE A marine term referring to loading freight into ships' holds. Everything for support and fastening of articles to be stowed, as anchor or boat stowage.

STOWAGE FACTOR Ratio of a cargo's cubic measurement to its weight, expressed in cubic feet to the ton or cubic meters to the tonne, used in order to determine the total quantity of cargo that can be loaded in a certain space

STOWAGE INSTRUCTIONS Imperative details about the way certain cargo is to be stowed, given by the shipper or his agent.

STOWAGE PLAN Diagrammatic sketch of vessel showing location of cargo as stowed in the vessel's hold(s).

STOWAWAY A person illegally aboard and in hiding.

STR Steamer.

STRADDLE CARRIER   Mobile truck equipment with the capacity for lifting a container within its own framework.

STRADDLE CARRIER/STRAD   A self-propelled, steerable vehicle on wheels, open in the middle, that can straddle a container or container on chassis, then lift and move it from one place to another in a container yard. Capable of straddling a single row of containers, stacked two to five containers high. Derived from the method used by old lumber carriers in moving lumber and timber around a lumberyard.

STRADDLE CRANE/STACKER/HIGH PILER   A crane running on tracks or wheels, usually spanning an open area, rail tracks, or containers. Capable of straddling several rows of container, three to four high. *See also* Transtainer.

STRAIGHT BILL OF LADING   A nonnegotiable bill of lading that states a specific identity to whom the goods should be delivered. *See* Bill of Lading.

STRAIGHT RUN GASOLINE (RAW GASOLINE)   A gasoline that is obtained directly from crude by fractional distillation.

STRAIGHT TRUCK   Vehicle that carries cargo in a body mounted to its chassis, rather than on a trailer towed by the vehicle.

STRAIGHT UP AND DOWN   When the anchor cable is vertical from hawse pipe to water.

STRAIN   Alteration in shape or dimensions resulting from stress. The lengthening or distortion of a member due to stress.

STRAINER BOX   Unit prior to cargo pump through which cargo flows to remove debris and objects, which might damage the cargo pump.

STRAKE   A course or row of shell, deck, bulkhead, or other plating.

STRAKE, BILGE   A term applied to a strake of outside plating running in the way of the bilge.

STRAKE, BOTTOM   Any strake of plating on the bottom of a ship that lies between the keel and the bilge strakes.

STRAND   A number of yarns or wires twisted together that may be twisted into rope. Rope may be designated by the number of strands composing it. Rope is commonly three stranded. A vessel run ashore is said to be stranded.

STRANDING   Running a vessel aground.

STRAP   A ring of rope made by splicing the ends and used for slinging weight holding the parts of a block together, etc. A rope, wire, or iron binding encircling a block and with a thimble seized into it for taking a hook.

STRAPPING   Measuring storage tanks and cargo carriers for capacity.

STRATEGIC PLANNING   Matching an institution's internal strengths and weaknesses with the full range of its external threats and opportunities, then devising goals and objectives and a plan of action for the institution. Usually done for a one-to-five year period.

STRATEGIC VARIABLES   The variables that effect change in the environment and logistics strategy. The major strategic variables include the economy, population, energy, and government.

STRATIGRAPHIC TRAP A structural formation in which the oil producing formation pinches out and disappears up the structure, forming an impervious layer of cap rock.

STREAM To put out and slack out a hawser to a towed unit.

STRENGTH MEMBER Any plate or shape that contributes to the strength of the vessel. Some members may be strength members when considering longitudinal strength but not when considering transverse strength and vice versa.

STRESS Force per unit area. The intensity of the force that tends to alter the form of a solid body; also the equal and opposite resistance offered by the body to a change of form.

STRETCH The leg between two points.

STRETCH WRAP An elastic, thin plastic material that effectively adheres to itself, thereby containing product on a pallet when wrapped around the items.

STRETCHERS Athwartship, movable pieces against which the oarsmen brace their feet in pulling a small boat.

STRIKES, RIOTS AND CIVIL COMMOTION (SR&CC) A term referring to an insurance clause excluding insurance loss caused by labor disturbances, riots and civil commotions or any person engaged in such actions.

STRINGER A fore and aft member used to give longitudinal strength to shell plating. According to location stringers are called hold stringers, bilge stringers, side stringers, etc.

STRINGER PLATE Deck plate at outboard edge of deck, connected to the shell of a ship by welding or with an angle; also, web of built-up side stringers.

STRINGPIECE The heavy square timber lying along the top of the piles forming a dock front or timber pier. A small apron between the edge of the pier and the transit shed that is wide enough for passage but not for cargo operations.

STRIPPER SUCTION FOOT A round casting that sits in a position similar to the main suction foot.

STRIPPER SUCTION VALVES Control the stripper suction lines.

STRIPPING The removal of the last few gallons of liquid from the bottom of the tank. Unloading a container (devanning).

STRONGBACK Portable supporting girders for hatch covers; a rig used in straightening bent plates; a bar for locking cargo ports.

STRONG LOW OR STRENGTHENING LOW Low pressure system in which the winds are at least gale force or are likely to reach gale force or higher as the central pressure of the low drops.

STRUM BOX The enlarged terminal on the suction end of a pipe and forming a strainer that prevents the entrance of material likely to choke the pipe.

STRUT Outboard support for propeller tail shaft, used on ships with more than one propeller.

STUD A bolt threaded on both ends, one end of which is screwed into a hole drilled and tapped in the work, and is used where a through bolt cannot be fitted.

STUDDING The vertical timbers or framing of a wooden deckhouse, fitted between the sill and the plate.

STUFFING The loading of a container.

STUFFING BOX A mechanical seal to prevent fluid leaks around pump shafts or reach rods. A fitting designed to permit the free passage or revolution of a rod or a pipe while controlling or preventing the passage by it of water, steam, etc.

STW Said to Weigh.

SU Set Up.

SUB Subject To.

SUBMARINE Beneath the surface of the sea. A vessel that is capable of service both below and on the surface of the water.

SUBMERSIBLES Vehicles suitable for deep diving applications such as repair work on undersea cables. One such type is the Pisces.

SUBROGATE (INS) To put in place of another, i.e., when an insurance company pays a claim it is placed in the same position as the payee with regard to any rights against others.

SUBROGATION (INS) The legal process by which an insurance company seeks from a third party who may have caused the loss, recovery of the amount paid to the insured.

SUBROGATION WAIVER (INS) A waiver by the named insured giving up any right of recovery against another party. Normally an insurance policy requires that subrogation (recovery) rights be preserved.

SUBSIDY The economic benefit granted by a government to producers of goods or services often to strengthen their competitive position.

SUBSTITUTE SERVICE Substitution of a land movement for a portion of a normally all water service.

SUBSTRETCH Part of a stretch. To distinguish between a stretch and a part thereof.

SUCL Set Up Carload.

SUCTION Attraction of the stern towards bank caused by drop of water level at inshore side of stern.

SUE & LABOR CLAUSE A provision in marine insurance obligating the Assured to do things necessary after a loss to prevent further loss and to act in the best interests of the insurer.

SUFFERANCE WHARF A wharf licensed and attended by Customs authorities.

SULCL Set Up in Less Than Carload.

SUMMER TANKS Tanks on outboard sides of expansion trunks when oil tankers had such an arrangement. They were reserve spaces that could be filled with oil to bring vessel to the loading mark in summer.

SUNK FORECASTLE, SUNK POOP A forecastle or poop deck that is raised only a partial deck height above the level of the upper or weather deck.

SUPERCARGO Person employed by a shipowner, shipping company, charterer of a ship or shipper of goods to supervise cargo-handling operations. Often called a port captain.

SUPERSTRUCTURE The upper portion of the ship. A structure extending all the way across the ship, built immediately above the uppermost complete deck; *see* House.

SUPERSTRUCTURE DECK A partial deck above the main, upper, forecastle, or poop deck, and not extending out to the side of the ship.

SUPPLEMENTAL CARRIER A for-hire air carrier having no time schedule or designated route; the carrier provides service under a charter or contract per plane per trip.

SUPPLEMENTAL MANIFEST a manifest used to add subsequent pages to a previously issued manifest

SUPPLIER FINANCING Arrangement where the seller/supplier of goods allows the buyer an extended period of time after shipment to pay for the goods.

SUPPLY CHAIN A logistical management system, which integrates the sequence of activities from delivery of raw materials to the manufacturer through to delivery of the finished product to the customer into measurable components. "Just in Time" is a typical value-added process.

SUPPLY CHAIN MANAGEMENT The integration of the supplier, distributor, and customer logistics requirements into one cohesive process to include demand planning, forecasting, materials requisition, order processing, inventory allocation, order fulfillment, transportation services, receiving, invoicing, and payment.

SUPPLY VESSEL A specialty vessel characterized by a forward house and long low after deck, usually providing support to the offshore oil industry.

SURCHARGE An extra or additional charge.

SURETY (INS) A term loosely used to describe the business or surety ship or bonds. Surety ship is an arrangement whereby one party becomes answerable to a third party for the acts of neglect of a second party; the party in a surety arrangement who holds himself responsible for the acts of another.

SURETY BOND (INS) A bond in which the surety agrees to answer to the obligee for the nonperformance of the principal (known as the obligor).

SURFACE TRANSPORTATION BOARD (STB) The U.S. federal body charged with enforcing acts of the U.S. Congress that affect common carriers in interstate commerce. STB replaced the Interstate Commerce Commission (ICC) in 1997.

SURGE Unsteady fore and aft motion of a ship in a seaway, generally caused by waves and/or weather conditions.

SURGE GEAR Name used in Pacific Northwest towing for the chain bridle and pendant. Every foot of chain weighed 150 pounds.

SURGE PRESSURE Surge pressure is caused by an abrupt change in the flow velocity in a pipeline, which, as a shock wave, can result in a quick and substantial increase over normal pipeline pressure.

SURTAX An additional extra tax.

SURVEY In cargo insurance, an examination of damaged property to determine the cause, extent, and value. In hull insurance, an inspection of the ship to help determine its insurability or, after a loss, the cause and extent of damage.

SURVEYOR A specialist who conducts surveys of cargo or hulls or cargo losses.

SUS Initials of Saybolt Universal Seconds. *See* Saybolt Universal Viscosity.

SV Sailing Vessel.

SWAB A rope mop.

SWAD Saltwater Arrival Draft.

SWAGE To bear or force down. An instrument having a groove on its under side for the purpose of giving shape to any piece subjected to it when the swage is struck by a hammer.

SWALLOW The larger opening in a block, above or below the sheave, through which the fall leads.

SWAMP To sink by filling with water.

SWAP BODY *See* Swop Body.

SWASH BULKHEAD Longitudinal or transverse nontight bulkheads fitted in a tank to decrease the swashing action of the liquid contents. Their function is greatest when the tanks are partially filled. Without them the unrestricted action of the liquid against the sides of the tank would be severe. A plate serving this purpose is called a swash plate.

SWASH PLATE Baffle plate in tank to prevent excessive swashing.

SWDD Saltwater Departure Draft.

SWEAT BATTENS Permanent dunnage attached to the side of the ship to aid in ventilation.

SWEDISH WIRE ROPE A retrieving wire and fiber line, strong and flexible, used on U.S. West Coast barges between the tow pendant and bridles and the barge (also called spring lay wire rope).

SWEET CRUDE OIL Crude oil containing less than 0.05 cubic feet of dissolved hydrogen sulfide per 100 gallons making it unnecessary for any chemical treatment for the removal of sulfur or sulfur compound.

SWELL Waves that have left the wind fetch area where they are created and have become more rounded in shape and regular in period. The heave of the sea.

SWING ANCHORS The anchors set to each side of the dredging project and to which the swing wires are attached.

SWING SHIP The evolution of swinging a ship's head through several compass points to obtain compass errors for making a deviation table.

SWING WIRES   The cables that run from anchors located to both sides of the dredging project through sheaves located on the dredge ladder to winching equipment on the dredge. These cables are responsible for pulling the dredge suction through the bottom material. The cable on one side is activated to move the dredge suction in that direction; the spud arrangement is changed and the opposite swing wire is used to pull the dredge suction in the opposite direction.

SWITCH ENGINE   A railroad engine that is used to move railcars short distances within a terminal and plant.

SWITCH TRANSACTIONS   The practice of exporting (or importing) goods through an intermediary country to final destinations. This is done when the destination country is short of U.S. dollars and is willing to exchange for the destination country's currency or goods. Switch transactions must be performed within the various laws concerning export licenses.

SWITCHING COMPANY   A railroad that moves railcars short distances; switching companies connect two mainline railroads to facilitate through movement of shipments.

SWITCHING COSTS   Costs incurred in changing suppliers or marketplaces. Net markets often seek to re-architect procurement, search, and other processes so buyers stay put, a key reason switching costs are higher in business-to-business than consumer e-commerce. *See* Churn.

SWIVEL   A special link constructed in two parts that revolve on each other, used to prevent fouling due to turns or twists in chain, etc.

SWL   Safe Working Load. The maximum weight or load that the ship's gear will support with safety.

SWOP BODY   Separate unit without wheels to carry cargo via road sometimes equipped with legs to be used to carry cargo intermodal within Europe. The advantage is that this unit can be left behind to load or discharge while the driver with the truck/chassis can change to another unit. These units are not used for sea transport.

SYNCHRONOUS ROLLING   Occurs when the rolling period of the vessel is the same as the wave period; a condition to be avoided.

SYNDICATE POLICY   A policy issued on behalf of a group of companies sharing a risk or class of risks. A syndicate policy carries the names of all the participating companies and usually designates the share of the liability assumed by each company.

SYNDICATE (S)   In Lloyd's Insurance, a group of individuals or companies who assume risk on behalf of their clients.

SYNERGY   The simultaneous joint action of separate parties that, together, have greater total effect than the sum of their individual effects.

SYNTHETIC DETERGENT   *See* Detergents. The term "synthetic" is used to distinguish the newer chemical cleaners from the older ones, such as soaps.

SYNTHETIC FUELS   Indicates fuels manufactured from sources other than crude petroleum (such as shale or coal).

SYSTEM   A set of interacting elements, variable, parts, or objects that are functionally related to each other and form a coherent group.

T

T1 Goods that are not in free circulation are assigned the EC Customs code T1. High speed Internet line carrying 1.2 megabits per second of data.

T2 Goods that are in free circulation are assigned the EC Customs code T2.

TABERNACLE A watertight structure for stowing gear and housing winches. Also called a mast table.

TABLE OF DENIAL ORDERS The TDO is a list of individuals and firms that have been disbarred from shipping or receiving U.S. goods or technology. Firms and individuals on the list may be disbarred with respect to either controlled commodities or general destination (across-the-board) exports. The list is published in the Export Administration Regulations.

TACHOGRAPH An electronic device that records the road speed and the engine RPMs (revolutions per minute) on a truck and tells a lot about the vehicle that has been driven.

TACK To bring a ship up into the wind and around so as to catch it from the other side, meanwhile trimming the sails accordingly.

TACKLE An assembly of ropes and blocks, (pronounced take'l). Tackles are used to secure a mechanical advantage that is, to enable the lifting of a heavy object by the exertion of a force considerably less than the weight of the object.

TAFFRAIL The rail around the top of the bulwark or rail stanchions on the after end of the weather deck, be it upper, main, raised, quarter, or poop.

TAFFRAIL LOG The log mounted on the taffrail and consisting of a rotator, a log line, and a recording device.

TAG LINE A steadying line.

TAIL Rear of a container or trailer opposite the front or nose.

TAIL (INS) This term has been used to describe both the exposure that exists after expiration of a policy and the coverage that may be purchased to cover that exposure. On "occurrence" forms a claims tail may extend for years after policy expiration, and the losses may be covered. On "claims made" forms tail coverage may be purchased to extend the period for reporting covered claims beyond the normal policy period.

TAILGATE Rear of trailer or straight truck.

TAIL SHAFT Short section of propeller shaft extending through stern tube and carrying propeller.

TAKE A TURN To pass a turn around a belaying pin or cleat and hold on.

TAKE IN To haul onboard a line or piece of equipment; to lower and furl sails.

TALL TRACK A stub end track, usually at the end of a yard, kept clear of standing cars to allow space for rail equipment to switch or to exit from a ladder or body track.

TALLYMAN   A person who records the number of cargo items together with the condition thereof at the time it is loaded into or discharged from a vessel.

TALLY SHEET   List of cargo, incoming and outgoing, checked by tally clerk on dock.

TANDEM   More than one tug towing side by side, or one ahead of the other, or more than one unit in a single tow.

TANDEM AXLE SHIFTABLE BOGIE   Two-wheeled axled bogie that can be shifted to predetermined locations on the chassis.

TANDEM AXLE TRAILER   A trailer or semitrailer that has two axles at the rear.

TANK, SETTING   Fuel oil tanks used for separating entrained water from the oil. The oil is allowed to stand for a few hours until the water has settled to the bottom, when the latter is drained or pumped off.

TANK, WING   Tanks located well outboard adjacent to the side shell plating, often consisting of a continuation of the double bottom up the sides to a deck or flat.

TANK BARGE   A basic type of barge for the transportation of liquid bulk commodities. Some tank barges have independent cylindrical tanks to carry liquid bulk cargoes whereas others use the entire midship shell of the vessel's hull as a cargo tank divided by bulkheads. Any tank vessel not equipped with means of self-propulsion.

TANK CAR   Railcars designed to haul bulk liquid or gas commodities.

TANK CLEANING   Cleaning out and clearing of gases from the cargo tanks on a tanker. Automatic mechanical tank washing machinery is used to jet high-pressure hot or cold water around the tank. Portable machines may also be used that enter the tank through circular apertures in the deck.

TANK CONTAINER   These containers are suitable for carrying a variety of goods. They are constructed of stainless steel and are maintained to food quality status as they are primarily dedicated to the carriage of potable spirits. Tank containers have capacities of 20,000 and 24,000 litres.

TANK DECK   The section of deck over the cargo tanks.

TANKER   A ship specially constructed or converted to carry bulk liquid cargo: crude petroleum, petroleum product, and chemical tankers, LNG and LPG tankers, wine, molasses, and whaling tankers. Also, a ship for moving dry or liquid bulk commodities. In U.S. Census Bureau International Commerce data, it only refers to liquid bulk.

TANKERMAN   Any person holding a certificate issued by the Coast Guard attesting to his competency in the handling of flammable or combustible liquid cargo in bulk.

TANK FARM   Storage facility for bulk petroleum products consisting of storage and transloading tanks as well as related facilities including marine truck and rail docks, loading racks, pumping units, and associated piping.

TANKS Compartments for liquid or gas, either built into ship's structure as double-bottom tanks, peak tanks, deep tanks, etc., or independent of it and supported by an auxiliary foundation.

TANKSHIP Any tank vessel that is self-propelled.

TANK TOP Lowest deck, top plate of the bottom tanks. On freighters, the bottom of the cargo hold, which is the top of the double-bottom tanks. On tankers, this is the main deck access point to the tanks and includes an ullage opening (port).

TANK VESSEL Any vessel specially constructed or converted to carry liquid bulk cargo in tanks.

TAPERING RATE A rate that increases with distance but not in direct proportion to the distance the commodity is shipped.

TAPS Trans Alaska Pipeline Service. The bugle call for out lights.

TAR A sailor.

TARE WEIGHT The weight of packing material, containers, or strapping without the goods to be shipped. Net weight plus tare equals gross weight.

TARGET'S MOTION TREND An early indication of the target's predicted motion. Used only in connection with ARPA performance standards.

TARGET'S PREDICTED MOTION The indication on the display of a linear extrapolation into the future of a target's motion, based on measurements of the target's range and bearing on the radar in the recent past. Used only in connection with ARPA performance standards.

TARIFF (TRF) A publication setting forth the charges, rates, and rules of transportation companies.

TARIFF ACT OF 1930 Title VII of the Tariff Act of 1930, as amended, provides for the imposition of antidumping duties on imported merchandise found to have been sold in the United States at "less than fair value," if these sales have caused or are likely to cause material injury to, or materially retard the establishment of, an industry in the United States.

TARIFF ANOMALY A tariff anomaly exists when the tariff on raw materials or semimanufactured goods is higher than the tariff on the finished product.

TARIFF ESCALATION A situation in which tariffs on manufactured goods are relatively high, tariffs on semi-processed goods are moderate, and tariffs on raw materials are nonexistent or very low.

TARIFF QUOTAS Application of a higher tariff rate to imported goods after a specified quantity of the item has entered the country at a lower prevailing rate.

TARIFF RATES In transportation, a list or scale of prices and charges for various transportation services. In a port, a list or scale of port services (for example, wharfage and dockage).

TARIFF SCHEDULE A comprehensive list of the goods that a country may import, and the import duties applicable to each product.

TARIFF SCHEDULES OF THE U.S. ANNOTATED Effective 1979 to January 1989, the U.S. import statistics were initially collected and compiled in terms of the commodity classifications in the Tariff Schedules of the United States Annotated (TSUSA), an official publication of the U.S. International Trade Commission embracing the legal text of the Tariff Schedules of the United States (TSUS) together with statistical annotations. This publication was superseded by the Harmonized Tariff Schedule of the United States Annotated for Statistical Reporting Purposes (HTSUSA) in January 1989.

TARIFF SERVICE The type of service required, such as house to house, pier to pier, pier to house, etc.

TARPAULIN Heavy canvas used as a protective covering over the hatches.

TATTOO A bugle call preparatory to taps, an inked pattern on the skin.

TAUNT Said of a vessel having lofty spars.

TAUT The condition of a rope, wire, or chain when under sufficient tension to cause it to assume a straight line, or to prevent sagging to any appreciable amount. With no slack. Strict as to discipline.

TBN To Be Named.

TC Time Charter.

TCP Time Charter Party.

TD OR T/D Time Definite. Normally a guaranteed delivery time with assumed liabilities if delivery is not made by a "guaranteed" time. Note: Normal cargo insurance rarely covers "guaranteed" delivery by a set time without explicit approval of Underwriters.

TDO *See* Table of Denial Orders.

T&E Transportation and Exportation. Customs form used to control cargo movement from port of entry to port of exit, meaning that the cargo is moving from one country, throughout the United States, to another country.

TEE BAR A rolled or extruded structural shape having a cross section shaped like the letter T.

TEETH Directly towards the wind.

TELEGRAPH An apparatus, either electrical or mechanical, for transmitting orders, as from a ship's bridge to the engine room, steering gear room, or elsewhere about the ship.

TELEMETERING A method for transmitting technical information from a remote site to a central location for analyzing and processing.

TELEMOTOR A device for operating the valves of the steering engine from the pilothouse by means of either fluid pressure or electricity.

TELEPORT An array of large-scale satellite communication dishes located in an area with little or no electronic interference designed to send and receive large volumes of commercial data via satellite; some port agencies are promoting and developing these facilities.

TELEX Used for sending messages to outside companies. Messages are transmitted via Western Union, ITT, and RCA.

TEMPERATURE RECORDER   A device to record temperature in a container while cargo is en route.

TEMPLATE   A mold or pattern made to the exact size of a piece of work that is to be laid out or formed and on which such information as the position of rivet holes and size of laps is indicated. Common types are made of paper or thin boards.

TEMPORARY IMPORTATION UNDER BOND (TIB)   When an importer makes entry of articles brought into the United States temporarily and claimed to be exempt from duty under Chapter 98, Subchapter XIII, Harmonized Tariff Schedule of the United States, a bond is posted with Customs that guarantees that these items will be exported within a specified time frame (usually within one year from the date of importation). Failure to export these items makes the importer liable for the payment of liquidated damages for breach of the bond conditions. *See* 19 CFR 10.31. The Temporary Importation Under Bond (TIB) is usually twice the amount of duties and other payments the importer would otherwise be required to pay. Merchandise imported under TIB is usually for sales demonstration, testing, or repair.

TENDER   A vessel is tender when its center of gravity is high, making it careen easily, i.e., it is top heavy. It returns slowly to the upright position, with relatively little force. Also, the offer of goods for transportation or the offer to place cars or containers for loading or unloading. *See also* Stiff.

TENDER SHIP   A ship that possesses very little stability or metacentric height, offering a relatively comfortable ride due to its slow return to the vertical. Cruise ships are renown for this condition. *See* Crank Ship.

TENON   The end of a piece of wood cut into the form of a rectangular prism, designed to be set into a cavity or mortise of a like form in another piece.

TENOR   Time and date for payment of a draft. Time at which a draft indicates it is payable, e.g., "at sight," "60 days after the bill of lading date," or "on May 31, 2001."

TENSILE STRENGTH   The measure of a material's ability to withstand a tensile, or pulling, stress without rupture, usually measured in pounds or tons per square inch of cross section.

TENSION   Stress caused by pulling. Tensile stress is a result of two forces acting in opposite directions on the same line. When tensile stress is applied to a material, it tends to pull the material apart, lengthening it in the process.

TENSION WINCH   A self-stowing winch fitted with a device that may be set to adjust automatically the tension on a mooring line by controlling the amount of power being fed to the operating driving unit.

TERMINAL   A shore facility where tankers are berthed for the purpose of loading or discharging petroleum cargo. An assigned area in which containers are prepared for loading into a vessel, train, truck or airplane or are stacked immediately after discharge from the vessel, train, truck, or airplane.

TERMINAL CHARGE A charge made for a service performed in a carrier's terminal area.

TERMINAL DELIVERY ALLOWANCE A reduced rate that a carrier offers in return for the shipper or consignee tendering or picking up the freight at the carrier's terminal.

TERMINAL HANDLING CHARGE (THC) THC is a charge assessed against the cargo interests by the steamship line to recover ocean carrier costs allegedly related to port and terminal expenses. These costs include outlays for chassis rental, equipment inspection/maintenance and repair, port assessments, grounding and mounting containers, gate formalities and documentation processing, longshoremen's wages and fringe benefits, etc. THC applies over and above the ocean transportation costs and is collected from the party named in the carrier's tariff, which is usually the consignee at destination, unless the shipment is prepaid.

TERMINAL INTERCHANGE RECEIPT Interchange receipt between trucker and carrier; document showing condition of container/equipment at the time of interchange.

TERMINAL OPERATOR The enterprise responsible for the operation of facilities for one or more modes of transportation.

TERMINAL PASS A document provided to the delivering carrier by the terminal operator to allow admission into the operator's facility.

TERMINAL RECEIPT A document used to accept materials or equipment at a terminal. This provides the delivering carrier with proof of delivery and the terminal with a verification of receipt.

TERMINAL RECEIVING CHARGE (TRC) Charge assessed by the terminal for cargo being delivered for export.

TERMS OF DELIVERY All the conditions agreed upon between trading partners regarding the delivery of goods and the related services. Note: Under normal circumstances, the INCO terms are used to prevent any misunderstandings.

TERMS OF FREIGHT All the conditions agreed upon between a carrier and a merchant about the type of freight and charges due to the carrier and whether these are prepaid or are to be collected.

TERMS OF SALE The point at which sellers have fulfilled their obligations so the goods in a legal sense could be said to have been delivered to the buyer. There are shorthand expressions that set out the rights and obligations of each party when it comes to transporting the goods. Here are 13 terms of sale in international trade as reflected in the recent amendment to the International Chamber of Commerce Terms of Trade (INCOTERMS), effective July 1990: exw, fca, fas, fob, cfr, cif, cpt, cip, daf, des, deq, ddu and ddp.

CFR (Cost and Freight): A term of sale where the seller pays the costs and freight necessary to bring the goods to the named port of destination, but the risk of loss or damage to the goods, as well as any additional costs due to events occurring after the time the goods have been delivered onboard the vessel, is transferred from the seller to the buyer when the goods pass the ship's rail in the port of shipment. The CFR term requires the seller to clear the goods for export.

CIF (Cost, Insurance, and Freight): A term of sale where the seller has the same obligations as under the CFR but also has to procure marine insurance against the buyer's risk of loss or damage to the goods during the carriage. The seller contracts for insurance and pays the insurance premium. The CIF term requires the seller to clear the goods for export.

CIP (Carriage and Insurance Paid To): A term of sale that means the seller has the same obligations as under CPT, but with the addition that the seller has to procure cargo insurance against the buyer's risk of loss or damage to the goods during the carriage. The seller contracts for insurance and pays the insurance premium. The buyer should note that under the CIP term the seller is required to obtain insurance only on minimum coverage. The CIP term requires the seller to clear the goods for export.

CPT (Carriage Paid To): A term of sale that means the seller pays the freight for the carriage of the goods to the named destination. The risk of loss or damage to the goods, as well as any additional costs due to events occurring after the time the goods have been delivered to the carrier, is transferred from the seller to the buyer when the goods have been delivered into the custody of the carrier. If subsequent carriers are used for the carriage to the agreed upon destination, the risk passes when the goods have been delivered to the first carrier. The CPT term requires the seller to clear the goods for export.

DAF (Delivered At Frontier): A term of sale that means the sellers fulfill their obligation to deliver when the goods have been made available, cleared for export, at the named point and placed at the frontier, but before the Customs border of the adjoining country.

DDP (Delivered Duty Paid): "Delivered Duty Paid" means that the seller fulfills his obligation to deliver when the goods have been made available at the named place in the country of importation. The seller has to bear the risks and costs, including duties, taxes and other charges of delivering the goods thereto, clear for importation. While the EXW term represents the minimum obligation for the seller, DDP represents the maximum.

DDU (Delivered Duty Unpaid): A term of sale where the seller fulfills his obligation to deliver when the goods have been made available at the named place in the country of importation. The seller has to bear the costs and risks involved in bringing the goods thereto (excluding duties, taxes and other official charges payable upon importation) as well as the costs and risks of carrying out customs formalities. The buyer has to pay any additional costs and to bear any risks caused by failure to clear the goods for in time.

DEQ (Delivered Ex Quay [Duty Paid]): A term of sale that means the DDU term has been fulfilled when the goods have been available to the buyer on the quay (wharf) at the named port of destination, cleared for importation. The seller has to bear all risks and costs including duties, taxes, and other charges of delivering the goods.

DES (Delivered Ex Ship): A term of sale where the seller fulfills his/her obligation to deliver when the goods have been made available to the buyer onboard the ship, uncleared for import at the named port of destination. The seller has to bear all the costs and risks involved in bringing the goods to the named port destination.

EXW (Ex Works): A term of sale that means the seller fulfills the obligation to deliver when he or she has made the goods available at his/her premises (i.e., works, factory, warehouse, etc.) to the buyer. The seller is not responsible for loading the goods in the vehicle provided by the buyer or for clearing the goods for export, unless otherwise agreed. The buyer bears all costs and risks involved in taking the goods from the seller's premises to the desired destination. This term thus represents the minimum obligation for the seller.

FAS (Free Alongside Ship): A term of sale that means the seller fulfills his obligation to deliver when the goods have been placed alongside the vessel on the quay or in lighters at the named port of shipment. This means that the buyer has to bear all costs and risks of loss of or damage to the goods from that moment.

FCA (Free Carrier): A term of sale that means the seller fulfills their obligation when he or she has handed over the goods, cleared for export, into the charge of the carrier named by the buyer at the named place or point. If no precise point is indicated by the buyer, the seller may choose, within the place or range stipulated, where the carrier should take the goods into their charge.

FOB (Free Onboard International Use): An international term of sale that means the seller fulfills his or her obligation to deliver when the goods have passed over the ship's rail at the named port of shipment. This means that the buyer has to bear all costs and risks of loss or damage to the goods from that point. The FOB term requires the seller to clear the goods for export.

FOB (Freight Allowed): The same as FOB named inland carrier, except the buyer pays the transportation charge and the seller reduces the invoice by a like amount.

FOB (Freight Prepaid): The same as FOB named inland carrier, except the seller pays the freight charges of the inland carrier.

FOB Vessel: Seller is responsible for goods and preparation of export documentation until actually placed aboard the vessel.

TERRITORIAL SEA   The zone off the coast of a nation immediately seaward from a baseline. Complete sovereignty is maintained over this coastal zone by the coastal nation, subject to the right of innocent passage to the ships of all nations. The United States recognizes this zone as extending 4.8 km (3.0 miles) from the baseline.

TERRORISM REINSURANCE ACT OF 2001 (TRIA)   Requires that terrorism insurance be quoted for land transits as well as ocean portions of shipments.

TEST HEAD   The head or height of a column of water that will give a prescribed pressure on the vertical or horizontal sides of a compartment or tank in order to test its tightness or strength or both.

TETHER   Line from bow of towing vessel to the stern of the towed vessel. This allows the tug to act as a rudder.

TETRAETHYL LEAD   A volatile lead compound, $Pb(D_2H_3)4$, that when added in small proportions to gasoline increase the octane rating.

TETRAETHYL LEAD SUSCEPTIBILITY   *See* Lead Susceptibility.

TEU   Twenty-Foot Equivalent Unit. It is used as a standard measure of a containership's container carrying capacity in terms of an $8 \times 8 \times 20$ foot size container. Also, a means of expressing containers of various sizes, such as 40 or 48 foot, in equivalent units.

THAT'S HIGH   An order to cease hoisting.

THC   Terminal Handling Charge.

THEFT & PILFERAGE (TP) (T&P)   Associated with loss to cargo from theft of all or a portion of the shipment.

THERMAL CONTAINER   A container built with insulating walls, doors, floor, and roof by which heat exchange with the environment is minimized thus limiting temperature variations of the cargo.

THERMAL CRACKING   The process of cracking by heat or by heat and pressure.

THERMAL VALUE   Calories per gram or Btu per pound produced by burning fuels.

THERMOCLINE   The meeting boundary of two layers of ocean water off different temperatures. This boundary tends to bend or scatter sonar signals.

THIEF   A sampling apparatus so designed that a liquid sample can be obtained within ½ inch of the bottom of a tank.

THIEVING   Taking a sample from the bottom of a tank, primarily to determine the amount of free water present. Also, commonly used to mean measuring the amount of water at the bottom of a tank by means of a tape and bob, or by a gauging pole (measured from the bottom of the tank to the bottom of the cargo).

THIMBLE   A pear-shaped metal ring, grooved on the outside to take rope around it. It protects the inside of an eye splice from wearing out.

THIRD-PARTY LOGISTICS (3PL)   Supply of logistics-related operations between traders by an independent organization.

THOLES   The pins in the gunwale of a boat that are used for oarlocks.

THREAD   The spiral part of a screw.

THRESHOLD LIMIT VALUE (TLV)   The highest concentration of a harmful substance in the air to which it is believed a person may be exposed for eight hours per day for an indefinite period without danger to health.

THROUGH BILL OF LADING Bill of lading covering receipt of goods at the premises of the owner of the cargo for delivery to the ultimate consignee located beyond the port of discharge. Used when transportation involves two or more connecting carriers.

THROUGH CHARGE The total rate from point of departure to point of destination. It may be a joint rate or a combination of rates (air cargo). Synonym: Through Rate.

THROUGH RATE The total rate from the point of origin to final destination.

THROUGH ROUTE The total route from point of departure to point of destination (air cargo).

THROUGHPUT The amount of cargo that reasonably can be expected to be processed, given the physical facilities available, the operating conditions present, and the business conditions characteristic of the trade in which the terminal is engaged.

THROUGHPUT CAPACITY The estimated total tons of cargo that can be processed and handled through a port terminal or berthing facility in the course of one year.

THROUGHPUT CHARGE The charge for moving a container through a container yard off or onto a ship.

THROUGH TRANSPORT Movement of goods by transport mode that overcomes traditional obstacles of geographical or government origin. For example, container inspected and sealed by Customs at factory travels across frontiers without further inspection until arrival at destination.

THROW MAT A mat used to prevent chafing; specifically the mat placed between a vessel's side and spur shore shoe.

THRUST BEARING Bearing on propeller line shaft that relieves the engine from the driving force of the propeller and transfers this force to the structure of the ship.

THWARTS The boards extending across a rowboat just below the gunwale to stiffen the boat and to provide seats.

THWARTSHIPS At right angles to the fore and aft line.

TIB *See* Temporary Importation Under Bond.

TIDES The periodic variation in the surface level of the oceans and bays, gulfs, inlets, and tidal regions of rivers, caused by the gravitational attraction of the sun and moon.

TIE BACK A timber or steel cable, rod or channel iron, I beam, U beam, or other form running horizontally from a retaining wall to an anchor pile or dead man to compensate for the outward thrust of the fill.

TIE PLANK The fastening holding the ship from sliding down the ways; also called solepiece.

TIE PLATE A single fore and aft course of plating attached to deck beams under wood deck to give extra strength.

TIER Barges grouped in a single line. There may be up to five tiers in a single river tow.

TILLER Arm attached to rudder head for operating rudder.

TILT TRANSPORT Road transport whereby the cargo area is protected against the elements by means of a tilt made of canvas or other pliable material.

TIME BAR Time after which legal claims will not be entered/accepted.

TIME CHARTER A contract for leasing between the ship owners and the lessee. It would state, for example, the duration of the lease in years or voyages.

TIME DEFINITE (TD OR T/D) Normally a guaranteed delivery time with assumed liabilities if delivery is not made by a "guaranteed" time. Note: Normal cargo insurance rarely covers "guaranteed" deliver by a set time without explicit approval of Underwriters.

TIME DRAFT A draft that matures either a certain number of days after acceptance or a certain number of days after the date of the draft.

TIME/SERVICE RATE A rail rate that is based upon transit time.

TIME SHEET Statement, drawn up by the ship's agent at the loading and discharging ports, which details the time worked in loading and discharging the cargo together with the amount of laytime used.

TIME TABLES A time schedule of departures and arrivals by origin and destination; typically used for passenger transportation by air, bus, and rail.

TIME/VOLUME CONTRACT An agreement between a shipper and a carrier that provides discounted rates for carrying cargo in exchange for a guaranteed volume of cargo over a stipulated time.

TIPPING CENTER *See* Center of Flotation.

TIR Transport International aux par la Route. Road transport operating agreement among European governments and the United States for the international movement of cargo by road. Display of the TIR carnet allows sealed container loads to cross national frontiers without inspection.

TIR (EIR) Trailer Inspection (or Interchange) Report. Same as an Equipment Interchange Report, used to document damage and condition of containers and chassis.

TL Trailer Load. Total. Truck Load.

TLO Total Loss Only.

TOE The edge of a flange on a bar.

TOFC Trailer on Flatcar. The movement of a highway trailer on a railroad flatcar. Also known as piggyback.

TOGGLE PIN A pin having a shoulder and an eye worked on one end, called the head, and whose other end, called the point, has its extremity hinged in an unbalanced manner so that after being placed through a hole it forms a T-shaped locking device to keep the pin from working out or being withdrawn without first bringing the hinged portion into line with the shaft of the pin.

TOLERANCE An allowable variation from a specified limit.

TOLLS *See* Wharfage.

TOLUENE (TOLUOL) An aromatic hydrocarbon $C_6H_5CH_3$, the principle component of TNT.

TOMMING Shoring that forces cargo down against the deck.

TON The short or net ton is 2,000 pounds. Also, the long ton is 2,240 pounds.

TON MILE A unit used in comparing freight earnings or expenses. The amount earned from the cost of hauling a ton of freight one mile. Also, the movement of a ton of freight one mile.

TONGUE AND GROOVE The term applied to a plank or board that has one edge cut away to form a projection, or tongue, and the opposite edge cut out to form a groove, the tongue of one plank fitting into the groove of the adjoining plank.

TONNAGE A measure of the internal volume of spaces, within a vessel in which 100 cu foot is 1 ton. Gross tons includes a ship's internal volume, excluding such spaces as the double bottom, peak or deep tanks used only for water ballast, open-ended poop, bridge or forecastle, certain light and air spaces, skylights, anchor and steering gears spaces, the wheelhouse, toilets, and certain passenger spaces. Net tonnage is the gross tonnage less certain additional spaces such as officer and crew spaces, chart room, and percentage of the propelling machinery spaces.

TONNAGES Short: 2,000 pounds. Long: 2,240 pounds. Metric: 2,204.6 pounds.

TONNE (METRIC TON) 1,000 kilograms (2,204 pounds).

TONS Expressed in maritime trade as "long," "short," or "metric." A long ton equals 1,016 kilograms or 2,240 pounds. A short ton equals 2,000 pounds. A metric ton equals 100 kilograms or 2,204.6 pounds.

TOP To raise or lift up the boom.

TOP A BARGE The act of spinning a barge around end for end.

TOP AIR DELIVERY A type of air circulation in a container. In top air units, air is drawn from the bottom of the container, filtered through the evaporator for cooling, and then forced through the ducted passages along the top of the container. This type of airflow requires a special loading pattern.

TO PAY AS TOTAL LOSS (INS) Used in ancillary insurances relating to the cargo (e.g., increased value) when the Assured is not required to show evidence of loss or interest and can claim on the policy if he can show that a corresponding loss has been settled on the main cargo policy.

TOP BREADTH The width of vessel measured across the shelter deck.

TOP HAMPER The spars and rigging above the decks.

TOP HEAVY Too heavy aloft.

TOPLIFT A type of forklift with a spreader device for lifting containers from the top.

TOPOGRAPHIC Graphic delineation of manmade and natural features of a site, showing relative location and elevation on a map or chart.

TOPPED CRUDE Crude oil from which some of the lighter constituents have been removed by distillation.

TOPPING   Removal of volatile fractions by distillation.

TOPPING LIFT   A rope or chain extending from the head of a boom or gaff to a mast, or to the vessel's structure, for the purpose of supporting the weight of the boom or gaff and its loads and permitting the gaff or boom to be raised or lowered.

TOPPING OFF   At loading, the process of bringing a tank up to a predetermined ullage.

TOPSIDE   Portion of the side of the hull that is above the designed waterline. On or above the weather deck.

TORQUE   The moment of a system of forces that causes rotation, as of a shaft or a rudderstock.

TOSCA   Toxic Substance Control Act. An extra release that is needed for chemicals, hazardous material, etc. Not a charge by customs, but brokers may charge extra to get the release.

TOTAL COST ANALYSIS   A decision-making approach that considers total system cost minimization and recognizes the interrelationship among system variables such as transportation, warehousing, inventory, and customer service.

TOTAL LOSS (INS)   This can be actual total loss or constructive total loss, where the cost of damage repair exceeds the value of the property insured.

TOTAL QUALITY MANAGEMENT (TQM)   A management approach championed by Demming in which managers constantly communicate with organizational stakeholders to emphasize the importance of continuous quality improvement.

TOUGH   An elongation of the isobars around a low. Inclement weather often occurs in a trough. This term is also applied to weather patterns found in the upper air.

TOUGHNESS   A measure of the ability of a metal to withstand a sudden shock.

TOW   To pull through water; vessels towed.

TOWAGE   The charge made for towing a vessel.

TOWBOAT   A powerful shallow draft vessel designed to push tow barges or larger vessels between ports and landings over inland waterway navigation channels.

TOW HOOK   A simple hook with remote release as used on European harbor tugs.

TOW MOTOR   A small gasoline powered vehicle for towing laden trailer.

TOW PINS   Extensions up from the taffrail on either side of the vessel to keep the towline on the vessel's centerline.

TOW TRACTOR   A tractive unit used to tow containers on chassis.

TOW WINCH   A single drum tow winch with vertical automatic cable threader or guide. The open chock on the right gives a good lead for lines running to the gypsyhead. A hand brake is shown on the left. Power may be electric, hydraulic, or diesel.

TOWING MASTER   A person with considerable expertise, other than the tug captain, who has been placed in charge of a tug or group of tugs, usually handling a very difficult tow.

TOXICITY   The level of poison of a substance.

T&P   Theft and Pilferage.

TPI   Tons Per Inch immersion. Number of tons necessary to change the mean draft of a vessel one inch; varies with draft.

TPND   Theft, Pilferage, and Nondelivery.

TQM   *See* Total Quality Management.

TRACE   The act of searching for a missing shipment.

TRACING   Determining a shipment's location during the course of a move.

TRACK   The path of a vessel. The recommended route to be followed when proceeding between predetermined positions.

TRACKING   The process of observing the sequential changes in the position of a target, to establish its motion. Used only in connection with ARPA performance standards.

The function of maintaining status information, including current location of cargo, cargo items, consignments, or containers either full or empty.

TRACK & TRACE   Usually a computer-based monitoring system that tracks the movement of goods in real time along the supply chain.

TRACTION   The power to grip or hold to a surface while moving without slipping.

TRACTIVE UNIT   The front (or towing) part of an articulated vehicle.

TRACTOR   Unit of highway motive power used to pull one or more trailers/containers.

TRACTOR TUG   A general reference to any tug fitted with a cycloidal or rudder propeller propulsion system. *See* Water Tractor.

TRADE   A geographic area or specific route served by carriers.

TRADE ACCEPTANCE   A time or a date draft that has been accepted by the buyer (the drawee) for payment at maturity.

TRADE LANE   The combination of the origin and destination points.

TRADE LOSS   A loss, usually small in amount, specific to certain kinds of cargo and which, because it is expected, is uninsurable. For example, seepage or evaporation of liquid from wooden casks.

TRADES   The practically steady winds found in the tropics and blowing towards the equator N.E. in the northern and S.E. in the southern hemisphere.

TRAFFIC   Movement of shipping; persons and property carried by transport lines.

TRAFFIC LANE   An area within definite limits inside which one-way traffic is established.

TRAFFIC MANAGEMENT   The buying and controlling of transportation services for a shipper or consignee, or both.

TRAFFIC SEPARATION SCHEME   Shipping corridors, marked by buoys, that separate incoming from outgoing vessels. Improperly called sea lane.

TRAILER   The truck unit into which freight is loaded as in tractor-trailer combination. *See* Container.

TRAILER ON FLATCAR (TOFC)   "Piggybacking" highway trailers on specially equipped rail flatcars.

TRAILING SUCTION HOPPER DREDGE   A self-propelled vessel with pumps and other apparatus for removing bottom materials while underway, storing the materials temporarily in hoppers aboard the vessel, then steaming to a disposal site to dispose of the dredged materials.

TRAMP   Irregular service afforded by vessels, other than tankers, that are chartered or otherwise hired for the carriage of goods on special voyages. Service is not predetermined or fixed. Most of the cargo is dry bulk, but also includes general cargo moved in ship odd lots.

TRAMP LINE   An ocean carrier company operating tramp steamers not on regular runs or schedules.

TRAMP VESSEL   A vessel not operating under a regular schedule.

TRANSFER   Movement of cargo between ship/shore, ship/ship, or barge/shore.

TRANSFER CARGO   Cargo arriving at a point by one flight and continuing by another flight (air cargo).

TRANSFER RISK   Risk incurred by the seller of goods that, due to the fact that his country has a negative balance of payments, no foreign exchange (U.S. dollars or other "hard" currency) may be available to the buyer when he is ready to pay for the goods.

TRANSFERABLE LETTER OF CREDIT   Type of letter of credit that names a middleman as beneficiary and allows him to give another party, the actual supplier, certain rights to present documents and receive payment under the letter of credit. Transfer must be affected by a bank authorized to do so by the issuing bank and involves notifying the transferee (called the "second beneficiary") of what documents he must present. The documents must be the same as those required in the letter of credit itself, but the price of the goods may be reduced and the middleman's name may be required to be listed in the transferee's invoices as the buyer, thereby allowing the middleman to substitute invoices at a higher price and receive the difference without disclosing the name of the actual end-buyer. The transferring bank is not obligated to pay documents presented under the transfer. Such obligation remains with the issuing bank.

TRANSFERRING CARRIER   A participating carrier who delivers the consignment to another carrier at a transfer point (air cargo).

TRANSFORMER OIL   An oil used in transformers to conduct heat, soften and protect the insulation, and reduce oxidation.

TRANSIT CARGO   Cargo between outwards customs clearance and inwards customs clearance. Cargo arriving at a point and departing from the same through flight (air cargo).

TRANSIT CLAUSE (INS)   A clause in the Institute Cargo Clauses, specifying the attachment and termination of cover.

TRANSIT PRIVILEGE   A carrier service that permits the shipper to stop the shipment in transit to perform a function that changes the commodity's physical characteristics, but to still pay the through rate.

TRANSIT SHED   Building or other structure located on or adjacent to a wharf, designed for the short-term storage of merchandise in transit. Usually associated with breakbulk cargo. Also, a building on a breakbulk general cargo wharf for the purpose of providing temporary accommodations and sorting space for cargo being transferred to or from a vessel.

TRANSIT SHIPMENT   A shipment passing between one port and another, or between a port and a final destination.

TRANSIT TIME   A time period for cargo to move between two points (i.e., from a consignor to a consignee). Total transit time is usually calculated by adding the sea time between two given ports, the port handling time, the inland movement time, and half of the service frequency.

TRANSIT ZONES   A form of free trade zone are ports of entry in coastal countries that are established as storage and distribution centers for the convenience of a neighboring country lacking adequate port facilities or access to the sea. A transit zone is administered so that goods in transit to and from the neighboring country are not subject to the Customs duties, import controls, or many of the entry and exit formalities of the host country. Transit zones are more limited facilities than a foreign trade zone or a free port.

TRANSMITTAL LETTER   Contains a list of the particulars of the shipment, a record of the documents being transmitted, and instructions for disposition of these documents. Any special instructions are also included.

TRANSOM   A seat or couch built at the side of a stateroom or cabin, having lockers or drawers underneath.

TRANSOM, TRANSOM BOARD   The board forming the stern of a square-ended rowboat or small yacht.

TRANSOM FRAME   The last transverse frame of a ship's structure. The cant frames, usually normal to the round of the stern, connect to it.

TRANSPONDER   A device (chip) used for identification that automatically transmits certain coded data when actuated by a special signal from an interrogator.

TRANSPORT   To move traffic from one place to another.

TRANSPORTATION AND EXPORTATION ENTRY   A form declaring goods that are entering the United States (for example from Canada) for the purpose of exportation through a United States port. Carriers and any warehouse must be bonded.

TRANSPORTATION ASSOCIATION OF AMERICA   An association that represents the entire U.S. transportation system, carriers, users, and the public; now defunct.

TRANSPORTATION & EXIT (T&E)   Allows foreign merchandise arriving at one port to be transported in bond through the U.S. to be exported from another port, without paying duty.

TRANSPORTATION METHOD   A linear programming technique that determines the least-cost means of shipping goods from plants to warehouses or from warehouses to customers.

TRANSPORTATION REQUIREMENTS PLANNING (TRP)   Using computer technology and information already available in MRP and DRP databases to plan transportation needs based on field demand.

TRANSPORT DOCUMENTS   *See* Shipping Documents.

TRANSPORTER   An electric vehicle moving on rails, with hydraulic lifting rams, that lifts and transports barges between the elevator and cargo holds of a Seabee mother vessel.

TRANSPORT INTERNATIONAL BY ROAD (TIR)   A set of rules following a Customs convention to facilitate the international, European transport of goods by road with minimal interference under cover of TIR carnets.

TRANSPORT SERVICES   Services offered by the transport provider.

TRANSSHIP   To transfer goods from one transportation line to another, or from one ship to another ship. Sometimes this is referred to as "Relay."

TRANSSHIPMENT   Refers to the act of sending an exported product through an intermediate country before routing it to the country intended to be its final destination. A shipment under one bill of lading, whereby sea (ocean) transport is "broken" into two or more parts. The port where the sea (ocean) transport is "broken" is the transshipment port. Transfer of cargo from one means of transport to another for on carriage during the course of one transport operation. Customs: Customs procedure under which goods are transferred under Customs control from the importing means of transport to the exporting means of transport within the area of one Customs office, which is the office of both importation and exportation.

TRANSSHIPMENT PORT   Place where cargo is transferred to another carrier.

TRANS-SIBERIAN LANDBRIDGE (TSR)   Overland route from Europe to the Far East via the Trans Siberian Railway (TSR).

TRANSTAINER   The registered trade name of a yard gantry or bridge crane manufactured by Pacific Coast Engineering Company (PACECO). *See also* Portainer.

TRANSVERSE   At right angles to the ship's fore and aft centerline.

TRANSVERSE BULKHEAD   A large watertight bulkhead, which runs from the keel to the main deck athwartship.

TRANSVERSE CONSTRUCTION   Method of constructing vessels that provide large open areas for the stowage of large solid objects such as containers.

TRANSVERSE FRAMES Athwartship members forming the ship's "ribs."

TRANSVERSE METACENTER *See* Metacenter.

TRAVELING MANIFEST A manifest of all cargoes aboard a vessel that must be available for inspection at the vessel's first port of call. Corrections to the manifest must be made at the first port. This manifest is then certified by Customs and travels with the vessel through the remainder of its ports of call.

TRAWLER A fishing vessel specifically designed to drag a net through the water to harvest fish. Not to be confused with trolling.

TRAWLING To fish or catch with a large net dragged along the bottom of a fishing bank.

TRC Terminal Receiving Charge. Charge assessed by the terminal for cargo being delivered for export.

TREADS The stops or horizontal portions of a ladder or staircase upon which the foot is placed.

TREENAILS Wooden pins employed instead of nails or spikes to secure the planking of a wooden vessel to the frames.

TRESTLES Steel tripods placed under the forward end of semi trailers.

TRF *See* Tariff.

TRIA *See* Terrorism Reinsurance Act.

TRICE To haul up.

TRICING LINE A line used for suspending articles.

TRICK The period of time during which the steersman remains at the wheel.

TRIM To shift ballast to make a ship change its position in the water. The difference between the forward draft and the after draft.

TRIM CALCULATOR A device that calculates quickly the trim of a vessel after loading or discharging.

TRIMMING TABLES Tables that calculate change of mean draft and change of trim after loading, discharging, or shifting of weights.

TRIP To let go. *See* Voyage.

TRIP COVER (INS) Term denoting coverage for one "trip" or "voyage."

TRIP LEASE Leasing a company's vehicle to another transportation provider for a single trip.

TRIP RECORDER Cab-mounted device that electronically or mechanically records data such as truck speed, engine rpm, idle time, and other information useful to trucking management.

TRIPPING BRACKETS Flat bars or plates placed at various points on deck girders, stiffeners, or beams as a reinforcement to prevent their free flanges from tipping.

TRIPPING LINE A line used for capsizing the sea anchor.

TROLLEY Athwartship movement of container crane on LASH vessels.

TROLLING To fish with a baited line trailed behind a slowly moving boat.

TROPICAL DEPRESSION Cyclone that originates over the tropical ocean and may be the early stage of a hurricane or typhoon. Winds up to 33 knots.

TROPICAL STORM   More intense tropical cyclone in which the winds are 34 knots through 63 knots.

TRP   *See* Transportation Requirements Planning.

TRUCK   The flat circular piece of wood secured at the top of the highest mast or at the top of a flagstaff. Also, class of automotive vehicles of various sizes and designs for transporting goods.

TRUCK LOAD (TL)   The quantity of freight required to fill a trailer, usually more than 10,000 pounds.

TRUCKMEN'S LIABILITY FORM (INS)   *See* Motor Truck Cargo.

TRUCK TRAILER   A combination consisting of a tractive unit and a draw bar trailer.

TRUE COURSE   The apparent heading of a target obtained by the vectorial combination of the target's relative motion and ship's own motion. Expressed as an angular distance from north. Used only in connection with ARPA performance standards.

TRUE MOTION DISPLAY   The position of own ship on such display moves in accordance with its own motion. Used only in connection with ARPA performance standards.

TRUE SPEED   The speed of a target obtained by the vectorial combination of its relative motion and own ship's motion. Used only in connection with ARPA performance standards.

TRUNION   The hinge at the connection of the dredge ladder and the dredge. The trunion allows the ladder to pivot in a vertical plane.

TRUNK   A vertical or inclined space or passage formed by bulkheads or casings, extending one or more deck heights, around openings in the decks, through which access can be obtained and cargo, stores, etc., handled or ventilation provided without disturbing or interfering with the contents or arrangements of the adjoining spaces. Also main line, primary line of transport.

TRUNK LINES   Oil pipelines used for the long-distance movements of crude oil, refined oil, or other liquid products.

TRUNKING   Movement of containers between terminal and carrier's inland facilities.

TRUST RECEIPT   Release of merchandise by a bank to a buyer while the bank retains title to the merchandise. The goods are usually obtained from manufacturing or sales purposes. The buyer is obligated to maintain the goods (or the proceeds from their sales) distinct from the remainder of the assets and to hold them ready for repossession by the bank.

TSA   Transportation Security Administration.

TSR   *See* Trans-Siberian Landbridge.

TSS   Traffic Separation System.

TSUSA   *See* Tariff Schedules of the United States.

T/T   Telegraphic Transfer. Wire funds.

TTL   Total.

TUG BOAT   A powerful small vessel designed for towing larger vessels.

TUGMASTER   Brand name of tractor unit used in ports to pull trailers. They are equipped with a fifth wheel or a gooseneck type of coupling.

TUMBLE HOME   The inward slope of a ship's side, usually above the designed waterline. The decreasing of a vessel's beam above the waterline as it approaches the rail. Opposite of flare.

TURBINE GAS   An engine in which the heat energy in a gas is converted to rotational energy by the gas impinging on a series of blades on revolving discs. The gas turbine unit normally consists of compression, heating, and expansion cycles.

TURBOCHARGER   A turbine driven air compressor powered by the exhaust gases from the parent internal combustion engine. The compressor has a compression ratio of up to 1:3:5, increases the power developed by the I.C. engine by up to two and a half times, rotates at 10,000 to 24,000 rpm and is a major source of noise (+100 dB). In highly rated engines with high bmep's, ratios of up to 1:6 may be required in which case two turbochargers are fitted in series to provide two-stage turbocharging, but this arrangement is not widely fitted today.

TURNAROUND   Period of time required by a vessel to make one complete round trip between two ports and complete preparations to resume the cycle. The time it takes between the arrival of a vessel and its departure.

TURNBUCKLE   A link with two threaded bars inserted in opposite ends. Twisting the link draws the bars together. Used for tightening purposes, such as the securing of deck cargo, or securing standing rigging to dock.

TURNING CIRCLE   Standard maneuver carried out as a measure of the efficiency of the rudder.

TURN OF THE BILGE   Curved section between the bottom and side of the ship.

TURNOUT   A switch and accompanying section of track allowing the diversion of rolling stock from one track to another.

TURN TO   To report for duty.

TURN TURTLE   To capsize.

TURRETS   Turrets are constructed so as to revolve about a vertical axis usually by means of electrical or hydraulic machinery.

TW   'Tween Decker.

'TWEEN DECKS   The space between any two adjacent decks; also called between decks. The mid-level deck within a cargo hold.

TWENTY-FOOT EQUIVALENT UNIT (TEU)   TEU is a measure of a ship's cargo-carrying capacity. One TEU measures 20 feet × 8 feet × 8 feet—the dimensions of a standard twenty-foot container.

TWIST LOCK CONES   Stacker cones that can be pivoted by a lever in order to lock them in position and thus lock one container on top of another or to the deck.

TWIST LOCKS   A set of four twistable bayonet-type shear keys used as part of a spreader to pick up a container or as part of a chassis to secure the containers.

TWO BLOCK   When the two blocks of a tackle have been drawn as close together as possible.

TWO-WAY PALLET   A pallet so designed that the forks of a forklift truck can be inserted from two sides only.

TWO-WAY ROUTE   An area within definite limits inside which two way traffic is established.

TYNE POCKETS (TP)   Two enclosed pockets at bottom of containers for lifting by forklift.

TYPE OF CARGO   An indication of the sort of cargo to be transported, (e.g., breakbulk, containerized, RO/RO).

TYPE OF EQUIPMENT   The type of material used, e.g., 40-ft container, four-way pallet, or mafi trailer.

TYPE OF LOAD INDICATOR   A general reference or a classification of loads of cargo like "FCL," "LCL," "unpacked" and even ship's convenience container, though this is rarely used nowadays.

TYPE OF MEANS OF TRANSPORT   The type of vehicle used in the transport process, e.g. wide-body aircraft, tank truck, or passenger vessel.

TYPE OF MOVEMENT   Description of the service for movement of containers. Note: The following type of movement can be indicated on B/L and manifest: all combinations of FCL and LCL and breakbulk and RO/RO. While only on the manifest, combinations of house, yard, and CFS can be mentioned.

TYPE OF PACKING   Description of the packaging material used to wrap, contain, and protect goods to be transported.

TYPE OF TRANSPORT   The indication whether the carrier or the merchant effects and bears the responsibility for inland transport of cargo in containers, i.e., a differentiation between the logistical and legal responsibility. Note: Values are carrier haulage and merchant haulage, while in this context special cases are carrier-nominated merchant haulage, and merchant-nominated carrier haulage.

TYPE OF VESSEL   The sort of vessel used in the transport process, e.g., container, RO/RO, or multipurpose.

TYPHOON   A hurricane in the western Pacific Ocean.

U

UBIQUITY   A raw material that is found at all locations.

UCC   Uniform Commercial Code.

UCP   Uniform Customs and Practice for Documentary Credits, published by the International Chamber of Commerce. This is the most frequently used standard for making payments in international trade, e.g., paying on a letter of credit. It is most frequently referred to by its shorthand title: UCP No. 500. This revised publication reflects recent changes in the transportation and banking industries, such as electronic transfer of funds.

UFC   Uniform Freight Classification.

ULCC   Ultra Large Crude Carriers. Tankers larger than 300,000 dwt.

ULD   *See* Unit Load Device.

ULLAGE   The distance from the top of a tank to the top of a liquid or the space not filled with liquid in a drum or tank.

ULLAGE HOLE   A small hole cut in the large cover on top of a tank to allow access for measuring liquid cargo in the tank by tape measure or other mechanical means.

ULLAGE PORTS   Ten-inch diameter, watertight access ports to cargo tanks used to measure liquid level and monitor loading and discharge; must be equipped with flame screens.

ULLAGE TABLES   Calibrated tables, one for each tank, giving the amounts of oil in barrels for various ullages.

ULLAGES   Measurements taken with a steel sounding tape from the lip of the ullage hole to the surface of the liquid, and read to the nearest quarter of an inch.

ULTIMATE CONSIGNEE   The ultimate consignee is the person located abroad who is the true party in interest, receiving the export for the designated end use.

ULTIMATE STRENGTH   Stress necessary to achieve the failure of the material. The ultimate strength of mild steel in tension is approximately 30 tons psi and in shear, 22 tons psi.

ULTRA LARGE CRUDE CARRIER   An incredibly large tanker designed solely to carry crude oil. ULCC can be over 1,200 feet long, draw 100 feet and have abeam of 200 feet, usually over 300,000 deadweight tons.

UMBRELLA   The metal shield in the form of a frustum of a cone, secured to the outer casing of the smokestack over the air casing to keep out the weather.

UMBRELLA LIABILITY POLICY (INS)   A liability policy designed to provide liability protection above and beyond that provided by standard liability contracts.

UMBRELLA RATE   An ICC ratemaking practice that held rates to a particular level to protect another mode's traffic.

UNBEND   To cast adrift or untie.

UNCLAIMED FREIGHT   Freight that has not been called for or picked up by the consignee or owner.

UNCONFIRMED LETTER OF CREDIT   Letter of credit that has not been confirmed.

UNCTAD   United Nations Conference on Trade and Development.

UNDERCARRIAGE   A supporting frame or structure of a wheeled vehicle.

UNDERCARRIER   A carrier in a conference or consortium who carries less cargo than the allotment distributed to him.

UNDERCHARGE   To charge less than the proper amount.

UNDER INSURANCE (INS)   A condition in which not enough insurance is carried to cover the insurable value, and, especially, to satisfy a coinsurance clause.

UNDER MANNED   Insufficient number of crew; shorthanded.

UNDER RUN   To haul a boat under a hawser; to raise up the bight of a hose, to empty it of water. To place a shackle, hook, and line under a cable and back the rig so as to clear or run toward an anchor or other object.

UNDERTOW   A current off shore in a surf zone.

UNDERWAY   Said of a vessel when not at anchor, nor made fast to the shore, nor aground.

UNDERWRITER (INS)   A person trained in evaluating risks and determining the rates and coverages that will be used for them. An agent, especially a life insurance agent, who might qualify as a "field Underwriter."

UNDG NUMBER   *See* United Nations Dangerous Goods Number.

UN/EDIFACT   United National EDI for Administration, Commerce, and Transport. EDI Standards are developed and supported by the UN for electronic message (data) interchange on an international level.

UNFAIR BUSINESS PRACTICES   A general standard used in U.S. transportation law to connote an activity considered detrimental to U.S. commerce and that can be prevented by action of regulatory agencies.

UNIFORM COMMERCIAL CODE   U.S. statute covering the rights and obligations of the various parties involved in the purchase and sale of goods. The UCC includes coverage of drafts and other negotiable instruments, documents of title, transfers of funds between banks, and security interests in assets as well as draft collections (in Article 4) and letters of credit (in Article 5).

UNIFORM CUSTOMS & PRACTICES FOR DOCUMENTARY CREDITS (UCP)   Rules for letters of credit drawn up by the Commission on Banking Technique and Practices of the International Chamber of Commerce in consultation with the banking associations of many countries. *See* Terms of Payment.

UNIFORM RULES FOR COLLECTIONS   International standards of draft collection practice established for bankers by the International Chamber of Commerce. The Uniform Rules are not law but are more properly viewed as a handbook for banks used to establish common understanding of terminology and expectations.

UNIFORM WAREHOUSE RECEIPTS ACT   The act that sets forth the regulations governing public warehousing. The regulations define a warehouse manager's legal responsibility and define the types of receipts he or she issues.

UNIT LOAD   Packages loaded on a pallet, in a crate, or any other way that enables them to be handled at one time as a unit.

UNIT TRAIN   A train of a specified number of railcars, perhaps 100, that remain as a unit for a designated destination or until a change in routing is made. Also, a train transporting a single commodity or type of cargo from one source (shipper) to one destination (consignee). For coal and other bulk cargos, usually the integrity of unit trains is maintained after unloading at the destination and the emtpies (still coupled in the same order) are returned for subsequent loading.

UNITED NATIONS CONFERENCE ON TRADE & DEVELOPMENT (UNCTAD)   A United Nations agency whose work in shipping includes the liner code involving the sharing of cargoes between the shipping lines of the importing and exporting countries and third countries in the ratio 40:40:20.

UNITED NATIONS DANGEROUS GOODS NUMBER (UNDG)   The four-digit number assigned by the United Nations Committee of Experts on the Transport of Dangerous Goods to classify a substance or a particular groups of substances. Note: The prefix "UN" must always be used in conjunction with these numbers.

UNITED STATES RAILWAY ASSOCIATION   The planning/funding agency for Conrail; created by the 3-R Act of 1973.

UNITIZATION   The consolidation of a quantity of individual items into one large shipping unit for easier handling. Loading one or more large items of cargo onto a single piece of equipment, such as a pallet.

UNITIZE   To consolidate several packages into one unit; carriers strap, band, or otherwise attach the several packages together.

UNITIZED CARGO   Individual items of cargo, which are strapped, glued, or shrink-wrapped together to make one solid unit.

UNIT LOAD DEVICE (ULD)   Refers to airfreight containers and pallets.

UNIT PACKING LIST (UPL)   A form listing all cargo loaded into a container. Also referred to as a container load plan, container manifest, container flat manifest, unit load list, stuffing manifest, and unit load plan.

UNLOADING   Removal of a shipment from a container to a platform or warehouse.

UNMOOR   To heave up one anchor, leaving the other down.

UNRIG   To take the rigging off a vessel.

UNSATURATED HYDROCARBON   Hydrocarbon having a deficiency of hydrogen.

UNSEAWORTHINESS   The state or condition of a vessel when it is not in a proper state of maintenance, or if the loading equipment or crew, or in any other respect is not ready to encounter the ordinary perils of sea.

UNSHIP To take apart or to remove from its place.

UNSTABLE EQUILIBRIUM Exists when G is above M. Vessel does not tend to return to an erect position after being inclined but, for small angles, tends to continue inclination.

UNWATCHED Said of a lighthouse not tended.

UNWORKED PENETRATION The penetration at 77°F of a sample of grease that has received only the minimum handling in transfer from sample can to test apparatus and has not been subjected to the action of a grease worker.

UP ANCHOR The order to weigh the anchor and get underway.

UP BEHIND An order to cease pulling and slack up roundly so that gear may be belayed.

UPPER DECK Generally applied to the uppermost continuous weather deck.

UPPER EXPLOSIVE LIMIT (UEL) The maximum concentration of vapor in air, which forms an explosive mixture.

UPPER WORKS Superstructures or deck erections located on or above the weather deck. Sometimes applied to the entire structure above the waterline.

UPTAKE A metal casing connecting the boiler smoke outlet with the inner smokestack. It conveys the smoke and hot gases from the boiler to the stack.

URBAN MASS TRANSPORTATION ADMINISTRATION An agency of the U.S. Department of Transportation responsible for developing comprehensive mass transport systems for urban areas and for providing financial aid to transit systems.

USAGE CHARGE Title 46, Code of Federal Regulations, Part 515 et seq., that regulates U.S. Marine Terminal Operators recognizes, in Section 515.6 (d) (8), that a charge may be established for: "The use of terminal facility by any rail carrier, lighter operator, trucker, shipper or consignee, its agents, servants, and/or employees, when it performs its own car, lighter or truck loading or unloading, or the use of said facilities for any other gainful purpose for which a charge is not otherwise specified."

USANCE Time allowed for payment of foreign drafts.

USC Unless Sooner Commenced.

USCG United States Coast Guard.

U.S. CONSULAR INVOICE A document required on merchandise imported into the United States.

USDA U.S. Department of Agriculture. A government agency that regulates functions of specific imported merchandise, e.g., plants and plant products, domestic animals, serums and by products, etc.

USER FEES In harbor management, the authority by law to charge a fee against vessels that benefit from the use of newly developed channels, proceeds to be used to offset the cost of the nonfederal share of the project.

UTR PARKING An area for parking utility tractors (yard hostlers), which are not in use in the container yard.

UU Unless Used

UUIWCTAUTC Unless Used In Which Case Time Actually Used To Count.
U/W (INS) Underwriter.

V

VACUUM PUMP A pump that evacuates the air from equipment or tanks.

VAL. Value

VALENCE The combining capacity of one atom of an element as compared with that of an atom of hydrogen.

VALIDATED EXPORT LICENSE A document issued by the U.S. government, which authorizes the export of commodities for which written authorization is required by law.

VALIDATION Authentication of B/L and when B/L becomes effective.

VALUABLE CARGO A consignment that contains one or more valuable articles (air cargo).

VALUATION CHARGES Transportation charges to shippers who declare a value of goods higher than the value of the carriers' limits of liability.

VALUATION CLAUSE Provides basis for determining insured value of a shipment under the Open Cargo policy.

VALUE ADDED This measures regional output in the same sense that "Gross Domestic Product (GDP)" measures national output; it is the difference between the value of goods and services purchased as production inputs and the value of goods and services produced. Value added consists of wages, state and local taxes, and "other value added." The latter includes nonwage employee compensation, profit type income (other than proprietor's), net interest, and capital consumption allowances.

VALUE ADDED TAX (VAT) A form of indirect sales tax paid on products and services at each stage of production or distribution, based on the value added at that stage and included in the cost to the ultimate customer.

VALUE FOR CUSTOMS PURPOSES ONLY The U.S. Customs Service defines "value for Customs purposes only" as the value submitted on the entry documentation by the importer that may or may not reflect information from the manufacturer but in no way reflects Customs appraisement of the merchandise.

VALUE-OF-SERVICE PRICING Pricing according to the value of the product being transported; third degree price discrimination; demand-oriented pricing; charging what the traffic will bear.

VALUE SURCHARGE A surcharge for the carriage of cargo having a value in excess of a specified amount per kilogram (air cargo).

VALUTA Designation for foreign means of payment (Devisen, drafts) exclusive coins.

VALVE A mechanical device used for controlling or shutting off the passage of a fluid or gas into or out of a container or through a pipeline.

VAN Container.

VANE   A fly made of bunting and carried at the masthead or truck, which, being free to rotate on a spindle, indicates the direction of the wind.

VANG   Ropes secured to the outer end of a cargo boom, the lower ends being fastened to tackles secured to the deck, used for guiding and swinging and for holding the boom in a desired position. Also applied to ropes secured to the after end of a gaff and led to each side of the vessel to steady the gaff when the sail is not set.

VANNING   A term for stowing cargo in a container.

VAPOR   The gaseous form of a substance that is normally a liquid or solid when it is at atmospheric pressure and room temperature. One or more of the components of petroleum when in the vapor phase.

VAPOR EXPLOSIVE RANGE   *See* Explosive Limits.

VAPORIZATION   Conversion of a liquid to its vapor, such as the conversion of water into steam.

VAPOR LOCK   Malfunctioning of carburetor and fuel feed systems of internal combustion engines caused by evolution of bubbles of vapor from the gasoline.

VAPOR PRESSURE   The outward pressure of a mass of vapor at a given temperature when enclosed in a gas tight vessel. It is an index to the volatility of the liquid from which the vapor was produced. (Reid Method of Determination) A small amount of oil to be tested is placed in a container affixed with pressure gauges. The container is sealed and then heated to 100°F. The vapor pressure on the gauge is the Reid Vapor Pressure.

VARIABLE COST   Costs that vary directly with the level of activity within a short time. Examples include costs of moving cargo inland on trains or trucks, stevedoring in some ports, and short-term equipment leases. For business analysis, all costs are either defined as variable or fixed. For a business to break even, all fixed costs must be covered. To make a profit, all variable costs must be recovered.

VARNISH   *See* Lacquer.

VAST   An order to cease.

VAT   *See* Value Added Tax.

VCPO   *See* Value for Customs Purposes Only.

VEER   To slack off and allow to run out; said of a change of direction of wind.

VELOCITY METER   A device that detects the rate of movement of the mixture in the dredge system.

VENDEE   Buyer.

VENDOR   A firm or individual that supplies goods or services; the seller.

VENDOR-MANAGED INVENTORIES (VMI)   A customer service strategy used to manage inventory of customers to lower cost and improve service.

VENTILATED CONTAINER   A container designed with openings in the side and/or end walls to permit the entrance of outside air when the doors are closed. The ventilation arrangement is such that the ingress of water is prevented. These are primarily designed for the coffee trade.

VENTILATION The ability for gases to be routed into or out of a particular area onboard a vessel. Natural and forced by power. The process of providing fresh air to the various spaces and removing foul or heated air, gases, etc., from them. This may be accomplished by natural draft or by mechanical means, particularly the replenishment of oxygen for breathing purposes.

VENTILATION SHUTDOWN Automatic ventilation motor shutdown switch located on the bridge.

VENTILATOR COWL A swiveled opening at the top of a ventilator.

VENTILATORS, BELL MOUTHED OR COWL Terminals on open decks in the form of a 90-degree elbow with enlarged or bell-shaped openings, so formed as to obtain an increase of air supply when facing the wind and to increase the velocity of air down the ventilation pipe.

VENTING The procedure for release of gas or intake of air from and to the cargo tanks. *See* Gas Vent Lines.

VENTURE An undertaking, such as one voyage of a vessel.

VERTICAL CENTER OF GRAVITY (VCG) The vertical height of the center of gravity of a compartment above its bottom, or of the center of gravity of a vessel above its keel.

VERTICAL KEEL Row of vertical plates extending along center of flat plate keel. Sometimes called center keelson.

VERTICAL ZONE An area of the vessel between adjacent bulkheads.

VERY LARGE CRUDE CARRIER (VLCC) A big tanker, over 150,000 deadweight tons.

VES. Vessel.

VESSEL CROSSING A vessel proceeding across a fairway/traffic/lane/route.

VESSEL INWARD A vessel, which is proceeding from sea to harbor or dock.

VESSEL LEAVING A vessel that is in the process of leaving a berth or anchorage. (When she has entered the navigable fairway, she will be referred to as an outward, inward, crossing, or turning vessel).

VESSEL MANIFEST The international carrier is obligated to make declaration of the ship's crew and contents at both the port of departure and arrival. The vessel manifest lists various details about each shipment by B/L number. Obviously, the B/L serves as the main source from which the manifest is created.

VESSEL OUTWARD A vessel that is proceeding from harbor or anchorage to seawards.

VESSEL PRODUCTIVITY The amount of cargo-ton miles traveled by a cargo ship in one year; as port time decreased with the growth of containerization, vessel productivity increased.

VESSEL SHARE AGREEMENT (VSA) An agreement signed by two or more operators. There is no joint capital investment in ships or equipment. Shipping companies share vessels and costs.

VESSEL SUPPLIES FOR IMMEDIATE EXPORTATION (VSIE) Allows equipment and supplies arriving at one port to be loaded on a vessel, aircraft, etc., for its exclusive use and to be exported from the same port.

VESSEL TURNING A vessel making large alteration in course; such as to stem the tide when anchoring, or to enter, or proceed, after leaving a berth or dock.

VESSEL'S CONVENIENCE (VC) Carrier loads and stows a commodity for the convenience of the vessel, at carrier's own expense and risk.

VETTING INSPECTION Safety inspection performed by a private contractor in order to assist operator in complying with IMO and Coast Guard regulations.

VHF Very High Frequency type of radiotelephone.

VIRTUAL RISE OF G Caused by the "swinging" motion of water in a slack tank.

VISCOSIMETER An apparatus for determining viscosity.

VISCOSITY The property of a fluid, which indicates its resistance to flow. Viscous oils are fuel oils, asphalt and heavy crudes.

VISCOSITY INDEX A measure of the temperature coefficient of viscosity of a lubricating oil as expressed by the relationship between its viscosity at 100°F and its viscosity at 210°F.

VISCOUS NEUTRALS The heavier distillates ordinarily used for blending purposes or in the manufacture of straight lubricants such as turbine oils and light motor oils.

VISOR A small inclined awning running around the pilot house over the windows or air ports to exclude the glare of the sun or to prevent rain or spray from coming in the openings when the glazed frames are dropped or opened. They may be of canvas or metal.

VIZ Namely. Used in tariffs to specify commodities.

VLCC Very Large Crude Carrier (refers to vessels of between 150,000 DWT and 300,000 DWT).

VMI *See* Vendor-Managed Inventories.

VOICE TUBE A tube designed for the carriage of the human voice from one part of the ship to another. In its simplest form the voice tube system includes a speaking connection between the pilothouse and engine room only. In large war vessels the system becomes very complicated. Voice tubes are generally made up to about four inches in diameter and fitted with appropriate speaking and listening terminals. Telephones have largely replaced them.

VOID POLICY (INS) One that is inadmissible as evidence in a court of law (e.g., P.P.I. policy).

VOIT SCHNEIDER Form of vertical axis propeller where the propeller blades are vertical and of aerofoil shape.

VOLATILE LIQUID   A liquid that vaporizes readily at ambient temperatures.

VOLATILITY   The tendency for a liquid to vaporize. A measure of the propensity of a substance to change from the liquid or solid state to the gaseous state. A volatile liquid is one that readily vaporizes at comparatively low temperatures.

VOLATILITY ALLOWANCE   The largest difference in container availability taking into account past peaks in net demand after having removed the trend in container demand during the repositioning trade-off period.

VOLUME   Size or measure of anything in three dimensions.

VOLUME CHARGE   A charge for carriage of goods based on their volume (air cargo).

VOLUME OF DISPLACEMENT   The volume of water displaced by a floating object; weight of this volume of water is equal to the weight of the object.

VOLUTE   A term most usually applied to springs in which successive coils are a progressively increasing (or decreasing) diameter and arranged also with some spacing axially. The resulting geometrical arrangement may be described as a conical spiral or conical helix. It is a spring configuration that results in a spring having a progressively increasing rate with increasing deflection and also facilitates having a large number of coils within a moderate overall length, successive coils being able to enter each other as compression proceeds.

VOUCHER   A receipt, entry, or other document that establishes the accounts.

VOYAGE   The trip designation (trade route and origin/destination) identifier, usually numerically sequential.

VOYAGE CHARTER   A contract whereby the ship owner places the vessel at the disposal of the charterer for one or more voyages, the ship owner being responsible for the operation of the vessel.

VOYAGE NUMBER   Reference number assigned by the carrier or his agent to the voyage of the vessel.

VPC   Vehicle Processing Center where automobile accessories are added, damage is repaired, etc.

VPD   Vessel Pays Dues/Duties.

VRP   Vessel Response Plan.

VSA   Vessel Sharing Agreement.

VSIE   *See* Vessel Supplies for Immediate Exportation.

VTS   Vessel Traffic Service system. Organized approach, using radar and other communication equipment, to advise or control ship traffic in critical areas.

W

WAGES This includes wages, salaries, and proprietors' incomes only. They do not include nonwage compensation (such as pensions, insurance, and health benefits).

WAGES NET OF TAXES These are not equal to wages minus the total state and local taxes, because only taxes directly attributable to households are deducted from wages to obtain the net result. Total state and local taxes, however, include taxes on businesses.

WAIST The amidships section of the main deck; the portion of the deck between the forecastle and quarterdeck.

WAITING PERIOD (INS) A period of time between the beginning of a disability and the date benefits begin.

WAITING TIME The period of time between the moment at which one is ready for an activity to start and the moment at which this activity can actually begin.

WAIVE (INS) To forego; to refrain from insisting upon application of an insurance deductible under specific conditions.

WAIVER CLAUSE Clause in a marine insurance policy stating that no acts of the insurer or insured in recovering, saving, or preserving the property insured, shall be considered a dismissal from or acceptance of abandonment. A clause that entitles both Underwriter and Assured to take measures to prevent or reduce loss without prejudice to the rights of either party.

WAKE A vessel's track; behind.

WALES The side planking on a wood ship lying between the keel and the deck edge.

WALKING SPUD A spud positioned on the centerline of the dredge and mechanized in such a manner that the dredge can be repositioned without lifting the spud.

WARDROOM A room or space on shipboard set aside for use of the officers for social purposes and also used as their mess or dining room.

WAREHOUSE A place for the reception, delivery, consolidation, distribution, and storage of goods or cargo. Also, a building in which goods may be stored over such a period of time as necessary to make further distribution.

WAREHOUSE ENTRY Document that identifies goods imported when placed in a bonded warehouse. The duty is not imposed on the products while in the warehouse but will be collected when they are withdrawn for delivery or consumption.

WAREHOUSE KEEPER Party who takes responsibility for goods entered into a warehouse.

WAREHOUSE RECEIPT Receipt for products deposited in a warehouse.

WAREHOUSE TO WAREHOUSE An export/import policy clause that provides protection from the shipper's warehouse and during ordinary course of transit to the consignee's warehouse.

WAREHOUSE WITHDRAWAL FOR IMMEDIATE EXPORTATION (WDEX) Allows merchandise that has been withdrawn from a bonded warehouse at one U.S. port to be exported from the same port without paying duty.

WAREHOUSE WITHDRAWAL FOR TRANSPORTATION (WDT) Allows merchandise that has been withdrawn from a bonded warehouse at one port to be transported in bond to another port, where a superseding entry will be filed.

WAREHOUSE WITHDRAWAL FOR TRANSPORTATION EXPORTATION (WDT&E) Allows merchandise that has been withdrawn from a bonded warehouse at one port to be transported in bond through the U.S. to be exported from another port, without paying duty.

WAREHOUSING The storing of goods or cargo.

WARP The act of moving a vessel broadside, or one end of a vessel broadside, by heaving on a line to a laid out anchor or to the dock.

WARPING Moving a ship alongside a pier using winches, without ship's engines.

WARPING BRIDGE Bridge at after end of hull, used while docking a ship; also called docking bridge.

WARPING DRUM *See* Gypsy.

WARRANTY (INS) A statement by the Assured, the truth of which determines the validity of the insurance contract. A warranty may relate to matters existing at or before the issuance of the policy (affirmative warranty). Or it may be an undertaking by the Assured that something be done or omitted after the policy takes effect and during its continuance (promissory warranty).

WAR RISK Separate insurance coverage for loss of goods resulting from any act of war. This insurance is necessary during peacetime due to objects, such as floating mines, left over from previous wars. War Risk Insurance in the United States is underwritten exclusively through the American Cargo War Risk Reinsurance Exchange, a group formed to share the extreme losses possible.

WARSAW CONVENTION The Convention for the Unification of Certain Rules Relating to International Carriage by Air, signed at Warsaw, 12 October 1929, or that Convention as amended by the Hague Protocol, 1955, stipulating obligations or parties and limitations and/or exonerations of carriers (air cargo).

WASH DOWN AREAS Areas of a container yard specifically designed with apparatus to wash and clean containers and equipment.

WASH PLATE Plates fitted fore and aft to check the rush of bilge water from side to side when the ship is rolling.

WASH PORT *See* Freeing Port.

WASTE Cotton yarn used for cleaning purposes.

WASTE CUBE Where the cargo does not completely fill or fit the capacity, or where the weight load limit of a container is reached in advance of the volumetric limit, thus leaving empty space in the container; sometimes called breakage.

WATCH AND WATCH Two watches alternating on deck.

WATCH CAP A canvas cover secured over a funnel when not in use. Sailor's headgear, being a pliable, woolen type, capable of covering the ears in cold weather.

WATCH HO! WATCH! The word passed along from forward to aft in heaving the deep-sea lead as a warning that the line is running out.

WATCHING PROPERLY An aid to navigation on its assigned position exhibiting the advertised characteristics in all respects.

WATCH OFFICER An officer taking his turn as officer of the engineering watch.

WATERBORNE AGREEMENT (INS) A market understanding whereby Underwriters cover goods against war risks only when they are on the overseas vessel. This rule is relaxed only in the case of goods in a transshipping port for a short period awaiting onward carriage.

WATER BREAKER A small cask carried in ship's boats for drinking water.

WATER-DEPENDENCY In harbor management, the policy expressed in federal and state laws that scare shore-land space should be reserved for uses that are dependent on a shoreline location.

WATER FOG Very fine droplets of water generally delivered at a high pressure, through a fog nozzle.

WATERFRONT REVITALIZATION In harbor management, the renovation, re-use, or redevelopment of obsolete shore-land industrial area for urban-oriented residential, retail, or recreational uses.

WATER JET PROPULSION The main engine drives a seawater pump, ejecting instead of a propeller a jet of water astern. Jet propulsion is less susceptible to underwater damage, than a propeller, particularly for inshore operation, and is safer if divers or swimmers are involved.

WATERLINE The line of the water's edge when the ship is afloat; technically, the intersection of any horizontal plane with the molded form of the ship. A term used to describe a line drawn parallel to the molded baseline and at a certain height above it, as the 10-foot waterline. It represents a plane parallel to the surface of the water when the vessel is floating on an even keel, i.e., without trim. In the body plan and the sheer plan it is a straight line, but in the plan view of the lines it shows the contour of the hull line at the given distance above the base line. Used also to describe the line of intersection of the surface of the water with the hull of the ship at any draft and any condition of trim.

WATER LOGGED Filled or soaked with water but still afloat.

WATER MONKEY A clay jar for keeping water cool.

WATERPLANE   The plane defined by the intersection of the water in which a vessel is floating with the vessel sides.

WATERPLANE COEFFICIENT   A coefficient of fineness that expresses the relationship between the area of the waterplane and a rectangle having the length and breadth of the vessel at that waterplane.

WATER'S EDGE   The surface of the water.

WATERSHED   A fitting on the outside of the shell of a ship over an air port, a door, or a window to prevent water that runs down the ship's side from entering the opening. One over an airport is also called a brow or a port flange.

WATER SPRAY   Water divided into coarse drops by delivery through a special nozzle.

WATERTIGHT   So constructed as to prevent the passage of water.

WATERTIGHT BULKHEAD   A bulkhead (wall) strengthened and sealed to form a barrier against flooding in the event that the area on one side of it fills with liquid.

WATERTIGHT COMPARTMENT   A space or compartment within a ship having its top, bottom, and sides constructed in such a manner as to prevent the leakage of water into or from the space unless the compartment is ruptured.

WATERTIGHT DOORS   Heavy hinged doors that are installed between watertight compartments below the main deck and on the main deck to weather decks. Watertight doors below the main deck that are to remain open must be equipment with remotely actuated closing devices; watertight doors to weather decks must have a mechanical closing system that ensures equal pressure against the penetrations knife edge. *See* Dogs.

WATERTIGHT FLAT   Short section of watertight deck, forming a step in a bulkhead or the top of a watertight compartment or water tank.

WATERTIGHT TRANSVERSE BULKHEAD   A bulkhead that has no openings through it and extends from tank top up to the main deck, built to control flooding.

WATER TRACTOR   A special type of tug built with cyclodial or rudder propeller power. The propulsion may be located near the middle of the vessel or aft. These tugs can tow from either end.

WATERWAY   A narrow passage along the edge of the deck for the drainage of the deck. A gutter.

WATERWAY BAR   An angle or flat bar attached to a deck stringer plate forming the inboard boundary of a waterway and serving as an abutment for the wood deck planking.

WAY   Movement through the water.

WAY POINT   A mark or place at which a vessel is required to report to establish its position. (Also known as reporting point or calling in point).

WAYBILL (WB) OR (W/B)   A document prepared by a transportation line at the point of a shipment; shows the point of the origin, destination, route, consignor, consignee, description of shipment, and amount charged for the transportation service. It is forwarded with the shipment or sent by mail to the agent at the transfer point or waybill destination. Abbreviation is WB. Unlike a bill of lading, a waybill is NOT a document of title.

WAYS   Timbers, etc., on which a ship is built or launched.

W/B   Waybill.

WCCON   Whether Customs Cleared Or Not.

WEAK FRONT   Weather front that has winds less than about 20 knots and that is disappearing with time. A strong front may become a weak one as it tries to push through a stationary ridge of high pressure. Some cloudiness and light precipitation may still occur.

WEAK HIGH   High-pressure system that is incapable of keeping weather fronts from passing through it. Central pressure of a weak high will usually be 1,020 mb or less.

WEAK LOW   Low-pressure system with winds less than gale force. Central pressure is usually above 1,000 mb.

WEAR & TEAR   Loss or deterioration resulting from ordinary use.

WEATHER DECK   Uppermost continuous deck with no overhead projection having watertight openings. A term applied to the upper, awning, shade, or shelter deck, or to the uppermost continuous deck, exclusive of forecastle, bridge, or poop that is exposed to the weather.

WEATHER EYE   To keep a weather eye is to be on the alert.

WEATHER SIDE   The windward side.

WEATHER WORKING DAY   A day when reasonable weather conditions prevail to allow normal working to the vessel.

WEB   The vertical portion of a beam, the athwartship portion of a frame; the portion of a girder between the flanges.

WEB FRAME   A built-up member consisting of a web plate, to the edges of which are attached single or double bars if riveted, or a faceplate, if welded.

WEDGES   Wood or metal pieces shaped in the form of a sharp V, used for driving up or for separating work. They are used in launching to raise the vessel from the keel blocks and thus transfer the load to the cradle and the sliding ways.

WEEPING   A slight leak.

WEIGH   To lift anchor off the bottom.

WEIGHT, LEGAL   Net weight of goods, plus inside packing.

WEIGHT BREAK   The shipment volume at which the LTL charges equal the TL charges at the minimum weight.

WEIGHT CARGO   A cargo on which the transportation charge is assessed on the basis of weight.

WEIGHT CHARGE   The charge for carriage of goods based on their weight (air cargo).

WEIGHT-LOSING PRODUCT CHARACTERISTICS   A product that loses weight during the production process must therefore be processed as near to its origin as possible. The finished product that weighs less is transported.

WEIGHTS AND MEASURES   Measurement ton: 40 cubic feet.

Net Ton or Short Ton: 2,000 pounds.

Gross Ton or Long Ton: 2,240 pounds.

Metric Ton Kilo Ton: 2,204.6 pounds.

Cubic Meter: 35.314 cubic feet.

WEIGHT TON   A ton of 1,000 kilos.

WEIGHT UNIT QUALIFIER   The unit of measure that the user wants to see for weight.

WELDING   Making a joint of two metal parts by fusing the metal in between them or by forging together at welding heat.

WELL   Space in bottom of a ship to which bilge water runs so that it may be pumped out.

WELL CAR   Also known as stack car. A drop frame rail flatcar.

WELL DECK   The apparent indentation in a main deck between the foc's'le and the house.

WESTERLY   True wind direction from the NW to SW sector.

WESTERN HEMISPHERE TRADE CORPORATION   A domestic (U.S.) corporation whose business is done in any country of North, South, or Central America or the West Indies, and which usually receives certain tax advantages.

WETDOCKS   A basin for mooring vessels that is separated from the main water body by a tidal gate, thus allowing the basin water level to remain stationary and protecting vessels from waves.

WET GAS   A gas containing a relatively high proportion of readily condensable constituents.

WETLAND   An area having one or more of the following three attributes:

• At least periodically the substrate is dominated by hydrophytes or plants that grow in water or saturated earth;

• The substrate is predominantly hydric soils, or those that are frequently wet and sometimes anaerobic, or without oxygen;

• The substrate is nonsoil and is either saturated with or covered by shallow water at some time during the growing season. Typical vegetated wetlands include marshes, swamps, bogs, bottomlands, and tundra.

WETTED SURFACE   That part of the external hull of a ship below the deep load line.

WHALE BACKS   Specially constructed steel pallets suitable for mechanical forklift handling.

WHARF   A shore side facility, which extends out into deeper water to which ships secure. Place for loading or unloading vessels. The term is also used specifically for a berthing structure of open piling construction, aligned parallel with the shoreline and referred to as a marginal wharf.

WHARFAGE   Charge assessed by a pier or dock owner against freight handled over the pier or dock or against a steamship company using the pier or dock; charge for the use of berthing space.

WHEEL   Nickname for propeller; steering gear control.

WHEEL ROPES   The ropes connecting the steering wheel with the drum of the steering gear.

WHELPS   Iron pieces bolted to the wooden barrel of a windlass to prevent the chain from cutting the barrel.

WHERE AWAY   A call in answer to the report of a lookout that an object has been sighted.

WHIP   To bind the end of a piece of line so it will not unravel. A line used for hoisting light weights. Usually used with a single fixed block.

WHIPPING   Turns of small cord wound around the end of a rope to prevent its unlaying.

WHISKERS   Horizontal spars of wood or iron projecting on each side of the bowsprit and to give spread to the job boom guys. Also the bands of light that appear near the running lights in fog or other conditions of restricted visibility.

WHITE CAP   The white froth on the crests of waves.

WHITE OILS OR WHITE PRODUCTS   Term applied to substantially colorless, tasteless, and odorless oils, covering a wide range of viscosities.

WHITE SPIRIT   Highly refined distillate within a distillation range of about 300–390°F (150–200°C).

WHOLESALER   An intermediary between manufacturers and retailers in various activities such as promotion, warehousing, and the arranging of transport and or distribution.

WIBON   Whether In Berth or Not.

WIDE BERTH   At a considerable distance.

WIDE BODY   An aircraft with two aisles, such as a Boeing 747 or Airbus A340.

WIFPON   Whether In Free Practique Or Not.

WIG WAG   A code indicated by sweeps of a flag to the right, left, or front.

WILD CAT   The large toothed wheel of the windlass that catches the anchor chain and carries it over the windlass.

WILLIWAW   A term borrowed from the Cape Horn area to describe sudden gusts of wind that occur in narrow, fjord-like passages.

WINCH   An engine, usually electric or steam driven, secured on deck, and fitted with drums on a horizontal axis, which are used for hoisting or lowering cargo. A hoisting or pulling machine fitted with a horizontal single or double drum. A small drum is generally fitted on one or both ends of the shaft supporting the hoisting drum. These small drums are called gypsies, niggerheads, or winch heads. The hoisting drums either are fitted with a friction brake or are directly keyed to the shaft. The driving power is usually steam or electricity, but hand power is also used. A winch is used principally for the purpose of handling, hoisting, and lowering cargo from a dock or lighter to the hold of a ship and vice versa. Aboard a dredge winches are the equipment that maneuvers the various cable systems. There are normally five winches: one for each spud, one for each swing wire, and one for the ladder wire.

WINCH HEAD   Auxiliary drum fitted on the end of a Windlass used to haul rope or cable.

WINDLASS   The powered apparatus used to hoist and lower heavy anchor chains, hawsers, etc. It may be either vertical or horizontal like a winch.

WIND SCOOP   A scoop-shaped fitting of sheet metal, which is placed in an open-air port with the open side forward for the purpose of catching air and forcing it into a cabin, stateroom, or compartment.

WINDWARD   In the general direction from which the wind blows: in the wind, on the weather side.

WINDY BOOKING   A freight booking made by a skipper or freight forwarder to serve space but not actually having a specific cargo at the time the booking is made. Carriers often overbook a vessel by 10 to 20 percent in recognition that "windy booking" cargo will not actually ship.

WING, WINGING   A term used to designate structural members, compartments, sails, and objects on a ship that are located a considerable distance off the fore and aft centerline.

WING BALLAST TANK   Tank, usually located in the upper 'tween deck on either side of the engine room casing, which is especially valuable in raising the center of gravity of a light ship. These tanks also serve to dampen the period of roll of a vessel. Any weights "winged out" increase the "mass moment of inertia" of a vessel, thus dampening rolling.

WINTER LIGHT   A light that is maintained during those winter months when the regular light is extinguished. It is of lower candlepower than the regular light but usually of the same characteristic.

WINTER MARKER   An unlighted buoy without sound signal, used to replace a conventional buoy when that aid to navigation is endangered by ice.

WIP   *See* Work In Progress.

WIPON   Whether In Port Or Not.

WIRE ROPE   Steel wires twisted together for the purpose of securing a ship to shore or for lifting cargo; called cable ashore.

WITH AVERAGE   Provides a broader cover than Free of Particular Average (FPA), in that the partial losses by perils of the sea are recoverable if they reach a certain percentage of the insured value. Losses less than this amount are paid only if the vessel meets with a specified accident.

WITH PARTICULAR AVERAGE (WPA) (INS)   Partial loss or damage to goods is insured. Many have a minimum percentage of damage before payment. May be extended to cover loss by theft, pilferage, delivery, leakage, and breakage.

WITHOUT BENEFIT OF SALVAGE (INS) A term in a marine insurance policy, whereby the Underwriters forgo their subrogation rights. A policy incorporating such a term is deemed to be a gambling policy in law, and is therefore invalid in a court of law.

WITHOUT PREJUDICE (WP) (INS) The claim is paid on this occasion, although the Underwriter feels it does not attach to the policy, but this action must not be treated as a precedent for future similar claims.

WITHOUT RECOURSE Negotiation of a draft, or other negotiable instrument, or letter of credit documents without the normal warranty on the part of the seller of the instrument/documents that the obligor named in the instrument (the "drawee," "payor," or "maker") will pay. Although the seller is still responsible for the genuineness of the instrument and documents, the purchaser takes on the credit risk of being able to collect payment from the obligor when due. Unless negotiation is without recourse, the purchaser of the instrument/documents has the right to recover the face amount from the seller if the obligor fails or refuses to pay for any reason.

WLTOHC Waterline-To-Hatch Coaming.

WM Weight and Measure. The basis for assessing freight charges. Also known as "worm." The rate charged under WM will be whichever produces the highest revenue between the weight of the shipment and the measure of the shipment.

Similar to MTC. A basis for determining charges by weight or measure. *See also* Weights and Measures.

WOG Without Guarantee.

WORK IN PROGRESS (WIP) Parts and subassemblies in the process of becoming completed assembly components. These items, no longer part of the raw materials inventory and not yet part of the finished goods inventory, may constitute a large inventory by themselves and create extra expense for the firm.

WORK PERMIT A document issued by an authorized person permitting work to be done in a defined area. *See* Hot Work Permit.

WORKED PENETRATION The penetration at 77°F of a sample of grease that has been worked or mechanically kneaded prior to transfer to test apparatus.

WORKING TRACK In an ITF, track used for loading or unloading containers from railcars.

WORLDSCALE An index representing the cost of time chartering a tanker for a specific voyage at a given time. The index is given at Worldscale 100, which represents the price in dollars per ton for carrying the oil at that rate. The negotiated rate will be some percentage of the index value.

WORM, WORM SHAFT A threaded shaft designed to engage the teeth of a wheel lying in the plane of the shaft axis. This type of gear is used for the transmission of heavy loads at low speed.

WORMING   The laying of a small rope or worm along the lay of a larger rope to bring the surface of the rope more nearly round for the purpose of parceling or serving.

WP   Weather Permitting. Time during which weather prevents work. *See* Without Prejudice.

WPA   With Particular Average.

WPD   Weather Permitting Day.

WRENCH   A hand tool used to exert a twisting strain, such as setting up bolts, nuts, etc.

WRIC   Wire Rods In Coils.

WTL   Western Truck Lines.

WWD   Weather Working Days.

WWR   When, Where Ready.

WYE   Track configuration in shape of a capital letter "Y," used to "turn around" a complete train consisting of engine and some number of railcars.

X

X-RAY Method of inspecting containers or other cargo. High frequency electromagnetic ray of short wavelength, capable of penetrating most solid substances.

Y

Y/A York/Antwerp Rules.

YARD A term applied to a spar attached at its middle portion to a mast and running athwartship across a vessel as a support for the square sail, signal halyards, lights, etc. Also, a classification, storage, or switching area.

YARD AIR Air compressors and distribution system installed in a yard so railcar air brake systems can be charged prior to arrival of motive power. Reduces time required for brake tests and departure of outbound trains.

YARDARM Outer end of a yard.

YARD CART A four-wheeled draw bar trailer used for shunting containers around a yard.

YARD CHASSIS Used within a container terminal to transfer containers to and from consolidation and dissemination areas and the container marshalling area or between vessels and the yard storage area.

YARD DOLLY A nonself-propelled, wheeled device, similar to a dolly used to carry containers around a yard or area.

YARD GANTRY CRANE *See* Straddle Crane.

YARD TRACTOR A tractive unit—usually unlicensed—for moving containers within a terminal. Sometimes called a hustler or tug.

YARN Twisted fibers that may be twisted further into strands.

YAW To steer wildly or out of the line of the course, as when running with a heavy quartering sea; the oscillation of a vessel about a vertical axis approximately through the center of gravity.

YEOMAN An individual in charge of secretarial and administrative duties.

YIELD Transport revenue derived per unit of traffic carried in transportation.

YIELD BUCKET The remaining slot capacity for a trade/voyage in a certain port of loading after deduction of the allowance for specific contracts.

YIELD MANAGEMENT The process of maximizing the contribution of every slot, vessel, trade and network. Basically it should be seen as the process of allocating the right type of capacity to the right kind of customer at the right price as to maximize revenue or yield.

YIELD POINT The stress at which a piece of material under strain yields markedly, becoming permanently distorted without increase of load.

YOKE A frame or bar having its center portion bored and keyed or otherwise constructed for attachment to the rudderstock. Steering leads to the steering gear are connected to each end of the yoke for the purpose of turning the rudder. Yoke lanyards are lines extending from the ends of the yoke to the stern sheets of a small boat for use in steering.

YORK ANTWERP RULES OF 1974 Established the standard basis for adjusting general average and stated the rules for adjusting claims.

Z

ZODIAC A rubber dinghy. An inflatable craft for the transport of people.

ZONE Area, belt, or district extending about a certain point defined for transport and/or charge purpose.

ZONE HAULAGE RATE The rate for which the carrier will undertake the haulage of goods or containers between either the place of delivery and the carrier's appropriate terminal. Such haulage will be undertaken only subject to the terms and conditions of the tariff and of the carrier's combined transport bill of lading.

ZONE OF RATE FLEXIBILITY Railroads may raise rates by a percentage increase in the railroad cost index. The railroads could raise rates by six percent per year through 1984 and four percent thereafter.

ZONE OF RATE FREEDOM Motor carriers may raise or lower rates by ten percent without ICC interference. If the rate change is within the zone of freedom, the rate is presumed to be reasonable.

ZONE OF REASONABLENESS A zone or limit within which air carriers may change rates without regulatory scrutiny, if the rate change is within the zone, the new rate is presumed to be reasonable.

ZONE PRICE The constant price of a product at all geographic locations within a particular zone.

ZULU Time based on Greenwich Mean Time.

BIBLIOGRAPHY

Business Logistics/Supply Chain Management, 5th Ed., Ronald H. Ballou, Prentice-Hall, Upper Saddle River, N.J., 2004

Contemporary Logistics, 8th Ed., Paul R. Murphy Jr., Donald F. Wood, Prentice-Hall, Upper Saddle River, N.J., 2004

Contemporary Transportation, 5th Ed., Donald F. Wood, James C. Johnson, Prentice Hall, Upper Saddle River, N.J., 1996

Designing and Managing the Supply Chain, 2nd Ed., David Simchi-Levi, Philip Kaminsky, Edith Simchi-Levi, McGraw-Hill, New York, N.Y., 2003

International Logistics: Global Supply Chain Management, Douglas Long, Kluwer Academic Publishers, Dudrecht, Netherlands, 2003

Intro to Transportation Engineering, 2nd Ed., James H. Banks, McGraw-Hill, New York, N.Y., 2002

Purchasing and Supply Management, 12th Ed., Michiel R. Leenders, Harold E. Fearon, Anna E. Flynn, P. Fraser Johnson, McGraw-Hill, Irwin, New York, N.Y., 2002

The Shadow Organization in Logistics, Jo Ellen Gabel, Ph.D., Saul Pilnick, Ph.D., Council of Logistics Management, Oak Brook, Ill., 2002

Traffic Management: Planning, Operations and Control, John E. Tyworth, Joseph L. Cavinato, C. John Langley, Jr., Addison-Wesley Pub. Co., Reading, Mass., 1987

Transportation, 4th Ed., Robert C. Lieb, Thomas Learning Customs Publishing, Cincinnati, Oh., 1994

Transportation, 5th Ed., John J. Coyle, Edward J. Bardi, Robert A. Novack, Thompson Learning, New York, N.Y., 2000

World Class Supply Management: The Key to Supply Chain Management, 7th Ed., David N. Burt, Donald W. Dobler, Stephen L. Starling, McGraw-Hill, Irwin, New York, N.Y., 2003

ABOUT THE AUTHORS

Capt. Jeffrey W. Monroe, MM

Captain Jeffrey Monroe, Master Mariner, is Director of the Department of Ports and Transportation for the City of Portland, Maine. In that capacity he supervises the development and operations of the Port of Portland, Portland International Jetport, and coordinates the city's surface transportation program.

Prior to joining the city he was Deputy Port Director for the Massachusetts Port Authority, Director of the Center for Maritime Training and Associate Professor at the Massachusetts Maritime Academy, Executive Director of the Governor's Commission on Commonwealth Port Development under Governor Weld of Massachusetts, and Assistant Professor and first director of the Center for Simulated Marine Operations at the State University of New York. His professional experience also includes positions as Director of Marine Operations for Oceanic Marine Management and all capacities as deck officer including master in the U.S. Merchant Marine.

Capt. Monroe is a 1976 graduate of Maine Maritime Academy and earned a master's degree from the State University of New York in transportation management. He holds an Unlimited Master Mariner's license and has numerous professional certifications.

In 1999, Captain Monroe was appointed by Secretary of Transportation Rodney Slater as the Vice Chairman of the U.S. Coast Guard Navigation Safety Advisory Committee. He is also a maritime historian and preservationist and was former chairman of the Maritime Industry Museum in New York.

Captain Monroe is married to the former Linda Mallik of Cleveland and has a daughter Michelle, a licensed merchant marine officer, and son Michael, an Honors Program Business School graduate of Boston College. He has resided with his family in Cape Elizabeth, Maine, for the last 24 years.

Captain Robert Stewart Ph. D.

Captain Robert Stewart, Ph. D., is currently the Chair of the Business Administration Department at the California Maritime Academy, a Campus of the California State University system.

Captain Stewart is a 1975 graduate of the United States Merchant Marine Academy at Kings Point, NY. He has sailed in a number of capacities aboard various U.S. merchant vessels including a variety of tank vessels, container and breakbulk vessels, as well as tugs and oil field support vessels.

During his tenure at the Maritime Academy, Captain Stewart served in many different roles, including Lecturer, Chair of the Mraine Transportation Department, as well as various shipboard roles of Training Officer, Navigator, Chief Mate, and Training Captain aboard two different training vessels designated as the *Golden Bear.*

Captain Stewart has earned a Masters Degree in Public Administration from Cal State University at Hayward and a doctorate in Public Administration from Golden Gate University of San Francisco, California. He currently carries an Unlimited Masters license with all relevant STCW certifications and other professional certificates.

Captain Stewart is married to the former Cynthia Crowther of Sunnyvale, California, and has a son and two daughters. Captain Stewart has resided with his family in Vallejo for the last 22 years.

 CORNELL MARITIME PRESS

American Merchant Seaman's Manual
    William B. Hayler, Editor in Chief, ISBN 0-87033-549-9

Applied Naval Architecture
    Robert B. Zubaly, ISBN 0-87033-475-1

Behavior and Handling of Ships
    Henry H. Hooyer, ISBN 0-87033-306-2

Business of Shipping
    Lane C. Kendall and James J. Buckley, ISBN 0-87033-526-X

Cornell Manual, The
    John M. Keever, ISBN 0-87033-559-6

Diesel Engines
    Leo Block, P.E., ISBN 0-87033-418-2

Formulae for the Mariner
    Richard M. Plant, ISBN 0-87033-361-5

Handbook of Rights and Concerns for Mariners
    Roberto Tiangco and Russ Jackson, ISBN 0-87033-530-8

Marine Cargo Operations
    Robert J. Meurn and Charles L. Sauerbier, ISBN 0-87033-550-2

Marine Engineering Economics and Cost Analysis
    Everett C. Hunt and Boris S. Butman, ISBN 0-87033-458-1

Marine Radionavigation and Communications
    Jeffrey W. Monroe and Thomas L. Bushy, ISBN 0-87033-510-3

Marine Refrigeration and Air-Conditioning
    James A. Harbach, ISBN 0-87033-565-0

Master's Handbook on Ship's Business
Tuuli Anna Messer, ISBN 0-87033-531-6

Modern Marine Engineer's Manual, Volume I
Everett C. Hunt, Editor in Chief, ISBN 0-87033-496-4

Modern Marine Engineer's Manual, Volume II
Everett C. Hunt, Editor in Chief, ISBN 0-87033-537-5

Modern Marine Salvage
William I. Milwee, Jr., ISBN 0-87033-471-9

Modern Towing
John S. Blank, 3rd, ISBN 0-87033-372-0

Nautical Rules of the Road
B. A. Farnsworth and Larry C. Young, ISBN 0-87033-408-5

Primer of Towing
George H. Reid, ISBN 0-87033-563-4

Real Time Method of Radar Plotting
Max H. Carpenter and Wayne M. Waldo, ISBN 0-87033-204-X

Shiphandling for the Mariner
Daniel H. MacElrevey and Daniel E. MacElrevey, ISBN 0-87033-558-8

Shiphandling with Tugs
George G. Reid, ISBN 0-87033-354-2

Stability and Trim for the Ship's Officer
William E. George, ISBN 0-87033-564-2

Survival Guide for the Mariner
Robert J. Meurn, ISBN 0-87033-444-1

Tanker Operations
Mark Huber, ISBN 0-87033-528-6

U.S. Regulation of Ocean Transportation
Gerald H. Ullman, ISBN 0-87033-470-0

Vessel Traffic Systems
Charles W. Koburger, Jr., ISBN 0-87033-360-7

Watchstanding Guide for the Merchant Officer
Robert J. Meurn, ISBN 0-87033-409-3

ISBN-13: 978-0-87033-569-3
ISBN-10: 0-87033-569-3

51995